INTRODUCTION TO
THEORETICAL LINGUISTICS

INTRODUCTION TO THEORETICAL LINGUISTICS

JOHN LYONS

Professor of General Linguistics
University of Edinburgh

CAMBRIDGE
AT THE UNIVERSITY PRESS
1969

Published by the Syndics of the Cambridge University Press
Bentley House, 200 Euston Road, London N.W.1
American Branch: 32 East 57th Street, New York, N.Y.10022

© Cambridge University Press 1968

Standard Book Numbers:
521 05617 9 clothbound
521 09510 7 paperback

First published 1968
Reprinted 1969 (twice)

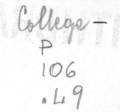

Printed in Great Britain
at the University Printing House, Cambridge
(Brooke Crutchley, University Printer)

CONTENTS

NOTE

Explanatory notes, bibliographical references and suggestions for further reading for chapters 1 to 10 are given in *Notes and References*, pp. 482–9.

PREFACE

My purpose in writing this book has been to provide a relatively self-contained introduction to the most important trends in contemporary linguistic theory. Although the book is intended primarily for students of linguistics, I hope that it will also prove useful to students of psychology, anthropology, sociology, biology, computer science, and a number of other disciplines which are concerned, in various ways, with the analysis of human language, as well as to students of literature and the 'humanities', with which linguistics (or 'philology') has an association of longer standing. I should like to think that the book will be of some interest also to the general reader who wishes to learn something of modern linguistics.

This is an introductory book in the sense that it does not presuppose any previous training in the subject. But it does assume that the reader—especially the reader whose educational background, like my own, is more in the 'humanities' than in mathematics and 'science'—is prepared to make a certain intellectual effort with respect to the use of symbols and formulae. Few subjects suffer more than linguistics from the separation of the 'sciences' and the 'humanities' that is still maintained in the curricula of most of our schools and universities. For contemporary linguistic theory draws simultaneously, and in roughly equal measure, upon the more traditional approach to language that is characteristic of the 'humanities' and the more 'scientific' approach that has developed recently in connexion with advances that have been made in formal logic, computer science and automata theory. Readers of a 'literate' rather than a 'numerate' turn of mind may be discouraged by the proliferation of arcane symbols and formulae in certain sections of the book. Let them take heart from the thought that they probably have a considerable advantage over their 'numerate' brethren in their intuitive appreciation of the nuances of language, and perhaps also in their knowledge of the historical and philosophical background. Both groups of readers, I trust, will benefit from an occasional excursion into the other's territory.

Every textbook must be selective. Let me say something, therefore, about the scope and emphasis of the present book. I have restricted its coverage to what, by common consent, is most central to linguistic theory—phonetics and phonology, grammar and semantics: I have said nothing about stylistics, and very little about the acquisition of language by children, the role of language in society or the historical development of languages. Nor have I said anything about the actual or potential applications of linguistics—in the teaching of languages, in speech therapy, in language-planning, in machine-translation and information-retrieval, etc. I have deliberately given less space to phonetics and phonology, and more space to semantics than most other textbooks of linguistics; and I have been far more sympathetic to traditional grammar than the majority of linguists are.

As far as the theory of syntax is concerned, I have adopted a generative, and in particular a transformational, point of view. I have given a reasonably full account of Chomsky's system of transformational grammar, since this is currently the most familiar and the most highly developed system; and I have made certain tentative suggestions of my own (with due warning to the reader) in the later chapters. I may have ground a few axes here and there elsewhere in the book also, but I have not done so deliberately.

It remains for me to acknowledge my indebtedness to those who have assisted me most directly in the writing of this book. When I first became interested in linguistics, I had the inestimable good fortune to come under the personal supervision of four inspiring teachers: W. Sidney Allen, C. E. Bazell, F. W. Householder and R. H. Robins. There is much in the present book that I first learned from them, although they will, no doubt, disagree with many of the views that I now hold. I should like them to look upon this book as a tribute from their pupil. The other friends and colleagues who have influenced my views in linguistics are too numerous to mention here: I hope that they too will find some satisfaction in the book and that they will be tolerant of its shortcomings. Michael H. Black, of the Cambridge University Press, kindly read a good deal of the book in typescript and made numerous editorial suggestions. Most of the book was typed by Sandra Morton and Margaret Ramsay. My colleagues, E. K. Brown and E. C. Fudge, and my wife have helped me with the correction of proofs. To all of them I express my appreciation of this very valuable assistance. Finally, I must acknowledge here the patience and understanding shown by my wife and daughters while this book was being written.

Edinburgh, 1 January 1968   J. L.

1

LINGUISTICS: THE
SCIENTIFIC STUDY OF LANGUAGE

1.1 Introductory

1.1.1 *Definition of linguistics*

Linguistics may be defined as the scientific study of language. This definition is hardly sufficient to give the reader any positive indication of the fundamental principles of the subject. It may be made a little more revealing by drawing in greater detail the implications contained in the qualification 'scientific'. For the moment, it will be enough to say that by the scientific study of language is meant its investigation by means of controlled and empirically verifiable observations and with reference to some general theory of language-structure.

1.1.2 *Linguistic terminology*

It is sometimes suggested that the terminology, or 'jargon', of modern linguistics is unnecessarily complex. This is a criticism which need not detain us long. Every science has its own technical vocabulary: it is only because the layman takes on trust the established sciences, and especially the 'natural' sciences, that he does not question their right to furnish themselves with special vocabularies. The technical terms used by linguists arise in the course of their work and are easily understood by those who approach the subject sympathetically and without prejudice. It should not be forgotten that most of the terms which the non-linguist employs to talk about language ('word', 'syllable', 'letter', 'phrase', 'sentence', 'noun', 'verb', etc.) originated as technical terms of traditional grammar and are no less 'abstract' in their reference than the more recent creations of linguists. If the contemporary linguist requires different terms, instead of, or in addition to, those familiar to the layman, this is accounted for partly by the fact that the non-technical employment of many of the terms of traditional grammar has rendered them insufficiently precise for scientific purposes and partly by the simple

[1]

fact that modern linguistics has in certain respects advanced beyond traditional grammar in its attempt to construct a general theory of language-structure. The technical terms employed in this book will be introduced gradually, with full explanation and as far as possible with reference to traditional terms of general currency. As we shall see, the use of a special vocabulary eliminates a good deal of ambiguity and possible misunderstanding in the discussion of language.

1.1.3 *Objective approach to language*

The chief difficulty facing the person who comes new to the study of linguistics is that of being prepared to look at language objectively. For language is something we tend to take for granted; something with which we are familiar from childhood in a practical, unreflecting way. And, as has often been observed, it requires a particularly strong effort to look at familiar things afresh. Nor is it merely our intuitive or practical familiarity with language that stands in the way of its objective examination. There are all sorts of social and nationalistic prejudices associated with language, and many popular misconceptions fostered by the distorted version of traditional grammar that is frequently taught in the schools. To free one's mind of these prejudices and misconceptions is indeed difficult; but it is both a necessary and a rewarding first step.

1.1.4 *History of linguistics*

Nothing is more helpful to the layman or student making his first acquaintance with the science of linguistics than some knowledge of the history of the subject. Many of the ideas about language which the linguist will question, if he does not abandon them entirely, will seem less obviously self-evident if one knows something of their historical origin. This is true not only of a good deal that is taught formally at school, but also of much that at first sight might appear to be a matter of downright common sense; for, as Bloomfield has remarked of the common-sense way of dealing with linguistic matters, 'like much else that masquerades as common sense it is in fact highly sophisticated, and derives, at no great distance, from the speculations of ancient and medieval philosophers'. As instances of 'common-sense' attitudes to language which derive from what Bloomfield refers to as 'the speculations of ancient and medieval philosophers' one may cite the commonly-held belief that all languages manifest the same 'parts of speech' (in the form in which this belief is usually held and expressed). The traditional theory of 'the parts of speech', and the standard definitions of classical grammar, reflect, as we shall see in due course, ancient and medieval attempts to force together the categories of grammar, logic and metaphysics. Other commonly held views about language derive not so much from philosophical speculation as from the subordination of grammar to the task of interpreting written texts, and especially to that of interpreting works written in Greek and Latin by the classical authors.

But the history of linguistics is of interest today not only in so far as it enables us to free ourselves of certain commonly held misconceptions about language. Linguistics, like any other science, builds on the past; and it does so, not only by challenging and refuting traditional doctrines, but also by developing and reformulating them. As an aid to the understanding of the principles and assumptions governing modern linguistics a knowledge of the history of the subject has therefore a positive, as well as a negative, contribution to make. This point will be abundantly illustrated in the course of the book. It is stressed here because many recent works on linguistics, in describing the great advances made in the scientific investigation of language in the last few decades, have neglected to emphasize the continuity of Western linguistic theory from earliest times to the present day.

It may also be pointed out here that what is generally referred to as 'traditional grammar' (and we shall continue to use this term) is much richer and more diversified than is often suggested in the cursory references made to it by many modern handbooks of linguistics. Much of the earlier history of Western linguistic thought is obscure and controversial. This is mainly due to the fact that most of the original sources have disappeared: from what has survived it is clear that, although one can trace a continuous line of development from Plato and the Sophists to the medieval Schoolmen, throughout this period there were many individual grammarians who were capable of original thought. A definitive and comprehensive history of 'traditional grammar' is yet to be written. Although the necessarily brief outline of the history of linguistics which follows is intended primarily as an introduction to the present state of the subject, we shall try, as far as possible, to relate past developments in linguistic theory to the social conditions and the philosophical ideas current at the time.

1.2   Traditional grammar

1.2.1   *Philosophical origins of traditional grammar*

Traditional grammar, like so many other of our academic traditions, goes back to Greece of the fifth century before Christ. For the Greeks 'grammar' was from the first a part of 'philosophy'. That is to say, it was a part of their general inquiry into the nature of the world around them and of their own social institutions.

1.2.2   *'Nature' and 'convention'*

The Greek philosophers debated whether language was governed by 'nature' or 'convention'. This opposition of 'nature' and 'convention' was a commonplace of Greek philosophical speculation. To say that a particular institution was 'natural' was to imply that it had its origin in eternal and immutable principles outside man himself (and was therefore inviolable); to say that it was 'conventional' implied that it was merely the result of custom and tradition (that is, of some tacit agreement, or 'social contract', among the members of the community—a 'contract' which, since it was made by men, could be broken by men).

   In the discussion of language, the distinction of 'nature' and 'convention' was made to turn principally upon the question whether there was any necessary connexion between the meaning of a word and its form. Extreme adherents of the 'naturalist' school, like Cratylus, whose views Plato reports in his dialogue of that name, maintained that all words were indeed 'naturally' appropriate to the things they signified. Although this might not always be evident to the layman, they would say, it could be demonstrated by the philosopher able to discern the 'reality' that lay behind the appearance of things. Thus was born the practice of conscious and deliberate etymology. The term itself (being formed from the Greek stem *etymo*-signifying 'true' or 'real') betrays its philosophical origin. To lay bare the origin of a word and thereby its 'true' meaning was to reveal one of the truths of 'nature'.

   Various ways were recognized in which the form of a word might be 'naturally' appropriate to its meaning. First of all, there was the relatively small set of words, like *neigh*, *bleat*, *hoot*, *crash*, *tinkle*, etc. (to use examples from English rather than Greek), which to some degree or other were 'imitative' of the sounds they referred to.

A different, though related, category comprised words (*cuckoo*, *peewit*, etc.) which were 'imitative' of a particular kind of sound, but which denoted the source of the sound, rather than the sound itself. In both cases there is an obvious 'natural' connexion between the physical form of the word and what it signifies. The technical term employed for words belonging to these two categories, and still used in this sense, was *onomatopoeia*. This was simply the Greek word for 'the creation of names'. The fact that it was restricted by grammarians to words which 'imitate' the sounds they denote reflects the view maintained by the Greek 'naturalists' (particularly the Stoic philosophers) that such words form the basic set of 'names' from which language has developed. The fundamental relationship between a word and its meaning was that of 'naming'; and originally words were 'imitative' of the things they named. Onomatopoeic words formed the nucleus of the vocabulary.

But relatively few words are onomatopoeic. Others were demonstrated to be of 'natural' origin by reference to one or more of their constituent sounds. Certain sounds were held to be suggestive, or 'imitative', of particular physical qualities, or activities, being classified as 'smooth', 'harsh', 'liquid', 'masculine', etc. For instance, one might maintain, in the spirit of the 'naturalists', that l is a liquid sound, and that therefore the words *liquid, flow*, etc., contain a sound which is 'naturally' appropriate to their meaning. The modern term for this kind of relationship between the constituent sounds of words and their meaning, in so far as it is asserted to be a feature of language, is *sound-symbolism*.

After taking full account of onomatopoeia and sound-symbolism, the Greek etymologists were still left with very many words to explain. At this point they invoked various principles in terms of which words could be derived from, or related to, one another; and these were codified in time as the traditional principles of etymology. We shall not go into these principles here, except to mention that they fall into two types. First, the meaning of a word might be extended by virtue of some 'natural' connexion between the original and the secondary application: cf. the *mouth* of a river, the *neck* of a bottle, etc. (These are examples of *metaphor*, one of the many terms introduced by the Greeks which have passed into traditional grammars and works on style.) Second, the form of a word might be derived from that of another by the addition, deletion, substitution and transposition of sounds (granted some 'natural' connexion in the meanings of the two words). It is only by a very free and uncontrolled use of the second set of principles, operating upon the form of a word, that the 'naturalists' could maintain their position, claiming to be able to derive all words from a primary set of words of 'natural' origin.

1.2.3 *Analogists and anomalists*

The dispute between 'naturalists' and 'conventionalists' was to endure for centuries, dominating all speculation about the origin of language and the relationship between words and their meaning. Its importance for the development of grammatical theory is that it gave rise to 'etymological' investigations which stimulated and maintained the interest of scholars in classifying the relationships between words. For good and ill, it set the study of grammar in the framework of general philosophical inquiry.

For reasons that need not be discussed here, the controversy between the 'naturalists' and the 'conventionalists' developed rather later (from about the second century B.C.) into a dispute as to how far language was 'regular'. In Greek, as in English, although there are many obvious instances of 'regular' patterns in the language, there are also many exceptions. As an example of a 'regular' pattern in English, take *boy*: *boys*, *girl*: *girls*, *cow*: *cows*, etc. This is an instance of one kind of 'regularity' in language discussed by the founders of traditional grammar. Other types will be illustrated below. The Greek words for regularity and irregularity in this sense of these terms are 'analogy' and 'anomaly'; those who maintained that language was essentially systematic and regular are generally called 'analogists', and those who took the contrary view are referred to as 'anomalists'.

It is to be observed that the term 'analogy' is also being used here in the more particular sense of a mathematical 'proportion', according to which we say, for instance, that the proportion 6:3 equals the proportion 4:2, 2:1, etc. (The term 'proportion' comes from the Latin translation of the Greek word *analogia*.) 'Analogical' reasoning was widely applied by Plato and Aristotle, and their followers, in the study of the sciences. On the basis of a proportion like *boy*: *boys*, we can form 'analogically' thousands of other words: *cow*: *cows*, *girl*: *girls*, etc.; given either *cow* or *cows*, we can 'solve' the equation *boy*:*boys* = *cow*:*x* or *boy*:*boys* = *x*:*cows*.

The analogists devoted their energies to the establishment of the various models with reference to which the regular words of the language could be classified (the traditional term 'paradigm' is merely the Greek word for 'model' or 'example'). The anomalists did not deny that there were regularities in the formation of words in language, but pointed to the many instances of irregular words for the formation of which analogical reasoning is of no avail (*child*:*children*, etc.) and also to the multiplicity of different 'analogies' that had to be recognized for words of the same class (this is more striking for Greek or Latin than for English). They also drew attention to the fact that the relationship between the form of a word and its meaning was frequently 'anomalous': for instance the names of the cities *Thebes* or *Athens* are plural nouns in Greek, although they denote single cities; one of the Greek words for 'child' (*paidíon*) is neuter in gender, although children must be either male or female (cf. the German word *Kind*, which is also neuter: examples of this kind of 'anomaly' could be given from many languages). Another example of 'anomaly' was afforded by the existence of synonymy (two or more words with the same meaning) and homonymy (one form with two or more meanings). If language were really a product of human 'convention' one would not expect to find 'irregularities' of these various kinds; and if they existed they should be corrected. The anomalists maintained that language, a product of 'nature', was only partly susceptible of description in terms of analogical patterns of formation, and that due attention had to be given to 'usage', however 'irrational' a particular fact of 'usage' might be.

That the dispute between the 'analogists' and the 'anomalists' was not settled once and for all by the Greeks is hardly surprising. In the first place, the distinction between *descriptive* and *prescriptive* (or *normative*) grammar was not clearly drawn (that is to say, the distinction between describing how people actually speak and write and prescribing how they ought to speak and write: we shall discuss this distinction in some detail later: cf. 1.4.3). Consequently the 'analogist' would tend to 'correct' any apparent 'anomalies' with which he might be confronted rather than change his ideas about the nature of language. Secondly, and more importantly, since 'irregularities' can only be determined with reference to the 'regularities' from which they differ, what is 'irregular' from one point of view, from another may be regarded as 'regular'. Any general dispute as to whether language is 'regular' or not involves the further question: what are in fact the 'regular' patterns? The controversy between the 'analogists' and the 'anomalists' was not therefore, as is sometimes suggested, a pointless dispute resulting from the perverse refusal of both sides to recognize the obvious fact that there are both 'analogies' and 'anomalies' in language. It was at most a dispute as to what constitutes 'regularity' in language and how much of the apparent 'irregularity' can be shown, by further analysis, to be describable in terms of alternative patterns.

The history of the controversy between the 'analogists' and the 'anomalists' is far from clear. Its earlier development is known only from fragments, and from quotations and comments in the works of later authors; and it is possible that the later writers (in particular Varro, a Roman grammarian of the first century B.C.) may have exaggerated the differences between the two parties to the controversy. Whatever their theoretical pronouncements, both the 'analogists' and the 'anomalists' admitted that there were certain regularities in language, and both contributed to the systematization of grammar. Indeed it was the Stoics, usually said to be 'anomalists', who laid the foundations of traditional grammar in connexion with their 'etymological' work. And the Alexandrian 'analogists' built upon these. Such differences as we find between the Stoics and the Alexandrians can generally be explained in the light of their difference of purpose. The Stoics were interested primarily in the philosophical problem of the origin of language, in logic and in rhetoric; the Alexandrians in literary criticism. Moreover, as we shall see, the Alexandrian scholars were working upon the literary texts of the past; where there was no recorded 'usage' to refer to they invoked the principle of 'analogy' to supply the want of this. Later grammarians, responsible for the codification of what we now call traditional grammar, recognized both 'analogy' and 'usage' ('anomaly') as theoretical principles. However, this did not really solve the problem since, on the one hand, when one is looking for regularities in language, one is frequently faced with alternative ways of relating words and sentences, and, on the other, there still remains the question whose 'usage' is to be taken as correct. Modern linguistics may claim to have made some progress in the solution of these questions, as we shall see, but not to have solved them definitively. The controversy between 'analogists' and 'anomalists' is still with us.

1.2.4   *Alexandrian period*

With the establishment of the great library in the Greek colony of Alexandria at the beginning of the third century B.C. that city became the centre of intense literary and linguistic research. The manuscripts of the authors of the past, and in particular those containing the text of the Homeric poems, had by now become intolerably corrupt. By comparing different manuscripts of the same works the Alexandrian scholars of the third and second centuries B.C. sought to restore the original text and to decide between genuine and spurious works. Since the language of the classical texts differed in many respects from the contemporary Greek of Alexandria, the practice grew up of publishing commentaries on the texts and grammatical treatises elucidating the various difficulties that might trouble the reader of the earlier Greek poets. Admiration for the great literary works of the past encouraged the belief that the language in which they were written was itself inherently 'purer', more 'correct', than the current colloquial speech of Alexandria and the other Hellenistic centres. The grammars produced by Hellenistic scholars came therefore to have a double purpose: they combined the aim of establishing and explaining the language of the classical authors with the desire to preserve Greek from corruption by the ignorant and unlettered. This approach to the study of language fostered by Alexandrian classicism involved two fatal misconceptions. The first concerns the relation between written and spoken language; the second has to do with the manner in which languages develop. They may both be referred to what I will call the 'classical fallacy' in the study of language.

From the beginning Greek linguistic scholarship had been concerned primarily with the written language. (The term 'grammar', which the Greeks applied to the study of language, bears witness to this: it is derived from the word for 'the art of writing'.) No consistent distinction was drawn between sounds and the letters used to represent them. In so far as the difference between the spoken and the written language was perceived at all, the tendency was always to consider the former as dependent on, and derived from, the latter. The Alexandrian concern with literature merely reinforced this tendency.

The second misconception inherent in the Alexandrian approach to the study of language was the assumption that the language of the fifth-century Attic writers was more 'correct' than the colloquial speech of their own time; and in general that the 'purity' of a language is maintained by the usage of the educated, and 'corrupted' by the illiterate. For more than two thousand years this prejudice was to reign unchallenged. It is all the harder to eradicate in that the terms in which the assumption is usually expressed—'purity' and 'correctness'—are taken as absolutes. It should be clear, however, that these terms have no meaning except in relation to some selected standard.

The assertion that the language of Plato is a 'purer' form of Greek than, let us say, that of some illiterate artisan of Alexandria is therefore not so much false as either meaningless or tautological. We shall return to this point and to a more detailed discussion of the relation between written and spoken language towards the end of the present chapter (cf. 1.4.2).

1.2.5 *Greek grammar*

We may now look at some of the more important particular features of the grammatical analysis of their own language carried out by the Greeks. To those who have been familiar from their school-days with the various grammatical categories employed in traditional descriptions of Greek, it might very well appear that the recognition of just these categories and no others would impose itself immediately upon anyone who set himself the task of analysing the language. Even the most superficial knowledge of the history of Greek grammatical scholarship shows us that this is not true. The particular analysis reflected in standard school-grammars of Greek was so far from being self-evident that it took some six centuries to elaborate (from the fourth century B.C. to the second century A.D.). Moreover it is not the only analysis possible, and is perhaps not even the best. In any case, it could not reasonably be said that slightly different ways of describing the language favoured by some of the Greek grammarians are necessarily inferior to that which was eventually standardized and handed to posterity as *the* grammar of Greek. In the following brief account of the historical development of the traditional grammatical framework the various categories recognized by the Greeks and their successors will not be discussed in any detail. Such discussion will be postponed until the ground has been prepared in subsequent chapters.

Protagoras, one of the earliest and most influential of the fifth-century Sophists, is credited with the distinction of three *genders* in Greek. It is Plato (*c.* 429–347 B.C.) who, as far as we know, first explicitly distinguished beteeen *nouns* and *verbs*. It may be noted, however, that the two classes of words defined by Plato as 'nouns' and 'verbs' were not co-extensive with the classes to which these labels were given in the later systems of analysis upon which our school-grammars are based. As defined by Plato, 'nouns' were terms that could function in sentences as the subjects of a predication and 'verbs' were terms which could express the action or quality predicated. (Roughly speaking, the *subject* of a predication names the thing about which something is said, and the *predicate* is that part of the sentence which says something about the thing named by the subject: cf. 8.1.2.)

Two things may be observed. First, the definition of the major grammatical classes, 'nouns' and 'verbs', was made on logical grounds: i.e. as constituents of a proposition. Second, what we now call verbs and adjectives were put together in the same class. Even when later Greek grammarians abandoned the classification established by Plato, they did not replace it with the tripartite system into nouns, verbs and adjectives, with which we are familiar, but substituted another bipartite system, which brought together what we call nouns and adjectives. Little attention was given at first to words which were not members of the major classes.

It was not until medieval times that the division of words into nouns, verbs and adjectives was made. Aristotle (384–322 B.C.) kept the Platonic distinction between 'nouns' and 'verbs', but added to these a further distinct class. These were the 'conjunctions'; by this term Aristotle meant all those words which were not members of the major classes, 'nouns' and 'verbs'. He also took over from his predecessors the threefold classification of gender. He observed, however, that the names of many 'things' (the term employed by Protagoras to label the third gender) were grammatically either 'masculine' or 'feminine' in Greek, and he introduced the term 'intermediate' to refer to the third gender. (Later, that which was neither 'masculine' nor 'feminine' was called, quite simply, 'neither'; and it is the Latin translation of this which has given us the traditional term 'neuter'.) A more significant advance made by Aristotle was his recognition of the category of *tense* in the Greek verb: that is to say, he noted that certain systematic variations in the forms of the verb could be correlated with such temporal notions as 'present' or 'past'. His teaching on this point, however (though more explicit than Plato's), is far from clear.

Of the several different 'schools' of Greek philosophy, it was the Stoics who gave the most attention to language. The reason for this lay in their belief that right conduct was a matter of living in harmony with 'nature' and that knowledge consisted in the conformity of our ideas with the real things in 'nature', of which these ideas are, or should be, the image. Language was therefore central to Stoic philosophy, and, in particular, to the part to which they gave the term 'logic', but which included also what we should call epistemology and rhetoric, as well as grammar. One of the first and most fundamental distinctions they made was that between form and meaning, 'that which signifies' and 'that which is signified'. But the Stoics did not take language to be a direct reflection of 'nature'. For the most part they were 'anomalists', insisting on the lack of correspondence between words and things and on the illogicalities of language. Earlier members of the 'school' distinguished four parts of speech ('noun', 'verb', 'conjunction', 'article'); later members five (by separating 'common nouns' and 'proper nouns'). The adjective was classed with the noun. The classification of what we now call *inflexion* (e.g. the relationship between such forms, in English, as *boy, boys*, or *sing, sang, sung*) was greatly developed by the Stoics. It was they too who gave to the term *case* the sense which it has preserved in standard grammatical usage ever since, distinguishing between the true form of the noun, the 'upright' case (what we now refer to as the nominative), and the 'oblique' cases, which they regarded as deviations from the upright. They realized that another factor in addition to time was involved in determining the form of Greek verbs; namely, the completion or non-completion of the action expressed by the form in question. They distinguished between the *active* and the *passive*; and between *transitive* and *intransitive* verbs.

The Alexandrian scholars carried further the work of the Stoic grammarians. And it was in Alexandria that what we now call the 'traditional' grammar of Greek was more or less definitively codified. Unlike most of the Stoics, the Alexandrian grammarians were 'analogists'; and their search for regularities in language led them to establish 'canons', or patterns, of inflexion. The grammar of Dionysius Thrax (late second century B.C.) was, to the best of our knowledge, the first comprehensive and systematic grammatical description to be published in the western world. In addition to the four Stoic parts of speech Dionysius recognized also the *adverb*, the *participle* (so called because of its 'participation' in both nominal and verbal characteristics), the *pronoun*, and the *preposition*. All Greek words were classified in terms of *case, gender, number, tense, voice, mood*, etc. (cf. chapter 7). Dionysius did not deal explicitly with syntax, the principles according to which words were combined into sentences. This part of the grammatical description of Greek was carried out some three centuries later, less systematically, however, by Apollonius Dyscolus (second century A.D.).

1.2.6 *The Roman period*

We have now traced briefly the development of grammar among the Greeks. Less need be said about the work of the Latin grammarians. It is a matter of common knowledge that in every sphere of Roman scholarship, art and literature, Greek influence was supreme. From the second century B.C., and in some cases earlier, the Roman aristocracy enthusiastically adopted Greek culture and Greek methods of education. Their children were brought up to speak, read and write Greek as well as Latin, and frequently went to complete their education in one of the great Hellenistic centres of philosophy and rhetoric. It is hardly surprising therefore to find that the Latin grammarians were almost wholly dependent on their Greek models. The influence of both the Alexandrians and the Stoics can be seen in Varro's work on the Latin language (first century B.C.). And at Rome, as in Greece, grammatical studies remained subservient to philosophy, literary criticism and rhetoric. The controversy between 'analogists' and 'anomalists' was kept alive and, with other grammatical points, was the subject of a good deal of dilettante discussion. Caesar himself wrote a grammatical treatise *On Analogy* (which he dedicated to Cicero) in the midst of his military campaigns in Gaul.

The Roman grammarians followed their Greek models not only in their general assumptions about language, but also in points of detail. A typical Latin grammar was organized, as was the grammar of Dionysius Thrax, in three sections. The first section would define the scope of grammar as the art of correct speech and of the understanding of the poets, and would deal also with letters and syllables. The second section would treat of the 'parts of speech' and give, in greater or less detail, the variations they underwent according to tense, gender, number, case, etc. Finally there would be a discussion of good and bad style, warnings against common 'faults' and 'barbarisms', and examples of the recommended 'figures of speech'.

In dealing with the 'parts of speech' the Latin grammarians made only such minor modifications as the differences between Greek and Latin forced to their attention. The fact that the two languages are very similar in their general structure doubtless encouraged the view that the various grammatical categories elaborated by the Greek scholars—the 'parts of speech', case, number, tense, etc.—were universal and necessary categories of language. This view was to be maintained explicitly by medieval grammarians.

The later period of Latin grammatical scholarship, the period of

Donatus (*c.* A.D. 400) and Priscian (*c.* A.D. 500), like the Alexandrian period, was an age of classicism. The grammars of Donatus and Priscian, intended as teaching grammars and used as such through the Middle Ages and as late as the seventeenth century, set out to describe not the language of their own day, but that of the 'best writers', especially Cicero and Virgil, and thus perpetuated what I have called the 'classical' fallacy in the approach to linguistic description.

1.2.7. *Medieval period*

A dominant feature of the medieval period in Europe was the important place occupied by Latin in the educational system. All personal advancement, both secular and clerical, depended upon a sound knowledge of Latin. For Latin was not only the language of the liturgy and the scriptures, but also the universal language of diplomacy, scholarship and culture. Since it was now a foreign language which had to be learnt at school for important practical, as well as cultural, purposes, a large number of manuals were written to assist the schoolboy in the mastering of it. Most of these were based upon the grammars of Priscian and Donatus. And Latin was not merely a foreign language; it was primarily a written language. In so far as it was spoken, each country developed its own pronunciation. And this fact could not but have reinforced the traditional view of the primacy of the written language.

Many advances were made in the grammatical analysis of Latin by medieval scholars and have become part of what we now think of as traditional grammar. Far more important, however, than the details of the grammatical analysis of Latin carried out by the scholars of the later Middle Ages were the philosophical presuppositions which they brought into the study of language.

The thirteenth century saw a flowering of scholarship in all its branches: it was the period of the great scholastics, who, under the influence of the newly-accessible works of Aristotle and other Greek philosophers, set out to reduce all sciences, including grammar, to a set of propositions whose truth could be demonstrated conclusively by deduction from first principles. The scholastic philosophers, like the Stoics, were interested in language as a tool for analysing the structure of reality. It was therefore the question of meaning, or 'signification', to which they attached the greatest importance. Indeed, so many works were produced with the title 'The Modes of Signifying' (*De modis significandi*) that the grammarians of the period are often referred to collectively as 'modistae'. Inspired with the scholastic ideals of science as a search for universal and invariant causes, they deliberately attempted to derive the categories of grammar from the categories of logic, epistemology and metaphysics; or rather, to derive the categories of all four sciences from the same general principles. But in doing this, it should be noted, they took it for granted that the grammatical categories to be found in the works of Donatus and Priscian were in general valid. Their objection to Donatus and Priscian (and this objection was in fact made explicitly) was not that the Roman grammarians had inaccurately described the facts of Latin grammar, but that they had not accounted for these facts scientifically, that is by deducing them from their 'causes'.

It was the task of scientific, or 'speculative', grammar to discover the principles whereby the word, as a 'sign', was related on the one hand to the human intellect and on the other to the thing it represented, or 'signified'. It was assumed that these principles were constant and universal. For how else could language be the vehicle of true knowledge? According to the speculative grammarians the word did not directly represent the nature of the thing it signified; it represented it as existing in a particular way, or 'mode'—as a substance, an action, a quality, etc.—and it did this by having the forms of the appropriate part of speech. Grammar was therefore a philosophical theory of the parts of speech and their characteristic 'modes of signifying'. (The term 'speculative' is worth noting. It must not be taken in its modern sense, but in the more particular sense deriving from the view that language is like a 'mirror', Latin *speculum*, which gives a 'reflection' of the 'reality' underlying the 'phenomena' of the physical world. The Stoics had employed the same metaphor.)

It is easy enough to say that the method of definition employed by the scholastic grammarians is circular and their views on grammar self-evidently false. They were certainly more ready than we are to assume that the modes of signifying necessarily coincided with the modes of 'being' and 'understanding'. But before we dismiss their linguistic speculations as unworthy of our attention (as is often the tendency) it would be as well to consider whether it is merely the terminology of the time which we find unacceptable or incomprehensible. Statements such as the following are often quoted as if obviously absurd and needing no further discussion: 'Grammar is substantially the same in all languages, even though it may vary accidentally'; 'Whoever knows grammar in one language also knows it in another so far as its substance is concerned. If he cannot, however, speak another language, or understand those who speak it, this is because of the difference of words and their formations which is accidental to grammar'. The first quotation is from Roger Bacon (1214–94), and the second from an anonymous scholar of the same period. We may be tempted to reject these statements out of hand on the basis of our experience of foreign languages. Surely, we exclaim, the grammatical differences between French and English, or Russian and English, are not just 'accidental' and unimportant; and we tend to attribute the scholastic view of the universality of grammar to the unique position occupied by Latin throughout the Middle Ages and the low status of the vernacular languages, many of which were in any case derived from, or strongly influenced by, Latin. The privileged position of Latin was doubtless an important factor in the development of universal grammar. But the scholastic view of language was not abandoned at the Renaissance with the new interest in the vernaculars and their use in literature. What the scholastic statements which I have quoted mean, when they are stripped of their metaphysical expression in terms of 'substance' and 'accidents', is merely this: all languages will have words for the same concepts and all languages will manifest the same parts of speech and other general grammatical categories. This view may be true or false; we shall return to this question in due course (cf. chapters 7 and 8). But it is a view which, in the form in which it has just been put, would be accepted by many of those who most vociferously proclaim their emancipation from the fetters of scholasticism.

1.2.8   The Renaissance and after

The Renaissance scholars certainly thought that they were making a radical break with the scholastic tradition. Petrarch and his followers ridiculed the language of the schoolmen for its 'barbarism', and took Cicero's usage as their model of good Latin style. From Cicero too they derived their ideal of 'humanism'—this term (Cicero's *humanitas*) being synonymous with 'civilization' and opposed to 'barbarism'. Holding that the literature of classical antiquity was the source of all 'civilized' values, they concentrated their energies upon the collection and publication of the texts of the classical authors; especially after the invention of printing in the late fifteenth century, which made possible the wide and rapid distribution of accurate texts. Once again grammar became an aid to the understanding of literature and to the writing of 'good' Latin. Erasmus himself (in 1513) published a Latin syntax based on Donatus. Greek also became the object of intense study, and, somewhat later, Hebrew. Thus it was that the 'humanists' handed on to succeeding generations of scholars the languages and literature of three cultures.

The vernacular languages of Europe began to attract the notice of scholars even before the Renaissance: we have a seventh-century grammar of Irish, a twelfth-century grammar of Icelandic and a thirteenth-century grammar of Provençal, not to mention Aelfric's comparison of Latin and Anglo-Saxon (tenth century) and a number of observations about Basque which go back to the tenth century. Several grammars of French were produced for travelling Englishmen in the fourteenth and fifteenth centuries. With the Renaissance, heralded in this respect by Dante's *De vulgari eloquentia*, interest in the vernacular languages developed enormously, and grammars were written in great numbers. In fact, the whole classical conception was extended to the modern languages of Europe. Language still meant the language of literature; and literature, when it became the object of academic study in our schools and universities, continued to mean the work of the 'best authors' writing in the accepted genres—Dante in that of the Virgilian epic, Milton in a more Homeric strain, Racine in the vein of Sophocles, and so on. It is true that a more satisfactory academic approach to literature has developed nowadays, and authors are no longer classified by the normative canons of Alexandria and the Renaissance. Yet the study of grammar in the language departments of our schools and universities still tends to be classical in spirit.

The ideals of 'speculative' grammar were revived in France in the seventeenth century by the teachers of Port Royal. In 1660 they published their *Grammaire générale et raisonnée*, the aim of which was to demonstrate that the structure of language is a product of reason, and that the different languages of men are but varieties of a more general logical and rational system. The Port Royal grammar had an immense influence both in France and abroad, and the 'Age of Enlightenment' was to see the publication of many such works. All these 'rational' grammars worked within the confines of the classical tradition and produced no new linguistic theories.

No more striking evidence of the endurance of the classical tradition in the study of language could be given than the definitions to be found in the most recent editions (1932) of the dictionary and grammar of the French Academy, which, since its foundation by

Richelieu (in 1637), has been charged with the task of establishing authoritatively the vocabulary and grammar of French. Grammar is defined as 'the art of speaking and writing correctly'; its object is to discover the relations holding between the elements of language, whether these relations be 'natural' or 'conventional'; the grammarian's task is to describe 'good usage', that is the language of those educated persons and writers who write 'pure' French, and to defend this 'good usage' from 'all causes of corruption, such as the invasion of the vocabulary by foreign words, technical terms, slang, and those barbarous expressions which are constantly being created to satisfy the dubious needs of trade, industry, sport, advertising, etc.'; as for the rules of grammar, these are not arbitrary, but 'derive from the natural tendencies of the human mind'.

There exists no official body whose function it is to legislate authoritatively about English usage. Nevertheless, the literary and philosophical prejudices embodied in the French Academy's definitions quoted above, the origin of which can be traced in Greece and Alexandria, are hardly less prevalent in the English-speaking countries than they are in France.

The true followers of the classical and scholastic grammarians are not those who seek to preserve intact the whole framework of classical grammar, but rather those who carry out free and critical inquiry into the role and nature of language within the context of present-day scientific thinking, and with the more extensive knowledge of languages and cultures that is now available. As we shall see in the course of this book, many of the insights into the structure of language obtained by the classical grammarians were valuable and revealing, but demand reformulation in more general and more empirical terms.

1.2.9   Wider influence of the Greco-Roman tradition

Throughout this section the term 'traditional grammar' has been employed, as is customary, to refer to that tradition of linguistic analysis and linguistic theory which originated in Greece, was further developed in Rome and in medieval Europe, and was extended to the study of the vernacular languages at the Renaissance and afterwards. This, the Greco-Roman tradition of linguistic analysis (as it may be called for convenience), influenced the descriptions of certain non-European languages even before the Renaissance. The grammar of Dionysius Thrax was translated into Armenian in the fifth century

A.D., and somewhat later into Syrian. Subsequently, the Arab grammarians drew upon the Syrians, and they also came more directly into contact with the Greco-Roman tradition in Spain. And the Hebrew grammarians were influenced by the Arabs. So it was that the native grammatical descriptions of Armenian, Syrian, Arabic and Hebrew were already strongly influenced by the Greco-Roman tradition even before these languages attracted the attention of European scholars at the Renaissance.

1.2.10 *The Indian tradition*

Before turning our attention to the period of 'Comparative Philology' in the next section, we must look briefly at one other tradition of grammatical analysis which has exercised considerable influence upon the development of modern linguistics: this is the Indian, or Hindu, tradition.

The Indian grammatical tradition is not only independent of the Greco-Roman but also earlier, more diverse in its manifestations and in some respects superior in its achievements. Pāṇini (?fourth century B.C.), acknowledged as the greatest of the Indian grammarians, mentions a large number of predecessors, and it may be assumed that he is working in a tradition which started some centuries before him. As for the diversity and extent of Indian grammatical work: about twelve different schools of grammatical theory have been recognized in the Indian tradition (most, if not all, to some degree dependent on Pāṇini), and there are about a thousand separate grammatical works preserved.

Although Indian grammar and Greco-Roman grammar were, as far as we know, independent of one another, both in their origins and in their development, there are certain points of similarity. In India, as in Greece, there was a controversy about the 'natural' or 'conventional' status of language; and just as the Alexandrian scholars, dealing with the classical texts of the past, produced glossaries and commentaries to explain words or constructions which were no longer current in contemporary Hellenistic Greek, so the Indian grammarians compiled glossaries and commentaries on the sacred Hindu texts, the earliest of which, the Vedic hymns, were composed some centuries earlier; and the distinction between what we may call 'nouns' and 'verbs' in Sanskrit was drawn in much the same way as it was drawn by Plato for Greek, that is to say in terms of a distinction between 'subject' and 'predicate'. (The Sanskrit grammarians also recognized two other parts of speech, which we may translate as 'preposition' and 'particle'.)

There are two respects in which Indian linguistic work may be held to be superior to Western traditional grammar: first in phonetics, and second in the study of the internal structure of words. Indian grammatical studies seem to have had their origin in the necessity of preserving intact, not only the text, but also the pronunciation of the Vedic hymns, the precise and accurate recitation of which is held to be essential to their efficacy in Hindu ritual. The Indian classification of speech sounds was more detailed, more accurate and more soundly based upon observation and experiment than anything achieved in Europe (or elsewhere as far as we know) before the late nineteenth century, when the science of phonetics in Europe was in fact strongly influenced by the discovery and translation of the Indian linguistic treatises by Western scholars. In their analysis of words the Indian grammarians went well beyond what might be thought necessary for the original purpose of preserving the language of the sacred texts. And Pāṇini's grammar is not in fact specifically devoted to the language of the Vedic hymns, but to the language of his own day.

Pāṇini's grammar of Sanskrit has frequently been described, from the point of view of its exhaustiveness (within the limits which it sets itself: i.e. mainly with regard to the structure of words), its internal consistency and its economy of statement, as far superior to any grammar of any language yet written. The main part of the grammar, which is a highly technical work and can be interpreted only with the aid of the commentaries of his successors, consists of about 4,000 rules (some of them extremely short) and lists of basic forms ('roots'), to which reference is made in the rules. The rules are ordered in sequence in such a way that the scope of a particular rule is defined or restricted by the preceding rules. Further economy is achieved by the use of abbreviations and symbols.

As we shall see in the following section, the discovery of Sanskrit by Western scholars was one of the principal factors in the development of comparative philology in the nineteenth century. This was not simply a matter of being brought into contact with the Sanskrit language, but also of becoming acquainted with the Indian grammatical tradition. There are many aspects of nineteenth-century linguistics which are clearly derived from the practice or theory of the Indian grammarians. But the influence of Pāṇini's principles (exhaustiveness, consistency and economy) is to be seen even more clearly in some of the most recent work in linguistics.

1.3 Comparative philology

1.3.1 'Language-families'

It is a well-known fact that different languages resemble one another in different degrees. Speaking very generally, we may say that resemblances between languages are of two kinds: resemblances of vocabulary and resemblances of grammatical structure. If we compare English and German, for example, we shall find many words, in all parts of the everyday vocabulary of the two languages, which are similar in form and meaning (*son*: *Sohn*, *mother*: *Mutter*, *brother*: *Bruder*, *six*: *sechs*, *seven*: *sieben*, *have*: *habe*, *must*: *muss*, *can*: *kann*, etc.). There are far fewer instances of vocabulary resemblances between English and Russian; and very few indeed between English and Turkish, or English and Chinese (if we discount 'international' scientific terminology). Moreover, in the case of the languages I have mentioned, the degree of vocabulary resemblance is supported by the degree of grammatical resemblance. German and English are more alike in their grammatical structure than are Russian and English, and still more alike than are Turkish and English, or Chinese and English. These facts are a matter of experience and observation, immediately obvious to anyone who sets out to learn, or simply examines, the languages in question. The facts are explained by saying that English and German are closely related; that English and Russian are more distantly related; and that English and Turkish, or English and Chinese, are (as far as we can tell) totally unrelated.

In this context the term 'relationship' is being used, as is customary in linguistics, to refer to a historical, or 'genetic', relationship. To say that two languages are *related* is equivalent to saying that they have developed from some earlier single language. This is otherwise expressed by saying that they belong to the same *family* of languages. Most of the languages of Europe and many languages of Asia belong to what is called the *Indo-European* family. Within this wider family, however, there are many different branches, or sub-families: *Germanic*, comprising German, English, Dutch, Swedish, etc.; *Slavonic*, comprising Russian, Polish, Czech, etc.; *Romance* (the term used for languages deriving from Latin), comprising French, Italian, Spanish, etc.; *Greek*; *Indo-Iranian*, comprising Sanskrit (with its medieval and modern descendants), Persian, etc.; *Celtic*, comprising Gaelic (Irish and Scottish), Welsh, Breton, etc. This is far from being a complete list of the distinct branches, let alone of the individual

languages, but it will suffice to give the reader an idea of the extent
of the Indo-European family. Other major language-families (to
mention but a few) include *Semitic* (Hebrew, Arabic, etc.), *Finno-
Ugrian* (Finnish, Hungarian, etc.), *Bantu* (Swahili, Kikuyu, Zulu,
etc.), *Altaic* (Turkish, etc.), *Sino-Tibetan* (Chinese, Tibetan, etc.)
and *Algonquian* (including a number of American Indian languages).

To have established the principles and methods used in setting up
these, and other, language-families and, what is more important, to
have developed a general theory of language change and linguistic
relationship was the most significant achievement of nineteenth-
century linguistic scholarship. The term 'comparative philology',
which I shall use to refer to this period of linguistics and to its
characteristic aims and methods, is one which came to replace the
earlier and less satisfactory 'comparative grammar' in the course of
the nineteenth century and which, though less commonly used these
days by linguists themselves (who tend to prefer 'comparative and
historical linguistics'), is not infrequently met in general books on
language and, like many other unsuitable terms, has been perpetuated
in the titles of university chairs and departments and of prescribed
courses of study. The important thing to notice is that 'philology' in
this context has no connexion with textual criticism and literary
scholarship, quite separate branches of study for which the term
'philology' is also used, though less commonly in Great Britain and
America than in Europe.

1.3.2 'Scientific' linguistics

It is usually said that the nineteenth century saw the birth of the
scientific study of language in the western world. And this statement is
true, if we give to the term 'scientific' the sense it generally bears
today; it was in the course of the nineteenth century that facts of
language came to be carefully and objectively investigated and then
explained in terms of inductive hypotheses. It should not be forgotten,
however, that this conception of science is of quite recent development.
The speculative grammar of the scholastics and of their philosophical
successors at Port Royal was scientific according to their understanding of what constituted sure knowledge. Their causal demon-
strations of why languages were as they are were based on principles
assumed to be universally valid. The difference between this way of
looking at linguistic questions and that which resulted in the im-
mensely fruitful period of comparative philology was not so much

that the latter was more respectful of the 'facts' and more careful in its observation and collection of them (this is effect, rather than cause), but by the end of the eighteenth century there had developed a general dissatisfaction with *a priori* and so-called 'logical' explanations and a preference for historical reasoning.

1.3.3 Evolutionary point of view

The change of outlook that led to the adoption of the historical point of view was general and was not confined to the study of language. The abandonment of *a priori* reasoning had first taken place in the so-called 'natural' sciences. Later this attitude was extended to the study of human institutions as well. It was observed that all human institutions—laws, customs, religious practices, economic and social groups, and languages—were continually changing, and it was no longer felt to be satisfactory to explain their state at a particular time in terms of abstract principles, but rather in terms of their development from some previous different state by adaptation to changing external conditions. The 'providential' theory of history of the general Christian tradition had been increasingly challenged, and was replaced by evolutionary and secular theories of human development.

1.3.4 A wider range of languages

As we have seen, the Renaissance had already brought about a far greater interest in the contemporary languages of Europe, in addition to promoting the more intensive study of Greek, Latin and Hebrew. From the sixteenth century onwards, dictionaries and collections of sample texts came to be published exemplifying more and more languages, including (in a limited way) some of the languages of the Middle and Far East and even of America. Various attempts were made to group languages into families; but most of these attempts were vitiated by the assumption that, since Hebrew was the language of the Old Testament, it was the source from which all other languages were to be derived.

1.3.5 Romanticism

Of particular importance in the study of language was the new spirit of romanticism which developed at the end of the eighteenth century, particularly in Germany, as a reaction against the classicism and avowed rationalism of the previous age. The leaders of the romantic movement rejected the view that the canons of literary excellence had been fixed for all time by the classical tradition. Their interest in German antiquities led to the publication and study of texts and glossaries of the older Germanic languages (Gothic, Old High German, and Old Norse). Herder (1744–1803) maintained that there was an intimate connexion between language and national character. Following him, the statesman and polymath Wilhelm von Humboldt (1767–1835) gave more definite form to this thesis, saying that each language had its own distinctive structure, which reflected and conditioned the ways of thought and expression of the people using it. This belief in the connexion between national language and national character, which took firm root in Germany, later gave rise to a good deal of extravagant and mischievous speculation in which the notions of 'race' and 'language' were inextricably confused (notably with respect to the term 'Aryan'). At the period we are discussing it promoted not only an interest in the earlier stages of the German language, but a more general enthusiasm for linguistic variety itself and a readiness to consider all languages, however 'barbarous', on their own terms. It is no accident that German scholars were pre-eminent among the founders of comparative philology.

1.3.6   Discovery of Sanskrit

At the end of the eighteenth century it was discovered that Sanskrit, the ancient and sacred language of India, was related to Latin and Greek and to other languages of Europe. This discovery was made independently by several scholars. Of these the most influential was the British orientalist, Sir William Jones, who declared (in 1786), in words that have since become famous, that Sanskrit bore to Greek and Latin 'a stronger affinity both in the roots of verbs and in the forms of grammar than could possibly have been produced by accident: so strong indeed that no philologer could examine them at all without believing them to have sprung from some common source, which perhaps no longer exists'. It is not difficult to recapture the feeling of excitement and wonder which this discovery kindled in the minds of classically-trained Western scholars. They had long been aware of the similarities that existed between Greek and Latin. But they also knew of the strong and lasting cultural and political ties which had united Greece and Rome; and this might seem to account for the resemblances between the two languages. By the end of the eighteenth century enough information was available about languages of different structures for scholars to realize immediately that the resemblances observed between the classical languages of Europe and Sanskrit were so striking as to demand an explanation.

1.3.7 *Importance of Indo-European languages*

Once the imagination of scholars had been fired by discoveries in the field of the Indo-European languages and their permanent interest secured by the development of what were felt to be sound principles of comparison, it was natural that they should direct their attention to the determination of other language families, some of which I have mentioned above. However, the Indo-European family has, and perhaps always will have, pride of place in the historical and comparative study of languages. This is not because of any intrinsic qualities of the Indo-European languages themselves. The reason is simply that many of the Indo-European languages have very ancient written records, going back hundreds and even thousands of years. Since related languages are for the most part divergent forms of some earlier single language, the further back we go in time the less difference will we find between the languages being compared. Although some of the relationships within the Indo-European family could be demonstrated from the evidence of the modern spoken languages, the details of these relationships could certainly not have been worked out without the help of the older texts.

1.3.8 *'Loan-words'*

So far I have talked as though a certain degree of resemblance in vocabulary and grammar—a degree of resemblance greater than can reasonably be attributed to chance—were a sufficient proof of relationship. This is an over-simplification; it takes no account of what is referred to technically, though perhaps misleadingly, as *borrowing*. It is a well-known fact that languages in geographical or cultural contact 'borrow' words from one another quite freely; for words tend to travel across geographical and linguistic boundaries together with the object or custom to which they refer. Much of the resemblance in the vocabularies of different languages may therefore be due to their having borrowed words either from one another or from some third language. We have only to think of the vast numbers of words of Greek and Latin origin in the vocabularies of modern European languages to see the force of this point. (It may be noted that, if we use the term 'borrowing' here to refer, not only to words which have been taken directly from the classical languages, but also to words which have been created in recent times by the deliberate combination of parts of Greek and Latin words, then we must say that most modern scientific terms, as well as the names of such modern inventions as the telephone, television, automobile, cinema, etc., have been indirectly borrowed from Greek and Latin.) Borrowing from the classical languages explains many of the more obvious similarities in the words of different modern European languages. In addition, these languages have all borrowed from one another in different degrees and at different periods of history, and continue to do so. With our knowledge of the languages involved and of the general development of European culture, we have little difficulty in recognizing most of the *loan-words* in the vocabularies of modern European languages. It is clear, however, that if we were unable to identify the loan-words, and so discount them in our calculations, we should very probably overestimate the degree of relationship holding between the languages in question. The founders of comparative philology were well aware that words pass easily from one language to another, but had no sure way of distinguishing loan-words from the rest of the vocabulary. For this reason, they tended to rely particularly upon grammatical resemblances as evidence of linguistic relationship and to be cautious in invoking resemblances between words except where these were found in the 'basic' vocabulary of the languages concerned—the most essential words, those which are learned earliest and used constantly. We now know that the grammar of a language can also be influenced by that of another language with which it is in contact; and, although it is undeniable that what may be called 'cultural' words are more prone to borrowing than others, it is doubtful whether there is any particular set of words so basic in a language that they are immune from replacement by borrowing. However, this question is less important than it might seem to be. For, in the case of those languages which have been most successfully investigated from a comparative point of view, the vague notion of resemblance has been abandoned in favour of the more precisely definable concept of *systematic correspondence*.

1.3.9 *'Grimm's law'*

Instances of partly systematic correspondences between the sounds of equivalent words in different languages had been noted by the earliest comparative philologists. In 1822, Jacob Grimm, following the Danish scholar, Rasmus Rask, pointed out, for example, that the Germanic languages frequently had: (i) an f where other Indo-European languages (e.g. Latin or Greek) had a p; (ii) a p where other languages had a b; (iii) a 'th-sound' where other languages had a t; (iv) a t where other languages had a d; and so on according to the following (partial and somewhat simplified) table for Gothic (the earliest Germanic language for which we have substantial records), Latin, Greek and Sanskrit:

Table 1

Gothic	f	p	b	θ	t	d	h	k	g	
Latin	p	b	f	t	d	t	c	g	h	
Greek	p	b	ph	t	d	th	k	g	kh	
Sanskrit	p	b	bh	t	d	dh	ś	j	h	

(Notice that θ in the transcription of Gothic denotes the voiceless fricative 'th-sound', found in such English words as *thick, thin*, etc., as distinct from the corresponding voiced fricative of e.g. *then, there*, etc.; and that th, ph, kh, dh, bh used in the transcription of Greek and Sanskrit denote aspirated stops: for the distinction between fricatives and aspirated stops, cf. 3.2.6.) Instances of words which illustrate some of these correspondences are: Go. *fotus*, L. *pedis*, Gk. *podós*, Skt. *padas* ('foot'); Go. *taíhun*, L. *decem* (n.b. the Latin *c* represents a 'k-sound'), Gk. *déka*, Skt. *daśa* ('ten'). Grimm explained such correspondences by postulating a 'sound-shift' in a prehistoric period of Germanic whereby the original Indo-European 'aspirate' consonants (bh, dh and gh) became unaspirated (b, d and g), the original voiced consonants (b, d and g) became voiceless (p, t and k) and the original voiceless consonants (p, t and k) became 'aspirates' (f, θ and h). It should be observed that the formulation of the correspondences given here is not quite accurate as a restatement of what Grimm said about the Germanic 'sound-shift': it substitutes the modern terms 'voiced' and 'voiceless' (cf. 3.2.6) for the traditional terms of classical grammar employed by Grimm and, more important, it distinguishes

phonetically between the original Indo-European and the later
Germanic 'aspirates'; moreover, it leaves out of consideration the
later 'High German Sound-Shift', which Grimm regarded as part of
the same general process working itself out over many centuries.
Also, our formulation is imprecise in that it gives only a partial
account of the correspondences between Gothic and the other
languages. However, it conveys the essence of what later came to be
known as 'Grimm's law'—the most famous of all the 'sound-laws'
established by comparative philologists—and is sufficient for our
present purpose.

Grimm and his contemporaries saw that there were many exceptions to such generalizations as those we have summarized in the
table of correspondences given above. They observed, for instance,
that, although the word for 'brother' was completely 'regular' in the
development of the consonants (cf. Go. broθar: L. frater; b = f,
θ = t), the word for 'father' was only partially so (cf. Go. fadar:
L. pater; f = p, but d = t). They were not troubled by exceptions of
this kind, for they had no reason to believe that sound-change was
'regular'. Grimm himself remarked: 'The sound-shift succeeds in
the majority of cases, but never works itself out completely in every
individual case; some words remain in the form they had in the older
period; the current of innovation has passed them by.'

1.3.10   The 'Junggrammatiker'

Some fifty years later, a strikingly different principle was proclaimed
by a group of scholars who saw themselves as revolutionaries and
rejoiced in the label which their opponents contemptuously applied
to them—the 'Junggrammatiker' (the 'Young Grammarians' or
'Neogrammarians'). As expressed by Wilhelm Scherer (1875), the
principle is this: 'The sound changes which we can observe in docu-
mented linguistic history proceed according to fixed laws which
suffer no disturbance save in accordance with other laws.' The claim
that all sound-change could be accounted for by laws which operate
without exceptions was highly controversial, but now appeared more
reasonable than it would have done in Grimm's day. Between 1820
and 1870 an enormous amount of research had been devoted to the
investigation of sound-change in the different branches of the Indo-
European languages; and at the end of this period various brilliant
discoveries were made which had the effect of explaining many of the
apparently 'irregular' correspondences noticed by earlier scholars.

1.3.11 '*Verner's law*' *and other* '*sound-laws*'

In 1875, the Danish scholar, Karl Verner, published a particularly influential article in which he was able to demonstrate that correspondences such as Gothic d = Latin t (in, e.g. Go. *fadar* = L. *pater*), though exceptional in terms of 'Grimm's law', were perfectly regular if this 'law' was modified to take account of the place of the accent in corresponding Sanskrit words (marked in the following table by ''):

Table 2

Sanskrit	*bhrătar-*	*pitár-*
Gothic	*brōðar*	*fadar*
Latin	*frāter*	*pater*

Verner assumed that Sanskrit had preserved the place of the earlier Indo-European word-accent, and that the Germanic 'sound-shift' had taken place before the accent was shifted to word-initial position in some prehistoric period of Germanic. On this assumption, occurrences of d (which, between vowels, may have been a voiced fricative; i.e. pronounced like the th of English *father*) could be explained by the following 'law': the voiceless 'aspirates' resulting from 'Grimm's law' (f, th, h) were preserved if the preceding syllable bore the accent (hence Go. *brōðar*, etc.), but otherwise were voiced (as b, d, g, respectively: hence Go. *fadar*, etc.). It may be added that the identification of the medial consonants in the English words *father* and *brother* is due to developments particular to English; they were distinguished in Old English, and they are distinguished in modern German (cf. *Vater*: *Bruder*), although they have changed phonetically as a result of the 'High German Sound-Shift', which was comparatively recent and applied only to German.

In addition to 'Verner's law', a number of other important 'sound-laws' were established at about the same time which accounted successfully for some of the more troublesome exceptions to the general correspondences holding between the various Indo-European languages. The general effect of these 'sound-laws' was to give scholars a much clearer idea of the relative chronology of developments within the different branches of Indo-European and to increase their confidence in the principle of regularity in sound-change. Although this principle met with violent and widespread opposition

when it was first proclaimed by the 'Junggrammatiker' it came to be
accepted by the majority of comparative philologists towards the end
of the nineteenth century.

The methodological significance of the principle of regularity in
sound-change was tremendous. By concentrating their attention on
the exceptions to the 'laws' which they established it forced scholars
either to formulate these 'laws' more precisely (in the way that
'Grimm's law' was made more precise by 'Verner's law') or to
provide a satisfactory explanation for those words which had not
developed in accordance with the 'laws' whose conditions they
appeared to fulfil.

1.3.12   *Exceptions explained by 'borrowing'*

Many apparent exceptions to the 'sound-laws' could be explained as
loan-words, borrowed from some neighbouring related language or
dialect after the operation of the 'law' which they appeared to violate.
An example is one of the Latin words for 'red', *rufus*, which has an f
where comparison with words in other Indo-European languages and
the relevant 'sound-law' set up for Latin (we shall not go into the
details here) would lead us to expect a b. And there is another Latin
word for 'red', *ruber*, which has the expected b (it has a different
ending; but this does not concern us here). The existence of the
'doublets', and the difference between them, is plausibly explained
on the assumption that Latin borrowed *rufus* from one of the
neighbouring closely related dialects in which, as we know from other
evidence, the f was a regular development.

1.3.13   *Role of analogy*

The second main factor which the 'Junggrammatiker' invoked to
account for exceptions to their sound-laws was what they referred to
as *analogy*. It had long been recognized that the development of
language had frequently been influenced by the tendency to create
new forms 'by analogy with' the more common or more regular
patterns of formation in the language—by the same tendency that
underlies, for instance, the English-speaking child's production of
forms like *flied, goed, tooths* (for *flew, went* and *teeth*). Since this
tendency was thought to have the effect of introducing into the
language 'incorrect' forms, it was regarded as one of the factors
responsible for the 'corruption' of the language in a degenerate and

illiterate age. And it was thought that, just as parents and teachers should correct the false analogical formations of children, so should grammarians correct the 'false analogies' of adult speakers which threatened to gain wider currency. With the increased attention that was devoted to the historical and prehistorical development of the classical and vernacular languages of Europe in the course of the nineteenth century, it came to be realized that 'analogy' was a major factor in the development of languages at all periods and could not be attributed merely to periods of decline and corruption.

The influence of analogy and its explanatory force in the case of exceptions to the 'sound-laws' can be illustrated by reference to a certain class of nouns in Latin. Consider, for example, the nominative and genitive singular of the Greek word *génos*, the Latin *genus* and the Sanskrit *janas* (words which are related to the English *kin* and which can be translated as 'family', 'race', 'species', etc.): Gk. *génos*, *génous*, L. *genus*, *generis*, Skt. *janas*, *janasas*. On the basis of the correspondences exemplified in these (and many other) words the following sound-laws can be set up for the development of the reconstructed, 'original' Indo-European *s:

(i) in Sanskrit, the 'original' *s is preserved (in all cases relevant to the present example);

(ii) in Greek, the 'original' *s
   (a) is preserved before and after consonants and in word-final position,
   (b) becomes h in initial position (cf. Gk. *heptá*, L. *septem*, Skt. *sapta*, Eng. *seven*), and
   (c) disappears between vowels (hence *genesos → géneos, → génous*);

(iii) in Latin, the 'original' *s
   (a) is preserved before and after consonants, and also in word-initial and word-final position, and
   (b) becomes r between vowels (hence *genesis → generis*).

The forms of Gk. *génos* and L. *genus* are therefore 'regular' in their development. The asterisk is used, in accordance with the customary practice of comparative philologists, to distinguish 'reconstructed' sounds or forms from the sounds or forms actually attested in the recorded texts. Although we are concerned here only with the development of Indo-European *s, the examples are 'regular' also in terms of the sound-laws set up for the other consonants, as well as for the vowels, of Indo-European. But in both Greek and Latin there are 'exceptions' to the 'sound-laws'. To take a Latin example: in the classical authors we find a difference in the form employed for the nominative singular of the word for 'honour'—in general, the earlier authors have *honos* and the later authors *honor*—whereas they all agree in the form of the other 'cases', *honoris*, *honorem*, etc. The forms *honoris*, *honorem*, etc., are 'regular' (from **honosis*, **honosem*, etc.) in terms of the 'laws' given above; so also is *honos* (**s* is preserved in word-final position). Now there are many nouns in Latin in which the r has developed 'regularly' from an Indo-European **r*: *cultor*, *cultoris*, *cultorem*, etc. The form *honor* may be explained therefore as an 'analogical' replacement of *honos*, which had the effect of bringing *honor*: *honoris*, etc. into line with *cultor*: *cultoris*. In fact, the word *honor* is only one example from a large class of Latin nouns of the same type (cf. *amor*, 'love'; *labor*, 'work'; *timor*, 'fear'; etc.); to be contrasted with them are such monosyllabic nouns as *flōs*: *flōris* ('flower'), *mōs*: *mōris* ('custom'), etc., in which the 'regular' s was preserved in the nominative singular of the classical Latin forms. (For those readers who know Latin it may be pointed out that the account of the development of these words given here has been simplified somewhat in that it has made no reference to the length of the vowel o in the endings; 'analogy' is relevant here also.)

Some of the 'laws' set up by the 'Junggrammatiker' and their followers were of extraordinarily limited scope; many implausible 'analogies' were suggested; and forms were frequently assumed to have been borrowed without any indication of the dialect from which they might have been borrowed. In the light of the research carried out in the field of historical and comparative linguistics over the last eighty years, we can now see that the distinction made by the 'Junggrammatiker' between 'sound-laws', 'borrowing' and 'analogy' was drawn too sharply: certain sound-changes may have their origin in one word or a small set of words 'borrowed' from a neighbouring dialect and may then spread 'by analogy' into a wider class of words. After this has happened, it may be possible to describe the change ('macroscopically' as it were) by means of a general 'law'. But this does not mean that the change in question has taken place as a result of some 'law' operating upon language from without.

1.3.14　*Positivist outlook of nineteenth-century linguistics*

The notion of 'evolution', although it was by no means a new concept, was one of the dominant ideas of nineteenth-century thought. It was an idea which was enthusiastically taken up by the romantic movement in its reaction to the classical tradition. With the publication of Darwin's *Origin of Species* (1859) and the substitution of the principle of natural selection for the notion of purpose or design, not only was evolutionary biology offered the possibility of adopting the prevailing mechanistic, or positivist, outlook of the 'natural' sciences, but the whole idea of 'evolution' was thought to have been put on a sounder 'scientific' footing. There are many particular features of nineteenth-century linguistic thought which can be attributed to the influence of evolutionary biology which need not be dealt with here. What must be stressed is the fact that the apparent success of the positivist outlook in biology tended to promote the search for 'laws' of 'evolution' in all the social sciences. In their attempt to construct a theory of language-change on the basis of what were conceived as the sound positivist principles of the 'exact' sciences the 'Junggrammatiker' were merely falling into line with the social scientists of the time. Contemporary linguistics is no longer committed to a positivist conception of science; and, as we shall see, it is no longer predominantly concerned with the 'evolution' of languages.

1.3.15 *Comparative philology and general linguistics*

Comparative linguistics (as a branch of general linguistics) is an explanatory science. It sets out to explain the evident fact that languages change and that different languages are related to one another in different degrees. The changes that languages undergo and the different degrees of relationship between languages are accounted for in terms of hypotheses which, like any other scientific hypotheses, are subject to revision as a result of the discovery of new evidence or of the adoption of a new way of looking at, and systematizing, the evidence. The 'Indo-European' hypothesis has been continually modified for both of these reasons. We now give a rather different interpretation to the term 'evolution' from that given to it by certain nineteenth-century scholars; we may understand the terms 'sound-law', 'reconstruction' and 'analogy' somewhat differently; we may recognize more clearly than our predecessors that language-change is not simply a function of time, but also of social and geographical conditions; and we may admit that languages can, under certain conditions, 'converge' as well as 'diverge' in the course of time. However, none of these modifications is sufficient to invalidate completely either the methods or the earlier conclusions of comparative linguistics.

Since we are not concerned in this book with the history of linguistics for its own sake, we shall not go further into the principles of the comparative method as these were elaborated in the course of the nineteenth and twentieth centuries. We will conclude this section by making explicit the main ways in which comparative philology has contributed to the formation of the attitudes and assumptions characteristic of contemporary theoretical linguistics.

One of the most immediate and most important effects of the nineteenth-century concern with the 'evolution' of languages was the realization that developments in the forms of words and phrases in the written texts and inscriptions of the past could generally be explained on the basis of attested or postulated changes in the corresponding spoken language (in terms of 'sound laws'). The earliest comparative philologists inherited the classical view, that the written language was in some sense prior to the spoken, and continued to describe sound-change in terms of changes in the constituent 'letters' of words. However, it was soon appreciated that any systematic account of language-development must give theoretical and practical recognition to the principle that letters (in an alphabetic writing-system) are merely symbols for the sounds in the corresponding spoken language. As we shall see in the following section, it is one of the fundamental assumptions of modern linguistics that sound, not writing, is the primary medium of language. Comparative philology gave a powerful impetus to the development of phonetics (which was also influenced by the theories of the Indian grammarians: cf. 1.2.10), which contributed, in its turn, to the formulation of more general and more satisfactory 'sound-laws'.

No less important was the gradual development, from the middle of the nineteenth century, of a more correct understanding of the relationship between 'languages' and 'dialects'. Intensive study of the history of the classical and modern languages of Europe made it quite clear that the various regional 'dialects', far from being imperfect and distorted versions of the standard literary languages (as they were frequently thought to be), had developed more or less independently. They were no less systematic—they had their own regularities of grammatical structure, pronunciation and vocabulary—and they were no less suitable as tools for communication in the contexts in which they were used. It became clear, in fact, that the differences between 'languages' and closely-related 'dialects' are for the most part political and cultural, rather than linguistic. From a strictly linguistic point of view, what are customarily regarded as 'languages' (standard

Latin, English, French, etc.) are merely 'dialects' which, by historical 'accident', have become politically or culturally important. From this point of view, for example, it was linguistically 'accidental' that the 'dialect' of Rome and the surrounding area should have spread with the growth of the Roman empire and become the 'language' we call Latin: there is nothing in the structure of Latin itself to account for this development. Of course, the use of a particular 'dialect' for literature, administration, philosophy and a wide range of other purposes and activities may have the result that this 'dialect' will develop a commensurately wide vocabulary, incorporating all the distinctions necessary for it to operate satisfactorily in this way. This is a different matter; and it is the effect, not the cause, of the importance achieved by the speech of a particular community. In general, the standard languages of various countries have originated in the 'dialects' spoken by the socially-dominant or governing classes in those countries.

A further point that has become clear as a result of the investigation of regional 'dialects' (in the branch of linguistics referred to as dialectology, or dialect-geography) is the impossibility of drawing a sharp line of demarcation between 'dialects' of the same or neighbouring languages. In those areas of the world where there have been frequent changes of political boundaries or where the principal lines of trade and communication cross political boundaries, what is generally regarded as a dialect of one language may shade more or less imperceptibly into a dialect of another. For example, there are dialects spoken on both sides of the Dutch–German border which are equally close to (or equally remote from) both standard Dutch and standard German. If we feel that they must be dialects of either the one or the other language, we are victims of the traditional view of the relationship between 'language' and 'dialect'. It may be added that judgements on questions of this kind are only too frequently influenced by political or nationalist prejudice.

The assumption that all languages have the same grammatical structure (cf. 1.2.7) is no longer generally accepted by linguists. One reason for its abandonment derives from the demonstration by nineteenth-century comparative philologists that all languages are subject to continuous change; in particular, that classical Greek and Latin were, from a linguistic point of view, merely stages in a process of continuous development, and that much of their grammatical structure could be accounted for in terms of reduction or expansion of an earlier system of grammatical distinctions. It was realized that different languages, and different chronological stages of the same language, might vary considerably in grammatical structure; and it was no longer possible to assert that the traditional framework of grammatical categories was essential to the functioning of human language. This conclusion was reinforced by the investigation of a far wider range of languages than those that were accessible to earlier scholars who had maintained the universal validity of traditional grammatical theory. As we shall see, current linguistic theory rests on far more general assumptions than those of traditional grammar.

1.3.16 'Analogy' and 'structure'

The reader cannot fail to have been struck by the fact that, whereas the traditional grammarian regarded 'analogy' as the principle of regularity in language, the comparative philologist of the late nineteenth century tended to look upon it as one of the main factors that inhibited the 'regular' development of language (cf. 1.2.3). This paradox can now be resolved. If we are primarily concerned with the establishment of a theory of language-change, as were most of the nineteenth-century scholars, we may overlook the fact that, not only the differences, but also the identities in the speech of successive generations need to be accounted for. If the child learning English uses the form *comed*, rather than *came*, or *tooths*, rather than *teeth*, it is presumably because he has acquired an understanding of the principles whereby the past tense of most verbs and the plural of most nouns in English are formed: he has learned some of the regularities, or some of the rules, of the language. If the child did not succeed in acquiring an understanding of these principles of regular formation, he would never be able to do more than repeat, parrot-wise, utterances of the language which he has previously heard around him. We do not say that he 'knows' the language, until he is capable of constructing new utterances which are recognized as normal and can be understood by other speakers of the language.

The important point is that language is patterned, or *structured* (we shall come back to this term in the following chapter), on a number of different levels. In every language there are regular principles according to which sounds combine with one another to form words, and regular principles according to which the sounds may be pronounced somewhat differently in different positions of the word or sentence. At the same time there are regularities in the formation of words and sentences from the point of view of their grammatical function. There is nothing anomalous about the form *came*, considered solely from the point of view of its pronunciation: cf. *lame*, *maim*, *game*, *same*, etc. What is irregular about *came* is its relationship to *come*, by contrast with *love*: *loved*, *jump*: *jumped*, etc. Because forms like *came* stand outside the regular patterns of grammatical formation, they will tend to be regularized as the language is transmitted from one generation to the next. So much was clear to the 'Junggrammatiker'. But they drew a sharp distinction between the 'physical' medium in which language was manifest—its sounds—and the 'psychological' aspects of grammatical structure; and they assumed that only the 'physical' was subject to 'laws' of regular development. We now know that the way in which sounds combine with one another to form words and sentences cannot be explained solely, or even primarily, in terms of the 'physical' nature of these sounds. The principle of analogy is no less relevant to the formation of regular groups of sounds in particular languages than it is to the formation of grammatical 'paradigms' (cf. 1.2.3). The child must learn the one, just as he must learn the other.

The process of change in language can be looked upon as the replacement of one system of 'analogies' and 'anomalies' with another. Changes may be brought about either by such 'external' causes as borrowing or by the 'internal' factor of 'structural pressure'. By structural pressure is meant the tendency to regularize the 'anomalies' in accordance with the general patterns of the language. Since changes may be taking place simultaneously at different levels of the language-system, the result is not necessarily the gradual elimination of all irregularity. For example, the change of s to r between vowels in prehistoric Latin was a matter of regular development (cf. 1.3.13). It may have started in just one or two words, and then spread 'by analogy'; whether the change took place in all words simultaneously or not, the outcome was a somewhat different system at the level of the permissible combinations of sounds (s no longer appearing between vowels). But this new regularity at the level of sounds, as we have seen, created such grammatical 'anomalies' as *honos*: *honoris*, etc., by contrast with *cultor*: *cultoris*, etc. And these 'anomalies' were subsequently regularized by structural pressure at the grammatical level (*honor*: *honoris*). It is because the changes at different levels of the system are not always in phase, because conflicting principles of analogy may be operative at the same time, and because particularly frequent forms (e.g. *came*, *went*) are resistant to regularization, that languages never achieve a state of anomaly-free equilibrium. Not all these points have been illustrated here. But enough may have been said to make it clear that even the irregularities in language may originate from what were once regularities, however paradoxical this may appear; and also that analogy, or pattern, or structure, is the dominating principle, without which languages could not be learned or used to say things which had not been said before. Recognition of the different levels of structure, or patterning, in language carries us into the third of our chronological periods in the history of linguistics—the period of twentieth-century 'structural linguistics'.

1.4   Modern linguistics

1.4.1   *Ferdinand de Saussure*

If any one person is to be called the founder of modern linguistics it is the great Swiss scholar, Ferdinand de Saussure, whose lectures (reconstructed from the notes of his students after his death) were published in 1915 as *Cours de linguistique générale*. Many different schools of linguistics can be distinguished at the present time, but they have all been directly or indirectly influenced (in various degrees) by de Saussure's *Cours*. Although we shall have occasion to refer to some of these different 'schools' in later chapters of this work, we shall make no general attempt to assess their contribution to the development of the subject over the last fifty years. In this section, we will in fact abandon the principle of chronological sequence entirely. Instead, we will list the most important features which distinguish modern linguistics as a whole from the linguistics of previous periods.

1.4.2   *Priority of the spoken language*

As we have already seen (cf. 1.2.4 and 1.2.8), the traditional grammarian tended to assume that the spoken language is inferior to and in some sense dependent upon the standard written language. In conscious opposition to this view, the contemporary linguist maintains (though with certain important qualifications which we shall introduce presently) that the spoken language is primary and that writing is essentially a means of representing speech in another medium.

The principle of the priority of the spoken language over the written implies, first of all, that speech is older and more widespread than writing. It is sometimes asserted that speech cannot be 'proved' to be older than writing. But this is true only if the term 'proof' is made to bear a far greater load than we generally require it to bear in questions of historical fact. We know of no system of writing with a history of more than some six or seven thousand years. On the other hand, there is no group of people known to exist or to have existed without the capacity of speech; and many hundreds of languages have never been associated with a writing-system until they were committed to writing by missionaries or linguists in our own day. It seems reasonable to suppose therefore that speech goes back to the origins of human society.

The relative antiquity of speech and writing is, however, of secondary importance. Far more relevant to understanding the relation between speech and writing is the fact that all systems of writing are demonstrably based upon units of spoken language. (In some cases it is necessary to go back to an earlier form of a particular language or to some other language from which the writing-system was borrowed; but this does not invalidate the principle.) In the description of spoken language, the linguist generally finds that he must recognize units of three different kinds (as well as many others, of course): 'sounds', 'syllables' and 'words'. Now, all commonly-used systems of writing take one or other of these units as basic; *alphabetic* systems being based on 'sounds', *syllabic* on 'syllables', and *ideographic* on 'words'. Granted that all three 'layers' are present beforehand in spoken language, it is easy enough to explain the derivation of each of the main systems of writing from a different 'layer' of the spoken language. Although a particular alphabet or a particular syllabary may be more suitable for certain languages than for others, there is no correlation between the general structure of different spoken languages and the type of writing-system used to represent them. Spoken Turkish did not change as a result of the replacement of the Arabic script by the Roman in 1926; and no modification of spoken Chinese is implied by the present government's proposal to introduce an alphabetic script in place of the traditional ideographic system.

For historical reasons (usually as a result of sound-change or of borrowing from other languages with different orthographic conventions) certain words may be distinguished in their written, but not their spoken, form: instances of such words (traditionally called *homophones*) are *great* and *grate*, *meat* and *meet*, *seen* and *scene*, in English. Conversely, words that are written in the same way may be pronounced differently: English examples of such forms (which we may refer to as *homographs*) are the words written *lead* and *read* (which may rhyme with either *bleed* or *bled*). The longer the period during which a language has been committed to writing (and used for literature and administration) the greater will be the discrepancy between spelling and pronunciation, unless, of course, this discrepancy has been corrected periodically by spelling reforms. Throughout history, scribal traditions have tended to be conservative: this conservatism is partly explained by the prevalence of the 'classical' view of language-change as 'corruption' (cf. 1.2.4); and it has been reinforced, in modern times, by the standardization of spelling for printing.

There are more important differences between spoken and written language than those brought about by the development of homophony and homography. No writing-system represents all the significant variations of pitch and stress which are present in spoken utterances; and the conventions of punctuation to distinguish different kinds of sentences (e.g. the use of an exclamation-mark or question-mark, rather than a full-stop) and the practice of italicizing words for emphasis constitute, at best, an indirect and imperfect means of supplying this deficiency. Moreover, in the typical situations in which the written language is used there is no direct, face-to-face confrontation of writer and reader; information which might be carried by the gestures and facial expressions accompanying speech must therefore be conveyed verbally. The fact that there are invariably such differences as these between speech and writing means that written language cannot be regarded as *merely* the transference of spoken language to another medium.

In the case of particular languages the principle of the priority of speech over writing must be qualified even further. In a literate society, especially in one that is educated to a knowledge and an appreciation of the writings of the past, the written and the spoken language may develop at different rates and may come to diverge from one another considerably in vocabulary and grammar. Modern French affords a particularly striking example of this. Not only is there a good deal of homophony between grammatically unrelated forms (cf. *cou* 'neck', *coup* 'blow', etc., *coût* 'cost', which are all pronounced alike), but many of the grammatically related forms (e.g. the singular and plural of the same noun or verb), though spelled differently, are not distinguished at all in the spoken language (cf. *il pense* and *ils pensent*, 'he thinks' *v.* 'they think'). As a result there are many French sentences which are ambiguous when spoken (and taken out of context), although they are perfectly clear in the written form (cf. *il vient toujours à sept heures*: *il vient toujours à cette heure*, 'he always comes at seven o'clock': 'he always comes at this time'). More important than homophony is the fact that certain verbal forms, notably the 'simple past' tense forms (e.g. *donna* 'gave', *répondit* 'answered', etc.) and the past subjunctive *qu'il donnât* 'that he should give', etc.), have disappeared from spoken French and are learned by French children, to be used thereafter only in writing, when they go to school. In addition to these differences of grammatical structure, there are many differences of vocabulary: as in English, there are many words and expressions which would be regarded as 'bookish' if they were used in conversation, and many others which do not appear in written French (except, of course, in the written representation of conversation in a novel or a play). In other words, written and spoken French (to a greater degree than written and spoken English) are learned and used by educated Frenchmen as partially independent languages. Written and spoken Chinese are even more independent of one another, since what are conventionally referred to as different 'dialects' of Chinese (Mandarin, Cantonese, etc.) are written in essentially the same way. Educated speakers of Mandarin and Cantonese are thus able to communicate with one another in writing, although they may not be able to do so in speech.

Although facts such as these lead us to modify the principle of the priority of the spoken language, they do not oblige us to abandon it entirely. For it is only exceptionally that a written language becomes completely independent of the spoken language from which it originally derived. This happened notably in the case of Latin, which was used for centuries in Europe as the language of religion, administration and scholarship (and is still used in this way by the Catholic Church). The Latin of scholars, priests and diplomats in medieval and Renaissance Europe was a 'dead' language; it was not their normal medium of everyday discourse, learned 'naturally' in childhood, but a language which they learned and used for restricted purposes. Moreover, it was essentially an unchanging, written language (based on the 'living', spoken Latin of many centuries before); and, when spoken, drew constantly and deliberately upon the written works of the past. As we have seen, the peculiar status of Latin in medieval and Renaissance Europe tended to confirm the scholars of the time in their acceptance of the classical principle of the priority of the written language (cf. 1.2.7). Other well-known examples of 'dead' languages which continued to be used for religion or scholarship are Sanskrit, Byzantine Greek and Old Church Slavonic.

In discussing the relationship between written and spoken language (which, as we have seen, is by no means a simple relationship and varies considerably in the case of different languages), we have said nothing about the different 'styles' that must be distinguished in dealing both with spoken and with written language. When the traditional grammarian maintained the principle of the priority of the written language, he was, of course, thinking primarily of the language of literature (rather than, for instance, the language of telegrams, newspaper-headlines or public notices); and he would tend to say that the literary language was the 'noblest' or most 'correct' form of the language. We may now take up the discussion of this question. We will return to the principle of the priority of the spoken language in the following chapter (cf. 2.2.6).

1.4.3   *Linguistics is a descriptive, not a prescriptive, science*

The traditional grammarian tended to assume, not only that the written language was more fundamental than the spoken, but also that a particular form of the written language, namely the literary language, was inherently 'purer' and more 'correct' than all other forms of the language, written and spoken; and that it was his task, as a grammarian, to 'preserve' this form of the language from 'corruption'. There are several different points here, but they may all be treated conveniently under the distinction to be drawn between prescriptive and descriptive linguistics.

The first question to be discussed is that of 'purity' or 'correctness'. It should be evident that there are no absolute standards of 'purity' and 'correctness' in language and that such terms can only be interpreted in relation to some standard selected in advance. We can say that a foreigner has made a mistake because he has said something which would not be said by a native speaker. We can also say, if we wish, that some speaker of a regional dialect of English has produced an 'incorrect' or 'ungrammatical' form because this form is not in conformity with the patterns of standard English: but we are now assuming that he ought to have been speaking standard English in that particular situation. To assert that any linguistic form is 'correct' or 'incorrect' *because* it is at variance with some other form taken (explicitly or implicitly) as the standard is therefore tautological. Each socially or regionally differentiated form of the language has its own standard of 'purity' and 'correctness' immanent in it. Once this is realized and accepted, the way is clear to a more satisfactory description of languages. Whether the speech of one region or of one social group should be taken as the standard for wider use (e.g. as the basis for a literary language), is a question of a different order. The linguist's first task is to *describe* the way people actually speak (and write) their language, not to *prescribe* how they ought to speak and write. In other words linguistics (in the first instance at least) is *descriptive*, not *prescriptive* (or normative).

The second point to be made has to do with the notion that linguistic change necessarily involves 'corruption'. All languages are subject to constant change. This is an empirical fact, explicable in terms of a number of factors, some of which, as we saw in the previous section, are now more or less well understood. Nor is it in the least a matter for regret that languages should change in the several ways in which they do. All living languages, it may be assumed, are of their nature efficient and viable systems of communication serving the different and multifarious social needs of the communities that use them. As these needs change, languages will tend to change to meet the new conditions. If new terms are required they will be incorporated in the vocabulary, whether by 'borrowing' them from other languages or by forming them from existing elements in the vocabulary by the productive resources of the language; fresh distinctions may be drawn and old distinctions lost; the same distinctions may come to be expressed by different means. In denying that all change in language is for the worse, we are not of course implying that it must be for the better. What we are saying is merely that any standard of evaluation applied to language-change must be based upon a recognition of the various functions a language 'is called upon' to fulfil in the society which uses it.

It should be stressed that in distinguishing between description and prescription, the linguist is not saying that there is no place for prescriptive studies of language. It is not being denied that there might be valid cultural, social or political reasons for promoting the wider acceptance of some particular language or dialect at the expense of others. In particular, there are obvious administrative and educational advantages in having a relatively unified literary standard. It is important, however, to realize two things: first, that the literary standard is itself subject to change; and second, that from the point of view of its origin the literary standard is based generally upon the speech of one socially or regionally determined class of people and, as such, is no more 'correct', no 'purer' (in any sense that the linguist can attach to these terms) than the speech of any other class or region. If the literary standard has a richer vocabulary (that is to say, if those who do a good deal of reading and writing have a larger vocabulary) this is because, through literature, we may enter vicariously into the lives of many societies, including those of the past, and share in their diverse experiences.

In condemning the literary bias of traditional grammar, the linguist is merely asserting that language is used for many purposes and that its use in relation to these functions should not be judged by criteria which are applicable, only or primarily, to the literary language. The linguist is not denying that there is a place in our schools and universities for the study of the literary purposes to which language is put. Still less is he claiming to enter the field of literary criticism. This point has often been misunderstood by critics of linguistics.

1.4.4   *The linguist is interested in all languages*

This principle is merely a generalization of the preceding one. It is still fairly common to hear laymen talking about 'primitive' languages, and even repeating the myth that there are some peoples whose language consists of a couple of hundred words supplemented by gestures. The truth is that every language so far studied, no matter how 'backward' or 'uncivilized' the people speaking it, has proved on investigation to be a complex and highly developed system of communication. Moreover, there is absolutely no correlation between the different stages of cultural development through which societies have 'evolved' and the 'type' of language spoken in these stages of cultural development. If there is any truth at all in the nineteenth-century speculations about the development of languages from structural complexity to simplicity, or from simplicity to complexity, this is not recoverable from the study of any of the thousands of different languages spoken throughout the world today. Most linguists these days refrain from speculating about the origin and development of language in general terms. They have found that the study of all languages on equal terms is rewarding. The results of such study have so far thrown no light on the more general question of the origin and development of language in the remote past of mankind.

It may be necessary to learn another language, or at least a specialized vocabulary, in order to study a particular subject or talk satisfactorily about it. If anyone wants to understand Greek philosophy or scholastic philosophy, for example, he must learn Greek or medieval Latin (or at least, by diligent and intelligent study of commentaries and expositions, come to understand the significance of the key-terms—and this is a way of learning, indirectly, a certain small part of the languages). He may then find that it is impossible to discuss the questions that exercised the Greek and scholastic philosophers at all adequately except by using their terminology. It may thus be said that his own language, say modern English, is 'poorer' than Greek or Latin, since it does not provide him with the necessary distinctions in this particular field. This might seem to run counter to the assumption that all languages are efficient and viable systems of communication serving the needs of the community in which they operate. But the contradiction is only apparent. The number of distinctions one can draw in classifying the features of 'the world' is in principle infinite. Only those that are of importance in the life of a particular community will be given recognition in the vocabulary of that community. The fact that we do not have in normal colloquial English terms to refer to some of the concepts of ancient philosophy is merely a reflection of the fact that most of us do not discuss problems of ancient philosophy: if we did, the terms would have been created for this. Whether we choose to say that the extended specialized vocabularies that are used by different sub-groups for different specialized purposes (e.g. discussing nuclear physics or heraldry) are part of English depends upon the way in which we define 'English' (we shall have more to say about this later). The point is that no language can be said to be intrinsically 'richer' than another: each is adapted to the characteristic pursuits of its users.

The linguist's concern (in principle) with all languages derives from the proclaimed aims of his subject: the construction of a scientific theory of the structure of human language. All recorded and observable instances of language serve as data to be systematized and 'explained' by the general theory.

1.4.5 *Priority of synchronic description*

One of the most important of the many conceptual and terminological distinctions introduced into linguistics by de Saussure was his distinction between the *diachronic* and the *synchronic* study of language. (The distinction is sometimes drawn by opposing 'historical' to 'descriptive'. This is a different sense of the term 'descriptive' from that which is intended when 'descriptive' is opposed to 'prescriptive': cf. 1.4.3. For that reason, it is preferable to use the technical terms coined by de Saussure.) By the diachronic study of a particular language is meant the description of its historical development ('through time'); for example, a diachronic study of the English language might treat of its development from the time of our earliest records to the present day, or might cover some more limited period of time. By the synchronic study of a language is meant the description of a particular 'state' of that language (at some 'point' in time). It is important to realize that synchronic description is not restricted in principle to the analysis of modern spoken language. One can carry out a synchronic analysis of 'dead' languages provided that there is sufficient evidence preserved in the written records that have come down to us. The description of a 'dead' language will necessarily be less complete than the description of a modern spoken language, simply because it is impossible to check the validity of certain statements made about the language by appealing to native speakers as a source of further evidence. But there are many 'dead' languages for which there exists enough material for a reasonably comprehensive synchronic description.

As we have seen, nineteenth-century linguistics ('comparative philology') was primarily concerned with the diachronic (cf. 1.3.1). The principle of the priority of synchronic description, which is characteristic of most twentieth-century linguistic theory, implies that historical considerations are irrelevant to the investigation of particular temporal 'states' of a language. The application of this principle may be illustrated by means of a famous analogy used by de Saussure. In this analogy (which he drew upon to make a number of different theoretical points) de Saussure compared languages to games of chess.

In the course of a game of chess the state of the board is constantly changing, but at any one time the state of the game can be fully described in terms of the positions occupied by the several pieces. It does not matter by what route (the number, nature or order of the moves) the players have arrived at the particular state of the game: this state is describable *synchronically* without reference to the previous moves. So it is with language, said de Saussure. All languages are constantly changing; and just as the state of the chess-board at some particular time can be described without reference to the particular combination of moves that has brought the game to that point, so can the successive, or socially and geographically delimited, states of a language be described independently of one another.

An example will make clear the several points involved. In Latin of the classical period up to six 'cases' of the noun were distinguished by a difference of ending (cf. Table 9, in 7.4.2). The different cases marked the different kinds of relation holding between words in a sentence. In later Latin, as a result of an increasing use of prepositions and certain 'sound-changes' which reduced the number of distinct endings, a system gradually developed in which no more than two cases of the noun were distinguished: a 'nominative' and an 'oblique' case, the former being used for the subject of the sentence and the latter for the object of a transitive verb or of a preposition. This is the situation that is found in Old French. However, the difference between the two cases was not marked in all types of nouns (and adjectives). In fact the following three main noun-classes can be set up for the oldest period in French:

		I	II	III
Sing.	Nom.	*murs*	*porte*	*chantre*
	Obl.	*mur*	*porte*	*chanteur*
Plur.	Nom.	*mur*	*portes*	*chanteurs*
	Obl.	*murs*	*portes*	*chanteurs*

(The reason for the development in words of class III of a difference of stem in the nominative singular is the difference in the historical development of stressed and unstressed vowels of Latin: *chantre* is from Latin *cántor*, *chanteur* from *cantórem*.) If we compare the different classes, we shall see that in words of Class I the presence or absence of the ending s cannot be taken as marking the form for either case or number independently. It is only in construction with other words that *murs* can be recognized as either singular (and nominative) or plural (and oblique). By contrast in words of class II the s can be regarded as marking *portes* as plural and its absence as marking *porte* as singular, there being no indication of case in the internal structure of words of this class. Between the eleventh and fourteenth centuries the whole of the French nominal (and adjectival) system was regularized on the pattern of the class II words, with the result that the distinction between the nominative and the oblique cases disappeared and the final s came to be the mark of the plural. (The distinction between the two cases in the singular endured a little longer in words of class III—*chantre*: *chanteur*, *maire*: *majeur*, *pastre* (*pâtre*): *pasteur*, etc.—but finally this disappeared also as a grammatical feature, although in some instances the two forms have been preserved in modern French as 'doublets', i.e. as different words each with its own singular and plural.) When nouns such as

fils ('son'), *Georges*, *Louis*, etc., preserved what was, from the
historical point of view, the s of the old nominative singular, they lost
the contrasting form without s (Old French has the contrast *fils*: *fil*
in the singular). The result of the change that took place between the
two periods was the development of the system still reflected in
traditional French orthography in which, by and large, number is
marked in the noun (and adjective) by the presence or absence of s,
and case plays no part.

We may now interpret the example in the light of de Saussure's
analogy. There are two states of the language in question. The
historical development of the later system cannot be understood
except by reference to the earlier, but the facts of the historical
development are clearly not relevant to an understanding of how the
later system worked. It would be absurd to suggest, for instance, that
the relation of *portes* to *porte* in the later period was different from
that of *murs* to *mur*. Each state of the language can, and should, be
described on its own terms without reference to what it has developed
from or what it is likely to develop into. Although the words in the
two different states of the language are identical in form (in order to
simplify the exposition we may assume this to be so), the grammatical
relationship between them is quite different. The pieces, as it were,
are the same, but the positions they occupy on the board have
changed. (In modern spoken French the state of the board is different
again: the distinction between singular and plural in the noun is
generally made, if at all, not in the form of the word itself, but in a
number of different ways, including the form of the accompanying
definite article, agreement of the verb, 'liaison' before a word beginning with a vowel, etc. We have already seen that there is considerable difference between the structure of modern spoken and written
French: cf. 1.4.2.)

Relatively few speakers of a language know very much about its
historical development; and yet, learning the language 'naturally' as
children, they come to speak it according to certain systematic
principles, or 'rules', 'immanent' in the utterances they hear about
them. It is the task of synchronic linguistic description to formulate
these systematic 'rules' as they operate in the language at a particular
time. (It may be that the way in which the rules are integrated in the
system of description will reflect particular historical processes in the
development of the language. If so this is an important fact about
the structure of language. But it does not affect the general principle of
the priority of the synchronic, since the native speakers of a particular

language are able to learn and apply the 'rules' of their language without drawing upon any historical knowledge.) With regard to those few members of a speech-community who do have some knowledge of previous states of the language, the following argument would seem to apply. Either their specialized knowledge has some effect upon the way they speak the language, or it does not. If it affects their usage, so that their speech is in some respect different from (presumably more 'archaic' than) that of other members of the community, it is to that extent a different language; and will not therefore fall within the scope of a description of the more typical usage of the speech-community. And if it has no noticeable effect upon their normal speech, it is even more clearly irrelevant to the synchronic description. In either case, therefore, synchronic analysis is independent of such knowledge of the history of the language as may exist in the speech-community.

The principle of the priority of synchronic description is generally taken to carry the further implication that diachronic description presupposes the previous synchronic analysis of the various 'states' through which languages have passed in their historical development. Since we are not primarily concerned with historical and comparative linguistics, we will not go further into this question. There is, however, one important point that must be made here.

The convenient terminological distinction between synchronic and diachronic description must not be understood to imply that time is itself the determining factor in language-change. Strictly speaking, change in language is never 'a function of time' in this sense. There are many different factors, both within a language and external to it, which may determine its development from one synchronic 'state' to another; and the passage of time merely allows for the complex interaction of these various factors. Furthermore, one must bear in mind that the notion of diachronic development (language-change) is most usefully applied *macroscopically*—that is to say, in the comparison of 'states' of a language relatively far removed from one another in time. One would be quite mistaken if one were to assume that the language of a particular 'speech-community' at a particular time is completely uniform, and that language-change is a matter of the replacement of one homogeneous system of communication by another equally homogeneous system at some definite 'point' in time.

The 'speech-community' is always made up of many different groups, and the speech of the members of these groups will reflect in various ways (in pronunciation, grammar and vocabulary) differences of age, place of origin or prolonged residence, professional interest, educational background, and so on. Any particular member of the speech-community belongs of course simultaneously to many such linguistically-relevant groups. In addition to the differences in the language which derive from the existence within the community of various social groups, there are also important differences of 'style' which relate to the various functions of language and the different social situations in which the language is used: such differences as can be referred to the distinction of 'formal' and 'colloquial', etc. It is customary (except in works devoted specifically to this question) to abstract from synchronic variation in language, either by restricting the description of a language to the speech of a particular group using a particular 'style', or by describing the language in terms of such generality that the description is valid (in intention at least) for all 'varieties'. Some degree of 'idealization' is involved in either of these two procedures, and this may be necessary at the present stage of linguistic theory. It is important to realize, however, that much of the difference between two diachronically-determined 'states' of a language may be present in two 'varieties' of the language existing at the same time. From the *microscopic*, as distinct from the *macroscopic*, point of view it is impossible to draw a sharp distinction between diachronic 'change' and synchronic 'variation'.

1.4.6 *The structural approach*

The most characteristic feature of modern linguistics—one which it shares with a number of other sciences—is 'structuralism' (to use the label which is commonly applied, often pejoratively). Briefly, this means that each language is regarded as a *system of relations* (more precisely, a set of interrelated systems), the elements of which— sounds, words, etc.—have no validity independently of the relations of equivalence and contrast which hold between them. (The reader may well have observed that the key terms 'system' and 'relation' have already been used in the discussion of de Saussure's distinction of the synchronic and diachronic. In fact, de Saussure drew this distinction as a consequence of his conviction that every language, at a given time, constitutes an integrated system of relationships.)

The more particular implications of structuralism may be left for the following chapter. Here it is sufficient to remark that there is no conflict between the peculiarly abstract approach to the study of language, which is characteristic of modern, 'structural' linguistics, and more 'practical' approaches. However abstract, or 'formal', modern linguistic theory might be, it has been developed to account for the way people actually use language. It derives from, and it is validated or refuted by, empirical evidence. In this respect linguistics is no different from any other science; and the point would not be worth stressing, if it were not the case that some linguists, out of sympathy with current developments, have seen a necessary opposition between what have been called 'formalism' and 'realism' in the study of language.

1.4.7 *'Langue' and 'parole'*

At this point, it will be convenient to introduce, for future reference, de Saussure's distinction between *langue* and *parole*. (English equivalents have occasionally been proposed, but most scholars have continued to use the French terms employed by de Saussure. Chomsky has recently drawn roughly the same distinction in terms of linguistic 'competence' and 'performance' with respect to particular languages.)

The distinction is intended to eliminate an ambiguity in the use of the word 'language'. Suppose we were to propose as a provisional definition of 'English' the following: the English language may be defined as the set of utterances produced by speakers of English when they are speaking English. We see the ambiguity immediately. When we say of someone that he 'speaks English' (or is a 'speaker of English') we do not imply that he is actually 'speaking English' on any one occasion. It would be quite reasonable to say of a parrot, in the appropriate circumstances, that it 'is speaking English', but not that it 'speaks English'. Let us follow de Saussure, and say that all those who 'speak English' (or are 'speakers of English') share a particular *langue* and that the set of utterances which they produce when they are 'speaking English' constitute instances of *parole*.

A number of questions now arise. What is the relationship between *langue* and *parole*? Which, if either, does the linguist claim to be describing when he writes the grammar of 'English' (or of any other 'language')? De Saussure's own answer to both of these questions was very largely determined by his adherence to the psychological and sociological theories of Durkheim; and we need not go into these details. It suffices, for the present, to have posed the problem and to have introduced de Saussure's terms.

The relationship between *langue* and *parole* is very complex, and somewhat controversial. For the moment, we may be content with the statement that all members of a particular language-community (all those who speak a particular language, e.g. English) produce utterances, when they are speaking that language, which, despite their individual variations, are describable in terms of a particular system of rules and relations: in some sense, they have the same *structural* characteristics. The utterances are instances of *parole*, which the linguist takes as evidence for the construction of the underlying common structure: the *langue*. It is therefore the *langue*, the language-system, which the linguist describes. We shall see later that a distinction must be made between 'utterances' and 'sentences'; and that the description of a 'language' is, in principle, a two-stage operation. The utterances of a particular 'language' (what speakers actually produce, when we say that they 'are speaking the language') can be described only indirectly, and at the present time very inadequately, on the basis of a prior description of the sentences of the 'language'. This distinction between utterances and sentences is fundamental in most modern linguistic theory. But we can develop certain preliminary notions without invoking it. Although we shall use the terms 'sentence' and 'utterance' more or less synonymously throughout the next three chapters, the reader should bear in mind that the relationships we are describing hold within what will later be established as sentences (units of *langue*), not utterances (instances of *parole*).

2

THE STRUCTURE OF LANGUAGE

2.1 Introductory

2.1.1 'Sounds' and 'words'

If we were to ask a non-linguist what are the ultimate units of language, the building-blocks, so to speak, out of which utterances are constructed, he might well reply that the ultimate units of language are 'sounds' and 'words'. He might add that words are made up of sequences of sounds, each sound being represented, ideally, by a particular letter of the alphabet (in the case of languages customarily represented by a system of alphabetic writing); and that, whereas the words of a language have a meaning, the sounds do not (their sole function being to form words). These several propositions underlie the traditional view of language reflected in most grammars and dictionaries: the grammar gives rules for the construction of sentences out of words, and the dictionary tells us what the individual words mean. In the following chapters, we shall have occasion to examine critically the terms 'sound', 'word', 'meaning' and 'sentence' which figure in these general statements about language. However, for the purpose of the present preliminary discussion of the structure of language, we may leave these terms undefined. Certain distinctions will be indicated in the course of this chapter and will be made explicit later.

2.1.2 Phonology, grammar and semantics

The traditional view of language incorporates the notions of *composition* (a more complex unit is composed of simpler, or smaller, units: a word is composed of sounds, a phrase of words, a clause of phrases, a sentence of clauses, and so on) and of *correlation* (each word is correlated with one or more meanings). If we use the term 'level' for the former and the term 'plane' for the latter we may say that, according to the model of language-structure which we have provisionally adopted, every language can be described in terms of two *planes*: 'form' and 'meaning', or preferably (for the traditional terms

3 [53] LIT

have various conflicting interpretations in linguistics) *expression* and *content*. And the expression-plane of language can be described in terms of (at least) two *levels*: that of sounds and that of words. To introduce now the terms generally used by linguists: the sounds of a given language are described by *phonology*; the form of its words and the manner of their combination in phrases, clauses and sentences by *grammar*; and the meaning, or content, of the words (and of the units composed of them) by *semantics*.

2.1.3 The 'double articulation' of language

Linguists sometimes talk of the 'double articulation' (or 'double structure') of language; and this phrase is frequently understood, mistakenly, to refer to the correlation of the two planes of expression and content. What is meant is that the units on the 'lower' level of phonology (the sounds of a language) have no function other than that of combining with one another to form the 'higher' units of grammar (words). It is by virtue of the double structure of the expression-plane that languages are able to represent economically many thousands of different words. For each word may be represented by a different combination of a relatively small set of sounds, just as each of the infinitely large set of natural numbers is distinguished in the normal decimal notation by a different combination of the ten basic digits.

2.1.4 'Level' versus 'plane', 'expression' versus 'content'

Having recognized the two planes of expression and content and the two levels of phonology and grammar we have not, of course, advanced at all beyond the traditional view of the structure of language. We must now see what it is that characterizes the more modern approach to the study of language to which it is customary to attach the label 'structural linguistics'.

2.2 Substance and form

2.2.1 Structure of the vocabulary

Few people these days would maintain that the correlation of a particular word and a particular meaning is other than conventional. The long controversy between the 'naturalists' and the 'conventionalists' may be considered closed (cf. 1.2.2). But the very means by which the conventionality of the relationship between 'form' and 'meaning' (between *expression* and *content*) is demonstrated, namely the citation from different languages of quite different words referring to the same thing or having the same meaning (e.g. *tree* in English, *Baum* in German, *arbre* in French), tends to encourage the view that the vocabulary of any given language is essentially a list of names associated by convention with independently existing things or meanings.

And yet one soon comes to realize, in learning a foreign language, that there are distinctions of meaning made in one language that are not made in another; that learning the vocabulary of another language is not simply a matter of acquiring a fresh set of labels to attach to familiar meanings. To take an example: the English word *brother-in-law* can be translated into Russian as *zjatj, shurin, svojak,* or *deverj*; and one of these four Russian words, *zjatj,* must sometimes be translated as *son-in-law*. From this it should not be concluded, however, that the word *zjatj* has two meanings, and that in one of its meanings it is equivalent to the other three. All four words in Russian have a different meaning. It so happens that Russian brings together (under *zjatj*) both sister's husband and daughter's husband, but distinguishes wife's brother (*shurin*), wife's sister's husband (*svojak*) and husband's brother (*deverj*). So there is really no word which means 'brother-in-law' in Russian, just as there is no word which means 'zjatj' in English.

Every language has its own semantic *structure*. To the degree that the meanings of one language can be brought into one-to-one correspondence with those of another we will say that the two languages are *semantically isomorphic* (have the same semantic structure). The degree of semantic isomorphism between different languages varies considerably. In general (this point will be discussed and exemplified more fully in the chapter on semantics: cf. 9.4.6), the structure of the vocabulary of a particular language will reflect the distinctions and equivalences which are of importance in the culture of the society in which the language operates. The degree of semantic isomorphism between any two languages will therefore depend very largely upon the amount of overlap there is in the culture of the two societies using those languages. Whether there are, or could be, two languages whose vocabularies are to no degree whatsoever isomorphic with one another is a question with which we need not be concerned. We can at least allow for the possibility that all the meanings recognized by a given language are unique to that language and have no validity or relevance outside it.

2.2.2   Substance and form

De Saussure and his followers account for the differences in the semantic structure of different languages in terms of a distinction between *substance* and *form*. By the *form* of the vocabulary (or the form of the content-plane: cf. 2.1.4) is meant the abstract structure of relationships which a particular language imposes, as it were, on the same underlying substance. Just as the same lump of children's clay can be fashioned into objects of different shapes and sizes, so the *substance* (or medium) within which distinctions and equivalences of meaning are drawn can be organized into a different form in different languages. De Saussure himself conceived of the substance of meaning (the substance of the content-plane) as the whole mass of thoughts and emotions common to mankind independently of the language they speak—a kind of nebulous and undifferentiated conceptual medium out of which meanings are formed in particular languages by the conventional association of a certain complex of sounds with a certain part of the conceptual medium. (The reader should note that in this section the terms 'substance' and 'form' are being employed in the sense in which they were introduced into linguistics by de Saussure: cf. 4.1.5.)

2.2.3   Semantic structure exemplified with colour-terms

There is much in de Saussure's account of semantic structure that may be attributed to outdated psychological theories and rejected. The whole notion of a conceptual substance independent of language and culture is of doubtful validity. Indeed, many philosophers, linguists and psychologists today would be reluctant to admit that meanings can be described satisfactorily as ideas or concepts in the mind. The notion of substance can be illustrated, however, for certain words at least, without the postulation of an underlying conceptual medium. It is an established fact that the colour-terms of particular languages cannot always be brought into one-to-one correspondence with one another: for example, the English word *brown* has no equivalent in French (it would be translated as *brun, marron*, or even *jaune*, according to the particular shade and the kind of noun it qualifies); the Hindi word *pilā* is translated into English as *yellow*, *orange* or even *brown* (although there are different words for other shades of 'brown'); there is no equivalent to *blue* in Russian—the words *goluboj* and *sinij* (usually translated as 'light blue' and 'dark blue', respectively), refer to what are in Russian distinct colours, not different shades of the same colour, as their translation into English might suggest. To make the point as generally as possible, let us compare part of the English vocabulary with part of the vocabulary of three hypothetical languages: A, B and C. For simplicity, we will restrict our attention to the area of the spectrum covered by the five

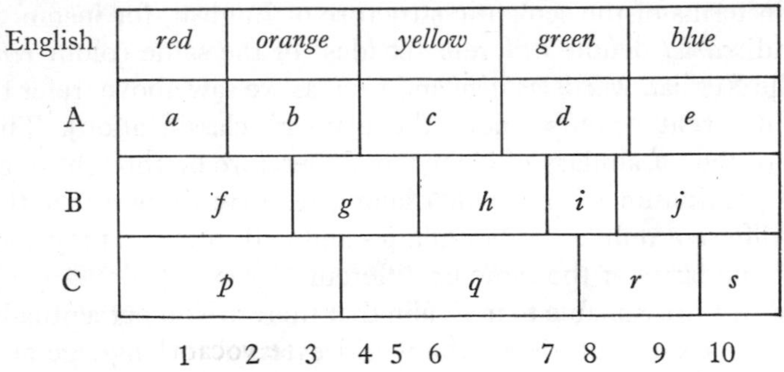

English	red	orange	yellow	green	blue
A	a	b	c	d	e
B	f	g	h	i	j
C	p		q	r	s

1 2 3 4 5 6 7 8 9 10

Fig. 1.

terms: *red, orange, yellow, green, blue*. We will assume that the same area is covered by the five words a, b, c, d and e in A, by the five words f, g, h, i and j in B and by the four words p, q, r and s in C (see Fig. 1). From the diagram, it is clear that language A is semantically isomorphic with English (in this part of its vocabulary): it has the same number of colour-terms, and the boundaries between the area of the spectrum covered by each of them coincide with the boundaries of the English words. But neither B nor C is isomorphic with English. Although B has the same number of terms as English, the boundaries come at different places in the spectrum; and C has a different number of terms (with the boundaries in different places). In order to appreciate the practical implications of this, let us imagine that we have ten objects (numbered 1 to 10 in Fig. 1), each of which reflects light at a different wavelength, and that we wish to group them according to their colour. In English, object 1 would be described as 'red' and object 2 as 'orange'—they would differ in colour; in language A they would also differ in colour, being described as a and b, respectively. But in B and C they would be described by the same colour-term, f or p. On the other hand, objects 2 and 3 would be distinguished by B (as f and g), but brought together by English and by A and C (as 'orange', b and p). From the diagram it is clear that there are many cases of non-equivalence of this kind. It is not being maintained, of course, that the speakers of B cannot see any difference in the colour of objects 1 and 2. They will presumably be able to distinguish them in much the same way as the speakers of English can distinguish objects 2 and 3, by referring to them as *reddish-orange* and *yellow-orange*. The point is that the primary classification is different; and the secondary classification rests upon and presupposes the primary (in terms of the semantic structure of English, for instance, *crimson* and *scarlet* denote different 'shades' of the same colour *red*, whereas the Russian words *goluboj* and *sinij*, as we saw above, refer to what are different colours under the primary classification). The substance of the vocabulary of colour may therefore be thought of as a physical continuum within which languages may draw either the same or a different number of boundaries and within which they may draw the boundaries at the same or different places.

It would be unreasonable to maintain that there are no perceptually discrete objects and features of the world external to language and independent of it; that everything is amorphous until it is given form by language. At the same time it is clear that the manner in which objects, flora and fauna, etc., are grouped together under particular words may vary from language to language: the Latin word *mus* refers to both mice and rats (as well as to certain other rodents); the French *singe* refers to both apes and monkeys; and so on. A rather more abstract notion of substance is required to bring facts of this kind within the scope of the Saussurean explanation of semantic structure. And there is quite clearly no possibility of accounting for the vocabulary of kinship in terms of the imposition of form upon an underlying physical substance. Only a limited number of words can be described in terms of their reference to contiguous areas within a physical continuum. And we shall see later that even the vocabulary of colour (which is frequently cited as one of the clearest examples of what is meant by the imposition of form on the substance of the content-plane) is rather more complex than is commonly supposed (cf. 9.4.5). The additional complexities do not affect the points that have been made in this section. It is sufficient that for at least some parts of the vocabulary one may postulate an underlying substance of content.

But the notion of semantic structure is independent of the assumption of substance. As the most general statement of what is meant by semantic structure—a statement which applies to all words, whether they refer to objects and features of the physical world or not—we may adopt the following formulation: the semantic structure of any system of words in the vocabulary is the network of semantic relations that hold between the words in the system in question. The nature of these relations we must leave for the chapter on semantics. The important point to notice in the definition of semantic structure that has just been given is that it makes use of the key-terms *system* and *relation*. Colour-words (like kinship-words, and many other sets of words in the vocabularies of languages) constitute an organized system of words which are related to one another in a certain way. Such systems are isomorphic if they have the same number of terms in them and if the terms are related in the same way.

2.2.4 *'Language is form, not substance'*

Before discussing the distinction of substance and form with respect to the expression-plane of language (where it is in fact of more general validity), it might be helpful to return briefly to de Saussure's analogy of the chess-game. First of all, it may be pointed out that the actual material out of which the chess-pieces are made is irrelevant to the operation of the game. They can be made of any material at all (wood, ivory, plastic, etc.), provided that the physical nature of the material is such as to maintain the significant differences of shape between the pieces in the conditions under which the game is normally played. (This last point, the physical stability of the material, is obviously important; it was taken for granted, rather than stressed, by de Saussure. Chess-pieces carved out of ice would not do, if the game was to be played in a heated room.) Not only is the material out of which the pieces are made irrelevant; so also are their particular shapes. All that is necessary is that each piece should be identifiable as one which by the rules of the game moves in a particular way. If one of the pieces is lost or broken, we can replace it with some other object (a coin or a piece of chalk, for example) and establish the convention that the substituted object will be treated for the purposes of the game as the piece it represents. The relationship between the shape of a piece and its function in the game is a matter of arbitrary convention. Provided that the conventions of interpretation are accepted by the participants, the game can be played equally well with pieces of any shape. If we draw the implications of the analogy in respect of the expression-plane of language, we shall come closer to understanding one of the fundamental principles of modern linguistics: to put it in de Saussure's own terms, *language is a form, not a substance*.

2.2.5 *'Realization' in substance*

As we saw in the previous chapter, the spoken language is prior to the written (cf. 1.4.2). In other words, the primary substance of the expression-plane of language is sound (in particular, that range of sound which can be produced by the human speech organs); and writing is essentially a technique for transferring the words and sentences of a language from the substance in which they are normally *realized* to the secondary substance of shape (visible marks on paper or stone, etc.). Further transference from the secondary to a tertiary substance is also possible, as, for instance, in the transmission of messages by teleprinter. The fact that this kind of transference can be carried out (one is tempted to call it 'transubstantiation') means that the structure of the expression-plane of language is very largely independent of the substance in which it is realized.

For simplicity, let us first of all consider the case of languages which make use of an alphabetic system of writing. We will assume that the sounds of the language are in one-to-one correspondence with the letters of the alphabet used to represent them (in other words, that each sound is represented by a different letter and each letter represents always the same sound). If this condition is met, there will be neither homography nor homophony—there will be one-to-one correspondence between the words of the written language and the words of the spoken language; and (on the simplifying assumption that sentences are composed of words, and nothing more) all the sentences of the written and spoken language will also be in one-to-one correspondence. The written and spoken language will therefore be isomorphic. (That the written and spoken language are never completely isomorphic, as we have seen already, is irrelevant to the argument at this point. To the degree that they are not isomorphic they are different languages. This will be one of the implications of the principle that language is form, not substance.)

To prevent confusion, we will use square brackets to distinguish sounds from letters (this is a standard notational convention: cf. 3.1.3). Thus [t], [e], etc., will denote sounds, and *t*, *e*, etc., will denote letters. We may now introduce a distinction between *formal units* and their *substantial realization* as sounds and letters. When we say that [t] is in correspondence with *t*, [e] with *e*, and in general that a particular sound is in correspondence with a particular letter, and *vice versa*, we can interpret this to mean that neither the sounds nor the letters are primary, but that they are both alternative realizations of the same formal units, which of themselves are quite abstract elements, independent of the substance in which they are realized. For the purpose of the present section let us call these formal units 'expression-elements'. Using numbers to refer to them and putting the numbers between slants, we may say that /1/ denotes a certain expression-element, which might be realized in *phonic substance* by the sound [t] and in *graphic substance* by the letter *t*; that /2/ denotes another expression-element, which might be realized by [e] and *e*; and so on.

Now it is clear that, just as the chess-pieces can be made out of various kinds of material, so the same set of expression-elements can be realized, not only in sound and shape, but in many other kinds of substance. For instance, each element could be realized by a light of a different colour, by a particular gesture, by the emission of a characteristic odour, by exerting pressure of a certain degree of intensity on the hand, and so on. It might be possible in fact to construct a system of communication within which each expression-element is realized by a different kind of substance—a system within which, for example, /1/ might be realized by a sound (of any kind whatsoever), /2/ by a light (of any colour), /3/ by a gesture of the hand, etc. However, we may neglect this possibility and concentrate rather upon the realization of expression-elements by means of differences in one homogeneous substance. This is far more typical of human language. Although spoken language may be associated with various conventional gestures and facial expressions, these gestures and expressions do not realize formal units of the same level as those realized by the constituent sounds of the accompanying words: that is to say, a particular gesture does not combine with sounds to make a word in the way that two or more sounds combine to make a word.

In principle, the expression-elements of language may be realized in any kind of substance, provided that the following conditions are satisfied. (*a*) The sender of a 'message' must have available the necessary apparatus for the production of the significant differences in the substance (differences of sound, shape, etc.), and the receiver of the message must have the apparatus necessary for the perception of these differences: in other words, the sender (speaker, writer, etc.), must have the requisite 'encoding' apparatus and the receiver (hearer, reader, etc.) must have the appropriate 'decoding' apparatus. (*b*) The substance itself, as the medium within which the differences are drawn, must be sufficiently stable to maintain the differences between the realizations of the expression-elements under the normal conditions of communication long enough for the transmission of messages between the sender and the receiver.

2.2.6   The substance of spoken and written language

Neither of these conditions requires much comment. Nevertheless, a brief comparison of speech and writing (more precisely, of phonic and graphic substance) might be helpful from the point of view of (a) their availability and convenience, and (b) their physical stability or durability.

In their speculations about the origins of human language many linguists have suggested that sound was a more convenient medium for the development of language than any of the available alternatives. By contrast with gestures or any other substance within which differences are perceived by the sense of sight (a very highly-developed sense in human beings), sound does not depend upon the presence of a source of light and is not so frequently obstructed by objects which lie in its path: it is therefore equally well suited for communication by day and by night. By contrast with various kinds of substance dependent upon the sense of touch for the production and perception of distinctions within them, sound does not require that the sender and receiver should be in very close proximity; and it leaves the hands free for other tasks. Whatever other factors may have influenced the development of human speech, it is clear that phonic substance (that range of sound which can be produced by the human speech organs and falls within the normal range of human hearing) satisfies the conditions of availability and convenience fairly well. Relatively few human beings are physically unable either to produce or to perceive differences of sound. Phonic substance also satisfies the condition of physical stability well enough for what one must assume to have been the most normal and most necessary form of communication in primitive societies.

Graphic substance differs somewhat from phonic substance in respect of convenience and availability: it requires the use of some implement or other, and does not leave the hands free for the performance of various co-operative tasks.

Far more important, however, are the differences between the two kinds of substance with regard to durability. Until recent times (with the invention of the telephone and sound-recording equipment), it was a characteristic of phonic substance that it did not serve as a very reliable medium for communication unless the sender and the receiver were present in the same place at the same time. (Oral tradition and the employment of a third person as a messenger were dependent upon memory.) Of themselves, as it were, sound-sequences died away and, if they were not 'decoded' on the spot, were lost for ever. But with the invention of writing an alternative and more durable medium was made available for 'encoding' language. Although writing was less convenient (and was therefore not used) for communication of a more ephemeral kind, it made possible the transmission of messages over considerable distances and also their preservation for future reference. These differences in the conditions under which speech and writing were, and still are, most typically employed—the one in unreflecting, face-to-face communication, the other in more carefully composed texts intended to be read and understood without the aid of all the clues in the immediate situation—go a long way towards explaining both the origin of writing in the first place and many of the subsequent divergences between written and spoken languages. As we have already seen, these differences are such that it would be inaccurate to say of languages with a long history of literacy behind them that writing is *merely* the transference of speech to an alternative substance (cf. 1.4.2). Granted the differences in the physical stability of phonic and graphic substance and their importance in the historical development of written and spoken languages, it remains true that both kinds of substance are sufficiently stable to maintain the perceptual differences between the sounds or shapes which realize the expression-elements in the conditions under which speech and writing are customarily employed.

2.2.7 *Arbitrariness of substantial realization*

We may turn now to the second of the points which de Saussure made about the substance in which language is realized: just as the shape of the chess-pieces is irrelevant to the operation of the game, so also are the particular distinctions of shape or sound whereby the expression-elements of language are identified. In other words, the association of a particular sound or letter with a particular expression-element is a matter of arbitrary convention. The point may be illustrated from English. Table 3 gives, in column (i), six of the expression-elements of English, numbered arbitrarily from 1 to 6; column (ii) gives their normal orthographic realizations, and column

Table 3

Expression-elements

(i)	(ii)	(iii)	(iv)	(v)	(vi)
/1/	t	[t]	p	[p]	e
/2/	e	[e]	i	[i]	b
/3/	b	[b]	d	[d]	d
/4/	d	[d]	b	[b]	p
/5/	i	[i]	e	[e]	t
/6/	p	[p]	t	[t]	i

Words

(vii)	(viii)	(ix)	(x)	(xi)
A	'bet'	dip	[dip]	dbe
B	'pet'	tip	[tip]	ibe
C	'bit'	dep	[dep]	dte
D	'pit'	tep	[tep]	ite
E	'bid'	deb	[deb]	dtp
F	'bed'	dib	[dib]	dbp

(iii) their realizations as sounds. (For simplicity, we will assume that the sounds, [t], [e], etc., are not further analysable and realize the minimal expression-elements of the language, as they are found, for example, in the words written *bet, pet, bid,* etc. Although this assumption will be questioned in the following chapter, the argument is unaffected by any subsequent modifications we may feel obliged to make.) Let us now establish a different arbitrary convention according to which /1/ is realized orthographically by *p*, /2/ by *i*, and so on; cf. column (iv). As a result, the word A (which means 'bet', and was formerly written *bet*) will now be written *dip*, the word B will be written *tip*, and so on: cf. columns (vii), (viii) and (ix). Quite clearly, every word and sentence of written English that is distinguished under the normal conventions of the orthography is distinguished under the new conventions. The language itself is totally unaffected by the change in its substantial realization.

The same argument applies with respect to the spoken language (but with certain limitations which we will introduce presently). Suppose that the expression-element /ɪ/ were realized in phonic substance as [p], /2/ as [i], and so on: cf. column (v). Then the word that is now written *bet* (and might still be written *bet*, since there is obviously no intrinsic connexion between the letters and the sounds) would be pronounced like the word that is now written *dip* (although it would still mean 'bet'); and so on for all other words: cf. column (x). Once again, the language itself is unchanged by this alteration in its substantial realization.

2.2.8 *Priority of the phonic substance*

There is, however, an important difference between the graphic and the phonic realization of language; and it is this difference which compels us to modify the strict Saussurian principle that the expression-elements are completely independent of the substance in which they are realized. Whereas there is nothing in the shape of the letters *d*, *b*, *e*, etc., which prohibits their combination with one another in any way we choose to select, certain combinations of sounds are un-pronounceable. For example, we might decide to adopt for the written language the set of realizations listed in column (vi) of the table, so that word A would be written *dbe*, word B *ibe*, and so on: cf. column (xi). The letter-sequences of column (xi) can be written or printed no less easily than those of column (ix). By contrast, such sound-complexes as would result from the substitution of [d] for [b], of [t] for [i] and of [p] for [d] in the word for 'bid' (the word E) would be unpronounceable. The fact that there are limits upon the pronounce-ability (and audibility) of certain groups or complexes of sounds means that the expression-elements of language, or rather their combinations, are partly determined by the nature of their primary substance and the 'mechanisms' of speech and hearing. Within the range of possibilities left open by the limits imposed by the condition of pronounceability (and audibility) each language has its own combinatorial restrictions, which may be referred to the phonological structure of the language in question.

Since we have not yet drawn a distinction between phonetics and phonology (cf. chapter 3), we must be content here with a rather imprecise statement of the point at issue. We will take for granted the classification of sounds into consonants and vowels; and we will assume that this classification is valid both in general phonetic theory and also in the description of the combinatorial possibilities for particular languages, including English. Now, the substitution of [p] for [t], of [e] for [i], etc. (cf. column (iv)), would not affect the pronunciation of the language, because (amongst other things) it holds constant under the substitution the consonantal and vocalic nature of the sounds. This not only guarantees the pronounceability of the resultant spoken words, but also respects their phonological structure (as words of English) in terms of the ratio of consonants to vowels and the way in which these two classes of sounds combine with one another. It should be clear, however, that other substitutions might be made which, though they might maintain pronounceability, would alter the balance of consonants and vowels and their patterns of combination in words. Nevertheless, provided that all the words of spoken English are kept distinct under the new system for realizing the expression-elements, the grammatical structure of the language would be unchanged. It is therefore in principle possible for two (or more) languages to be grammatically, but not phonologically, isomorphic. Languages are phonologically isomorphic if, and only if, the sounds of the one are in one-to-one correspondence with the sounds of the other and corresponding classes of sounds (e.g. consonants and vowels) conform to the same principles of combination. One-to-one correspondence between sounds does not imply identity. On the other hand, as we have seen, the principles of combination are not wholly independent of the physical nature of the sounds.

The conclusion to be drawn from the argument of the preceding two paragraphs supports the principle that the spoken language is to be given priority over the written language in general linguistic theory (cf. 1.4.2). The patterns of combination to which the letters conform in the written language are totally inexplicable in terms of the shapes of the letters, whereas they are at least partly explicable in terms of the physical nature of the sounds in the corresponding spoken words. For example, u and n are related to one another in shape in precisely the same way as d and p. But this fact is completely irrelevant to the combination of these letters with one another in the written words of English. Far more relevant is the fact that the letters in question are in partial correspondence with the sounds of the spoken language. The study of the substance of sound is therefore of more central concern to the linguist than is the investigation of graphic substance and writing-systems.

2.2.9 Combination and contrast

The only properties that expression-elements have, considered in abstraction from their substantial realization, are (i) their *combinatorial function*—their capacity to combine with one another in groups or complexes which serve to identify and distinguish words and sentences (and we have just seen that the combinatorial properties of the expression-elements of language are in fact partly determined by the nature of their primary substance, sound) and (ii) their *contrastive function*—their difference from one another. It was the second of these properties that de Saussure had in mind when he said that the expression-elements (and, more generally, all linguistic units) are essentially negative in nature: the principle of *contrast* (or opposition) is fundamental in modern linguistic theory. The point may be illustrated with reference to Table 3 on p. 64. Each of the expression-elements (numbered from 1 to 6 in the table) contrasts with, or is in *opposition* with, each other element that could occur in the same position in English words, in the sense that the substitution of one element for another (more precisely, the substitution of the substantial realization of one element for the substantial realization of another) will have the effect of changing one word into another. For instance, the word A (*bet*) is distinguished from the word B (*pet*) in that it has /3/ rather than /6/ initially, A is distinguished from C (*bit*) in that it has /2/ rather than /5/ medially, and A is distinguished from F (*bed*) in that it has /1/ rather than /4/ in final position. On the basis of these six words, we can say that /1/ is in contrast with /4/, /2/ with /5/, and /3/ with /6/. (By bringing other words forward for comparison we should of course be able to establish other contrasts and other expression-elements.) As a formal unit, and within the limits of the sample of the language we are considering, /1/ can be defined as 'that element which is not /4/, and which combines with either /2/ or /5/ and either /3/ or /6/'; and all the other elements in the table can be defined similarly. In general, any formal unit can be defined (i) as being distinct from all other elements which contrast with it, and (ii) as having certain combinatorial properties.

2.2.10 Discreteness of expression-elements

Certain important principles may now be introduced on the basis of the distinction between form and substance. Let us take for the purpose of illustration the contrast between /3/ and /6/, which is maintained in the spoken language by the difference between the sounds [b] and [p]. As we have seen, the fact that it is this particular difference in sound, rather than some other, is irrelevant to the structure of English. It should also be noticed that the difference between [b] and [p] is not absolute, but relative. That is to say, what we have been referring to as 'the sound [b]' or 'the sound [p]' are ranges of sound; and there is in fact no determinate point at which the '[b]-range' begins and the '[p]-range' ends (or *vice versa*). From the phonetic point of view, the difference between [b] and [p] is a matter of continuous variation. But the difference between the expression-elements /3/ and /6/ is absolute—in the following sense. The words A and B (*bet* and *pet*), and all other words of English kept apart by the occurrence of either /3/ or /6/, do not gradually change into one another in the spoken language as [b] is gradually varied towards [p]. There might be some point at which it is impossible to tell whether A or B was intended, but there is no word of English which is in some sense half-way between the two with respect to its grammatical function or meaning and is identified by a sound midway between [b] and [p]. From this it follows that the expression-plane of language is constructed of discrete units. But these discrete units are realized in physical substance by ranges of sound within which there is the possibility of considerable variation. Since the expression-units must not be confused with one another in their substantial realization as sounds, there must be some 'safety-margin' between the range of sounds which realizes one and the range of sounds which realizes another. Certain contrasts may be lost in the course of time or may not be maintained in all words by all speakers of a language. This fact may be accounted for by assuming that the contrasts in question fall below the 'threshold' of importance in the number of utterances of the language they keep distinct. It does not mean that the difference between certain pairs of expression-elements is relative, rather than absolute.

2.2.11   *Grammatical and phonological words*

We are now in a position to eliminate an ambiguity in the term 'composition', as it was used in the previous section. It was said that words were composed of sounds (or letters) and that sentences, clauses and phrases were composed of words (cf. 2.1.1). It will now be clear that the term 'word' is ambiguous. In fact, it is customarily used in a number of different senses, but here we need distinguish only two.

As formal, grammatical units, words may be regarded as totally abstract entities, whose only properties are that they have a particular contrastive and combinatorial function (what the principles of contrast and combination are for grammatical units we shall discuss later). But these *grammatical* words are realized by groups or complexes of expression-elements, each of which (in the spoken language) is realized by a particular sound. We may refer to the complexes of expression-elements as *phonological* words. That such a distinction is necessary (and we will return to it later: cf. 5.4.3) is evident from the following considerations. First of all, the internal structure of a phonological word is in general irrelevant to the fact that it realizes a particular grammatical word. For example, the grammatical word A (which means 'bet': cf. the table on p. 64) happens to be realized by the complex of expression-elements /321/; but it might equally well be realized by a complex of different expression-elements, not necessarily three in number. (Notice that this is not the same point as that made earlier about the realization of the expression-elements. A phonological word is not composed of sounds, but of expression-elements.) Furthermore, the grammatical and phonological words of a language are not necessarily in one-to-one correspondence. For instance, the phonological word which we may identify by its normal orthographic representation, *down*, realizes at least two grammatical words (cf. *down the hill*: *the soft down on his cheek*): they are different grammatical words because they have different contrastive and combinatorial functions in sentences. An instance of the converse of this phenomenon is afforded by the alternative realizations, which may be written *dreamed* and *dreamt*, of one and the same grammatical word (the past tense of a particular verb). It may be pointed out in passing that the two phenomena that have just been exemplified are commonly treated as kinds of homonymy and synonymy (cf. 1.2.3). We have made no appeal to the meaning of the words in the argument presented above, but only to their grammatical function and to their phonological realization. To summarize the points that have been made: grammatical words are realized by phonological words (and there is no presupposition of one-to-one correspondence); and phonological words are composed of expression-elements. It is clearly possible to distinguish yet a third sense of the term 'word', according to which we would say that the English word written *cap* and the French word *cap* are identical: they are the same in (graphic) substance. But we are not generally concerned with the substantial identity of words in linguistics. The relationship between the grammatical word and its substantial realization in sound or shape is indirect, in the sense that it is handled through the intermediate level of phonology.

2.2.12 'Abstractness' of linguistic theory

The considerations of this section might seem to be remote from all practical concerns. This is not so. It is the rather abstract approach to the study of language made possible by the distinction of substance and form that has given us a greater understanding of the historical development of languages than was possible in the nineteenth century and has led, more recently, to the construction of more comprehensive theories of the structure, the acquisition and the use of human language. And such theories have been put to eminently practical purposes in the development of more efficient means of teaching languages, in the construction of better systems of telecommunication, in cryptography and in the design of systems for the analysis of languages by computer. In linguistics, as elsewhere, abstract theory and practical application go hand in hand; but the theory is prior to its application and is justified independently by its contribution to our greater understanding of the subject-matter it deals with.

2.3   Paradigmatic and syntagmatic relations

2.3.1   The notion of distribution

Every linguistic unit (with the exception of the sentence: cf. 5.2.1) is to a greater or less degree restricted with respect to the contexts in which it can occur. This fact is expressed by saying that every linguistic unit (below the level of the sentence) has a characteristic *distribution*. If two (or more) units occur in the same range of contexts they are said to be *distributionally equivalent* (or to have the same distribution); if they have no contexts in common they are *in complementary distribution*. Between the two extremes of total equivalence and complementary distribution there are two kinds of partial equivalence that we need to recognize: (*a*) The distribution of one unit may *include* (without being totally equivalent to) the distribution of another: if x occurs in all the contexts in which y occurs, but there are some contexts in which y but not x occurs, then the distribution of y includes the distribution of x. (*b*) The distribution of two (or more) units may *overlap* (or intersect): if there are some contexts in which both *x* and *y* occur, but neither *x* nor *y* occurs in all the contexts in which the other occurs, then *x* and *y* are said to have an overlapping distribution. (To those readers who are familiar with certain elementary notions of formal logic and mathematics, it will be clear that the various kinds of distributional relationship that hold between linguistic units can be brought within the scope of class-

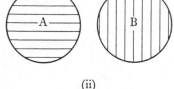

(i)

Distributional
equivalence

(ii)

Complementary distribution

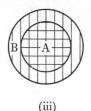
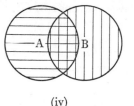

(iii)

Distributional inclusion

(iv)

Overlapping distribution

Fig. 2. Distributional relations (*x* occurs in the set of contexts A, and B is the set of contexts in which *y* occurs).

logic and set-theory. The fact that this is so is highly relevant to the study of the logical foundations of linguistic theory. What one might refer to loosely as 'mathematical' linguistics is now a very important part of the subject. Although we cannot go into the details of the various branches of 'mathematical linguistics' in the present elementary treatment of linguistic theory, we shall make reference to some of the more important points of contact as the occasion arises.)

It should be emphasized that the term 'distribution' is applied to the range of contexts in which a linguistic unit occurs only in so far as that range of contexts can be brought within the scope of a *systematic* statement of the restrictions determining the occurrence of the unit in question. What is here meant by 'systematic' may be explained by way of an example. The elements /l/ and /r/ of English are at least partially equivalent in distribution (for the convention of oblique strokes, cf. 2.2.5): both may occur in a number of otherwise phonologically-identical words (cf. *light*: *right*, *lamb*: *ram*, *blaze*: *braise*, *climb*: *crime*, etc.). But many of the words in which one of the elements occurs cannot be matched with otherwise phonologically-identical words in which the other occurs: there is no word *srip* to match *slip*, no *tlip* to match *trip*, no *brend* to match *blend*, no *blick* to match *brick*, and so on. However, there is an important difference between the non-occurrence of words like *srip* and *tlip*, on the one hand, and of words like *brend* and *blick*, on the other. The first pair (and others like them) are excluded by certain general principles which govern the phonological structure of English words: there are no words which begin with /tl/ or /sr/ (the statement could be made in more general terms, but this formulation of the principle will suffice for our present purpose). By contrast, no such systematic statement can be made about the distribution of /l/ and /r/ which would account for the non-occurrence of *blick* and *brend*. Both elements are found elsewhere in the contexts /b-i.../ and /b-e.../: cf. *blink*: *brink*, *blessed*: *breast*, etc. From the point of view of their phonological structure *brend* and *blick* (unlike *tlip* and *srip*) are acceptable words of English. It is a matter of 'chance', as it were, that they have not been given a grammatical function and a meaning, and put to use in the language.

The point that has just been illustrated by means of a phonological example applies also at the grammatical level. Not all combinations of words are acceptable. Of the unacceptable combinations, some can be accounted for in terms of a general distributional classification of the words of the language, whereas others must be explained by reference to the meaning of the particular words or to some other fact specific to them as individual words. We shall return to this question in a later chapter (cf. 4.2.9). For the purpose of the present argument, it is sufficient to observe that distributional equivalence, total or partial, does not imply absolute identity in the range of contexts in which the units in question occur: what it implies is identity in so far as the contexts are specified by the phonological and grammatical regularities of the language.

2.3.2   *Free variation*

As we saw in the previous section, every linguistic unit has both a contrastive and a combinatorial function. Now it is clear that two units cannot be in contrast unless they are at least partially equivalent in distribution (for units that are in complementary distribution the question of contrast does not arise). Units which occur, but are not in contrast with one another, in a given context are *in free variation*. For example, the vowels of the two words *leap* and *get* contrast in most contexts in which they both occur (cf. *bet*: *beat*, etc.), but are in free variation in the alternative pronunciations of the word *economics*. Both in phonology and in semantics, one must be careful not to confuse free variation (equivalence of function in context) with distributional equivalence (occurrence in the same range of contexts). What is meant by free variation and contrast will depend upon the nature of the units to which the terms are applied and the point of view from which they are regarded. As we have seen, two expression-elements are in contrast if the substitution of one for the other in the same context produces a different word or sentence; otherwise they are in free variation. But words (and other grammatical units) may be looked at from two different viewpoints. It is only when one is concerned with their grammatical function (roughly speaking, whether they are nouns, verbs or adjectives, etc.) that the notions of contrast and free variation are interpreted in terms of distributional equivalence; and this is because there is a direct connexion between grammatical function and distribution (cf. 4.2.6). Although there is also some connexion between the meaning of a word and its distribution, neither is completely determined by the other; and for that reason the two notions are theoretically distinct. In semantics free variation and contrast are to be interpreted as 'sameness and difference of meaning'. (It is more usual, however, to employ the traditional term 'synonymy', rather than 'free variation', in semantics.)

2.3.3 *'Paradigmatic' and 'syntagmatic'*

By virtue of its potentiality of occurrence in a certain context a linguistic unit enters into relations of two different kinds. It enters into *paradigmatic* relations with all the units which can also occur in the same context (whether they contrast or are in free variation with the unit in question); and it enters into *syntagmatic* relations with the other units of the same level with which it occurs and which constitute its context. To return to the example used in the previous section: by virtue of its potentiality of occurrence in the context /-et/ the expression-element /b/ stands in paradigmatic relationship with /p/, /s/, etc.; and in syntagmatic relationship with /e/ and /t/. Likewise,

/e/ is in paradigmatic relationship with /i/, /a/, etc., and in syntagmatic relationship with /b/ and /t/. And /t/ is related paradigmatically with /d/, /n/, etc., and syntagmatically with /b/ and /e/.

Paradigmatic and syntagmatic relationships are also relevant at the word-level, and indeed at every level of linguistic description. For example, by virtue of its potentiality of occurrence in such contexts as *a...of milk*, the word *pint* contracts paradigmatic relations with such other words as *bottle, cup, gallon*, etc., and syntagmatic relations with *a, of* and *milk*. In fact, words (and other grammatical units) enter into paradigmatic and syntagmatic relations of various kinds. 'Potentiality of occurrence' can be interpreted with or without regard to the question whether the resultant phrase or sentence is meaningful; with or without regard to the situations in which actual utterances are produced; with or without regard to the dependencies that hold between different sentences in connected discourse; and so on. We shall have more to say later about the different conditions that can be imposed upon the interpretation of the term 'potentiality of occurrence' (cf. 4.2.1, on the notion of 'acceptability'). Here it must be emphasized that all linguistic units contract syntagmatic and paradigmatic relations with other units of the same level (expression-elements with expression-elements, words with words, etc.); that the *context* of a linguistic unit is specifiable in terms of its syntagmatic relations; and that the range of contexts in which it is said to occur, as well as the extent of the class of units with which it is said to be paradigmatically related, will depend upon the interpretation explicitly or implicitly attached to 'potentiality of occurrence' (or 'acceptability').

This last point has been formulated in what might appear to be an unnecessarily devious manner. It will become clear later that one of the advantages of this formulation is that it enables us to draw the distinction between grammatical sentences and meaningful sentences, not in terms of the combination of grammatical units in the one case and of semantic units ('meanings') in the other, but in terms of the degree or kind of 'acceptability' that is preserved by various combinations of the same units.

2.3.4   *The interdependence of paradigmatic and syntagmatic relations*

Two important points must now be made about paradigmatic and syntagmatic relations. The first of these, which (together with distinction of substance and form) might be taken as the defining characteristic of modern, 'structural' linguistics, is as follows: linguistic units have no validity independently of their paradigmatic and syntagmatic relations with other units. (This is a more specific formulation of the general 'structural' principle that every linguistic unit has a certain place in a system of relationships: cf. 1.4.6.) To illustrate from the level of expression-elements: In our earlier discussion of such words as *bet*, *pet*, etc., in English, it was assumed that all these words were realized as sequences of three expression-elements (just as they are all written as sequences of three letters by the orthographic conventions of the language). We may now verify this assumption. Let us suppose, contrary to the facts, that there were words whose realization in sound was identical with that of *put*, *tit*, *cat*, *pup*, *tip*, *cap*, *puck*, and *tick*, but no words realized ('pronounced') like *but*, *pet*, *pit*, *bit*, *cut*, *gut*, *kit*, *duck*, *cab*, *cad*, *kid*, *cud*, etc. What is being assumed (to put it in rather imprecise phonetic terms) is that all the phonological words realized as complexes of three sounds can be described, from the point of view of their substantial realization (i.e. as phonetic words), as sequences of consonant + vowel + consonant (where the consonants are [p], [t] or [k] and the vowels [u], [i] and [a]—for simplicity, we have assumed no other consonants or vowels), but that the only combinations of consonant and vowel possible in first and second position of the sequence are [pu], [ti] and [ka]. Given this situation, it is clear that [u], [i] and [a] do not realize three distinct expression-elements of the language since they are not in paradigmatic relationship (and, *a fortiori*, not in contrast). Just how many expression-elements would be recognized in a situation of this kind (and it is not at all untypical of what is found in language) depends upon certain more particular phonological principles which we will discuss later. We might say that in each word there are only two positions of contrast, of which the first is 'filled' by one of three consonant-vowel complexes and the second by one of three consonants: we might therefore recognize six expression-elements (realized as /1/: [ka], /2/: [pu], /3/: [ti], /4/: [p], /5/: [t] and /6/: [k]). Alternatively, we might recognize four expression-elements, of which three are realized by the consonants [p], [t] and [k], occurring in initial and final position, and the fourth, which occurs in medial position, is realized by a vowel, the phonetic quality of which is determined by the preceding consonant. The point is therefore that one cannot first establish the elements and then state their permissible combinations. The elements are determined by taking account simultaneously of their paradigmatic and syntagmatic relations. The reason why we recognize three positions of contrast in the English words *bet, pet, bit, pit, bid, tip, tap*, etc., is that paradigmatic and syntagmatic relations can be established at three points. We shall see that the interdependence of the paradigmatic and syntagmatic *dimensions* is a principle that holds at all levels of language-structure.

2.3.5 'Syntagmatic' does not imply 'sequential'

The second important point is the following: syntagmatic relations do not necessarily presuppose an ordering of units in linear sequence, such that the substantial realization of one element must precede the substantial realization of another in time. Compare, for instance, the two Chinese words *hào* ('day') and *hǎo* ('good'), which differ from one another phonologically in that the first has what is conventionally referred to as 'the fourth tone' (/ˋ/, realized as a fall in the pitch of the syllable from high to low) and the second has 'the third tone' (/ˇ/, realized as a variation in the pitch of the syllable from medium to low and back to medium). The two elements, /ˋ/ and /ˇ/, are in paradigmatic contrast in the context /hao/; that is to say, in this context (and many others) they enter into the same syntagmatic relations. If we say that one word is to be analysed phonologically as /hao/ + /ˋ/ and the other as /hao/ + /ˇ/, it is obviously not being implied that the substantial realization of the tone follows the substantial realization of the rest of the word. Language-utterances are spoken in time and can therefore be segmented into a sequence of successive sounds or complexes of sounds. But whether or not this time-sequence is relevant to the structure of the language depends once again upon the paradigmatic and syntagmatic relations of the linguistic units and not, in principle, on the successivity of their substantial realizations.

Relative sequence is one of the potentialities of the phonic substance (as it is also one of the derivative potentialities of graphic substance under the conventions of left-to-right, right-to-left or up-to down writing) which may or may not be actualized. The application of the principle may be illustrated conveniently from the grammatical level. English is a language with what is commonly called 'fixed word order', and Latin a language with 'free word order'. (In fact, the word-order of English is not completely 'fixed' and the word-order of Latin is not completely 'free', but the difference between the two languages is sufficiently clear for the purpose of the present illustration.) In particular, an English sentence consisting of a subject, a verb and an object (e.g. *Brutus killed Caesar*) will normally be spoken (and written) with the substantial realizations of the three units in question sequentially-ordered as subject + verb + object, and the permutation of the two nouns or noun-phrases will have the effect of rendering the sentence ungrammatical or converting it into a different sentence: *Brutus killed Caesar* and *Caesar killed Brutus* are different sentences; although *The chimpanzee ate some bananas* is a sentence, *Some bananas ate the chimpanzee* (we will assume) is not. By contrast, *Brutus necavit Caesarem* and *Caesarem necavit Brutus* are alternative substantial realizations of the same sentence ('Brutus killed Caesar'), as are *Caesar necavit Brutum* and *Brutum necavit Caesar* ('Caesar killed Brutus'). The relative order in which words occur in the Latin sentence is therefore grammatically irrelevant, although of course the words cannot be spoken other than in one order or another.

2.3.6 *Sequential and non-sequential syntagmatic relations*

Let us now make the point in a more general way. For simplicity, we will assume that we are dealing with two classes of units (or tentatively-established units), the members of each class being in paradigmatic relationship with one another. The classes are X, with a and b as members, and Y, with p and q as members: using a standard notation for expressing class-membership,

$$X = \{a, b\}, \quad Y = \{p, q\}.$$

(These equations may be read as follows: 'X is a class whose members are a and b', 'Y is a class whose members are p and q'.) The substantial realization of each unit is represented by the corresponding italic letter (*a* realizes a, etc., and X and Y are variables standing for the realizations of the units), and we will assume that these substantial realizations cannot occur simultaneously (they might be consonants and vowels, or words), but are sequentially-ordered relative to one another. There are three relevant possibilities: (i) the sequence may be 'fixed' in the sense that, say, X necessarily precedes Y (i.e. *ap, aq, bp, bq* occur, but not *pa, qa, pb, qb*); (ii) the sequence may be 'free' in the sense that both XY and YX occur, but $XY = YX$ (where ' = ' means 'is equivalent to'—equivalence being defined for the particular level of description); (iii) the sequence may be 'fixed' (or 'free') in the different sense that both XY and YX occur, but $XY \neq YX$ (' $\neq$ ' means 'is not equivalent to'). It may be observed in passing that the three possibilities are not always distinguished in discussing such questions as word-order. Of the three possibilities, the last two are the simplest to handle from a theoretical point of view. In the case of (ii), since XY and YX are not in contrast, the units a, b, p and q, as they are realized in such sequences as *ap* or *pa*, are in a *non-sequential syntagmatic relationship* (this is the situation with respect to the words in a language with free word order). In the case of (iii), since XY contrasts with YX, the units are in a *sequential syntagmatic relationship* (this is the situation with respect to the adjective and noun, for certain adjectives, in French). It is in the case of (i), which is extremely common, that confusion is likely to arise. Since YX does not occur, the members of the classes X and Y cannot be sequentially-related at that level. On the other hand, at some point in the description of the language, we must specify the obligatory sequence of their realizations in substance; it may therefore serve the purpose of economy in the integration of one level with another if instances of (iii) are assimilated with instances of (ii). It was by tacit appeal to this principle that we said earlier that English words like *bet*, *pet*, etc., had the phonological structure of consonant + vowel + consonant (using the terms 'consonant' and 'vowel' for classes of expression-elements). That some of the syntagmatic relationships between the expression-elements in English are sequential is clear from the comparison of such words as *pat*, *apt*, *cat*, *act*, etc. Although the sequence CCV (consonant + consonant + vowel: the consonants in question being realized as [p], [t], [k], [b], [d] and [g]) does not occur, both CVC and at least some instances of VCC do, as we have just seen. At the same time there are systematic restrictions upon the co-occurrence of consonants in VCC: for example, a word that would be realized in substance as [atp] or [atk] is systematically excluded; so, too, are [akk], [app], [att]. English therefore exemplifies both (i) and (iii) in the phonological structure of the words we have been considering. By assimilating them to the same sequentially-ordered formulae we simplify the statement of their substantial realization. It should be stressed, however, that this does not mean we must not also bring out the difference between such 'accidental' gaps in the English vocabulary as [git] or [ped] and such systematically-excluded 'words' as [pti] or [atp] (cf. 2.3.1).

Further discussion of the question of sequence would be out of place at this point. We shall return to it in later chapters. But before we continue with the exposition, it should be emphasized that the whole of the present discussion has been deliberately restricted by the assumption that all units in syntagmatic relationship co-occur on equal terms and that there are no groupings within complexes of such units. The discussion may also appear to have been based on the additional assumption that units are necessarily realized each by one and only one isolable segment or feature of the phonic substance. This is not the case, as we shall see later. The two general points that have been made are these: (1) the paradigmatic and the syntagmatic dimensions are interdependent, and (2) the syntagmatic dimension is not necessarily time-ordered.

2.3.7 'Marked' and 'unmarked'

So far we have recognized only two possibilities for units in paradigmatic relationship: that they should be in contrast or in free variation. It is frequently the case that of two units in contrast (and for simplicity we may restrict ourselves to two-term contrasts) one will be positive, or *marked*, the other being neutral, or *unmarked*. What is meant by these terms may be made clear by way of an example. Most English nouns have a plural and a singular form which are related, as are *boys*: *boy*, *days*: *day*, *birds*: *bird*, etc. The plural is positively marked by the final *s*, whereas the singular is unmarked. Another way of expressing what has just been said would be that in a given context the presence of a particular unit is in contrast with its absence. When this situation holds it is usually the case that the unmarked form is more general in sense or has a wider distribution than the marked form. And it has become customary to employ the terms 'marked' and 'unmarked' in a rather more abstract sense, such that the marked and unmarked members of a contrasting pair are not necessarily distinguished by the presence and absence of a particular overt unit. For instance, from the semantic point of view the words *dog* and *bitch* are unmarked and marked for the contrast of sex. The word *dog* is semantically unmarked (or neutral), since it can be applied to either males or females (*That's a lovely dog you've got there: is it a he or a she?*). But *bitch* is marked (or positive), since it is restricted to females and may be used in contrast with the unmarked term to determine the sense of the latter as negative, rather than neutral (*Is it a dog or a bitch?*). That is to say, the unmarked term has a more general sense, neutral with respect to a certain contrast; its more specific negative sense is derivative and secondary, being a consequence of its contextual opposition with the positive (non-neutral) term. It follows from the particular relationship that holds between the words *dog* and *bitch* that, whereas both *female dog* and *male dog* are perfectly acceptable, both *female bitch* and *male bitch* are semantically anomalous, the one being tautological and the other contradictory. This notion of 'marking' within paradigmatic oppositions is extremely important at all levels of language-structure.

2.3.8 Syntagmatic length

One final general point may be made here with respect to the relationship between the paradigmatic and the syntagmatic dimensions. If there is a given set of units to be distinguished in terms of their composition out of 'lower-level' elements, then (independently of certain statistical considerations, which we shall discuss in their following section) the 'length' of each 'higher-level' unit, measured in terms of the number of syntagmatically-related elements in the complex which identifies it, will be inversely proportionate to the number of elements in paradigmatic contrast within the complex. Let us suppose, for example, that in one system there are just two expression-elements (which we will refer to as 0 and 1) and that in another system there are eight expression-elements (which we will number from 0 to 7); and for simplicity, since this assumption does not affect the general principle, let us assume that all combinations of the expression-elements are permissible by the 'phonological' rules governing the two systems. If there are eight 'phonological' words to be distinguished within the first (binary) system, each of the words will be at least three elements long (000, 001, 010, 011, 100, 101, 110, 111), whereas each of the eight words can be distinguished by a single occurrence of a different element of the second (octal) system (0, 1, 2, 3, 4, 5, 6, 7). If there are sixty-four words to be distinguished, then complexes at least six elements long will be required by the binary system, and complexes at least two elements long by the octal system. In general, the minimal number of 'higher-level' units that can be distinguished by a set of 'lower-level' elements syntagmatically related in complexes is determined by the formula: $N = p_1 \times p_2 \times p_3 ... p_m$ (where N is the number of 'higher-level' units; where m is the number of positions of paradigmatic contrast for the 'lower-level' elements; and where p_1 denotes the number of elements in paradigmatic contrast in the first position, p_2 denotes the number of elements in paradigmatic contrast in the second position, and so on to the mth position). It will be observed that this formula does not presuppose either that the same elements can occur in all positions or that the number of elements in paradigmatic contrast is the same in all positions. The simple illustration given above for a binary and an octal system, within which all elements occur in all positions and all syntagmatic combinations are possible, is therefore merely a special case which falls within the scope of the more general formula:

$$2 \times 2 \times 2 = 8, \quad 2 \times 2 \times 2 \times 2 = 16, \text{ etc.,}$$

and

$$8 = 8, \quad 8 \times 8 = 64, \quad 8 \times 8 \times 8 = 512, \text{ etc.}$$

The reason why we chose to compare a binary system (with two elements) and an octal system (with eight elements) is that 8 is an integral power of 2: it is 2 to the power 3, rather than 2 to the power 3·5 or 4·27, etc. And this brings out clearly the relationship between paradigmatic contrast and syntagmatic 'length'. Other things being equal, the minimal length of our binary words will be three times that of our octal words. We shall make use of this particular numerical relationship in the following section. And we shall make appeal to the more general principle that distinctions can be made either syntagmatically or paradigmatically in later chapters, especially in the chapter dealing with semantics.

It should be observed that the notion of 'length' that has just been discussed is defined in terms of the number of positions of paradigmatic contrast within a syntagmatic complex. It is not necessarily bound to temporal sequence. This point (which follows from what was said earlier in this section: cf. 2.3.6) will be of considerable importance in the subsequent discussion of phonological, grammatical and semantic structure.

2.4 Statistical structure

2.4.1 Functional load

Not all paradigmatic contrasts are of equal importance in the functioning of language. They may vary considerably in respect of their *functional load*. To illustrate what is meant by this term we may consider some contrasts within the phonological system of English.

There are very many words of spoken English that are distinguished in their substantial realization by the occurrence of [p] rather than [b] in the same context (cf. *pet*: *bet*, *pin*: *bin*, *pack*: *back*, *cap*: *cab*, etc.); and, on the basis of this contrast, we may establish an opposition between /p/ and /b/, which, for the present at least, we may regard as two minimal expression-elements of the language (by a 'minimal' unit is meant one that is not further analysable). Since there are many words that are distinguished by the opposition of /p/ and /b/, the contrast between these two elements has a high functional load. Other contrasts have a lower functional load. For example, there are relatively few words that are kept apart from one another in their substantial realization by the occurrence of one rather than the other of the two consonants that occur in the final position of *wreath* and *wreathe* (the symbols for these two sounds in the International Phonetic Alphabet are [θ] and [ð] respectively: cf. 3.2.8); and there are very few, if any, that are kept apart by the occurrence of the initial sound of *ship* rather than the second consonantal sound of *measure* or *leisure* (these two sounds are symbolized as [ʃ] and [ʒ] respectively in the International Phonetic Alphabet). The functional load of the contrasts between /θ/ and /ð/ and between /ʃ/ and /ʒ/ is therefore much lower than that of the contrast /p/: /b/.

The importance of functional load is obvious. Misunderstanding will tend to occur if the speakers of a language do not consistently maintain those contrasts which serve to distinguish utterances which differ in meaning. Other things being equal (and we will return to this condition in a moment), the higher the functional load the more important it is that the speakers should learn the particular contrast as part of their 'speech-habits' and should subsequently maintain it in their use of the language. It is to be expected therefore that children will tend to learn first those contrasts which have the highest functional load in the language which they hear about them; and, as a consequence of this fact, that contrasts with a high functional load will be correspondingly resistant to disappearance in the transmission of the language from one generation to the next. Investigation of the ease with which children master the contrasts in their native language and the study of the historical development of particular languages lend some empirical support to these expectations. In each case, however, there are additional factors which interact with, and are difficult to isolate from, the operation of the principle of functional load. We shall not go into these other factors here.

The precise quantification of functional load is complicated, if not made absolutely impossible, by considerations excluded above under the proviso 'other things being equal'. First of all, the functional load of a particular contrast between expression-elements will vary according to the *structural position* they occupy in the word. For example, two elements might contrast frequently at the beginning of a word, but only very rarely at the end of a word. Do we simply take an average over all the positions of contrast? The answer to this question is not clear.

Secondly, the importance of a particular contrast between expression-elements is not just a function of the number of words they distinguish: it also depends on whether the words themselves can occur and contrast in the same context. To take the limiting case: if A and B are two classes of words in complementary distribution, and if each member of A differs in its substantial realization from a member of B solely in that it has the element /a/ where the corresponding word of B has /b/, it is clear that the functional load of the contrast between /a/ and /b/ is nil. So the functional load of a particular contrast must be calculated for words which have the same or an overlapping distribution. It is also clear that any 'realistic' measure of the importance of a particular contrast should take account, not simply of the distribution of the words as specified by the rules of the grammar, but of the actual utterances in which the words might be confused if the contrast were not maintained. How often, for instance, or in what circumstances, would an utterance such as *You'd better get a cab* be confused with *You'd better get a cap*, if the speaker failed to make the distinction in the final consonants of *cab* and *cap*? The answer to this question is evidently relevant to any precise quantification of the functional load of the contrast in question.

Finally, the importance of a particular contrast would seem to be related to its *frequency of occurrence* (which is not necessarily determined by the number of words it distinguishes). Let us assume that the three expression-elements, /x/, /y/ and /z/, occur in the same structural position of words of the same distributional class. But let us further suppose that, whereas the words in which /x/ and /y/ occur are in frequent contrast in the language (they are high-frequency words), the words in which /z/ occurs have a low frequency of occurrence (although they might be equally numerous in the vocabulary). If a speaker of the language failed to acquire the contrast between /x/ and /z/, he would be less severely handicapped in communication than he would be if he failed to acquire the contrast between /x/ and /y/. The functional load of the latter contrast is, *ex hypothesi*, higher than that of the former.

The considerations of the previous paragraphs demonstrate the difficulty of arriving at any precise measure of functional load. So far, the various measures that have been proposed by linguists cannot lay claim to the precision that their mathematical sophistication might appear to invest them with. Nevertheless, we must allow a place in our theory of language-structure for the undoubted importance, both synchronic and diachronic, of the concept of functional load. For it is still possible to say of certain contrasts that they have a higher load than others, even if we cannot say by how much.

2.4.2 Information-content and probability of occurrence

Another important statistical notion has to do with the amount of *information* carried by a linguistic unit in a given context; and this also is determined by (or is generally held to be determined by) its frequency of occurrence in that context. The term 'information' is here being employed in the specialized sense it has acquired in communication-theory, which we will now explain. The information-content of a particular unit is defined as a function of its *probability*. To take the simplest case first: if two or more units are equiprobable in a given context, they each have the same information-content in that context. Probability is related to frequency in the following way. If two, and only two, equiprobable units may occur, x and y, each of them will occur (on average) in just half the instances of the context in question: each has a probability, *a priori*, of $\frac{1}{2}$. The probability of a particular unit x is denoted by p_x. Thus, in the present instance, $p_x = \frac{1}{2}$ and $p_y = \frac{1}{2}$. More generally, each of n equiprobable units $(x_1, x_2, x_3, \ldots, x_n)$ has a probability of $\frac{1}{n}$. (It will be observed that the sum of all the probabilities in the set of units is 1. This holds independently of the more particular assumption of equiprobability. A special case of probability is 'certainty'. Units which cannot but occur in a given context have a probability of 1.) If the units are equiprobable, each of them carries the same amount of information.

More interesting, since they are more typical of language, are unequal probabilities. Suppose, for example, that two, and only two, units occur, x and y; and that x occurs twice as often, on average, as y: then, $p_x = \frac{2}{3}$ and $p_y = \frac{1}{3}$. The information-content of x is half that of y. That is to say, information-content is *inversely proportionate* (and, as we shall see, logarithmically related) to probability: this is the fundamental principle of information-theory.

At first sight, this principle may appear somewhat surprising. But consider first the limiting case of complete predictability. In written English, the letter u approximates very closely to complete predictability when it follows q; if we disregard certain borrowed words and proper names, we may say that it is completely predictable (it has a probability of 1). Similarly, the word *to* has a probability of 1 in such sentences as *I want...go home, I asked him...help me* (assuming that only one word is permitted in the contexts in question). If it were decided to omit the *u* (in *queen, queer, inquest,* etc.) or the word *to,* in the contexts referred to, no information would be lost (here we see the connexion between the general and the more specialized sense of the word 'information'). Since the letter *u* and the word *to* are not in paradigmatic contrast with any other units of the same level which might have occurred in the same context, they have a probability of 1 and their information-content is 0: they are *totally redundant.* Consider now the case of the two-term contrast where $p_x = \frac{2}{3}$ and $p_y = \frac{1}{3}$. Neither is totally redundant. But it is clear that the omission of *x* is of less consequence than the omission of *y*. Since *x* is twice as probable as *y*, the receiver of a message (knowing the *a priori* probabilities) would stand twice as good a chance on average of 'predicting' where *x* had been omitted as he would of 'predicting' where *y* had been omitted. Redundancy is therefore a matter of degree. The redundancy of *x* is twice that of *y*. In general, the more probable a unit is, the greater its *degree of redundancy* (and the lower its information-content).

2.4.3 *Binary systems*

Information-content is usually measured in *bits* (the term is derived from 'binary digits'). Any unit with a probability of $\frac{1}{2}$ conveys one bit of information; any unit with a probability of $\frac{1}{4}$ carries 2 bits of information; and so on. The convenience of this measure of information-content will be clear if we consider the practical problem of 'encoding' a set of units (which we will first of all assume to be equiprobable) as groups of binary digits. In the previous section, we saw that each of a set of eight units could be realized as a distinct group of three binary digits (cf. 2.3.8). This fact rests on the relationship between the number 2 (the *base* of the binary system of calculation) and 8 (the number of units to be distinguished): $8 = 2^3$. More generally, if N is the number of units to be distinguished, and m is the number of positions of contrast in the groups of binary digits required to distinguish them, then $N = 2^m$. The relationship between the number of paradigmatic contrasts at the 'higher' level (N) and the syntagmatic length of groups of 'lower'-level elements (m) is therefore logarithmic: $m = \log_2 N$. (The logarithm of a number is the power to which the base of the numerical system must be raised in order to arrive at the number in question. If $N = x^m$, then $m = \log_x N$: 'if N equals x to the power m, then m equals the logarithm to the base x of N'. It will be remembered that in decimal arithmetic, the logarithm of 10 is 1, of 100 is 2, of 1000 is 3, etc.: that is, $\log_{10} 10 = 1$, $\log_{10} 100 = 2$, $\log_{10} 1000 = 3$, etc. If information-theory had been based on the decimal, rather than the binary, system of measurement, it would have been more convenient to define the unit of information in terms of a probability of $\frac{1}{10}$.) It should be clear to the reader that the equation, $N = x^m$, given here, is a special case of the equation $N = p_1 \times p_2 \times p_3 ... p_m$, introduced in 2.3.8. The equation $N = x^m$ holds when there is the same number (x) of elements in paradigmatic contrast at each of the positions in the syntagmatic group.

The reason why information-content is generally measured in bits is simply that many physical systems for the storage and transmission of information operate on a binary principle: they are *two-state systems*. For instance, information may be coded on magnetic tape (for processing by a digital computer) as a sequence of magnetized or unmagnetized positions (or groups of positions): each position is in one of two possible states, and may therefore carry one bit of information. Again, information might be transmitted (as, for instance, in Morse code) as a sequence of 'impulses', each of which can take one of two values: short or long in duration, positive or negative in electrical charge, etc. Any system which makes use of an 'alphabet' of more than two elements can be encoded into a binary system at the source of transmission and decoded into the original 'alphabet' when the message is received at its destination. This is what happens when messages are transmitted by teleprinter. That information-content should be measured logarithmically to the base 2, rather than logarithmically to some other numerical base, is a consequence of the fact that communications-engineers customarily work with two-state systems. Whether the principle of binary 'coding' is directly relevant to the study of languages under their more normal conditions of 'transmission' between speaker and hearer, is a matter of considerable dispute among linguists. It is certainly the case that many of the most important phonological, grammatical and semantic distinctions in language are binary, as we shall see in later chapters; and we have already seen that one of the two terms of a binary contrast can frequently be regarded as positive, or marked, and the other as neutral, or unmarked (cf. 2.3.7). We shall not enter here into the question whether all linguistic units can be reduced to complexes of hierarchically-ordered binary 'choices'. The fact that many units (at all levels of language-structure) are reducible in this way means that the linguist should be accustomed to thinking in terms of binary systems. At the same time, it should be realized that the fundamental concepts of information-theory are quite independent of the particular assumptions of binarism.

2.4.4 Unequal probabilities

Since each binary digit can carry no more than one bit of information, a group of m binary digits can carry a maximum of m bits. So far we have assumed that the higher-level units to be distinguished are equiprobable. Let us now consider the more interesting and more typical case, where the probabilities are unequal. For simplicity, we will take a set of three units, a, b and c, with the following probabilities: $p_a = \frac{1}{2}$, $p_b = \frac{1}{4}$, $p_c = \frac{1}{4}$. The unit a carries 1 bit, and b and c each carry 2 bits of information. They might be encoded in a binary system of realization as a: oo, b: o1 and c: 1o (with 11 left unassigned). But if the digits were transmitted in sequence along some channel of communication and if each digit took the same length of time to send and receive, this would be an inefficient convention of encoding to adopt. For a would take up as much of the capacity of the channel as b and c, although it carries only half as much information. It would be more economical to encode a as one digit, say 1, and to distinguish b and c from a by encoding them with the contrasting digit, o, in the first position: b and c would then be distinguished from one another in the second position of contrast (which is of course empty for a). Thus a: 1, b: oo and c: o1. This second convention makes the most economical use of the capacity of the channel, because it maximizes the amount of information carried by each group of one or more digits. Since a, which occurs twice as often as b and c, is transmitted in half the time, the maximum number of messages can be transmitted in the shortest time (on the assumption that the messages are long enough or numerous enough to reflect the average frequencies of occurrence). In fact, this simple system represents the theoretical ideal: each of the three units, a, b and c, carries an integral number of bits of information and is realized by that number of distinctions in substance.

2.4.5 Redundancy and noise

The theoretical ideal is never achieved in practice. First of all, the probabilities of the units will generally lie between, rather than correspond with, the terms in the series $1, \frac{1}{2}, \frac{1}{4}, \frac{1}{8}, \frac{1}{16}, \dots, \frac{1}{2^m}$. For example, a particular unit might have a probability of $\frac{1}{5}$: it will therefore convey $\log_2 5$—approximately 2·3—bits of information. But there is no such thing as 0·3 of a distinction in substance: distinctions in substance are absolute, in the sense explained above (cf. 2.2.10). And if we use three digits to identify a unit with a probability of $\frac{1}{5}$, we thereby introduce redundancy into the substantial realization. (The average redundancy of the system can be minimized to whatever point is considered desirable; and the mathematical theory of communication is primarily concerned with this question. But we need not go into the more technical details here.) The important point is that some degree of redundancy is in fact desirable in any system of communication. The reason is that, whatever medium is used for the purpose of transmitting information, it will be subject to various unpredictable physical disturbances, which will obliterate or distort part of the message and thus lead to the loss of information. If the system were free of redundancy, the information lost would be irrecoverable. The term used by communication-engineers for random disturbances in the medium, or channel of communication, is *noise*. The optimum system, for a particular channel, is one in which there is just enough redundancy to enable the receiver to recover the information lost as a result of noise. It should be observed that the terms 'channel' and 'noise' are to be interpreted in the most general sense. They are not restricted to acoustically-based systems, still less to the systems constructed by engineers (telephone, television, teleprinter, etc.). The distortions produced in one's handwriting by writing in a moving train can be attributed to 'noise'; so too can the distorting effects on speech of a cold in the head, drunkenness, distraction and lapse of memory, etc. (Misprints are one of the effects of noise in the 'encoding' of the written language: they are frequently unnoticed by the reader, because the redundancy of most written sentences is high enough to counteract the distorting influence of random errors. Misprints are more serious in a string of figures, any combination of which is *a priori* possible. This fact is recognized by the practice of accountants, who deliberately introduce redundancy into their ledgers by requiring that the totals of different columns should balance. And the convention that cheques should specify the amount to be paid in both words and figures makes it possible for banks to detect, if not to correct, many of the errors caused by noise of one kind or another.) As far as the spoken language is concerned, the term 'noise' can be taken to include any source of distortion or misunder-standing, whether this be attributable to the imperfect performance of the speaker and hearer or to the acoustic conditions of the physical environment in which the utterances are produced.

2.4.6 Summary of general principles of information-theory

From the early 1950s communication-theory (or information-theory) has exerted a powerful influence on a number of different sciences, including linguistics. The fundamental principles may be summarized as follows:

(i) All communication rests upon the possibility of *choice*, or selection from a set of alternatives. In the chapter on semantics we shall see that this principle provides us with an interpretation of the term 'meaningful' (in one of its senses): a linguistic unit, of whatever level, has no meaning in a given context if it is completely predictable in that context.

(ii) Information-content varies inversely with probability. The more predictable a unit is, the less meaning it has. This principle is in accord with the commonly-expressed view of writers on style, that clichés (or 'hackneyed expressions' and 'dead metaphors') are less effective than more 'original' turns of phrase.

(iii) The redundancy in the substantial realization of a linguistic unit (its 'encoding') is the difference between the number of distinc-tions in substance required to identify it and its information-content. A certain degree of redundancy is essential in order to counteract noise. Our previous discussion of the stability of the substance in which language is realized, and of the necessity of some 'safety margin' between the realizations of contrasting elements, can also be brought within the scope of the more general principle of redun-dancy (cf. 2.2.10).

(iv) The language will be more efficient (in terms of information-theory) if the syntagmatic length of units is inversely related to their probability. That some such principle is indeed operative in language is suggested by the fact that the most frequently-used words and expressions tend to be shorter. This was first observed empirically, rather than deduced as a testable consequence of theoretical prin-ciples; and a particular formula known as 'Zipf's law' (after its originator) has been worked out to express the correlation between length and frequency. (We shall not give 'Zipf's law' here or discuss its mathematical and linguistic basis; it has in any case been modified by more recent work.) At the same time, it must be recognized that the length of a word in letters or sounds (in the sense in which we have been employing the term 'sound' so far) is not necessarily a direct measure of syntagmatic length. We will return to this point. It is extremely important, and it has not always been stressed in statistical treatments of language.

2.4.7   Diachronic implications

Languages, as they develop through time and 'evolve' to meet the changing needs of the societies that use them for communication, can be regarded as *homeostatic* (or 'self-regulating') systems, the state of a language at any one time being 'regulated' by two opposing principles. The first of these (which is sometimes referred to as the principle of 'least effort') is the tendency to maximize the efficiency of the system (in the particular sense of 'efficiency' explained above): its effect is to bring the syntagmatic length of words and utterances closer to the theoretical ideal. The other principle is 'the desire to be understood': this inhibits the shortening effect of the principle of 'least effort' by introducing redundancy at various levels. As a consequence, it is to be expected that the changing conditions of communication will tend to keep the two tendencies in balance. If the average amount of noise is constant for different languages and different stages of the same language, it would follow that the degree of redundancy in language is constant. Unfortunately, it is impossible (at present at least) to verify the hypothesis that languages keep these two opposing principles in 'homeostatic equilibrium'. The reasons for this will occupy us presently. Nevertheless, the hypothesis is suggestive. Its general plausibility is supported by 'Zipf's law'; and also by the fact (pointed out long before the era of information-theory) that words tend to be replaced by longer (and more 'colourful') synonyms, especially in colloquial usage, when frequent use has robbed them of their 'force' (by reducing their information-content). The extreme rapidity with which 'slang' expressions are replaced can be accounted for in these terms.

So too can the phenomenon of 'homonymic conflict' and its dia-chronic resolution (which has been abundantly illustrated by Gilliéron and his followers). 'Homonymic conflict' may arise when the opera-tion of the principle of 'least effort' may concur with other factors determining sound-change to reduce, or eliminate, the 'safety margin' between the substantial realizations of two words and so produce homonymy. (The term 'homonymy' is commonly used to refer to either homophony or homography these days: cf. 1.4.2. Here it is of course homophony.) If the homonyms are more or less equally probable in a large number of contexts, the 'conflict' will tend to be resolved (or inhibited) by the replacement of one of the words. A well-known example is the disappearance from standard Modern English of the word *quean* (originally meaning 'woman', and later 'hussy' or 'prostitute') which was brought into 'conflict' with *queen* by the loss of the earlier distinction between the vowels realized orthographically as *ea* and *ee*. The most famous example of 'homonymic conflict' in the literature is probably the case of the words for 'cat' and 'rooster' in the dialects of south-west France. Distinguished as *cattus* and *gallus* in Latin, they had both developed, as a result of sound-change, into [gat]. The 'conflict' was resolved by the replacement of [gat] = 'rooster' with various other words, including the local variants of *faisan* ('pheasant') or *vicaire* ('curate'). The substitution of the second of these presumably rested upon some previous connexion in 'slang' usage between 'rooster' and 'curate'. There is a very rich literature on the subject of 'homonymics'. (References are given in the notes.)

2.4.8 *Conditional probabilities of occurrence*

As we have seen, the occurrence of a particular unit (a sound or letter; an expression-unit; a word; etc.) may be totally or partially determined by its context. We must now clarify this notion of contextual determination (or conditioning), and draw out its implications for linguistic theory. For simplicity, we will first of all restrict our attention to the consideration of contextual determination as it operates within syntagmatically-related complexes of units on the same level of language-structure; that is to say, we will for the present neglect the all-important point that the complexes of lower-level units realize higher-level units which themselves have contextually-determined probabilities.

We will use the symbols x and y as variables, each standing for a particular unit or syntagmatically-related group of units; and we will assume that x and y are themselves in syntagmatic relationship. (For example, at the level of expression-units x might stand for /b/ or /b/ + /i/, and y for /t/ or /i/ + /t/; at the level of words x might stand for *men* or *old* + *men*, and y for *sing* or *sing* + *beautifully*.) Both x and y will have an average, *a priori*, probability of occurrence: p_x

and p_y, respectively. So too will the combination $x+y$ which we will symbolize as p_{xy}.

In the limiting case of statistical independence between x and y, the probability of the combination $x+y$ will be equal to the product of the probabilities of x and y: $p_{xy} = p_x \times p_y$. This fundamental principle of probability theory may be illustrated by means of a simple numerical example. We will consider the numbers from 10 to 39 (inclusive), and let x and y stand for 2 and 7, in the first and second position of their decimal representation: the combination of x and y will therefore stand for the number 27. Within the range of numbers we are considering (on the assumption that each of the thirty numbers is equiprobable) $p_x = \frac{1}{3}$ and $p_y = \frac{1}{10}$. If we were to 'think of a number between 10 and 39' and to ask someone to guess which number we had in mind, his chance of guessing correctly (without further information) would be one in thirty: $p_{xy} = \frac{1}{30}$. But suppose that we told him that the number was a multiple of 3. Clearly, his chance of guessing correctly would now improve to one in ten. More important from our point of view (since we are considering the probability of one digit in the context of the other), the choice of one of the two digits is no longer statistically independent of the choice of the other. The probability of y, given that $x = 2$, is $\frac{1}{3}$, since there are only three multiples of 3 within the range (21, 24, 27); and the probability of x, given that $y = 7$, is 1, since there is only one multiple of 3 that ends in 7 within the range. We may symbolize these equations as $p_y(x) = \frac{1}{3}$ and $p_x(y) = 1$. The *conditional probability* of occurrence of y in the context of x is $\frac{1}{3}$, and the conditional probability of x given y is 1. (The two expressions 'in the context' and 'given' are to be understood as equivalent; both are used in works on statistical linguistics.) To generalize from the example: if $p_x(y) = p_x$ (that is, if the probability of x in the context of y is equal to its *a priori*, unconditioned, probability), x is statistically independent of y; if however, the occurrence of x is rendered more or less probable by the occurrence of y—if either $p_x(y) > p_x$ or $p_x(y) < p_x$—then x is 'positively' or 'negatively' conditioned by y. The extreme case of 'positive' conditioning is, of course, total redundancy, with $p_x(y) = 1$ (y presupposes x); and the extreme case of 'negative' conditioning is, 'impossibility', with $p_x(y) = 0$ (y precludes x). It is important to realize that contextual conditioning may be either 'positive' or 'negative' (in the sense in which these terms have been used here); and also that the probability of x given y is not always, indeed rarely, equal to the probability of y given x.

Various kinds of conditioning must be distinguished, if the results of any statistical analyses are to be of significance for linguistics. As we saw above, syntagmatic relations may be sequential or non-sequential; conditioning may therefore be *sequential* or *non-sequential*. When x and y are sequentially-related, $p_x(y)$ is *progressive* if y precedes x, and *regressive* if y follows x. Independently of whether the conditioning is progressive or regressive, x and y may be contiguous (next to one another in a sequentially-ordered syntagmatic complex); in this case, if x is conditioned by y, $p_x(y)$ is *transitional*. Many popular accounts of the statistical structure of language tend to give the impression that the conditional probabilities operative at all levels of language-structure are necessarily sequential, transitional and progressive. This is clearly not so. For example, the conditional probability of a particular noun as subject or object of a particular verb in Latin is unaffected by the relative order with which the words occur in temporal sequence (cf. 2.3.5); the occurrence of the prefixes *un-* and *in-* in English (in such words as *unchanging* or *invariable*) is regressively conditioned; the occurrence of a particular expression-unit at the beginning of a word may be 'positively' or 'negatively' conditioned by the occurrence of a particular expression-unit at the end of a word (or conversely); and so on.

Of course, it is in principle possible to calculate the conditional probability for any unit relative to any context. The important thing is to choose the context and the direction of conditioning—that is, to calculate $p_x(y)$ rather than $p_y(x)$—in the light of what is already known of the general syntagmatic structure of the language. (A certain class of units, X, may presuppose or allow the occurrence of another syntagmatically-related class of units, Y, at a particular position relative to it (it may also preclude the occurrence of a third class, Z.) Given that this is so, one may then calculate the conditional probability of a particular member of the class, Y.) The results will be of statistical interest if, and only if, $p_x(y)$ or $p_y(x)$ is significantly different from p_x and p_y.

2.4.9 *Positional probabilities for English consonants*

Probabilities can also be calculated for particular structural positions. For example, three sets of probabilities are given in Table 4 for each of twelve consonants in spoken English: (i) their *a priori* probability averaged over all positions; (ii) their probability in word-initial position before vowels; and (iii) their probability in word-final

Table 4. *Probabilities of selected English consonants*
in different positions of the word

	(i) 'Absolute'	(ii) Initial	(iii) Final
[t]	0·070	0·072	0·105
[n]	0·063	0·042	0·127
[l]	0·052	0·034	0·034
[d]	0·030	0·037	0·039
[h]	0·026	0·065	—
[m]	0·026	0·058	0·036
[k]	0·025	0·046	0·014
[v]	0·019	0·010	0·048
[f]	0·017	0·044	0·010
[b]	0·016	0·061	0·0005
[p]	0·016	0·020	0·008
[g]	0·015	0·027	0·002

position after vowels. It will be observed that there are some striking differences between the frequency with which particular consonants occur in different positions of the word. For example, of the units listed [v] is the least frequent in word-initial position, but the third most frequent in word-final position; on the other hand, [b] is the third most frequent in word-initial position, but the least frequent in word-final position (apart from [h], which does not occur at all finally: n.b. we are talking of sounds, not letters). Others (like [t]) have a high probability, or (like [g] and [p]) a low probability for both positions. It will also be observed that the range of variation between the highest and the lowest probability is greater for the end of the word than it is for the beginning. Facts of this kind find their place in a description of the statistical structure of phonological words in English.

It was said earlier (with reference to 'Zipf's law': cf. 2.4.6.) that the number of sounds or letters in a word is not a direct measure of its syntagmatic length in terms of information-theory. The reason is of course that not all sounds or letters are equiprobable in the same context. If the probability of a phonological or orthographic word were directly related to the probabilities of its constituent expression-elements, it would be possible to derive the probability of the word by multiplying together the probabilities of the expression-elements for each of the structural positions in the word. For example, given that x is twice as probable as y in initial position and a is twice as probable as b in final position, one would expect xpa to be twice as frequent as either ypa or xpb and four times as frequent as ypb. That this expectation is not fulfilled in particular instances is evident from the consideration of a few words in English. The expression-elements realized by [k] and [f] are more or less equally probable initially, but the word *call* is far more frequent than *fall* (according to various published frequency-lists for English words); although the element realized by [t] has about fifty times the probability of that realized by [g] in word-final position, the word *big* occurs with about four times the frequency of *bit*; and so on.

The probabilities for initial and final position used in these calculations (cf. Table 4) are probabilities based on the analysis of continuous text. This means that the occurrence of a particular consonant in relatively few high-frequency words may outweigh the occurrence of another in very many low-frequency words (cf. the remarks made in 2.4.1, in connexion with the concept of 'functional load'). The consonant [ð], which occurs initially in such words as *the, then, their, them,* etc., in English, illustrates the effect of this weighting. In initial position, it is the most frequent of all consonants, with a probability of about 0·10 (compared with 0·072 for [t], 0·046 for [k], etc.). But it occurs in only a handful of different words (less than thirty in modern usage). By contrast initial [k] is found in many hundreds of different words, although its probability in continuous text is less than half that of [ð]. Comparison of all the words in English realized as consonant + vowel + consonant (which in itself is a very common structure for English phonological words) shows that in general there are more words with a high-frequency initial and final consonant than there are words with a low-frequency initial and final consonant, and also that the former tend to be of more frequent occurrence. At the same time, it must be stressed that certain words are far more frequent or far less frequent than one might predict from the probabilities of their constituent expression-elements.

2.4.10 *'Layers' of conditioning*

Although we have so far discussed the question of contextual determination with reference to the conditional probabilities holding between units of the same level, it is clear that the occurrence of a particular expression-element is very largely determined by the contextual probability of the phonological word of which it forms a part. For example, the three words written *book*, *look* and *took* are all of frequent occurrence: they differ from one another phonologically (and orthographically) solely in the consonant which appears in the initial position. From the point of view of the grammatical structure of English, the possibility of contrast between the three words in actual utterances is relatively small (and it is totally unrelated to the probabilities of the initial consonants). The word *took* stands apart from the other two in a number of ways, the most important of these being that it realizes the past tense of a verb. It therefore occurs more freely with such words and phrases as *yesterday* or *last year* than do *look* and *book* (where the phonological words corresponding to *took* are the words written *looked* and *booked*); it can have *he*, *she* or *it* or a singular noun as subject (*he took*, etc., but not *he look* or *he book*, etc.); and it cannot occur with *to* preceding it (e.g. *I am going to took* is unacceptable). But *book* and *look* also differ from one another grammatically. Each of them may be used as a noun or a verb in the appropriate context (it must not be forgotten that a phonological word may realize more than one grammatical word: cf. 2.2.11). Although *look* is far more frequent as a verb and *book* as a noun, this difference is of small account compared with such non-statistical grammatical facts as the following: as a verb *book* (i.e. 'make reservations', etc.), but not *look*, may take a noun or noun-phrase as its direct object (*I will book my seat, He is going to book my friend for speeding*: the word *look* is impossible here); and *look* normally takes a 'prepositional phrase' (*I will look into the matter, They never look at me*: here *book* is impossible). It would seem to be the case that in the majority of English utterances produced by speakers in their everyday use of the language the confusion of *book* and *look* is precluded by grammatical constraints of one kind or another. And this is quite typical of minimally-contrasting phonological words in English.

But let us now consider the relatively small set of utterances in which both *look* and *book* are grammatically acceptable. It is quite easy for a speaker of English to devise, and on occasion he will produce or hear, such utterances. An example might be *I looked for the theatre*: *I booked for the theatre*. If we assume, for the sake of the argument, that all but the initial consonant of the words *booking* or *looking* is 'transmitted' to the hearer without significant distortion by 'noise' in the 'channel', he is faced with the problem of 'predicting', on the basis of the redundancies in the language and in the situation of utterance, which of the two words was intended by the speaker. (For simplicity, we will suppose that *cooked*, etc., are impossible, or highly improbable, in the particular situation.) Although *looked* may be assumed to occur far more frequently than *booked* in any representative sample of (British) English, it is quite clear that the occurrence of *theatre* raises the probability of *booked* considerably. Whether *booked* or *looked* is more probable with *for the theatre*, it would be very hard to say. But in any particular situation either one may be more highly determined than the other. This is evident from a comparison of the following two longer utterances:

(i) *I looked for the theatre, but I couldn't find it.*
(ii) *I booked for the theatre, but I have lost the tickets.*

The word *booked* would appear to be contextually precluded in (i) and *looked* in (ii). But the situation itself, including any previous conversation, might also have introduced various 'presuppositions', the determining force of which is as strong as that of *but* and *couldn't find* in (i) and *but* and *tickets* in (ii). If this is so, the hearer will already be 'conditioned' by these presuppositions to 'predict' (that is, in fact, to hear) *looked* rather than *booked* (or the converse) in the shorter 'frame' *I -ooked for the theatre*. For the present, we may refer to these probabilities, which derive from the co-occurrence of one word with another and the 'presuppositions' of the particular situation of utterance, as 'semantic'. (In later chapters we will distinguish other levels of acceptability within what we are here calling 'semantics'.)

Our example has been drastically over-simplified: we have recognized only three levels of conditioning (phonological, grammatical and semantic), and we have assumed that only one expression-unit has been lost, or distorted, through 'noise'. These simplifications do not, however, affect the general conclusion of the argument. When it comes to the discussion of particular utterances, it must be recognized that the semantic probabilities outweigh the grammatical and the grammatical outweigh the phonological. Since it is impossible (in the present state of linguistic research at least) to identify all the semantically-relevant factors in the external situations in which particular utterances occur, it is also impossible to calculate the probability, and therefore the information-content, of any part of them. This is one of the points that was stressed in our earlier discussion of functional load and information-theory (cf. 2.4.1).

2.4.11   *A dilemma and its methodological resolution*

Two apparently contradictory principles have been maintained in this section: first, that statistical considerations are essential to an understanding of the operation and development of languages; second, that it is in practice (and perhaps also in principle) impossible to calculate precisely the information carried by linguistic units in actual utterances. This apparent contradiction is resolved by recognizing that linguistic theory, at the present time at least, is not, and cannot, be concerned with the production and understanding of utterances in their actual situations of use (except for a relatively small class of language-utterances which can be handled directly in this way: cf. 5.2.5), but with the structure of sentences considered in abstraction from the situations in which actual utterances occur.

3

THE SOUNDS OF LANGUAGE

3.1 Introductory

3.1.1 *Phonetics and phonology*

So far we have been taking for granted the traditional view of language, according to which sentences are composed of words and words of 'sounds' (cf. 2.1.1). In the course of our discussion of substance and form in the previous chapter we saw that the term 'sounds' is potentially ambiguous. We must now clear up this ambiguity.

If the linguist is asked whether two 'sounds' are the same or different, or how many 'sounds' there are in a given language, he must know whether the question is one of substance or form; whether these 'sounds' are to be regarded as physical entities which can be described without knowing to what language they belong or whether they are to be described in terms of such differences and similarities of sound as are functional in the language (by 'functional' is to be understood 'relevant for the purpose of communication'). In the first case he will give a *phonetic* description of what he hears or analyses instrumentally; in the second he will give a *phonological* description.

3.1.2 *Speech-sounds*

Let us now distinguish, provisionally, between the terms 'speech-sound' and 'phoneme'. A *speech-sound* is any phonetically distinct unit of sound; that is to say, any unit of sound produced by the speech-organs that can be distinguished by the phonetician from all other units of sound produced by the speech-organs. Since there is practically no limit to the number of different speech-sounds that can be produced by the human speech-organs and distinguished by the phonetician, it follows that the speech-sound is somewhat indeterminate in nature. Individual phoneticians will differ in expertise; and even with the various instrumental techniques now available for measuring the acoustic properties of sound, there is in the last resort room for minute differences and discrepancies. The fact is that there is no natural limit to the divisibility of the range of sounds used in speech. The point at which the phonetician stops distinguishing different speech-sounds is dictated either by the limits of his own capacities and those of his instruments or (more usually) by the particular purposes of the analysis. For some purposes he will wish to draw more refined distinctions than for others. According to the degree of refinement in representation which he seeks to achieve he will use what is called a 'broader' or a 'narrower' transcription. (There are, of course, any number of intermediate stages between 'broadest' and 'narrowest'.) Let me give some examples.

In English, p, t and k in certain positions of the word are slightly aspirated (that is, pronounced with an accompanying slight puff of breath); in other positions, after s for example, they are unaspirated (cf. *top*: *stop*, *pot*: *spot*, etc.). In a broad transcription, therefore, the phonetician might well use the same letter (or other symbol) to represent both the English speech-sounds (as indeed the alphabet used for English generally does), although they are quite easily distinguishable, phonetically. Again, in English there are two main 'l-sounds', impressionistically referred to as 'clear' and 'dark': the former occurs before vowels, the latter before consonants and at the end of words (cf. *leaf*, *late*: *feel*, *field*). A narrow transcription would mark the difference between the 'clear' and the 'dark' l; a broad transcription might not.

3.1.3 Phonemes and allophones

A discussion of broad transcriptions brings us naturally to the notion of the *phoneme*. To return to the example of the English p, t and k: the reason why we can represent both the aspirated and the un-aspirated consonants with the same symbol in broad transcription is that the distinction between the aspirated and the unaspirated variety never has the function of keeping apart different words in English (this is a very crude, and partly inaccurate, statement of a principle that will be treated more fully later); it is not a *functional* difference: it is a phonetic difference, but not a phonological, or phonemic, difference of English (for the present, we shall not distinguish between the terms 'phonological' and 'phonemic'). In other languages (for example, in some Northern Indian languages and in most dialects of Chinese) the distinction between aspirated and unaspirated conso-nants is functional, or phonemic. And there are phonemic differences of English that play no role (though they may occur, as speech-sounds) in other languages. For example, in certain languages the distinction between the speech-sounds d and t, b and p, g and k, etc. (between what the phonetician describes as voiced and voiceless consonants) is not a phonemic difference—for instance, p, t and k might occur at the beginning and end of words and b, d and g only in the middle of words. In cases of this kind we say that the phonetically distinguishable pairs of speech-sounds are positional variants, or *allophones*, of the same phoneme. They are called positional variants because the occurrence of one rather than another of the phonetic variants of a particular phoneme is determined by the position of the phoneme in the word.

It will now be clear why the word 'sounds' is ambiguous, and why a distinction must be made between the units of phonetic description (speech-sounds), on the one hand, and the units of phonological description (phonemes), on the other. In order to distinguish speech-sounds from phonemes in the transcription of utterances, it has become customary to put symbols standing for the latter between obliques and the the former between square brackets; and we shall follow this convention throughout. We might say, for instance, with reference to the example used above, that /p/, /t/ and /k/ have as allophones [p], [t] and [k] in initial and final position and [b], [d] and [g] in medial position. A fuller treatment of the concept of the phoneme in modern linguistic theory will be given presently. We must first discuss some of the general principles of phonetic analysis.

3.2 Phonetics

3.2.1 *Different branches of phonetics*

Phonetics is not to be regarded as just an ancillary tool for the linguist and the student of foreign languages. As practised today, it is a highly developed science, incorporating parts of physiology and physics, but with its own conditions of relevance, its own methods of investigation and experiment, and its own technical vocabulary.

Speech-sounds are often described non-technically in subjective, and largely meaningless, terms, as 'harsh', 'guttural', 'soft', 'flat', etc. They can be described objectively from three main points of view: (1) in terms of the manner of their production by the human speech-organs; (2) in terms of the acoustic properties of the sound-waves travelling between speaker and hearer; and (3) in terms of their physical effects upon the human ear and its associated mechanisms. This yields a threefold division of the subject into *articulatory*, *acoustic* and *auditory phonetics*.

3.2.2   Auditory phonetics

The auditory classification of speech-sounds has not yet been carried very far; and for practical purposes, at the present time, phonetics can be regarded as being made up of two main branches: articulatory and acoustic phonetics. It would be impossible in the space available here to give anything like a satisfactory treatment of either of these branches. All one can hope to do is to provide a brief account of the general principles of classification and theory.

3.2.3   Articulatory phonetics

The oldest, and still the most common, method of phonetic description is that made in terms of 'articulation' by the speech-organs. What the phonetician, for convenience and from his own particular point of view, calls 'the organs of speech' do not, it is true, form a primary physiological system. Most of the speech-organs (the lips, the teeth, the tongue, the vocal cords, the nose, the lungs, etc.) serve some other purpose also, which, in man as in the other animals, can be considered as biologically primary. However, the speech-organs are legitimately considered by the phoneticians as a unitary, interconnected system. Individual differences in the speech-organs of different persons (apart from obvious physical defects) have no significant effect on the kind of sounds produced. The difference between a boy's voice and a man's, or between a man's and a woman's, is not generally relevant in speech. Nor is it true, although it is often said, that the speech-organs of certain 'races' are physically adapted to the production of certain sounds rather than others. 'Inability' to produce certain sounds is generally a result of environmental factors in childhood, the main factor being that of learning one's native language as one hears it pronounced.

3.2.4   Voice and pitch

Most phoneticians divide speech-sounds into *consonants* and *vowels*. This classification depends upon a prior distinction of voiced and voiceless sounds. *Voice* is produced by the regular vibration of the vocal cords in the larynx, or 'Adam's apple'. The rate of vibration depends on the degree of tension, and this governs the *pitch* of the resulting sound. (Pitch is usually treated as a concomitant feature of the sounds produced, rather than as an integral part of them.) Vowels are defined (in articulatory terms) as voiced sounds in the formation of which the air passes through the pharynx and the mouth without obstruction (by the tongue, lips, teeth, etc.). All speech-sounds other than vowels are defined to be consonants. Consonants are therefore rather heterogeneous. Indeed, a number of phoneticians would deny that the distinction between vowels and consonants is as fundamental as it is usually said to be. Not only are there such apparently paradoxical sounds as 'voiceless vowels', but voicing may be complete or partial and the term 'obstruction' is far from being as precise as it might appear at first sight. Supplementary criteria of different kinds must be brought to bear in the case of partially obstructed sounds to decide whether they are to be classed as vowels or consonants. These are points we need not dwell upon. They are mentioned here in order to support the view, which will be stressed throughout this section, that sound as produced by the human speech-organs is a continuum within which there are perhaps no 'natural' absolute categories.

3.2.5 *Vowels*

Vowels are generally classified in terms of three main articulatory dimensions: the degree to which the mouth is opened (*close* v. *open*); the position of the highest part of the tongue (*front* v. *back*); and the position of the lips (*rounded* v. *spread*, or *unrounded*). Thus, a certain sound may be described as a close, front, rounded vowel (e.g. the vowel in the French word *lune*); another as close, front, unrounded (e.g. that of the French *si* or of the English word *sea*). The terms 'close', 'front', etc., are not of course used absolutely. Each of the three dimensions represents a continuum and, in principle, is infinitely divisible. The vowel of the French word *si*, for instance, is closer than that of the English word *sea* (as well as being different in certain other respects). What has been done for the purpose of classification is to establish a set of so-called 'cardinal' vowels; that is (to quote Daniel Jones, the originator of this system of classification) 'a set of fixed vowel-sounds having known acoustic qualities and known tongue and lip positions'. Although Jones talks of the 'known acoustic qualities' of the cardinal vowels, the system is primarily, and to the extent that it is objective, one of articulatory classification. The principle followed is that of first defining a set of articulatory extremes (the 'closest possible front vowel', 'the openest of the back vowels', etc.) and then selecting intermediate positions in such a way that 'the degrees of acoustic separation are approximately equal'. The judgement of the intervals of 'acoustic separation' is subjective (though of course that of a brilliant and highly skilled phonetician). Now that the value of each of the cardinal vowels has been fixed and Daniel Jones's own recording of them has been analysed instrumentally their acoustic properties are, within certain limits, known objectively. That the cardinal vowel-system is in the last resort arbitrary does not make it any the less useful or scientific: the values of the cardinal vowels are fixed in the International Phonetic Alphabet (IPA), and by reference to them as a standard of measurement trained phoneticians can satisfactorily describe the vowels of any language, to a greater or less degree of precision according to need.

In addition to the three articulatory variables which the phonetician selects as basic in the classification of vowels, there are several others which he customarily treats as secondary modifications of what is taken to be the 'normal' pronunciation. For instance, vowels are assumed to be pronounced 'normally' without the passage of air through the nose. If the nasal passage is kept open during the production of the vowel so that air passes out from both the mouth and the nose, the vowel is said to be *nasalized*; it is regarded, and represented by the IPA, as a modification of the corresponding non-nasalized vowel (cf. [a]: [ã]).

3.2.6 *Consonants*

Consonants fall into several different, interesting categories. They may be *voiced* or *voiceless*; and *oral* or *nasal*. If the obstruction in the air passage is complete, the resulting sounds are described as *stops* (or plosives); if the obstruction is only partial, but produces friction, they are called *fricatives* (or spirants). The place at which the obstruction occurs is referred to as the point of articulation: the lips, the teeth, the alveolae (or teeth ridge), the palate (i.e. the hard palate), the velum (or soft palate), the uvula, the pharynx, the glottis—these are the principal points of articulation to which recognition is given in the IPA. The organ (or that part of it) which is brought into contact with (or close to) the point of articulation is called the articulator: in most cases this is some part of the tongue, which for the purpose is regarded as being made up of four parts—the apex (or tip), the blade, the middle, the dorsum (or back). Apical consonants are those in which the tip of the tongue acts as articulator; dorsal consonants those in which the articulator is the back of the tongue. Most of the traditional terms used by phoneticians are interpreted under the tacit assumption that certain articulators are normally associated with particular points of articulation: for instance, the term 'dental' is used for sounds (e.g. [t], [d]) which are produced by bringing the *tip* of the tongue into contact with, or close to, the (upper) teeth; the term 'velar', on the other hand, is used for sounds (e.g. [k], [g]) which are produced by contact, or friction, between the *back* of the tongue and the soft palate. In other cases the term employed is a compound label specifying the articulator and the place of articulation: thus 'labiodental' denotes sounds (e.g. [f], [v]) which result from contact, or friction, between the (upper) teeth and the (lower) lip. And, if necessary, further terms can be freely created on the same pattern. Consonants may be classified then in terms of a number of different articulatory variables (we have mentioned only some of them). For example, according to the conventions of the IPA, [p] is a bilabial, voiceless, oral, stop; [b] is a bilabial, voiced, oral, stop; [f] is a labio-dental, voiceless, (oral) fricative; [m] is a bilabial, (voiced) nasal, stop; [t] is a dental (or alveolar), voiceless, oral stop; [n] is a dental (or alveolar), (voiced) nasal stop; and so on. Perceptible deviations from what are taken to be the 'normal' points of articulation are described as being 'advanced' or 'retracted'. For instance, the initial sounds of the English words *key* and *car* are phonetically different: they would commonly be described as an 'advanced' and 'retracted' (or 'front' and 'back') variety of [k]. This does not mean that they are different 'species' of some natural 'genus' of sounds, but only that the roof of the mouth and the surface of the tongue are conventionally divided by phoneticians into a smaller, rather than a larger, number of regions.

3.2.7 *Articulatory variables: 'long' and 'short' components*

So far we have talked as if speech were made up of sequences of physically discrete units. This is not the case. Speech consists of continuous bursts of sound of varying length, within which the only physical breaks are at points where the speaker pauses to take breath. What the phonetician calls speech-sounds are abstracted by him from the continuous streams of sound according to some explicit or implicit criteria of demarcation. Simplifying the question somewhat, we may say that the number of speech-sounds recognizable in a continuous stretch of speech is determined by the number of successive distinct states of the speech-organs: a change in the state of the speech-organs may be defined as a perceptible change in at least one of the recognized *articulatory variables*. It follows that certain of the variables may keep the same value throughout a number of successive states of the speech-organs. Consider the two English words *cats* and *cads*, which may be written, in a broad transcription, as [kats] and [kadz]. It will be observed that the phonetic notation used here represents the difference between the two words as the sum of the differences between two distinct speech-sounds (i.e. [t]: [d] and [s]: [z]). In fact the difference lies in only one of the articulatory variables (we may neglect the difference in the vowels): in [kats] the portion of the word occurring after the vowel is voiceless; in [kadz] it is voiced (this is something of a simplification; but it does not affect the point being made). We can distinguish therefore between two kinds of phonetic components, which may be conveniently called 'short' and 'long' according to whether they occupy one or more than one position. It is important to observe that the same articulatory component may be long or short in different phonetic sequences. For example, in the word *under* the component of voicing extends over the whole word, and that of dental contact over two positions [nd], whereas nasality is confined to only one position [n]; in the word *omnipotent*, however, nasality is a long component, in [mn], and it is the shift from labial to dental (more precisely, alveolar) contact which leads us to distinguish between the positions occupied by the speech-sounds [m] and [n].

Certain articulatory components, notably voice and nasality, being unaffected by the presence or absence of obstruction in the mouth, may enter into the formation of both consonants and vowels. For example, the relations that hold between the vowels written as [a̧], [a] and [ã] in the International Phonetic Alphabet (IPA) are identical with those that hold between the consonants [p], [b] and [m]; [t], [d] and [n]; [k], [g] and [ŋ]: the first member of each set of three is neither voiced nor nasalized, the second is voiced but not nasalized, and the third is both voiced and nasalized. This point may be illustrated by means of a hypothetical example. Let us suppose that in a given language there are three words which may be transcribed phonetically as (*a*) [pa̧ta̧k], (*b*) [badag] and (*c*) [mãnãŋ]. There are five articulatory variables involved: three points of articulation— (i) labial, (ii) dental and (iii) velar contact—and two components

which may enter into the formation of both consonants and vowels—
the presence or absence of (iv) voice and (v) nasality. The phonetic
relationships between the three words can be represented by means
of the two-dimensional matrices given in Fig. 3, in which the
horizontal dimension is used for temporal succession and the vertical
dimension for the specification of the 'positive' or 'negative' value
for each of the five relevant articulatory variables: the 'positive'
value (voiced, rather than voiceless; nasal, rather than oral; dental,
rather than either labial or velar, contact; etc.) is marked with a
horizontal broken line; and the 'negative' value is left unmarked.
These matrices are absolutely equivalent to the more usual alphabetic
transcriptions: (a) [pa̯ta̯k], (b) [badag], (c) [mãnãŋ].

	(a)	(b)	(c)
Labial	–	–	–
Dental	–	–	–
Velar	–	–	–
Nasal	·		———
Voiced		———	———
	p a̯ t a̯ k	b a d a g	m ã n ã ŋ

Fig. 3. Note that, since 'labial', 'dental' and 'velar' imply obstruction at
these points of articulation (the articulatory components of the vowels are
not given—they are assumed to be constant in value), the distinction of
vowels and consonants, and hence the recognition of five states of the speech
organs, is clear from the absence of obstruction in two portions, and the
presence of obstruction in three portions, of each word.

In the case of [pa̯ta̯k], [badag] and [mãnãŋ] it is clear that the
presence or absence of voice and nasality are long components
running from the beginning to the end of each word (it will be
recalled that the small circle put under a vowel marks it as voiceless
and the 'tilde' (˜) placed over a vowel marks it as nasalized, and that,
unless they are specified as voiceless, vowels are assumed to be
voiced, as 'normally'); it is also clear that the sequence of obstructed
and unobstructed segments distinguishes consonants and vowels, and
in this case the number of speech-sounds. Careful consideration of
this example and generalization of the facts implicit in it should lead
us to the conclusion that such expressions as 'a [p]-sound', 'an

[m]-sound', etc. are convenient, but potentially misleading, ways of saying 'a stretch of sound which is characterized at a particular place by labiality, occlusion, voicelessness and lack of nasality', 'a stretch of sound characterized at a particular place by labiality, occlusion, voice and nasality', etc. (to mention only a few of the relevant articulatory variables). The alphabetic system of transcription customarily used by phoneticians, and used here in citing the examples, is therefore a far from perfect system for the transcription of speech. A more satisfactory system might be one which gave a direct representation of each of the overlapping articulatory components of any given stretch of speech and explicitly marked the relative lengths of the components. As it is, anyone who wishes to read phonetic transcriptions with understanding must first learn to 'de-alphabetize' them, mentally substituting for each of the symbols the simultaneous articulatory components they imply and then combining these components with one another in sequence according to the principles illustrated above.

This question has been discussed at some length because it is not always stressed sufficiently, and is sometimes not even mentioned, in elementary and popular treatments of language. Only too often the impression is given that speech is composed of sequences of discrete and independent speech-sounds, and that these speech-sounds are the ultimate units of articulatory phonetic analysis. We shall see presently that the distinction that has been made here on phonetic grounds between short and long components is one which can be made also on phonological grounds.

3.2.8   Phonetic alphabets

The reader will now readily appreciate the following point. The International Phonetic Alphabet (IPA) is based upon the Roman alphabet. Moreover, the phonetic values assigned to the letters were established before the necessity of distinguishing between phonetics and phonology had been clearly recognized. The IPA betrays its origins in the inconsistency with which it represents certain articulatory features and in its assumptions of 'normality' and 'abnormality'. In general, the letters were defined to have the values of the 'sounds' they denoted in one or more of the major European languages using the Roman alphabet; some letters which were redundant, e.g. *x*, as used in English, etc. (= [ks]) and *c*, as used in English and French, etc. (= [k] or [s]), were given a different phonetic interpretation; and a certain number of new symbols (borrowed from the Greek alphabet or specially designed for the purpose) were introduced, e.g. [θ] and [ð] to represent the initial 'sounds' of the English words *thick* and *there*. Although the inventors of the IPA and those responsible for its further development have shown great ingenuity, as well as a commendable attention to the requirements of typographical clarity, in the design of new symbols for the alphabet, there was clearly a practical limit to the number of totally distinct symbols that could be constructed. So the IPA has from the outset made provision for the use of diacritics in addition to letters. The diacritics are employed, as we saw earlier, either to give a 'narrower' transcription than is possible by using the letters alone or to show that a certain 'sound' is pronounced in a manner which the conventions of the IPA regard as 'abnormal'.

The distinction that is made in the IPA system between letters and diacritics can be misleading. Almost inevitably it suggests that the differences between the sounds represented by distinct letters are more fundamental than those marked by diacritics. For example, voiced and voiceless oral stops are represented by distinct letters ([d]: [t], [b]: [p], [g]: [k], etc.); but as we have seen, vowels and nasal consonants are assumed to be voiced unless marked as voiceless by means of a special diacritic. From the point of view of articulatory description, as we have seen above, the relationship between [d] and [t] is the same as that between [a] and [ą] or between [n] and [ṇ]. The conventions of the IPA might tend to suggest, or support, the notion that, whereas [d] and [t] are two quite different 'sounds', the voiceless [ą] and [ṇ] are merely less common variants of the more 'normal' voiced [a] and [n]. There are many inconsistencies. Nevertheless, the IPA remains a very useful tool for the phonetician; for its conventions have been carefully defined and have been accepted by phoneticians of many different countries.

There are other alphabetic systems of phonetic transcription besides the IPA. Some of these have the advantage that they can be typed on a standard typewriter, and are for this reason preferred by many authors, especially in America. It should not be thought, however, that any important difference of principle distinguishes the various phonetic alphabets in common use. All the remarks which have been made above about the IPA apply to phonetic alphabets in general.

3.2.9   *Acoustic phonetics*

It is in the field of *acoustic phonetics* that the most striking developments have taken place since the Second World War. With the aid
of various kinds of electronic equipment, the most widely used of
which is the sound spectrograph, it is now possible to analyse the
complex sound waves produced in speech into their component
frequencies and relative amplitudes as these vary continuously
through time. Furthermore, considerable progress has been made in
what is called *speech-synthesis*: the artificial reconstruction of recognizable utterances in particular languages by producing sound waves
at the frequency-bands that have been found to be of particular
importance in human speech and combining these in the appropriate
way. We shall not go into the principles of acoustic phonetics. All that
is required in a book of this nature is some brief indication of the
results that have been achieved and their implications for linguistic
theory.

First of all, acoustic analysis has confirmed (if confirmation was
needed) that speech is not made up of a sequence of discrete 'sounds'.
The determinable components of the sound-waves produced when we
talk are of varying lengths and overlap one another in the time-
sequence. Rather more surprisingly perhaps, the factors identified by
acoustic analysis are not always relatable in a very straightforward
manner to the factors traditionally regarded as criterial in the distinction of different speech-sounds by the articulatory phonetician. The
acoustic analysis of vowels in terms of their constituent *formants*
(i.e. the two frequency-bands at which there is the maximum concentration of energy) correlates quite well with their description in terms
of the articulatory dimensions of front *v.* back and close *v.* open; the
articulatory feature of rounding can also be identified acoustically.
So too can voice and nasality; as well as obstruction and friction. It is
the acoustic identification of the place of articulation that presents the
greatest difficulty. From the acoustic point of view, it would appear
that the distinction between consonants produced at different places
of articulation is carried mainly by contextual and transitional features
in the sound-wave, rather than by some features inherent in the
consonants themselves.

Although it has long been known that what is perceptually the
same sound can, in certain instances, be produced by a different
combination of 'articulations', it was probably assumed by most
phoneticians until recently that the articulatory distinctions were

for the most part maintained by the sound-waves as these were transmitted for analysis by the auditory system of the hearer. It is now realized that the transmission of speech is rather more complex.

Allowance must be made for *feedback*. In the case of speech, we are not dealing with a system of sound-production and sound-reception in which the 'transmitter' (the speaker) and the 'receiver' (the hearer) are completely separate mechanisms. Every normal speaker of a language is alternately a producer and a receiver. When he is speaking, he is not only producing sound; he is also 'monitoring' what he is saying and modulating his speech, unconsciously correlating his various articulatory movements with what he hears and making continual adjustments (like a thermostat, which controls the source of heat as a result of 'feedback' from the temperature readings). And when he is listening to someone else speaking, he is not merely a passive receiver of sounds emitted by the speaker: he is registering the sounds he hears (interpreting the acoustic 'signal') in the light of his own experience as a speaker, with a 'built-in' set of contextual cues and expectancies. For this reason, therefore, the primary medium of language (the substance of the expression-plane: cf. 2.2.8) is perhaps not rightly conceived in wholly physical terms (in the narrowest sense of the term 'physical'). The phonic data is not just sound as it might be treated by the physicist, but sound as 'filtered' and categorized by human beings in their use of language. In other words, the phonic medium of language has a psychological, as well as a purely physical, aspect. It is possible that this psychological aspect of the medium may yet be reducible to a rather more complex physical description of the properties of sound. But this should not be taken for granted.

It may be pointed out here that the principle of 'feedback' is not restricted to the production and reception of physical distinctions in the substance, or medium, in which language is manifest. It operates also in the determination of phonological and grammatical structure. Intrinsically ambiguous utterances will be interpreted in one way, rather than another, because certain expectancies have been established by the general context in which the utterance is made or by the previous discourse (cf. 2.4.5, on redundancy).

3.3 Phonology

3.3.1 *The phoneme*

In the previous section a distinction was made between the phonetic and the phonological analysis of language. The principles underlying phonetic analysis have now been discussed in sufficient detail, and we may look a little more closely at the concept of the *phoneme*, which has been introduced as the unit of phonological description.

3.3.2 *Complementary distribution of allophones*

We may begin our further discussion of the theory of the phoneme from the point we reached earlier at which we distinguished between phonemes and 'speech-sounds' (cf. 3.1.2). Two phonetically different 'sounds' in the same environment which have the effect of distinguishing different words are recognized as different phonemes. Thus, for example, [l] and [r] are different phonemes in English because they distinguish numerous pairs of words, such as *lamb : ram, lot : rot, light : right,* etc. We may refer to these phonemes as /l/ and /r/, respectively. (It will be recalled that square brackets are being used for phonetic symbols and oblique strokes for phonemic symbols, according to the general practice of linguists.) There are many languages in which [l] and [r] either do not both occur or do not both occur in the same environment with the effect of distinguishing different words. In such languages (e.g. in Chinese and Japanese) the difference between [l] and [r] is not phonemic. Phonetic units that never occur in the same environment (and therefore cannot distinguish different words) are said to be in *complementary distribution* (cf. 2.3.1). The example of the 'clear' and 'dark' [l] in English has already been given: the 'clear' [l] occurs only before vowels and the phoneme /y/, and the 'dark' [l] before all other consonants and at the end of words. The phonetically distinct 'clear' and 'dark' [l] are recognized therefore as positional variants, or allophones, of the same phoneme. There is no reason to consider the distinction between [l] and [r] as more 'naturally' phonemic than that between the 'clear' and 'dark' [l]. This is a contingent fact of English. Not only are there languages in which [l] and [r] are in complementary distribution and recognized by the phonologist as allophones of the same phoneme, but there are also languages (e.g. Russian and certain dialects of Polish) in which the distinction between a 'clear' and 'dark' [l] is phonemic. It may be observed in passing that the application of the principle of complementary distribution will generally correlate pretty well with the phonetically-untrained native speaker's judgement about what is and what is not the same 'sound'. This may be attributed to the fact that the native speaker has learned to respond to certain phonetic differences as functional in his language and to neglect others as irrelevant for the purpose of communication.

3.3.3 *Phonetic similarity of allophones*

Implicit in what has been said so far is a further condition for grouping different speech-sounds into a smaller set of phonemes. It is clearly not a sufficient condition for their allocation as variants of the same phoneme that speech-sounds should be in complementary distribution. To return to yet another earlier example, the voiceless stop consonants of English are pronounced differently in different environments, with slight aspiration in some cases and without any aspiration in others. This means that each of the set of aspirated stops (let us write them in a narrow transcription as [ph], [th], [kh]) is in complementary distribution with each of the set of unaspirated stops (let us write these as [p], [t], [k]). Why not group [ph] with [t] or [k], rather than with [p]? Notice that, provided the conventions of phonetic interpretation are made clear, /top/: /spop/ and /pot/: /stot/ are no less adequate representations of the contrasts between the words normally written *top*: *stop* and *pot*: *spot*, than are /top/: /stop/ and /pot/: /spot/. All we have to do, if we choose to make the identifi-cations implied in the first way of transcribing the words, is to associate with the phonemes /t/ and /p/ the following conventions of phonetic interpretation: /t/ and /p/ are realized phonetically as [th] and [ph] in initial and final position, and as [p] and [t], respectively, when they occur after /s/. However, no phonologist describing English would make this particular set of identifications. And there are a number of reasons why he would not. The first, and most important, supplementary criterion (to which most linguists would give as much weight as they do to the condition of complementary distribution) is that of *phonetic similarity*. And it is this criterion that has been implicit in the discussion of the various examples brought forward to illustrate the difference between speech-sounds and phonemes. [ph] and [p], rather than [ph] and [t], are considered as allophones of the same phoneme /p/ because phonetically they are more similar to one another than [ph] and [t] (which are also in complementary distri-bution).

It will be clear from our discussion of the principles of phonetic analysis that whether or not two speech-sounds are similar is not a question that admits of a simple answer. It follows from the multi-dimensional nature of the sounds used in human speech that they may be alike in some respects and unlike in others. This means that the phonologist analysing a particular language may be faced with alternative possibilities. Is a voiceless, unaspirated stop more like a voiced, unaspirated stop or a voiceless, aspirated stop? This is a question that confronts the linguist analysing English. For [p], [t] and [k] are in complementary distribution not only with [ph], [th] and [kh], but also with [b], [d] and [g], which never occur after /s/ in the same word. As long as we confine our attention to just this isolated problem, then neither of the two possible solutions forces itself upon us as more reasonable than the other. (We must be careful not to assume that [ph] and [p] are phonetically more similar simply because the International Phonetic Alphabet represents them as two kinds of [p]. This point has been stressed in the preceding section.) In fact the linguist never considers such problems in isolation from the rest of the analysis. If we take a general view of the phonology of English, we shall see that the opposition of voiced and voiceless consonants is one of greater importance in the language than that of the opposition of unaspirated and aspirated consonants. Not only are stops distinguished in certain positions by the presence or absence of voice (*bet*: *pet*, etc.), where they are also distinguished by the absence or presence, respectively, of aspiration; but other consonants (frica-tives and affricates: *leave*: *leaf, jeep*: *cheap*, etc.) are distinguished by the presence or absence of voice, and here there is no question of an opposition between aspirated and unaspirated variants of a pair of phonemes. This being so, it is doubtless preferable to consider the lack of aspiration in [p] *vis-à-vis* [ph] as a matter of allophonic variation, rather than its lack of voice *vis-à-vis* [b]. It should be realized, however, that this decision has not, and could not have, been made on the grounds simply of phonetic similarity.

3.3.4   *Free variation in phonology*

It may happen that two phonetically different units occur, but do not contrast, in the same environment: that is to say, the substitution of one for the other does not produce a different word, but merely a different 'pronunciation' of the same word. In this case the phoneti-cally different units are said to be *in free variation* (cf. 2.3.2). For example, the 'glottal stop' (a sound produced by first bringing the vocal cords together and then releasing them so that there is a sudden escape of air: the IPA symbol for this sound is [ʔ]) is a free variant of /t/ at the end of a syllable before a consonant in what is called the (standard) 'Received Pronunciation' of English. Most speakers who use this kind of pronunciation are probably not conscious of the fact that they have two alternative pronunciations of such words as *fortnight*, etc., according to whether they are speaking more or less formally and deliberately, whereas they are well aware of the occurrence of the same speech-sound as a 'substandard' variant of /t/ before vowels in, for example, the 'Cockney' pronunciation of words like *city*. It may also happen that alternative pronunciations of a word are current involving a difference that is generally phonemic in the language. For example, the word *economics* is sometimes pronounced with the vowel found in *bet* and sometimes with that of the word *beat*; the word *either* is sometimes pronounced with the vowel of *beat* and sometimes with that of *bite*. And there are many such alternatives, often in the speech of the same person, in English. However, this would not normally be described as allophonic free variation. The fact that the difference of the vowels serves to distinguish at least some words in English means that it is always recognized as phonemic. This is by virtue of the principle which is sometimes expressed in the words 'once a phoneme, always a phoneme'. Moreover, it is not possible to give an account of the sporadic fluctuation of phonemes of the kind exemplified here other than by listing the words in which it is to be found. From this point of view, the difference between the two pronunciations of *economics*, *either*, etc., is, as it were, 'accidental': it is not part of the regular phonological structure of the language. In this respect it differs from the kind of free variation mentioned above (between [t] and the glottal stop) where we were able to state concisely, and in phonological terms (that is to say, without reference to the particular words, but in terms of the categories of phonemes preceding and following the free variants) the conditions under which it takes place.

3.3.5 *Neutralization in phonology*

A more common phenomenon than free variation between phonemes in phonologically definable conditions is the so-called *neutralization* of the distinction between them in certain positions. This may be explained by means of a commonly-used example. In many languages, including German, Russian, Turkish, there is a phonemic distinction between voiced and voiceless consonants in most positions of the word, but at the end of words voiced consonants do not occur. Thus, both the German words *Rad* ('wheel', 'bicycle') and *Rat* ('council', 'advice') are pronounced alike, namely as [raːt]. (Many speakers of German distinguish this pair of words, *Rad* and *Rat*, in terms of the length or quality of the vowel. But the point being made is unaffected by this fact.) The normal orthography takes account of the fact that in the forms of words in which the same consonants occur in non-final position the distinction between the voiced and voiceless member of the pair is consistently made: cf. *zum Rade* [raːdə] *verdammen* ('to condemn to torture on the wheel') and *meinem Rate* [raːtə] *folgen* ('follow my advice'). The distinction between voiced and voiceless consonants, i.e. between /d/ and /t/, /b/ and /p/, etc., is said to be 'neutralized' in final position; and this is a phonological statement about the language.

However, there are several different ways of treating this kind of neutralization. Some linguists would say that it is the phoneme /t/ that occurs finally in both *Rad* and *Rat* and account for the change of /d/ to /t/ manifest in the relation between *Rade* and *Rad* in a section of linguistic description intermediate between grammar and phonology (to which the name *morphophonemics* is given: this is the approach followed in many standard American textbooks and published analyses of languages). Another school would say that the fact that certain phonological oppositions are 'neutralizable', whereas others are not, in a given language constitutes such an important and basic feature of the phonology of the language as to justify the recognition of two different kinds of phonological unit. Linguists who take this line of approach (principally the so-called 'Prague school') recognize in addition to the phonemes, which preserve their distinctive function in all positions, also what are termed *archiphonemes* restricted to the positions of neutralization. A common and convenient way of symbolizing archiphonemes is by the use of capital letters: thus /T/ is an archiphoneme in German, as distinct from /d/ and /t/, which are phonemes and do not occur in final position. A word like *Tod* ('death') would be transcribed /toD/; that is to say, in a manner which makes it clear that the unit which occurs finally is of a different order from that which occurs initially. Phonetically speaking, the speech-sounds that occur at the beginning and end of this word are the same (up to a certain degree of narrowness in transcription). Whether or not they are phonologically the same is a question that can only be answered with reference to a particular theory of phonology. The linguist who accepts the principle 'once a phoneme, always a phoneme' will say that they are. The linguist who draws a distinction between phonemes and archiphonemes will say that they are not. We shall look further into some of the theoretical differences underlying these different answers later in this chapter. Enough has been said here to arouse in the reader the suspicion (which will become stronger as we advance further in the subject) that the 'facts' which a linguist discovers about the structure of a particular language are not entirely independent of the theories with which he approaches it in the first place.

3.3.6 *Syntagmatic relations between phonemes*

In our discussion of phonological theory so far, we have been concerned solely with the *paradigmatic* dimensions of speech (cf. 2.3.3). We have said that /p/, /b/, /l/, etc., are different phonemes in English because they are in paradigmatic *contrast* in various contexts. (This notion of 'contrast' has already been treated, from a more general point of view, in the previous chapter: cf. 2.2.9). In the word *pet*, for example, we may say that the phoneme /p/ occurs in the initial position, where it is in contrast with /b/, /l/, etc. (cf. *bet*, *let*, etc.); that the phoneme /e/ occurs in the second position, where it is in contrast with /i/, /o/, etc. (cf. *pit*, *pot*, etc.); and that the phoneme /t/ occurs in final position, where it is in contrast with /k/, /n/, etc. (cf. *peck*, *pen*, etc.). The word *pet* may, therefore, be represented as a sequence of three phonemes: /p/+/e/+/t/, abbreviated to /pet/. (The reasons why the phonemes are said to be sequentially-ordered have been discussed above: cf. 2.3.6.)

For simplicity, let us assume that three, and only three, phonemes are in contrast in the context /-et/, namely, /p/; /b/ and /l/: that three, and only three, are in contrast in the context /p-t/: namely, /e/, /i/ and /o/: and that three, and only three, are in contrast in the context /pe-/; /t/, /k/ and /n/. On the basis of this assumption, we can construct the following two-dimensional matrix, in which the vertical columns represent the sets of phonemes in contrast in each of the three positions:

$$\begin{array}{ccc} /p/ & /e/ & /t/ \\ /b/ & /i/ & /n/ \\ /l/ & /o/ & /k/ \end{array}$$

The horizontal dimension represents the possibility of *syntagmatic* combination (cf. 2.3.3). The matrix may be interpreted in the following way: at any of the positions of paradigmatic contrast in the word /pet/, which is given in the top row of the matrix, one may substitute another of the phonemes from the second or third row, and the result will be a different English word. The matrix summarizes, therefore, the facts described in the previous paragraph. It tells us that the following seven syntagmatic combinations of phonemes constitute English words: /pet/, /bet/, /let/, /pit/, /pot/, /pen/ and /pek/.

Under this interpretation of the matrix, we have taken the word *pet* as 'focal'; and we have held constant two of its constituent phonemes as the context for paradigmatic substitution. But we may also interpret the matrix in such a way that no particular word is taken as 'focal' in this sense. Many other English words can be accounted for, if we allow any phoneme from the first column to combine syntagmatically with any phoneme from the second and third columns: cf. *bin, bit, lick, lock*, etc. (to put the words in their standard orthographic form). But this extension will also admit certain combinations which do not constitute English words: e.g. /bik/ or /lon/. At this point, we must decide whether such combinations are systematically excluded by virtue of some general restrictions upon the combination of English phonemes with one another. If no such restrictions can be established, we will say that forms like /bik/ and /lon/ are phonologically acceptable 'words' of English, which have not been 'actualized', as it were, by the language and invested with a particular meaning and a particular grammatical function. 'Non-actualization', in this sense of the term, contributes to the redundancy of utterances (cf. 2.4.5).

The determination of the phonological structure of a language may be thought of, then, in the following way. Every language has a vocabulary of 'actual' words, each of which in the first instance may be taken as phonologically 'regular' (conforming to certain systematic principles of combination operating upon the constituent phonemes). The linguist's task is to account for their phonological 'regularity'. (For simplicity of exposition, we are deliberately restricting the discussion of phonological structure at this point by assuming that phonology is concerned solely with the formation of words, independently of their occurrence in sentences.) Given a set of 'actual' words, the linguist will describe their phonological structure in terms of rules which specify the permissible combinations of classes of phonemes, each member in the class being in contrast with every

other. For example, let us say that each column of phonemes in the
matrix given above constitutes a class, as follows: $X = \{/p/, /b/, /l/\}$,
$Y = \{/e/, /i/, /o/\}$, $Z = \{/t/, /n/, /k/\}$. We may now formulate a rule
which says that any member of X may combine with any member of
Y and Z (in that order). The rule, as we have just seen, will not only
account for the phonological regularity of such 'actual' words as *pet*,
bet, *lit*, *lick*, *peck*, etc.; but it will also admit as regular a number of
non-occurrent 'words'.

Let us now assume that we have established a whole set of rules of
this kind, each of which accounts for the 'regularity' of a class of
English words of different phonological structure, but each of which
also defines as phonologically regular many non-occurrent 'words'.
By contrast with the 'actual' words of English, the non-occurrent
'words' also defined as regular by the same phonological rules may
be called 'potential'. In addition there will be many combinations of
phonemes (e.g. /pta / or /atp/: cf. 2.3.6) which are explicitly or
implicitly excluded by the phonological rules, and are defined as
irregular.

3.3.7 *'Actual' and 'potential' phonological words*

It might be thought that the ideal system of phonological rules would
be one which successfully defined as regular all the words actually
used by the speakers of the language, and no others. But quite apart
from the practical impossibility of formulating rules of this kind, it is
theoretically undesirable that one should attempt to eliminate the
distinction between the 'actual' and the 'potential'. We shall return
to this question in connexion with the principles of generative
grammar (cf. 4.2.2). Here it is sufficient to point out that any attempt
to identify the 'regular' with the 'actually occurrent' in phonology
would fail in two equally important respects.

The vocabulary of most languages will contain a number of words
which are phonologically 'irregular' in the sense that they do not
conform to the patterns of formation characteristic of the majority of
words in the language: they may have been borrowed from other
languages and may not have been 'assimilated' fully, or they might be
'onomatopoeic' (cf. 1.2.2). Although the linguist, as a matter of
principle, tends to assume at the outset that all the words used by the
speakers of a language are phonologically 'regular', he will be
prepared to revise this assumption in the case of particular words, if
he finds that he is unable to bring them within the scope of the rules

he sets up for the majority of the words in the vocabulary. And he will the more readily treat them as 'irregular', when native speakers of the language agree that there is something 'unusual' or 'alien' about them.

But the identification of the 'actual' and the 'regular' also fails in another respect. Many of the non-occurrent combinations of phonemes would be accepted by native speakers as more 'normal' than others; they are, not only easily pronounceable, but in some way similar in form to other words of the language. The phonological description of the language should reflect (although it should not necessarily be determined by) feelings of this kind. It is noticeable, for instance, and it has often been pointed out, that writers of nonsense verse (like Lewis Carroll or Edward Lear) will create 'words' which almost invariably conform to the phonological structure of actual words in the language; and the same is true of brand-names invented for manufactured products. The ideal system of phonological rules for a language will therefore be one which correctly characterizes as regular, not only those combinations of phonemes which constitute the majority of words in the vocabulary, but also many others, which native speakers of the language might accept as 'possible', or 'potential', words. Needless to say, there might be considerable dispute as to the 'correctness' of the characterization. The point is that 'regularity' cannot be defined except in terms of the rules which specify the permissible combinations of the phonological units. And this point is valid at all levels of linguistic description (cf. 4.2.13).

3.3.8   Distinctive features

So far we have assumed that the phonemes of a language are not susceptible of further analysis: that they are minimal expression-elements (to use the terminology of the previous chapter, cf. 2.2.5). This assumption is still made in most of the standard textbooks of linguistics, although it was challenged over thirty years ago by Trubetzkoy, Jakobson and other members of the Prague school. Their approach to phonology has recently been gaining ground, not only in Europe, where it has always had many adherents, but also in America.

According to Trubetzkoy and his followers, the phoneme is further analysable into *distinctive features*. Consider, for example, the following nine phonemes of English: /k/, /g/, /ŋ/, /t/, /d/, /n/, /p/,

/b/, /m/. Typical instances of words in which they occur, in initial and final position, are:

Table 5

/k/	kill,	lack	/p/	pet,	cap	/t/	top,	cat
/g/	gull,	peg	/b/	bid,	hub	/d/	doll,	kid
/ŋ/	—	song	/m/	man,	ham	/n/	net,	pan

The gap in the row for /ŋ/ is accounted for by the fact that this phoneme does not occur in word-initial position. Under the interpretation of phonemic theory outlined above each of these nine phonemes is totally different from all the others. Phonetic considerations are relevant to the question of allophonic variation (i.e. to the grouping together of speech-sounds in complementary distribution as contextually-determined variants of the same phoneme: cf. 3.3.3), but not to the relations which hold between one phoneme and another. To quote Hockett: '...it must constantly be remembered that a phoneme in a given language is defined *only in terms of its differences from the other phonemes in the same language*'. The Prague school phonologists would amend this statement by defining each phoneme in terms of both its similarities and its differences with respect to other phonemes in the same language.

In the case of the nine consonantal phonemes of English illustrated above we can recognize seven *features*, or components, to which we can give the following names (derived from a partial description of their allophones in terms of articulatory phonetics): velar, labial, dental (or alveolar); voiceless, voiced; oral, nasal. Of these, the distinction between voiced and voiceless can be regarded as a distinction between the presence or absence of the feature of voice; and the distinction between nasal and oral as a distinction between the presence or absence of nasality. If we treat the velar, labial and dental-alveolar components as independent features, each of which is either present or absent, we can analyse the nine consonants in terms of five two-valued variables. The variables are La (labial), Ve (velar), De (dental or alveolar), Vo (voice), Na (nasality), and the two values are positive (presence) and negative (absence). We will use the binary digits 1 and 0 to indicate these positive and negative values (cf. 2.4.3).

Given these notational conventions, we can represent each of the nine phonemes as a column of values in a two-dimensional matrix

Table 6. *Articulatory features of English stop consonants*

	/k/	/g/	/ŋ/	/p/	/b/	/m/	/t/	/d/	/n/
La	o	o	o	I	I	I	o	o	o
Ve	I	I	I	o	o	o	o	o	o
De	o	o	o	o	o	o	I	I	I
Vo	o	I	I	o	I	I	o	I	I
Na	o	o	I	o	o	I	o	o	I

Table 7. *Distinctive features of English stop consonants*

	/k/	/g/	/ŋ/	/p/	/b/	/m/	/t/	/d/	/n/
La				+	+	+			
Ve	+	+	+						
De							+	+	+
Vo	−	+		−	+		−	+	
Na	−	−	+	−	−	+	−	−	+

(cf. Table 6). For example, the column for /k/ reads (from top to bottom) as 01000, the column for /g/ as 01010, and so on. It will be observed that every phoneme is distinguished from every other by at least one value of the five variable features.

We must now recognize a distinction between *functional* and *non-functional* values. The phonological contrast between /k/ and /g/ is maintained solely by the negative or positive value of the variable *Vo*; so too, is the contrast between /p/ and /b/, and between /t/ and /d/. The opposition of voiceless v. voiced is therefore a minimal functional contrast within the English oral stop consonants: it is a *distinctive feature*. On the other hand, /ŋ/ is opposed to both /k/ and /g/, /m/ to both /p/ and /b/, and /n/ to both /t/ and /d/, by the positive value of *Na* (nasality); but the fact that the nasal consonants (/ŋ/, /m/ and /n/) are also realized with voice can be regarded as irrelevant to the phonological structure of English. Nasality presupposes, or determines, the occurrence of voice in the phonetic realization of English words: there are no words which are distinguished by the occurrence of a voiceless nasal, rather than a voiced nasal, in the same position of paradigmatic contrast. In this sense, voice is non-functional when it combines with nasality. Similarly, since there are no consonants which are both labial and velar, both labial and dental, both dental and velar, etc., the positive specification of *La*, *Ve* or *De* in any column of the matrix determines the negative value of the other two. We may therefore construct a new matrix in which ' + ' will be used for 'positive', ' − ' for negative, and the absence of either ' + ' or ' − ' for 'non-functional' (cf. Table 7). Each of the nine phonemes we have been discussing is now distinguished from the others in terms of either two or three distinctive features.

The advantage of this approach is that it enables us to state more systematically and more economically restrictions upon the distribution of particular classes of phonemes. For example, although there are many words of English which have /sp/, /sk/ or /st/ in the first two positions (e.g. *spot*, *skip*, *step*), there are none which begin with /sb/, /sg/, or /sd/. Quite clearly, this is not an 'accidental' coincidence in the combinatorial properties of /p/, /k/ and /t/, on the one hand, and of /b/, /g/ and /d/, on the other. There are not six independent 'facts' to be described at this point, but simply one: 'in the context /s-/ the distinction between the voiced and voiceless consonants is non-functional.' And there are many other contexts in which we would wish to say that a particular opposition between one set of phonemes and another is non-functional.

3.3.9 *'Grimm's law' reformulated in terms of distinctive features*

Furthermore, in the diachronic description of languages, developments in the phonological system, which would otherwise be accounted for in terms of 'sound-laws' operating independently upon particular phonemes, can often be more satisfactorily stated in terms of distinctive features. In fact, this kind of formulation was implicit in what was said about 'Grimm's law' in the first chapter (cf. 1.3.9). It is made explicit in Fig. 4 below, in which + *As* stands for 'aspiration' (as against − *As*, absence of aspiration) and + *Fr* stands for 'friction (partial obstruction, characteristic of fricatives, as against total obstruction, characteristic of stop consonants: cf. 3.2.6). This is an over-simplified representation of 'Grimm's law'; and it incorporates certain assumptions about the reconstructed Indo-European consonant system which we need not discuss here. But it will serve for the purpose of illustration.

First of all, it will be noted that what may be regarded as the same speech-sounds (e.g. [p], [g]) are described in terms of different distinctive features in the two systems labelled 'Indo-European' and 'Germanic'. For example, in the former system, [p] opposes [b] as voiceless *v.* voiced, and it opposes [bh] as unaspirated *v.* aspirated. In the 'Germanic' system, [p] opposes [f] as non-fricative *v.* fricative, and it opposes [b] as voiceless *v.* voiced. The presence or absence of aspiration is taken as distinctive for 'Indo-European' (but not for

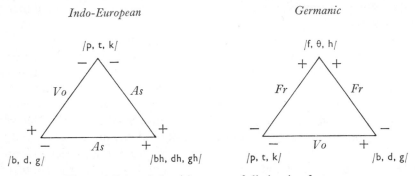

Fig. 4. 'Grimm's law' in terms of distinctive features.

'Germanic'), and the presence or absence of friction is regarded as distinctive in 'Germanic' (but not in 'Indo-European'). The features labial, dental and velar are not indicated, since they remain constant in value between the two stages (i.e. from the phonological point of view, /f/ is regarded as a labial and [h] as a velar). In terms of this analysis, 'Grimm's law' may be stated by means of three 'rules' operating upon the distinctive features: (i) $-Vo \rightarrow +Fr$, (ii) $+Vo \rightarrow -Vo$, (iii) $+As \rightarrow -As$. This does not mean that there were three independent and chronologically-separated developments. For simplicity, however, we may describe it as if the phonetic changes in the realization of the phonemes took place in the following order. (i) In certain positions, notably at the beginning of the word, /p/, /t/, /k/ come to be realized as [f], [θ] and [h] (or [x]). This means that they are now distinguished phonetically from /b/, /d/ and /g/ both as voiceless *v.* voiced and as fricative *v.* non-fricative. At this hypothetical stage of the language (on the basis of the simplifying assumptions we are making here) 'voiceless and fricative' may be regarded as the complex phonetic realization of the value of one phonologically-distinctive feature. (ii) But, subsequently or concomitantly, /b/, /d/ and /g/ come to be realized, phonetically, without voice. As a consequence the opposition between /p/ and /b/, etc., is realized phonetically as [f] *v.* [p], etc. (iii) And, subsequently or concomitantly, aspiration, which was formerly distinctive in /b/ *v.* /bh/, etc., becomes non-functional (and is lost), when these pairs of consonants are distinguished by the opposition of voice.

This summary of the diachronic development also illustrates the important fact that the same speech-sounds may realize different combinations of distinctive features in different languages. For example, [p] has been assigned the values − *Vo* and − *As* in 'Indo-European', and the values − *Fr* and − *Vo* in 'Germanic'. (It may be that, in each case, one of the two values is non-functional. We will not discuss this question, since it would require a rather extensive treatment of the 'Indo-European' and 'Germanic' phonological systems; and the evidence is not always easy to interpret.)

A further point can now be made in relation to this example. The reader may have been puzzled by the apparently unmotivated shift from a phonetic to a phonological description of 'Grimm's law' in the course of the previous paragraph. As we saw in the first chapter 'Grimm's law' did not in fact operate independently of the phonological context in which the consonants occurred. It was 'inhibited', first of all by the accentual conditions described by Verner (cf. 1.3.11), and also by the occurrence of a preceding /s/ in word-initial position. Consequently, a certain number of the voiceless fricatives which resulted from the *phonetic* change [p] → [f], etc., were subsequently voiced (and realized either as voiced stops or voiced fricatives—in either case, they were identical with the consonants which resulted from [bh] → [b], etc.); and the word-initial groups [sp], etc., did not develop into [sf], etc., but were phonetically unchanged. It is for this reason that we say that the *phonological* system changed. This point may be illustrated by means of the following schematic representation of what is assumed to have taken place. The 'words' have been deliberately constructed in order to demonstrate the principles involved without the introduction of extraneous complications:

> Stage 1   Stage 2
> (1) [béda] → [peta]
> (2) [péba] → [fepa]
> (3) [spéda] → [speta]
> (4) [dépar] → [tefar]
> (5) [depár] → [tebar]
> (6) [pébhar]→ [febar]

It will be observed that the place of the accent is given for stage 1. This is to take note of 'Verner's law', according to which in (4) the [p] develops to [f], but in (5) it becomes [b]. As a result, whereas at stage 1 (4) and (5) had the same consonant in medial position and thus differed from (6), at stage 2 (5) and (6) share the same medial consonant and together differ in this respect from (4). And, whereas at stage 1 the consonant that occurs after [s] in (3) is phonetically identical with that which occurs initially in (2), at stage 2 it is identical with the initial consonant of (1). If therefore we describe each system independently of the other, we will say that the distribution of the phonemes is quite different. However, if the phonetic changes had taken place without affecting the syntagmatic and paradigmatic relations of any phoneme relative to any other, we would say that the two systems, despite their phonetic realization, were phonologically *isomorphic* (cf. 2.2.1).

3.3.10   *'Neutralization' in relation to 'marked' and 'unmarked' terms*

In the discussion of the stop consonants in English, we said that the distinction between $+ Vo$ and $- Vo$ was non-functional in the context /s-/ (cf. 3.3.8). It will be clear that this is a somewhat different sense of the term 'non-functional' from the sense in which it was employed a little earlier, when we said that the distinction between $+ Vo$ and $- Vo$ was non-functional in combination with $+ Na$ (cf. 3.3.8). In the one case, the presence or absence of voice is rendered non-functional by the simultaneous occurrence of a particular distinctive feature as a component of the same phoneme; in the other, its redundancy is determined by the context in which the phoneme in question occurs. Contextually-determined redundancy of this kind is described as *neutralization*: the opposition of voice is neutralized in the context /s-/. As we have seen, the Prague school phonologists would say (in earlier statements of the theory at least) that it is not the phoneme /p/ which occurs in the word *spot*, but the archiphoneme /P/ (cf. 3.3.5).

The notion of neutralization is important (not only in phonology, but also in grammar and semantics), because it correlates with the distinction of *unmarked* and *marked* terms of an opposition (cf. 2.3.7). In general, it is the unmarked term which occurs in a position of neutralization. We tacitly took account of this fact in the assignment of the values 'positive' and 'negative' in Table 7. (The assignment of values in the discussion of the 'Indo-European' and 'Germanic' systems is more problematical, and may be treated with some reserve.)

The presence of voice, rather than the 'presence' of voicelessness, was taken as the 'positive' value of the feature in question because it is the voiceless stop consonants which realize the archiphonemes in positions of neutralization: e.g. /s-/.

3.3.11 Recent developments in distinctive-feature theory

Recent developments in distinctive-feature theory (associated mainly with the names of Jakobson and Halle) have been characterized by three main tendencies. The first is the attempt to establish a relatively small set of distinctive features for the analysis of the phonological structure of all languages. The second is the tendency to interpret the phonetic correlates of the distinctive features (their realization in substance: cf. 2.2.5), not in articulatory terms, as we have done here, but in terms of acoustically-based categories (more precisely, perhaps, in terms of categories which can be given an acoustic as well as an articulatory interpretation). The third is the tendency to analyse all contrasts in terms of one or more binary (or two-valued) features. This might involve, for example, the recognition that /p/ and /k/ share some positive or negative value which distinguishes them from /t/, instead of saying, as we have said above, that each of the three differs from the other two by having a positive feature (*La*, *Ve* or *De*) which the other two not only lack, but could not possibly have, under the standard interpretation of such articulatory-phonetic terms as 'labial', 'dental' and 'velar'.

The three tendencies listed in the previous paragraph might be summarized as: (i) universalist, (ii) acoustically-based, and (iii) binarist. All three are highly controversial at the present time; and it would be inappropriate to do more than mention them in an elementary book of this nature. For further discussion, reference may be made to the more technical works cited in the notes.

3.3.12 Prosodic analysis

We must now refer briefly to yet a third approach to phonology. This is generally referred to as *prosodic analysis*: it has been practised mainly by Firth and his followers in London over the last twenty years. It differs from other theories of phonology in that it gives no place at all to the phoneme, whether as a minimal unit of analysis or as a complex of distinctive features. Otherwise, as we shall see, it has a certain affinity with Prague school phonology. We will use Turkish for the purpose of exemplification. This has the advantage that we can simultaneously illustrate the phenomenon of *vowel harmony*, which is found (in one form or another) in very many languages; and it will make the Turkish examples used in the grammatical sections of the book easier to follow.

3.3.13 *Vowel-harmony in Turkish*

The current orthography for standard literary Turkish recognizes eight vowels: *i, ï, ü, u, e, a, ö* and *o*. (Here and elsewhere in this book, we shall use *ï* in place of the undotted form which is normally used in Turkish orthographic practice.) These eight vowels can be described in terms of the following three articulatory oppositions: high *v.* low, back *v.* front, rounded *v.* unrounded (cf. 3.2.5). For simplicity we will regard low as 'negative' with respect to high (*Hi*), front as the 'negative' of back (*Ba*), and unrounded as the 'negative' of rounded (*Ro*); but this attribution of 'positive' and 'negative' values should not be taken here as implying anything about the status of these terms as marked or unmarked. Since each of the eight vowels is in contrast with all the others in monosyllabic words, they may be regarded as eight distinct phonemes, analysable into distinctive features as indicated in Table 8.

Table 8. *The vowel-phonemes of Turkish*

	/i/	/ï/	/ü/	/u/	/e/	/a/	/ö/	/o/
Hi	+	+	+	+	−	−	−	−
Ba	−	+	−	+	−	+	−	+
Ro	−	−	+	+	−	−	+	+

However, it is a characteristic of Turkish that the principle of 'vowel-harmony' operates throughout the word, in the following sense: (i) all the syllables of the word take the same 'value' for the feature *Ba*; and (ii) the feature *Ro* can take the value 'positive' only in the first syllable of the word and in suffixes which have a high vowel (+*Hi*). There are a number of exceptions to this formulation of the general principles. They fall into two main classes: (*a*) borrowed words (e.g. *salon*, 'drawing-room', which has +*Ro* in the second syllable and −*Ro* in the first, *kitap*, 'book', which has −*Ba* in the first syllable and $+Ba$ in the second), and (*b*) words containing 'non-harmonic' suffixes (e.g. *sev-iyor*, 'he loves', where the first vowel of *-iyor-* is 'harmonic', in that it has $-Ba$ and $-Ro$ like *sev-*, but the second is not: it has $+Ba$ and $+Ro$). Both classes of words are phonologically 'irregular' in terms of the general structure of Turkish (cf. 3.3.7). It is customarily said that the values of Ba and Ro are determined by the value they have in the preceding syllable; and there is certainly good reason to assert that vowel-harmony is 'progressive', rather than 'regressive', in Turkish (cf. 2.4.8, for this sense of 'progressive' conditioning). Alternatively, however, we might say that it is neither one nor the other. Instead we can define Ba and Ro not as distinctive features of phonemes, but as *prosodies* of the word. We can think of them as being 'switched' to a particular value throughout the domain of their operation (in the case of Ba and $-Ro$ this is the whole word, in the case of $+Ro$ it is the first syllable: and the occurrence of an irregular 'non-harmonic' vowel 'resets' the 'switch', as it were). By contrast, Hi can take the value 'positive' or 'negative' independently in all syllables. We will now distinguish $+Hi$ and $-Hi$ as *phonematic units* (n.b. not 'phonemes') and symbolize them as 'I' and 'A', respectively.

The effect of this distinction between prosodies and phonematic units is to attribute to the Turkish word a two-dimensional phonological structure. The sequence of phonematic units constitutes the segmental 'infrastructure' of the word, whereas the prosodies form its 'superstructure'. This can be represented notationally in various ways. The system we will use here, for typographical simplicity, is somewhat unconventional. We will put the phonematic units within parentheses and prosodies outside the parentheses: thus $+Ba$, $-Ro$ (kIzlArImIzdAn). The orthographic form of this word, hyphenated to show the grammatical units out of which it is composed, is *kïz-lar-ïmïz-dan* ('from our daughters'). It will be observed that the phonetic realization of the vowel in each syllable of the word is determined in part by the phonematic unit A or I which occurs there and in part by the prosodies $+Ba$ and $-Ro$ which extend over the whole word. The main advantage of this two-dimensional phonological analysis of Turkish is that it gives a more correct impression of the number of phonological contrasts that are possible within the word.

If each of the eight vowels is regarded as being in contrast with all the others, independently in all syllables of the word, this implies that the number of possible vowel sequences in a Turkish word of n syllables is 8^n. But the number of regular sequences is in fact 4×2^n;

i.e. $2 \times 2(2^n)$. This will be clear from the statement of the principles of vowel-harmony given above; and it is reflected in the two-dimensional prosodic analysis. There are four classes of words determined by the two values of each of the prosodic 'variables': (1) $+Ba$, $+Ro$; (2) $-Ba$, $+Ro$; (3) $+Ba$, $-Ro$; and (4) $-Ba$, $-Ro$. And each of these classes contains words of one or more syllables, which may be extended, as the word $k\ddot{i}z = +Ba$, $-Ro$ (kIz) was extended above, by the addition of further syllables. In principle, since there is the possibility of either A or I in each syllable, for every value of n (where n is the number of syllables in the resultant word), there are 2^n phonologically-regular sequences of phonematic units. There are therefore 4×2^1 ($= 8$) different 'sequences' of vowels in mono-syllabic words; 4×2^2 ($= 16$) two-vowel sequences; 32 three-vowel sequences; and so on. Once we take note of the difference in the 'domains' of contrast for phonematic units and prosodies the formula $2 \times 2(2^n)$ can be interpreted as an instance of the more general formula $N = p_1 \times p_2 \times p_3 \ldots p_m$ given in 2.3.8.

For the benefit of those readers who are not familiar with Turkish, the following list of six words may be helpful for the interpretation of the statements made above about vowel-harmony:

gözleriniz	$-Ba$, $+Ro$ (gAz-lAr-In-Iz)	'eye-*plural*-your-*plural*' = 'your eyes'
kollarïmïz	$+Ba$, $+Ro$ (kAl-lAr-Im-Iz)	'arm-*plural*-my *plural*' = 'our arms'
adamlarïn	$+Ba$, $-Ro$ (AdAm-lAr-In)	'man-*plural*-of' = 'of (the) men'
evlerinde	$-Ba$, $-Ro$ (Av-lAr-I(n)-dA)	'house-*plural*-his-in' = 'in their house'
kolum	$+Ba$, $+Ro$ (kAl-Im)	'arm-my' = 'my arm'
gözümüz	$-Ba$, $+Ro$ (gAz-Im-Iz)	'eye-my-*plural*' = 'our eyes'

A prosodic representation of the words is given in the second column, together with an indication of the way in which the words are composed by the 'agglutination' (cf. 5.3.7) of smaller grammatical units. It will be observed that the phonematic structure of these smaller grammatical units remains constant (lAr, Im, etc.). By virtue of their occurrence in words of one prosodic class rather than another, they are realized phonetically in different ways: e.g. [ler] *v.* [lar]; [im] *v.* [ïm] *v.* [um] *v.* [üm] (the orthographic representation in the first column is 'broadly' phonetic: cf. 3.1.2).

3.3.14 *'Multidimensional' nature of prosodic analysis*

One of the main differences, then, between phonemic analysis and prosodic analysis is that the former represents words (and utterances composed of words) as a *unidimensional* sequence of elements (phonemes), the latter as a *multidimensional* structure composed of prosodies and phonematic units. It is multidimensional, rather than simply two-dimensional, because there may be several 'layers' of prosodies operating over 'domains' of different lengths (pairs of consonants, syllables, words, and even groups of words or whole utterances): there is no space to illustrate all these possibilities here. The phonematic units are like phonemes in the sense that they are regarded as discrete units ordered serially, or sequentially, in the unidimensional sequence of phonemes (and archiphonemes).

3.3.15 *Difference between various 'schools' of phonology*

There are many other important similarities and differences between the various approaches to phonology that have been developed in recent years. It should be emphasized, however, that they all rest upon the prior acceptance of the notion of contrast, or opposition, and the recognition that the paradigmatic and syntagmatic 'dimensions' of language are interdependent. The differences between the various 'schools' of phonology can frequently be accounted for in terms of the more particular assumptions which they accept, often for purely methodological reasons.

3.3.16 *Phonology and grammar*

Of these assumptions only one need be mentioned here. For a number of years, many linguists (including Bloch, Harris and Hockett, who did so much to establish the principles and procedures characteristic of the 'orthodox' American approach to phonemics) held that phonological analysis must precede and be independent of grammatical analysis. This assumption, or methodological principle, was never universally accepted (even in America). Nowadays, most, if not all, linguists would agree that it imposes an unnecessarily strong and undesirable restriction upon the theory of language. If anything, it reverses the order of precedence, since the notion of contrast can only apply to words which are capable of occurring in the same context (cf. 2.4.10). The occurrence of words is determined partly by their grammatical function (as nouns, verbs, etc.) and partly by their meaning. It follows, therefore, that two words whose grammatical function prohibits their occurrence in the same context cannot be in phonological contrast. And it is frequently the case that a quite different set of phonological contrasts is relevant for different grammatical classes.

This is true of Turkish. It has already been mentioned that in Turkish (as in Russian and German: cf. 3.3.5) the contrast of voiced *v*. voiceless is neutralized for stop consonants in word-final position. However, it is also neutralized for the majority of suffixes that are added to words in the process of 'agglutination' illustrated above. For example, the suffix meaning 'in' or 'at' (which was written as -dA- in the prosodic representation of the word *evlerinde*) does not contain a voiced dental stop, but a dental stop which is neutral with respect to voice. Whether it is realized as [d] or [t] is determined by its occurrence in a voiced or voiceless environment. (This is a somewhat inaccurate statement of the conditions, but it will suffice.) The point is that the phonological structure of words may be partly determined by their grammatical structure. Although it has been merely mentioned, rather than discussed or fully illustrated, in this section, it will be taken for granted throughout the rest of this book.

3.3.17   *Limited coverage of phonology in present treatment*

Whole areas of phonology have been left untouched in the very brief treatment of the subject that has been presented here. Nothing has been said about stress and intonation in phrases and utterances; nothing about the various functions that tone may serve in different languages; and nothing about the status of the syllable as a phonological unit. For an account of these and other topics, reference should be made to the works cited in the bibliographical notes. In the following chapters we shall be concerned with grammar and semantics.

4

GRAMMAR: GENERAL PRINCIPLES

4.1 Introductory

4.1.1 'Grammar'

The term 'grammar' goes back (through French and Latin) to a Greek word which may be translated as 'the art of writing'. But quite early in the history of Greek scholarship this word acquired a much wider sense and came to embrace the whole study of language, so far as this was undertaken by the Greeks and their successors. The history of western linguistic theory until recent times is very largely the history of what scholars at different times held to fall within the scope of 'grammar' taken in this wider sense.

4.1.2 Inflexion and syntax

More recently the term 'grammar' has developed a narrower interpretation. As used nowadays, it tends to be restricted to that part of the analysis of language which was handled in classical grammar under the headings of inflexion and syntax. The traditional distinction between inflexion and syntax, which rests on the acceptance of the individual word as the fundamental unit of language may be formulated as follows: inflexion treats of the internal structure of words, and syntax accounts for the way in which words combine to form sentences. For the present, we may continue to take the notions of 'word' and 'sentence' for granted. Grammar, we will say, gives rules for combining words to form sentences. It thus excludes, on the one hand, the phonological description of words and sentences, and, on the other, an account of the meaning that particular words and sentences bear. This, it may be observed, is also the sense in which the non-linguist usually intends the word 'grammatical' to be understood when he says that such-and-such a combination of words or the form of a particular word is 'grammatical' or 'ungrammatical'.

4.1.3   *'Notional' grammar*

Modern grammatical theory is frequently said to be 'formal', in contrast with traditional grammar, which was 'notional'. According to Jespersen, a distinguished representative of an older school of grammarians standing between the traditional and the modern approach to grammatical analysis, 'notional' grammar starts from the assumption that there exist 'extralingual categories which are independent of the more or less accidental facts of existing languages' and are 'universal in so far as they are applicable to all languages, though rarely expressed in them in a clear and unmistakable way'. Whether there are any universal 'categories' of grammar which hold for all languages (the 'parts of speech', 'tense', 'mood', etc.) in the sense in which Jespersen and traditional grammarians understood the term is a question that we will discuss later (cf. 7.1 ff.). For the present we shall assume that there are not (or, at least, that there may not be); and in making this assumption we shall be adopting the 'formal' approach to grammatical analysis.

It should be noticed that this is a rather special use of the term 'formal' and has nothing to do with the distinction of 'form' and 'substance' which we made in an earlier chapter (cf. 2.2.2). It differs too from the more general scientific use according to which a formal, or formalized, theory is one in which theorems may be derived from a set of basic terms and axioms by the application of explicit rules of inference. As we shall see later, recent developments in linguistics have gone a considerable way towards formalizing grammatical theory in this more general sense of the term 'formal'. For the moment, the term 'formal' may be taken to imply the rejection of 'notional' assumptions: in other words, formal grammar makes no assumptions about the universality of such categories as the 'parts of speech' (as they were traditionally defined) and claims to describe the structure of every language on its own terms. A more positive indication of what linguists have had in mind when they have used the term 'formal' in opposition to 'notional' will be given in the following section.

4.1.4   *Semantic considerations in grammar*

The 'formal' approach to grammatical description has frequently been understood to carry the further implication that semantic considerations are irrelevant both in the determination of the units of grammatical analysis and in the establishment of rules for their permissible combination in sentences of the language. The proposal to make the theory and practice of grammar independent of questions of meaning has been responsible for the most interesting and most fertile developments in modern grammatical theory. But it has often been mistakenly assumed that linguists who refuse to admit considerations of meaning in grammar take up this position because they have no interest in semantics. This is not so. Nor is it because they believe that semantic analysis is necessarily more subjective than phonological or grammatical analysis. The reason is simply that the grammatical structure of a language and its semantic structure tend to be highly, but not totally, congruent with one another. As soon as the linguist becomes seriously interested in semantics, he must see that nothing but advantage can come from the methodological separation of semantics and grammar. As long as it is maintained that every identity or difference of grammatical structure must be matched with some corresponding identity or difference of meaning (however subtle and difficult to determine) there is a danger that either the grammatical description or the semantic, or both, will be distorted.

Furthermore, it should be noted at this point that the methodological separation of grammar and semantics refers only to the way in which the description of the language is presented. It does not mean that the linguist will deliberately refuse to take advantage of his knowledge of the meaning of sentences when he is investigating their grammatical structure. We shall see later that the fact that a particular sentence is ambiguous (has two or more different meanings) is often an indication that it should be assigned two or more different grammatical analyses (cf. 6.1.3). But we shall also see that ambiguity of itself is insufficient to justify a difference in the grammatical analysis.

4.1.5 *The term 'formal'*

It is unfortunate that the term 'formal' (like many other terms employed by linguists) is used in so many different senses in the literature of the subject. It would be easy enough to avoid such terms. However, anyone who becomes interested in linguistics must sooner or later learn to adjust his interpretation of words like 'formal' according to the context in which he meets them. This adjustment becomes easier when one knows something about the historical development of the subject. For that reason, we shall frequently give a brief account of the etymology or historical development of the more important technical terms when the notions they are associated with come up for discussion. As far as the word 'formal' is concerned, it should be remembered that it is commonly used in the following senses: (i) with reference to the phonological and grammatical structure of language, *in contrast with the semantic* (by virtue of the traditional distinction between the 'form' of a word and its 'meaning': cf. 2.1.2); (ii) with reference to the phonological, grammatical *and* semantic structure of language as distinct from the 'medium' in which language is realized or the conceptual or physical continuum 'structured' by the lexical elements of language (in this sense it is opposed to 'substantial': by virtue of the Saussurian distinction of 'substance' and 'form', cf. 2.2.2); (iii) as equivalent to 'formalized' or 'explicit', in contrast with 'informal' or 'intuitive'; (iv) in opposition to 'notional', in the sense in which this latter term has been illustrated above with the quotation from Jespersen. Of these four senses, (i) and (iv) are not always distinguished in the literature: when linguists talk about 'notional' grammar, they tend to assume that any universal categories postulated by the grammarian will necessarily be based on meaning. (Whether this is a valid assumption or not we will not discuss at this point: we merely draw attention to the fact that it is often taken for granted that 'notional' implies 'semantically-based'.) It is sense (ii), which is in direct conflict with sense (i), that tends to cause the most confusion.

For the sake of completeness, one should perhaps mention that in the very recent literature a somewhat different opposition has been introduced by Chomsky, in his discussion of the universal properties of language. This is a distinction between 'formal' and 'substantive' universals (n.b. 'substantive', not 'substantial'). Roughly, this rests upon a distinction between the nature of the rules used by the linguist in the description of languages and the elements (linguistic units or classes of units) to which reference is made in the rules. If one holds, for example, that there is a fixed set of distinctive features, a particular selection of which is combined in various ways in the phonological systems of different languages (cf. 3.3.11), one may say that these distinctive features constitute the *substantive* universals of phonological theory. By contrast, any condition imposed upon the manner in which the phonological rules operate or the way in which the phonological units combine with one another according to the specification of the rules is a *formal* universal of phonological theory. The postulate of unidimensionality, for instance, could be regarded as a formal universal of 'orthodox' phonemic theory (cf. 3.3.14).

Chomsky's use of 'formal' is related to sense (iii) of the previous paragraph. The universal categories of traditional grammar (in particular the 'parts of speech') cannot be described as either 'formal' or 'substantive', in any very strict application of this distinction, since the rules of traditional grammar were not explicitly formalized. However, it is probably true to say, with Chomsky, that they were defined primarily in 'substantive' terms. It should be noticed, however, that the traditional definitions of the 'parts of speech' frequently included some specification of their combinatorial properties. We shall return to this question in a later chapter (cf. 7.6.1 ff.).

These terminological remarks are intended to assist the reader who may have read, or who may go on to read, other works on linguistic theory. In this book, the term 'formal' will be employed only in senses (iv) and (iii), that is to say, in opposition to 'notional', on the one hand, and to 'informal', on the other: the transition from one sense to the other will be made in the course of the present chapter. When the noun 'form' is used in a technical sense, it will be clearly distinguished by its juxtaposition with either 'meaning' or 'substance': cf. (i) and (ii) above.

4.2 Formal grammar

4.2.1 *'Acceptability'*

We must now try to characterize modern grammatical theory a little more positively than we have done so far.

We may begin by invoking the notion of 'acceptability'. 'Acceptable' is a primitive, or pre-scientific, term, which is neutral with respect to a number of different distinctions that will be made later, including the distinction that is drawn traditionally between 'grammatical' and 'meaningful' (or 'significant'). It is a more primitive term than either 'grammatical' or 'meaningful' in the sense that, unlike these terms, it does not depend upon any technical definitions or theoretical concepts of linguistics. An acceptable utterance is one that has been, or might be, produced by a native speaker in some appropriate context and is, or would be, accepted by other native speakers as belonging to the language in question. It is part of the linguist's task, though not the whole of it, to specify as simply as possible for the language he is describing what sentences are acceptable, and to do this in terms of some general theory of language-structure.

In the description of a modern spoken language the linguist will usually have available a collection of recorded utterances (his 'data', or 'corpus') and he will also be able to consult native speakers of the language (his 'informants'). He may of course be his own informant if he is describing his own language; but in this case he must be on his guard against the danger of producing for description a corpus of material which includes only such sentences as satisfy his preconceived ideas about the structure of the language. As the description proceeds the linguist can obtain further utterances of various kinds from his informants, and so extend the corpus; and he can check with them the acceptability of sentences which he himself constructs in order to test the generality of his tentative rules. If he finds that his informants will not accept as a natural or normal sentence some utterance which satisfies the rules of acceptability which he has so far established, then he must, if possible, revise the rules so that they exclude the 'sentence' in question, whilst still allowing all the acceptable sentences for which they were set up in the first place. In the case of the so-called 'dead' languages, like Latin, it is of course impossible to verify one's rules by checking with native speakers the acceptability of all the sentences accounted for by the rules. For this reason a description of one of the classical languages will inevitably be incomplete in certain respects. However, the adequacy of the description will be proportionate to the amount and variety of the material upon which it is based.

At first sight it might appear that the term 'acceptable', as it has been employed here, is redundant and introduces unnecessary complications. It might be thought that to say that a given utterance is acceptable is to say no more than that it has at some time been produced by a native speaker and that it would be possible, in principle, for a linguist, or team of linguists, to collect all the sentences of a language and put them in the corpus. But this view is erroneous. The term 'acceptable' not only has the advantage of stressing the operational connexion between the linguist's 'raw material' and its ultimate source of control in the reactions of native speakers. It also emphasizes the fact that the linguist must account not only for the utterances which have actually occurred in the past, but also for very many others which might equally well have occurred and might occur in the future. This was generally taken for granted and occasionally made explicit by traditional grammarians. More recently, in their desire to avoid the pitfalls of prescriptive grammar (cf. 1.4.3), many linguists have declared that their descriptions of a particular corpus of material are valid only for the sentences actually occurring in the corpus and carry no implications as to what other sentences might be produced by native speakers of the language in question. But this attitude, however well-intentioned, is, as we shall see, both theoretically and practically untenable.

4.2.2 *The sentences of a language may be unlimited in number*

Every native speaker of a language is able to produce and understand, not merely those sentences which he has at some time heard before, but also an indefinitely large number of new sentences which he has never heard from other speakers of the language. It seems probable, in fact, that most of the sentences produced by native speakers, apart from a limited set of 'ritual' utterances (like *How do you do?*, *Thank you!*, etc.), are 'new' sentences in this sense. And the 'new' sentences will satisfy the same operational test of acceptability to other native speakers as 'old' sentences, which might have been produced simply from memory. They will exhibit the same regularities and can be accounted for by the same rules. In other words, it is the class of potential utterances which we must identify as the sentences of the language. And the number of potential utterances in any natural language is unlimited. Any given collection of utterances, however large, is but a 'sample' of this unlimited set of potential utterances. If the sample is not only large, but representative of the totality of potential utterances, it will, *ex hypothesi*, manifest all the regularities of formation characteristic of the language as a whole. (The distinction made here between the 'sample' and the language as a whole is essentially the distinction drawn by de Saussure between 'parole' and 'langue': cf. 1.4.7.) It is the linguist's task therefore in describing a language to establish rules capable of accounting for the indefinitely large set of potential utterances which constitute the language. Any linguistic description which has this capacity of describing actual utterances as members of a larger class of potential utterances, is said to be *generative* (for further discussion of this term, cf. 4.2.13). We shall see that if rules are established to account for the acceptability of any representative sample of utterances, the same rules will necessarily account for a much larger set of utterances not in the original corpus, unless the application of the rules is very severely, and 'unnaturally', restricted. Moreover, if certain rules with particular properties are incorporated into the description, it will be capable of accounting for an infinite, but specified, set of acceptable utterances. In this respect therefore a generative description will reflect, and indeed can be thought of as 'explaining', the native speaker's ability to produce and understand an indefinitely large set of potential utterances.

4.2.3 'Layers' of acceptability

The question which now confronts us is this: How much of acceptability, or what kind of acceptability, falls within the scope of the grammar, and how much is to be accounted for by other parts of the linguistic description or by disciplines outside linguistics? It seems clear that utterances can be acceptable or unacceptable in various ways or in various degrees. We might say of a foreigner's English, for example, that it is 'grammatically' acceptable (or correct), but that his 'accent' is faulty and marks him immediately as a non-native speaker of the language. We might say of certain sentences (as Russell did, for instance, of the sentence *Quadruplicity drinks procrastination*) that they are 'grammatical', but 'meaningless'; we might wish to say the same of the nonsense verse of Lewis Carroll, but for somewhat different reasons. Then there are other kinds of acceptability and unacceptability, which have nothing to do with whether an utterance is meaningful or not. Fairy-tales and science fiction provide many instances of sentences which would be unacceptable in 'everyday' English. Again, some utterances, though meaningful, would be regarded by certain people or in certain circumstances as 'blasphemous' or 'obscene': this we may refer to, loosely, as 'social acceptability'. In what follows we shall neglect 'social acceptability'.

4.2.4 'Idealization' of the data

When we say that two people speak the same language we are of necessity abstracting from all sorts of differences in their speech. These differences, reflecting differences of age, sex, membership of different social groups, educational background, cultural interests, and so on, are important and, in principle at least, are to be accounted for by the linguist. However, in the speech of any persons who are said to 'speak the same language' there will be what may be described as a 'common core'—a considerable overlap in the words they use, the manner in which they combine them in sentences and the meaning which they attach to the words and sentences. The possibility of communication depends upon the existence of this 'common core'.

For simplicity of exposition, we shall assume that the language we are describing is uniform (by 'uniform' is meant 'dialectally and stylistically' undifferentiated): this is, of course, an 'idealization' of the facts (cf. 1.4.5) and that all native speakers will agree whether an utterance is acceptable or not. We shall also assume that the 'odd' sentences which one might find in children's stories or science fiction are describable in terms of an extension of the description which accounts primarily for more 'normal' utterances. We shall concentrate therefore upon the distinction of phonologically acceptable and grammatically acceptable, on the one hand, and of grammatically acceptable (grammatical) and semantically acceptable (meaningful) on the other.

4.2.5 *Phonological and grammatical acceptability*

In the preceding section we saw that every language has its own phonological structure, describable in terms of a set of units (phonemes or phonological units of diverse kinds according to the nature of the language and the model of analysis adopted by the linguist) and a statement of their possibilities of combination. A certain amount of unacceptability (including much of what is popularly referred to as 'accent') can be accounted for at the phonological, or even the phonetic, level. If we were to produce a large set of sequences of phonological units, each sequence being constructed in accordance with the rules of combination established by phonological analysis of the language in question, we should find that only an infinitesimal fraction of the resulting 'utterances' were acceptable to a native speaker. This point is readily illustrated by means of an English example. For simplicity we may assume that the orthography of English exactly reflects the phonological structure of the language. This assumption, though of course false, does not affect the validity of the point we are illustrating.

Let us take as our example the following English sentence: *iwantapintofmilk*. (It is printed without spaces to indicate that for the moment we are considering it simply as a sequence of letters, each of which is assumed to represent one phonological unit; there is of course no pause between the words in the normal pronunciation of the corresponding spoken utterance.) Making use of our knowledge of the permissible sequences of English letters, we might try the effect of substituting single letters and groups of letters at different places in our model sentence. We know, for instance, that *s* may follow *i* and precede *a* (cf. *isangasongofsixpence*); but **isantapintofmilk* is not an acceptable sentence. (Throughout this and the following sections we shall use an asterisk before a word or sentence to denote unacceptability. This is now standard practice in linguistics. In historical and comparative studies the asterisk generally denotes an unattested, or 'reconstructed', word or phonological unit (cf. 1.3.13).) Nor is **iwantapinkofmilt*, or **ipindawantopfilk*, although none of these 'utterances' can be excluded by virtue of the phonological structure of English. Even if we were to work out over a large body of text, not only the permissible pairs, triples, quadruples, etc., of letters, but also the probabilities of occurrence of particular letters relative to their neighbours (such calculations have been carried out for English and for certain other languages, and the results have been used in cryptography and in the design of communication channels for the transmission of written messages), this would not help us very much in our attempt to construct other acceptable sentences of English by substituting single letters or groups of letters in the model sentence. The fact is that certain 'blocks' of letters within the language form 'higher-level' units at the boundaries of which the probabilities of occurrence of single letters relative to one another are of little significance in determining which 'blocks' can combine with one another to form acceptable utterances.

More relevant than the general probability of occurrence of *w* after *i* and before *a* is the fact that *w* forms part of the 'block' *want*. From one point of view this can be considered as a permissible sequence of letters in English; from another point of view it must be considered as a unit, for which other 'blocks' may be substituted to produce further acceptable utterances: *idrinkapintofmilk*, *itakeapintofmilk*, etc. And *i* is also a 'block': the fact that it is composed of only one letter is irrelevant. No other single letter may be substituted for it in the present environment to produce a different acceptable utterance, but only such other 'blocks' as *we*, *they*, *thejoneses*, etc. What we have been calling 'blocks' of letters we may now recognize, provisionally at least, as words of the language. (To simplify the argument, we will here neglect the fact that some 'blocks' which we might substitute for *I* in the present example are not single words, but combinations of words, like *The Joneses*, *They all*, etc. At this point the reader may wish to refer again to the section dealing with the 'double articulation' of the expression-plane: cf. 2.1.3.)

4.2.6 *Distributional approach to grammatical description*

It will be observed that we have been brought to the traditional view that English sentences are 'structured' on two levels, that of letters (or phonological units) and that of words, without explicitly invoking the notion of meaning. What we have done is to distinguish a phonological (or orthographic) component of acceptability from the rest of acceptability and to leave the rest (or 'residue') of acceptability to be analysed into other 'higher-level' components. It is of course true that the utterances *I want a pint of milk, I drink a pint of milk,* etc. (we may now insert the spaces between the words) are meaningful when used in an appropriate context. Moreover, they are different in meaning; and their difference of meaning is properly described as a function of the meanings of the constituent words, *want, drink,* etc. But so far we have not taken account of these facts; and we shall not do so within the theory of grammar that is being presented here. They will be handled by the theory of semantics. All that we have done in principle is to construct a set of acceptable sentences by placing different words in the same 'frame', or context. The whole set of contexts in which a linguistic unit may occur is its *distribution* (cf. 2.3.1). What is being developed here, therefore, is the distributional approach to grammatical analysis.

We have now advanced to the point at which we can say that phonology accounts for the acceptability and unacceptability of utterances, so far as this can be done, by means of rules or formulae which specify permissible combinations of the phonological units of the language under description and that grammar 'takes over', as it were, at the 'higher' level, accounting for acceptability in terms of permissible combinations of words.

4.2.7 *Interdependence of phonology and grammar*

At this stage in the argument, it should be pointed out that we are still working with the assumption that sentences are composed of words and that words are composed of phonological units (or letters, if we are dealing with the written language). Both of these assumptions will be modified later. (The argument would be made somewhat more complicated, but it would not be invalidated, if we were to introduce the modifications here.) It should also be mentioned that, although we have talked as though grammatical description will necessarily come after (but be independent of) phonological analysis, this need not be the case (cf. 3.3.16). Grammar and phonology are established as theoretically distinct levels of linguistic structure. But the phonological and the grammatical structures of particular languages are usually interdependent (in different ways and in different degrees). It will be the linguist's task in describing a given language to account for this interdependence, where it exists (as it will also be his task to account for such interdependence as may hold between the grammatical and the semantic structure of the language).

4.2.8 *A simple example of distributional analysis*

We are still far from having arrived at a satisfactory account of grammatical description. For we have not yet said how the acceptable combinations of words are to be specified. Listing all the acceptable sequences of particular words is out of the question, since, as we have seen, no natural language can be regarded as a limited set of sentences. In the case of a closed corpus of material it would be possible of course to compile a list of all the phonologically (or orthographically) different sentences and then to decide the question of acceptability by reference to the list. But this would not only be unrevealing, in the sense that it would not contribute to our understanding of the native speaker's ability to produce 'new' sentences. It would not even be the most economical way of describing the given text. If we pursue the matter a little further, we shall see why.

In a reasonably large and representative sample of the sentences of a language there will be a considerable overlap in the distributions of different words. For example, not only could *beer, water, gin*, etc., be substituted for *milk* in *I drink a pint of milk*, but the same set of words could occur in many of the other environments in which *milk* can occur. Likewise *they, we* and *you* can be substituted for *I*, and *buy take, order*, etc., for *drink* in many other environments than the one in the model sentence. Words that can generally be substituted for one another in many different sentences can therefore be grouped into *distributional classes* by virtue of this fact.

Let us assume that we have a corpus of material for analysis consisting of the following seventeen 'sentences': *ab, ar, pr, qab, dpb, aca, pca, pcp, qar, daca, qaca, dacp, dacqa, dacdp, qpcda, acqp, acdp*. Each different letter represents a different word: the symbolic notation is used for reasons of generality, and also to make clear that at this point we are not directly invoking semantic considerations. (Since acceptability is assumed to be preserved by the operation of substitution and since 'acceptability' includes 'meaningfulness', it may appear that we are guilty of equivocation here. We are working towards, but still have not reached, the distinction of 'grammatical' and 'meaningful'.) It will be seen that a and p have certain environments in common (cf. $-r$, $pc-$, $dac-$), and so do b and r (cf. $a-$, $qa-$), and d and q (cf. $dac-a$, $-aca$, $ac-p$), but that c has a unique distribution ($a-a$, $p-a$, $p-p$, $qa-a$, $da-a$, $da-p$, etc.) in the sense that no other 'word' occurs in any of the environments in which c occurs. Let us now put a and p into a class X, and substitute the class-label X at each place where either a or p occurs (the sentences which differ only in that where one has a the other has p being reduced formulaically to one class of sentences): Xb, Xr (ar, pr), qXb, dXb, XcX (aca, pca, pcp), qXr, $qXcX$, $dXcX$ ($daca$, $dacp$), $dxcqX$, $dXcdX$, $qXcdX$, $XcqX$, $XcdX$. Let us now group b and r into a distributional class Y, and d and q into a class Z. Substituting Y for b and r, and Z for d and q, we get: (1) XY, (Xb, Xr); (2) ZXY (qXb, qXr, dXb); (3) XcX; (4) $ZXcX$ ($qXcX$, $dXcX$); (5) $ZXcZX$ ($dXcqX$, $dXcdX$, $qXcdX$); (6) $XcZX$ ($XcqX$, $XcdX$). We can thus account for the sentences of our corpus in terms of six structural formulae specifying the acceptable sequences of classes of words (c being a one-member class). These formulae are *linear* (in a sense to be explained later: cf. 6.1.1).

For the present we may be content with the description of the sentences of our corpus in terms of their linear structure—that is to say, in terms of the following formulae, or rules:

(1) XY
(2) ZXY
(3) XcX
(4) $ZXcX$
(5) $ZXcZX$
(6) $XcZX$

Each of these rules may be thought of as describing a distinct *sentence-type*. (The fact that it is possible to reduce these sentence-types to subtypes by invoking the principles of constituent-structure is irrelevant at the present stage of the exposition: cf. 6.1.2 ff.) It will be observed that this system of rules satisfactorily accounts for the acceptability of the seventeen sentences of the corpus (it defines them as *grammatical*). But it does so only by including the occurrent sentences as members of a total set of forty-eight sentences. (The number 48 is obtained by applying the formula given in 2.3.8 to each of the six sentence-types and summing the totals. There are

$2 \times 2 = 4$ sentences of type (1), $2 \times 2 \times 2 = 8$ sentences of type (2), $2 \times 1 \times 2 = 4$ sentences of type (3), 16 sentences of type (4), 8 of type (5) and 8 of type (6): $4+8+4+16+8+8 = 48$.) The language described by this grammar therefore contains exactly 48 sentences. The thirty-one non-occurrent sentences must either be allowed as acceptable or excluded, if for any reason it is decided that they must be excluded, by means of additional rules prohibiting certain combinations of particular words. The additional rules would obviously much complicate the 'grammar'. In this sense, therefore, the most economical way of describing the given text is one which represents it as a random sample of seventeen sentences from the total set of forty-eight sentences which constitute the language. And the 'grammar' we have set up to describe the text is generative in the sense explained above (cf. 4.2.2). We will say that it *generates*, or *characterizes*, the language of the text, assigning to each of the sentences that occur in the 'sample' (as well as to those which do not occur in the 'sample') a particular *structural description*: *pr* is a sentence of structure XY, *pcda* of structure $XcZX$, etc.

In the case of this restricted artificial 'language', used for the purpose of exemplification, only seven distinct words occur, and there are in the corpus only seventeen simple sentences out of a total of forty-eight which the grammar generates. With a natural language the situation is of course far more complex. The number of individual words will run into many thousands; their distributional classification will not be so straightforward and certainly cannot be carried out in the manner illustrated. Moreover, there will be a number of different types of sentences to be accounted for, including sentences of considerable complexity. However, these facts do not affect the principle. The words of natural languages can be grouped into distributional classes (and, in practice, as we shall see, always have been by grammarians); and the distributional classes established for particular positions in one type of sentence are generally valid for particular positions in other, and more complex, types of sentences. Grammar, as it is understood here, is nothing other than the description of the sentences of a language in terms of the combination of words (and phrases, etc.) by virtue of their membership of distributional classes. It is a kind of algebra in which the 'variables' are word-classes and the 'constants', or the 'values' taken by the variables in particular sentences, are individual words.

In order to see that this yields, in principle, the kind of description which would normally be called 'grammatical', we need only interpret the example with reference to English. Let a = *men*, p = *women*, b = *live*, r = *die*, c = *love*, d = *old*, q = *young*. In other words, let the class X include all those words which are usually referred to as 'plural nouns'; let Y be the class of 'intransitive verbs'; c, the class of 'transitive verbs'; and Z, the class of 'adjectives'. Our statement of the permissible combinations of word-classes implies that sentences such as *Men die, Old men love young women*, etc., which would be described in traditional grammar as instances of a simple 'subject'–'predicate' construction, are grammatically acceptable, while **Die men* or **Old love young men women*, etc., are not.

4.2.9 *Grammatical classes*

In traditional grammatical theory the 'parts of speech' (nouns, verbs, adjectives, etc.) were defined, ostensibly, in 'notional' terms ('a noun is the name of any person, place or thing', etc.). But, as we shall see in a later chapter (cf. 7.6.1 ff.), traditional grammarians have tended to confuse two different questions in their discussion of the 'parts of speech'. The first, which is the question which concerns us here, is that of establishing the conditions under which a certain word may be said to belong to a particular grammatical class: 'Is the word *men* a member of class X or class Y?' In practice, this was always determined in terms of the distribution of the word—its potentiality of occurrence in sentences relative to the occurrence of other words in the same sentences. In this respect, modern linguistics has merely given recognition, within the theory of grammar, to the distributional principle by which traditional grammarians were always guided in practice. The theoretical acceptance of this principle distinguishes 'formal' from 'notional' grammar. The second question has to do with the *naming* of the grammatical classes (once their *membership* has been established on 'formal' grounds): 'Is X appropriately called the class of "nouns"?' From the point of view of 'formal' grammar, any label is as good as any other; and the traditional terms, 'noun', 'verb', 'adjective', etc., are neither more nor less satisfactory for the purpose than any other terms would be.

We shall see later that it may be possible to define such terms as 'noun' or 'verb' in a way that both respects their traditional 'notional' interpretation and also makes them applicable in the 'formal' analysis of different languages. But this question will not be pursued at this point. For the present we will assume that the terms 'noun', 'verb', 'adjective', etc., and other traditional terms of grammar,

have no 'notional' (or universal) application, but denote distributionally justifiable grammatical classes to which any arbitrary labels
might have been given.

We are now in a position to discuss, in a preliminary way, the
distinction between 'grammatical' and 'meaningful'. (We shall,
however, return to this question at various places later in the book.)
For simplicity, we shall restrict our attention at this point to one class
of English sentences (all of which will be described here in a deliberately simplified manner). The class in question may be illustrated by
the following examples, assumed to be acceptable:

    (1) *The dog bites the man*
    (2) *The chimpanzee eats the banana*
    (3) *The wind opens the door*
    (4) *The linguist recognizes the fact*
    (5) *The meaning determines the structure*
    (6) *The woman undresses the child*
    (7) *The wind frightens the child*
    (8) *The child drinks the milk*
    (9) *The dog sees the meat*

In a traditional grammatical description of English, all these sentences
would be defined as simple sentences of subject–predicate structure.
Furthermore, it would be asserted that (in all the instances of the
class of sentences we are at present concerned with) the subject is a
phrase (i.e. a unit made up of more than one word) composed of an
Article (here *the*, 'the definite article') and a *Noun* (e.g. *dog*), and (as
is normally the case in English) it precedes the predicate; and that the
predicate is a phrase composed of a (transitive) *Verb* (e.g. *bites*)
followed by the object of the verb, the object being a phrase composed
of an *Article* and a *Noun* (e.g. *man*). Various other statements would
also be made about the particular class of sentences illustrated above:
that the subject and the verb agree in 'number' (i.e. if the subject-
noun is singular, the verb is also singular, but if the subject-noun is
plural, then the verb is plural: thus *The dog bites* v. *The dogs bite*);
that the verb is 'inflected' for 'tense' (i.e. *bites* is 'present', *bit* is the
corresponding 'past tense' of the same verb, and so on). All these
various points can be more or less satisfactorily interpreted within the
framework of modern 'formal' grammar (cf. especially chapters 7
and 8). For the moment, however, we shall work solely with the three
word-classes articles, nouns and verbs. The article may be regarded
as a one-member class, containing the word *the*; it will be abbreviated

here as T. The class of nouns and the class of verbs, abbreviated as N and V, contain several thousands of words, including those which occur in the 'actual' sentences listed above:

$N = \{dog, man, chimpanzee, banana, wind, door, linguist, fact,$
$meaning, structure, child, milk, meat, \ldots\}$

$V = \{bites, eats, opens, recognizes, determines, undresses,$
$frightens, drinks, sees, \ldots\}$

Given this tentative distributional classification of particular words of English (and it will be observed that we are, by implication, restricting ourselves to the consideration of sentences in which only 'singular' nouns and 'present-tense' verbs occur), we may propose the following grammatical rule (which assumes a purely linear structure: cf. 6.1.1):

$$\Sigma_1: T+N+V+T+N$$

The symbol 'Σ' ('sigma') stands for 'sentence': the Greek letter is employed rather than the Roman 'S' (practice varies in this respect in current work in linguistics) in order to emphasize the difference of 'status' in grammatical theory between sentences and the units out of which sentences are constructed, e.g. words (cf. chapter 5). The sub-script numeral attached to Σ indicates that the rule accounts for only one class of sentences. The choice of the numeral is purely arbitrary.

The rule may be read as follows: 'Any combination of words which results from the substitution of one member of the appropriate word-class, chosen at random from the word-lists in the *lexicon* of the language, in place of the symbols T, N and V at each position of the linear formula $T+N+V+T+N$ is a sentence of type 1.' The grammatical rule presupposes, therefore, not only a lexicon (or dictionary) in which all the words of the language are given the appropriate grammatical classification as N, V or T, but also one or more rules of *lexical substitution* for the replacement of the word-class symbols with words. The existence of such rules we may take for granted at this point: they will be discussed in the following section. Given the grammatical rule proposed above and the associated lists specifying the members of the grammatical classes, all the sentences in our 'sample' are defined to be grammatical, with the structural description $T+N+V+T+N$.

We have said that N and V might have several thousand members. To simplify the arithmetical calculation and yet obtain some reason-able indication of the number of English sentences that would be generated by the single rule given above, let us assume that each of the two classes, N and V, contains exactly one thousand (10^3) members. On this assumption, the proposed rule generates no more and no less than $1 \times 10^3 \times 10^3 \times 1 \times 10^3 = 10^9$ (one thousand million) sentences, each with the same structural description. This is but one rule, and it accounts for a very simple class of very short English sentences.

It is therefore a very comprehensive rule. It is comprehensive in the sense that it undoubtedly generates an enormous number of acceptable sentences. But it is perhaps too comprehensive, since it also generates (and defines to be grammatical) very many sentences which would fail to pass the test of acceptability in normal circumstances of use. (The condition 'in normal circumstances', however indeterminate it might be in application, cannot be omitted. For example, many 'normally' unacceptable 'sentences' are deliberately introduced in the context of linguistic discussion, and in similar 'abnormal' circumstances.) Since all the sentences generated by the proposed rule are thereby defined as grammatical, we must *either* amend the rule to exclude some of the sentences which we consider to be unacceptable *or* account for their unacceptability, if it can be accounted for in the total description of the language, in terms of the incompatibility of the meanings of particular subclasses of words (or in some other way). These two alternatives are not, in fact, mutually exclusive, as we shall see. But let us first consider the implications of the first alternative within the framework of 'formal' grammar.

4.2.10 *Subclassification*

One obvious way of amending the proposed grammatical analysis is to subdivide the classes N and V and formulate, not one new rule, but a whole set of different rules. Let us therefore reclassify the vocabulary as follows:

$$N_a = \{dog,\ man,\ chimpanzee,\ linguist,\ child,\ wind,\ \ldots\}$$
$$N_b = \{banana,\ door,\ milk,\ meat,\ \ldots\}$$
$$N_c = \{fact,\ meaning,\ structure,\ \ldots\}$$
$$V_d = \{eats,\ bites,\ frightens,\ undresses,\ sees,\ \ldots\}$$
$$V_e = \{recognizes,\ determines,\ sees,\ eats,\ \ldots\}$$
$$V_f = \{determines,\ \ldots\}$$

Before we proceed, a number of points should be stressed in connexion with this reclassification. First, the way in which we have arrived at the particular decisions incorporated in it is, in principle, irrelevant. It is not being suggested here that linguistic theory can, or should, yield a set of procedures for the determination, or 'discovery', of the distributional classes referred to in the grammatical rules. What matters is whether one classification rather than another enables the grammarian to formulate a set of rules which will include the maximum number of acceptable sentences and the minimum number of unacceptable sentences among the total set of sentences which the grammar generates. (There are additional considerations, which we will discuss later with reference to the distinction of 'strong' and 'weak' adequacy: cf. 6.5.7. They may be disregarded at this point.) The second point to notice is that the new subclasses, despite the use of subscripts, are now assumed to be totally unrelated to one another. In other words, N_a, N_b and N_c are subclasses of N only in the 'accidental' sense that we have gone from an earlier tentative grammatical classification to a later tentative classification. In principle, what we have done is to construct a completely new classification of the vocabulary and a completely new grammar for the language we are describing. As we shall see in the following section, it is possible to revise the notion of distributional classification with which we are at present operating in such a way that N_a, N_b, N_c can be regarded as subclasses of the wider class N, and V_d, V_e and V_f as subclasses of V. Finally, it should be observed that we have introduced a certain amount of multiple membership: *determines* occurs in both V_e and V_f, and *sees* in both V_d and V_e. Apart from anything that might be said against the double classification of these words, this has the undesirable consequence that within the present framework *sees* in a sentence like *The child sees the banana* is, from the grammatical point of view, a quite different element from *sees* in such sentences as *The child sees the meaning*. We shall return to this problem also in the next section.

Given the new classification of the words we are concerned with, we will substitute for the previous rule a whole set of rules (each one, it should be noticed, defining a completely different sentence-type):

(a) Σ_1: $T + N_a + V_d + T + N_a$ (cf. *The dog bites the man*)

(b) Σ_2: $T + N_a + V_d + T + N_b$ (cf. *The chimpanzee eats the banana*)

(c) Σ_3: $T + N_a + V_e + T + N_c$ (cf. *The linguist recognizes the fact*)

(d) Σ_4: $T + N_c + V_f + T + N_c$ (cf. *The meaning determines the structure*)

Although these four rules suffice to generate the nine sentences of the 'sample' (and very many others), it will be evident that further rules are now required to account for other sentences composed of the words used in the 'sample' which we might wish to regard as acceptable (*The banana frightens the linguist*, etc.). The reader is invited to construct some additional rules and also to extend the lists of words given above.

The most important point that arises in connexion with the revision of the grammatical rules is this: the distinction between the grammatical and the ungrammatical sentences of English has now been redefined. Such combinations of words as *The banana bites the meaning*, *The structure drinks the chimpanzee*, etc., which we will assume to be unacceptable as utterances of English, are now defined to be ungrammatical. On the other hand, there are many other unacceptable utterances which would be allowed by the rules as grammatical: *The chimpanzee drinks the door*, *The dog undresses the wind*, etc.

In principle, we might hope to make the classification of words and the system of rules progressively more detailed, making continual adjustments until it becomes capable of generating the maximum number of acceptable sentences and the minimum number of unacceptable sentences. With each successive modification—and this is the theoretical import of the illustration—the limits of grammaticality are redefined for the language being described. From the 'formal' (*v.* 'notional') point of view, grammaticality is nothing more than acceptability to the extent that this can be brought within the scope of a particular set of rules and a particular classification of the lexical and grammatical elements in the language. (For the present, the distinction between 'lexical' and 'grammatical elements' that has been slipped in at this point may be disregarded: 'lexical and grammatical elements' may be interpreted as 'words'.)

4.2.11 *Indeterminacy of grammar*

In describing a given language, the linguist will draw the limits of grammaticality at a particular point. His decision to draw these limits at one place rather than another, if the decision is made consciously after weighing the various alternatives that present themselves, will tend to be determined by two main factors. The first may be referred to as the principle of 'diminishing returns'. It is possible to go a lot further with the distributional subclassification of words than would have been thought feasible, or even desirable, by traditional grammarians. But sooner or later, in his attempt to exclude the definitely unacceptable sentences by means of the distributional subclassification of their component words, the linguist will be faced with a situation in which he is establishing more and more rules, each covering very few sentences; and he will be setting up so many overlapping word-classes that all semblance of generality is lost. This is what is meant by the principle of 'diminishing returns': there comes a point (and where this point is might be legitimate matter for dispute) at which the increase in the complexity of the rules is too 'costly' in proportion to its 'yield', a relatively small increase in the coverage of acceptable and unacceptable sentences. But the second factor is no less important. Since the sentences of the language being described are so numerous (and, as we shall see later, for both practical and theoretical reasons we may wish to say that they are infinite in number), one cannot hope to decide for every sentence generated by the grammar that it is definitely acceptable or unacceptable. In fact, one does not have to go very far with the grammatical description of any language before one finds disagreement among native speakers about the acceptability of sentences generated by the rules tentatively established by the grammarian. There is therefore a real, and perhaps ineradicable, problem of indeterminacy with respect to acceptability and unacceptability.

It would seem to follow from these considerations that the grammatical structure of any language is in the last resort indeterminate. It is not only that linguists will differ in their interpretation of what constitutes the optimum degree of generality in the scope of the rules and in their evaluation of the acceptability of particular sets of sentences. There is the additional problem that the generation of one set of sentences of a particular type may make the generation of other sentences of a different type extremely difficult to handle within the theoretical framework established for the first set. Some instances of the problems which arise will be given in a later chapter (cf. 8.3.6 ff.). It may be that they will be lessened, and even eliminated, by advances in grammatical theory that are now being made: but at the present time they seem to be rather intractable. We may therefore restate as a general principle which governs all grammatical description (and it will be unaffected by anything that is said in subsequent chapters about the nature and manner of operation of grammatical rules) the following fact: whether a certain combination of words is or is not grammatical is a question that can only be answered by reference to a particular system of rules which either generates it (and thus defines it to be grammatical) or fails to generate it (and thereby defines it to be ungrammatical).

Most writers on grammatical theory, including those who have made major contributions to the development of transformational grammar (in particular, Chomsky), would seem to reject this principle. They suggest that the grammatical structure of any language is determinate and is known 'intuitively' (or 'tacitly') by native speakers. This appears to be an unnecessarily strong assumption. It is undoubtedly the case that native speakers will agree that certain sets of utterances 'belong together', or are 'similar' or 'different' in some way. These 'intuitions', in so far as they are ascertainable, are an important part of the linguist's data; and he will try to account for them by distinguishing various kinds of acceptability (or well-formedness) and various kinds of relatedness between sentences. But he need not assume that there will be any very direct correspondence between the 'intuitions' of the speakers and the statements made by the linguist.

One should not exaggerate the difference of opinion between linguists on this question. To assert that the grammatical structure of language is *in the last resort* indeterminate is not the same as to assert that no part of the grammatical structure is determinate. There are many combinations of words (e.g. *They likes she, *The dog bite the man*, etc.) which all linguists will characterize immediately, not only as unacceptable, but also as 'ungrammatical' (without necessarily producing a set of grammatical rules). One can say that their immediate reaction is based on an 'intuitive' awareness of the grammatical structure of standard English; one can equally well say that the combinations in question infringe principles of such generality in utterances of standard English that any grammar would necessarily have to take account of them. It is with respect to the less general principles that alternative grammars might differ in their characterization of sentences as grammatical and ungrammatical. And the 'intuitions' of linguists and speakers of the language tend to be unreliable and inconsistent at this point anyway.

4.2.12   *'Grammatical' and 'meaningful'*

As we saw earlier in this section, it seems reasonable to distinguish different kinds of acceptability. The traditional distinction between 'grammatical' and 'meaningful' (not to mention the other kinds of acceptability referred to earlier) is not affected by the conclusion we have just reached: that the limits of grammar are ultimately indeterminate; or rather, that each grammar defines its own limits and, in that sense, makes them determinate. When we say that a certain utterance is ungrammatical (by reference to a given grammar), we are not implying that it is not also unacceptable for other reasons. Of some unacceptable combinations of words we will say that they are grammatical, but meaningless; of others that, although they are both grammatical and meaningful, they would not normally occur, because the occasion for saying what they 'express' could hardly arise. Of yet another class of combinations of words we might be inclined to say that they are both ungrammatical and meaningless. At one end of the 'continuum' of acceptability there are to be found certain combinations of words whose acceptability or unacceptability is accounted for only by the grammar (cf. *He gives, They give* v. **He give, *They gives*). At the other end of the continuum the grammatical description is of no avail. But there will be many utterances in the description of whose acceptability or unacceptability both a grammatical account and an explanation in terms of the meaning of the component words will be valid: and it is this fact which gives to the 'notional' definitions of certain grammatical classes the considerable degree of validity that they have in certain languages ('verbs of motion', 'masculine noun', 'locative phrase', etc.). We will return to this question of the correlation between the grammatical and the semantic classification of words in the next section.

4.2.13 *The term 'generative'*

But first we must say something more about the terms 'generate' and 'generative', since they have often been misunderstood. The first point to be stressed is the negative one: a generative grammar is not necessarily a transformational grammar (cf. 6.6.1). The terms 'generative' and 'transformational' are frequently confused, because they were introduced into linguistics at the same time by Chomsky. (The term 'transformation' was also used by Harris in roughly the same sense as it was used by Chomsky.) By Chomsky and his followers the term 'generative' is usually understood to combine two distinguishable senses: (i) 'projective' (or 'predictive'); and (ii) 'explicit' ('formal' *v.* 'informal'). It has been employed in both of these senses in the course of this section.

It was first introduced in the sense of 'projective' (or 'predictive'): to refer to any set of grammatical rules which, explicitly or implicitly, described a given corpus of sentences by 'projecting' them upon, or treating them as a 'sample' of, a larger set of sentences. A grammar of this kind is 'predictive' in that it establishes as grammatical, not only 'actual' sentences, but also 'potential' sentences. It is important to realize that most of the grammars that have ever been written throughout the history of linguistics are generative in this first sense of the term. There would be no reason to stress this point, were it not for the fact that the distinction between prediction and the prescription of normative standards of 'correct usage' is not always appreciated (cf. 1.4.3).

But the term 'generative' was subsequently used in this section in a rather particular sense of 'explicit' (cf. 'generate', 'characterize', 4.2.8). This approximates to, and indeed derives from, one of the senses in which the term 'generate' is employed in mathematics. Let us consider, in a non-technical way, a statement such as the following: 'The number 2 *generates* the set, or series, of numbers 2, 4, 8, 16, 32, ...' This set of numbers, which is infinite, can be ordered into a series, as illustrated in the statement, of 'ascending powers of 2', the number 2 being the base of the series. Every number generated by the base satisfies the function 2^n (where 2 is the base and n is a variable ranging over the natural numbers, 1, 2, 3, 4, ...). Any number of whatever magnitude either belongs to the set generated by 2 in the sense defined or it does not; whether it belongs to the set ('the powers of 2') is *decidable*. The *decision-procedure*, for any given number, might take the following form: generate the series in question up to or beyond the magnitude of the particular number, testing for identity with each of the numbers generated by the base. In this way we might decide, for instance, that 9 is not in the set, since it does not equal 2, 4, 8 or 16 (the first number in the series greater than 9). Furthermore, in order to emphasize the grammatical analogy, one might say that each number in the set is generated with a particular 'structural description': the 'structural description' of 64, for instance, is '2^n, where $n = 6$'.

When we say that a grammar generates the sentences of a language we imply that it constitutes a system of rules (with an associated lexicon) which are formulated in such a way that they yield, in principle, a decision-procedure for any combination of the elements of the language (let us call them 'words' at this juncture) in more or less the above sense. Furthermore, the grammar not only 'decides' whether a given combination is grammatical or not (by generating or failing to generate a combination of symbols which can be tested for 'identity' with the utterance in question); but it provides for each grammatical combination at least one structural description. (We shall see later that sentences with more than one structural description are defined to be grammatically ambiguous: cf. 6.1.3.)

This second, more or less mathematical, sense of the term 'generate' presupposes, for its applicability to grammar, a rigorous and precise specification of the nature of the grammatical rules and their manner of operation: it presupposes the *formalization* of grammatical theory. In the course of this section, we have therefore moved from 'formal' *v.* 'notional' to 'formal' *v.* 'informal' in our interpretation of the term 'formal grammar'. This transition reflects the historical development of grammatical theory over the last ten or fifteen years.

4.2.14 *'Distribution' and 'discovery procedures'*

The principles of distributional analysis (which we have been taking to be definitive for 'formal' *v.* 'notional' grammar) were most thoroughly and extensively discussed by Harris, especially in *Methods in Structural Linguistics* (published in 1951, but written a few years earlier). Harris and other American linguists at the time developed these principles within the framework of 'procedural' linguistics: a set of assumptions about the nature of linguistic theory and methodology which was not universally accepted then and is still less generally accepted now. In particular, it was assumed that the proper task of 'structural linguistics' was to formulate a technique, or procedure, which could be applied to a corpus of attested utterances and, with the minimum use of the informant's judgements of 'sameness' and 'difference', could be guaranteed to derive the rules of the grammar from the corpus itself. For this reason, the term 'distribution', and the term 'structuralist', has, for purely historical reasons, come to be associated with the view that it is possible to formulate 'discovery procedures' for the establishment of the rules of particular grammars on the basis of attested utterances. It should be clear that the term 'distribution' is used in this book without any of these adventitious implications. It should also be realized that the work of Harris and his colleagues, with its strong tendency towards rigorous formulation of distributional principles, served as the foundation upon which generative grammar has been built, since the publication of Chomsky's *Syntactic Structures* in 1957.

4.3 Grammar and lexicon

4.3.1 *Analysis and synthesis*

As we saw in the previous section, every grammar presupposes a *lexicon* (or dictionary) in which the words of the language are classified according to their membership of the distributional classes referred to in the grammatical rules.

Both the grammar and the lexicon can be looked upon from two different points of view, according to whether the linguist is concerned with the *analysis* ('recognition') of a corpus of utterances or the *synthesis* ('production') of grammatical sentences. Although practical convenience may dictate that the lexicon and the grammar be organized in a somewhat different way, according to whether they are being employed for 'recognition' or 'production', it is important to realize that they are themselves neutral with respect to this distinction. Any corpus of attested utterances can only be described satisfactorily as a 'sample' of the sentences the grammar generates (cf. 4.2.8). There is therefore no opposition between generative and 'descriptive' grammar.

However, the fact that grammar is neutral, in principle, with respect to analysis and synthesis does not mean that the adoption of one point of view rather than the other will not have any practical consequences. If the grammar is to be used for synthesis, it will be convenient to have the lexicon organized in such a way that, given a particular word-class symbol (e.g. N, 'noun'), one can readily find the members of the class in question for the operation of the lexical-substitution rules (cf. 4.3.2). One obvious way of doing this is to organize the lexicon as a set of lists, each of the following form

$$N = \{man,\ boy,\ chimpanzee,\ \ldots\}$$

On the other hand, if we are engaged upon the analysis of a given text, it will be easier to work with a master list in which the words are ordered according to some principle (e.g. alphabetically) which enables us to find quickly any individual words occurring in the sentences being analysed and discover their grammatical properties, e.g.

> *beauty: Noun*
> *die: Noun, Verb*
> *warm: Adjective, Verb*

Our conventional dictionaries are of this second type. Traditional grammarians did not usually compile lists of the first type except for 'irregular' forms (which they might put in the grammar, as well as listing them alphabetically in the dictionary). They assumed the possibility of constructing lists of words for the purpose of 'synthesis' on the basis of the meaning of particular words and the definitions of the 'parts of speech'. Some recent generative grammars, or grammatical sketches, provide partial lists for each word-class (and we shall discuss the nature of these lists below). The difference between the two kinds of lexicon is not one of principle, but simply one of convenience of reference. Modern generative grammars of the kind referred to have been more concerned to establish the grammatical classes required in the description of the language they are dealing with than exhaustively to classify all the words in these languages. If all the words of the language are not classified appropriately in the lexicon, the grammar will not be generative in the sense referred to as 'explicit' (cf. 4.2.13).

One consequence of the adoption of the point of view of analysis rather than synthesis may be mentioned here. If the linguist knows that his description of a particular language is going to be used only for the analysis of recorded material (this is the case, for example, in some of the projects which have as their aim the automatic analysis of written texts for the purpose of machine-translation or library-classification and the retrieval of information), he can afford to make a less exhaustive classification of the lexicon and a less complete grammatical description of the language.

For example, there are very many English nouns which end in *ness* (e.g. *goodness*, *correctness*, etc.). Most of these, like the two instances just cited, can be 'derived' from adjectives (e.g. *good*, *correct*, etc.). Without going into the nature of 'derivation' at this point (cf. 5.4.2), we can say one word, a noun, may be derived from another, an adjective, by means of the following formula: $A_x + ness = N_y$. (This may be read as follows: 'Any word composed of a member of word-class A_x and *ness* is a member of word-class N_y.') Since this is a very productive derivational rule of English, we may assume that it is included in the grammar; and all the words ending in *ness* which can be derived by means of the formula may be removed from the lexicon.

Now, if we are concerned with synthesis, we must decide which adjectives belong to the class A_x: whether, for instance, this class includes *true* and *strong*, so that *trueness* and *strongness* (in addition to, or rather than, *truth* and *strength*) would be generated as grammatical or excluded as ungrammatical. But a 'recognition' grammar need not wait upon this decision. Then it would be quite reasonable to work with the more general rule $A + ness = N_y$. ('Any word which occurs in a sentence at a position in which N_y is permissible, and which can be analysed into A and *ness* is to be accepted by the recognition programme.') If *trueness* and *strongness* were to turn up in the texts being analysed they would be analysed and accepted as grammatical; if not, the question is irrelevant. (The words *truth* and *strength* would be listed in the lexicon or analysed in terms of other rules. The example that has been used here comes from an actual computer programme which successfully analysed very many English derivational formations.)

There is no difference of principle associated with the difference of viewpoint. Whether it is used for analysis or synthesis, the formula $A + ness = N_y$ generates the same set of words (assuming that it makes reference to the same list of adjectives). But, if one is concerned solely with analysis, one can afford to set one's sights lower. One can deliberately generate (in the abstract, mathematical sense of 'generate'—and this is the sense in which the term must always be interpreted) a set of sentences which includes many that one would normally wish to exclude, on the assumption that they will not occur anyway. To exclude sentences which one assumes will not occur would add considerably to the 'cost' (cf. 4.2.11). This principle of 'cost-effectiveness' has frequently been applied in automatic language-analysis by computer, since the principle of 'diminishing returns' has a very direct economic interpretation (in terms of the additional time required for programming, extra running time for the computer, etc.).

But one must forestall a possible misunderstanding in connexion with analysis and synthesis. The fact that the grammar is neutral between the two does not imply that analysis is simply the converse of synthesis (or *vice versa*). It should not be supposed that a computer programme, for instance, might work 'downwards' through a set of rules (and from the grammar to the lexicon) in the 'production' of sentences and 'upwards' through the same set of rules (and from the lexicon to the grammar) in the 'recognition' of a given corpus of material. Both 'production' and 'recognition', whether by speakers and hearers of a language or by a computer programme designed to simulate their 'behaviour' in the use of language, would seem to involve 'feedback' from one process to the other (cf. 3.2.9). Little progress has yet been made in the investigation of this problem from a psychological point of view; and a certain amount of 'psycholinguistic' research has been vitiated by a failure to realize that 'generative' does not mean 'productive'. Hence this cautionary paragraph.

4.3.2   *Lexical substitution rules*

We may now return to our discussion of the structure of the lexicon. For simplicity, we shall continue to operate with our very simple notion of grammatical rules. Although this will be revised in subsequent chapters, the revision will have no effect upon the general points made here. Let us therefore return to the first rule used in the previous section:

$$\Sigma_1 : T + N + V + T + N$$

and the word-classes it presupposes

$$T = \{the\}$$
$$N = \{man, dog, chimpanzee, \ldots\}$$
$$V = \{bites, eats, opens, \ldots\}$$

The process of lexical substitution (the insertion of particular words at the positions established by the grammatical rule: cf. 4.2.9) can be described as follows: For each occurrence of a grammatical-class symbol in the structural description of a sentence put any member of the class referred to, taking this member from the class listed in the lexicon. (When all the grammatical-class symbols have been replaced, or 'rewritten', by means of the repeated application of this principle of lexical substitution, the 'output' of the generative system is a sentence with a specified structural description.) The operation of lexical substitution can be formalized by means of the following rule

$$X \to x \mid x \in X$$

'Rewrite X, where X is a variable ranging over ("taking as its values") all the grammatical classes referred to in the generative system (e.g. T, N or V), as x, where x is any member of the class X.' The repeated application of this lexical-substitution rule would convert $T + N + V + T + N$ into a sentence like *The dog bites the man*, which is represented in the *tree-diagram* in Fig. 5. (It will be observed that the distinction between the part of the 'output' which comes from the grammatical rule and the part which comes from the lexicon is represented in the distinction between solid and broken lines in the tree-diagram. This is a useful convention, which we will adhere to throughout the present work.)

Since the lexical-substitution rule operates in the same way independently of the 'value' taken by X, we can look upon the lists of words as a set of rules appended to the grammar and thus dispense

with the generalized lexical-substitution rule. In taking this view
(which we shall presently revise) we shall be following the practice
of Chomsky and the earliest writers on generative grammar. Let us
therefore organize the lexicon in the following form:

$$T \rightarrow \{the\}$$
$$N \rightarrow \{man, \, dog, \, chimpanzee, \, \ldots\}$$
$$V \rightarrow \{bites, \, eats, \, opens, \, \ldots\}$$

The arrow may be interpreted as an instruction to replace, or
'rewrite', the element occurring to the left of the arrow with one of
the elements listed to the right of the arrow: e.g. '$y \rightarrow z$' would mean
'rewrite y as z (under the conditions governing the system of rules)'.
Any system of rules, each of which is cast in this form (the manner of
their operation will be discussed in greater detail in chapter 6) will
be referred to as a *rewrite-system* (or system of rewriting rules).

We will now use the rewriting arrow for the grammatical rule also,
and integrate the grammatical rule and the lexical-substitution rules
in the one system:

(1) $\Sigma \rightarrow T + N + V + T + N$

(2) $T \rightarrow \{the\}$

(3) $N \rightarrow \{man, \, dog, \, chimpanzee, \, \ldots\}$

(4) $V \rightarrow \{bites, \, eats, \, opens, \, \ldots\}$

This is a very simple generative grammar, which we will now extend to
accommodate a certain amount of subclassification of the word-classes.

It was pointed out in the previous section that, within the framework of assumptions with which we were working in our discussion
of formal grammar, any reclassification of the words in the lexicon
yielded, not subclasses of the original wider classes, but *entirely
unrelated* new classes. From the grammatical point of view, this
inadequacy may be remedied by the inclusion of additional rules, as
follows

$$N \rightarrow \{N_a, \, N_b, \, N_c\}$$
$$V \rightarrow \{V_d, \, V_e, \, V_f\}$$

We must now amend the lexical-substitution rules (increasing their
number). Thus, the new grammar-and-lexicon takes the following
form:

(1) $\Sigma \rightarrow T + N + V + T + N$

(2) $N \rightarrow \{N_a, \, N_b, \, N_c\}$

(3) $V \rightarrow \{V_d, V_e, V_f\}$

(4) $N_a \rightarrow \{man, dog, chimpanzee, \ldots\}$

(5) $N_b \rightarrow \{banana, door, milk, \ldots\}$

(6) $N_c \rightarrow \{fact, meaning, structure, \ldots\}$

(7) $V_d \rightarrow \{eats, bites, frightens, \ldots\}$

(8) $V_e \rightarrow \{recognizes, \ldots\}$

(9) $V_f \rightarrow \{determines, \ldots\}$

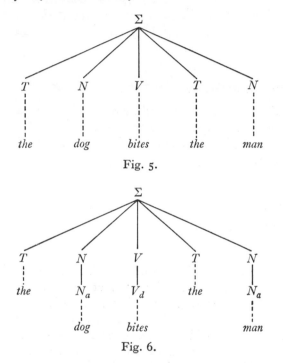

Fig. 5.

Fig. 6.

This system of rules formalizes *within the grammar* the fact that N_a, N_b and N_c are subclasses of N (the members of the subclasses are 'nouns') and V_d, V_e and V_f are subclasses of V (the members are 'verbs'). There is consequently an additional 'layer' of grammatical structure introduced by the system for the purpose of formalizing this fact (cf. Fig. 6, which represents the additional 'layer' by means of the branches of the 'tree' connecting N and N_a and V and V_d). However, it does so by allowing as grammatical the very combinations of subclasses that the process of subclassification was designed to prohibit. (There is no restriction in the above set of rules to prevent the selection of, say, N_b in the second position, of V_d in the third position, and of N_c in the fifth position.)

What is involved here is the principle of syntagmatic conditioning, or compatibility, between one subclass of words and another: what is generally referred to as *lexical selection*. At this point, we are concerned with the structure of the lexicon, and we will not go into the grammatical aspects of this. Let us simply assume that an appropriate formalization is available (making use of 'context-sensitive' rules: cf. 6.5.1) which will enable us to preserve the notion of subclassification, expressed in rules (2) and (3), and yet to generate the desired combinations of subclasses.

4.3.3 *Grammatical features*

We may now envisage a more and more detailed subclassification of the vocabulary of the language (to the point of 'diminishing returns'). The grammar might be extended, for example, to include such further rules as

$$N_a \rightarrow \{N_{a1}, N_{a2}\}$$
$$N_b \rightarrow \{N_{b1}, N_{b2}\}$$
$$N_{a1} \rightarrow \{N_{a11}, N_{a12}\}$$

etc.

Each successive subclassification of this kind implies an increase in the number of lexical-substitution rules at the end of the grammar. Moreover, it will be evident that this formalization is based upon a very particular (and, as we shall see, false) assumption about the grammatical structure of language. The rules divide the vocabulary into *hierarchically-ordered* classes and subclasses (cf. Fig. 7), such that N_{a11} and N_{a12} are totally included in N_{a1}, N_{a1} is totally included in N_a, and N_a is totally included in N; and so on. This assumption was made in the earliest generative grammars which adopted the rewrite-system of formalization (introduced into linguistics by Chomsky).

It is unsatisfactory in two respects. First, it leads to a large number of separate lists of words in the lexicon, with a commensurately high degree of multiple-membership (cf. 4.2.10). Second, and more important, it makes the formulation of the grammatical rules more complicated than the 'facts' would suggest is necessary. To quote

Chomsky: 'The difficulty is that this subcategorization [i.e. the sub-classification of the vocabulary] is typically not strictly hierarchic, but involves cross classification. Thus, for example, Nouns in English are either Proper (*John, Egypt*) or Common (*boy, book*) and either Human (*John, boy*) or non-Human (*Egypt, book*)...But if the sub-categorization is given by rewriting rules, then one or the other of these distinctions will have to dominate, and the other will be unstatable in the natural way.' For instance, if the class of Nouns is

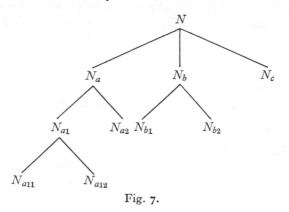

Fig. 7.

first divided into Proper Nouns and Common Nouns, then each of these in turn divided into a Human and non-Human subclass, the only way in which a rule can be formulated to refer to all Human nouns is by making it refer to both of the *completely unrelated* classes Proper–Human and Common–Human (since there is no list of Human Nouns in the lexicon). Chomsky goes on to point out: 'As the depth of the analysis increases [i.e. with successive subclassifi-cation], problems of this sort mount to the point where they indicate a serious inadequacy in a grammar that consists entirely of rewriting rules.'

We shall not discuss the revision of the *grammatical* rules which Chomsky has proposed in order to solve these problems: in this chapter we are working with a very simple system. As far as the lexicon is concerned the effect of 'cross-classification' is clear. It means that each word must be indexed in a way that makes it possible to select, for instance, any 'human' noun (regardless of whether it is 'proper' or 'common'), any 'concrete' noun (regardless of whether it is 'animate' or 'inanimate'), and so on. The technical term which has come to be associated with this kind of classification, or 'indexing', is *feature* (cf. the use of the term 'feature' in phonology, with which there is a certain parallelism). Every word, we assume, must be listed in the lexicon (which can now no longer take the form of a set of rewrite-rules included in the grammar) with a set of features, as follows:

> *boy:* [common], [human], [masculine], ...
> *door:* [common], [inanimate], ...

The rule, or rules, of lexical substitution will then be formulated in a manner which makes it possible to select a particular word according to one or more specified features. At what point in the generative system the lexical-substitution rules will apply is a disputed question. It should be observed, however, that, although we must now abandon the view of the lexicon which represented it as a set of rules of the form $N_a \rightarrow \{boy, \ldots\}$, our more general rule still holds (cf. 4.3.2):

$$X \rightarrow x \mid x \in X$$

('rewrite X as x, where x is a member of the word-class X'). The difference is that now X is that class of words which satisfy a particular feature-specification. For example, if the sentence generated by the grammar calls for a 'common, human, masculine' noun, then X is the class composed of all the words in the lexicon which include among their grammatical features [common], [human] and [masculine]: e.g. *boy*. But there is no list of this composite class.

4.3.4 *Implications of congruence in grammatical and semantic classification*

We may now take up a further point. Although it is hardly relevant to the understanding of generative grammar as this is represented so far in the published literature, it is beginning to assume some importance in connexion with certain proposals that have been made recently for the formalization of semantics. As we shall see in later chapters, there is good reason to believe that the integration of grammar and semantics will bring about some *rapprochement* between 'formal' and 'notional' grammar. For that reason, it is especially important not to lose sight of the general principles.

The terms used for the features mentioned in the previous paragraphs ('proper', 'common', 'animate', 'masculine', etc.) were described as *grammatical*. We have not abandoned the principle that such terms, when they denote classes of words referred to by the grammatical rules, are labels for what are assumed to be distribution-ally-based classes. However, the labels that have been employed at this point (which derive from 'notional' grammar) obviously carry with them certain semantic implications. We have already referred to the congruence which holds, in various degrees, between the grammatical and the semantic structure of language; and we shall come back to this question later. It may be assumed that most of the grammatically 'animate' nouns will denote human beings or animals, that most 'masculine' nouns will denote males, and so on. But the classification of words in terms of such features as 'animate' or 'masculine' will often conflict with a classification based on the meaning of the words (cf. chapter 7). This is well-recognized, and it is the main reason why most linguists have turned away from 'notional' grammar.

At the same time, it should be clearly understood that in a compre-hensive description of a language the lexicon will include both grammatical and semantic information for every word that is listed there. It is not inconceivable that the semantic information should be organized in such a way that it then becomes possible to derive part of the grammatical information (required for the operation of the grammatical rules) from the statement of the meaning of the word *whenever there is congruence between the grammatical and the semantic classification*. Let us suppose, for example, that the word *man* is given in the lexicon with a statement of its meaning (in whatever form this might take) and let us further suppose that from this information it is possible to derive by a statable rule the fact that *man* (in at least one of its meanings) denotes a male, adult, human being (n.b. this does not imply that the meaning of *man* is 'male, adult, human being': this proviso is important in view of what will be said in the chapters on semantics). Given this fact, we can derive from it the *grammatical* classification of the word *man* as [masculine], [human], which implies [animate], etc. This is a grammatical classification, because it is designed to account for such distributional facts as the use of the forms *who* v. *which*; *he, him, his* v. *she, her* v. *it, its*, etc. For example, **The man which came...*, or **The man washed her own shirt* must be excluded as unacceptable, and we will assume as ungrammatical.

At first sight, it might appear that this proposal to derive the grammatical classification of a word from a statement of its meaning contradicts the principles of formal grammar discussed in the previous section. This is not so, provided that we respect the following important condition: any general rule that is established for the derivation of grammatical features from the statement of the meaning of a word given in the lexicon is inhibited by the overt specification of the word with a *contradictory* feature. Let us assume, for example, that all words denoting human beings are grammatically [human], and that this also implies that they are [animate]; further, that they are [masculine] if they denote males, and [feminine] if they denote females. This is the general principle, which will apply if there is no contradictory grammatical classification associated in the lexicon with a given word. We will now state (and assume the grammatical apparatus for the formalization of this statement) that [inanimate] contradicts [animate]. Since the word *man* does not have any contradictory grammatical features associated with it in the lexicon, the general rules for the conversion of semantic information into grammatical will apply correctly.

But the word *child* might be entered in the lexicon with the feature [inanimate], in order to allow such sentences as *The child ate its dinner*. One realizes immediately, however, that the facts are far more complicated than this simple technique can handle. Such sentences as *The child ate his dinner* and *The child ate her dinner* are also acceptable. We might therefore introduce a distinction between [inanimate] and [neuter]. Normally, [inanimate] (whether it is specified in the grammatical information or derived for a particular word from an analysis of its meaning) will imply [neuter]; and [animate] will imply either [masculine] or [feminine], the choice being left free if the noun is not determined as one or the other. But we might consider the possibility of entering *child* as both [animate] and [neuter]. In this case, we must set up the grammatical rules in such a way that the selection of either *he* or *she* on the basis of [animate] is not inhibited by the presence of [neuter]; and, conversely, that the selection of *it* on the basis of [neuter] is not inhibited by the presence of [animate]. The situation is in fact rather more complicated than we have indicated here. But the general principles are not affected by the additional complexity.

The proposal that has just been outlined has not yet been implemented in any of the published literature (as far as I am aware). But it has much to recommend it; and its implementation might well result from developments that have been taking place recently in 'componential' semantics (cf. 10.5.1 ff.). At the same time, it must be stressed that the proposal is not only highly speculative at the present time, but any attempt to implement it would entail a rather radical revision of the formalization of generative grammar as this has been developed by Chomsky and his followers. Various suggestions have been made recently by other authors which, for other reasons, would tend to imply that this revision is necessary; and reference to these will be made in the notes appended to later sections of this book. However, in the body of the book we shall follow (in general, if not always on points of detail) the main line of development in the theory of generative grammar, as this has been traced by Chomsky and those working most closely with him.

4.3.5 Summary

In this chapter, we have introduced the notion of 'generative grammar'; and we have deliberately simplified the treatment of grammatical rules, in order to concentrate upon the more general principles. We have also maintained the view that sentences are constructed by the simple operation of taking words from the lexicon (according to their grammatical classification) and combining them in sequence. Furthermore, we have not distinguished consistently between 'sentence' and 'utterance', since we have tacitly assumed that the grammar (supplemented by the rules of phonology and their phonetic interpretation in the substance of sound) generates sentences which are 'identical' with the potential utterances of the language. Modifications will be introduced on all these points in the course of the next two chapters. Before we return to the further development of the generative framework, we must discuss the nature of sentences and other grammatical units.

5
GRAMMATICAL UNITS

5.1 Introductory

5.1.1 *Words, sentences, morphemes, phrases and clauses*

Traditional linguistic theory operates with two fundamental units of grammatical description: the *word* and the *sentence*. Both of these units are given practical recognition in the conventions of different writing systems. For instance, in the various alphabetic systems employed for European languages, as well as for many other languages throughout the world, sentences are separated from one another by using special marks of punctuation (full-stop, question-mark, exclamation-mark) and by capitalizing the first letter of the first word in each sentence; and, within sentences, words are separated from one another by spaces. For this reason, the educated layman is familiar with the terms 'word' and 'sentence', and uses them freely in talking about language.

So far we have been employing the terms 'word' and 'sentence' without definition or explanation. We must now examine these terms in the light of the general principles discussed in the previous chapter, taking account of the implications that 'word' and 'sentence' carry in everyday usage and in traditional grammatical theory.

For reasons which will be explained later in this chapter, the classical grammarians were little concerned with the analysis of words into smaller elements. However, it is clear that, in many languages at least, such elements exist. For instance, the English word *unacceptable* is made up of three smaller units, each of which has a characteristic distribution: *un*, *accept*, and *able*. Moreover, these are minimal units in the sense that they cannot be analysed further into distributionally-classifiable units of English. Such minimal units of grammatical-analysis, of which words may be composed, are customarily referred to as *morphemes*.

We have therefore three different units of grammatical description to consider in this chapter: sentences, words and morphemes. Intermediate between the word and the sentence, two other units are commonly recognized by grammarians: phrases and clauses. Traditionally, the distinction between the two was formulated somewhat as follows: any group of words which is grammatically equivalent to a single word and which does not have its own subject and predicate is a *phrase*; on the other hand, a group of words with its own subject and predicate, if it is included in a larger sentence, is a *clause*. The distinction between phrases and clauses was not always drawn clearly or consistently in the analysis of particular sentences. Theoretically, the traditional distinction between phrases and clauses amounts to a distinction between word-like and sentence-like groups of words within sentences; for the sentence itself, as we shall see, was traditionally defined in terms of 'subject' and 'predicate'. The phrases and clauses of traditional grammar are therefore secondary units defined in terms of their grammatical equivalence to the primary units, words and sentences. We shall have little to say about phrases and clauses from the point of view of modern grammatical theory in this book (but cf. 5.5.1, 6.2.10).

The relation between the five units of grammatical description (in languages for which all five are established) is one of *composition*. If we call the sentence the 'highest' unit and the morpheme the 'lowest', we can arrange all five units on a scale of *rank* (sentence, clause, phrase, word, morpheme), saying that units of higher rank are composed of units of lower rank. Alternatively, we can say that units of higher rank can be analysed (or 'decomposed') into units of lower rank.

Many older books on language devoted a good deal of space to discussing which of the two traditional primary units of grammatical description, the word or the sentence, it to be regarded as 'basic': does the grammarian first of all identify words and then account for the structure of sentences in terms of the permissible combinations of words, or does he start by recognizing the sentences in his material and then analyse these sentences into their constituent words? We shall not go into this question here. For the present, we will assume that the grammar of a language is neutral with respect to the question whether one works 'up' or 'down' the scale of rank, just as it is neutral to the distinction of analysis and synthesis (cf. 4.3.1).

5.1.2 *The utterance*

One reason why linguists no longer argue whether the sentence or the word is more 'basic' is that they now realize, more clearly than did their predecessors, that neither words nor sentences, nor indeed any of the other units of linguistic description, are 'given' in the unanalysed material. When the linguist sets out to describe the grammar of a language on the basis of a recorded corpus of material, he starts with a more primitive notion than that of either the word or the sentence (by 'primitive' is meant 'undefined within the theory', 'pre-theoretical'). This more primitive notion is that of the *utterance*. Just as 'acceptability' is a more primitive notion than 'grammaticality' or 'significance' (cf. 4.2.1), so 'utterance' is more primitive than 'word', 'sentence', 'morpheme', etc., in that its application does not rest upon any technical definitions or postulates of the science of language. The utterance has been defined by Harris as 'any stretch of talk, by one person, before and after which there is silence on the part of that person'. It must be remembered that we are not dealing here with the formal definition of some linguistic unit, but with a pre-scientific description of the linguist's data. 'Silence' and the other terms used to characterize and delimit utterances are to be understood with the tolerance customarily granted to everyday non-scientific discourse. Furthermore, we must not assume that there will necessarily be a high degree of correspondence between utterances and sentences, or indeed between utterances and grammatical units of any one particular type. As Harris goes on to say, 'The utterance is, in general, not identical with the "sentence" (as that word is commonly used), since a great many utterances in English, for example, consist of single words, phrases, "incomplete sentences", etc. Many utterances are composed of parts which are linguistically equivalent to whole utterances occurring elsewhere.'

5.2   The sentence

5.2.1   *Bloomfield's definition of the sentence*

Bloomfield's definition of the sentence will serve as a starting-point for our discussion. According to Bloomfield a sentence is 'an independent linguistic form, not included by virtue of any grammatical construction in any larger linguistic form'. He exemplifies his definition with the following utterance: *How are you? It's a fine day. Are you going to play tennis this afternoon?*; and goes on to say, 'whatever practical connexion there may be between these three forms there is no grammatical arrangement uniting them into one larger form: the utterance consists of three sentences'. The point of Bloomfield's definition can be stated more concisely as follows: *the sentence is the largest unit of grammatical description*. A sentence is a grammatical unit between the constituent parts of which distributional limitations and dependencies can be established, but which can itself be put into no distributional class. This is equivalent to saying that the notion of distribution, which is based on substitutability, is simply not applicable to sentences. Consider Bloomfield's example. Unless we take the wider context into account, it is pointless to talk of substituting other forms for, say, *It's a fine day*. And even if we do take into account the wider context, what Bloomfield calls the 'practical connexions' between the three sentences could not be brought within the scope of general rules of distributional selection. Not only are the constituent elements of the sentence *It's a fine day* not predictable from the wider context; it is not even possible to say that a statement, rather than a question, is bound to occur. *How are you?*, *It's a fine day.*, *Are you going to play tennis this afternoon?*, are all distributionally independent of one another; and for that reason they are recognized as three distinct sentences.

5.2.2 'Derived' sentences

A few examples may now be given of various kinds of utterances or parts of utterances which are traditionally regarded as sentences, although they are not distributionally independent in the sense in which we have been using the term 'distribution'. First of all, we may consider utterances which contain pronouns of 'personal' reference (*he, she, it, they*, in English). An utterance like *He'll be here in a moment* presupposes the previous occurrence of some masculine noun or noun-phrase (e.g. *John, the milkman*, etc.) to which the pronoun *he* refers. The distributional restrictions on the occurrence of 'personal' pronouns which are traditionally formulated by saying that *he* (*him, his*) 'stands for' masculine singular nouns, *she* (*her*) for feminine singular nouns, *it* (*its*) for neuter singular nouns, and *they* (*them, their*) for plural nouns, may operate over very long utterances (and indeed over several different utterances by several speakers). However, if, as is generally the case, the utterances can be segmented into stretches which are distributionally independent of one another in all respects apart from the selection of the 'personal' pronouns, these stretches may be regarded as 'derived' sentences within which nouns have been replaced with pronouns (masculine, feminine, etc., as appropriate) by secondary grammatical rules. This is what is implied by the traditional term 'pronoun' (a grammatical element of variable reference which 'stands for' some noun previously given, explicitly or implicitly, in the context). And it is clear that in order to under-stand a 'derived' sentence, like *He'll be here in a moment*, the hearer must be able to substitute for the pronoun *he* the correct noun or noun-phrase which it 'replaces'.

As another example of distributional constraints running over a sequence of what would be normally regarded as separate sentences we may consider the 'indirect discourse' construction in Latin. This construction is seen in its simplest form in a sentence such as *Dico te venisse in Marci Laecae domum* (from Cicero: 'I assert that you came into Marcus Laeca's house'), where the segment *te venisse in...domum* is the 'indirect' form (in the 'accusative and infinitive' construction) of the 'direct' form *(tu) venisti in...domum*. It is not at all uncommon in Latin authors for a whole speech to be put in 'indirect discourse' with each segment in it that is traditionally regarded as a separate sentence (and punctuated as such) marked as dependent on some previous 'verb of saying' by the occurrence of the 'accusative and infinitive' (and other features). This phenomenon, which may be called 'extended indirect discourse', is also found in English (and many other languages). Take for instance a passage such as the following: *The prime minister said that he deeply regretted the incident. He would do everything he could to ensure that it did not happen again. On the following day he would confer with his colleagues. He was confident that...* Once again, passages of this kind are best accounted for in two stages: first of all, by describing a set of independent sentences in their 'direct' form (*I deeply regret...*; *I will do every-thing I can...*; *Tomorrow I will confer...*; *I am confident that...*) and then, by specifying the secondary grammatical rules which will transpose each of these sentences into the corresponding 'indirect' form when they occur in sequence after a 'verb of saying'.

5.2.3 *'Incomplete' sentences*

Finally, we may consider the case of what are traditionally called 'incomplete' or 'elliptical' sentences. This category has recently come in for a lot of criticism from linguists, who have pointed out (correctly, but irrelevantly) that, when such utterances occur in a particular context, they are perfectly comprehensible, and from this point of view can hardly be called 'incomplete'. One must distinguish between contextual completeness and grammatical completeness.

There are many utterances of normal, everyday conversation which are dependent for their internal form on the preceding utterances of the same speaker or the person with whom he is conversing. An example might be *John's, if he gets here in time*, which could hardly occur except immediately after a question which 'supplied' the words required to make it into what would traditionally be regarded as a 'complete' sentence. For instance, it might occur after *Whose car are you going in?*, but not after *When are you going there?* An utterance like *John's, if he gets here in time* is therefore grammatically 'incomplete', since it is not itself a sentence (it is not distributionally independent) and yet it can be derived from a sentence which is constructed by adding to the utterance various elements 'given' in the context: *We are going in John's car, if he gets here in time.*

Somewhat different is the case of an utterance such as *Got the tickets?* At first sight it might appear that there is no reason to call this an 'elliptical' sentence at all, a shortened form of the sentence *Have you got the tickets?*, since it can be interpreted without reference to any previously occurring utterance. It is probable that the simplest way of accounting for the utterance in question is by deriving it by means of a rule which deletes *Have you* from sentences beginning *Have you got*... For in this way we can account for the fact that it will be understood to 'contain' the pronoun *you* and also for the form of the reply *Yes, I have* (*got them*). The difference between this example and the one considered in the previous paragraph is, however, quite clear. Although they are both 'elliptical', shorter forms of some longer version of the same sentence, they are 'elliptical' in a different sense. *John's, if he gets here in time* is grammatically incomplete; that is to say, it is not a sentence, and therefore is not to be described directly by the grammar, but by supplementary rules (if such rules can be established) which account for the deletion of contextually-determined elements in the sentences from which the utterances of connected discourse are derived. On the other hand, *Got the tickets?* (in British English at least) is a sentence (and in that sense it is 'complete'); the ellipsis that is involved in its derivation from the alternative version of the same sentence *Have you got the tickets?* is purely a matter of grammar and is independent of the wider context. Similarly, the grammatical rules of English must allow for the generation of such grammatically equivalent (but perhaps stylistically distinct) forms as *don't* and *do not*, *can't* and *cannot*, etc., occurring in otherwise identical sentences. Traditional grammarians often failed to distinguish between grammatical and contextual completeness.

5.2.4   *Two senses of the term 'sentence'*

The sentence is the maximum unit of grammatical analysis: that is, it is the largest unit that the linguist recognizes in order to account for the distributional relations of selection and exclusion that are found to hold in the language he is describing. It will be clear from the discussion of the examples given above (which could be multiplied) that distributional relations frequently hold across the boundaries of segments of utterances which would normally be regarded as separate sentences. This would appear to be a contradiction. It may be resolved, however, by distinguishing two senses of the term 'sentence'. As a grammatical unit, the sentence is an abstract entity in terms of which the linguist accounts for the distributional relations holding within utterances. In this sense of the term, utterances never consist of sentences, but of one or more segments of speech (or written text) which can be put into correspondence with the sentences generated by the grammar. On the other hand, the segments themselves are often referred to as sentences, as for instance by Bloomfield, when he says that the utterance *How are you? It's a fine day. Are you going to play tennis this afternoon?* 'consists of three sentences'. In the case of segments which are distributionally independent (such as the three segments into which Bloomfield divides his utterance) it is tempting to say that the grammar generates them directly without recourse to the more abstract grammatical units. But, as we have seen, the correspondence between sentences and the segments referred to them is often far less straightforward. It would seem to be preferable therefore to restrict the term 'sentence' (as traditional grammarians did, though perhaps not explicitly or consistently) to the more abstract sense suggested here. To invoke de Saussure's distinction explained above (cf. 1.4.7), utterances are stretches of *parole* produced by native speakers out of sentences generated by the system of elements and rules which constitute the *langue*. The linguist describes instances of *parole* by establishing the *langue* and relating them to it in the simplest way. Having made this point, we shall continue to follow the normal practice of linguists by saying that utterances are composed of sentences. This form of expression is to be understood in the way explained here.

5.2.5 *'Ready-made' utterances*

At this point we should perhaps mention a further category of utterances or parts of utterances which resemble 'incomplete' sentences in that they do not correspond directly to sentences generated by the grammar, but differ from them in that their description does not involve the application of the rules established to account for the vast mass of more 'normal' utterances. These are what de Saussure has called 'ready-made utterances' ('locutions toutes faites'): expressions which are learned as unanalysable wholes and employed on particular occasions by native speakers. An example from English is *How do you do?*, which, though it is conventionally punctuated as a question, is not normally interpreted as such; and unlike genuine questions beginning *How do you...*, constructed by means of the productive rules of English grammar, it cannot be matched with corresponding sentences of the form *I — very well, How does he — ?, He — beautifully*, etc. Another 'ready-made' English expression is *Rest in peace* (as a tombstone inscription) which, unlike for example *Rest here quietly for a moment*, is not to be regarded as an instruction or suggestion made to the person one is addressing, but a situationally-bound expression which is unanalysable (and which does not require any analysis) with reference to the grammatical structure of contemporary English. The stock of proverbs passed on from one generation to the next provides many instances of 'ready-made utterances' (cf. *Easy come easy go*; *All that glisters is not gold*; etc.). From a strictly grammatical point of view such utterances are not profitably regarded as sentences, even though they are distributionally independent and thus satisfy the definition of the sentence given above. Their internal structure, unlike that of genuine sentences, is not accounted for by means of rules which specify the permissible combinations of words. However, in a total description of the language, which brings together the phonological and the grammatical analysis, they might be classified as (grammatically unstructured) sentences, since they bear the same intonation contour as sentences generated by the grammar. Apart from this fact, they are to be accounted for simply by listing them in the dictionary with an indication of the situations in which they are used and their meaning.

In addition to those 'ready-made' expressions which may serve as complete utterances and which permit no extension or variation, there are others which are grammatically unstructured, or only partially structured, but which can yet be combined in sentences according to productive rules. Examples are: *What's the use of -ing...?*; *Down with —!*; *for —'s sake.* There is no generally accepted term for such elements. We will refer to them as schemata. Schemata, it will be observed, may be of different ranks. *What's the use of -ing...?* and *Down with —!* are sentence-schemata (and so belong to the only class of grammatical units which concerns us in this section). An indefinitely large number of sentences can be generated from them by 'filling' the vacant 'slot' in the schema with a member of the appropriate grammatical class: thus, *What's the use of worrying?*, *What's the use of getting everything ready the night before?*, *Down with the King!*, *Down with the Sixth Republic!* On the other hand, *for —'s sake* is a phrase-schema; and the grammar must not only account for the class of elements which can 'fill the slot' in the schema (*for his sake*, *for my mother's sake*, etc.), but must also classify the resultant phrase according to its distribution in sentences (*I did it for —'s sake*, etc.).

5.2.6 *Different types of sentences*

In traditional grammar, sentences are classified into different *types* in two ways: first of all by function, as statements, questions, exclamations and commands; and secondly according to their structural complexity, as simple or compound. Complex sentences are made up of a number of simple sentences (which when incorporated as constituents of larger sentences are, by virtue of this fact, called *clauses*). Thus: *I saw him yesterday and I shall be seeing him again tomorrow* is a complex sentence. Complex sentences are divided into: (*a*) those in which the constituent clauses are grammatically *co-ordinate*, no one being dependent on the others, but all being, as it were, added together in sequence, with or without the so-called co-ordinating conjunctions (*and, but*, etc.); and (*b*) those in which one of the clauses (the 'main clause') is 'modified' by one or more *subordinate* clauses grammatically dependent upon it and generally introduced (in English) by a subordinating conjunction (*if, when*, etc.). Subordinate clauses are subdivided by function as nominal, adjectival, adverbial, etc.; and further as temporal, conditional, relative, etc. We shall not go into the details of this classification here. The notion of grammatical dependence has been given a distributional interpretation in this section; and the other notions, of 'function' and 'modification', whereby sentences may be classified into various types will be treated from a distributional point of view in a later chapter (cf. 6.4.1).

There is one general point which must be made before we temporarily leave the question of sentence-types. The 'formal' approach to grammatical description adopted in this book and accepted by most linguists today implies a rejection of any attempt to categorize sentences 'notionally' in advance of their classification in terms of internal structure (that is, in terms of the distributional relations holding between their parts). It must not be assumed in advance that every language will have formally differentiated patterns of sentence-structure for each of the four major sentence-types (statements, questions, exclamations, commands) recognized in traditional grammar. What must be done, as we have insisted in the previous chapter, is first to establish for each language independently the grammatical units and patterns of combination valid for that language, and only then, if at all, to give them such labels as 'statement', 'question', etc., in terms of their semantic or contextual correlations. Traditional grammar recognized four main sentence-types because Greek and Latin had four formally distinct patterns of sentence-construction which could be classified, roughly, into the four semantic categories of statements, questions, exclamations, and commands. The doctrine that these four types are universal grammatical categories, like the doctrine that the 'parts of speech' are universal features of language, was part of the wholesale transference of the particular details of Greek and Latin to the plane of the theoretically necessary and *a priori* categories assumed by the medieval 'speculative' grammarians and their successors.

5.2.7 *Phonological criteria*

The criterion of distributional independence is not always sufficient of itself to segment an utterance uniquely into a determinate number of sentences. (It will be remembered that utterances are said to be composed of sentences only with the reservations set forth earlier in this section.) Take for example the utterance *I shouldn't bother if I were you I'd leave it till tomorrow*. The segment *if I were you* is not distributionally independent (and so is not a sentence), since it presupposes, generally at least, another segment (either preceding it or following it) in the same utterance containing *would, should, 'd*, etc. Both the segment preceding *if I were you* and the segment following it satisfy these conditions of distributional presupposition, so that the utterance can be divided into two sentences in two different ways; *I shouldn't bother if I were you.|I'd leave it till tomorrow*, and *I shouldn't bother.|If I were you I'd leave it till tomorrow.* In deciding between these two possibilities in any particular case we should have recourse to other considerations, principally to the criteria of potential pause and intonation. Distributionally defined sentences in English which present no problems of demarcation have a characteristic intonation pattern and may be set off from one another when they occur in sequence in the same utterance by pauses of greater or less duration. Hence, in the total description of English the sentence, which is defined primarily in grammatical terms, is also to be recognized as the domain of the phonological features summed up in the term 'intonation'. Since this is so, it makes for a simpler total description of the language if the phonological features in question are allowed to determine the cases, such as the one exemplified above, left undecided by the strictly grammatical criteria. It is, of course, theoretically conceivable that in a particular language the domain of intonation should be quite differently established (as a given number of syllables, for example) and correspond to no grammatically delimited unit. However, it is probably the case that in all languages the sentence is the unit at which there is the greatest 'congruence of levels', particularly between the phonological and grammatical levels of description. It may be mentioned here that what are traditionally referred to as complex sentences made up of co-ordinate clauses would not be recognized as single sentences, but as sequences of separate sentences, on purely grammatical criteria. An utterance such as *I saw him yesterday and I shall be seeing him again tomorrow* would be segmented by the test of distributional independence into two sentences (the break coming between *yesterday* and *and*). However, the supplementary criteria of potential pause and intonation will distinguish utterances in which two or more consecutive sentences are to be taken as clauses in a single sentence or as independent sentences. Orthographical practice reflects the distinction in such cases: cf. *I saw him yesterday. And I shall be seeing him again tomorrow*, on the one hand, and *I saw him yesterday and I shall be seeing him again tomorrow*, on the other.

5.3   The morpheme

5.3.1   *Word and morpheme*

In the discussion of the other two 'primary' units of grammatical analysis, the word and the morpheme, we are faced with the difficulty that, whichever one we take first, we must presuppose some knowledge of the other. Most modern treatments of grammatical theory have glossed over this difficulty by defining the morpheme as the minimal unit of grammatical analysis (which is the definition we will provisionally adopt) and then failing to point out that the general practice of linguists is not always consistent with this definition, but is conditioned equally by some explicit or implicit reference to the word as a grammatical unit. The reasons for this ambivalence or equivocation are historically explicable and will become clear in the course of our discussion. We shall then see that neither words nor morphemes (as these terms as generally applied by linguists) are universal features of language, although it would be possible to make them so by definition. However, in order to make either one or the other of the two units universal, we should have to make a more radical break with the past than most linguists have been prepared to do so far. Although we will deal mainly with the morpheme in this section and with the word in the next, there will necessarily be a certain measure of overlap between the two sections.

5.3.2 *Segmentability of words*

We have described morphemes as minimal units of grammatical analysis—the units of 'lowest' rank out of which words, the units of next 'highest' rank, are composed (cf. 5.1.1). By way of example, we said that the English word *unacceptable* is composed of three morphemes, *un, accept, able*, each one of which has a particular distribution and also a particular phonological (and orthographical) form, or 'shape'. We must now draw a distinction between the morphemes themselves, as distributional units, and their phonological (or orthographical) 'shape'.

Whether a word can be divided into smaller grammatical segments is a matter of degree. The words *boy-s*; *jump-s, jump-ed, jump-ing*; *tall-er, tall-est*; etc. can be segmented into their constituent parts no less readily than *un-accept-able*; and so can the majority of English nouns, verbs and adjectives. Such words, we will say, are *determinate with respect to segmentation*. But there are many other English nouns, verbs and adjectives which either cannot be segmented at all or are only partially determinate with respect to segmentation. Examples are: the irregular plurals *men, children, mice, sheep*, etc.; the 'strong' verbs *went, took, came, run, cut*, etc.; the irregular comparatives and superlatives *better, best, worse, worst*. These words all present problems of segmentation, different in degree or in kind. For instance,

7   LIT

men stands in the same grammatical relationship to *man* as *boys* does to *boy* (as *boys* is the plural of the singular form *boy*, so *men* is the plural of the singular *man*); and there is at least some phonological (and orthographical) resemblance between *men* and *man* which could be made the basis for segmenting *men* into two parts. The same is true for *mice* and *mouse* (notice that here the orthographical difference is greater than the phonological). On the other hand, although *worse* and *went* stand in the same grammatical relationship to *bad* and *go* as do *taller* and *jumped* to *tall* and *jump*, there is no phonological resemblance at all between *worse* and *bad* or between *went* and *go*. Words such as *worse* or *went* cannot be segmented into parts. Linguists have exercised considerable ingenuity in arguing for one 'solution' rather than another to the problem of words that are indeterminate with respect to segmentation and even for the 'segmentation' of such words as *worse* and *went*. We shall not discuss these 'solutions' here since they are motivated by certain methodological assumptions which are less general than the assumptions we are making in the present work. It suffices for our purpose to have drawn attention to the fact that, in some languages at least, there are words which cannot be segmented into parts, except arbitrarily, although these words belong to the same grammatical class as other words which are segmentable.

5.3.3   *The morpheme as a distributional unit*

Now there is nothing in the definition of the morpheme to imply that it must always be an identifiable segment of the word of which it is a constituent. To say that *worse* is composed of two morphemes, one of which it shares with *bad* (and *worst*) and the other of which it shares with *taller*, *bigger*, *nicer*, etc., is equivalent to saying that *worse* differs from *taller*, *bigger*, *nicer*, etc. in grammatical function (that is, in its distribution throughout the sentences of English) in the way that *bad* differs from *tall*, *big*, *nice*, etc. (and *worst* from *tallest*, etc.). This is commonly expressed as a proportion of grammatical, or distributional, equivalence (cf. the original sense of 'analogy': 1.2.3).

> *bad* : *worse* : *worst* = *tall* : *taller* : *tallest*

This proportion expresses the fact that, for example, *worse* and *taller* (as well as *bigger*, *nicer*, etc.) are grammatically alike in that they are comparative forms of the adjective—they can occur in such sentences as *John is worse* (*taller*, etc,) *than Michael, It is getting worse* (*taller*, etc.) *all the time*. *Worse* and *taller* (as well as *bigger*, *nicer*, etc.) differ from one another, however, in that they cannot occur in exactly the same set of sentences—for instance, as traditional grammarians would say, they cannot 'qualify' exactly the same set of nouns. In so far as the class of nouns which can be qualified by a particular adjective is grammatically determined (and here we touch upon a point to which we shall return presently), this feature of their distribution is accounted for by postulating a particular morpheme as a component of one adjective and another morpheme as a component of another adjective which 'qualifies' a different class of nouns.

In order to make this point clear, let us first put in symbolic form the distributional proportion we have just set up, representing each different word with a different letter, and factorize this as we would any other algebraic proportion:

$$A : B : C = D : E : F$$

Factorizing (and employing arbitrary symbols) we obtain:

$$ax : bx : cx = ay : by : cy$$

That is to say, each word is factorized into two components; all the words on the left-hand side of the equation have the component x, and all the words on the right-hand side the component y; with regard to their other component (a, b or c) the first word on the left-hand side agrees with the first word on the right-hand side, the second word on the left-hand side agrees with the second word on the right-hand side, and so on. The components, or distributional factors, of the words are morphemes.

By factorizing the distribution of words in this way we can account for their occurrence in sentences in terms of the distribution of their component morphemes: the distribution of a word is the product of the distribution of the morphemes of which it is composed.

5.3.4 *Morpheme and morph*

It is clear that from this point of view the question whether words can be segmented into parts or not is quite irrelevant. The morpheme is not a segment of the word at all; it has no position in the word (for example, in the analysis of A into its component morphemes we could just as well put xa as ax), but merely its 'factorial' function. When the word can be segmented into parts, these segments are referred to as *morphs*. Thus the word *bigger* is analysable into two morphs, which can be written orthographically as *big* and *er* (with the orthographical conventions of English accounting for the additional 'linking' *g*) and in a phonological transcription as /bɪg/ and /ə/. Each morph *represents* (or is the exponent of) a particular morpheme.

The distinction that we have drawn here between morphs and morphemes can be expressed in terms of de Saussure's distinction of *substance* and *form* (cf. 2.2.2). Like all grammatical units, the morpheme is an element of 'form', 'arbitrarily' (cf. 2.2.7) related to its 'substantial' realization on the phonological (or orthographical) level of the language. As we have seen, morphemes may be represented directly by phonological (or orthographical) segments with a particular 'shape' (that is, by morphs), but they may also be represented in the substance of the language in other ways. In order to refer to morphemes, it is customary to use one of the morphs which represents the morpheme in question and to put it between braces. Thus {*big*} is the morpheme which is represented in phonological substances by /bɪg/ and in orthographic substance by *big*; and the word *went* (phonologically /went/), which cannot be segmented into morphs, represents the combination of the two morphemes {*go*} and {*ed*}. Although we shall follow this convention, it must be realized that the particular notation chosen to refer to morphemes is a matter of arbitrary decision. We might just as well number the morphemes and say, for instance, that {207} is represented by /bɪg/ (or *big*); and that {1039} + {76} is represented by the substantially unitary form /went/ (or *went*).

5.3.5 *Allomorphs*

A further point may now be made with regard to the relationship between morphemes and morphs. It frequently happens that a particular morpheme is not represented everywhere by the same morph, but by different morphs in different environments. These alternative representations of a morpheme are called *allomorphs*. For example, the plural morpheme in English, which we may refer to as {*s*}, is regularly represented by the allomorphs /s/, /z/ and /ɪz/. These are *phonologically conditioned*, in the sense that the selection of any one is determined by the phonological form of the morph with which it is combined. The rule is as follows: (i) if the morph representing the noun morpheme with which {*s*} is combined to form the plural ends with a 'sibilant' (/s/, /z/, /ʃ/, /ʒ/, /tʃ/, /dʒ/), {*s*} is represented by /ɪz/ (cf. /bʌsɪz/, *buses*; /saizɪz/, *sizes*; /fiʃɪz/, *fishes*; /garaːʒɪz/, /garaːdʒɪz/, *garages* (n.b. the variation in the phonological representation of this word by speakers of standard British English); /batʃiz/, *batches*; etc.); (ii) otherwise, if (*a*) the morph ends in one of the voiced phonemes (including the vowels), {*s*} is represented by /z/ (cf. /dogz/, *dogs*; /bedz/, *beds*; /laiz/, *lies*; etc.) and if (*b*) the morph ends in a voiceless (consonant) phoneme, {*s*} is represented by /s/ (cf. /kats/, *cats*; /bets/, *bets*; etc. (It will be observed that the orthographical conventions of English distinguish only two of these three allomorphs, with -*s* standing for both /s/ and /z/ and -*es* standing for /iz/. The present tense singular morpheme, which we can refer to as {*z*} (in order to distinguish it from the morpheme {*s*} which forms the plurals of English nouns) is regularly represented by the same three allomorphs as {*s*}. And the statement of the phonological conditioning of their occurrence is identical: cf. the verbs (i) /fiʃiz/, *fishes*; /kætʃiz/, *catches*; etc.; (ii) /digz/, *digs*; /ebz/, *ebbs*, etc.; and (iii) /kiks/, *kicks*; /sips/, *sips*; etc. The past tense morpheme of English, {*ed*}, is also regularly represented by three phonologically-conditioned allomorphs: /t/, /d/ and /id/. The rule governing their distribution is as follows: (i) /id/ occurs after morphs ending in alveolar stops (i.e. after /t/ and /d/) (cf. /wetid/, *wetted*; /wedid/, *wedded*, etc.); elsewhere, (ii) /d/ occurs after voiced phonemes (including the vowels and the nasals) and (iii) /t/ after voiceless phonemes (cf. (ii) /sægd/, *sagged*; /lʌvd/, *loved*; /moud/, *mowed*; /maind/, *mined*; etc. and (iii) /sækt/, *sacked*; /pʌft/, *puffed*, etc.). In fact, the allomorphic variation associated with the regular representations of all the three morphemes discussed here, {*z*}, {*s*} and {*ed*}, can be subsumed under a more general rule whereby the appropriate morph is generated from an underlying invariant morph, neutral with respect to voicing, which is syllabified (as /iz/ or /id/) when combined with a morph ending in 'the same sound' (i.e. for the purpose of this rule, all the sibilants are considered to 'contain the same sound' as the underlying 's-sound' representing both {*s*} and {*z*} and both /t/ and /d/ to 'contain the same sound' as the underlying alveolar sound representing {*ed*}). It will be obvious that a rule of this kind can be stated in terms of prosodic or distinctive feature analysis more readily than with reference to a phonemic analysis of English: cf. 3.3.8 ff.

The limiting case of allomorphic variation is found where no generalization can be made, in terms of phonological structure or in any other terms, about the selection of a particular allomorph. This situation can be illustrated from English. In addition to the three regular allomorphs of the English plural morpheme {*s*} one might also establish the form /ən/ which is to be found in the word *oxen*, /oksən/. Since all other morphs ending in /ks/ which represent noun-morphemes in English have the regular /iz/ in the plural (cf. /boksiz/, *boxes*; /foksiz/, *foxes*, etc.), the occurrence of /ən/ in /oksən/ is not phonologically conditioned. In fact, it is not determined by any feature of the morpheme {*ox*} or the morph /oks/ which can be brought within the scope of any general statement about the structure of English. It is true that the plural nouns *children* and *brethren* also end in /ən/. But whereas *oxen* presents no problems of segmentation, since it can be analysed into two morphs, /oks/ and /ən/, the former of which is identical with the morph representing the singular *ox* (and in this respect *oxen* is like the regular plurals in English), the recognition of /ən/ in *children* and *brethren* would leave us with two morphs, /tʃildr/ and /breðr/, neither of which is identical with the morph representing the singular of these nouns (even granting that *brethren* has a singular in modern English) and neither of which occurs elsewhere in the language. Since the formation of the word *oxen* is an irregular fact of English, which, despite the segmentability of the word into two constituent morphs, can only be handled by an *ad hoc* 'rule' applying to this one instance, there is little point in recognizing /ən/ as an allomorph of {*s*} in the description of contemporary English.

The reader may be tempted to think that the elaboration of such subtle distinctions as those we have drawn in this section between morpheme, morph, and allomorph is something of an idle, scholastic pastime which serves no useful purpose. But such distinctions are essential if we wish to construct a general theory of language-structure. As we shall see, in certain languages words can generally be segmented into parts (morphs), in others they cannot; in some languages the morphs each tend to represent a single minimal grammatical unit (a morpheme), in others they do not; and in some languages each morpheme is usually represented by a segment of constant phonological form, whereas in others certain morphemes are represented by a set of alternant morphs (allomorphs) the selection of which in particular environments may be conditioned by phonological or grammatical factors.

It is true that a good deal of what is often regarded as phonologically-conditioned allomorphic variation may be eliminated from the description by adopting a prosodic or distinctive-feature analysis for the phonology. But grammatically-conditioned variation of allomorphs cannot be eliminated in this way, and only a certain amount of phonologically-conditioned variation. The concept of the allomorph is therefore useful. It is, however, the distinction between the morpheme and the morph, between the grammatical unit and its 'substantial' representation, which is particularly important. For it is by making this distinction that we can bring out clearly both the grammatical similarity and the formational difference between such words as *went* and *killed*, or *worse* and *bigger*. In the purely grammatical part of the description both the 'regular' and 'irregular' forms can be handled alike: {*go*}+{*ed*}, {*kill*+*ed*}; {*bad*}+{*er*}, {*big*}+{*er*}; etc. The difference between the 'regular' and 'irregular' forms is seen at that point in the description where words as purely grammatical units are 'embodied', as it were, in phonological (or orthographic) substance. In the case of the regular forms, like *killed*, rules can be set up to combine morphs (and one now sees the advantage, from the point of view of total description of the language, of using the morph to stand for the morpheme—a convention which was described above as purely arbitrary). These rules are of very general applicability, and, in many cases, their scope can be left open by employing a formulation which says, in effect, but more formally: 'any forms which are not accounted for by one of the special rules are to be handled by the following general rule(s) according to the following conditions'. The irregular words are handled by special rules of restricted scope, applying in the limiting case to one and only one word: e.g. '{*go*}+{*ed*} is realized by *went*'. One means of ensuring that both the 'regular' and the 'irregular' forms are handled appropriately is by ordering the rules in such a way that the rule of limited scope is applied first, where applicable, and then the rules of general applicability, whose scope may now be left totally unrestricted.

5.3.6 *Isolating, agglutinating and inflecting languages*

Now that we have distinguished between morpheme, morph and allomorph, we can draw upon these distinctions in the exemplification of some of the differences between languages referred to in the previous paragraph. Languages are frequently classified into structural *types* (in terms of a system of classification which originated in the nineteenth century) as *isolating, agglutinating* and *inflecting* (or 'fusional').

An isolating (or 'analytic') language is defined as one in which all words are invariable. (Since we are for the present taking the concept of the word for granted, we shall postpone to the following section the question whether there is any need to distinguish between the word and the morpheme in the description of isolating languages.) Chinese is often cited as a well-known example of the isolating type of language; but nowadays scholars appear to agree that many Chinese words are composed of more than one morpheme, and Vietnamese is said to be a more 'typical' isolating language than Chinese. Whether a language is isolating or not is obviously a matter of degree. Granted the recognition of words and morphemes for the language in question, the average degree of 'isolation' can be expressed as a ratio of the number of morphemes over the number of words: the lower the ratio, the more highly isolating is the language (a ratio of 1·00 being characteristic of the 'ideal' isolating language). Average ratios which have been calculated over a body of continuous text for a number of languages show that, for instance, English (with a ratio of 1·68) is more 'analytic' than Sanskrit (2·59) or the highly 'synthetic' Eskimo (3·72). These figures, it must be remembered, give average ratios over running text. Since a language might be, and frequently is, relatively isolating with respect to certain classes of words and relatively synthetic with respect to other classes of words, the ratios might be quite different if they were calculated over all the words in the language with each word counted once.

5.3.7   *Turkish: an 'agglutinating' language*

It is the distinction between agglutinating and inflecting languages (both types being 'synthetic') which is more interesting for our present purpose. An agglutinating language is one in which words are typically composed of a sequence of morphs with each morph representing one morpheme. Turkish may be taken as an example which approximates very closely to the 'ideal' of the agglutinating type. In Turkish the plural morph is {*ler*}, the possessive morph ('his', 'her', 'its') is {*i*}, and the 'ablative' morph is {*den*}. There are many other morphs which are added to nouns in Turkish; but these will serve to illustrate the nature of 'agglutination'. *Ev* ('house') is the 'nominative', singular form; *evler* ('houses') is 'nominative', plural; *evi* is singular, possessive ('his/her house'); *evleri* ('his/her houses', 'their house(s)') is plural, possessive; *evden* ('from the house') is ablative, singular; *evlerden* ('from the houses'); *evinden* ('from his/ her house') is singular, possessive, ablative; and *evlerinden* ('from his/her houses', 'from their house(s)') is plural, possessive, ablative. (The insertion of *n* between *i* and *den* is automatic and regular.) The first thing to notice is that each of the three morphs representing, respectively, the plural, the possessive and the ablative morphemes, {*ler*}, {*i*} and {*den*}, preserve their phonological identity and are immediately recognizable; they are, as it were, simply 'stuck on' ('agglutinated') in sequence. Consequently, Turkish words are, in general, readily segmented into their constituent morphs: *ev-ler-i(n)-den*, etc.

A second and no less important feature of Turkish is that in a particular word each morph represents just one morpheme. These two features, (i) determinacy with respect to segmentation into morphs (cf. 5.3.2), and (ii) the one-to-one correspondence between morph and morpheme, are characteristic of 'agglutinating' languages. It should be noticed, however, that the two features are independent of one another: as we shall see below, a language may manifest either one without the other. It should also be observed that the one-to-one correspondence between morph and morpheme referred to here is to be understood as holding within a given word: certain Turkish morphs (including {*i*}) may represent different morphemes in different classes of words, in the same way as, for instance, the English morphs /s/, /z/ and /iz/ represent the present singular morpheme in verbs and the plural morpheme in nouns. The degree to which languages employ this kind of multiple representation of morphemes by single morphs (which is the converse of the representation of one morpheme by many allomorphs) varies considerably.

5.3.8 *Latin: an inflecting language*

Let us now take Latin as an example of a language of the 'inflecting' type. Generally speaking, Latin words cannot be segmented into morphs; rather, they can only be segmented into morphs at the price of arbitrariness, inconsistency and the proliferation of allomorphs. Take, for instance, the words *domus* ('house'; nominative singular), *domī* ('of the house'; genitive, singular), *domum* (accusative, singular), *domō* ('from the house'; ablative, singular), *domī* ('houses'; nominative, plural), *domōrum* (genitive, plural), *domōs* (accusative, plural), *domīs* (ablative, plural). We might be tempted to analyse these forms into *dom*, on the one hand, and *us*, *ī*, *um*, *ō*, *ōrum*, *ōs*, *īs*, on the other; and this is what some grammarians do. But let us now bring forward for comparison another set of words of a very common type: *puella* ('girl'; nominative, singular), *puellae* (genitive, singular), *puellam* (accusative, singular), *puellā* (ablative, singular), *puellae* (nominative, plural), *puellārum* (genitive, plural), *puellās* (accusative, plural), *puellīs* (ablative, plural). What principle of segmentation should we follow here? If we try to match the 'endings' of the two types as far as possible, we should doubtless segment the forms into *puell* and *a*, *ae*, *am*, *ā*, *ārum*, *ās*, *īs* (with *īs* being the only morph common to the two types of nouns). But if we segment *puella*, *puellae*, etc., in this way, we should certainly be left with the uncomfortable feeling that, since *a* or *ā* is found in all forms of the second type except *puellīs* and is never to be found in the first set of forms, *domus*, etc., we ought perhaps to recognize two allomorphs: *puell* (which combines only with *īs*) and *puella* (which combines with 'zero', in the nominative singular, and with *e*, *m*, *a*, *arum*, *as*: n.b. the long vowel *ā* has now been resolved into a sequence of two instances of the short *a*). This is attractive enough as far as it goes. Similarly, we could recognize two allomorphs for the first type, *dom* and *domo* (with a third 'pseudo-allomorph', *domu*, accounted for as a variant of *domo* which occurs before consonants), and thus identify the accusative singular morph (*m*) and the accusative and genitive plural morphs of both types (vowel lengthening + *s*, and vowel lengthening + *rum*). But we should still be left with a number of allomorphs for the endings of the two types of nouns: 'zero' and *s* (or *us*, or indeed *os*) for the nominative singular, etc. And, as anyone who has any acquaintance with Latin knows, we have yet to take account of the other three regular types of formation (traditionally called 'declensions'), not to mention the numerous irregular nouns. What may seem a reasonable procedure when just two types are compared would no longer seem so when these other types are brought into the picture. It is no doubt because Latin (and Greek) words are not readily segmentable into morphs that their formation was handled in a quite different way by the classical grammarians. The traditional manner of dealing with the formation of words in Latin (and Greek) was to classify them into types ('declensions' for nouns and adjectives, 'conjugations' for verbs) and to set up for each type a table, or 'paradigm', giving all the forms for one chosen member of the type. It was then left to the person using the grammar to construct the forms for other members of the type by reference to the appropriate 'paradigm' (the term 'paradigm' derives from the Greek word for 'pattern' or 'example'). That is to say, the classical grammarians did not establish rules, but merely 'patterns', of formation. Some recent grammars of Latin (and also of Greek) have kept the traditional 'paradigms', but have superimposed upon the traditional method of handling 'inflexion' some attempt to segment words into 'stems' and 'endings'. In doing so, they have frequently been influenced by historical considerations. According to the hypotheses of the comparative philologists of the nineteenth century and their successors a good deal of Latin (and Greek) 'inflexion' can be plausibly explained as being due to the coalescence of once distinct morphs. This is largely irrelevant in the synchronic analysis of the language. We cannot get away from the fact that Latin (and Greek) words do not lend themselves to segmentation into morphs.

The impossibility of segmenting Latin words neatly or consistently into morphs illustrates one feature of the language which makes it 'inflecting' (or 'fusional'), rather than 'agglutinating'. (It should be observed that the term employed here is *inflecting*, not *inflexional*. 'Inflexion' is used for both 'fusional' and 'agglutinating' languages: cf. 5.4.2.) The other, more important, feature is the lack of any correspondence between such segments of the word as we might recognize and morphemes (assuming that the morpheme is still defined as 'minimal grammatical unit'). Even if we were to segment *domus, domī*, etc., into the morph *dom* (or the allomorphs *dom, domo*) and a set of 'endings', *us* (or *s*), *ī, ōrum* (or vowel lengthening +*rum*), etc., we could not say that one part of *us* (or *s*) represents {singular} and another part {nominative}; that part of *ī* represents {singular} and another part {genitive}; and so on. We should have to say that *us* (or *s*) represents simultaneously {singular} and {nominative}; that *ī* represents simultaneously either {singular} and {genitive} or {plural} and {nominative}; etc. The difference between Latin and Turkish in this respect is striking.

5.3.9 *No 'pure' types*

It must be realized that the recognition of three 'types' of languages, by the opposition of 'analytic' to 'synthetic' (which is in any case a question of degree, as we have seen), and then, within 'synthetic', of 'agglutinating' to 'inflecting' does not imply that any one language will fall neatly into one 'type'. Still less does it imply (as certain nineteenth-century linguists maintained) that there is necessarily any 'evolutionary' law which governs the historical development of languages from one 'type' to another. As Sapir has put it: 'A linguist who insists on talking about the Latin type...as though it were necessarily the high-water mark of linguistic development is like the zoologist that sees in the organic world a huge conspiracy to evolve the race-horse or the Jersey cow.' The *typological* classification of languages into 'inflecting' or 'agglutinating' is only one of many ways in which languages can be classified according to their structure. Turkish, though largely 'agglutinating', is to some degree 'inflecting'; and Latin provides instances of 'agglutination'. And both languages are in part analytic. English, we as have seen, is fairly 'analytic', having a large number of single-morpheme words: *man, book, go, tall, good,* etc. As for the 'synthetic' words in English some are 'agglutinative' (*books, taller,* etc.); others are 'semi-agglutinative' (or 'semi-inflecting') in that they are partly or wholly indeterminate with respect to segmentation (cf. *men, mice, worse,* etc.) or contain segments which represent simultaneously more than one minimal grammatical unit. As an instance of the latter kind of 'semi-agglutination' consider the forms /z/, /s/ and /iz/ (orthographically, *s* and *es*), which we earlier regarded as allomorphs of the present singular 'morpheme' {z}. These endings, which may be reduced to a single underlying 'sibilant' ending, represent simultaneously both singular and 'third person' (cf. the verbs *jump-s, love-s, fish-es,* etc.). There are few instances of fully 'inflecting' words in English (satisfying both the conditions mentioned above). One such instance is the 'third person singular of the verb *to be*'. This form, *is*, might be segmented into *i* (an allomorph of {be}) and the regular *s*, but there is little point in doing so, since *i* occurs nowhere else as an allomorph of {be}.

There is yet another kind of 'semi-agglutination'. The same morph may represent different grammatical units either in different positions of the same word or in different words of the same class. This happens on a small scale in many languages, including Turkish and English. For example, in English the same morph (or allomorphs: /s/, /z/, /iz/) represents 'third person, singular (present)' in verbs and {plural} in nouns, as we have already seen. And the morph *er* is found both in the comparative form of adjectives (*tall-er,* etc.) and in 'agent' nouns formed from verbs (*run(n)-er, read-er,* etc.). This kind of 'semi-agglutination' (if it may be so called) is what was described above as the multiple representation of morphemes by single morphs. It is particularly characteristic of various so-called 'Austronesian' languages (Sundanese, Tagalog, Malay, etc.).

5.3.10 *Inconsistency between theory and practice*

It should now be clear that the relationship between the morpheme and the morph is not a purely grammatical relationship. The words of Latin can be analysed into their distributional 'factors' as easily as can the words of Turkish. The difference between the 'inflecting' and the 'agglutinating' (and the various kinds of 'semi-agglutinating') languages is not therefore one of grammatical structure; it is a difference in the way in which the minimal grammatical units are represented in the phonological (or orthographical) form of the word. It should also be clear, from our discussion of the various ways in which minimal grammatical units are represented in different languages, that the distinction of morpheme and morph is forced upon us, in the first instance, by the fact that not all languages are 'agglutinating' or 'inflecting' and, more particularly, by the fact that there are languages which do not conform to the 'ideal' of either 'type' (indeed there is probably no purely 'agglutinating' or purely 'inflecting' language). If all 'synthetic' languages were purely 'agglutinating' the morpheme would be a minimal grammatical unit of constant phonological shape, and we could account directly for the combination of morphemes into words. On the other hand, if all 'synthetic' languages were fully inflecting, we should have no use for the morph (which is by definition a phonological segment of a word representing a morpheme). It is because many languages are partly 'agglutinating' and partly 'inflecting' that the distinction between morpheme and morph must be made.

In the case of languages that are mainly 'agglutinating' (and most languages of the world are said to approximate to the 'agglutinating' type) the distinction is undoubtedly useful. As we have seen, it enables us to account for the distribution of grammatically equivalent words in the same way in the grammar (*boys*: {*boy*}+{*s*}, *oxen*: {*ox*}+{*s*}, *mice*: {*mouse*}+{*s*}, *sheep*: {*sheep*}+{*s*}, etc.) and then, in the 'conversion' of these words into their phonological form, to set up general rules of 'direct transcription' for the regular, 'agglutinating' forms and special, more complex rules (of the kind required for 'inflecting' languages) for the conversion of the irregular, non-agglutinating forms.

However, with regard to languages that are mainly 'inflecting', we must now face a problem which has so far only been implicit in our discussion of this 'type'. We have observed that such segments (granted their recognition as segments) as *a* (or 'zero') in *puella*, and *us* (or *s*) in *domus* do not represent minimal grammatical units, such as {singular} or {nominative}, but the combination {singular + nominative}. On our definition of the morpheme as the minimal grammatical unit (which is the definition to which most linguists, in theory, adhere) it is such elements as {singular} and {nominative} which are morphemes. Yet most linguists who have dealt with the morphemic analysis of Latin have regarded *a* and *us* as allomorphs of 'the nominative singular morpheme'. This is the inconsistency between theory and practice to which we referred at the beginning of the present section. The reason for the inconsistency is doubtless the historical one that the morpheme was first established for those languages in which the formation of words could be described in terms of the combination of phonologically constant segments (this is the sense in which the concept was employed by the Sanskrit grammarians); later the morpheme was defined as a more 'abstract', distributional unit, and this led to the distinction of morpheme and morph. In Latin there is a conflict between these two conceptions of the morpheme. If we define the morpheme as the minimal grammatical unit, then it cannot simultaneously be a unit functioning in the formation of words in Latin; if on the other hand we define it as a formational segment of the word, then it is not a minimal grammatical unit in Latin (or a universal concept of linguistic theory).

5.4   The word

5.4.1   *Morphology and syntax*

The word is the unit *par excellence* of traditional grammatical theory. It is the basis of the distinction which is frequently drawn between morphology and syntax and it is the principal unit of lexicography (or 'dictionary-making').

According to a common formulation of the distinction between morphology and syntax, *morphology* deals with the internal structure of words and *syntax* with the rules governing their combination in sentences. The very terms 'morphology' and 'syntax', and the way in which they are applied, imply the primacy of the word. Etymologically speaking, 'morphology' is simply 'the study of forms' and 'syntax' the theory of 'putting together': it was taken for granted by traditional grammarians that the 'forms' treated in grammar are the forms of words and that words are the units which are 'put together', or combined in sentences. In older books on language, the distinction between morphology and syntax is sometimes represented in terms of a distinction between 'form' and 'function'. This also rests upon the implied primacy of the word: according to their 'function' in the sentence, which is accounted for by the rules of syntax (with reference to such notions as 'subject', 'object', 'complement', etc.), words are said to assume a different 'form', and the different 'forms' are handled by morphology.

5.4.2 *Inflexion and derivation*

Although the term 'morphology' is now sufficiently well-established to be called 'traditional', it is not in fact a term employed in classical grammar. The term which opposes 'syntax' in classical grammar is 'inflexion'. The standard reference grammars of Greek and Latin, and the grammars of modern languages which are based on classical principles, are generally divided into three sections, not two: namely, into inflexion (or 'accidence'), derivation (or 'word-formation'), and syntax. But these three sections are not regarded as being of equal importance to the grammarian. Whereas some hundreds of pages may be devoted to inflexion and syntax, there will usually be not more than half-a-dozen or so pages on derivation. The reason for this disproportionate treatment is that there is really no place in classical grammar for derivation. *Inflexion* is defined in classical grammatical theory somewhat as follows: inflexion is a change made in the form of a word to express its relation to other words in the sentence. And in the grammars of particular languages the section on inflexion will describe the 'declensions' of nouns, adjectives, and pronouns, and the 'conjugations' of verbs, according to selected models of formation, or 'paradigms'. The section on *derivation* will list various processes whereby new words are formed from existing words (or 'roots'): adjectives from nouns (*seasonal* from *season*), nouns from verbs (*singer* from *sing*), adjectives from verbs (*acceptable* from *accept*), and so on. That any space at all is allotted to derivation is an awkward, and theoretically inconsistent, gesture in recognition of the fact that some words can be further analysed into components even if the rules in the main body of the grammar have nothing to say about the function or distribution of these components.

It was in the nineteenth century that the term 'morphology' was introduced into linguistics to cover both inflexion and derivation. (The term itself appears to have been invented by Goethe and to have been first applied, in biology, to the study of the 'forms' of living organisms; as we saw in the first chapter, from the middle of the nineteenth century linguistics was very much influenced by evolutionary biology.) The reason why a section on derivation was grafted on to grammars of the western classical languages at this period was that the comparative philologists, to a considerable extent influenced by the Sanskrit grammatical treatises now available to them, had become interested in the systematic study of the formation of words from a historical point of view. And it was realized that inflexional and derivational processes had a good deal in common.

But in classical grammar the distinction between inflexion and derivation is absolutely fundamental. Whereas *singing* is but a form of the word *sing*, syntactically determined, *singer* is a different word with its own set of forms, or 'paradigm' (cf. 1.2.3). The fact that from the point of view of their formation both *singing* and *singer* can be regarded as being composed of a 'root' (or 'stem'), *sing*, and a suffix, *ing* or *er* (the one process of formation being hardly less productive than the other in English) is obscured by the difference of treatment imposed by the presuppositions of classical grammatical theory. Standard dictionaries of English (and of most other languages), which are based upon the assumptions of classical grammar, list derivational forms as distinct words, but not the regular inflexional forms, which can be constructed by reference to the 'paradigms' set out in a conventional grammar of the language. In later chapters it will become clear that much of what is traditionally referred to as derivation can be, and ought to be, integrated with the syntactical rules of English in a generative grammar of the language. For the present, however, we may leave the question of derivation and look more closely at the concept of the 'word'.

5.4.3 *Ambiguity of the term 'word'*

The term 'word' has been used in the preceding paragraphs in three quite different senses. The first two senses are readily distinguished in terms of the notion of 'realization' (cf. 2.2.11). Just as we must distinguish between the morph as the phonological (or orthographical) representation of the morpheme, so we must distinguish between phonological (or orthographical) words and the grammatical words which they represent. For example, the phonological word /sæŋ/ and the corresponding orthographic word *sang* represent a particular grammatical word, which is traditionally referred to as 'the past tense of *sing*'; whereas the phonological word /kʌt/ and the corresponding orthographic word *cut* represent three different grammatical words: 'the present tense of *cut*', 'the past tense of *cut*', and the 'past participle of *cut*'. It has already been mentioned that phonological and orthographic words in English are generally in one-to-one correspondence with one another in the sense that they represent the same set of (one or more) grammatical words (cf. the examples just given). But there are some instances of (*a*) one–many or (*b*) many–one correspondence between phonological and grammatical words: cf. (*a*) /poustmən/: *postman, postmen*; /miːt/: *meat, meet*, etc. (*b*) /riːd/, /red/: *read* ('the present tense of *read*', 'the past tense of *read*'; n.b. /red/ is also in correspondence with the orthographic word *red*, and /riːd/ with the orthographic word *reed*). Many other languages besides English, whose spelling conventions are popularly said to be only partly 'phonetic' (in a non-technical usage of the term 'phonetic'), provide similar examples of one–many or many–one correspondence between phonological and orthographic words (cf. 1.4.2).

5.4.4 Word and 'lexeme'

There is a third, more 'abstract', usage of the term 'word'. It was this usage that we employed above when we said, for instance, that in traditional grammar 'whereas *singing* is but a form of the word *sing*... *singer* is a different word, with its own set of forms, or "paradigm"'; and the same, more 'abstract' sense was implicit in our reference to *sang* as 'the past tense of *sing*'. Modern linguists have tended to neglect, or even to condemn, this more 'abstract' usage. Bloomfield, for example, says that the school tradition is 'inaccurate' in referring to units like *book, books*, or *do, does, did, done*, as 'different forms of the same word'. But it is Bloomfield himself who is here guilty of inaccuracy. It is up to us to decide which way we wish to define the term 'word'. The important thing is to keep the three senses apart. Modern linguists have not always done this consistently and as a result they have frequently misinterpreted traditional grammatical theory. It is, of course, the more 'abstract' sense that the term 'word' bears in classical grammar. However, since most linguists now employ the term 'word' to refer to such phonological or orthographic units as /sæŋ/ or *sang*, on the one hand, or to the grammatical units they represent, on the other (and indeed do not always distinguish even between these two senses), we shall introduce another term, *lexeme*, to denote the more 'abstract' units which occur in different inflexional 'forms' according to the syntactic rules involved in the generation of sentences. Notationally, lexemes will be distinguished from words by the use of capitals. Thus the orthographic word *cut* represents three different inflexional 'forms' (i.e. three different grammatical words) of the lexeme CUT.

In later sections of this book, we shall use the term 'lexeme' only when it might not be clear from the context which sense of 'word' is intended. It is unfortunate that modern linguistics has not followed the traditional practice of defining the word to be the more 'abstract' unit.

5.4.5 *'Accidence'*

It is worth while dwelling for a moment on the implications of the term 'form' as it is employed in traditional grammar. We have already seen that the opposition drawn by de Saussure between 'substance' and 'form' is to be distinguished from the Aristotelian and scholastic opposition of these terms. We shall not go into the details of Aristotelian metaphysics with its rich terminology of distinctions ('substance', 'matter', 'form', 'essence', 'existence', etc.), but it must be realized that classical grammar rests upon metaphysical assumptions of a more or less Aristotelian kind. In particular, it presupposes the distinction between the 'essential' and the 'accidental' properties of an object. For instance, it is part of the 'essence' of man (let us say) to be intelligent and to have two legs; whereas it is 'accidental' that particular men should have red hair or blue eyes. Similarly, the words that occur in sentences have particular 'accidental' properties (e.g. nouns are either singular or plural, verbs are in the present, past or future tense, and so on); and the grammarian's 'paradigms' (and lists of irregularities) describe the 'forms' of words of different classes. Lexemes (the 'words' of traditional grammar) are the underlying invariant units considered in abstraction from their 'accidental' properties: lexemes are 'substances' which occur in various 'accidental' 'forms'. It is this conception, it will be observed, which underlies Roger Bacon's view quoted above (1.2.7): 'Grammar is substantially the same in all languages, even though it may vary accidentally.' And it is this conception which explains the traditional term 'accidence' for what we are calling 'inflexion': strictly speaking, words are 'inflected' (i.e. they vary their 'form') according to their 'accidence' (from the Latin *accidentia*, 'accidental properties'). And the classical grammarians assumed that the 'accidental' properties of lexemes, like the 'accidental' properties of everything else in the universe, could be classified under a restricted set of 'categories' (cf. 7.1.1). A more extended treatment of the basis of classical grammar than can be given in an introductory work of this kind would show that it was not always possible to apply the Aristotelian system consistently to the description of language. The present brief account will be sufficient for the elucidation of the traditional concept of the 'word'. And, as we shall see, the traditional view of the 'word' (or lexeme), when stripped of its metaphysical implications, merits a more sympathetic consideration than it has received from most modern linguists.

5.4.6 *Orthographic words*

We may now take up the question of the word and its status in general linguistic theory. We have already seen that it is the word, rather than the lexeme, which has engaged the interest of most modern linguists, although they have not generally distinguished between these concepts. With the habits of reading and writing drilled into us at school and sustained by continuous practice thereafter, it is perhaps difficult for us to think of utterances except as being composed of words. But the ability to break utterances up into words is not only characteristic of educated and literate speakers of a language. Sapir tells us that uneducated American-Indian speakers, with no experience of writing any language at all, when asked to do so, were perfectly capable of dictating to him texts in their own language 'word by word', and had little difficulty in isolating words from utterances and repeating them to him as units. Whatever else we may say about the word as a linguistic unit, we must reject the view which has sometimes been advanced that 'primitive languages' do not have words. The habit of reading and writing, especially in a complex, industrialized society like our own which is founded on literacy, may well reinforce the native speaker's consciousness of the word as an element of his language (and may also maintain certain inconsistencies: cf. *all right*, *altogether*); but it certainly does not create his ability to break utterances up into words in the first place.

5.4.7 *'Potential pause'*

It has been suggested that the word should be defined as 'any segment of a sentence bounded by successive points *at which pausing is possible*'. Even if we grant that this criterion of potential pause will in fact segment utterances into units which we should wish to regard as words, it should be considered as a procedural help to the linguist working with informants, and not as a theoretical definition. The fact is that speakers do not normally pause between words. Since the native speaker is able to actualize the 'potential pauses' in his utterances when he wishes to, even though he does not do this normally, it follows that the words must be identifiable as units in his language under the normal conditions in which he uses it. It is this functional unity of the word in the language as it normally operates that we must try to capture in our definition; and it is presumably the native speaker's consciousness of the word as a functional unit which also lies behind the recognition of the word in most systems of orthography.

5.4.8 *Semantic definition of the word*

One well-known definition of the word runs as follows: 'A word may be defined as the union of a particular meaning with a particular complex of sounds capable of a particular grammatical employment.' This definition, it will be observed, makes it a necessary condition that the word should be simultaneously a semantic, a phonological and a grammatical unit. Now it may well be true that all the units which we wish to regard as words in the description of a given language satisfy these three conditions. But they are certainly not the only units to satisfy them. Entire phrases, like *the new book*, have a definite meaning, a definite phonological shape and a definite grammatical employment. And so do distributionally limited segments of even higher rank. Some linguists have suggested that the definition can be made satisfactory by saying that words are the smallest segments of utterances which fulfil the three conditions. But this will not do either. The *un* and the *able* of *unacceptable* satisfy the three criteria. Yet they would not generally be regarded as words. Moreover, the word *unacceptable* is more or less synonymous with the phrase *not acceptable*; both can be analysed into three meaningful units (and three grammatical units: three morphemes each represented by one morph). We must conclude that semantic considerations are irrelevant in the definition of the word, as in the definition of other grammatical units. As for the phonological criterion: although, as we shall see later, words are phonologically delimited in various ways in many languages, such phonological features are never more than secondary correlations. We shall therefore concentrate upon defining the word in purely *grammatical* terms.

To simplify the discussion, for the present we will continue to assume, with the majority of linguists, that in all languages the morpheme is the minimum unit of grammatical analysis. The

question we have set ourselves therefore is this: how shall we define a
unit intermediate in rank between the morpheme and the sentence
and one which will correspond fairly closely with our intuitive ideas of
what is a 'word', these intuitive ideas being supported, in general, by
the conventions of the orthographic tradition?

5.4.9 'Minimal free form'

The first answer to be considered is Bloomfield's, which is probably
the most famous of all modern attempts to define the word in general
terms applicable to all languages. According to Bloomfield the word
is 'a minimum free form'. This depends upon the prior distinction of
'free' and 'bound' forms in the following sense: forms which never
occur alone as whole utterances (in some normal situation) are *bound*
forms; forms which may occur alone as utterances are *free* forms. Any
free form no part of which is itself a free form is, by Bloomfield's
definition, a word. It will be evident to the reader that this definition
applies, in so far as it does apply, to phonological words rather than
grammatical words. Bloomfield did not distinguish clearly between
these two concepts.

There is no doubt that Bloomfield's definition will cover a good
number of the forms in different languages that we should wish to
recognize as words. And it would account satisfactorily for the native
speaker's ability to actualize the 'potential pauses' between such
forms as are covered by the definition when they occur in the stream
of speech. But, as Bloomfield himself pointed out, the definition will
not capture certain forms that have traditionally been considered as
independent words: e.g. *the* or *a* in English. Such forms are not likely
to occur as whole utterances in any normal situation of language use.
(Clearly the word *the* might be said as a whole utterance in reply to
someone doing a crossword-puzzle and asking for 'a three-letter word
beginning with *th*'; or in reply to the inquiry 'Did you say "*a*" or
"*the*"?' In all such contexts linguistic forms are being 'mentioned'
rather than 'used': and in contexts of 'mention' linguistic units of
every rank and level can occur as whole utterances.) Bloomfield is, of
course, aware of this difficulty; but, instead of making a stand on his
primary criterion and saying that, despite their traditional classification, such forms as *the* and *a* are not in fact words, he introduces a
supplementary criterion of 'parallelism' with forms which are
classified as words by the first criterion of freedom of occurrence.
The and *a* occur in the same environments in sentences as *this* and *that*

(cf. *the man, a man, this man, that man,* etc.); *this* and *that* may occur as minimal free forms, and so are classified as words; therefore *the* and *a* are words.

Although Bloomfield's definition of the word in terms of 'freedom' and 'bondage' has been accepted by many eminent linguists, it can hardly be regarded as satisfactory. We must not lose sight of the primary object of grammatical description: to generate sentences from which can be derived the utterances and potential utterances of the language being described. All questions of classification must be subordinated to this purpose. We may assume that, in general, sentences are composed of many morphemes; and that the word is a unit, 'below' the rank of sentence, composed, typically, of a number of morphemes. But to call a particular 'complex' of morphemes a 'unit' implies that these morphemes are in greater 'cohesion' than other groupings of morphemes in the sentence which are not recognized as words; that sentences can be generated more satisfactorily by taking into account (at least) two different principles of composition, one of which determines the combination of morphemes into 'complexes' (which we will call grammatical words) and the other the combination of words into sentences. Now, as a matter of empirical fact it may be true that the set of 'minimal free forms' will generally correspond in all languages to the set of phonological units representing grammatical words; but, if so, this fact presumably depends upon and reflects the structural 'cohesion' of the word in sentences, and is of only indirect concern to the grammarian. Like the criterion of 'potential pause', that of occurrence as a 'minimum free form' is at best a procedural aid to the linguist working with informants. Let us now look a little more closely therefore at some of the features involved in what has been referred to as the 'cohesion' of the word as a grammatical unit.

5.4.10 'Internal cohesion' of the word

The grammatical 'cohesion' of the word (regarded as a combination of morphemes) is commonly discussed in terms of two criteria: 'positional mobility' and 'uninterruptability'. The first of these may be illustrated with reference to the following sentence, which we have segmented into morphemes (or morphs):

> *the-boy-s-walk-ed-slow-ly-up-the-hill*
> 1   2   3   4   5   6   7   8 9   10

The sentence may be regarded as a combination of ten morphemes, which occur in a particular order relative to one another. However, various permutations are possible, if we start from the order in which the morphemes occur in the sentence cited above: *slow-ly-the-boy-s-walk-ed-up-the-hill, up-the-hill-slowl-y-walk-ed-the-boy-s*, etc. Substituting the numbers for these two other possibilities, we get (in place of 1 2 3 4 5 6 7 8 9 10):

    6 7 1 2 3 4 5 8 9 10
    8 9 10 6 7 4 5 1 2 3

There are other possible permutations which will yield an acceptable English sentence. The point is, however, that under all the permutations certain pairs or triples of morphemes will behave as 'blocks', not only occurring always together, but also in the same order relative to one another: there is no possibility of the sequence 3 2 1 (**s-boy-the*), or 5 4 (**ed-walk*). One of the characteristics of the word is that it tends to be internally stable (in terms of the order of the component morphemes), but positionally mobile (permutable with other words in the same sentence). Clearly, this characteristic is far more striking in languages with a 'free word-order' (cf. 2.3.5).

It is worth pointing out that positional mobility and internal stability are independent of one another. Suppose, for example, we found a language in which the order of words was fixed, but the order of morphemes within words freely subject to permutation. This may be indicated symbolically as follows (taking *A*, *B* and *C* to be words):

A	*B*	*C*
1 2 3	4 5 6	7 8 9 10
2 3 1	6 4 5	10 9 8 7
3 2 1	5 6 4	9 7 8 10
2 1 3	4 5 6	9 10 7 8

Here, it is the order of the intermediate units relative to one another which is 'fixed', by contrast with the 'freedom' of order within the intermediate units (one might say that the sentence is 'internally stable' at the word-rank, whereas the morphemes are 'positionally mobile' within words). To illustrate from English: this situation would hold if, for example, not only *The-girl-s have-be-en-eat-ing apple-s* were acceptable, but also **Girl-the-s en-have-be-eat-ing s-apple*, etc. (We have here taken *the girls* to be one word, and also *have been eating*: in terms of the present criterion, this is correct.) So far (to the best of my knowledge) no language has been found which manifests this particular feature. As we have already seen, 'free' order tends to be found, if at all, at the higher ranks (cf. 2.3.6). This is an empirical fact about the structure of language. The converse situation, which we have just envisaged, is not only logically conceivable, but it would define the word as a structural unit of language no less clearly than the common phenomenon of relatively 'free' word-order.

But we have said that positional mobility and internal stability are independent of one another. Once again we may illustrate from English. The criterion of positional mobility would fail to define the 'definite article', *the*, as a word: it cannot be moved from one place in the sentence to another independently of the noun it 'modifies'. In this respect, it is like the so-called 'postpositive' articles of Swedish, Norwegian, Rumanian, Bulgarian, Macedonian, etc. ('postpositive' simply means 'following', rather than 'preceding': cf. 'postposition' *v.* 'preposition', 7.4.7): e.g. Rumanian *lup* 'wolf': *lupul* 'the wolf', Macedonian *grad* 'city': *gradot* 'the city'. It is the criterion of 'interruptability' (or 'insertability') which distinguishes the English article as more 'word-like' than the Rumanian or Macedonian article. It is possible to 'interrupt' (or 'insert' within) the sequence *the-boy*, whereas it is not possible to 'interrupt' the sequence *grad-ot* or *lup-ul*: by 'interruptability' is meant the possibility of inserting other elements, more or less freely, between the morphemes or 'blocks' of morphemes. For example, between *the* and *boy* one may insert a whole sequence of other elements: *the big strong strapping boy*, etc.

The fact that one criterion, but not the other, applies to the English article implies that, even if it is taken to be a word, it is not so 'fully' a word as other elements to which all the relevant criteria apply. There are many marginal cases in various languages which have been much discussed in the literature.

5.4.11 *Phonological correlations*

In many languages the word is phonologically marked in some way. For instance, a great number of languages have what is called a word-accent: in such languages every word is 'accented' (this may be a matter of stress or pitch, or both) on one and only one syllable. The accent may be 'free' (as in English or Russian), in the sense that the syllable on which it falls is not generally determined by the phonological structure of the word or its grammatical classification; or 'restricted' (the accent is restricted to one of the last three syllables in both Classical and Modern Greek); or 'fixed', with reference to the beginning or end of the word or to some other feature. Examples of well-known languages with a fixed accent are: Latin, where the place of the accent is generally determined by the length of the penultimate syllable; Polish, where the accent (generally) occurs on the next to the last syllable; Turkish, where it (generally) occurs on the last syllable; and Czech, where it falls on the initial syllable of the word. To mention just two other ways in which words may be phonologically delimited: 'vowel-harmony' in Turkish and Hungarian operates throughout words, but not beyond (cf. 3.3.13); and in many languages a more restricted set of phonological units occur at the beginning or end of words than in other positions. For all languages with a word-accent it is true (in general) that there will be the same number of words in an utterance as there are accents; and in the case of languages with a fixed accent the boundaries between words may be determined by reference to the syllables on which the accent falls. However, the very fact that we can say that there are exceptions to the general rules governing the place of the accent (that, for instance, the Russian word *ne*, 'not', is never stressed; that the reflexive forms of the verb in Polish have the accent on the same syllable as in the corresponding unreflexive forms; that such Turkish forms as *gitmiyordu*, 'he was not going', or *askérken* 'when (he was) a soldier', are words despite the place of the accent and their partial violation of the rules of 'vowel-harmony') shows that the accent is not the primary defining feature of the word in these languages. We could hardly determine the place of the Polish or Turkish accent with respect to the beginning or end of the word, if the word-boundaries themselves were determined solely by reference to the place of the accent! The partial 'congruence' of the phonological and grammatical levels by virtue of the double status of the word as both a grammatical and phonological unit is therefore a common, though not a universal, feature of languages. There are languages (a notable instance is French) where whatever congruence there is between phonological and grammatical structure seems to hold over units of higher rank than the word.

5.4.12 *Independence of criteria*

For a fuller account of the various features by means of which the grammatical 'cohesion' of the word may be established, and also of the different ways in which words may be phonologically marked in different languages, reference may be made to the works cited for this section in the bibliographical notes. Enough has been said in the preceding paragraphs to show that the grammatical criteria are independent of one another, and that phonological criteria are not only independent of one another, but necessarily subordinate to the grammatical. It follows from these facts that what we call 'words' in one language may be units of a different kind from the 'words' of another language; and yet the application of the term 'word' is not entirely arbitrary, since the relevant features whereby words are established for different languages all tend to support their identification as structural units.

Since the criteria for the establishment of words apply not only independently of one another, but also independently of the criteria whereby morphemes are defined as minimal grammatical units, in certain languages the same units may be simultaneously both words and morphemes. For instance, in English the morphs /nais/, /boi/, /wont/ (orthographically, *nice, boy, want*) represent simultaneously the morphemes 'nice', 'boy', and 'want' and (on the assumption that this is in fact the correct analysis of these forms) grammatical words composed each of one morpheme. As we have already seen (5.3.6), a one-to-one ratio of morphemes to words is the defining characteristic of 'isolating' languages.

5.5 The notion of 'rank'

5.5.1 *'Rank' is a surface-structure notion*

In this chapter we have given a very brief account of the primary units of grammatical analysis and the way in which the terms applying to them have been defined in modern linguistics. As we have seen, the sentence and the word (in the sense of 'lexeme': cf. 5.4.4) were the main units with which traditional grammar operated, the phrase and the clause being defined, not always consistently, in terms of them. The morpheme has replaced the word as the minimal unit of grammatical analysis in many modern treatments of linguistic theory; but few linguists have adhered in practice to a theoretically consistent definition of the morpheme.

At the beginning of the chapter, we said that the relationship between sentences, clauses, phrases, words and morphemes was one which could be expressed by saying that a unit of 'higher' *rank* was composed out of units of 'lower' rank. The term 'rank' has been taken from Halliday; other linguists use 'level' (e.g. Pike) or 'stratum' (e.g. Lamb) in roughly the same sense. Various attempts have been made to formulate a consistent theory of grammatical structure based on the notion of 'composition' (notably by the three authors mentioned in the previous sentence). We shall not discuss these theories here, but simply refer the reader to the works cited in the notes.

In the next chapter, we shall adopt a transformational approach to grammatical description. One consequence of this is that we shall be led to the distinction of what will be referred to as the 'deep' and the 'surface' structure of sentences. It will then appear that such distinctions as can be drawn consistently between units of different rank (and it is undeniable that sentences have a grammatical structure that can be described appropriately in such terms) are drawn with respect to the surface structure.

5.5.2 *An illustration*

There is no reason to believe, or to make it a theoretical requirement, that the rules of the grammar must be organized in such a way that one set of rules (say) generates words out of morphemes, that another set of rules then combines these words into phrases, that a third set of rules generates clauses out of phrases, and finally that a fourth set of rules generates sentences out of clauses. Within a transformational framework, much of the importance that has been attached in the past to the definition of units of different ranks disappears. We are no longer committed to the necessity of saying that every sentence must be analysable without residue into units of one rank or another.

To give just one example at this point. There is a large class of adjectives in English, exemplified by *red-haired, blue-eyed, one-legged*, etc., which quite clearly 'contain' three morphemes (as the term 'morpheme' is generally applied): e.g. {*red*}+{*hair*}+{*ed*}. In each case, two of the constituent morphemes may be regarded as words, e.g. *red* and *hair*. They are free forms, and they satisfy the various other criteria that have been proposed for the definition of the word (cf. 5.4.6 ff.). From one point of view, it might be desirable to regard *red-haired* as one word: in particular, for the purpose of integrating the grammar and phonology in the determination of the distribution of stress. (Most English words have one primary stress; and the 'complex' adjectives we are discussing would seem to satisfy this criterion.) On the other hand, *red-haired* 'contains' two words and a bound morpheme. Furthermore, there would seem to be some sense in which the bound morpheme {*ed*} is 'added' to the phrase *red hair*:

there is no form *haired*, which we can combine at a higher rank with *red*. Problems of this kind cease to be worrying if we accept that adjectives like *red-haired* can be generated by the grammar in a sequence of operations which are not constrained by the requirements of linguistic theory to follow the principle that units of 'higher' rank are composed of an integral number of units of 'lower' rank.

With these remarks, we can embark upon our further discussion of grammatical structure. We shall continue from the point we reached in the previous chapter. But we shall no longer maintain the view that the vocabulary of a language is a set of words, listed in the lexicon, which are combined into sentences by means of rules operating directly upon word-classes.

6

GRAMMATICAL STRUCTURE

6.1 Immediate constituents

6.1.1 *Concatenation and linearity*

In our treatment of the general principles of 'formal grammar' in chapter 4, we deliberately adopted the view that all sentences had a simple *linear* structure: i.e. that every sentence of the language could be satisfactorily described, from the grammatical point of view, as a *string* (or sequence) of *constituents* (which we assumed to be words).

As an abstract illustration of what is meant by the term 'string' (which is the technical term used in mathematical treatments of the grammatical structure of language) we may consider the following instances:

$$a+b+c+d$$

The plus-sign is employed here (other conventions of notation are also to be found in the literature) to indicate *concatenation* ('chaining together'). The string results from the combination of the constituents, or elements, in a particular order. What the order denotes depends upon the interpretation given to the system in its application to particular phenomena. In the case of natural languages, the left-to-right ordering of the constituents in the string may be thought of as reflecting the time-sequence (from earlier to later) in spoken utterances or the left-to-right ordering of written sentences in the conventions used for English and most languages of the world today. At the same time, it should be realized that the same abstract principle of linear ordering might also be used for other purposes in the description of language. Indeed, there is no reason why linear ordering should not be interpretable in different ways in different parts of a grammar. We tacitly assumed, in chapter 4, that the combination of words resulting from the application of a grammatical rule constituted a string, with the order of the concatenated words being determined by the order in which the words occur in sentences of the language.

It was pointed out in chapter 2 (cf. 2.3.5) that the notion of syntagmatic relationship did not necessarily presuppose an ordering of the elements between which the relationship held: and instances were given of both sequential and non-sequential combinations of elements. It is important to realize that a string is a particular kind of *syntagm*, as concatenation is a particular kind of *combination*. If the data suggested that we should, we might formalize the theory of grammatical structure in terms of a non-concatenating system of rules which generated not strings of elements, but unordered sets (between the members of which there held certain relations of syntagmatic presupposition, dependency, etc.). For example, a *rewrite-rule* (cf. 4.3.2) of the form

$$X \rightarrow a+b+c+d$$

might be interpreted (the plus-sign now no longer indicating concatenation) to mean solely that X is a syntagm composed of the unordered combination of elements a, b, c and d. Although most of the discussion in this chapter will take for granted the restriction to concatenating systems of rewrite-rules, the point should be borne in mind. Some of the rules suggested in a later chapter will be non-concatenating. But before we continue with the more formal discussion, we must say something about the historical background.

6.1.2   *Immediate constituents*

Most modern textbooks of linguistics attach great importance to what is called *immediate constituent analysis*. The term 'immediate constituent' was introduced by Bloomfield (1933), as follows: 'Any English-speaking person who concerns himself with this matter, is sure to tell us that the immediate constituents of *Poor John ran away* are the two forms *poor John* and *ran away*; that each of these is, in turn, a complex form; that the immediate constituents of *ran away* are *ran*... and *away*...; and that the constituents of *poor John* are ...*poor* and *John*.'

There is an obvious parallelism between immediate constituent analysis and the traditional procedure of 'parsing' sentences into 'subject' and 'predicate', and each of these, where appropriate, into words, phrases and clauses of various types. Bloomfield's sentence might be described as a simple sentence whose subject is a noun-phrase, made up of the noun *John* 'modified' by the adjective *poor*, and whose predicate is a verb-phrase, consisting of the verb *ran* 'modified' by the adverb *away*. Underlying both approaches to grammatical analysis is the view that sentences are not just linear sequences of elements, but are made up of 'layers' of *immediate constituents*, each lower-level constituent being part of a higher-level constituent. The analysis of a sentence into its several 'layers' of constituents can be represented graphically in a number of ways. We may use brackets: [(*Poor John*) (*ran away*)]. Or we may construct a *tree-diagram* (cf. Fig. 8).

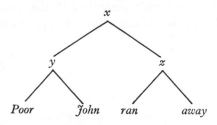

Fig. 8. Bloomfield's immediate constituents.

These two methods of representation are equivalent. (The symbols x, y and z are employed here merely for convenience of reference to the diagram.) The tree-diagram given above is to be interpreted as follows: the ultimate constituents of the sentence (the elements out of which the sentence is constructed) are *poor*, *John*, *ran* and *away*; the words *poor* and *John* are the immediate constituents of one construction, *poor John*, so the branches leading to them derive directly from one 'node' (y); the words *ran* and *away* are the immediate constituents of another construction, being related through the next-highest 'node' common to them both (z); and the two constructions *poor John* and *ran away* are the immediate constituents of the highest-level construction, the sentence itself, so they both derive directly from the 'node' x. It will be observed that neither in the representation of the constituent structure of the sentence by means of brackets nor in the equivalent tree-diagram have we incorporated the information that *poor* is an adjective, that *poor John* is a noun-phrase, etc. Nor have we taken account of the fact that *poor John* is 'subject' and *ran away* is 'predicate' or of the notion of 'modification'. In these respects our analysis of the sentence into its constituents differs from, and so far is 'poorer' than, the analysis that would be given in terms of the categories of traditional grammar.

One can distinguish three periods of development in the theory of constituent structure. Bloomfield himself did little more than introduce the notion and explain it by means of examples. He spoke of a 'proper analysis' of the sentence into constituents as 'one which takes account of the meanings'. His followers, notably Wells and Harris, formulated the principles of constituent analysis in greater detail and replaced Bloomfield's somewhat vague reference to 'taking account of the meanings' with explicitly distributional criteria. Finally, in the last few years, the theory of constituent-structure has been formalized and subjected to mathematical study by Chomsky and other scholars, who have given considerable attention to the nature of the rules required to generate sentences with the appropriate constituent-structure.

6.1.3   Grammatical ambiguity

One of the most cogent reasons for recognizing that sentences, and parts of sentences, have a non-linear constituent-structure is that it enables us to handle a large class of ambiguities at the grammatical level of description. If we compare the following three examples, we shall see that ambiguity may be a function either of the distributional classification of the elements or of the constituent structure, or of both together:

(a) *They can fish*

(b) *Beautiful girl's dress*

(c) *Some more convincing evidence*

In the case of the first example, (a) *They can fish* (cf. *They could fish, They may fish*, on the one hand, and *They canned fish, They eat fish*, on the other), the ambiguity is accounted for by the double classification of both *can* (as a modal auxiliary or a transitive verb) and *fish* (as an intransitive verb or a noun). Since the verb-phrase in an English sentence may consist of a transitive verb and a noun or of an intransitive verb with a preceding auxiliary (this is of course an over-simplified account), it follows that *They can fish* is analysable in two ways. There is, however, no difference of bracketing; under both interpretations the sentence is to be bracketed as *They (can fish)*. By contrast, the ambiguity of (b) *beautiful girl's dress* is to be accounted for, not in terms of the distributional classification of the elements (*beautiful, girl, dress*), but in terms of a difference of constituent-structure; under one interpretation, 'girl's dress which is beautiful', the words *girl's* and *dress* form a constituent; under the other, 'dress of (a) beautiful girl', it is *beautiful* and *girl* that are bracketed together to form a constituent. The third example combines both factors: the phrase (c) *some more convincing evidence* may be paraphrased, unambiguously, as either

(i) *some evidence which is more convincing*, or (ii) *some more evidence which is convincing*; in other words, it can be bracketed into constituents as either (i) *some* [(*more convincing*) *evidence*], or (ii) [(*Some more*) (*convincing evidence*)]. But correlated with this difference of constituent-structure there is also a difference in the distributional classification of the elements. This becomes clear, if we substitute *less* for *more* and *good* (or *bad*, etc.) for *convincing*: *some less convincing evidence* is not ambiguous, nor is *some more good evidence*, nor is *some better evidence*, nor is *some more evidence*. The word *more* belongs to (at least) two distributional classes: (i) like *less*, it combines with adjectives to form adjectival-phrases (however, its distribution is more restricted than that of *less*, since *more* is here in complementary distribution with the suffix *-er*: cf. *nicer* v. *more nice, etc.), and (ii) unlike *less*, it combines with a preceding *some* to form a 'modifier' of nouns and noun-phrases (cf. *some more evidence* v. **some less evidence*).

Ambiguity may be a function then either of constituent-structure or of the distributional classification of the ultimate (and intermediate) constituents; and this is the case not only for English, but for many other languages as well. We must therefore take account of both factors in the analysis of sentences. This can be done easily enough by labelling the bracketed structures or the 'nodes' of the tree-diagram. Thus:

$$\Sigma\{NP(A\ [poor] + N\ [John]) + VP(V\ [ran] + Adv\ [away])\}$$

There is no distinction associated with the different kinds of brackets used here. The employment of different brackets makes it easier to locate, visually, the corresponding left and right member of a pair of brackets. An equivalent tree-diagram (which is much easier to 'read') is given in Fig. 9.

We have now brought into the representation of the grammatical structure of sentences such as *Poor John ran away* the fact that *poor John* is a noun-phrase (*NP*) consisting of the adjective (*A*) *poor* and the noun (*N*) *John* and that *ran away* is a verb-phrase (*VP*) composed of the verb (*V*) *ran* and the adverb (*Adv*) *away*. And from now on we shall consider such information to be an integral part of the analysis of sentences in terms of their constituent-structure. We have still not introduced the traditional notions of 'subject' and 'predicate'. Nor have we yet said anything about 'modification'. In traditional grammatical theory the phrase *poor John* would be classed as a noun-phrase because it 'functions as', or 'does the work of', a noun in

8

sentences. This can be interpreted as meaning that phrases of the form adjective + noun have the same distribution in the sentences generated by the grammar as nouns; that *poor John*, *new car*, etc., can be freely substituted for *John*, *car*, etc., in any given sentence, and the result will be another grammatically acceptable sentence. This fact is accounted for in our analysis of such sentences as *Poor John ran away* by labelling the 'node' through which the adjective and the noun are related with the term 'noun-phrase'.

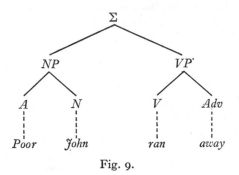

Fig. 9.

Before we develop further the notions of constituent-structure from a generative point of view, we must explain what is meant by the term 'grammatical ambiguity', as it has been used above. Consider all the noun-phrases in English of the form $A + N_1 + N_2$ (A = adjective, N = noun). Many of these are ambiguous; and their ambiguity can be resolved by specifying their constituent-structure as either $A + (N_1 + N_2)$ or $(A + N_1) + N_2$. Now, many of these phrases are not subject to misinterpretation when they are actually used in sentences, because either the rest of the sentence or the general context in which the language operates makes it certain, or at least very probable, that one interpretation rather than the other is the correct one. The phrase *fresh fruit market*, for instance, is hardly likely to be understood in the sense indicated by the bracketing *fresh (fruit market)*; conversely, the phrase *new fruit market* is not likely to be used in the sense of *(new fruit) market*. Let us assume, for the sake of the argument, that neither *fresh fruit market* nor *new fruit market* has more than one interpretation: from the semantic point of view, we will say that they are not ambiguous. Are they grammatically ambiguous? Is the constituent-structure *fresh (fruit market)*, in the one case, and *(new fruit) market*, in the other, grammatically acceptable? To answer these questions we must of course refer to some explicit grammar of

English. It is clear that, in general, the bracketing $A + (N_1 + N_2)$ is acceptable if the first noun can combine with the second (*fruit market*) and if the adjective can combine with the second noun (*new market*, ?*fresh market*); and the bracketing $(A + N_1) + N_2$ is acceptable if the first noun can combine with the second noun and if the adjective can combine with the first noun (*fresh fruit*, ?*new fruit*). The question therefore is essentially the same as that discussed above in connexion with the limits of grammar: the question of sub-classification with the two limiting factors of indeterminacy and of 'diminishing returns' (cf. 4.2.11). Any phrase of the form $A + N_1 + N_2$ will be given two grammatical analyses, unless the grammar and lexicon to which we refer prohibits explicitly the combination of the adjective in question with one or other of the nouns.

The notion of constituent-structure does not rest solely upon its capacity to handle ambiguities of the kind we have discussed. The main reason for regarding sentences as being composed of 'layers' of constituents is that in this way we can achieve a more economical and intuitively more satisfying description. This will be clear from the discussion which follows. It may be mentioned in passing that there are other kinds of ambiguity which can be accounted for by an essentially different kind of grammatical structure from that which we are at present considering. Some of these will be discussed later in this chapter (cf. 6.6.2).

6.2   Phrase-structure grammars

6.2.1   *'Phrase-structure'*

It is one thing to know where to put the brackets in a given sentence: it is quite a different matter to construct a system of generative rules of such a kind that they will explicitly assign the correct constituent-structure to sentences. Although many different systems of grammatical rules can be designed which will impose a constituent-structure analysis upon the sentences they generate, we shall restrict ourselves initially to the consideration of concatenating rewrite-systems of the type which Chomsky has made familiar. Such systems we will call *phrase-structure* grammars. By implication, 'constituent-structure grammars' will be a wider term.

6.2.2   *Rewrite-systems*

We may begin by providing a set of rewrite-rules (they are assumed to be concatenating: cf. 6.6.1) of the following form:

(1) $\Sigma \rightarrow NP + VP$

(2) $VP \rightarrow V + Adv$

(3) $NP \rightarrow A + N$

If these rules are applied in sequence in such a way that each rule (apart from the first) is used to replace, or 'rewrite', in the 'output' of the previous rules, whatever symbol occurs in the left-hand side of the rule with whatever symbols occur 'bracketed' after the arrow, we shall get by rule (1) the output

$\Sigma \{NP + VP\}$

and by the application to this of rule (2)

$\Sigma \{NP + VP(V + Adv)\}$

and, finally, by rule (3)

$\Sigma \{NP(A + N) + VP(V + Adv)\}$

That is, each rule brackets together the constituents which form the construction it defines, and labels the construction; and the structural layers are determined by the order in which the rules are applied. In the present instance the result would be the same if rule (3) were applied before rule (2). But rule (1) must be applied first, in order to produce the elements required for rules (2) and (3). The term occurring in the left-hand part of rule (1) of the grammar denotes the highest-level construction of which all other constructions generated by the grammar are constituents. We shall call this term ('sentence') the *initial symbol*. After the application of all the rules relevant in the generation of a particular type of sentence, the grammar will have 'produced' a bracketed 'string' of symbols (adjective, noun, verb, etc.), each of which denotes a class of elements in the lexicon. The symbols denoting lexical classes we shall refer to as *terminal symbols*, and bracketed strings of terminal symbols as *terminal strings*. If we now substitute for each of the terminal symbols in a terminal string a member of the lexical class it denotes, we shall get a sentence whose constituent structure is completely determined by the rules which generate the terminal string. Thus, if the lexicon contains the following information (cf. 4.3.1 ff.)

$N = \{John, \text{etc.}\}$

$V = \{ran, \text{etc.}\}$

$A = \{poor, \text{etc.}\}$

$Adv = \{away, \text{etc.}\}$

the three-rule grammar given above will generate such sentences as
Poor John ran away with their correct constituent-structure. Conversely, presented with this sentence and using a lexicon which is
organized more conveniently for analysis, i.e. in some such form as

> *away: Adv*
>
> *John: N*
>
> *poor: A*
>
> *ran: V*

we shall be able to replace each word of the sentence with its class-
symbol and then work through the rules of the grammar upwards and
from right to left until, if we arrive successfully at the initial symbol
in rule (1), we thereby recognize the sentence as being grammatically
acceptable and as having a certain constituent structure. It should be
stressed that the reason why it is possible to work through the rules
in either direction in the case of the present grammar is that it
conforms to certain general conditions (which we will not discuss here:
cf. 6.2.11). Independently of this particular property it is neutral with
respect to analysis and synthesis (cf. 4.3.1); and it formalizes the
notion of 'labelled bracketing' (cf. 6.1.3).

6.2.3   *Alternative rules*

Let us now extend the grammar, in order to make it capable of
'producing' and 'recognizing' sentences like *Old men love young
women*, in addition to such sentences as *Poor John ran away*. We can
do this by introducing rules which allow for alternative ways of
'rewriting' the element *VP* (verb-phrase). Thus:

> (1) $\Sigma \rightarrow NP + VP$
>
> (2a) $VP \rightarrow V_{intr} + Adv$
>
> (2b) $VP \rightarrow V_{tr} + NP$
>
> (3) $NP \rightarrow A + N$

It is to be understood that one of the subrules (2a) and (2b) must be
applied but that the choice between them is free. When we introduce

the possibility of choosing between (2 *a*) and (2 *b*) in the grammar, we must also change the classification of words in the lexicon:

$$V_{intr} = \{ran, \text{ etc.}\}$$
$$V_{tr} = \{love, kill, \text{ etc.}\}$$

Our grammar is still somewhat unsatisfactory in a number of ways. First of all, it will be observed that, although it correctly generates the sentences we started with, it also generates such unacceptable 'sentences' as **Poor John kill old women*. At some point we shall have to take account of the 'agreement' that holds in English between the 'subject' of the sentence and the verb (if the verb is in the 'present tense'). This question we shall leave for the moment (cf. 6.5.4). A second deficiency of the grammar is that, if each of the rules is applied where it is applicable, as we have so far assumed to be the case, the grammar will necessarily generate either five-word sentences, like *Old men love young women*, or four-word sentences, like *Poor John ran away*. It will not generate *John ran away, John ran, Men love young women, Old men love women*, etc. And it will not generate, for example, *Old men love young women passionately*.

6.2.4   *Optional and obligatory rules*

Suppose we now make rule (3) into two rules, viz.:

(3) $NP \rightarrow N$

(4) $N \rightarrow A + N$

specifying that, whereas rule (3) is *obligatory*, rule (4) is *optional*. The grammar will now generate *John ran away, Men love women, Old men love women, Men love young women*, etc.

Consider now the tree-diagrams (given in Fig. 10) representing the sentences generated by the rules set up so far, as exemplified by (i) *John ran away*, (ii) *Poor John ran away*, (iii) *Men love women*, (iv) *Old men love women*, (v) *Men love young women*, (vi) *Old men love young women*.

By reference to these tree-diagrams or to the rules by which they are constructed, we can see that all the sentences in question are subtypes of the *sentence-type* $\Sigma(NP + VP)$. In other words, at a certain level of analysis they are structurally identical. At a lower level, (i) and (ii) are identical with one another, but different in structure from (iii)–(vi); and so on. The introduction of optional rules and alternative rules therefore increases the power of the grammar, and also groups sets of constructions into subtypes of a common type.

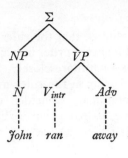

(i)

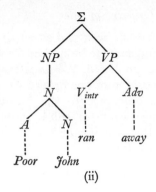

(ii)

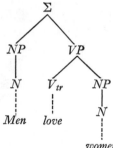

(iii)

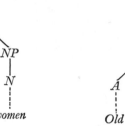

(iv)

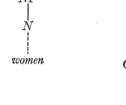

(v)

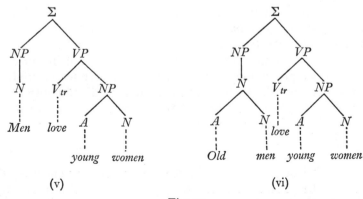

(vi)

Fig. 10.

(Note that the branch for NP→N has been omitted from (v) and (vi).)

6.2.5 *Ordering of rules*

In all that has been said so far, it has been assumed that the rules of the grammar are to be applied (where applicable) in the order in which they are numbered. We must look at this question more closely, for the imposition of one order rather than another upon the rules may make a difference to the output of the grammar. Consider the following system of rules, which is the same as that given earlier, except that a new rule (4) has been added: (rules (4) and (5) are optional rules):

$(1)\ \Sigma \rightarrow NP + VP$

$(2a)\ VP \rightarrow V_{intr} + Adv$

$(2b)\ VP \rightarrow V_{tr} + NP$

$(3)\ NP \rightarrow N$

$(4)\ N \rightarrow T + N$

$(5)\ N \rightarrow Adj + N$

It is assumed that the information $T = \{the\}$ is given in the associated lexicon. Since rules (4) and (5) are optional, the grammar will generate *men*, *the men*, *good men*, and *the good men*. But if rule (5) had been allowed to apply before rule (4), such unacceptable sequences as **good the men* would have been permitted as grammatical. Notice also that the place of rule (3) is important. If it were put before (2*b*), it would have to be repeated again after (2*b*), in order to provide for the expansion of the *NP* which results from $VP \rightarrow V_{tr} + NP$.

We have seen that the order of rules in a 'rewrite' constituent-structure grammar may be critical for two reasons: to prevent the generation of unacceptable sequences of elements and to achieve a reduction in the number of rules required. In certain instances, it might be desirable to allow a particular group of rules to apply in various orders in order to account for grammatical ambiguity of the kind referred to above (cf. 6.1.3). Take, for instance, an optional rule for the co-ordination of nouns of the form

$(6)\ N \rightarrow N + and + N$

If it is applied before rule (5) in the present system of rules, the output will be phrases like (*old men*) *and women* and *men and* (*old women*). But if it is applied after rule (5), the result will be phrases like *old* (*men and women*). The ambiguity of the sequence *old men and women*, that is as either (*old men*) *and women* or *old* (*men and women*), can be satisfactorily accounted for, therefore, in terms of a difference in the relative order of application of rules (5) and (6). It may be observed, however, that the bracketed phrase generated by the application of rule (6) after rule (5), *old (men and women)*, is semantically equivalent to *(old men) and (old women)*, which could be generated by a double application of rule (5) to the output of rule (6).

6.2.6 *Recursive rules*

The rule for the co-ordination of nouns is one that we should wish to be applicable not just once, but many times; indeed innumerable times. For it is possible to have phrases formed of indefinitely many nouns linked by *and*. The simplest way of handling these might seem to be by introducing into the grammar a set of alternative rules:

(6*a*) $N \rightarrow N + and + N$

(6*b*) $N \rightarrow N + and + N + and + N$

(6*c*) $N \rightarrow N + and + N + and + N + and + N$

etc.

However , this is clearly unsatisfactory since there is no upper limit to the number of constituent nouns that can be co-ordinated in this way in English. It is true that in a given text, or in the total set of utterances that have ever been produced, there will be some noun-phrase (or a number of noun-phrases) which contains more co-ordinated nouns than any other noun-phrase. It may also be true that there is very little likelihood of a noun-phrase being produced by a native speaker which includes more than this highest number of constituent nouns. The fact remains that, whatever number we decide upon as the upper limit, it will always be possible to produce a sentence containing a noun-phrase the number of whose constituent, co-ordinated nouns exceeds any alleged 'upper limit'. Therefore, since it is impossible in principle to list an infinite set of alternative rules, we may specify that rule (6) may be applied indefinitely many times. Rules that may be applied an indefinite number of times are called *recursive*. It is very probable that in all languages there are many constructions, the generation of which requires recursive rules. Other examples from English are the co-ordination of clauses in sentences (e.g. *He came in and he sat down and he said that...and he...*); and the modification of nouns with adjectives (e.g. *great big black...dog*).

If we wish to make our grammar a more 'realistic' model for the production of sentences and to construct it in such a way that it will generate more instances of recursive structures with two constituents than with three, more instances of structures with three constituents than with four, and so on, we can do this by assigning a particular probability to each number of times that the rules in question are to be applied (the probabilities being generated as an infinite series whose limit is zero). Probabilities could be assigned in the same way to each member of a set of alternative rules and to each optional rule in the grammar. But we must be careful not to confuse probability of occurrence with grammaticality. Although native speakers may hesitate about the acceptability of certain particular constructions of low frequency, it does not appear to be the case that they will always consider constructions with a high probability of occurrence to be more acceptable than constructions with a low probability of occurrence.

6.2.7 *Recursive co-ordinate structures*

The treatment of co-ordination by means of a recursive rule brings us to another problem. All rules of the type we are discussing in this section assign a bracketed structure to the constructions they generate; as we have seen, the different structural 'layers' are determined by the order of application of the 'rewrite' rules. Consider now a phrase like *Tom and Dick and Harry*. This sequence of words will be produced by a double application of rule (6) given above. But it will necessarily be generated as grammatically ambiguous: as either (*Tom and Dick*) *and Harry* or *Tom and* (*Dick and Harry*). (Noun-phrases containing more than three co-ordinated nouns can be generated in several different ways, and will therefore be described by the grammar as multiply ambiguous.) Although the bracketing (*Tom and Dick*) *and Harry* or *Tom and* (*Dick and Harry*) might well be intuitively satisfying in certain instances, we should normally wish to regard noun-phrases composed of three (or more) co-ordinated nouns as internally unbracketed. Constituent-structure grammars therefore present us with a dilemma with regard to the treatment of co-ordination. Recursive rules will fail to yield what is intuitively the correct structural description. Yet recursive rules are necessary in order to generate the infinity of such constructions. Here we merely point to the dilemma. (It has been much discussed in works dealing with transformational grammar.)

6.2.8 *Discontinuous constituents*

In all that has been said so far we have tacitly assumed that the constituents of a given construction will always occur next to one another in sentences. Consideration of a sentence such as *John called Bill up* shows that this is not so; in this sentence, *called...up* is a *discontinuous constituent*, enclosing the other constituent, *Bill*, with which it is in construction. Let us now compare the following three sentences, to see how they might be handled in a generative grammar:

(a) *John called up Bill*

(b) *John called Bill up*

(c) *John called him up*

The important thing to notice is that *called up* is optionally discontinuous when the object is a noun, but obligatorily discontinuous when the object is a pronoun (**John called up him*, with normal stress and intonation, is unacceptable). We will say, not only that *called up* is a constituent of all three sentences, but that, in some sense or at some more abstract level, all three sentences have the same constituent-structure; and we will introduce a supplementary rule (of a different kind from the constituent-structure rule) which will apply optionally to the terminal string 'underlying' (a) and (b) and obligatorily to the string 'underlying' (c), the effect of which will be to insert the 'object' between the two parts of the verb *called up*. In this way (provided that we can specify the conditions under which it applies—with what class of verbs, how the 'object' is identified, etc.) we shall be able to handle the problem of 'discontinuous constituents' satisfactorily.

A similar treatment suggests itself, and is much more generally applicable, in the case of languages with 'free word-order'. An example from Latin will make the point clear. The English sentence *Catullus loved Clodia* can be translated into Latin by any one of the following six sequences of words: (i) *Catullus Clodiam amabat*, (ii) *Catullus amabat Clodiam*, (iii) *Clodiam Catullus amabat*, (iv) *Clodiam amabat Catullus*, (v) *Amabat Clodiam Catullus*, (vi) *Amabat Catullus Clodiam*. (There are differences of emphasis or contextual presupposition associated with each of the six versions, but all six are acceptable.) The form of the word *Catullus* (rather than *Catullum*, *Catulli*, etc.) marks it as the subject, in the 'nominative' case; and the form of the word *Clodiam* (rather than *Clodia*, *Clodiae*, etc.) indicates that it is the object, in the 'accusative' case. The simplest way of generating the six alternative versions of the sentence would seem to be by means of a set of supplementary rules of permutation operating upon the same terminal string. If all word-order were completely 'free' in Latin, the supplementary rules would be quite simple. The fact that there are constraints upon the order of certain words in Latin sentences makes the question more complicated, but does not affect the principle being illustrated.

6.2.9 *'Supplementary' rules*

This brief discussion of discontinuous constituents and 'free' word-order has brought us to the view that the grammar of a language might include rules of two different kinds: on the one hand, phrase-structure rules and, on the other, what we have been calling 'supplementary' rules whose function it is to 'transform' the terminal strings generated by the constituent-structure rules into actual sentences (or, more precisely, into sequences of elements which are more directly relatable to sentences). We will return to this more 'abstract' view of constituent-structure in a later section (cf. 6.6).

6.2.10 *Complex sentences*

Within certain limits constituent-structure grammar can handle the formation of complex, as well as simple sentences (for the traditional distinction of simple and complex sentences, cf. 5.2.6). For example, a sentence such as *Bill was reading the newspaper when John arrived* might be generated by a system of 'rewrite' rules which included the following (and others which, for simplicity, we will omit):

(a) $\Sigma \rightarrow NP + VP$ (Time Adverb)

(b) Time Adverb $\rightarrow \begin{cases} \text{Preposition} + \text{Time Noun} \\ \text{Temporal Conjunction} + \Sigma \end{cases}$

It will be observed that Time Adverb is introduced as an optional constituent of the sentence by rule (a): the parentheses signify that it is optional. We will assume that rule (b) is optional: so that, if rule (b) is 'bypassed', Time Adverb will appear in the terminal string and be replaced in sentences by *yesterday*, etc. On the other hand, if rule (b) is applied and the option Preposition + Time Noun is taken, the final result will be *on Tuesday, in March* (further rules would be required to account for the occurrence of different prepositions with different subclasses of 'time nouns' and also for the generation of *last week*, etc.). It is, however, the option Temporal Conjunction + Σ which concerns us at this point. The selection of this option, with the appropriate development of the constituent sentence, will account for *when John came in* (and will classify it as a Time Adverbial, like *yesterday* or *on Tuesday*). The constituent-structure assigned to a sentence like *Bill was reading the newspaper when John came in* would be as illustrated in Fig. 11. The effect of permitting the inclusion of

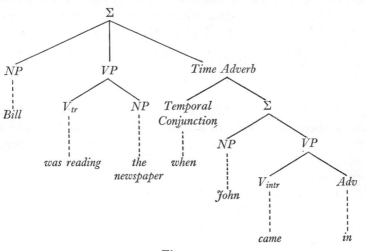

Fig. 11.

the initial symbol in the right-hand side of a 'rewrite' rule is to introduce the possibility of 'recycling' into the grammar. This feature is certainly required, in order to account for the 'embedding' of sentences (as clauses, or constituents of clauses) within other sentences: cf. *He said that...*, or *The man who...has just arrived.* At the same time, it is clear that sentence-embedding rules of the kind illustrated here are not capable of handling such features of complex sentences as what is traditionally called the 'sequence of tenses' in the constituent clauses (and so preventing the generation of such 'sentences' as **Bill was reading the newspaper when John has come in*). We shall have more to say about this and related questions in the following sections. It is sufficient for our present purpose to have shown how a 'rewrite' constituent-structure grammar might formalize the distinction that is traditionally drawn between simple and complex sentences: any sentence that is generated by a group of rules, at least one of which contains the initial symbol in the right-hand side is a *complex* sentence; all other sentences are *simple*.

6.2.11   *Formalization of context-free phrase-structure grammars*

All the constituent-structure rules given so far in this section have been of the general form A → B ('rewrite A as B', in the synthesis of sentences). Nothing has been said about the 'values' taken by A and B, except that the first rule of the system must have the initial symbol, Σ (Sentence), as A (i.e. on the left-hand side) and that the terminal symbols. (N, V_{tr}, V_{intr}, A, etc.), which occur in the strings generated by the grammar, denote lexical classes: $N = \{boy, girl, \ldots\}$, $V_{tr} = \{eat, kill, \ldots\}$, $V_{intr} = \{die, go, \ldots\}$, $Adj = \{good, old, \ldots\}$. Rules of the form A → B, which rewrite A as B without reference to the context of A, are referred to as *context-free* rules. (We return to this question in 6.5.1.)

The formal properties of context-free constituent-structure grammars have been intensively studied in the last few years. Chomsky and others have discussed the effect of ordering the rules in a system, of allowing both optional and obligatory rules, of introducing alternative subrules and of having recursive rules in the system. Furthermore they have pointed out that two important restrictions must be imposed upon the values of A and B in rules of the form A → B, if a grammar containing such rules is to be capable of assigning a unique structure to the sentence it generates: (i) A and B must not be identical (i.e. A must not be rewritten as itself); and (ii) A must be a single symbol, although B may be, and generally is, a string containing more than one symbol. Some scholars have worked with constituent-structure grammars which impose more particular limitations upon B, notably that it must consist of two and only two elements (e.g. $NP + VP$, or $V_{tr} + N$). For a fuller explanation of the implications of such restrictions the reader is referred to the more technical works cited in the notes.

6.2.12   *Weak and strong equivalence*

The most important result of this theoretical study of grammar (which draws upon research into the formalized systems of logic and mathematics) has been the demonstration that constituent-structure grammars with different formal properties may generate exactly the same set of sentences. Grammars which generate the same set of sentences are said to be *weakly equivalent*; grammars which not only generate the same sentences, but assign to them the same structural description are said to be *strongly equivalent*. To illustrate the difference between weak and strong equivalence we will consider briefly constituent-structure grammars of a somewhat different kind from the 'rewrite' systems discussed above: namely, 'categorial' grammars.

6.3 Categorial grammars

6.3.1 *Fundamental and derived categories*

Categorial grammars have their origin in the work of the Polish logician Ajdukiewicz (following Leśniewski); they have been further developed by Bar-Hillel, Lambek, and other contemporary logicians and linguists. (The choice of the term 'categorial' in this connexion is explained by particular developments in the history of logic and philosophy, which we will not go into here.)

In a categorial system there are just two *fundamental* grammatical categories, sentence and noun: we shall represent these as Σ and n, respectively. All lexical items other than nouns are given a *derived* categorial classification in the lexicon according to their potentiality for combination with one another or with one of the fundamental categories in the constituent-structure of sentences. The derived categories are *complex*, in the sense that they specify simultaneously (i) what other category the element in question can combine with in order to form a sentence-constituent, and (ii) the categorial classification of the constituent that results from this operation. To take a simple example: an element like *run* or *exist* (an 'intransitive verb') can combine with a noun (as 'subject') to form a sentence: e.g. *John ran* (we shall continue to disregard the question of tense and features of 'agreement').

6.3.2 *'Cancellation'*

In the 'quasi-arithmetical' notation of Bar-Hillel the categorial classification of elements like *run* can be expressed as a 'fraction' whose denominator denotes what other category *run*, etc. can combine with and whose numerator denotes the category of the resultant construction. Thus, the lexical classification of *run*, etc., as $\frac{\Sigma}{n}$ indicates that such elements combine with nouns to form sentences. Given this classification of *run* and given that *John* is a noun (n), we know that *John ran* is a grammatically well-formed sentence. We can determine this fact automatically by a simple rule of 'cancellation' similar to the arithmetical rules of cancellation: just as

$$y \times \frac{x}{y} = x, \quad \text{so} \quad n.\frac{\Sigma}{n} = \Sigma$$

(i.e. we 'cancel out' the numerator and denominator when they are identical and, in this case, we are left with Σ, which indicates that the expression is a sentence: the dot is being used here to represent linear concatenation). But the system must also be capable of excluding as ungrammatical such sequences as $\frac{\Sigma}{n}$.n (*Ran John*). We must therefore specify the *direction* in which an element combines, to the left or to the right. We will indicate this by means of an arrowhead attached to the horizontal 'fractional' line: thus $\overset{\Sigma}{\underset{n}{\leftarrow}}$ denotes an element which combines with a noun to the left to form a sentence; whereas, for example, $\overset{n}{\underset{n}{\rightarrow}}$ denotes an element (e.g. an 'adjective' like *poor*, *old*, etc.) which combines with a noun to its right to form a noun (or noun-phrase).

6.3.3   *More complex categories*

Derived categories may have, not only fundamental categories, but also derived categories as their numerator or denominator. For example, an 'adverb' combines with a 'verb' to its left to form a 'verb' (or verb-phrase); that is to say it combines to its left with an element which combines to its left with a noun to form a sentence (for simplicity we will consider only 'intransitive verbs', and we will disregard the fact that 'adverbs' may be given other categorial classifications as well). This is indicated by the 'fraction':

6.3.4   *Possible extensions*

The categorial system we have just described is a relatively simple one, but it is satisfactory enough for our purpose. It is *bidirectional*, in the sense that it allows for combination to either the left or the right: it could be extended in various ways (by permitting the occurrence of two or more concatenated categories in the denominator of a derived category; by permitting an element to combine both to the left and to the right simultaneously; and so on—we shall not go into the effect of such extensions here); and it could be restricted (made uni-directional) by allowing for combination in only one specified direction. It will also be observed that this categorial system, like the 'rewrite' system discussed above, cannot handle discontinuous constituents (cf. 6.2.8).

6.3.5 *Notational conventions*

At this point we will introduce a space-saving notational convention, which has no effect upon the formal capacity of the system. The convention is to write the 'fractions' as an ordered pair of bracketed symbols with the numerator coming first and the denominator second and an arrow over the denominator to indicate direction. By this convention *run* will be classified as $(\Sigma \overleftarrow{n})$, *poor* as $(n\overrightarrow{n})$ and an 'adverb' such as *away* as $\{(\Sigma \overleftarrow{n})(\Sigma \overleftarrow{n})\}$.

6.3.6 *'Categorial' analysis of constituent-structure*

We may now illustrate the operation of this simple bidirectional categorial grammar with reference to Bloomfield's sentence *Poor John ran away*. The categorial classification of all the lexical elements has been given in the previous paragraphs. We will write them under the words in the sentence:

$$\text{Poor} \quad \text{John} \quad \text{ran} \quad \text{away}$$
$$(n\overrightarrow{n}) \;.\; n \;.\; (\Sigma \overleftarrow{n}) . \{(\Sigma \overleftarrow{n})(\Sigma \overleftarrow{n})\}$$

Now for the 'cancellations'. It is clear that there are three possibilities at the first stage: (1 *a*) the 'cancellation' of *poor* with *John*; (1 *b*) of *John* with *ran*; and (1 *c*) of *ran* with *away*. But if (1 *b*) is selected, the result will be

$$(1\,b) \;\; (n\overrightarrow{n}) \;.\; \Sigma \;.\; \{(\Sigma \overleftarrow{n})(\Sigma \overleftarrow{n})\},$$

which establishes *John ran* as a sentence and leaves *poor* and *away* unaccounted for outside the sentence. If (1 *a*) is selected, at the next stage we will have

$$(1\,a) \;\; n \;.\; (\Sigma \overleftarrow{n}) \;.\; \{(\Sigma \overleftarrow{n})(\Sigma \overleftarrow{n})\}.$$

There are now two possibilities: and it is clear that, in order to analyse the sentences without residue, we must now cancel *ran* with *away* to yield

(2) n . $(\Sigma \overleftarrow{n})$;

and, finally

(3) Σ.

Alternatively, we might have first combined *ran* with *away* (1c), and then *poor* with *John*: in other words we might have cancelled the same elements, but in a different order.

6.3.7   *Comparison of phrase-structure and categorial analysis*

The operation of 'cancellation' reflects the notion of bracketing with which we are concerned in this section; it will be clear that the analysis of *Poor John ran away* which has just been given agrees with what Bloomfield said about the structure of this sentence: that it is composed of two immediate constituents, *poor John* and *ran away*, and that each of these consists of two immediate constituents, *poor* and *John*, on the one hand, and *ran* and *away*, on the other. Let us now compare the categorial analysis with an analysis in terms of the following 'rewrite' rules (cf. 6.2.2):

(1) $\Sigma \to NP + VP$

(2) $VP \to V_{intr} + Adv$

(3) $NP \to A + N$

From the composite tree-diagram given in Fig. 12, it will be clear that the two grammars are not only weakly equivalent (in that they generate the same set of sentences—the fact that we have put the categorial system in the form of a 'recognition' grammar and the 'rewrite' system in the form of a 'production' grammar is irrelevant to this issue: cf. 4.3.1); they are also equivalent with respect to the bracketing they assign to sentences like *Poor John ran away*. But they are far from being equivalent in all respects. First of all, it may be noted that the 'rewrite' system has two auxiliary symbols (NP and VP) in addition to the four terminal symbols which denote lexical classes (N, V_{intr}, A and Adv); so that, whereas the categorial analysis asserts that *poor John* is a phrase of the same category as *John* and *ran away* a phrase of the same category as *ran*, the 'rewrite' analysis does not. However, we could easily make the two systems equivalent with respect to this feature by substituting N for NP and V_{intr} for VP in the 'rewrite' rules (we will not go into the further implications of this revision). The main difference between the two systems lies in the fact that the categorial grammar, unlike the 'rewrite' grammar, regards one constituent in each construction as *dependent* upon the other: the categorial notation makes it clear which is the dependent constituent (the one with the more complex classification) and this is fundamental to the operation of 'cancelling'. The 'rewrite' system

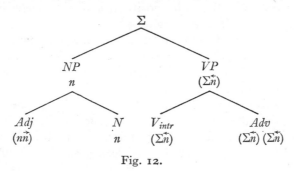

Fig. 12.

represents the notion of dependency only partially and indirectly: from a rule of the form $N \rightarrow A + N$ it can be inferred that A is dependent upon N, but in a rule like $\Sigma \rightarrow N + V_{intr}$ (or $\Sigma \rightarrow NP + VP$) no conclusions can be drawn about any relationship of dependency that might hold between the two constituents. This does not mean that the categorial system is necessarily better than the 'rewrite' system, but only that the two systems are not strongly equivalent. There may be reasons for preferring one analysis to the other; if so, we shall say that the grammar which assigns the preferred analysis is more *strongly adequate* than the grammar which does not. This is a separate question, to which we will return briefly later (cf. 6.5.7).

6.4 Exocentric and endocentric constructions

6.4.1 *Distributional interpretation*

We may now look a little more closely at the distributional basis for immediate constituent analysis. Constructions may be classified, according to their distribution and that of their constituents, into what are commonly called (in the terminology introduced by Bloomfield) *endocentric* and *exocentric* constructions. An endocentric construction is one whose distribution is identical with that of one or more of its constituents; and any construction which is not endocentric is exocentric. (In other words, exocentricity is defined negatively with reference to a prior definition of endocentricity, and all constructions fall into one class or the other.) For example, the now famous phrase *poor John* is endocentric, since it has the same distribution as its constituent *John*; any English sentence in which *John* occurs can generally be matched with another sentence in which *poor John* occurs in the same position; and, since *John* is a noun, *poor John* is described as a noun-phrase. On the other hand, *in Vancouver* is exocentric, since its distribution is different from that of either the preposition *in* or the noun *Vancouver*. The phrase *in Vancouver* has much the same distribution in English sentences as *there* and other adverbs (of place); therefore it is classified as an adverbial phrase (of place). These examples show that, although the distinction between endocentric and exocentric constructions is one that was not made as such in traditional grammar, the traditional notion of 'function' (according to which *poor John* is said to 'function as' a noun and *in Vancouver* as an adverb) can be given a natural interpretation in terms of the distribution of the elements in question.

It is often said that no construction has exactly the same distribution as any of its constituents; that the substitution of the construction for one of the constituents will result in a certain number of unacceptable utterances. This is doubtless true. But, as we saw in a previous chapter, by the distribution of an element we do not mean the totality of acceptable utterances in which the element occurs, but that set of utterances whose acceptability is accounted for by the grammatical description of the language, the limits to which this can be pushed being determined by what we have called the 'law of diminishing returns' (cf. 4.2.11). In this sense, therefore, any two elements either have or have not the same distribution; and constructions are either endocentric or exocentric. Any grammar of English will recognize many different (and overlapping) subclasses of nouns, verbs, adjectives, etc. For instance, a distinction will be drawn between 'countable' nouns and 'uncountable' (or 'mass') nouns (to handle the acceptability of *I like wine*, etc., and the unacceptability (except in cannibalistic circumstances) of **I like boy*, etc.); between 'human' nouns and 'non-human' nouns (to handle, *inter alia*, the distribution of *who*: *which*: cf. *the boy who...* and *the book which...*); between singular nouns and plural nouns (to handle 'agreement'; cf. *the boy is...* and *the boys are...*); between masculine, feminine and neuter nouns (to handle the 'reference' of *he, she, it*); and so on. When we say that two nouns have exactly the same distribution, we mean that they are given the same classification at the 'lowest' level of distributional subclassification that the grammar achieves. But we can say that two elements have the same distribution at various specified 'depths'. Thus, all nouns (and all noun-phrases and noun-clauses) have the same distribution at the relatively high level of classification for which the term 'noun' is used without further qualification. At a lower level two nouns might have a different distribution, one being 'animate' and the other 'inanimate', etc. The concepts of endocentricity and exocentricity are therefore to be used with respect to some specified 'depth' of subclassification.

6.4.2 *'Nesting' of endocentric constructions*

Endocentric constructions fall into main types: *co-ordinating* and *subordinating*. Co-ordinating constructions have the same distribution as each of their constituents taken separately. Thus *bread and cheese* and *coffee or tea* are co-ordinating noun-phrases. However, the two phrases belong to different subtypes, the first taking a plural verb and the second a singular verb (if, as here, each of the constituents is singular). Subordinating constructions have the same distribution as one of their constituents. Examples from English include: $A+N$ (*poor John*); $Adv+A$ (*awfully clever*); N (or NP)$+Adv$ (or adverbial phrase) (*the girl upstairs, the man on the bus*). The constituent whose distribution is the same as that of the resultant construction is called the *head*; the other constituent is the *modifier*. In subordinative constructions one modifier may be recursively 'nested' within another. For example, in *the man on the top of the bus* there are two constituents, *the man* (head) and *on the top of the bus* (modifier); *on the top of the bus* is an exocentric adverbial phrase consisting of the preposition *on* and the noun-phrase *the top of the bus*; *the top of the bus* is endocentric, its constituents being *the top* (head) and *of the bus* (modifier). Noun-phrases of the kind illustrated here can be extended more or less indefinitely: cf. *the man on the top of the bus in the park in the centre of the town on the top of the hill in the centre of the plain....*

The classification of the different types of construction that has just been given is based upon the work of Bloomfield and his followers; whereas the account of constituent-structure in terms of generative 'rewrite' rules which has taken up the greater part of this section derives mainly from the more recent treatment of the subject by Chomsky. It is to be noticed that, while Bloomfield talked always of the *classification* of constructions, Chomsky talks of the *generation* of constructions. As we have already seen (cf. 4.2.8), any analytic classification of the constructions of a language must also be synthetic (implicitly, if not explicitly). However, the change of outlook represented by the conscious and deliberate adoption of the generative approach has the practical effect of making the task of classification secondary to the main purpose of the grammar, the generation of sentences: the generative approach imposes limits on classification. For example, Bloomfield describes the English words *longlegs* and *butterfingers* as exocentric, 'because they occur both as singulars...and plurals (*that longlegs*)'. But this fact is sufficient to show that the forms in question are not constructions at all; they are to be entered in the lexicon as unanalysable wholes, as members of the appropriate distributional class, and are not to be generated by the grammar. The distribution of *longlegs*, unlike the distribution of *long legs* (in *He has long legs*) cannot be accounted for by any productive formational rules of modern English.

6.4.3   *Endocentricity in a phrase-structure grammar*

The distributional basis for the rules of a 'rewrite' constituent-structure grammar is clear enough. Every rule of the form $A \rightarrow B + C$ rests upon the distributional identity of A and $B + C$; more precisely, upon the inclusion of the distribution of $B + C$ in the distribution of A (identity being a special case of inclusion). The difference between identity and inclusion (or, in logical terms, between 'improper' and 'proper' inclusion) comes out in the distinction between rules which 'rewrite' all instances of A as $B + C$ and those which consist of a set of alternative subrules. For example, a rule such as $N \rightarrow A + N$ rests upon the distributional identity of *John* and *poor John*, of *man* and *old man*, etc. On the other hand, a rule such as

$$VP \rightarrow \begin{cases} V_{tr} + NP \\ V_{intr} \end{cases}$$

implies that the distribution of phrases like *eat meat*, on the one hand, and of words like *die*, on the other, is included in the distribution of the class of verb-phrases.

   The difference between endocentric and exocentric constructions, on the one hand, and between the two main subtypes of endocentric constructions (co-ordinating and subordinating), on the other hand, is manifest in the form of the 'rewrite' rules which account for the formation of these constructions. It should be noticed, however, that the notions of endocentricity, subordination, etc., have no systematic significance in a 'rewrite' grammar of the kind outlined above: that is to say, these notions are not invoked as such in the grammar. Moreover, since the effect of an obligatory rule (or set of subrules) is to 'rewrite' all instances of A as B+C it does not matter what A is called: after the operation of the rule, A disappears, except as the name of the higher 'node'. For example, the choice of the terms noun-phrase (NP) and verb-phrase (VP) in the first rule of the grammar

$$\Sigma \rightarrow NP + VP$$

is a perfectly arbitrary choice in a 'rewrite' constituent-structure grammar: for both NP and VP are obligatorily 'rewritten' as various other elements or constructions. (They might equally well be called Y and Z.) The relationship between noun-phrases, nouns and pronouns (of various subclasses) is not expressed by the nomenclature applied to them, as in 'classificatory' treatments, but by the fact of their deriving from some common 'node'. In respect of the notions of endocentricity and exocentricity, and of subordination and co-ordination, a categorial grammar might claim to be a truer formalization of the principles outlined by Bloomfield and developed by his successors, with a good deal of exemplification from many different languages. As we have seen, a categorial grammar takes as fundamental the notion of 'dependency' (which is generally to be equated with subordination); and the difference between endocentric and exocentric constructions is evident from the structure of the dependent category in a 'cancellation'—if the numerator and denominator are identical, the construction is endocentric; it not, it is exocentric (cf. above 6.3.2).

6.5   Context-sensitive grammars

6.5.1   *The term 'context-sensitive'*

We must now introduce a distinction between *context-sensitive* and *context-free* rules. (The terms 'context-restricted' and 'context-dependent' are used synonymously with 'context-sensitive' in the literature.)

All the rules given so far have been context-free, in the sense that the symbol appearing to the left of the rewrite-arrow was replaced in the 'output' of the rule as the symbol or string of symbols appearing to the right of the arrow in the statement of the rule. To take an example, the following rule (cf. 6.2.6)

$$N \rightarrow N + and + N$$

was interpretable as an instruction to 'rewrite' N as $N + and + N$ (optionally or obligatorily) in any string of symbols to which the rule was applied. In other words, the sole condition for the operation of the rule was the occurrence of N in the 'input' to the rule. For instance, given as alternative 'input' strings

(i) $X + N + Y$

(ii) $W + N + Z$

the 'output', after the operation of the rule in question, would be, in the one case,

$$X + N + and + N + Y$$

and in the other,

$$W + N + and + N + Z$$

The point is that there were no contextual restrictions imposed upon the operation of the rule.

Suppose, however, that we had formulated the rule in the following manner

$$N \rightarrow N + and + N / \text{in the context } X + \ldots + Y$$

This might be defined to mean that N was to be 'rewritten' (optionally or obligatorily) only if it occurred in the 'input' string with X immediately to its left and Y immediately to its right. In which case, the rule would apply to (i), but not to (ii). The specification of the contextual condition to the right of the oblique stroke in the above rule makes it a *context-sensitive* rule.

6.5.2 *Various kinds of context-sensitive grammars*

Very many different types and subtypes of context-sensitive rules can be formulated. We shall confine our attention to those which fall within the scope of phrase-structure grammars (formalized as a set of ordered or unordered, optional or obligatory, recursive or non-recursive, concatenating rules). Any such grammar that includes one or more context-sensitive rules is defined to be a *context-sensitive phrase-structure grammar*.

Within this class of grammars, one may distinguish those in which X and Y, in a rule of the kind that has just been given by way of exemplification, are restricted to cover only one symbol each; those in which either X or Y, or both, may refer to a string of more than one symbol; and so on.

We will tacitly assume that the class of context-sensitive grammars with which we are concerned here is defined by the condition that X and Y, in a rule of the following kind

$$A \to B/\text{in the context } X + \ldots + Y$$

may refer, each independently, to any finite number of concatenated symbols, but that A must be a single symbol. Furthermore, we will assume that B cannot be identical with A, and cannot be 'zero' (cf. 6.2.11). These conditions would allow the following rules as 'well-formed' within the system:

   (a) $P \to Q/\text{in the context } E + F + \ldots + G$

   (b) $P \to Q + R/\text{in the context } E + \ldots + G + H + K + L$

   (c) $P \to R + S + T/\text{in the context } G + \ldots + H$

   etc.

They would prohibit the inclusion in the grammar of rules such as the following:

   (d) $P \to P/\text{in the context } E + \ldots + F$

   (e) $P \to \emptyset/\text{in the context } E + \ldots + F$

Rule (d) is 'ill-formed' because it 'rewrites' P as itself (i.e. it breaks the condition that A and B must not be identical). Rule (e) contains the 'zero' symbol ($\emptyset$) immediately to the right of the arrow: this defines rule (e) as a *deletion-rule* ('rewrite P as zero' means 'delete P': the 'output' of rule (e), if it were allowed in the system, would be $E + F$, derived by the rule from the 'input' $E + P + F$).

It should be noticed that in the above rules some symbols are italicized, whereas others are not. The symbols printed in italics are *constants*, the others are *variables*. We shall return later to the distinction of constants and variables (cf. 6.6.6). For the purposes of this section, the difference is as follows: if a symbol occurs in any part of a rule as a *constant*, this means that the rule applies to occurrences of that particular symbol; if the symbol occurs as a *variable*, this means that the rule applies to any of the constants that are defined to fall within the class referred to by the variable.

In this section, the difference is relevant only to the extent that it distinguishes the actual rules of the grammar (which, we will assume, do not contain any variables) from an abstract specification of the format of the rules. In other words,

A → B/in the context X + ... + Y

is not a rule, but summarizes a whole class of rules, according to the 'values' defined as permissible for the variables A, B, X and Y. The conditions that restrict the scope of the variables have been given above.

6.5.3   *Context-sensitive grammars include context-free grammars*

If we add a further condition, we can define context-free phrase-structure grammars to be a subclass of context-sensitive grammars. The condition is that the 'value' of X and Y may be left unrestricted in rules of the form

A → B/in the context X + ... + Y

We will first distinguish, for purely terminological convenience, between the *null-value* (ø) and *positive values* (any permissible 'value', other than ø, that is assigned to a variable). Now, if it is specified, for a particular rule, that the contextual variables, X and Y, are *unrestricted* as to 'value' (each, independently, may be either positive in 'value' or null), the rule in question is context-free. If the 'value' of either X or Y is *restricted*, i.e. specified to be either null or positive, then the rule is context-sensitive.

To take a few examples. The following rules are all context-sensitive

(f) $P \rightarrow Q$/in the context ø + ... + ø

(g) $P \rightarrow Q$/in the context ø + ... + R + S

(h) $P \rightarrow Q$/in the context T + ... + ø

Rule (f) says, in effect, that P is to be 'rewritten' as Q only if it has no other symbol to its left and to its right in the 'input' string. (Normally, the only symbol that would satisfy this contextual condition is the initial symbol, Σ. But one might have a system of rules in which the initial symbol had been 'rewritten' as P.) Rule (g) says that P is to be 'rewritten' as Q, only when the 'input' string is $P + R + S$; and rule (h), that P is to be 'rewritten', only when it occurs in the final position of the 'input' string in question—$T + P$. These rules may also be put in another form (and frequently are in published grammars)

(f') $\emptyset + P + \emptyset \to \emptyset + Q + \emptyset$

(g') $\emptyset + P + R + S \to \emptyset + Q + R + S$

(h') $T + P + \emptyset \to T + Q + \emptyset$

Generalizing this format (by using A, B, X and Y are variables) we can say that all the rules of a context-sensitive grammar are of the form

$$X + A + Y \to X + B + Y$$

And a context-free rule of the form

$$A \to B$$

may be taken as a special case of a context-sensitive rule in which the 'values' of X and Y are unrestricted.

It is along these lines that the theory of phrase-structure grammars has been generalized to bring both context-free and context-sensitive rules within the same formal framework. We may now move on to a less abstract discussion of the implications of context-sensitivity in language.

6.5.4 *Concord and government*

One of the most obvious of the phenomena in language falling within the scope of the notion of 'context-sensitivity' is *concord* (or 'agreement'). We shall first of all give a fairly traditional account of the principles.

In many languages, the constituents of a particular syntactic construction are said to 'agree', or be 'in concord', with respect to such features as 'gender', 'number', 'case', 'person', etc. (The terms 'gender', 'number', etc., as well as the terms 'subject' and 'object', will be fully discussed from a theoretical point of view in chapters 7 and 8.) For example, in noun-phrases in French the article and the adjective must be in agreement with the noun in number ('singular' *v.* 'plural') and gender ('masculine' *v.* 'feminine'): cf. *un livre intéressant*, 'an interesting book', v. *une pièce intéressante*, 'an interesting play'; and *des livres intéressants*, '(some) interesting books' v. *des pièces intéressantes*, ('some) interesting plays'. Here *un* and *intéressant* are 'masculine, singular' in concord with *livre*; *une* and *intéressante* are 'feminine, singular' in agreement with *pièce*; *intéressants* is 'masculine, plural' in agreement with *livres*, and *intéressantes* 'feminine, plural' in concord with *pièces*; *des* is 'plural', but unmarked for the distinction of 'masculine' and 'feminine'. (For simplicity, we are referring to the concord-system of written French. We have already mentioned that written and spoken French are to a certain extent different languages: cf. 1.4.2.) As in French, so also in Italian, Spanish, German, Russian, Latin, and in many other languages of the world, the adjective must agree with the noun in constructions similar to the one illustrated. Again, in many languages, the verb must agree with either the subject or the object, or both, in number, gender or person. Part of the relatively complex gender-and-number concord of Swahili will be illustrated in the following chapter (cf. 7.3.5); and the 'ergative' concord-system of Eskimo will be referred to in the sections on 'transitivity' and 'ergativity' (cf. 8.1.6, 8.2.2).

By comparison with the languages mentioned in the previous paragraph, English has relatively little concord. Within noun-phrases it is only the demonstrative pronouns which agree with the noun they 'modify': cf. *this book, that book* v. *these books, those books*. However, concord is operative with respect to the verb in certain 'tenses' (more precisely, it is not simply 'tense' that is involved, but also 'mood' and 'aspect': cf. 7.5.1 ff.). The following simple sentences illustrate the principle, as it applies to English, that the verb is in agreement with the subject:

(1) *He goes* v. *I/You/We/They go*

(2) *He has gone* v. *I/You/We/They have gone*

(3) *He is going* v. *You/We/They are going* v. *I am going*

(4) *He/I was going* v. *You/We/They were going*

In the first two sentences, the person-and-number concord operates in the following manner: if the subject is 'third person, singular' (*he, she, it, someone*, etc., or a noun-phrase with a singular noun as its head, e.g. *John, the boy*), the verb is 'third person, singular'; whereas, if the subject is not 'third person, singular', the verb is in what we will refer to as the 'unmarked' form. In (3) and (4), which both contain what is traditionally called 'the verb *to be*' (here employed as an 'auxiliary verb'), concord operates somewhat differently: in (3), there is once again 'third person, singular' concord, but also 'first person, singular' concord (*I am*); and in (4), 'first person, singular' and 'third person, singular' fall together under subject–verb concord. With the 'simple past tense' of the verb (e.g. *went, loved*), there is no subject–verb concord: cf. *He/I/You/We/They went*, etc.

Concord, as illustrated above, is usually distinguished from *government* (or 'rection', in the usage of some authors). For example, in many languages the verb is said to 'govern' its object in a particular case: e.g. Latin (*Ego*) *amo te*, 'I love you', (*Ego*) *suadeo tibi*, 'I advise you' (*te* v. *tibi*, 'accusative' *v.* 'dative', are governed by, or *dependent on*, the verbs *amo* v. *suadeo*). In Latin (Russian, German, etc.), not only verbs, but also prepositions, may govern the noun, pronoun or noun-phrase dependent upon them in a particular case: e.g. *ad urbem*, 'to the city' (*ad* 'takes the accusative': *urbem*) *v. ab urbe*, 'from the city' (*ab* 'takes the ablative': *urbe*). For a fuller discussion of what is meant by such expressions as 'takes the ablative', cf. 7.4.1 ff.

It will appear from the above examples that the difference between concord and government lies in the fact that under concord two or more words or phrases are 'inflected' for the same category (e.g. number or person), whereas under government the *principal* and the *dependent* member of a syntactic construction do not both exhibit the same category: instead the dependent member is determined with respect to the relevant category (e.g. case) by the principal member.

We have just stated the difference between concord and government in a traditional manner; and it is a traditional distinction. In more recent grammatical theory, the distinction is frequently drawn with respect to the prior recognition of a distinction between endocentric and exocentric constructions (cf. 6.4.1). For instance, Hockett says that government is found 'only in exocentric constructions' (of a particular subtype): the Latin *ad urbem* is exocentric—it differs distributionally from its constituents, *ad* and *urbem*. Concord, on the other hand, 'is found in endocentric constructions, and in a tie that cuts across hierarchical [i.e. immediate-constituent] structure to link certain predicate attributes to subjects'. In other words, concord is found in both endocentric and exocentric constructions: the French *un livre intéressant* is endocentric, since its distribution is identical with that of *un livre*; but *Le livre est intéressant* (which also manifests concord between *livre* and *intéressant*), 'The book is interesting', is exocentric, because its distribution (in so far as the notion of distribution is relevant to sentences: cf. 5.2.1) differs from the distribution of *le livre*, on the one hand, and *est intéressant*, on the other.

Although what Hockett and other authors have to say in this connexion is correct as far as it goes, it should be pointed out that there is both a principal and a dependent member in constructions which manifest concord: it would be incorrect, for example, to maintain (as some linguists have maintained) that the person and number of the subject is determined by the person and number of the verb. It would be equally incorrect to say (and this view has been expressed even more frequently) that neither the subject nor the verb determines the other, but that both the subject and the verb manifest a category which pertains to the *construction* of which they are members. As we shall see later, number and person are nominal categories, which, if they are manifest in a given language, may be marked, inflexionally or otherwise, in the 'surface-structure' of the verb-phrase (cf. 7.2.6, 7.3.1). This is implicit in the traditional formulation of the facts: 'the verb agrees with the subject in number and person'. We shall assume that this view is correct in our discussion of context-sensitive rules in English in the following paragraphs. The distinction between 'surface-structure' and 'deep-structure' will be explained in a later section (cf. 6.6.1). Once we draw this distinction, it will become clear that the difference between concord and government (especially if it is made with reference to the notions of 'endocentric' and 'exocentric') is essentially a 'surface-structure' distinction.

6.5.5 *A context-free interpretation of subject–verb concord*

Let us now consider how we might generate some simple English sentences that manifest subject–verb concord. For simplicity, we will restrict our attention to transitive sentences in the 'present tense': examples are

(1*a*) *The dog bites the man*

(1*b*) *The dog bites the men*

(1*c*) *The dogs bite the man*

(1*d*) *The dogs bite the men*

(2*a*) *The chimpanzee eats the banana*

etc.

We will assume a lexical classification of the occurrent words: for simplicity, the lexicon may be regarded as a list of the members of the terminal classes of the grammar (T, N, V) similar to that given in chapter 4 (cf. 4.3.2).

Consider, now, the following context-free grammar:

(1) $\Sigma \rightarrow \begin{cases} NP_{sing} + VP_{sing} \\ NP_{plur} + VP_{plur} \end{cases}$

(2) $VP_{sing} \rightarrow V_{sing} + NP$

(3) $VP_{plur} \rightarrow V_{plur} + NP$

(4) $NP \rightarrow \begin{cases} NP_{sing} \\ NP_{plur} \end{cases}$

(5) $NP_{sing} \rightarrow T + N_{sing}$

(6) $NP_{plur} \rightarrow T + N_{plur}$

(7) $N_{sing} \rightarrow N + \emptyset$

(8) $N_{plur} \rightarrow N + s$

(9) $V_{sing} \rightarrow V + s$

(10) $V_{plur} \rightarrow V + \emptyset$

There are other ways of generating the sentences in question by means of context-free rules, but this set of rules will serve for the purpose of illustration. It is assumed that it would be supplemented by further rules for the phonological realization of the words occurring in sentences, such that $man + \emptyset$ is 'rewritten' as /man/, $man + s$ is 'rewritten' as /men/, $hit + \emptyset$ as /hit/, $hit + s$ as /hits/, and so on. It may be observed, in passing, that phonological realization rules of this kind (e.g. $hit + \emptyset \rightarrow$ /hit/) break one of the conditions imposed upon simple phrase-structure grammars above—they rewrite more than one symbol at once (cf. 6.2.11). The phonological realization rules must operate, of course, after the lexical-substitution rules (cf. 4.3.2). Throughout this book we have assumed that the lexical-substitution rules are outside the grammatical system properly so called.

Let us now interpret the grammatical rules that have just been given: a sample sentence with its structural description, in terms of this grammar, is represented in Fig. 13. The implication of the choice introduced by rule (1) is that there are two unrelated sentence-types, which we might call 'singular sentences' and 'plural sentences'. *The dog bites the men* is a 'singular sentence', and *The children drink the milk* a 'plural sentence', according to this interpretation of the grammar. In other words, number is defined to be a category of the sentence for subject–verb concord. But number is also introduced into the object noun-phrase by rule (4). The grammar, therefore, treats the choice between 'singular' and 'plural' in the subject-position of the sentence as something quite different from, and totally unrelated to, the choice between 'singular' and 'plural' in the object-position. It fails to represent the fact that number is a category of the noun-phrase (strictly speaking of the noun, or pronoun, rather than the noun-phrase: but we may neglect this difference here); that the choice between 'singular' and 'plural' is independently made in the subject-position and object-position; and that the prior determination of the subject as either 'singular' or 'plural' subsequently determines the verb as either 'singular' or 'plural' according to the principles of concord discussed above (cf. 6.5.4).

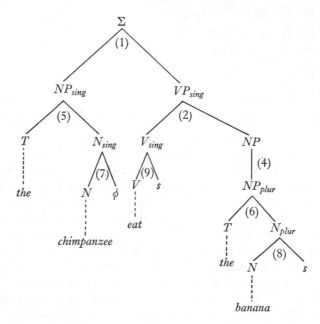

Fig. 13. Concord within a context-free grammar (the numerals attached to the branches refer to the rules of the grammar in 6.5.5).

6.5.6 *A context-sensitive interpretation of subject–verb concord*

Let us now suppose that we wish to formalize the fact that the number of the subject determines the number of the verb (within the framework of a phrase-structure grammar). One way of doing so would be as follows (and this is essentially the way adopted by Chomsky in *Syntactic Structures*: for reasons which we will not discuss here he puts the equivalent of rule (4) of the following system among the transformational rules of his grammar—but we are still operating without transformational rules):

(1) $\Sigma \to NP + VP$

(2) $VP \to Verb + NP$

$$(3) \quad NP \rightarrow \begin{cases} NP_{sing} \\ NP_{plur} \end{cases}$$

$$(4) \quad Verb \rightarrow \begin{cases} V+s/\text{in the context } NP_{sing}+\ldots \\ V+\emptyset/\text{in the context } NP_{plur}+\ldots \end{cases}$$

(5) $NP_{sing} \rightarrow T+N+\emptyset$

(6) $NP_{plur} \rightarrow T+N+s$

There are a number of differences between this set of rules and the set given in 6.5.5. It is shorter, with six rules rather than ten. Rules (5) and (6) analyse 'singular' and 'plural' noun-phrases into three constituents, of which one is an article, one a noun and the third a member of the category of number (either 'singular' or 'plural'). At the same time, it should be noticed that there is no formalization of the fact that the noun is the head of the noun-phrase. Although many other shortcomings of the analysis assigned to such sentences by a phrase-structure grammar can be remedied, as we shall see, by the introduction of transformational rules, this particular type of deficiency (and we will assume it is a deficiency) requires a rather more fundamental revision of the formalization (cf. 7.6.8).

For the moment, however, we are concerned solely with the question of context-sensitivity. The important point is that rule (1) defines all sentences generated by these rules to be sentences of the same type ($NP+VP$); rule (3) makes number a category of the noun-phrase, independently of the occurrence of the noun-phrase as subject or object; and rule (4) says that number in the verb (more precisely, in V: we will not go into the reasons why $Verb$ and V are distinguished in this set of rules) is determined by the number of the preceding noun-phrase. Rule (4) is a context-sensitive rule of the form $A \rightarrow B/\text{in the context } X+\ldots+Y$, where X is (in this case) assigned a positive 'value' and Y is left unrestricted (cf. 6.5.3). (It will be observed that the rule can be formulated in this way only within a system of concatenating rules: cf. 6.1.1. It is the left-hand noun-phrase, not the right-hand noun-phrase, which controls concord. Since the left-hand noun-phrase derives from the NP generated by rule (1) it may be interpreted, as we shall see later, as the subject rather than the object: cf. 7.6.2.) As far as it goes, therefore, the above system of six rules *correctly* formalizes the facts of concord in English (in this deliberately restricted class of sentences). The analysis of a sample sentence is given in Fig. 14.

It requires but little consideration to see that, as soon as we start

9

increasing the class of sentences generated by the grammar to include all the other kinds of concord referred to in 6.5.4, the number of rules required in a context-free grammar would increase considerably. There would be little difference in the number of rules added to the context-sensitive grammar. Independently of any evaluation of the two grammars in terms of economy of statement, however, we wish to say that the context-sensitive rules *correctly* formalize the facts of concord. This brings us to a discussion of the distinction between 'strong' and 'weak' adequacy.

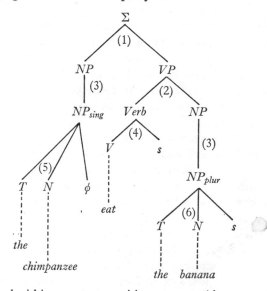

Fig. 14. Concord within a context-sensitive grammar (the numerals attached to the branches refer to the rules of the grammar in 6.5.6).

6.5.7 *Strong and weak adequacy*

We have already explained what is meant by strong and weak equivalence (cf. 6.2.12). Two or more grammars are weakly equivalent, if they generate the same set of sentences; they are strongly equivalent, if they generate the same set of sentences with the same structural description assigned to each sentence. The distinction between weak and strong adequacy is somewhat similar.

A grammar is said to be *weakly adequate* if it generates the set of sentences that one wishes to generate; a grammar is *strongly adequate* if it not only generates the desired set of sentences but also assigns to each sentence the *correct* structural description.

The term 'correct' is controversial, not to say tendentious. But it must be remembered that this definition of the difference between weak and strong adequacy carries with it absolutely no implications about the interpretation of 'correct': it does not even prejudge the question whether there are any standards of 'correctness'. However, we shall assume that, in certain cases at least, it is possible to say of two alternative descriptions of the same set of sentences that one description is 'more correct' than the other, or 'correct' in certain respects, even though we might not wish to say that any description is absolutely 'correct'.

It will be evident that the two sets of rules introduced in 6.5.5 and 6.5.6 are weakly, though not strongly, equivalent. There can be no doubt that the context-sensitive system is more strongly adequate (more 'correct') than the context-free system with regard to its characterization of the principles of subject–verb concord in English. It was for this reason that we deliberately introduced the notions of 'strong' and 'weak' adequacy at this point. The two grammars are readily comparable, because they are weakly equivalent and they both conform to the same general conditions imposed by the formalization of phrase-structure grammars (cf. 6.5.3).

6.6 Transformational grammar

6.6.1 Deep and surface structure

We may begin our discussion of transformational grammar with a quotation from Hockett: '...consider English *Atoms are too small to see by any possible technique* and *They are too much in love to see clearly*. The surface grammar of the two sentences is much the same, though not identical. But cutting across the surface grammar is a difference in the deeper connexions of *to see*. In the first sentence, *atoms* and *see* are related as they are in *You can't see atoms*; in the second, *they* and *see* are related as they are in *They see you*.' In the same chapter, Hockett says of the 'various layers of *deep grammar*' that lie 'beneath' the '*surface grammar*' (the 'one layer' which 'is immediately apparent to the analyst') that, although 'they have much to do with how we speak and understand', they 'are still largely unexplored, in any systematic way, by grammarians'.

By the time that Hockett's textbook appeared (1958), Chomsky and Harris had published works (1956 and 1957) in which proposals were made for the systematic analysis of both the surface structure and the deep structure of sentences by means of what they both called 'transformational' rules. Although Harris and Chomsky were working in close association (and in their publications each has acknowledged his debt to the other), they have from the outset developed the theory of 'transformational' grammar along different lines. More recently, the Soviet linguist, Shaumjan, has published a book (1965) in which yet a third system of grammatical analysis has been proposed making use of 'transformational' rules.

We shall not go into the differences between these theories here. It is important to realize, however, that there is a serious terminological problem in deciding what 'legitimately' counts as a *transformational* grammar. If we tried to formulate a definition of 'transformational' in such a way that it would apply to the theories of Chomsky, Harris and Shaumjan, then we should probably find that it also applied to many other theories of grammatical structure which are described by their authors as 'non-transformational'.

The purpose of this assertion (which is not intended to be polemical) is merely to draw the reader's attention to the fact that the term 'transformational' is strictly defined, but differently defined, in the formalizations proposed by Chomsky, Harris and Shaumjan.

The term 'transformational' has unfortunately engendered a good deal of unnecessary controversy and confusion in the recent literature of linguistics. If we use the term in a general and rather informal sense, rather than in the particular sense in which it is defined in any one theory, we can say, quite reasonably, that the 'deeper connexions' between sentences which 'cut across the surface grammar' (cf. the quotation from Hockett given above) are *transformational* relationships: this is a perfectly legitimate use of the term 'transformational'. Many of these transformational relationships between sentences are well-recognized in traditional grammar; but it is only recently that linguists have made any progress in accounting for them in an explicitly generative framework. Any grammar that claims to assign to each sentence that it generates both a deep-structure and a surface-structure analysis and systematically to relate the two analyses is a transformational grammar (whether it uses the label or not).

Of the many theories that are transformational in this wide, but quite reasonable, sense of the term, the best-known and so far the most highly-developed is that of Chomsky. In what follows, we shall therefore restrict our attention to the generative system which he and his associates have developed, and applied to the description of parts of the grammatical structure of many languages, over the last few

years. This system, like all others, has a number of known inadequacies. But so far it has proved itself capable of handling an im-
pressively large number of the 'deeper connexions' between sentences
that we have described as 'transformational'.

6.6.2 *Transformational ambiguity*

One reason for introducing the notion of 'bracketing' (or constituent-structure) into the theory of grammar is that it enables us to
account systematically for various kinds of grammatical ambiguity
(cf. 6.1.3). But there are many other ambiguous constructions in
different languages which depend upon the 'deeper connexions' we
have decided to call *transformational* rather than upon a difference of
'bracketing'.

Let us begin by taking a well-known example from traditional
grammar. The Latin phrase *amor Dei*, like its English translation *the
love of God*, is ambiguous (out of context). Traditional grammars of
Latin would say that the word *Dei* ('of God') is either a *subjective* or
objective 'genitive'. This is a transformational explanation of the
ambiguity: it implies that the phrase *amor Dei* is related to, and
indeed in some sense derivable from, two sentences: (i) a sentence in
which *Deus* (cited now in the 'nominative' case: cf. 6.2.9) is the
subject of the verb *amare* ('to love'); (ii) a sentence in which *Deum*
(cited now in the 'accusative') is the object of the verb *amare*. (From
our discussion of the traditional concept of the 'word' as a *lexeme*,
cf. 5.4.4, it will be clear that these statements can, and should, be
reformulated in terms of the lexemes DEUS and AMO.) Similarly, *the
love of God* is related to two sentences in English: (i) a sentence in
which *God* is the subject of the verb *love* (cf. *God loves mankind*);
(ii) a sentence in which *God* is the object of the verb *love* (cf. *Mankind
loves God*). The phrase might still be ambiguous in particular sentences:
It is the love of God which inspires men to work for their fellows.

One of Chomsky's most famous examples, the phrase *flying planes*
(in a sentence such as *Flying planes can be dangerous*), is ambiguous for
much the same reasons as *the love of God* is ambiguous: under one
interpretation *flying planes* is related to a sentence in which *planes* is
the subject of *fly* or *are flying*, under the other to a sentence in which
planes is the object of *fly* (cf. *Planes fly* v. *John flies planes*).

In traditional grammar, there is a distinction drawn between the
'participle' and the 'gerund'. In so far as this distinction applies in
English (and there are situations in which it is unclear) it might be

formulated as follows: (*a*) A *participle* is a word which is derived from a verb and used as an adjective. (*b*) A *gerund* is a word which is derived from a verb and used as a noun. This distinction is clearly relevant to the analysis of an ambiguous phrase like *flying planes*. If we consider the following two sentences (in which the principles of subject–verb concord 'disambiguate' the phrase in question)

(1) *Flying planes are dangerous*

(2) *Flying planes is dangerous*

the difference between the 'participle' and the 'gerund' comes out quite clearly. The verb *are* in (1) is 'plural' because its subject is *planes*, a plural noun, which is the head of the endocentric phrase *flying planes*: moreover, in (1) *flying* is distributionally equivalent to an adjective (e.g. *supersonic*). The recognition of a head and a modifier in *flying planes* in (2) is more problematical: but *flying* is nominal and the whole phrase is the subject (cf. *Flying is dangerous*). Traditional statements about the 'participle' and the 'gerund' are transformational in nature. We can interpret them to mean that a particular word (in the sense of 'lexeme': cf. 5.4.4) may be 'verbal' in one sentence and 'adjectival' in a transformationally-related phrase, or 'verbal' in one sentence and 'nominal' in a transformationally-related phrase. Without, for the moment, considering the nature of the rules which might account for these relationships, let us merely say that in (1) the phrase *flying planes* is to be derived by a rule which 'transforms' the structure underlying a sentence like *Planes are flying* and assigns to the resultant noun-phrase the derived structure of adjective + noun; and that in (2) the phrase *flying planes* is to be derived by transformational rule from the structure underlying a sentence like *John flies planes* and assigns to the resultant noun-phrase the derived structural description noun + noun (the first of the two nouns, if any, being the one that controls concord). If we now assume that the rules of the grammar generate sentences like (1) and (2) with both an *underlying* ('deep') and a *derived* ('surface') structural description, we have in principle explicated the 'subjective' and 'objective' interpretations of noun-phrases like *flying planes*.

Consider now a phrase like *eating apples*: this is also ambiguous. Under one interpretation (cf. *to eat apples* and *to fly planes*) it is structurally comparable with *flying planes* in (2). But the other interpretation, which is illustrated by

(3) *Eating apples cost more than cooking apples*

cannot be accounted for by saying that *apples* is in a 'subjective' relationship with *eating* in the deep structure of (3). The subjective interpretation of *eating apples* might be possible in somewhat unusual, or bizarre, situations in which apples are 'personified' (to use the traditional term). In such situations a sentence like the following

(4) *Apples eat with a hearty appetite*

would, presumably, be equally acceptable. Let us grant, however, that (4) is 'abnormal'; and that, whatever account we give of its 'abnormality', this account simultaneously explains the 'abnormality' of the 'subjective' interpretation of *eating apples*.

There are many phrases of the form $V+ing+N$ which are multiply-ambiguous: indeed, one might maintain that *flying planes* can be interpreted in the sense suggested by the paraphrase 'version' *planes for flying*. In the case of *flying planes*, this third interpretation is perhaps tautologous. It is quite likely, however, that any grammar which defines *eating apples*, etc., to have at least two deep-structure analyses will also assign at least three analyses to *flying planes*.

The reason why these phrases are said to be grammatically, and not just semantically, ambiguous is essentially the same as the reason given in 6.1.3. To illustrate this point with reference to another of Chomsky's examples (which is very similar to *the love of God* discussed above): a phrase like *the shooting of the hunters* is ambiguous (if it occurs in a context which does not 'disambiguate' it) because (*a*) *shoot* may be used both 'transitively' and 'intransitively' (more precisely, both 'transitively' and 'pseudo-intransitively': cf. 8.2.11), and (*b*) *the hunters* may occur in sentences containing the verb *shoot* as either the subject of the 'intransitive' (e.g. *The hunters shoot*) or the object of the 'transitive' (e.g. *John shot the hunters*). It is worth pointing out that the objective interpretation of the phrase *the shooting of the hunters* is closely related to passive constructions: cf. *The hunters were shot (by John)*. With a 'fully transitive' verb (i.e. with a verb which has an overt and specific object) phrases of the form *the V + ing of NP* do not normally admit of a subjective interpretation: they cannot be extended with an objective *of NP* (**the shooting of the hunters of the deer*). Instead, the subjective *NP* takes the 'possessive' suffix and the objective *NP* the preposition *of*: cf. *the hunters' shooting of the deer*. In a later chapter (cf. 8.2.3 ff.), we shall see that this is but one of many facts which suggest that in English (as in many languages) there is a particular relationship between the object of a transitive verb and the subject of a corresponding intransitive verb. For the present, however, we may be content with the informal account given above of the conditions which determine the ambiguity of phrases like *the shooting of the hunters*.

Let us now introduce the purely *ad hoc* convention (which is frequently used for this purpose in the literature) of employing numerical subscripts to identify the words and phrases which are said to be in correspondence in transformationally-related constructions. For example, we will say that a sentence like *John shoots the deer* has the form $NP_1 \, V_{tr} \, NP_2 (NP_1 = John; \, V_{tr}$ stands for a particular member of the class of transitive verbs, *shoot*; and $NP_2 = the$ *hunters*); and a sentence like *The hunters shoot* has the form $NP_1 \, V_{intr}$ ($NP_1 = $ the hunters, V_{intr} stands for a particular member of the class of intransitive verbs). Given this convention, we can say that a phrase of the form *the V + ing of NP* is *grammatically* ambiguous (and may or may not be semantically ambiguous) if, and only if, the grammar generates sentences of the form

and
$$(5) \; NP_1 V_{tr} \, NP_2$$
$$(6) \; NP_1 \, V_{intr}$$

and if (*a*) the *V* of *the V + ing of NP* is identical with a member of V_{tr} in (5) and a member of V_{intr} in (6), and (*b*) the *NP* of *the V + ing of NP* can occur both as NP_2 in (5) and NP_1 in (6). These conditions are satisfied in the case of *the shooting of the hunters*. But are they satisfied in the case of *the eating of the apples*? The verb *eat* (for simplicity, we will assume that the 'transitive' and the 'intransitive', or 'pseudo-intransitive', *eat* are instances of the 'same' verb, although this begs certain theoretical questions) occurs in sentences of the form represented in (5) and (6): cf. *John eats the apples* and *John is eating*. The phrase *the eating of the apples* is therefore interpretable 'objectively' (*the apples* is NP_2 in a transitive sentence with the verb *eat*). Whether it is defined as being 'subjectively' interpretable, from the syntactic point of view, will depend upon the generation or exclusion of a sentence like *The apples are eating*. The point is that a phrase like *the eating of the apples* manifests the same 'deep' relationship between *the apples* and *eat* as does the sentence (or non-sentence) *The apples are eating*. In other words, either the 'subjective' phrase *the eating of the apples* and sentence *The apples are eating* should both be generated as grammatical (and systematically related to one another in terms of their 'deep' structure) or they should both be excluded as ungrammatical. And their grammaticality or ungrammaticality will depend upon whether the noun *apple* and the verb *eat* are subclassified in the lexicon (by means of grammatical 'features': cf. 4.3.3) in such a way that the grammatical rules will admit or prohibit the combination of a noun with a given 'feature' (e.g. [inanimate]) as the subject of the verb-class of which *eat* is a member. (It is the same principle that is involved as was discussed in connexion with the constituent-structure analysis of *fresh fruit market* and *new fruit market* in 6.1.3).

6.6.3 *Neutralization and diversification in syntax*

Reference was made in an earlier chapter to the 'indirect discourse' construction in Latin (5.2.2). It was suggested (and this is a very traditional view) that a sentence like *Dico te venisse* (or its English translational equivalent *I say that you came*) should be generated in two 'stages': by first generating a sentence in its 'direct' form, (*Tu*) *venisti*, and then converting it into the 'indirect' form, *te venisse*, 'after' a 'verb of saying' (e.g. *dico*). This was a rather imprecise way of formulating the principle. We shall see later that, in Chomsky's system of transformational grammar, it is the 'deep' structure underlying (*Tu*) *venisti*, rather than this sentence itself, that is 'embedded' as the object of *dico* (for the term 'embedding', cf. 6.6.8).

It is well-known that the embedding of a transitive sentence in the 'indirect discourse' construction may lead to ambiguity in Latin. For example, (*a*) *Clodia amat Catullum*, 'Clodia loves Catullus', and (*b*) *Clodiam amat Catullus*, 'Catullus loves Clodia', are distinguished by the opposition of the 'nominative' and the 'accusative' case (cf. 7.4.2). But *Dico Clodiam amare Catullum* results from the embedding of either (*a*) or (*b*) as the object of *dico*; and, unless it is 'disambiguated' by the wider context, it is translatable into English as either 'I say that Clodia loves Catullus' or 'I say that Catullus loves Clodia'. (Word-order in Latin is irrelevant to the resolution of ambiguities of this kind.) The sentence is ambiguous, because both the subject and the object of the embedded sentence are in the 'accusative' case and, in this instance, each of the two nouns could be either the subject or object of *amare*. By contrast, a sentence like *Dico Horatium edere oleas*, 'I say that Horace is eating olives', is presumably not ambiguous; rather, it is ambiguous only if the underlying structure of *Horatium edere oleas* is relatable to that of *Horatium edunt oleae* ('The olives are eating Horace') as well as to that of *Horatius edit oleas* ('Horace is eating olives').

Let us now consider the 'indirect discourse' construction in Greek.

There are a number of alternative constructions. Of these we will mention only two: one that is very similar to the Latin construction and one that is similar to the English construction with *that*. Certain verbs require, or 'prefer', one construction rather than the other. But some verbs of 'saying' occur freely with both. For example:

$$aggélei \begin{cases} \text{(a)} & \textit{Kûron poreúesthai.} \\ \text{(b)} & \textit{hóti Kûros poreúetai.} \end{cases}$$

These are two alternative 'versions' of the same underlying structure; both are translatable as 'He announces that Cyrus is on the march'. In (a) *Kûron* is 'accusative' and *poreúesthai* is the 'infinitive'; in (b) *hóti* is an introductory particle, or conjunction, comparable with *that* in English, and *Kûros poreúetai* is identical in form with the 'direct discourse' simple sentence.

As we have seen, the distinction between *dico + Clodia amat Catullum* and *dico + Clodiam amat Catullus* (the plus-sign is here used as an *ad hoc* device to refer to what was described above as 'embedding') is *neutralized* in the surface-structure of *Dico Clodiam amare Catullum* (for the term 'neutralization', cf. 3.3.5). The Greek example illustrates the converse phenomenon, which (following Lamb, who might, however, describe the facts in a somewhat different framework) we may call *diversification*: two sentences may differ in surface-structure, but be identical in their deep-structure. (The English sentences *They denied the existence of God* and *They denied that God exists* also illustrate the phenomenon of diversification.)

Although we have so far discussed transformational relations with particular reference to neutralization and diversification (and we have deliberately adopted a traditional viewpoint), it must be emphasized that the distinction between surface structure and deep structure is independently justifiable. Traditional grammars of English would say that active and passive sentences (e.g. *John opened the door* and *The door was opened by John*) are syntactically-relatable, the object of the former 'becoming' the subject of the latter: this is a transformational statement, which implies a deep-structure identity or similarity. The relationship between active and passive sentences must be accounted for, whether this is a case of diversification or not (and opinions differ on this question). Furthermore, let us suppose, for the sake of the argument, that *the shooting of the hunters* (and all phrases of the form *the V + ing of NP*) are not ambiguous, but necessarily 'objective', and that *the hunters' shooting* (and all phrases of the form *NP's*

$V + ing$) are necessarily 'subjective'. We should still want the grammar to relate *the shooting of the hunters* to the transitive sentence NP_1 *shoot the hunters* and *the hunters' shooting* to the intransitive *The hunters shoot*.

The phenomena of syntactic neutralization and diversification, which are widespread in language, bring the distinction between deep and surface structure into sharper focus.

6.6.4 *PS-rules and T-rules*

Our discussion of transformational grammar has so far been very informal; and it has been more or less neutral with respect to various possible systems of rules which seek to formalize the relationship between deep structure and surface structure. At this point we will move on to consider the theory of grammatical structure which Chomsky developed in *Syntactic Structures*. Later in the section we will mention some of the more important modifications that have been introduced in the last few years.

For a number of reasons (not all of which have been mentioned above) Chomsky came to the view that 'notions of phrase structure are quite adequate for a small part of the language and that the rest of the language can be derived by repeated application of a rather simple set of transformations to the strings given by the phrase structure grammar. If we were to attempt to extend phrase structure grammar to cover the entire language directly, we would lose the simplicity of the limited phrase structure grammar and of the transformational development.'

Chomsky's proposal, therefore, was to split the syntax of the language into two parts: (i) a *phrase-structure component* (or *base-component*), containing rules of the form $X + A + Y \rightarrow X + B + Y$ (cf. 6.5.2), and (ii) a *transformational component*, containing 'supplementary' rules not necessarily constrained to the form of the phrase-structure rules. The transformational rules were to be 'supplementary' in the sense that they were to operate after, and upon the output of, the phrase-structure rules. Henceforth, we will use the abbreviations 'PS-rule' and 'T-rule' for rules of the base-component and transformational component, respectively. The PS-rules given in *Syntactic Structures* are as follows:

(1) $\Sigma \rightarrow NP + VP$

(2) $VP \rightarrow Verb + NP$

(3) $NP \rightarrow \begin{cases} NP_{sing} \\ NP_{plur} \end{cases}$

(4) $NP_{sing} \rightarrow T + N + \varnothing$

(5) $NP_{plur} \rightarrow T + N + s$

(6) $Verb \rightarrow Aux + V$

(7) $Aux \rightarrow C(M)\, (have + en)\, (be + ing)$

We have omitted the rules for lexical substitution from the PS-rules (cf. 4.3.2). Instead, we give Chomsky's sample lexicon in the following form (the difference is not relevant to any of the points being illustrated):

$T = \{the\}$

$N = \{man,\ ball,\ \dots\}$

$V = \{hit,\ take,\ walk,\ read,\ \dots\}$

$M = \{will,\ can,\ may,\ shall,\ must\}$

The only rule that requires any comment at this stage is (7): all the others conform to conventions used in previous sections. Rule (7) develops *Aux* (which has a mnemonic connexion with 'auxiliary verb') into a string of up to four elements: of these C is obligatory (and will be interpreted by a transformational rule to handle concord); the other elements on the right-hand side of rule (7) are optional, and each is independent of the other two. The output of rule (7) will therefore contain (in place of *Aux* in the output of rule (6)) one of the following eight strings:

    (i) C

   (ii) $C + M$

  (iii) $C + have + en$

  (iv) $C + be + ing$

   (v) $C + M + have + en$

  (vi) $C + M + be + ing$

 (vii) $C + have + en + be + ing$

(viii) $C + M + have + en + be + ing$

Other features of rule (7) will be explained later.

The output of the PS-rules is a *kernel string*. The reader must be careful not to confuse this term with *kernel sentence*. A kernel sentence (according to the system proposed in *Syntactic Structures*) is any sentence which is generated from a single kernel string without the application of any *optional* transformations. No sentences are generated without the application of at least a limited number of obligatory T-rules. This point is important, since it has frequently been assumed that kernel sentences (e.g. the simple, active, declarative sentences of English) were to be generated solely by the phrase-structure rules of a transformational grammar.

6.6.5 *The passive transformation*

We will illustrate the nature of the T-rules of *Syntactic Structures* with reference, first of all, to the generation of passive sentences in English. (The fact that Chomsky has modified his view of the relationship between active and passive sentences in his more recent work is not relevant to the points being made here.) The relevant T-rule, as given in *Syntactic Structures*, is as follows:

> *Passive* (optional)
>
> Structural Analysis: $NP - Aux - V - NP$
>
> Structural Change: $X_1 - X_2 - X_3 - X_4 \rightarrow$
> $$X_4 - X_2 + be + en - X_3 - by + X_1$$

(An alternative, less formal but equivalent, statement of the rule is as follows:

$$NP_1 - Aux - V - NP_2 \rightarrow NP_2 - Aux + be + en - V - by + NP_1$$

There is some significance in the distinction of dashes and plus-signs as concatenation symbols, but we need not go into this question.)

The first point to notice is that the above T-rule contains two parts: 'Structural Analysis' and 'Structural Change' (henceforth SA and SC, respectively). Unlike PS-rules, which apply to the output of the rule previously applied (whether optionally or obligatorily, recursively or non-recursively, with contextual restrictions or without, etc.), T-rules are defined to apply only to strings that are *analysable* in terms of the elements referred to in their SA. In the present instance, the transformation (the SC part of the rule) is restricted to strings which can be analysed into *NP*, *Aux*, *V* and *NP*. Each of these four elements is identified in the left-hand part of SC by means of the subscript attached to the symbol X: X_1 denotes the first element referred to in SA (i.e. *NP*); X_2 denotes *Aux*; etc. The transformation (defined in SC) has the following effects: (*a*) the first and the fourth elements are permuted; (b) by is attached to what is now the last NP in the string; and (c) be + en is attached to Aux. In other words, the effect of the transformation is precisely that suggested in the alternative, less formal, statement of the rule

$$NP_1 - Aux - V - NP_2 \rightarrow NP_2 - Aux + be + en - V - by + NP_1$$

We must now see what is meant by saying that a string is *analysable* in terms of the four elements NP, Aux, V and NP. Let us first run through the PS-rules in sequence, listing the strings that result from the application of each rule to the output of the previous rule (cf. 6.6.4):

By rule (1): $NP + VP$

(2): $NP + Verb + NP$

(3): $NP_{sing} + Verb + NP_{sing}$

(4): $T + N + \emptyset + Verb + T + N + \emptyset$

(6): $T + N + \emptyset + Aux + V + T + N + \emptyset$

(7): $T + N + \emptyset + C + M + have + en + V + T + N + \emptyset$

It will be observed that rule (3) was applied twice. Since NP_{sing} was selected for both positions in the output of rule (2), rule (4) was also applied twice, but rule (5) was inapplicable. In rule (7) *Aux* was rewritten as $C + M + have + en$ (i.e. as option (v) of the eight listed in 6.6.5 as possible under the notational conventions). The output of rule (7) is a *kernel string* of the type that underlies such corresponding active and passive sentences as *The man will have read the book* and *The book will have been read by the man.*

We now wish to apply the passive transformation to this string, provided that it is analysable in terms of the conditions specified in the SA part of the rule. Notice, first of all, that none of the elements referred to in the SA for the passive transformation occurs in the kernel-string. Furthermore, at no stage in the derivation of the kernel-string by the PS-rules did we meet the string $NP + Aux + V + NP$. Let us therefore run through the rules again; but this time we will generate the phrase-structure of the kernel string in question.

By rule (1) $\Sigma(NP + VP)$

(2) $\Sigma(NP + VP(Verb + NP))$

(3) $\Sigma(NP(NP_{sing}) + VP(Verb + NP(NP_{sing})))$

(4) $\Sigma(NP(NP_{sing}(T + N + \emptyset))$
$\qquad\qquad + VP(Verb + NP(NP_{sing}(T + N + \emptyset))))$

(6) $\Sigma(NP(NP_{sing}(T+N+\emptyset))$
$$+ VP(Verb(Aux+V)+NP(NP_{sing}(T+N+\emptyset))))$$

(7) $\Sigma(NP(NP_{sing}(T+N+\emptyset))+VP(Verb(Aux(C+M$
$$+have+en)+V)+NP(NP_{sing}(T+N+\emptyset))))$$

This is the phrase-structure of the kernel string underlying such sentences as *The man will have read the book* and *The book will have been read by the man*.

A labelled-bracketing of a string is referred to, technically, as a *phrase-marker*. Phrase-markers may also be represented by means of a tree-diagram with labelled nodes: cf. Fig. 15. We must now introduce two further notions: 'substring' and 'domination'.

A *substring* is any part of a string which is itself a string (of one or more elements). For example, the string $a+b+c$ is analysable in various ways into substrings: into the two substrings a and $b+c$, or $a+b$ and c, or into the three substrings a and b and c. The kernel string we are at present concerned with

$$T+N+\emptyset+C+M+have+en+V+T+N+\emptyset$$

can be analysed into very many different sets of substrings. What we want to know is whether any one set of substrings satisfies the conditions of analysability specified in the SA of the T-rule for the passive. We now need the notion of 'domination'.

A symbol *dominates* everything enclosed within the brackets opened immediately after the symbol in question in the phrase marker (or, equivalently, a symbol dominates everything which is traceable back to the node labelled with the symbol in question in the corresponding tree-diagram for the phrase-marker). Thus, in the phrase-marker we are considering: Σ dominates everything between the left-most and the right-most bracket; VP dominates $Verb$ $(Aux(C+M+have+en)+V)+NP$; and so on.

We can now define the notion of *structural analysability* as a condition for the application of T-rules. If a string (not necessarily a kernel string) is analysable (without remainder) into substrings, each of which is dominated in the phrase-marker for the string by a symbol referred to in the SA of the T-rule, then the string satisfies the conditions defined by the SA. If the T-rule in question is obligatory, it *must* be applied; if it is optional, it *may* be applied. The passive transformation is defined to be optional in the rule we are considering.

The (kernel) string in question satisfies the conditions for the application of the passive transformation. This will be clear from the following diagram (which may be interpreted with reference to the phrase-marker in Fig. 15):

$$\{T+N+\o\}+\{C+M+have+en\}+\{V\}+\{T+N+\o\}$$
$$NP_1 \quad - \quad Aux \quad -V- \quad NP_2$$

By the operation of the T-rule proper (in SC) the output will be another string (no longer a kernel string: cf. 6.6.4), which will then serve as the input, together with its associated phrase-marker, for further T-rules. If all the relevant obligatory T-rules are applied, but no more optional T-rules, the output of the generative system will be a passive sentence like *The book will have been read by the man.*

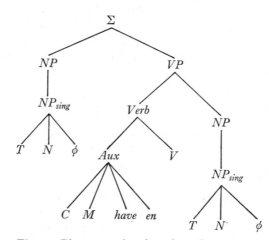

Fig. 15. Phrase-marker for a kernel sentence.

6.6.6   *Heterogeneity of T-rules*

We have gone into a certain amount of detail in our discussion of the notion of *analysability*; and this is essential to an understanding of Chomsky's formalization of transformational grammar. Many popular accounts of the theory (even when they are not factually incorrect or misleading) fail to give any indication of what is meant by the term 'transformational rule'.

One of the most striking features of the T-rules in *Syntactic Structures* is their *heterogeneity*. It is important to realize that the construction of even a partial transformational grammar for any language is a task of immense complexity; and there are many different factors which may influence the linguist in his decision to handle a particular feature by means of a T-rule rather than a PS-rule. As we shall see, not all the T-rules are 'inherently' transformational.

On the basis of our discussion of structural analysability, we may distinguish two different criteria which define a rule as 'inherently' transformational. The first may be summarized as follows: any rule which does not conform to the conditions imposed upon phrase-structure rules is transformational. Some of these conditions have been mentioned in an earlier section (cf. 6.2.11). If various formal restrictions of this nature are imposed upon the rules of the base-component of a transformational grammar, one may guarantee that the kernel-strings at least are *uniquely analysable* into substrings in terms of the conditions specified in the SA of a transformational rule.

The second criterion is somewhat different: a transformational rule is one which contains in the string of symbols to the left of the rewrite-arrow (or in the SA associated with the rule) at least one symbol which functions as a *variable*, which takes as its 'value' any one of the whole class of substrings dominated by that symbol in the phrase-marker associated with the string serving as input to the rule. For example, all the symbols (except V) in the SA of the passive transformation discussed above

$$SA: NP - Aux - V - NP$$

are variables in this sense. By contrast, V is a *constant*: it is a terminal symbol of the system of PS-rules given in 6.6.4, dominating no substring other than itself ('self-domination', in this sense, is a formal requirement of the system). This distinction between 'constants' and 'variables' (which may be regarded as a special case of the more general distinction drawn in 6.5.2) is fundamental to the definition of 'transformation' in Chomsky's system.

It is by virtue of their capacity to refer to classes of substrings, not simply to a given substring, that the transformational rules are more *powerful* than phrase-structure rules. The term 'powerful' is rather difficult to define, at least in a non-technical way. Let us be content with the statement that one rule is more powerful than another if it accounts for more 'facts' or accounts for them more 'correctly'. (Lurking behind this statement are various considerations of weak and strong adequacy: cf. 6.5.7.) In particular instances, it is easy enough to see what is implied by the term 'powerful'. We will give just one example.

The system of PS-rules given in 6.6.4 allows for the generation of only two substrings dominated by NP: $T+N+\emptyset$ and $T+N+s$

(e.g. *the boy* and *the boys*). But it is clear that in a more complete grammar of English the passive transformation will be required to permute noun-phrases of all kinds: cf. *The man who was here yesterday read a thousand books last year* and the corresponding passive 'version' *A thousand books were read last year by the man who was here yesterday.* Provided that all the rules of the grammar are correctly integrated in the generative system, both *the man who was here yesterday* and *a thousand books* will be analysed as 'constants' falling within the scope of the 'variables' NP_1 and NP_2; and the passive transformation will operate correctly. Other rules will account for the various possible positions of *last year*, the 'embedding' of *who was here yesterday* within the first NP of the string that serves as input to the transformational rule for the passive, etc. Apart from any other considerations, a rule containing variables (in this sense of the term) can handle whole classes of sentences which would otherwise require a lot of separate (and unrelated) phrase-structure rules.

If the grammar is transformational, in the sense that it includes some 'inherently' transformational rules operating upon the output of phrase-structure rules, then a number of other important factors come into play. Only two will be mentioned here. It might be decided, for instance, to transfer to the transformational component such 'complexities' as recursion and context-sensitivity (although these properties, of themselves, do not violate the conditions of analysability): for reasons which we need not discuss here, Chomsky made this decision, in principle, for the system proposed in *Syntactic Structures*. Another consideration has to do with the relative order in which the rules of the grammar are applied. A perfectly 'straightforward' phrase-structure rule may be required to operate upon the output of an 'inherently' transformational rule. If the system is formalized in such a way that the T-rules come after the PS-rules (and this is so in *Syntactic Structures*), then the 'straightforward' phrase-structure rule must be 'reclassified' as a T-rule, by virtue of the place it occupies in the grammar. (This is possible, because a constant can always be regarded as a variable with only one 'value'.) Considerations of this kind (and there are others) account for the heterogeneity of the transformational rules in grammars organized in terms of Chomsky's earlier formalization of the theory.

As we shall see, a number of modifications have recently been introduced into the system by Chomsky and others working upon the foundations of transformational theory. Analysability is guaranteed by somewhat different formal devices in the system recently proposed by Chomsky: but (to quote his own statement of the point) it remains 'the basic predicate in terms of which transformational grammar is developed'.

6.6.7 Subject–verb concord in a transformational grammar

At some point in the description of English we must account for the principles of subject–verb concord. We have already referred to these in connexion with the notion of context-sensitivity (cf. 6.5.6). We will now look briefly at the transformational rule which is introduced in *Syntactic Structures* to handle the concord of number ('singular' *v.* 'plural') that holds between the subject of the sentence and the verb. This will serve to illustrate some of the general points that have been made above about the nature of T-rules.

The rule (modified in one respect) is as follows:

Number transformation (obligatory)

SA: $X - C - Y$

SC: $C \rightarrow \begin{cases} s/\text{in the context } NP_{sing} + \dots \\ \varnothing/\text{otherwise} \end{cases}$

We now meet a different kind of SA from that which appeared in the passive transformation. X and Y are variables denoting any substrings of the input string without reference to their analysability; and C is a terminal symbol of the PS-rules given in 6.6.4. It is true that the contextual restriction for $C \rightarrow s$ makes reference to the non-terminal symbol NP_{sing}. But we might consider the possibility of including the present 'transformational' rule among the PS-rules. Notice that, if the PS-rules of 6.6.4 are applied in the following order (1), (2), (3), (6), (7), (4), (5), and if the rule for number-concord is applied after (7) and before (4), the effect is exactly the same as it would be if we applied the rule to a terminal string generated by the rules of 6.6.4 in the order in which they were listed there. The reader may verify this fact for himself.

There is, however, a very good reason why Chomsky puts the rule for number-concord at a particular place among the T-rules of *Syntactic Structures*. The principles of subject–verb concord in English apply both to active and to passive sentences: cf. *The men see the cows, The man sees the cows, The cow is seen by the men, The cow is seen by the man, The cows are seen by the men*, etc. If the passive transformation (which is an 'inherently' transformational rule) precedes the rule for number-concord, the latter can be formulated in such a way that it applies with respect to the number of the NP occurring to the left of C (the first element of Aux) in the input string.

Thus the kernel string

$$(1) \quad T+N+\text{ø}+C+M+have+en+V+T+N+s$$

(which is an instance of $NP_1 - Aux - V - NP_2$) will be transformed into

$$(1a) \quad T+N+\text{ø}+s+M+have+en+V+T+N+s$$

and $\quad$ (2) $\quad T+N+s+C+M+have+en+be+en$
$$+V+by+T+N+\text{ø}$$

(which is the corresponding $NP_2 - Aux + be + en - V - by + NP_1$, resulting from the application of the optional passive transformation) will be transformed by the rule for number-concord into

$$(2a) \quad T+N+s+\text{ø}+M+have+en+be+en$$
$$+V+by+T+N+\text{ø}$$

These are the strings underlying such sentences as *The man will have read the books* and the corresponding passive *The books will have been read by the man*.

Among the further transformational rules that must be applied to $(1a)$ and $(2a)$ are the rules for the attachment of the verbal suffixes and the marking of word-boundaries. We shall not give the rules (the reader should consult *Syntactic Structures*, pp. 39, 113: he will see that the rule for the 'auxiliary transformation' makes use of *ad hoc* variables). The effect of these rules is to convert $(1a)$ and $(2a)$ into

$$(1b) \quad \ldots M+s+ +have+ +V+en+ + \ldots$$

$$(2b) \quad \ldots M+\text{ø}+ +have+ +be+en+ +V+en+ + \ldots$$

(We have given only the $Aux - V$ portions of the strings. The double plus-sign is used in place of Chomsky's special boundary-symbol.)

Let us now apply the lexical substitution rules (cf. 4.3.2: there is some divergence here from the *Syntactic Structures* system, according to which the lexical items are the terminal symbols of the PS-rules), using a space to indicate the word-boundaries

$(1c)$ *the man + ø will + s have read + en the book + s*

$(2c)$ *the book + s will + ø have be + en read + en by the man + ø*

Further rules (in *Syntactic Structures* 'morphophonemic' rules) will now convert these strings into the correct phonological form:

$man + \emptyset \rightarrow$ /man/, $will + s \rightarrow$ /wil/, $read + en \rightarrow$ /red/, etc. Alternatively, for the written language, 'morphographemic' rules would convert the strings into

(1 d) *The man will have read the books*

(2 d) *The books will have been read by the man*

6.6.8 *Generalized transformations*

So far, in our discussion of the system of rules introduced by Chomsky in *Syntactic Structures*, we have assumed that only one terminal string will serve as input to the transformational component. However, the system also provides for the combination of two or more terminal strings (by the successive concatenation of pairs of strings) by means of optional *generalized* (or 'double-base') *transformations*. By contrast, T-rules operating solely upon one terminal string (and its subsequent transforms) are referred to as *singulary* (or 'single-base'). As we have seen, the singulary transformations of *Syntactic Structures* are specified as optional (e.g. the passive transformation) or obligatory (e.g. the number-concord transformation).

Generalized transformations fall into two classes: *embedding* and *conjoining* rules. There is a rough, but not exact correspondence, with the distinction sometimes drawn in traditional grammar (and rather difficult to apply in many instances) between complex and compound sentences (cf. p. 266). Among the many constructions that would be handled by means of an embedding rule, there are various 'nominalizations'. We have already discussed (in the earlier, more informal, parts of this section) sentences like *Flying planes are dangerous*. We said that *flying planes* was a noun-phrase in the surface structure of this sentence (and had the internal surface structure of adjective + noun, like *supersonic planes*), but that it was 'transformationally' related to the deep structure of *Planes fly* and *Planes are flying*. We can now say that the grammar generates a *matrix*-string (of the form $NP - be - A$) and a *constituent*-string (of the form $NP - V_{intr}$); and that the constituent-string is transformed ('nominalized') into an NP of the form $A + N$, and then embedded as the subject of the matrix $NP - be - A$.

We shall not go into the details of the formalization of embedding transformations. It was little more than adumbrated in *Syntactic Structures*; and the work that has been done since then has revealed a number of problems. The statement made in the previous paragraph was intended solely as a general indication of what is meant by the term 'embedding'. The main point is that an embedded structure (whether it be a phrase or a clause, according to the traditional distinction between these two kinds of 'secondary' units: cf. 5.1.1) is the transform of a string which could also serve as the underlying structure for a whole sentence, but which 'functions' as a constituent of another sentence. In a certain sense, it is a sentence within a sentence. The phrase-marker of the matrix-sentence, dominated by Σ, will therefore contain another instance of Σ dominated by the appropriate symbol for the 'function' performed by the constituent-sentence in the structure of the whole.

But conjoining transformations also combine sentences (more precisely, the structures underlying sentences) within a 'larger' sentence. The difference is (and this is the difference between 'complex', embedding, sentences and 'compound', conjoining, sentences in traditional grammar) that conjoining transformations do not subordinate one sentence, as a 'constituent', to the other or some part of the other, the 'matrix'. Both of the conjoined structures (assuming that only two underlying structures are involved in the operation of conjunction) preserve their 'sentential' status within the 'larger' sentence. The phrase-marker for the 'larger' sentence will therefore contain two (or more) instances of Σ, co-ordinate with one another, below the topmost Σ which dominates the whole phrase-marker. The most obvious (and *prima facie* the simplest) example of a sentence which results from the application of a conjoining transformation is a sentence with two co-ordinate clauses linked by a co-ordinating conjunction (e.g. *and*): cf. *Caesar advanced and Pompey retreated*.

6.6.9 *The present state of transformational grammar*

We began this section by saying that any grammar which claims to assign both a deep-structure analysis and a surface-structure analysis to the sentences it generates is a transformational grammar; and we saw that traditional grammars were transformational in this respect. They were also generative in the first of the two senses currently associated with this term (i.e. they were in principle 'projective', but they were not 'explicit': cf. 4.2.13).

Later in the section we restricted our attention to the best-known and most highly-formalized system of generative-transformational grammar that has so far been developed. This was the system introduced by Chomsky in *Syntactic Structures* (a relatively non-technical abridgement of previous work, for the most part unpublished, although it has circulated quite widely among linguists who have concerned themselves with formalized generative grammar). Many important theoretical questions have not been mentioned in this necessarily brief and fragmentary account of Chomsky's system. It has seemed preferable, in an introduction to linguistic theory, to concentrate upon such fundamental notions as 'structural analysability' and the nature of transformational rules, and to illustrate the operation of one or two simple rules in sufficient detail for the reader to appreciate the significance of the fundamental principles of the system.

It has also seemed preferable to illustrate these principles with reference to the earlier system of transformational grammar (as outlined in *Syntactic Structures*). One reason for this decision is that most of the detailed exemplification of transformational grammar so far published conforms, in general, to the earlier system of Chomsky. Another more important reason is that the major modifications which have recently been proposed by Chomsky and others derive from the serious attempts they have made over the last ten years to apply the earlier system to an ever wider range of syntactic relationships in language (some of which were not even handled 'informally' in traditional grammar). To understand the import of these modifications, one must first of all understand the earlier system.

Furthermore, there is a sense in which *Syntactic Structures* has not been superseded by later works. It was a book of revolutionary importance in the history of modern linguistics. In it, Chomsky did not amass a wealth of detail from many languages, but selected a few evident, and in a sense well-understood, facts about the structure of a very familiar language (English) and about the nature of language in general, and demonstrated, conclusively, that these facts could not be 'explained' within the framework of current linguistic theory. But in doing so, he set more rigorous standards of 'explanation' than linguists had hitherto been accustomed to. These standards are still somewhat controversial (although a good deal of the controversy is based on misunderstanding). But they have been accepted by many linguists, including some who have rejected the details of the formalization of grammatical theory developed by Chomsky. It is this fact which gives to *Syntactic Structures* its 'revolutionary' importance.

The principles of transformational grammar outlined and discussed in *Syntactic Structures* are simple enough (although it may require a certain effort to see the implications of the particular system of formalization). The application of these principles to the description of more than a fragment of the grammatical structure of any one language is far from simple. The use of T-rules in a generative grammar with a simple phrase-structure base-component leads to very serious problems in the specification of the order in which the T-rules (and in particular the generalized transformations of *Syntactic Structures*) operate relatively to one another. We have seen that the T-rules of the earlier system were very heterogeneous. The problem of analysability was solved for the kernel-strings by imposing certain restrictions upon the nature of the PS-rules in the base-component. But the problem was still there in the grammar. Since a T-rule could operate upon a string which resulted from the application of previous T-rules (involving permutations and deletions), and since (in theory) each T-rule transformed one phrase-marker (and not simply an unbracketed string) into another phrase-marker, it was necessary to establish the principles which govern the assignment of derived phrase-markers by particular types of T-rules. Although Chomsky and others concerned themselves with this problem from the outset, it is hardly discussed at all in *Syntactic Structures*; and it was never satisfactorily solved.

Over the last few years, many scholars have illustrated the problems of ordering T-rules in a grammar organized according to the system proposed in *Syntactic Structures*. Recently, Chomsky himself has modified the theory in a way which is designed to reduce, if not eliminate, these problems. Briefly (and this is not intended as a self-sufficient summary of the modifications), Chomsky's proposal amounts to the removal of generalized transformations from the grammar by introducing into the base-component optional recursive rules with Σ to the right of the rewrite-arrow. All transformations are then made singular and obligatory ('triggered off', in certain cases, by optional elements in the rules of the base-component) and ordered in such a way that they apply to constituent 'sentences' before embedding and to matrix 'sentences' after embedding (embedding, and conjoining, being controlled by the base-component rules).

Apart from reasons connected with the problem of ordering the rules, one of the principal motives for the revision of the system has been to integrate syntax with phonology and semantics. It has been tentatively suggested that the deep-structure analysis (generated by the base-component) is irrelevant for the operation of the phonological rules and that the surface-structure (resulting from the application to the deep-structure phrase-marker of the singular transformations) is irrelevant for the semantic interpretation of sentences. This is undeniably an attractive hypothesis; but its empirical validation, or refutation, will require a considerable amount of further detailed work. Until such work has been carried out and evaluated, both parts of the hypothesis must be treated with some degree of scepticism.

Although the irrelevance of surface structure to semantic analysis remains to be proved or disproved, most linguists who accept the validity of the distinction between deep grammatical structure and surface grammatical structure (including those who have described the relationship between the two in very different terms from Chomsky) assume that there is some particularly intimate connexion between deep syntax and semantics. We shall make the same assumption throughout this book.

In conclusion, one must make the following point. The evaluation of grammars that do not conform to the same system of formalization (or are unformalized) poses problems of a very different order from those posed by the evaluation of grammars that are weakly equivalent and formally comparable (cf. 6.2.12). The complexity of transformational grammars (and the term 'transformational' is now being used in its widest sense) is such that it becomes very difficult to compare transformational grammars of different types. It is also difficult to strike a balance between the conflicting claims of weak and strong adequacy with respect to many sets of sentences that we might wish to generate by means of a grammar of a particular type. In a later chapter of this book we shall mention some 'deep connexions' between sentences which Chomsky's theory of syntactic structure, in its present form, does not handle (as Chomsky himself has pointed out). It should be realized, however, that it is no difficult matter for a linguist (drawing upon the knowledge about language accumulated by his predecessors) to produce sets of sentences which he will correctly describe ('informally') as 'transformationally-related'. The problem is to give a systematic account of these relationships within the theoretical framework already established for other sets of sentences. If this cannot be done, one may be justified in modifying the framework. But the modification can then have the effect of making it impossible to handle the relationships which were satisfactorily accounted for by the previous system. This point should be borne constantly in mind during the more informal discussion of grammatical theory which follows.

7

GRAMMATICAL CATEGORIES

7.1 Introductory

7.1.1 *The term 'category' in traditional grammar*

So far we have adopted a purely 'formal' approach to grammatical analysis. In the present chapter we will discuss the traditional assumption that there exist certain 'notional' categories which are universal in the sense that they are common to all languages (cf. 4.1.3, 4.2.9). In particular, we shall be concerned with the traditional theory of the 'parts of speech' and such 'grammatical categories' traditionally associated with the parts of speech as person, tense, mood, gender, number and case. First of all, something must be said in this introductory section about the term 'grammatical category' and its traditional implications.

There is very little consistency or uniformity in the use of the term 'category' in modern treatments of grammatical theory. It is frequently employed, like 'class' or 'set', to refer to any group of elements recognized in the description of particular languages. Some authors refer to the 'parts of speech' as 'categories'; others, following the more traditional usage, restrict the application of the term to such features associated with the 'parts of speech' in the classical languages as have been mentioned above (person, tense, mood, etc.). And there are other—wider, narrower or quite different—technical senses in which the term has been employed. No attempt will be made here to give to the term 'grammatical category' a precise, technical interpretation. It is merely being used as a convenient heading for the chapter in which we will discuss certain important questions of traditional grammar in the light of more recent developments in general syntactic theory.

The term 'category' is but one of the many traditional terms used by linguists which owe their origin to the fact that western grammatical theory was developed on the basis of that particular philosophical system which, for the present purpose, we can refer to, somewhat loosely, as 'Aristotelian'. The term 'category' derives from a Greek word which is otherwise translated as 'predication' (in the logical, or philosophical, sense of 'attributing properties' to things). In Aristotelian (and scholastic) philosophy, the 'categories' were the different ways, or modes, in which predications could be made of things; and it was assumed that the different modes of predication represented differences in the objective world, the different modes of 'being'. Underlying the classification of the modes of predication and of 'being' was the assumption that the physical world consists of things ('substances') which have certain properties ('accidents'), initiate or undergo certain processes, stand in a certain relationship to one another, or have a certain extension or location in space or time. We shall not go into the details of the Aristotelian theory of the 'categories'. But two general points may be made. First, it should be noted that a fundamental distinction was drawn between the category of 'substance', on the one hand, and the other 'accidental' categories, on the other: the 'substance' was the individual thing in abstraction from its 'accidental' properties. Second, it was assumed by Aristotle and his followers, and stated explicitly by the medieval 'speculative' grammarians, that the structure of language reflected the structure of the world: that words signified things according to their mode of 'being', as 'substances' or 'accidents'. It was because of this correspondence between the modes of 'being' and 'signifying' that knowledge of the world was possible. The categories of 'being', 'signifying' and 'understanding' were congruent with one another; and the congruence of the three sets of categories was held to justify the intimate and indissoluble association of philosophy, grammar and logic.

7.1.2 'Matter' v. 'form': 'substance' v. 'accidents'

A further distinction of Aristotelian philosophy is relevant to the development of the traditional theory of the 'parts of speech' and the 'grammatical categories': this is the distinction that was drawn between 'matter' and 'form'. Every individual thing (that is, every 'substance') was said to consist of 'matter' (which we may think of as some physical material) and of the particular 'form' (the individuating principle) imposed upon this physical 'matter' which gave to the resulting thing its identity and internal stability. (The Aristotelian distinction of 'matter' and 'form', it will be observed, is very similar to the distinction drawn by de Saussure between 'substance' and 'form': cf. 2.2.2. As we have just seen, the traditional sense of the term 'substance' was quite different.)

Since language was both an object of analysis and also the instrument with which all philosophical analysis was carried out, the theory of the 'categories' has had a double effect upon traditional grammar. Not only were the elements of language themselves analysed in terms of 'matter' and 'form' and, as 'substances', classified with respect to their 'accidental' properties, but they were also grouped into classes ('parts of speech') according to their 'mode of signifying' the things, properties and relations to which they referred.

As we have already seen (cf. 5.4.1), the basic unit of grammatical analysis in traditional theory was the word (*dictio*, to use the Latin term). Each word, as a 'sign', was composed of a certain combination of sounds (*vox*) and meaning (*significatio*). The physical realization of the word (*vox*) was not an essential part of it, but merely the way in which that word happened to be pronounced, 'accidentally' and by 'convention' and 'usage', in a particular language. As a physical object the *vox* could be further analysed into its 'elements', sounds or letters. But the grammatical analysis proper began with the analysis of the ways in which words operated as 'signs', as instruments for the description and understanding of 'reality'; with their classification as 'parts of speech' and with the establishment of patterns (or 'paradigms') of 'declension' and 'conjugation'.

Words, like everything else that came within the scope of scientific inquiry, had to be described in terms of the traditional, definitive list of Aristotelian 'categories'. The 'substance' of the word had to be distinguished from its 'accidents'—the different forms it assumed according to its syntactic function and its particular 'mode of signifying'. Certain 'accidental' categories were typical and definitive for particular 'parts of speech': nouns were inflected for *case* (nominative, accusative, etc.) and *number* (singular, plural), and belonged to a particular *gender* (masculine, feminine, neuter); verbs were inflected for *tense* (present, past, future), *person*, *number*, etc.; and so on. What are traditionally referred to as 'the grammatical categories' are therefore the 'accidental' categories of grammatical theory; and this explains the older term 'accidence' (from the Latin *accidentia*) for what we now refer to as 'inflexional variation'.

Some of the 'accidental' grammatical categories, such as *tense* (derived from the Latin word for 'time'), could be referred without difficulty to the Aristotelian categories of predication. Others, such as *case*, were peculiar to language. What is important for our purpose is not a detailed understanding of the relation between the Aristotelian categories and the traditional 'grammatical categories', but merely an appreciation of the general relationship between them. The assumed universality of the Aristotelian categories of predication reinforced, or promoted, the further assumption that the 'grammatical categories' were universal features of human language: that every language necessarily manifested such categories as tense, number, case, etc.; and that these categories were typical of particular 'parts of speech'.

7.1.3 *'Major' and 'minor' parts of speech*

The 'parts of speech' themselves were also defined by reference to the Aristotelian 'categories' (independently of their inflexion according to such 'accidental' categories as case, tense, etc.). Nouns were defined, according to their 'mode of signifying', as words which referred to 'substances' (hence the term 'substantive'); adjectives as words which denoted 'qualities' and so on. The reader will doubtless be familiar with definitions of the 'parts of speech' cast in this traditional, 'notional' terminology. Later in this chapter we shall investigate the validity of such definitions.

The Aristotelian opposition of 'matter' and 'form' was also invoked by certain grammarians to distinguish between what we may refer to as *major* and *minor* 'parts of speech'. Only the major 'parts of speech' (nouns, verbs, adjectives and adverbs) were meaningful in the proper sense of the term: they 'signified' the objects of thought which constituted the 'matter' of discourse. The other 'parts of speech' (prepositions, conjunctions, etc.) did not 'signify' anything of themselves, but merely contributed to the total meaning of sentences by imposing upon them a certain 'form', or organization. This distinction recalls, on the one hand, that made by Aristotle between 'words' properly so called and 'conjunctions' (cf. 1.2.5) and, on the other, the distinction traditionally drawn between 'full' and 'empty' words in Chinese grammatical theory. It was taken up and given further currency by the grammarians of the Port Royal (cf. 1.2.8), and was used by Leibniz and many philosophers who have been influenced by him. The distinction is frequently drawn in modern treatments of grammatical theory in terms of 'lexical' and 'grammatical' meaning (cf. 9.5.1).

7.1.4 *Logic and grammar*

To conclude the present section, something must be said about the general influence of 'Aristotelian' logic upon traditional grammatical theory. It has frequently been asserted by philosophers that Aristotle's theory of 'categories', especially his distinction between 'substance' and 'accidence', is simply a reflection of the grammatical structure of Greek, and that if he had spoken a language with a very different grammatical structure he would have established a quite different set of 'categories' and possibly a different system of logic. On the other hand, grammarians are apt to say that some of the distinctions drawn in traditional grammar are purely 'logical' distinctions (for example, the distinction between proper nouns and common nouns) and cannot be justified for Greek and Latin. The fact that both these positions have been maintained suggests that the relationship between traditional grammar and 'Aristotelian' logic is far more complex than is commonly supposed. And this is, in fact, the case. As we shall see later in this chapter, recent developments in the theory of syntax (in particular, the distinction of 'deep' and 'surface' structure: cf. 6.6.1) may enable us to determine to what degree the 'categories' of logic and grammar are congruent with one another.

7.1.5 *Primary, secondary and functional categories*

For terminological convenience in the sections which follow, we shall refer to the 'parts of speech' as *primary* grammatical categories and such notions as tense, mood, case, etc., as *secondary* grammatical categories. The traditional syntactic notions of 'subject', 'predicate', 'object', etc., will be referred to as *functional* categories. For reasons which will become clear presently we will deal first with the secondary grammatical categories.

Most treatments of what we are calling, for convenience, the secondary grammatical categories give pride of place to the traditionally-recognized inflexional categories of Latin and Greek: *number*, *gender* and *case* for the noun; *person*, *tense*, *mood* and *voice* for the verb. It will be recalled that *case* was regarded as criterial for the noun and *tense* for the verb in traditional inflexional definitions of the parts of speech (cf. 1.2.5). The present treatment will follow the general practice by concentrating upon the categories of traditional grammar. We shall see that, although these categories are of fairly wide applicability, they require reformulation in the framework of modern generative grammar, which takes syntax as primary and regards inflexion as but one way of specifying syntactic relationships within sentences (cf. 5.4.2).

7.2 Deictic categories

7.2.1 *Deixis and the situation of utterance*

At this point we will introduce the notion of *deixis* to which we shall make frequent appeal in the discussion of grammatical categories. Every language-utterance is made in a particular place and at a particular time: it occurs in a certain spatio-temporal situation. It is made by a particular person (the speaker) and is usually addressed to some other person (the hearer); the speaker and the hearer, we will say, are *typically* distinct from one another (there may of course be more than one hearer) and moreover are *typically* in the same spatio-temporal situation. (There are many common situations of utterance which are 'untypical' in these respects: it is possible to 'talk to oneself'; and, if one is speaking on the telephone, the hearer will not be in the same spatio-temporal situation.) We will further assume that the typical utterance includes a reference to some object or person (which may or may not be distinct from the speaker and hearer, cf. *Have you finished yet?* : *Has he finished yet?*, etc.); for the present, we will call this object or person to which reference is made in the utterance the 'subject of discourse'. The utterance will therefore contain as many 'subjects of discourse' as there are lexical items in the utterance which refer to objects and persons.

The notion of *deixis* (which is merely the Greek word for 'pointing' or 'indicating'—it has become a technical term of grammatical theory) is introduced to handle the 'orientational' features of language which are relative to the time and place of utterance. The so-called 'personal pronouns' (*I, you, he*, etc.) constitute only one class of the elements in language whose meaning is to be stated with reference to the 'deictic co-ordinates' of the typical situation of utterance. Other elements which include a component of deixis are such adverbials of place and time as *here* and *there* ('in the vicinity of the speaker: 'not in the vicinity of the speaker') and *now* and *then* ('at the time of speaking': 'not at the time of speaking'). These are just the most obvious instances of the way in which the grammatical structure of language may reflect the spatio-temporal co-ordinates of the typical situation of utterance.

The typical situation of utterance is *egocentric*: as the role of speaker is transferred from one participant to another in a conversation, so the 'centre' of the deictic system switches (*I* being used by each speaker to refer to himself, *you* being used to refer to the hearer). The speaker is always at the centre, as it were, of the situation of utterance. It should also be observed that the participants in a situation of utterance not only assume the roles of speaker and hearer (we shall refer to these as *roles*). They may also stand in a certain linguistically-relevant relationship of *status* vis-à-vis one another (parent: child, master: servant, teacher: pupil, etc.). Status-relations interact with, and, in certain languages, may override the participant roles of speaker and hearer.

7.2.2 *Person*

The category of *person* is clearly definable with reference to the notion of participant-roles: the 'first' person is used by the speaker to refer to himself as a subject of discourse; the 'second' person is used to refer to the hearer; and the 'third' person is used to refer to persons or things other than the speaker and hearer. So much is straight-forward enough. There are, however, a number of points in the traditional treatment of the category of person which require clarification.

The 'third' person is to be distinguished from the 'first' and 'second' persons in several respects. The speaker and hearer are necessarily present in the situation, whereas other persons and things to which reference is made may not only be absent from the situation of utterance, they may be left unidentified. This means that the category of third person may combine with such other categories as 'definite' or 'indefinite' and 'proximate' or 'remote' (the category of 'proximity' being determined, as we shall see, by reference to the participants). The English pronouns *he*, *she* and *it* are definite, as against *someone*, *somebody* and *something*, which are indefinite. In Turkish the category of definiteness is obligatorily marked (by means of a suffix) in the pronouns of the first and second person (in the accusative) in the same way as it is marked, optionally, for nouns: cf. *ben-i*, 'me', *sen-i*, 'you', *kitab-i*, 'the book' v. *kitab*, 'a book'. But the English pronouns of first and second person are no less definite than the corresponding pronouns in Turkish. From the grammatical point of view, independently of their phonological realization, pronouns of first and second person are necessarily 'definite' (+def), whereas third person pronouns may be either 'definite' or 'indefinite' ($\pm$ def), if this distinction is actualized in the language in question. Furthermore, pronouns of the first and second person necessarily refer to human beings. (In fables and fairy-stories, animals and things are linguistically 'personified' and, when they are made to speak of themselves in languages whose gender-system makes this clear, it seems to be the case that they are automatically 're-categorized' as animate for the purpose.) Pronouns of the third person may refer to human beings, to animals and to things. This does not mean, of course, that these distinctions are syntactically relevant in the third person for all languages; merely that, if such distinctions are drawn in a particular language they will be neutral-ized in combination with first and second person. Finally, it seems reasonable to say that, whereas first and second person are the positive members of the category of person, third person is essen-tially a negative notion; unlike first and second person, it does not necessarily refer to participants in the situation of utterance. In many languages there is no overt recognition of what is traditionally called third person, merely the absence of the formal markers of first and second person.

Traditional terminology is rather misleading in the way in which it represents the combination of the categories of person and *number*. It is clear, for instance, that *we* ('first person plural') does not normally stand in the same relationship to *I* ('first person singular') as *boys*, *cows*, etc., do to *boy*, *cow*, etc. The pronoun *we* is to be interpreted as 'I, in addition to one or more other persons'; and the other persons may or may not include the hearer. In other words, *we* is not 'the plural of *I*': rather, it includes a reference to 'I' and is plural. According to whether the 'first person plural' pronoun includes a reference to the hearer or not, it is customary to distinguish between an 'inclusive' and an 'exclusive' use of the pronoun. Although this distinction is generally not relevant in English, there are many languages in which the distinction between the 'inclusive' and the 'exclusive' use of the 'first person plural' is drawn systematically in sentences of all types and realized as a distinction between two phonologically-unrelated pronouns. A distinction might also be made between an 'inclusive' and 'exclusive' use of the 'second person plural' (in a slightly different sense of 'inclusive' *v.* 'exclusive'). The English pronoun *you* may of course be either singular or plural (cf. *wash yourself* and *wash yourselves*). As a plural form, it may be either 'inclusive' (referring only to the hearers present—in which case it is the plural of the singular *you*, in the same sense as *cows* is the plural of *cow*) or 'exclusive' (referring to some other person, or persons, in addition to the hearer, or hearers). There may be good reason to suggest, therefore, that 'first' (*ego*) and 'second' (*tu*) are not of equal status in the category of person: that the primary distinction is between 'first' (+ *ego*: 'plus ego') and 'not-first' (− *ego*: 'minus ego') and that the distinction of 'second' and 'third' is secondary. If this is so, the correct syntactic analysis of the traditional singular personal pronouns of English in terms of their component deictic features would be as follows: *I* = [+ *ego*]; *you* (singular) = [− *ego*, + *tu*]; *he, she, it* = [− *ego*, − *tu*]. (*He, she* and *it* are further distinguished by the non-deictic features of gender. These features of gender are neutralized in English when person is combined with plural, *they* being neutral with respect to gender. This kind of neutralization is quite common: it is to be found, for instance, in Russian and German. By contrast, other languages, including French and Italian, maintain the distinction of gender in the plural personal pronouns. In French, for instance *il* 'he' and *elle* 'she' are matched in the plural by *ils* 'they' (masculine) and *elles* 'they' (feminine). But here there are neutralizations of a different sort which are operative. *Elles* is feminine in the sense that all the persons, or things, it refers to are feminine; *ils* is masculine in the sense that at least one of the persons, or things, referred to is masculine. In other words, masculine is here the dominant term of the gender system, as 'first' is the dominant term of the category of person.)

7.2.3 *Demonstrative pronouns and adverbs*

In this connexion one should mention the 'demonstrative pronouns' (e.g. *this, that: these, those*) and the 'situationally-bound adverbs of place' (e.g. *here, there*). It is evident that these forms 'include' an element of deixis; furthermore, that they are 'definite', rather than 'indefinite' (cf. *a, some* (...*or other*); *somewhere*), and that they are to be distinguished in terms of a category of 'proximity'. What is perhaps not so clear is that the category of *proximity* is typically determined in relation to the category of person. (Strictly speaking, both person and proximity are determined in relation to the elements of the typical situation of utterance.) Both *this* and *here* are to be interpreted as 'proximate' with respect to the speaker. It is to be noticed that, whereas English neutralizes the distinction between the 'second' and 'third' person in this category of 'proximity', there are languages for which this is not so. In both Latin and Turkish there is a three-term system of 'demonstrative' pronouns: Latin, *hic, iste, ille*; Turkish, *bu, şu, o*. The Latin *hic* and the Turkish *bu* correspond to the English *this*: they are 'first person demonstratives' (indicating proximity to the speaker). But Latin *iste* and *ille* and Turkish *şu* and *o* (which can generally be translated by the English *that*) are, respectively, 'second' and 'third person demonstratives'. *Iste* and *şu* indicate proximity to the hearer, whereas *ille* and *o* indicate remoteness from both speaker and hearer.

In many languages no distinction can be drawn between the 'demonstratives' and the 'third person pronouns'. This is the case, for example, in Turkish where *he, she* and *it* (if translated by a pronoun) would normally be translated with *o* (there is no gender in Turkish), and *they* with the plural form of the same 'demonstrative', *onlar*. In classical Latin (as in Greek), there was no 'third person pronoun' at all: where 'pronominal' reference was made to some 'subject of discourse' (other than the speaker or hearer), the appropriate 'demonstrative' was used—*hic, iste* or *ille* (in addition to these three and distinguished as to 'proximity' in relation to person, there was also the word *is*, which was not normally used for the grammatical subject, but in other syntactic positions was the most 'neutral' of the 'demonstrative pronouns', standing outside the category of 'proximity'). The 'third person pronouns' of the Romance languages (French, Italian, Spanish, etc.) have in fact developed from 'demonstrative pronouns'; and the same is true of the 'third person pronouns' of English and German. Moreover, in all these languages the 'definite article' (English, *the*; French, *le, la*; etc.) has also developed from what was originally a 'demonstrative pronoun'. This gives us the clue to the relationship between these three different 'parts of speech'. They all 'include' the feature 'definite': from this point of view *the man, this man, that man* contrast with *a man*, and *he* contrasts with *someone*. But *the man* and *he*, being undetermined with respect to proximity, are both in contrast with *this man* ('proximate') and *that man* ('remote'). The traditional separation of the 'articles', the 'personal pronouns' and the 'demonstrative pronouns' obscures these relationships.

7.2.4. *'Attraction' of person and number*

In this brief account of the category of person, it is impossible to pursue all the interesting additional distinctions that are to be found in particular languages. Reference should be made, however, to the phenomenon of 'attraction' and also to the 'honorific dimension' of the system of 'personal pronouns'. What is meant by 'attraction' in this connexion may be illustrated from Russian and French. A sentence such as *John and I arrived* might be translated into Russian and French respectively as *My s Ivanom priechali* (literally 'We with John arrived') and *Nous sommes arrivés avec Jean* (literally 'We arrived with John'). In both instances, it will be observed, the phrase 'with John' specifies the other person already included in the reference of the pronoun 'we'. 'Attractions' of this kind illustrate further the necessity of analysing the 'personal pronouns' which appear in the surface structure of sentences into their component features of deixis and number.

7.2.5 *'Honorific' distinctions*

The 'honorific' dimension is introduced to account for the differentiation of the personal pronouns in certain languages, not in terms of their reference to the *roles* of the participants in the situation of utterance, but in terms of their relative *status* or degree of *intimacy*. Well-known and obvious instances of this are to be found in a number of European languages (e.g. French, German, Russian, Italian, etc.) where the 'second person singular pronoun' is used in addressing children and friends (there are considerable differences in the conventions governing the application of the 'intimate' form in the various languages and they must be stated with reference to social class and other factors) and the 'second person plural' or some other pronominal form (e.g. Spanish *usted*) is used for more 'formal' reference to the hearer. It is important to realize that such uses of a 'plural' or 'third person' form to refer to the hearer do not invalidate the distinction of number in the 'second person' or the distinction of the 'second' and 'third' person in the singular. Not only is the recognition of these distinctions still required for the proper semantic interpretation of sentences containing the 'honorific' form of reference to the hearer, it is frequently required also in the statement of the syntactic rules for gender or number concord.

7.2.6 *Person and the verb*

Traditionally, person is regarded as a category of the verb; and it is certainly marked in the inflexional form of the verb or verb phrase in many languages. This fact may be illustrated with reference to the following Latin words: *amo* 'I love', *amas* 'you love', *amat* 'he, she loves'. In Latin, and in many other languages, there is normally no pronominal specification of the subject: *ego amo, tu amas*, etc., would be employed only when *ego* ('I'), *tu* ('you'), etc., are emphasized or contrasted with some other form, expressed or implied. On the basis of evidence such as this, it is frequently suggested that the selection of the pronoun, when it occurs, is controlled by the form of the verb: that *amo*, under conditions of emphasis, selects *ego*; that *amas* selects *tu*; and so on. This view is, however, mistaken, since it takes no account of the distinction between the 'surface' structure of sentences and their underlying 'deep' structure. In terms of the underlying, semantically-interpretable, structure of sentences, there is little difference between Latin and English. In both cases we must postulate an abstract 'pronominal' element (determined with respect to person and number) which is the subject of the verb and controls the rules governing the phonological realization of the verb in surface structure. This 'pronominal' element is not normally realized in Latin: in the generation of Latin sentences it is deleted, after the attachment of the features of person and number to the verb, whereas in English it is 'rewritten' by the rules of phonological realization as a 'personal pronoun' (*I*, *you*, etc.). As we have seen, the 'pronominal' element is also given a phonological realization in Latin under certain conditions of emphasis or contrast. And it is phonologically realized (as *me*, *te*, etc.) in other syntactic environments: cf. (*dixit*) *me amare*..., '(He said) that I was in love with...'. In general syntactic theory, person (like number) is only secondarily, and derivatively, a category of the verb; and that only in certain languages.

7.3   Number and gender

7.3.1   *Number and countability*

The most common manifestation of the category of *number* is the distinction between *singular* and *plural* (cf. *boy*: *boys*, etc.), which is found in many languages all over the world. This distinction clearly rests upon the recognition of persons, animals and objects which can be enumerated (as 'one' or 'more than one') and referred to, individually or collectively, by means of nouns. Number is therefore a category of the noun; we have already seen that it combines in a special way with the category of person to form 'personal pronouns' (which may be regarded as syntactically equivalent to nouns).

At first sight, it might appear that the application of the distinction between 'one' and 'more than one' is straightforward enough. It is important to realize, however, that what counts as 'one object', and

what as 'more than one object', 'a group of objects' or an unindividu-
ated 'mass of material', in the inanimate world at least, is to a
considerable degree determined by the lexical structure of particular
languages. For example, the English word *grape* is a 'countable' noun,
in the sense that it can be pluralized (*Will you have some grapes?*, *He
ate six grapes*), whereas the German *Traube* and the Russian *vinograd*
are 'mass' nouns (like the English word *fruit*). The French word *raisin*
may be used in the singular either as a 'mass' noun (*Vous voulez du
raisin?*) or as a 'collective' noun (*Prenez un raisin*—which is normally
to be translated, not as 'Have a grape', but 'Have some grapes'). By
contrast, French *fruit* and the Russian *frukt* are 'countable' (cf. *Have
some fruit*: *Prenez un fruit*). And in all the languages referred to here
certain words may be used either as 'mass' or 'countable' nouns
(cf. *Have some grapefruit*: *Have a grapefruit*). Examples like this
could be multiplied indefinitely, to demonstrate the point that the
lexical categorization of the world in terms of 'countable', 'collective' and 'mass' nouns varies considerably from language to language,
even when the languages in question do have such syntactically-
distinct subclasses.

7.3.2 *'Secondary recategorization'*

Over and above the primary categorization of nouns in such terms as
'countable', 'mass' and 'collective', there may be the possibility of
'secondary recategorization'. In English, for example, most 'mass'
nouns may be 'recategorized' as 'countable' in certain contexts (cf.
They drink three or four different wines at every meal). There may be
individual 'anomalies': it has often been pointed out that *oats*,
unlike *wheat*, *barley*, etc., is plural (cf. *these oats*: *this wheat*), but it is
nonetheless a 'mass', rather than a 'countable', noun. (Not only is it
impossible to singularize *oats*—to talk of *one oat as distinct from
*two oats—but its anomalous status creates a certain tension in respect
of 'secondary recategorization'. One might wonder whether *One oats
is very like another* is possible or not.) To be distinguished from a
word like *oats* are such 'plural only' forms as *scissors*, *trousers*, etc.;
and also certain 'collectives' like *committee*, *Government* (cf. *This
Government have/has decided...*, but not **These Government have
decided...*). Finally, there may be stylistic differences between the
usage of different groups in the speech-community. It is noticeable,
for instance, that hunters tend to use such words as *lion*, *elephant*,
buffalo, etc., as 'semi-mass' nouns: cf. *an elephant*, but also *a herd of*

elephant. Compare, for all styles of English, *a fish*: *a shoal of fish*; and contrast, on the one hand, *a cow*: *a herd of cows*, and, on the other, **a cattle*: *a herd of cattle*. The analysis of the category of number in particular languages may be a very complex matter.

The notion of 'countability' is inherent in the lexical structure of all human languages, since (as we shall see in our discussion of the 'parts of speech': cf. 7.6.1 ff.) the recognition of what is probably a universal primary category of language, the noun, presupposes the 'individuation' and enumeration of persons, animals and at least a certain number of perceptually-discrete objects. However, not all languages have a grammatical category of number. In Chinese and Vietnamese (and many other languages), the distinction between, for example, 'I wrote a letter' and 'I wrote some letters' can be made, if necessary, by means of a numeral or a word meaning 'several', but it may be equally well left unexpressed. Other languages (e.g. Classical Greek, Sanskrit and certain Slavonic languages) have a dual, in addition to a singular and plural (the dual being used to refer to two objects: cf. Greek *ámphō kheîre* 'both hands'—but in Greek there was considerable fluctuation in the use of the dual and the plural). Fijian and a few other languages are reported to have a trial (for reference to three objects) as well as a singular, dual and plural.

7.3.3 *Gender*

The traditional names for the three *genders* found in the classical Indo-European languages—'masculine', 'feminine' and 'neuter'—clearly reflect the association which traditional grammar established between sex and gender (cf. 1.2.5). But the term 'gender' itself derives from an extremely general word meaning 'class' or 'kind' (Latin *genus*): the three genders of Greek and Latin were the three main noun-classes recognized in the grammar. From the grammatical point of view, the nouns of Greek and Latin were classified into three genders in order to account for two distinct phenomena: (i) pronominal reference, and (ii) adjectival concord (or 'agreement'). For the same reasons, the nouns of French, Italian and Spanish are classified into two genders, the nouns of Russian and German into three genders, the nouns of Swahili into at least six genders, and so on. Gender plays a relatively minor part in the grammar of English by comparison with its role in many other languages. There is no gender-concord; and the reference of the pronouns *he*, *she* and *it* is very largely determined by what is sometimes referred to as 'natural' gender—for English, this depends upon the classification of persons and objects as male, female or inanimate. The operation of gender-concord will be illustrated below from Swahili.

7.3.4   'Natural' basis for gender

The first general point that must be made is that the recognition of gender as a grammatical category is logically independent of any particular semantic association that might be established between the gender of a noun and the physical or other properties of the persons or objects denoted by that noun. On the other hand, it is a matter of empirical fact that in most languages that have gender (defined as a classification of nouns for pronominal reference or concord) there is some 'natural', semantic basis for the classification. This is not necessarily sex. It may be shape, texture, colour, edibility—in short, any set of 'natural' properties. The degree of correspondence between the classification of nouns by grammatical gender and a classification of the persons and objects denoted by them according to the relevant 'natural' properties will vary considerably from language to language. It is well-known that in the Indo-European languages many words which denote inanimate objects are 'masculine' or 'feminine' in gender; to this degree 'natural' and grammatical gender fail to correspond.

7.3.5   Gender in Swahili

In Swahili (and other Bantu languages) the nouns are classified into genders according to the singular and plural prefixes attached to them. There are at least six genders in Swahili (and many more in some other Bantu languages). They may be illustrated by the following words:

  I. *mtu, watu* ('person', 'people')

  II. *kisu, visu* ('knife', 'knives')

  III. *mti, miti* ('tree', 'trees')

  IV. *nchi, nchi* ('country', 'countries')

  V. *jiwe, mawe* ('stone', 'stones')

  VI. *udevu, ndevu* ('single hair of beard', 'beard')

It will be observed that, although there are only five singular prefixes and five plural prefixes (*m-, ki-, n-, ji-, u-,* and *wa-, vi-, m-, n-, ma-,* respectively), the possibilities of combination yield six classes of nouns (cf. classes I and III, on the one hand, and IV and VI, on the other). Gender is relevant, not only for the selection of the correct singular or plural form of any given noun, but also for the determination of the verbs, adjectives and other modifiers in construction with it:

> *mtu amefika, watu wamefika* ('The man has arrived', 'The people have arrived')
>
> *kisu kimeanguka, visu vimeanguka* ('The knife fell', 'The knives fell')
>
> *mti umekauka, miti imekauka* ('The tree withered', 'The trees withered')
>
> *mtu mzuri yule, watu wazuri wale* ('That beautiful person', 'Those beautiful people')
>
> *miti mzuri ule, miti mizuri ile* ('That beautiful tree', 'Those beautiful trees')

From these examples it will be clear that there is gender-concord between the subject of the sentence and the predicate (cf. the first three pairs of sentences with the prefix-patterns *m- a-, wa- wa-*; *ki- ki-, vi- vi-*; *m- u-, mi- i-*: notice that in the case of class I in the singular and class III in both the singular and the plural the prefix on the verb differs from the prefix of the noun) and also between any noun and the adjectives and other modifiers dependent upon it within the same phrase (cf. the fourth and fifth pairs with the prefix-patterns *m- m- yu-, wa- wa- wa-*; *m- m- u-, mi- mi- i-*: the word-order in these phrases is noun-adjective-demonstrative).

The subject prefix is an obligatory part of the verb in Swahili, whether there is a noun present as the subject of the sentence or not: cf. *Amefika, Wamefika* ('He/She has arrived', 'They have arrived'). The subject prefixes therefore operate like pronouns; and they are determined by the gender of the nouns they refer to. For example, *kimeanguka* would be used in reference to a word of class II, but *umeanguka* in reference to a class III word. The verb may also have an object prefix: cf. *Amewaona, Ameviona, Amemiona*, etc. ('He saw them', where the prefixes *wa-, vi-, mi-*, etc. refer to nouns of classes I, II, III, etc.). Pronouns of the first and second person also occur in the same positions to mark the subject or object of the verb: cf. *Nimewaona, Umewaona, Tumewaona*, etc. ('I, you, we, etc., saw them'). The subject and object prefixes in the verb thus have a pronominal function (cf. 7.2.2) in addition to marking concord between the verb and the nouns actually present in the sentence.

Although there is no distinction of masculine and feminine in the Swahili classification of nouns, there is some 'natural' basis to the gender system. Most nouns denoting human beings fall into class I, words denoting inanimate objects into class II, names of trees, plants, etc., into class III, abstract nouns into class VI, and so on. There are many words whose classification appears arbitrary or anomalous, but this does not invalidate the statement that there is a considerable degree of correspondence between gender and a classification of nouns from a semantic point of view.

7.3.6 *Clash between 'natural' and 'grammatical' gender*

But the distinction between 'animate' and 'inanimate' nouns cuts across their classification by gender in Swahili, and in certain circumstances may be in conflict with it. There are a number of nouns denoting human beings which belong to classes other than class I. Being 'animate', they tend to determine the verbal prefixes according to the principle of selection for class I nouns (although they select the prefixes corresponding to their own gender-class in the adjectives and modifiers dependent upon them within a noun-phrase). This also holds for most nouns which refer to animals (though the majority of these words belong to class IV). In other words, there is a certain clash between 'natural' and 'grammatical' gender which is reflected in the syntax of the language. It may be worth pointing out that this is also true in the more familiar European languages with anomalous gender classifications. For instance, in French the word *professeur* is masculine, although it may refer to a man or a woman. The gender of the noun determines concord within the noun-phrase as masculine, regardless of whether the person referred to is male or female: *le nouveau professeur* ('the new teacher'). But when the noun *professeur* refers to a woman and an adjective which would normally be in concord with it occurs in the predicate, there is a clash between the masculine gender of the noun and the female sex of the person denoted by the noun. Neither the masculine form of the adjective (e.g. *beau*) nor its feminine form (*belle*) can be used appropriately in these circumstances without resolving, as it were, the 'conflict' between 'grammatical' and 'natural' gender. Neither *Le nouveau professeur est beau* (which necessarily refers to a man) nor **Le nouveau professeur est belle* (which is ungrammatical) is possible. The 'conflict' is resolved with a sentence like *Elle est belle, le nouveau professeur* ('She is beautiful, the new teacher'). The resulting construction, it will be observed, is very similar syntactically to the normal pattern in Swahili (and a number of other languages); the subject of the sentence is referred to both pronominally and by means of a noun. In both languages 'grammatical' gender is dominant within the noun-phrase; but 'natural' gender may prevail in pronominal reference and for concord with the predicate. This phenomenon, which is found in a number of languages, would suggest that grammatical cohesion is stronger in the noun-phrase than it is between subject and predicate. It also shows that there is indeed some 'natural' basis for the gender systems of the languages in question.

7.3.7 *Redundancy of gender*

From the semantic point of view, gender distinctions in the noun are usually redundant. For instance, the forms *la* and *ronde* (rather than *le* and *rond*) are determined by the feminine gender of the noun *table* with which they are in concord in the French phrase *la table ronde* ('the round table'). It is true that there are a few homonyms in French which are distinguished by their gender: e.g. *le mousse*: *la mousse* ('the cabin boy': 'the moss'). Although the occurrence of *le* rather than *la* with *mousse* would be sufficient to resolve any potential ambiguity between 'cabin boy' and 'moss', it seems clear that the two words would rarely be used in the same context. The functional load of the difference in gender is therefore negligible (cf. 2.4.1). This would seem to be true of most pairs of homonyms that have a different gender in French. It is probably true of the Indo-European languages generally.

Gender is semantically relevant, however, in the case of words which are traditionally described as having 'common gender'. For example, the French word *enfant* ('child') is inherently indeterminate with regard to gender, but is determined as either masculine or feminine according to the sex of the child referred to. Gender is also semantically relevant in the case of sets of words, such as the French pairs *le chien*: *la chienne* ('dog': 'bitch'), *le chat*: *la chatte* ('cat': 'female cat'), etc., where the formally-marked difference of gender is used systematically to make a particular difference of meaning. Compare, for example, the Spanish and Italian words for 'boy' and 'girl': *muchacho, muchacha*; *ragazzo, ragazza*. In Swahili, too, the use of one prefix rather than another may have the effect of determining the sense of a noun in a particular way. For example, if *-tu* occurs with class I prefixes (*m-, wa-*) it means 'person', but if it occurs with class II prefixes (*ki-, vi-*) it means 'thing': in other words,

-tu itself is neutral as between the senses 'person' and 'thing', but is determined as one or the other by giving it 'human' or 'inanimate' gender in a particular context. (This is no different in principle from the determination of the Italian word-stem *ragazz-* as either 'boy' or 'girl' according to the particular gender suffix that is attached to it.) But such instances are untypical. For most nouns, both in Indo-European and Bantu languages, gender is inherent. Where there is some correspondence between 'natural' and grammatical gender, it is usually the meaning of the noun which may be regarded as determining the gender, rather than the converse. It is in this sense that gender distinctions in nouns are semantically irrelevant (except for such instances of 'common gender' and formally-related sets of words as have been exemplified in this paragraph). And it is worth noting that the most common of the words that are semantically related in a manner that could be marked by gender tend to be completely different in phonological form: the absence of phonological correspondence that is found in the English or French pairs *boy*: *girl*, *garçon*: *fille* is more typical of the way the vocabulary is organized with respect to common words than is the parallelism of the Italian *ragazzo*: *ragazza*. Gender-concord is a 'surface-structure' phenomenon of certain languages (cf. 6.6.1). It is clearly the pronominal function of gender which is of primary importance in communication.

7.3.8 'Classifiers'

Rather similar to the category of gender is the system of noun-classification for the purpose of enumeration and individuation that is found in many languages of south-east Asia. In Chinese, for example, unless the noun itself denotes a unit of measurement (e.g. *nián*, 'year', *tiān*, 'day'), it must be preceded by a 'classifier' when it occurs with a numeral or a demonstrative (*zhè*, 'this'). Some of the classifiers are very general and may be regarded as semantically empty. Others are specific to certain classes of nouns, and they may even be used themselves elsewhere as nouns. It is as if the words *thing*, *person*, *animal*, *tree*, *fruit*, etc., in English were used in this way: so that, for instance, one would say *that person policeman*, *three tree banana* (for 'that policeman', 'three banana trees'); and the difference between 'three bananas' and 'three banana trees' would be made solely in the classifier—*three fruit banana*: *three tree banana*.

7.4 Case

7.4.1 *The term 'case'*

The nouns (as well as the pronouns and adjectives) of Greek and Latin were classified by traditional grammarians according to particular paradigms of *declension* for the *inflexional* categories of *case* and number. The terminology that has just been employed—'inflexion', 'case', and 'declension' (the word 'paradigm' simply meant 'pattern' or 'model': cf. 1.2.3)—testifies to the importance that traditional grammar has always attached to the category of case in the definition and classification of nouns. The Latin word *casus* (and the Greek word which it translates) means 'falling' or 'deviation'. Whatever might be the precise metaphorical origin of the technical sense of the term in grammatical theory (and there is some dispute about this), it is clear that variation in the forms of a lexeme according to the syntax of the language was regarded as deviation from its normal 'upright' form (cf. 1.2.5; for 'lexeme', see 5.4.4). The terms 'inflexion' and 'declension' are explained by the same metaphor. It was the Stoics who gave to the word 'case' the more particular sense that it has since borne in grammatical terminology (cf. 1.2.5). Case was the most important of the inflexional categories of the noun, as tense was the most important inflexional category of the verb. It is significant that the term 'case' (originally more or less synonymous with what was later called 'inflexion') was restricted to one particular inflexional category. The reason for this would seem to be that most of the other categories—gender, number, tense, person, etc.—could be related to a principle of semantic classification. Although each case of the noun was given a label suggestive of at least one of its principal semantic functions (e.g. the 'dative' was the case associated with the notion of 'giving', the 'ablative' was the case associated with 'removal', etc.), it was impossible to give a satisfactory general definition of the category of case itself in semantic terms. In effect, traditional definitions of the category of case for Latin and Greek (and other Indo-European languages) say little more than the following: of the two inflexional categories of the noun, one is number (definable in semantic terms and relatable to the Aristotelian category of quantity), the other is case. The category of case was, as it were, the most peculiarly grammatical of all the traditional categories of inflexion, for it had no counterpart in the sister sciences of logic, epistemology and metaphysics.

7.4.2 Case in Latin and Turkish

At this point it will be helpful to refer to three Latin paradigms illustrating some of the most common patterns of declension. The paradigms are set out in the traditional way in Table 9. We shall not discuss the origin and significance of the traditional names for the cases in Latin. It is sufficient to say that the most common function of the 'nominative' is to mark the subject of the sentence; the 'vocative' is the case of address; the 'accusative' is used to mark the object of a transitive verb; the 'genitive' is the case of 'possession'; the 'dative' marks the indirect object (e.g. the equivalent of *boy* would be in the dative and the equivalent of *book* in the accusative in the Latin translation of *I gave the boy a book*); and the 'ablative', has a variety of functions, including that of marking the 'instrument' with which something is done (e.g. the equivalent of *sword* in the translation of *I killed him with a sword*). It should also be noted: that particular classes of verbs may determine their objects in cases other than the accusative; that different prepositions select particular cases (most commonly the accusative or the ablative); and that the accusative and the ablative (with and without prepositions) have various

Table 9. *Three Latin declensions*

(The lexeme PUELLA 'girl' is feminine, LUPUS 'wolf' is masculine, BELLUM 'war' is neuter.)

Singular

Nominative	puella	lupus	bellum
Vocative	puella	lupe	bellum
Accusative	puellam	lupum	bellum
Genitive	puellae	lupī	bellī
Dative	puellae	lupō	bellō
Ablative	puellā	lupō	bellō

Plural

Nominative	puellae	lupī	bella
Vocative	puellae	lupī	bella
Accusative	puellās	lupōs	bella
Genitive	puellārum	lupōrum	bellōrum
Dative	puellīs	lupīs	bellīs
Ablative	puellīs	lupīs	bellīs

'adverbial' functions with respect to the distinctions of place and time. All these points will be of importance in the general discussion. We have started with Latin, since it exemplifies a number of more general and more particular features of the category of case in the Indo-European languages. As we shall see, the main problem in defining case as a grammatical category is that of deciding just how many of the more particular 'Indo-European' features we wish to preserve in the definition.

It has already been pointed out in an earlier chapter that case and number are 'fused' in Latin, in the sense that the inflexional suffixes (in those instances where there is determinacy of segmentation into stem and suffix) mark the noun simultaneously for a particular case and a particular number; furthermore, that the combination of a particular case and a particular number may be marked by a quite different suffix in different 'declensions' and the same suffix may mark different combinations of case and number. In short, Latin is 'fusional' with respect to inflexion in the noun (cf. 5.3.8). There is no reason to make it a defining condition of the category of case that, either alone or 'fused' with some other nominal category, it should subclassify nouns into various declensions. The syntactic functions of the cases in Turkish are very similar to the functions of the cases in Latin, but, as we have already seen, they are marked by a suffix which (under the general principles of vowel harmony) is segmentable and constant for all nouns. There is thus only one regular pattern of 'declension' in Turkish (cf. Table 10).

Six cases are traditionally recognized in the description of Latin. But there is no Latin noun in which all six cases are distinguished morphologically. For most declensions the nominative and the vocative forms are identical in both the singular and the plural: the principal exception to this generalization is illustrated by the declen-

Table 10. *Case and number in Turkish*

	Singular	Plural
Nominative	*ev*	*evler*
Accusative	*evi*	*evleri*
Genitive	*evin*	*evlerin*
Dative	*eve*	*evlere*
Locative	*evde*	*evlerde*
Ablative	*evden*	*evlerden*

sion of LUPUS—a very common paradigm. In some declensions there is no morphological distinction between the genitive and dative singular (cf. PUELLA), in others the dative and ablative singular are not distinguished (cf. LUPUS, BELLUM); in no Latin noun is the dative plural morphologically distinct from the ablative plural. The principle upon which the traditional paradigms are based seems to be this: six cases are recognized, because this is the minimum number of syntactically-relevant distinctions with which it is possible to state rules of selection valid for all declensions in both the singular and the plural. If all nouns were declined like LUPUS, it would be unnecessary to draw a distinction between the dative and the ablative; if all nouns were declined like BELLUM, there would no be need to distinguish the nominative, vocative and accusative; and so on. Within the traditional system of classification, it becomes possible to make such general statements as 'the case of "possession" is the genitive' (*puellae et lupī*, 'of the girl and the wolf'), 'the indirect object is in the dative' (*puellae et lupō*, 'to the girl and the wolf'), 'the preposition *a* selects the ablative' (*ā puella et lupō*, 'by the girl and the wolf'). But this general principle is not in fact applied consistently in most grammars of Latin. For there is at least one other case which must be recognized in the rules which relate the inflexion of nouns to the syntax of the sentence. This is the locative of 'place where'. Locative phrases of 'place where' in Latin are usually of the form preposition + ablative of the noun (e.g. *in rīpā*, 'on the bank'; *in oppidō*, 'in the town'). With a certain set of nouns, however, no preposition is used; and the form of the noun that occurs is identical with the genitive singular for most nouns that are declined like PUELLA, LUPUS and BELLUM (cf. *Romae*, 'in Rome'; *domī*, 'at home'), but for certain other declensions (which have not been illustrated) it is like the ablative. The rule for the selection of the locative case is usually stated in the form in which it has just been given. This is evidently inconsistent with the principle implicit in the determination of the six traditional cases. But this particular inconsistency is merely one of many. Its importance for general grammatical theory is that it shows quite clearly that syntactically-equivalent constructions may be realized by words or phrases which might be classified quite differently in terms of their 'surface structure'. Even if we were to say that there is a locative case in Latin which happens to be identical with the genitive or the ablative according to the declension and number of the noun, we should still have to identify, syntactically, such expressions as *Romae* ('locative') and *in oppidō* (preposition + ablative). Any general theory of case must recognize two facts: (i) that the same case may realize more than one syntactic function; and (ii) that a particular syntactic function may be realized by a variety of means in the same language—in particular, that there is a 'deeper' relationship between cases and prepositional phrases in Latin than the traditional analysis of inflexion would suggest. Both of these facts are relevant to the description of many other languages, both within and outside the Indo-European family.

7.4.3 *Interdependence of case and gender in Indo-European languages*

The traditional method of grammatical description, which did not proceed to the statement of the rules of syntax until the various inflexional forms had been classified and displayed in paradigms, might encourage us to believe that each case has a typical syntactic function, and that all the different cases of the noun occupy the same place, as it were, in the grammatical structure of a language. The case-systems we find, in the Indo-European languages and elsewhere, are far less symmetrical than they are made to appear in their traditional presentation. We have already seen that in Latin, case-distinctions are made in one declension that are not made in another, and that the traditional system of six cases rests upon the somewhat inconsistent application of a principle which might be described as postulating for all 'declensions' whatever distinctions of case are drawn in any one. But there is at least one point at which this principle tends to obscure a very important feature of the category of case, not only in Latin, but in the Indo-European languages generally. The distinction between a nominative and an accusative form is never made for neuter nouns in any of the Indo-European languages: the declension of BELLUM is typical in this respect. It is also typical in that, apart from its nominative/accusative plural (we may neglect the vocative for the moment), it is declined like the masculine LUPUS. This would suggest that the category of case is interdependent with the category of gender in the Indo-European languages. To the extent that gender is 'naturally' based, on animacy and sex, there are two distinctions involved, animate *v.* inanimate and feminine *v.* non-feminine. The difference between masculine and neuter in the nominative may be regarded as a consequence of the greater importance of the distinction between subject and object with respect to animate nouns. Since many inanimate nouns are either masculine or feminine, the distinction is drawn more or less redundantly for them. But the important point is that relatively few animate nouns are neuter. Even in languages without case-inflexion there is a strong connexion between animacy and subject-position: the principle is therefore one of very general application, and we shall return to it later (cf. 8.2.5). The same principle is even more clearly operative in Russian (and other Slavonic languages), where masculine and neuter nouns are related in essentially the same way as they are in Latin, but where the distinction between animate and inanimate is 'redrawn', as it were, for masculine nouns on the basis of the 'natural' criterion of animacy. The distinction between the subject-case and the object-case is made for masculine animate nouns by what is frequently described, rather misleadingly, as using the 'genitive' rather than 'accusative' (the latter being described as identical with the nominative for masculine and neuter nouns in conventional descriptions of Russian). The effect of this distinction between animate and inanimate in masculine nouns is to mark the object of a transitive verb as inflexionally different from the subject in that particularly important set of sentences in which both the subject and the object are animate: cf. *Ivan videl Borisa, Borisa videl Ivan* ('John saw Boris', where the *-a* marks *Borisa* as the object). By contrast, in *Boris videl stol, Stol videl Boris* ('Boris saw a/the table') the inanimate *stol* is unmarked inflexionally as the object of the verb *videl*. It is relatively uncommon for two inanimate nouns to be equiprobable as subject or object of the same transitive verb; and when this happens, the distinction can be made in a number of ways. The relative order of the two nouns is one of the ways in which, residually as it were, the syntactic distinction between subject and object may be drawn in Russian (and in a number of other languages, including Latin and Greek). We must therefore consider the relationship between word-order and case, as well as the relationship between prepositional phrases and case, in any general discussion of the category of case.

7.4.4 *Case and definiteness*

A further category which is interdependent with case in a number of languages is the deictic category of definiteness (marked in English by the article *the*). The Turkish 'accusative' is distinguished inflexionally from the 'nominative' only when the noun is definite (proper nouns, like personal pronouns, being inherently definite)—cf. *ev aldïm*, 'I bought a house': *evi aldïm*, 'I bought the house'. In Finnish, the converse situation holds: if definite, a singular noun may be in the 'nominative'; if it is indefinite, it will be in the 'partitive' (or 'genitive'). In making this point we are not only indicating once again that the traditionally-recognized case-inflexions of the noun do not necessarily have just one, or even a primary, syntactic function but also that definiteness, like animacy, tends to be interdependent with the syntactic distinction of subject and object even in languages without distinctions of case, like English.

7.4.5 *'Grammatical' functions*

In many treatments of the case-inflexions found in various languages a distinction is drawn between their 'grammatical' and their 'local' functions: the distinction is sometimes formulated in terms of an opposition between the more 'abstract' ('grammatical') and the more 'concrete' ('local') functions of particular cases. Of the 'grammatical' functions that have been recognized in the description of many languages, the following are of particular importance in the context of the present discussion:

    (i)   subjective ('nominative')

    (ii) objective ('accusative')

    (iii) indirect objective ('dative')

    (iv) adnominal 'possessive' ('genitive')

    (v) instrumental

    (vi) agentive

    (vii) comitative

In this section we will take for granted the general validity of most of these 'grammatical' functions, although we shall have occasion to examine them more closely later. It is important to realize that the functions themselves are not necessarily realized by case-distinctions in all languages. The labels in brackets after the first four terms in the list give the traditional names for the four cases which have these functions in the Indo-European languages—Latin, Greek, Sanskrit, German, Russian, etc. The reason why no labels are attached to the instrumental, agentive and comitative functions is that they are realized differently in different Indo-European languages. The following English sentences illustrate the application of the seven functions distinguished above:

    (1) *Bill died*

    (2) *John killed Bill*

(3 a) *John gave the book to Tom*

(3 b) *John gave Tom the book*

(4) *It is Harry's pencil*

(5) *John killed Bill with a knife*

(6) *Bill was killed by John with a knife*

(7) *John went to town with Mary*

In (1) *Bill* is the subject, in (2) and (5) *Bill* is the (direct) object; in (2), (3), (5) and (7) *John* is the subject; in both (3 a) and (3 b) *Tom* is the indirect object (n.b. the preposition *to* is normal with nouns, though not necessarily with pronouns, in the version exemplified by (3 a): there are many factors involved in the determination of the relative order of animate and inanimate nouns and of animate and inanimate pronouns, and there are certain dialectal differences); in (4) *Harry* is in the adnominal 'possessive' relationship with respect to *pencil*; in (5) and (6) *a knife* has the instrumental function; in (6) *John* is agentive; and in (7) *Mary* has comitative function ('in company with'). There are certain transformational relations between particular pairs of sentences: the object of the active (5) 'becomes' the subject of the corresponding passive (6), and the subject of (5) 'becomes' the agent in (6); the subject of the intransitive (1) 'becomes' the object of the transitive (2), given that the verbs *die* and *kill* are in a 'causative' relationship. Sentence (4) is also transformationally-related to *The pencil is Harry's* and *Harry has a pencil* (notice that definiteness and indefiniteness, as well as other factors, are involved in the distinction of these last two sentences). We will return to these several transformational relationships later, in the discussion of subject and object, active and passive, intransitive, transitive and causative. The term 'adnominal' should, however, be explained at this point.

It has long been recognized by grammarians that the term 'possessive' is semantically far too specific for the most typical function of the 'genitive'. Not only in Indo-European, but in many genetically-unrelated languages throughout the world, there is a striking parallelism (*a*) between the adjective and the 'genitive', on the one hand, and (*b*) between the 'genitive' and the subject and/or the object of a verb, on the other. The most typical function of what is called the 'possessive', or 'genitive', is to modify a noun, or noun-phrase, in an endocentric construction (for endocentric *v.* exocentric constructions, cf. 6.4.1), and this is also the most typical function of the adjective:

cf. *Harry's pencil, the red pencil.* It is this function to which the
traditional term 'adnominal' is given (as the term 'adverbial' is given
to the function of modifying the verb in an endocentric construction:
but the term 'adverb' was used far more widely in traditional
grammar). And the adnominal 'attributive' function of nouns and
adjectives is related to their 'predicative' function with 'the verb *to
be*': cf. *The pencil is Harry's*: *Harry's pencil, The pencil is red*: *the red
pencil*. So too the endocentric construction adnominal + nominalized
verb is transformationally-related to either the subject–predicate
construction or the object–verb construction. These are traditionally
distinguished as the subjective and objective 'genitive': cf. *Bill's
death, John's killing of Bill*: *Bill died, John killed Bill*: *Bill's murder
(by John)*: *Bill was murdered (by John)*. Here again one observes the
relationship between the object of the active and the subject of the
passive. In English, unlike Latin for instance, the adnominal subjective and objective functions have alternative realizations (which
are partly in free variation and partly in complementary distribution):
the 'genitive' *Bill's* and the 'prepositional phrase' *of Bill*. Only the
first of these is a case of the noun in the traditional sense of the term
case. In fact, even the English 'genitive' is at some remove from the
traditional conception of a case, since the inflexional suffix -*'s* is not
necessarily attached to the head-noun of the noun-phrase: cf. *the
queen of Sheba's beauty*. In the following chapter, we will endeavour
to relate adnominal function to subjective and objective function
within a more general framework.

   With the exception of the 'genitive' (*Bill's*) there are no case-
inflexions in the English noun. The distinction between subject and
object is marked in some of the personal pronouns (*I*: *me, he*: *him*,
etc.)—the object case also being used with prepositions (*to me, with
me*, etc.); but the distinction is not made for the inanimate, or neuter,
pronoun (*it*). Otherwise the 'grammatical' functions listed above are
marked in English by relative word-order or prepositions. The
sentences (1)–(7) illustrate this. In Latin, the instrumental case is the
'ablative', in Greek it is the 'dative', in Russian and Sanskrit it is a
case (distinct from the 'dative' in Russian and distinct from both the
'dative' and the 'ablative' in Sanskrit) to which the label 'instrumental' is given; in German a preposition is used. In Latin, the
agentive function is realized by a prepositional phrase ($\bar{a}$ + ablative), so
also in Greek and German; in Russian and Sanskrit the 'instrumental' case also marks the agent. In Latin, the comitative is
realized by a prepositional phrase (*cum* + ablative), so also in Greek,

Russian, German and Sanskrit. This very concise (and somewhat simplified) statement of the way the 'grammatical' functions are realized in a few Indo-European languages shows, first of all, that there is a similarity of function between the cases and prepositional phrases (with a particular preposition selecting a particular case-inflexion); and also that there is some overlap between the realizations of instrumental and agent on the one hand (cf. Russian and Sanskrit: and note that in English *by the knife* may be instrumental if there is no agent or active subject in the sentence), and between the instrumental and the comitative on the other (cf. *with the knife*: *with Bill*; the typically comitative construction in Latin is also found with instrumental function). There are two obvious ways of reacting to this 'overlap' of function: one is to say that the distinction between agentive and instrumental, or between instrumental and comitative, cannot be drawn sharply in general grammatical theory; the other is to say that the 'merging' that is found in particular languages (the traditional term for this is *syncretism*) rests upon the neutralization of the distinction at a more superficial level of the grammar or upon 'recategorization' in terms of animacy or some other syntactically-relevant notion. To illustrate this notion of *recategorization*: in a pair of sentences like *This is the man that killed Bill* and *This is the knife that killed Bill*, the phrases *the man* and *the knife* would appear to have the same syntactic function. One might maintain, however, that *the knife* is an instrumental which has been syntactically 're-categorized' (the traditional notion of 'personification' is here relevant) as an 'actor' rather than a 'thing', and that this is possible in English when there is no 'actor' overtly referred to as subject or agent. 'Notional' explanations of this kind, although they have been abused in the past, should not be condemned out of hand. In the present instance, the analysis finds some support in the fact that in the corresponding passive sentences *the man* and *the knife* are overtly distinguished as agent (*by*) and instrument (*with*): *This is the man that Bill was killed by*, *This is the knife that Bill was killed with*. If *This is the knife that Bill was killed by* is possible, it certainly suggests 're-categorization' of *the knife* as an agent.

7.4.6 *'Local' functions*

We may turn now to the so-called 'local' functions of the category of case. The term 'local' must be understood to include temporal as well as spatial distinctions, since these are commonly brought together in the 'orientational' systems associated with different languages (cf. 7.2.1): it is for this reason that many linguists prefer to talk of 'concrete', rather than 'local', case-distinctions. As we shall see, it is in connexion with the category of case that we find one of the strongest reasons for insisting upon the necessity of relating syntax to the spatiotemporal, 'orientational', framework within which language operates.

Table 11. *The so-called 'local' cases of Finnish*

'Interior'	Inessive	*talossa*	'in the house'
	Elative	*talosta*	'from (inside) the house'
	Illative	*taloon*	'into the house'
'Exterior'	Adessive	*talolla*	'at (*or* near) the house'
	Ablative	*talolta*	'from (outside) the house'
	Allative	*talolle*	'to (*or* towards) the house'
'General'	Essive	*talona*	
	Partitive	*taloa*	
	Translative	*taloksi*	

A relatively simple system of 'local' oppositions is found in Turkish: *eve*, 'to the house'; *evde*, 'in the house'; *evden*, 'from the house' (cf. Table 10, 7.4.2). The same three-way opposition of 'to': 'in/at': 'from' is combined in Finnish with what is traditionally referred to as 'exterior' *v*. 'interior' (cf. Table 11: except for the 'illative' and 'allative', it will be noted that the distinction between the 'exterior' and 'interior' cases is quite evidently marked by the 'agglutinating' suffixes -*l*- and -*s*-: we will refer to the 'general' cases presently). Other languages form more complex combinations of 'local' case-distinctions, involving either an 'absolute' or a 'relative' point of reference. By an 'absolute' point of reference is meant some feature of the environment (a particular river or mountain, for example) to which reference is made in indicating situation or direction ('upstream of', 'far from the mountain', etc.): case-distinctions of this kind are found in some Australian and American-Indian languages. Also to be included under the heading 'absolute' are such 'local' distinctions as 'north', 'south', 'east' and 'west': cf. Eskimo *anna*, 'the one in the north'; *qanna*, 'the one in the south', etc. By a 'relative' point of reference is meant some component of the typical situation of utterance which serves for the indication of situation or direction. The primary 'local' distinctions ('to': 'in/at': 'from') may be combined with a reference to either the speaker or the hearer by adding the appropriate case-distinctions to stems formed from the deictic 'demonstratives' (cf. the older English three-way opposition of *hither*, *here* and *hence*; *thither*, *there* and *thence*): this feature is found in very many languages. Such notions as 'to the left of' *v.* 'to the right of', or 'in front of' *v.* 'behind', may refer implicitly to the speaker, as the 'centre' of the typical situation of utterance, or explicitly, when they are marked by the inflexion of a particular noun ('behind the house') to some other 'relative' point of reference. It is worth noting that in many languages which express these 'local' distinctions by means of a set of nouns (comparable with *back* or *top* in the English 'complex prepositions' *at the back of*, *at the top of*) the nouns in question are those used otherwise to denote parts of the human body—'head', 'foot', 'back', 'face', etc. But even in those languages where the same, or similar, 'local' distinctions are made by means of case-inflexions (comparable with the Finnish marking of 'exterior' *v.* 'interior') it is clear that the application of these distinctions rests upon the transference to the explicit point of reference of a categorization primarily suited for orientation with respect to the participants in a typical situation of utterance.

The most general distinction to be recognized within the 'local' functions of the cases is *locative* v. *directional* ('in/at' *v.* 'to' or 'from'). Whether the resultant form has spatial or temporal reference will depend primarily upon the subclassification of the inflected noun: cf. 'in the house', 'from the house': 'in childhood', 'from childhood', which would be translated in a number of languages by single inflected words. The terms 'locative' and 'directional' themselves are to be interpreted (like 'local') as neutral with respect to the distinction of space and time; and the distinction between 'to' and 'from' is a secondary distinction within 'directional'.

The opposition of 'locative' and 'directional' may be regarded as a particular manifestation of a more general distinction between *static* and *dynamic*. We shall return to this point in our discussion of the category of *aspect* in the following section. Here it is sufficient to say that as location is to motion, so being in a certain state or condition is to change into (or from) that state or condition: in other words, there is a notional parallelism between such static expressions as '(be) in London', '(happen) on Tuesday', '(be) a teacher' and their dynamic counterparts '(go/come) to London', '(last) until Tuesday', '(become) a teacher'. Similarly, as location is to motion, so possession is to acquisition (and loss): as '(be) in London' is to '(have) a book', so '(go/come) to London' is to '(get) a book' (cf. 8.4.7).

If we use the general term 'state' to refer to location, quality, condition, possession, etc., we can draw a distinction between those states which are seen as permanently (or necessarily) associated with particular persons and objects and those states which are regarded as only temporarily (or contingently) associated with them. Now the use of the dynamic form (expressing motion, change of condition, acquisition or loss) presupposes that the state in question is *contingent* (i.e. 'non-essential' or 'accidental'), rather than *necessary*. Furthermore, this distinction between the contingent and the necessary is marked in the case-inflexion of predicative nouns and adjectives in certain languages. In Russian, for instance, the 'instrumental' case is used (except in the 'present tense') for contingent states of quality or condition: *ja byl/stal soldatom* ('I was/became a soldier'), whereas the 'nominative' is used for more permanent, or necessary, states. In Finnish, the 'essive' is employed in the static form for contingent, periodic or temporary states of quality or condition ('while he was a teacher', 'in his capacity as teacher', etc.), and the 'translative' in the dynamic counterpart of these ('he became a teacher'; also in such expressions as 'it turned blue', etc.). The distinction between the contingent and the necessary may also be relevant within the class of relationships to which we have given the name 'possession': if the 'possessed' item is contingently associated with the 'possessor', it is marked in some languages (notably in Chinese, and also in the Siouan family) as *alienable* ('capable of being given away'), whereas it is unmarked, or marked as *inalienable*, if it is necessarily associated with the 'possessor'. Typical instances of alienable and inalienable relationships would be 'John's book' and 'John's father' respectively.

From antiquity, grammarians have argued about the relationship between the 'local' and the 'grammatical' functions of the category of case (in this context 'local' means 'relating to place and time'). In the classical languages (and in many other languages), the 'local' and the 'grammatical' functions of a particular case are often hard to distinguish; so that it is tempting to say that one is derivable from the other, or that both are derivable from some more general principle which is neutral with respect to the spatiotemporal and the syntactic. This also holds for the 'local' and 'grammatical' functions of the prepositions in English (which, as we shall see, may be regarded as cases of the nouns they govern, if the term 'case' is not restricted to inflexional variation). One might reasonably wonder whether the 'sense' of *from* in *I am from London* (i.e. 'a native of London') or *I came from school* is synchronically unrelated to the 'sense' of *from* in *I got the book from John*; and the directional 'sense' of *to* in *I went to London* unrelated to the *to* of the indirect object in *I gave the book to John*. No language has yet been studied in sufficient detail from a generative point of view for it to be possible to say just how much of the coincidence between the more clearly 'local' and the more clearly 'grammatical' functions of cases and prepositions is synchronically relevant in a particular language. At the same time, certain points of coincidence across genetically-unrelated languages are so striking that they demand an explanation in general syntactic theory. One such point of coincidence, to which we will give some attention later, is the similarity between the directional and the indirect object in many languages (cf. *I went to London* and *I gave the book to John*, and note that in *I sent the book to John* one might hesitate as to whether *to John* is directional or indirect object).

7.4.7 *Prepositions*

Although the category of case is traditionally restricted to inflexional variation, it is clear that both the 'grammatical' and the 'local' functions discussed in the preceding paragraphs are logically independent of the way in which they are realized in particular languages. Furthermore, these 'grammatical' and 'local' functions may be realized in the same language partly by case-inflexions and partly by other means—most commonly by prepositions or postpositions, or by word-order. This means that the category of case cannot be discussed solely from a morphological point of view.

The difference between *prepositions* and *postpositions* is trivial; and many linguists would say that it is mere pedantry to maintain the terminological distinction. In the traditional theory of the 'parts of speech', as it was developed for the description of the classical languages of Europe, the term 'preposition' was employed to refer to that class of invariable words, or particles, which had a 'grammatical' or 'local' function and which, as it happens in Latin and Greek, tend to occur immediately before the noun or noun-phrase they modify. In many other languages (Turkish, Japanese, Hindi, etc.), particles with similar 'grammatical' or 'local' functions to those of the Latin, Greek or English prepositions occur after the noun they modify (cf. Turkish *Ahmet için*, 'for Ahmet'; Japanese *Tokyo e*, 'to

Tokyo'; Hindi *Ram ko*, 'to Rama'; etc.); and for this reason they are usually called 'postpositions'. Whether a particle occurs before or after its noun is a matter of small consequence in general grammatical theory: for convenience, we will therefore use the more familiar term 'preposition' to cover both classes of particles.

Whether the term 'case' should be extended beyond its traditional application, to include prepositions as well as inflexional variation, is also a question of little importance. The difference between inflexional variation and the use of prepositions is a difference in the 'surface' structure of languages. What is of importance, from the point of view of general linguistic theory, is the fact that the 'grammatical' and 'local' functions traditionally held to be inherent in the category of case can be no more sharply distinguished in those languages which realize them by means of prepositions than they can in languages in which they are realized inflexionally. It is the 'interpenetration' of the syntactic and the 'orientational' framework of language which has been especially emphasized in this section.

The fact that the 'grammatical' and the 'local' functions of case-inflexions and prepositions cannot be separated in many, or even in most, instances does not, however, imply that there is no validity at all in the traditional distinction of 'grammatical' and 'local' (or 'abstract' and 'concrete'). First of all, it should be observed that it is not generally possible to substitute one 'abstract' case-inflexion or preposition for another without making consequent changes elsewhere in the sentence. One cannot substitute a 'nominative' for an 'accusative' or 'genitive' in Latin, for example; just as one cannot substitute *he* for *him* or *his* in an English sentence. This fact can be taken as typical of what is implied by the term 'abstract' (or 'grammatical') in this connexion. By contrast, it is frequently possible to substitute an 'exterior' case for the corresponding 'interior' case in Finnish, just as it is possible to substitute *at* for *in*, or *to* for *into*, in English (*I'll meet you at/in the church, Let's go to/into the church*). The distinction between 'exterior' and 'interior' is therefore more 'concrete': it is not controlled by other syntactic variables in the sentence, and may convey, of itself, a difference of meaning. As an example of a 'local' distinction which is intermediate between the fully 'abstract' and the fully 'concrete' we may consider the opposition between the 'locative' and the 'directional': this is less 'abstract' than the distinction between 'subjective' and 'objective', but less 'concrete' than the distinction between 'exterior' and 'interior'. The preposition *at* cannot be substituted for *to* in a sentence like *He went to church* without also substituting a 'locative' verb (e.g. *was*) for the 'directional' *went*; in that respect the difference is 'abstract'. At the same time, it would be reasonable to maintain that the choice of both *went* and *to* or *was* and *at* is determined by the prior selection of a 'directional' rather than a 'locative' predicate at a 'higher' (or 'deeper') level. This is the analysis that will be adopted below (cf. 8.4.7). If it is correct, it implies that the distinction between 'locative' and 'directional' is a semantically-relevant, or 'concrete', distinction of 'deep' structure, but that the choice of *to* rather than *at*, or *into* rather than *in*, is grammatically-determined; and, of itself, it cannot carry a difference of meaning.

Although the difference between inflexional variation and the use of prepositions has been described above as a rather unimportant difference in the 'surface' structure of languages, there is perhaps some empirical reason to suggest that, if a language has both inflexional distinctions and prepositions, the former will tend to have a more 'abstract' and the latter a more 'concrete' function by reference to the criterion suggested above. This is certainly true of the Indo-European languages; and it seems to be true of many other languages with case-inflexions. Furthermore, it may also be true that, although word-order is commonly used as a means of distinguishing between the 'subject' and the 'object', or between the 'modified' element and the 'modifier', in a sentence, it rarely, or never, has the more 'concrete' function typical of prepositions. In this respect, word-order may be a more typically 'grammatical' device than inflexion, and inflexion more typically 'grammatical' than the use of prepositions.

7.5   Tense, mood and aspect

7.5.1   *Tense*

The term 'tense' derives (*via* Old French) from the Latin translation of the Greek word for 'time' (Greek *khrónos*, Latin *tempus*). The category of *tense* has to do with time-relations in so far as these are expressed by systematic grammatical contrasts. Three such contrasts were recognized by traditional grammarians in the analysis of Greek and Latin: 'past', 'present' and 'future'. And it has often been supposed that the same three-way opposition of tense is a universal feature of language. This is not so. In fact tense itself is not found in all languages; and, as we shall see, the opposition of 'past', 'present' and 'future' is not simply a matter of tense even in Greek and Latin. The essential characteristic of the category of tense is that it relates the time of the action, event or state of affairs referred to in the sentence to the time of utterance (the time of utterance being 'now'). Tense is therefore a *deictic* category, which (like all syntactic features partly or wholly dependent upon deixis: cf. 7.2.1) is simultaneously a property of the sentence and the utterance (cf. 5.2.4). Many treatments of tense have been vitiated by the assumption that the 'natural' division of time into 'past', 'present' and 'future' is necessarily reflected in language. Even Jespersen falls victim to this assumption in his discussion of tense in *The Philosophy of Grammar*.

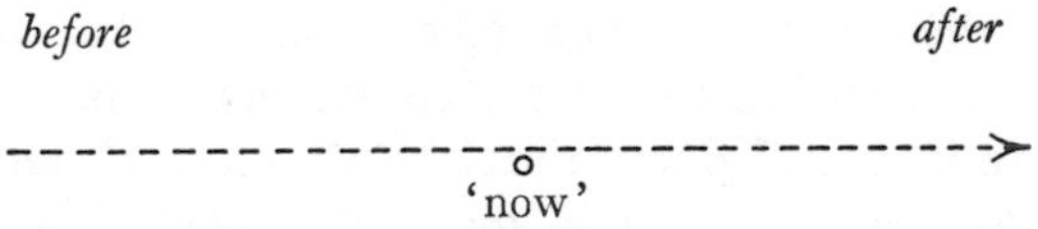

before   after

$$\text{-------------------}\underset{\text{'now'}}{\circ}\text{--------------} \rightarrow$$

Fig. 16. Time and tense.

Making reference to a diagram similar to that which is given in Fig. 16, he first of all establishes the 'present' as contemporaneous with the theoretical zero-point (the 'now' of the time of utterance), the 'past' as 'before-now' and the 'future' as 'after-now'. The 'primary' distinctions of 'past' and 'future' are then subdivided by Jespersen by means of a 'secondary' application of the notions 'before' and 'after': 'before-past', 'after-past', 'before-future' and 'after-future'. (As the 'theoretical zero-point', the 'present' is not subdivided.) The result is a seven-term 'notional' tense-system, partly or wholly realized in various languages.

But tense admits of categorization in many different ways. One might grant (as has often been suggested) that the directionality of time is given in 'nature' (as expressed by the arrowhead in the diagram in Fig. 16), but this may or may not be relevant to the analysis of tense in particular languages. Various categorizations are possible. The 'theoretical zero point' (the 'now' of utterance) might be included with either 'past' or 'future' to yield, on the one hand, a dichotomy between 'future' and 'non-future', or, on the other, a dichotomy between 'past' and 'non-past'. A different dichotomy (based on the distinction of 'now' and 'not-now' without reference to the directionality of time) could be 'present' *v.* 'non-present'. Other possible categorizations might depend upon the notion of 'proximity' (with or without reference to directionality): e.g. a dichotomy of 'proximate' *v.* 'non-proximate' (with respect to time of utterance), a trichotomy of 'now' *v.* 'proximate' *v.* 'remote'. And these distinctions might be combined in various ways, and not merely as suggested in Jespersen's scheme.

There is no space here to discuss, or even to illustrate, the wide variety of tense-systems that are found in different languages. Indeed, it would be difficult to do this satisfactorily quite apart from the limitations of space, since the analysis of tense, even in English, is a matter of considerable controversy. The major tense-distinction in English is undoubtedly that which is traditionally described as an opposition of 'past' *v.* 'present': e.g. *They jump*: *They jumped.* But this is best regarded as a contrast of 'past' *v.* 'non-past'. The reason is that, whereas the past tense does typically refer to 'before-now', the non-past is not restricted to what is contemporaneous with the time of utterance: it is used also for 'timeless' or 'eternal' statements (*The sun rises in the east*, etc.) and in many statements that refer to the future ('after-now'). In other words, a form like *jumped* is positively 'marked' as past, whereas *jump* (or *jumps*) is 'unmarked'. This analysis is supported, if not confirmed, by the fact that the opposition of past and non-past is realized systematically by suffixation of the first element of the verb-phrase: *jump*: *jumped*; *will jump*: *would jump*; *has jumped*: *had jumped*; *is jumping*: *was jumping*; *will have been jumping*: *would have been jumping*; etc.; and it is the one obligatory opposition of tense in the simple sentence.

What is traditionally described as the 'future' tense in English is realized by means of the 'auxiliary verbs' *will* and *shall* (the rules that are given for the choice between the two auxiliaries by normative grammarians being based, for the most part, upon certain pre-conceived ideas as to what ought to be the difference between them, rather than upon the usage of any group of English speakers). Although it is undeniable that *will* and *shall* occur in many sentences that refer to the future, they also occur in sentences that do not. And they do not necessarily occur in sentences with a future time reference. They are most appropriately described as modal (like *can, may, must*, etc.); and, in our discussion of the category of mood, we shall see that 'futurity' is as much a matter of mood as it is of tense. Even in the analysis of Greek and Latin (where the 'future', like the 'present' and the 'past', is realized inflexionally), there is some reason to describe the 'future tense' as partly modal.

7.5.2 *Mood*

Mood, like tense, is frequently realized by inflecting the verb or by modifying it by means of 'auxiliaries'. It is best defined in relation to an 'unmarked' class of sentences which express simple statements of fact, unqualified with respect to the attitude of the speaker towards what he is saying. Simple declarative sentences of this kind are, strictly speaking, non-modal ('unmarked' for mood). If, however, a particular language has a set of one or more grammatical devices for 'marking' sentences according to the speaker's commitment with respect to the factual status of what he is saying (his emphatic certainty, his uncertainty or doubt, etc.), it is customary to refer to the 'unmarked' sentences also (by courtesy as it were) as being 'in a certain mood'; and the traditional term for this 'unmarked' mood is *indicative* (or *declarative*).

Two classes of sentences tend to stand apart from all others by virtue of their modality. The first class comprises *imperative* sentences, which do not make statements at all, but express commands or instructions (*Come here!*, *Put your coat on!*, etc.). Since commands or instructions are generally issued directly to the hearer, what one might call the 'central' class of imperative sentences are associated with the 'second person'; and it is a rather striking fact that in very many languages which inflect the verb for person, number, tense, mood, etc. (including the Indo-European languages) the form of the verb which occurs in 'second person singular' imperative sentences is uninflected for all these categories (i.e. it is identical with the stem). Many linguists have taken this fact as evidence that giving commands, rather than making statements, is the more 'basic' function of language. Since it is not clear what is implied by 'basic' in this context, we will not go into the question. In any case, the distinction between giving commands and making statements cannot be sharply drawn. *I want you to come here* would normally be classed as a declarative sentence; and yet the corresponding utterance, in the right context, might be understood to express a command no less peremptory or authoritative than *Come here!*

Interrogative sentences also stand in contrast to declarative sentences by virtue of their modality. They are not traditionally regarded as modal, because in most languages (including Latin, Greek, English) the syntactic distinction between declarative and interrogative sentences is not associated with a difference of verbal inflexion or the selection of a particular auxiliary, but with the employment of various interrogative particles or pronouns, with a difference of word-order, or with intonation, together with the 'indicative mood'. Linguists do not usually speak of an 'interrogative mood', except in relation to those languages where questions are distinguished from modally 'unmarked' sentences by the same kind of syntactic devices as those which characterize other modally 'marked' sentences. But from a more general point of view, interrogative sentences are quite clearly modal; and they may be characterized by additional modalities which indicate the expectations of the speaker. For instance, three types of 'yes'–'no' questions are commonly recognized in the description of Latin: (i) 'open' questions (which do not indicate whether the speaker expects either 'yes' or 'no') with the suffix -*ne*; (ii) those expecting the answer 'yes', introduced by the particle *nonne*; and (iii) those expecting the answer 'no', introduced by *num*. There is a somewhat similar contrast in English between an 'open' question like *Is he here?* on the one hand, and *He's here, isn't he?*, or *He isn't here, is he?*, on the other. (By a 'yes'–'no' question is not meant one that *must* be answered with 'yes' or 'no', but one that *may* be so answered. For instance, *Did John come?*, but not *Who came?*, is a 'yes'–'no' question.)

It we turn now to other modalities, apart from command and interrogation, we find a large variety of ways in which the 'attitude' of the speaker is grammatically marked in different languages. At least three 'scales' of modality may be relevant. The first is the scale of 'wish' and 'intention'. This may be illustrated by the epitaph *Requiescat in pace*, 'May he rest in peace': the Latin 'subjunctive', *requiescat*, is in modal contrast with the 'indicative', *requiescit*, 'he rests'. (The Greek 'optative', which is distinct from the 'subjunctive', owes its name to the fact that one of its principal functions was conceived to be that of expressing wishes.) The second scale is that of 'necessity' and 'obligation': *I must go to London next week*, etc. The third is that of 'certainty' and 'possibility': *He may be here, He must be here*, etc. I have used the term 'scale' for these different modalities, because they may be categorized into a larger or smaller number of subdistinctions (e.g. 'certainty', 'probability', 'possibility', or 'stronger' and 'weaker', or different kinds of, 'obligation' and 'necessity'; and so on). Furthermore, particular languages may merge any two, or all three, of these scales of modality; or give no grammatical recognition to them at all. It should also be noted that there is an affinity between imperative sentences and the modalities of 'wish' and 'necessity', on the one hand, and between interrogative sentences and the modality of 'possibility', on the other. Indeed, an overtly interrogative sentence like *Will you come here?* (we will neglect the possibility of intonational differences) may be semantically equivalent to the imperative *Come here, will you?* (or simply *Come here!*) and can hardly be classified as being in one modality rather than another.

7.5.3 *Intersection of tense and mood*

The categories of mood and tense may 'intersect' in various ways. First of all, a particular modal distinction may be drawn in combination with one tense, but neutralized with another. For example, the distinction between the 'obligative' and the 'inferential' sense associated with the auxiliary verb *must* in English is neutralized in a non-past sentence like *He must come regularly* (which might be equivalent to either 'He has to come regularly' or 'I infer that he comes regularly'), but it is overtly drawn in the past: *He had to come regularly* v. *He must have come regularly*. (It is also worth observing that the neutralization of the 'obligative' and the 'inferential' *must* is not solely dependent upon tense. The ambiguity of *He must come regularly* depends upon the fact that it is determined as 'habitual' in aspect by the occurrence of the adverb *regularly*: by contrast, *He must come now* is determined as 'non-habitual', and it hardly admits of the 'inferential' interpretation. The category of aspect is discussed below.) There is a further distinction within the 'obligative' in English, which has to do with the acceptance or fulfilment of the obligation; and this is associated with the choice between *must* or *have to* (with certain differences between these two in the non-past) and *ought*. The distinction becomes clear if we compare the perfectly acceptable sentences *I ought to go to New York tomorrow but I'm not going to* or *He ought to have gone to New York yesterday but he didn't* with the unacceptable sentences **I must go to New York tomorrow but I'm not going to* or **He had to go to New York yesterday but he didn't*. There is, in other words, a difference in the modal presuppositions attached to the selection of *must/have to* and *ought*. Although these presuppositions are not dependent upon tense, they have the effect that from the past-tense sentence *He ought to have gone* the hearer will correctly infer that (as far as the speaker is aware) the person referred to did not in fact go, and from *He had to go* that he did in fact go. This distinction within the 'obligative' is sometimes rather misleadingly described in terms of a difference in the 'force' of the obligation, or in terms of a difference between 'duty' and 'necessity'.

Earlier in this section, it was suggested that the expression of 'futurity' in English (and in other languages) was as much a matter of mood as of tense. In the first place, it should be observed that sentences containing *will* and *shall* do not necessarily refer to the future. Among the definitely modal uses of *will* one may note the 'putative' (e.g. *He will be quite a big boy now*: to be distinguished from the 'inferential' *He must be quite a big boy now*) and the 'inductive', which (to quote Palmer) 'is used for "general" timeless truths, that may be proved inductively, of the kind illustrated by *Oil will float on water*'. In addition to the purely future sense of *shall*, there is also a more obviously modal use, the 'promissive': here the speaker puts himself forward as guarantor, as it were, of the truth or occurrence of the event he refers to (e.g. *You shall have your money by the end of the week*). There are other modalities associated with *shall* and *will*. Furthermore, not only have both 'verbs' developed historically from what were definitely modals in earlier stages of the language, but they are paradigmatically opposed to such other modals as *may*, *can* and *must* in present-day English syntax.

It is true that *will* and *shall* are commonly used in sentences referring to the future. But this may be regarded as a 'natural' consequence of the fact that statements made about future occurrences are necessarily based upon the speaker's beliefs, predictions or intentions, rather than upon his knowledge of 'fact'. It is noteworthy that in very many languages in which it is customary to recognize a future tense, this is also employed in sentences with modal implications similar to those mentioned above as characteristic of English sentences containing *will* and *shall*. We will give just a few examples. The French *Ça sera le facteur* (with the future *sera*) is used in exactly the same circumstances as the English *That will be the postman*. The Russian 'imperfective future' (e.g. *Ja ne budu rabotatj*, 'I won't work') may be used with implications of 'intention' or 'determination'. Even the Greek and Latin future tenses were modal in many of their uses; and their modality (by contrast with the 'present', i.e. non-past, and past tenses) is confirmed by two facts which relate the future 'tense' to the subjunctive mood: (i) in certain contexts the future may replace the subjunctive, and (ii) there is no 'future subjunctive' form in either language. Thus the traditional scheme of three tenses, with two moods for Latin and three moods for Greek (excluding the imperative in both instances), is not wholly satisfactory. For general syntactic theory, it may be taken as axiomatic that 'futurity' is a notion that cuts across the distinction of mood and tense.

Whether a language recognizes categories both of tense and mood is of course a matter for empirical investigation. According to Hockett: 'Hopi has three tenses: one used in statements of general timeless truth ("Mountains are high"), a second used in reports of known or presumably known happenings ("I saw him yesterday", "I'm on my way right now"), and a third used of events still in the realm of uncertainty, hence often where we would think of the event in the speaker's future ("He's coming tomorrow").' In view of what is said about the implications of these three 'tenses', one might well think that they would be more appropriately described as 'moods'. But the general point being made here is that mood and tense may 'intersect' in such a way that either one or the other label is equally appropriate. The same point may be illustrated by what Hockett says of Menomini (an American Indian language described by Bloom-field): 'Menomini has a five-way contrast, largely of the mode type [Hockett follows Bloomfield in preferring 'mode' to 'mood'], though semantically there are traces of tense-like meanings also: /piʔw/ "he comes, is coming, came": /piʔwen/ "he is said to be coming, it is said that he came": /piʔ/ "Is he coming? Did he come?": /piasah/ "so he *is* coming after all (despite our expectation to the contrary)": /piapah/ "but he was going to come! (and now it turns out that he is not!)".' One may note in passing that the form /piʔ/ could be described as being in 'the interrogative mood' (cf. 7.5.2).

We may note yet another way in which tense and mood may 'intersect'. There are many places in English where *would, should, could* and *might* are rightly described as past-tense forms corresponding to the non-past forms *will, shall, can* and *may* (with *had to* corresponding to both *must* and *have to*): cf. *I am going, I will go*: *He said that he was going, He said that he would go*, etc. But there are other sentences with *would, should*, etc., which have no reference to past time: e.g. *That would be a good place for a picnic, You should see a doctor, It could be true*, etc. In such sentences, the 'tense' distinction of non-past *v.* past would seem to subcategorize the modality in question in such a way that 'past' combines with mood to introduce a more 'tentative', 'remote' or 'polite' sense. In other words, 'tense' is here 'converted' into a secondary modality.

7.5.4 *The modality of subordinate clauses*

Our whole discussion of mood has been based so far upon the assumption of contrast between simple sentences. Something must now be said about the modality of subordinate clauses in complex sentences. The traditional term 'subjunctive' is revealing in this connexion: it comes from the Latin translation of the Greek word for 'subordinating', and shows that for the traditional grammarian the subjunctive was the mood of subordination *par excellence*. This point may be illustrated with reference to French, where (as in Greek and Latin) what is traditionally referred to as the subjunctive mood is obligatory in many constructions, and the indicative in others: e.g. *Je crois qu'il vient* v. *Je ne crois pas qu'il vienne* ('I think he is coming' v. 'I don't think he is coming'; *vient* is in the indicative and *vienne* in the subjunctive). In fact, there are very few contexts in which the indicative and the subjunctive are interchangeable in French. The subjunctive rarely occurs except in subordinate clauses, where its occurrence is very largely determined by the type of sentence of which the clause is a constituent, by the selection of a particular main verb, by negation, and by other factors. In other words, the indicative and the subjunctive forms of the verb are in almost complementary distribution.

The question now arises whether the French subjunctive is correctly described as a mood. More generally (since French is by no means unique in this respect), what is the connexion between mood and subordination? First of all, it should be noted that, in those contexts in which the selection of one form of the verb rather than another (e.g. *vienne* v. *vient*) is determined by other syntactic features of the sentence, the occurrence of one form rather than the other cannot of itself carry any distinction of modality. For instance, the occurrence of *vienne* rather than *vient* in *Je ne crois pas qu'il vienne* does not indicate any particular semantic distinction associated with the choice of the subjunctive *v.* the indicative: there is no choice open to the speaker in this context. Why, then, do we say that the verb *vienne* is in the subjunctive 'mood'? Why do we not say, using a more neutral term, that it is in the subjunctive 'form'?

Three relevant possibilities may be distinguished in the case of languages in which one set of verbal forms occurs mainly in subordinate clauses. (1) The distribution of a set of forms, A, and a set of forms, B, may be partly complementary and partly overlapping; and the distinction between them, in the contexts in which they contrast, may be modal. This situation obtains, though minimally, in French. One might contrast, for example, *Dieu vous bénit* (indicative, 'God blesses you') and *Dieu vous bénisse* (subjunctive, 'May God bless you'). In Latin and Greek there was a greater degree of contrast between the subjunctive and the indicative, but, as in French, the selection of one or the other was determined by other factors in the majority of subordinate clauses. (2) The occurrence of either A or B in subordinate clauses may correlate with a difference of modality which is also indicated elsewhere in the sentence. For instance, the negative sentence *Je ne crois pas qu'il vienne* expresses the speaker's doubt, in contrast to the relative assurance of the positive *Je crois qu'il vient*. (Actually, this difference in the modality of the two sentences is one which, in certain contexts, may be expressed solely by the selection of the indicative rather than the subjunctive. But this fact may be neglected for the purpose of illustration.) We may say, therefore, that in the case of *Je ne crois pas qu'il vienne* v. *Je crois qu'il vient*, the form of the verb is compatible with the modal context in which it occurs; in the same way, the form of the verb in *He came yesterday* is compatible with the time-reference of *yesterday*. (3) There may be no correlation at all between the occurrence of one set of forms rather than another and the modality of the context by which they are determined. In this situation one would not describe the difference between A and B as modal, even though one might quite reasonably use the term 'subjunctive' to refer to that set of forms which was more or less restricted to subordinate clauses. The subjunctive in Greek and Latin (as in French) is traditionally regarded as a mood because it satisfies both the first and second of the conditions described above; but the term 'subjunctive', of itself, carries no implications of modality.

7.5.5 *Aspect*

The term *aspect* (which is a translation of the Russian word *vid*) was first used to refer to the distinction of 'perfective' and 'imperfective' in the inflexion of verbs in Russian and other Slavonic languages. The term 'perfective' (or 'perfect') is reminiscent of that used by the Stoic grammarians for the somewhat similar notion of 'completion' found in Greek. As we have seen, the Stoics realized that something other than, and additional to, temporal reference of the kind indicated by tense was involved in the analysis of the Greek verbal forms (cf. 1.2.5). But this insight into what we now call 'aspect' was not taken over by the Alexandrians and their successors.

7.5.6   *'Perfective'* v. *'imperfective'*

The distinction between the perfective and the imperfective in Russian may be illustrated by means of the two sentences (i) *Ja pročital roman*, and (ii) *Ja čital roman*. Although each of these can be translated as 'I read a novel' (in answer to a question like 'What did you do last night?'), they are not equivalent in Russian. In (i) the perfective is used (*pro-čital*), and in (ii) the imperfective (*čital*). It is important to realize that the choice between one aspect and the other is not determined solely by the 'facts' of the situation being described. The perfective is the 'marked' term in the Russian aspectual system, and the imperfective is 'unmarked' by contrast with it. (This relation between the two aspects holds independently of the morphological derivation of the forms: many perfectives are derived by prefixation of the corresponding imperfectives, e.g. *pro-čital*: *čital*; in other instances, it is the imperfective which is derived from the perfective by suffixation, e.g. *za-pis-al* (perfective): *za-pis-yv-al* (imperfective), 'jotted down'.) The use of the perfective in (i) carries with it the positive implication that the 'action' of reading was completed (i.e. that the book was finished). But (ii) does not say whether the 'action' was completed or not; it merely tells us that the speaker spent some time reading a novel.

In Greek, as in Russian, the perfective is 'marked' by contrast with the imperfective. But there is a third term in the Greek aspectual system, the 'aorist', which, in certain syntactic positions, is in opposition with both the imperfective and the perfective; and this three-term system may well have been a feature of the Indo-European 'parent-language'. The Greek perfective is the most 'marked' of the three aspects: it is perhaps correct to say that, whereas the imperfective is 'unmarked' with respect to the perfective, the aorist is 'unmarked' with respect to the imperfective. As we have seen, the perfective *v.* imperfective opposition in Greek is one of 'completion'. It may be illustrated by means of the following sentence (taken from Plato's *Crito*): 'Now is no time to be deciding [imperfective, *bouleúesthai*] but to have already decided [perfective, *bebouleûsthai*].' The Greek perfective refers to the *state* which results from the completion of the action or process, so that the verb *bebouleûsthai* in the sentence just quoted might be translated, somewhat unnaturally but more revealingly for our present purpose, as 'to be in a state of decision'. The opposition between the imperfective and the aorist has to do with the duration of the action or process described. In contrast with the aorist *bouleúseasthai* ('to decide', with no indication as to whether the decision is momentary or not), the imperfective *bouleúesthai* means 'to be in the process of deciding'. The three-term opposition of perfective, imperfective and aorist in Greek is therefore the resultant of two binary distinctions: perfective (or completive) *v.* non-perfective, and durative *v.* non-durative. The aspectual notions of 'completion' and 'duration' are found, either together or singly, in many languages.

We shall not discuss any of the other notions that are customarily brought together under the term 'aspect': iterative (or frequentative), punctual (or momentary), habitual, inchoative (or inceptive), etc. To list just these few examples is sufficient to show that the category of aspect includes a wide variety of possible distinctions. Like tense-distinctions, these all have to do with time; but (as Hockett puts it) with the 'temporal distribution or contour' of an action, event or state of affairs, rather than with its 'location in time'. Aspect, unlike tense, is not a deictic category; it is not relative to the time of utterance.

7.5.7 *Aspect in English*

English has two aspects which combine fairly freely with tense and mood: the 'perfect' (e.g. *I have/had read the book, I will/would have read the book*) and the 'progressive' (*I am/was reading the book, I will/would be reading the book*). They also combine freely with one another (*I have/had been reading the book*)—unlike the two aspectual distinctions of Greek discussed above (which are in any case only roughly comparable). There are a number of other aspectual distinctions in English of more limited distribution, including the 'habitual' (which occurs only with the past tense: *I used to read*) and the 'mutative' (which is restricted to the passive: *I got killed*). For a detailed treatment of the category of aspect (and also of mood and tense) in English, reference may be made to a number of recent works listed in the bibliography. One or two points of more general theoretical interest may be mentioned here.

There are some verbs in English which do not normally occur with progressive aspect, even in those contexts in which the majority of verbs necessarily take the progressive form. Among the so-called 'non-progressive' verbs are *think, know, understand, hate, love, see, taste, feel, possess, own,* etc. The most striking characteristic that they have in common is the fact that they are 'stative'—they refer to a state of affairs, rather than to an action, event or process. Since the most common function of the progressive is to indicate duration, one might say that it is only 'natural' for stative verbs not to combine with the progressive: the implication of duration is already contained in the general meaning of these verbs. This is also true, it should be observed, of most predicative adjectives in English; a sentence like *The book is being very heavy* is abnormal, if not impossible. But there are some adjectives which occur with the progressive (of 'the verb *to be*'), when they refer to an activity rather than to a state or quality: *John is being very good now.* We shall return to this distinction between 'states' and 'activities' in our general discussion of the difference between verbs and adjectives below (cf. 7.6.4). Here it should be observed that all the 'non-progressive' verbs can in fact take the progressive aspect under particular circumstances. One of the occasions for the use of the progressive aspect with stative verbs in English is in fact to 'recategorize' them, *ad hoc*, as 'verbs of activity'. Even such a sentence as *I am having a headache*, unusual though it is, can be given an interpretation as 'activity' in the appropriate circumstances. It must also be noted that the 'non-progressive' verbs in English are not necessarily stative when they combine with either the past tense or one of the modals: e.g. *As soon as I saw him, I knew that there was something wrong*; *You will feel a slight pain when I insert the needle* (in these sentences the verbs *knew* and *feel* refer to an 'event'—to the beginning of a state, rather than to the state itself).

7.5.8 *Intersection of tense and aspect*

We have already seen that the distinction between tense and mood cannot be sharply drawn in English (or in other languages) with respect to future time. Aspect also 'merges' with both tense and mood. For example, the perfect is used with *just* to refer to the very recent past (*I have just seen him*); it forms a 'past-in-the-past' in reported speech (*He said he'd seen him the day before* may correspond to *I saw him yesterday* in the same way as *He said he was reading* corresponds to *I am reading*); and (to quote Palmer's formulation of this point) the past and the non-past perfective forms 'indicate periods of time that began before and continued up to a point of time, the present moment in the case of the present tense, and a point of time in the past in the case of the past tense'. All these features of the English perfect give support to the traditional view that, in certain circumstances at least, it is a secondary, or relative, tense, rather than an aspect. The progressive is not exclusively aspectual

either, but may have modal implications: in particular, it may express
intention (e.g. *I am going to London tomorrow*).

Tense, mood and aspect 'merge' into one another in many other
languages besides English. This is partly because certain notions, as
we have seen, might be classed equally well as modal, aspectual, or
temporal; and partly because more distinctions have to be recognized in the semantic analysis of these languages than are overtly
distinguished by the systematic morphological and syntactic contrasts
which we label as 'tense', 'mood' or 'aspect'. No one of the three
categories is essential to human language; and different languages vary
considerably in the way in which they group together or distinguish
temporal, modal and aspectual notions. It is only when these notions
are expressed by means of some such device as inflexion or the use of
particles that linguists tend to refer to them as *grammatical* notions.
There are many languages, for instance, in which temporal reference
is optionally, if at all, by means of *lexical* items like 'yesterday', 'tomorrow', etc., or 'now' and 'then'. This is not normally regarded as
tense. In much the same way, various modalities of the sentence can
be expressed in English by means of such adverbials as *certainly*,
probably, *perhaps*, etc., instead of, or in addition to, one of the modal
auxiliaries.

To conclude this section, it should be pointed out that the account
of tense, mood and aspect that has been given here has necessarily
been rather sketchy and over-simplified in places. In particular, we
have said nothing about the important fact that in any given context
the meaning of one of these grammatical categories may be more
precisely specified, or determined, by the adverbs or adverbial phrases
to which it is syntagmatically related in the sentence.

7.6 The parts of speech

7.6.1 *Alleged circularity of traditional definitions*

One of the criticisms most commonly made of the traditional definitions of the parts of speech is that they are circular. It is pointed out,
for example, that, if the class of nouns is defined, in 'notional' terms,
as that class of lexical items whose members denote persons, places
and things (and this is one way in which the noun was defined in
traditional grammar), the definition cannot be applied without
circularity to determine the status of such English words as *truth*,
beauty, *electricity*, etc. The circularity lies in the fact that the only

reason we have for saying that truth, beauty and electricity are 'things' is that the words which refer to them in English are nouns.

The criticism of circularity loses its force as soon as we take into account the distinction between 'formal' and 'notional' definitions, and the possibility that the 'notional' definitions of the parts of speech may be used to determine the names, though not the membership, of the major syntactic classes of English and other languages. Let us assume that we have established for English a set of syntactic classes, X, Y and Z (as well as a number of other classes) on 'formal', distributional grounds (cf. 4.2.9); and that the members of each of these classes are listed in the lexicon, or dictionary, associated with the grammar:

$$X = \{boy,\ woman,\ grass,\ atom,\ tree,\ cow,\ truth,\ beauty,$$
$$electricity,\ \ldots\}$$
$$Y = \{come,\ go,\ die,\ eat,\ love,\ exist,\ \ldots\}$$
$$Z = \{good,\ beautiful,\ red,\ hard,\ tall,\ \ldots\}$$

By reference to the lexicon, we can decide for each word in the language to what syntactic class or classes it belongs. It is true that not all the members of class X denote persons, places and things (if 'thing' is interpreted as 'discrete, physical object'). However, it may still be true that all (or the vast majority) of the lexical items which refer to persons, places and things fall within the class X; and, if this is so, we may call X the class of nouns. In other words, we have the 'formal' class X and a 'notional' class A; they are not co-extensive, but, if A is wholly or mainly included in X, then X may be given the label suggested by the 'notional' definition of A. It is for this reason that the lexical class which has as its members, not only *boy*, *woman*, etc., but also *truth*, *beauty*, etc., is appropriately called the class of nouns in English. Whether there exists any language in which the noun cannot be defined in this way is an empirical question. Most of the statements made by linguists to the effect that the noun is not a universal category of human language are vitiated by the failure to take note of the distinction between the criteria for membership and the criteria for naming the classes. In practice, linguists seem to have had little difficulty in deciding that one class, rather than another, in a particular language, is correctly identified as the class of nouns. As we shall see, the situation is somewhat different with respect to the other parts of speech recognized in traditional grammar. But in principle the distinction between 'formal' and 'notional' definition is applicable there too.

It is a more serious criticism that the criteria incorporated in the definitions are obviously language-dependent (or 'glossocentric'), in the sense that they do not apply outside a very narrow range of languages (including Latin and Greek, for which they were primarily established). This point may be illustrated with reference to the definitions of the noun, verb and preposition given by Dionysius Thrax (and taken over by most of his successors in the mainstream of the Western grammatical tradition: cf. 1.2.5): 'The *noun* is a part of speech having case-inflexions, signifying a person or a thing'; 'The *verb* is a part of speech without case-inflexion, admitting inflexions of tense, person and number, signifying an activity or a being acted upon'; 'The *preposition* is a word placed before all other parts of speech in word-formation and syntactic constructions'. The noun and the verb are defined, not only 'notionally' in terms of what they 'signify', but also in terms of their inflexional characteristics; whereas the definition of the preposition invokes the quite different property of relative position (in both morphological and syntactic constructions). First of all, inflexion is far from being a universal feature of language; secondly, languages that have inflexion do not necessarily manifest the categories of case, number and tense; and the sharp distinction that is drawn between cases and prepositions in traditional grammar cannot be sustained in general syntactic theory (cf. 1.2.5, 7.4.1, 7.4.7). The question that the definitions of Dionysius Thrax were intended to answer may be put in the following terms: Given that the sentences of the language have been segmented into words, to what class would each word be assigned? And the grammatical criteria for classification were mainly based upon the surface-structure properties of words.

It may be taken for granted that any general theory of the parts of speech which is intended to apply to more than a narrow selection of the world's languages must give explicit recognition to the distinction between deep and surface structure and must define the parts of speech, not as classes of words in surface structure, but as deep-structure constituents of sentences (cf. 6.6.1). For the remainder of this section, we shall be concerned with the question whether any, or all, of the traditional parts of speech can be defined in this way.

7.6.2 *Syntactic function of major parts of speech*

The distinction between deep and surface syntax was not made explicitly in traditional grammar. But it was implied, in part at least, by the assumption that all complex sentences, as well as various kinds of non-declarative sentences, clauses and phrases, were derived from simple, modally 'unmarked' sentences. Furthermore, the major parts of speech were associated with certain typical syntactic functions in simple sentences; and this was assumed by some grammarians to be a more important property of the parts of speech than their 'accidental', inflexional, characteristics in particular languages (cf. 7.1.2). It was asserted that every simple sentence is made up of two parts: a *subject* and a *predicate*. The subject was necessarily a noun (or a pronoun 'standing for' a noun). But the predicate fell into one of three types, according to the part of speech or parts of speech which occurred in it: (i) intransitive verb, (ii) transitive verb with its *object*, (iii) the 'verb *to be*' (or some other 'copula') with its *complement*. The object, like the subject, must be a noun. The complement must be either (*a*) an adjective, or (*b*) a noun.

The notions of 'subject', 'predicate', 'object' and 'complement' will be discussed in the following chapter. For the present, we will take them for granted; and we will assume that the statements made in the previous paragraph about their association with particular parts of speech are correct, for English at least. They may be illustrated by the following sentences:

(1) *Mary dances*

(2) *Mary cooks fish*

(3*a*) *Mary is beautiful*

(3*b*) *Mary is a child*

Omitting distinctions of tense, mood, aspect, countability and definiteness, we can generate these sentences with the appropriate structural descriptions by means of the following grammatical rules and associated lexicon:

Grammar	Lexicon
(i) $\Sigma \rightarrow A + X$	$A = \{Mary, fish, child, \ldots\}$
(ii) $X \rightarrow \begin{cases} B \\ C + A \\ D + Y \end{cases}$	$B = \{dance, \ldots\}$ $C = \{cook, \ldots\}$
(iii) $Y \rightarrow \begin{cases} E \\ A \end{cases}$	$D = \{be\}$ $E = \{beautiful, \ldots\}$

A diagrammatic representation of the underlying constituent-structure of these sentences is given in Fig. 17. It will be observed that *X* and *Y* are *auxiliary symbols*, the sole function of which is to label the nodes (cf. 6.1.3) and show that, whereas all four sentences are syntactically equivalent at the higher level, only (3*a*) and (3*b*) are

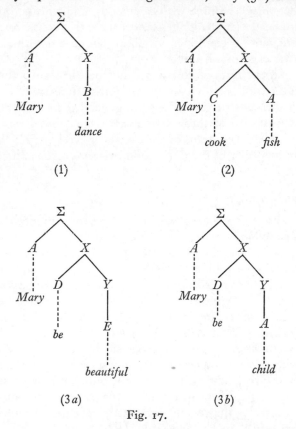

Fig. 17.

equivalent at the lower level of constituent-structure. Apart from the fact that we have employed the arbitrary symbols *A*, *B*, *C*, *D* and *E* in place of the traditional names for the parts of speech, the rules that have just been proposed formalize the traditional statements quoted above about the structure of various types of simple, declarative sentences. The question that now arises is whether it is possible to determine the traditional parts of speech or their functions solely on the basis of the constituent-structure relations that hold between the four types of sentences.

The answer to this question is clearly 'yes'. The class A is the class of nouns, since it is the one constituent class which all sentences have in common at the highest level of constituent-structure; B is the only class which combines directly with nouns (under the auxiliary node X) to form sentences, and is therefore the class of intransitive verbs; since the members of C combine with nouns (A), and with no other class, to form predicates (X), C is the class of transitive verbs; and D is the copula-class, since it combines with both nouns and with E, which is therefore the class of adjectives.

This argument rests of course on the specific assumptions incorporated in the traditional view of the syntactic function of the parts of speech. In the construction of a more general theory of the parts of speech, at least two of these assumptions must be challenged: the first has to do with the status of the copula or 'verb *to be*'; the second with the universality of the distinction between verbs and adjectives.

7.6.3   The 'verb to be'

It is a well-known fact that in many languages the sentences (3 *a*) *Mary is beautiful* and (3 *b*) *Mary is a child* would take the form 'Mary beautiful' and 'Mary (a) child'; that is to say, the predicative adjective or noun would be combined directly with the subject-noun without a *copula*. Even in the Indo-European languages the copulative function of 'the verb *to be*' appears to be of secondary development. The 'original' state of affairs is illustrated by contemporary Russian: *Marija krasivaja* ('Mary is beautiful') and *Marija rebënok* ('Mary is a child'), where *krasivaja* is the feminine form of the adjective in concord with *Marija* and *rebënok* is a noun (in the nominative case). In Latin and Greek 'the verb to be' was optional in such sentences. However, if we put them in the past tense (or in some other mood than the indicative), they would necessarily have the appropriate form of the 'verb *to be*' in Russian (*byla*, *budet*, etc.), and also in Latin (*erat*, etc.) and Greek (*ên*, etc.).

This fact suggests that the principal function of the copulative 'verb *to be*' in Russian, Greek and Latin is to serve as the *locus* in surface structure for the marking of tense, mood and aspect. ('Locus' is not a standard technical term. It is introduced to refer to the surface-structure element which 'carries' the overt marking of some syntactic distinction.) In other words, '*to be*' is not itself a constituent of deep structure, but a semantically-empty 'dummy verb' generated by the grammatical rules of Russian, Greek and Latin for the specification of certain distinctions (usually 'carried' by the verb) when there is no other verbal element to carry these distinctions. Sentences that are temporally, modally and aspectually 'unmarked' (e.g. 'Mary is beautiful') do not need the 'dummy' carrier.

This account of the function of the copula in Russian, Greek and Latin can be generalized for English and other languages, which have a 'verb *to be*' in sentences that are 'unmarked', as well as in those that are 'marked', for tense, mood and aspect.

One of the advantages of regarding the copulative 'verb *to be*' as a purely grammatical 'dummy' in English (like the 'dummy auxiliary' *do* in such sentences as *Do they come regularly?*, *He doesn't eat fish*, etc.) is that such noun-phrases as *the tall man* can be transformationally derived from the phrase-markers underlying such sentences as *the man is tall* without the need to delete the copula. Grammars of English which introduce *be* into the deep structure of sentences (cf. the rule $X \rightarrow D + Y$ in 7.6.2) will necessarily contain many transformational rules for the deletion of this element in a variety of positions in surface structure.

A more important point is that the 'verb *to be*' in such sentences as *Mary is beautiful* (unlike the verb *cook* in *Mary cooks fish*) is in contrast with only a limited set of other 'verbs', notably *become*. The occurrence of *become* rather than *be* depends upon the selection of the 'marked' rather than the 'unmarked' term in yet another grammatical opposition (of stative *v.* non-stative aspect). We will return to this point presently (cf. 8.4.7). For the moment, it is sufficient to have made a general case for the elimination of the 'verb *to be*' from the underlying constituent-structure of English. There is no doubt that a similar case could be made for other languages with a copulative 'verb *to be*'. We may turn now to the distinction between verbs and adjectives in general syntactic theory.

7.6.4 *Verb and adjective*

As we have already observed, adjectives were regarded as a subclass of 'verbs' by Plato and Aristotle, but as a subclass of 'nouns' by the Alexandrians and their successors; the tripartite distinction of nouns, verbs and adjectives (as independent parts of speech) was not established until the medieval period (cf. 1.2.5). This difference of attitude towards the adjective in Greek and Latin is readily explained in terms of the distinction between deep and surface structure. The principal reason for grouping the adjective and the noun together in Greek and

Latin is that they are both inflected for number and case. But the inflexion of the adjective is clearly a matter of surface structure: its number and case (and also its gender) are derived by the transformational rules of concord from the noun which it modifies. Otherwise the status of the adjective in Greek and Latin is not strikingly different from its status in English, where there is no concord between adjective and noun. Plato and Aristotle considered that the most typical function of both the adjective and the verb was that of predication, whereas the most characteristic function of the noun was that of naming the subject of the predication. It was for this reason that they grouped the adjective with the verb; and logicians have taken the same view. On the other hand, since the medieval period, most grammarians have drawn as sharp a distinction between the adjective and the verb as they have between the verb and the noun. We may therefore ask what, if anything, distinguishes the adjective from the verb in general syntactic theory? For simplicity, we will illustrate from English.

The two most obvious differences between the lexical classes in English traditionally referred to as adjectives and verbs both have to do with the surface phenomenon of inflexion. (1) The adjective, when it occurs in predicative position, does not take the verbal suffixes associated with distinctions of tense, mood and aspect; instead, a 'dummy verb' (*be, become*, etc.) is generated by the grammar to carry the necessary inflexional suffixes. Thus, *Mary is beautiful, Mary would have been beautiful*: *Mary dances, Mary would have danced*; but not **Mary beautiful-s* or **Mary would have beautiful-ed*, or **Mary is dance* or **Mary would have been dance*. (2) The verb is less freely transformed to the position of modifier in the noun-phrase; but when it does occur in this syntactic position, unlike the adjective, it bears the suffix -*ing*. Thus, *the beautiful girl*: *the singing girl*; but not **the beautiful-ing girl* or **the sing girl*.

In 'notional' treatments of the parts of speech, adjectives are frequently said to denote 'qualities', and verbs to denote either 'actions' or 'states'. But the difference between a 'quality' and a 'state' (if it is not entirely illusory) is less striking than the difference between an 'action' and a 'state'. One might well wonder, for example, whether *know, exist, happy, young*, etc. refer to 'states' or 'qualities'. There is no doubt, however, that *know* and *exist*, on the one hand, and *happy* and *young*, on the other, fall together grammatically. This question is decided for us by the criteria discussed in the previous paragraph. But there are many languages (e.g. Chinese) to which these criteria do not apply; and linguists tend to say that there is no adjective *v.* verb distinction in such languages, but rather a distinction between stative verbs and verbs of action.

A distinction between *stative verbs* and *verbs of action* is also relevant to English. As we have already seen, there are certain stative verbs in English which do not normally occur in the progressive form (cf. 7.5.7): by contrast with these, the majority of English verbs, which occur freely in the progressive, may be called verbs of 'action'. This aspectual difference between stative verbs and verbs of action is matched by a similar difference in English adjectives. Most English adjectives are stative, in the sense that they do not normally take progressive aspect when they occur in predicative position (e.g. *Mary is beautiful*, not **Mary is being beautiful*). But there are a number of adjectives which occur freely with the progressive in the appropriate circumstances (cf. *Mary is being silly now*). In other words, to be stative is normal for the class of adjectives, but abnormal for verbs; to be non-stative is normal for verbs, but abnormal for adjectives. The possibility of free combination with progressive aspect correlates with a number of other important features of English syntax: most notably, with the potentiality of occurrence in answer to a question like *What did she do?*, *What is she doing?*. Both *Mary danced* (*that's what she did*) and *Mary is being silly* (*that's what she's doing*) are possible answers to questions of this form, but not **Mary knows Greek* (*that's what she does*) or **Mary is beautiful* (*that's what she does*).

We talk about 'stative verbs' in English (as distinct from adjectives) and 'non-stative adjectives' (as distinct from verbs) because the aspectual contrast of stative *v.* non-stative in general coincides with, but in particular instances is in conflict with, the inflexional differences traditionally regarded as being of greater importance in the definition of the parts of speech. It is, however, the aspectual contrast which correlates, if anything does, with the notional definition of the verb and the adjective in terms of 'action' and 'quality'.

7.6.5 *The adverb*

A typical traditional definition of the adverb might run something like this: the adverb is a part of speech which serves as a modifier of a verb, an adjective or another adverb or adverbial phrase.

The first point to notice about this definition is the terminological one. The Latin prefix *ad-* (Greek *epi-*) may be translated as 'attached to and modifying'. But this is also the sense of 'adjective' (Greek *epithetos*). The adjective was the modifier *par excellence* of traditional grammar: it was 'attached to' and 'modified' the noun (and, for reasons that have already been discussed, it was regarded as a type of noun in the post-Aristotelian period). The adjective was therefore a nominal modifier (adnominal), and the adverb a verbal modifier (adverbial). But the definition given above makes reference to the 'modification' of adjectives as well as to the 'modification' of verbs. The point is that the traditional term 'adverb' (and indeed the definitions of Dionysius Thrax and Priscian) depended, implicitly, upon the earlier and wider sense of 'verb'. In other words, it pre-supposed that 'adjectives' and 'verbs' (in the narrower, more modern sense) were to be regarded as members of the same major syntactic class for the purpose of stating their combinatorial properties with respect to members of other major syntactic classes. We have already seen that 'adjectives' and 'verbs' have much in common, and that in many languages (including English) they are correctly brought together as members of the same deep-structure category.

The second point to notice about the definition of the adverb that we gave above is this: it implies that the adverb is a recursive category (more typically than the other parts of speech) in the sense that one adverb may modify another. For example, *extraordinarily* and *well* are both adverbs (of 'degree' and 'manner', respectively) in sentences like *Mary dances extraordinarily well* and *Mary cooks fish extraordinarily well*; and *extraordinarily* modifies *well* in the endocentric adverbial phrase *extraordinarily well*. It was on the basis of these combinatorial possibilities in simple sentences that both Jespersen and Hjelmslev constructed their theories of the parts of speech (independently of one another and with certain differences which, in the context of the present discussion, may be disregarded) some thirty years ago. We will give an outline of their views presently. But first we must say a little more about adverbs.

In traditional grammar, adverbs constitute a very heterogeneous class; and it is doubtful whether any general theory of syntax would bring together as members of the same syntactic class all the forms that are traditionally described as 'adverbs'. We will restrict our attention at this point to adverbs of 'manner' (as exemplified by *well* and *beautifully* in *Mary cooks fish well* and *Mary dances beautifully*).

Most adverbs of manner in English (and also in certain other languages) are distinct from, but morphologically-related to, 'adjectives' (cf. *beautifully*: *beautiful*). Furthermore, they are transformationally related to the corresponding 'adjectives' in a variety of parallel constructions: cf. *Mary is a beautiful dancer*: *Mary dances beautifully*. Since there would seem to be no possibility of paradigmatic opposition between the 'adverb of manner' and the 'adjective', they are to be regarded as contextually-determined variants of the same 'part of speech'. The attachment of the adverbial suffix -*ly* (in English) to 'adjectives' like *beautiful* (and the 'rewriting' of *good* as *well*) is to be handled by the rules which convert the deep-structure analysis into the surface structure of sentences. In other words, 'adverbial' refers to the modification of one verb (in the wider sense of this term) by another verb, the modifying verb being typically, but not necessarily (cf. *smilingly*, etc.), an 'adjective'. Not all 'adjectives' occur in 'adverbial' positions: cf. **The light shone greenly*, etc. Conversely, others occur as modifiers of nouns only in constructions which are transformationally derived from structures in which the 'adjective' has an 'adverbial' function: cf. *a rapid movement ← move rapidly*. But the majority of 'adjectives' in English modify both nouns and verbs in deep structure.

7.6.6 *A 'categorial' interpretation of the parts of speech*

In our discussion of the adverb, we made reference to the theories of the parts of speech put forward some years ago by Jespersen and Hjelmslev. These theories have tended to be neglected by most linguists in recent years (as part of the general lack of interest in 'notional' grammar). With the possibility of formalizing the distinction between deep structure and surface structure in transformational syntax, these theories have assumed a new importance in general syntactic theory. They have their roots in traditional grammar, and they were based on evidence from many languages.

We shall refer to Jespersen's formulation rather than Hjelmslev's (although, on points of detail, Hjelmslev's is somewhat subtler); but we will not use Jespersen's terminology, which is in conflict with the sense attached to particular terms elsewhere in this book and might lead to confusion. For Jespersen, nouns were categories of the *first degree*; verbs (including 'adjectives') were categories of the *second degree*; and adverbs categories of the *third degree*. This notion of what we are calling 'degree' is defined in terms of the combinatorial properties of the categories in question. Each category is modified, in the most typical simple structures, by a category of 'higher' degree. Nouns are modified by verbs (including 'adjectives'), which are therefore *adnominal* categories; verbs are modified by adverbs, which are therefore *ad-adnominal* categories; and adverbs are modified by other adverbs. No more than three degrees are required for the classification of the parts of speech (in any language referred to by either Jespersen or Hjelmslev), since there is no major category whose function it is to modify categories of the third degree.

It is worth pointing out here that this theory of 'degree' can be formalized very neatly in terms of categorial grammar (cf. 6.3.1): in fact, it was implicit in the early development of the notions of categorial grammar by Leśniewski and Ajdukiewicz. The noun is a fundamental category; all other parts of speech are derived, complex categories. Categories of the second degree combine with categories of the first degree (according to the principles of well-formedness which Ajdukiewicz called 'syntactic connectedness') to form sentences (or 'propositions'). Categories of the third degree combine with one another to form categories of the third degree.

For typographical simplicity, let us now introduce a numerical system of notation for the categorial representation of this notion of 'degree'. (The numerals may be defined to be equivalent to the 'fractional' expressions employed in our earlier references to categorial grammar.) We will use o (zero) for 'sentence', 1 for 'noun', 2 for 'verb' (including 'adjective'), and 3 for 'adverb'; and we will use 'primes' to indicate recursion, e.g. 3' ('three prime'), 3'' ('three double-prime'), etc. The underlying constituent-structure of a sentence like *Mary dances extraordinarily well* is given in terms of these numerical conventions in Fig. 18. It may be represented, equivalently, as $o(1 + 2(2 + 3(3 + 3')))$. The reader will observe that the system is assumed to be *non-directional*: given a complex category x composed of a pair of fundamental or derived categories, we can 'cancel' the 'denominator' (in the 'fractional' representation) of x with another category y, whether x and y are adjacent to one another or not in the surface structure of the sentence, and independently of the relative sequence of x and y in surface structure. In terms of the numerical notation, 3' cancels with 3 to yield 3, 3 cancels with 2 to yield 2, and 2 cancels with 1 to yield o.

We pointed out in an earlier section that (bidirectional) categorial grammars were weakly, but perhaps not strongly, equivalent to simple, context-free phrase-structure grammars (cf. 6.3.7). Neither categorial grammars nor simple phrase-structure grammars are sufficiently powerful for the total description of the syntax of any natural language. This has been proved by Chomsky (and others). So far no one has developed a transformational grammar with a categorial, rather than a phrase-structure, base-component. (Shau-mjan's theory comes closest to this conception; but it has certain other features which make it rather difficult to compare formally with Chomsky's theory of transformational syntax, and it has not yet been illustrated in detail.) Nevertheless, the notion of 'degree' has a good deal of support in the traditional theory of the parts of speech and in the application of this theory to the description of many languages

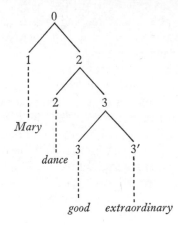

Mary dances extraordinarily well

Fig. 18. A categorial representation of underlying constituent-structure.

throughout the world. It is noticeable that much of the work now being published by a number of linguists (Lakoff, Rosenbaum, Fillmore, and others), though not by Chomsky himself, assumes the 'categorial' identity of the 'verb' and the 'adjective' in the deep structure of English. It is not inconceivable that further developments will justify the view that the base-component of a more adequate transformational grammar of English than is yet available will include a 'sub-component', the rules of which can be more elegantly formulated in terms of categorial grammar. There are, however, other features of deep structure which cannot be formalized by categorial grammars. We shall turn to these presently, drawing upon our discussion of the secondary grammatical categories and the parts of speech in this chapter. But first we must refer to an alleged inadequacy of categorial grammars.

7.6.7   *An alleged inadequacy of categorial grammars*

It has been suggested that categorial grammars have one serious inadequacy by comparison with phrase-structure grammars. The criticism is this. A categorial grammar will identify 'adjectives' and 'intransitive verbs' as members of the same major category (e.g. *beautiful* and *dance* in such sentences as *Mary is beautiful* and *Mary dances*), but will fail to relate 'transitive verbs' and 'intransitive verbs'. At first sight, this is a damaging criticism. But the relationship between 'transitive verbs' and 'intransitive verbs' is by no means as straightforward as current transformational theory would suggest. We must leave that question for a later chapter (cf. section 8.2). At this point we will draw attention to an equally serious inadequacy in the base-component formalized along the lines proposed by Chomsky in his most recent work. The point is that any theoretically satisfactory solution for phrase-structure grammar could be extended to categorial grammar; and it would automatically dispose of the criticism referred to above. Let us therefore turn our attention briefly to phrase-structure grammars, and the way in which they formalize the rules of the base-component of a transformational grammar.

7.6.8   *An inadequacy of phrase-structure grammars*

Consider the following rules:

(1) $\Sigma \rightarrow NP + Aux + VP$

(2) $VP \rightarrow V + NP$

(3) $VP \rightarrow V$

(4) $NP \rightarrow T + N$

Assuming a lexicon of the following kind

$N = \{man, doctor, \ldots\}$

$V = \{examine, leave, \ldots\}$

$T = \{the, a, \ldots\}$

and the necessary rules for the development of *Aux* (to handle tense, mood and aspect), for the assignment of number to the nouns and for the subsequent handling of subject–verb concord, the above phrase-structure rules will generate such sentences as *The doctor examines the man* $(T + N + V + s + T + N)$ and *The man leaves* $(T + N + V + s)$. There are various ways in which the relationship between 'transitive' and 'intransitive' verbs can be formalized in a phrase-structure grammar. The above set of rules does so by making them both members of the same major category (V) and distinguishing particular members of V, we will assume, by marking them in the lexicon with a *feature* (not shown above) which indicates whether the verb in question may or must have a following NP: cf. rule (2). This is essentially the technique developed by Chomsky in *Aspects of the Theory of Syntax*. (The earlier system of *Syntactic Structures* formalized the relationship between 'transitive' and 'intransitive' verbs quite differently.)

The point we wish to make here is simply this: the rules given above fail to formalize the fact that there is an essential, language-independent, relationship between N and NP and between V and VP. As far as the formalization of phrase-structure grammars is concerned, it is a matter of 'accidental' coincidence that linguists will include in their grammars of different languages rules which always expand NP into a string of symbols containing N and rules which always expand VP into a string of symbols containing V. In other words, phrase-structure grammars fail to formalize the fact that NP and VP are not merely mnemonically-convenient symbols, but stand for sentence-constituents which are necessarily nominal and verbal, respectively, because they have N and V as an obligatory major constituent. (Chomsky himself has recognized this particular inadequacy: he has indicated a possible solution, but this has not yet been developed in detail, and it is not referred to so far in the published literature.)

What is required, and what was assumed in traditional grammar, is some way of relating sentence-constituents of the form XP to X (where X is any major category: N, V, etc.). It would not only be perverse, but it should be theoretically impossible for any linguist to propose, for example, rules of the following form (for the base-component of English or of any other language):

$(1a)$ $\Sigma \to VP + Aux + NP$

$(2a)$ $NP \to V + VP$

$(3a)$ $NP \to V$

$(4a)$ $VP \to T + N$

The present system of formalization does not exclude rules like this; and they are equivalent, not only weakly, but perhaps also strongly, to the four rules given earlier. (This follows from the principles of phrase-structure grammar discussed in the previous chapter.)

If the problem can be solved for phrase-structure grammars, it can be solved also for categorial grammars. To take just the case of 'transitive' and 'intransitive' verbs: any lexical item with the categorial classification $(\Sigma n)/n$, e.g. a 'transitive' verb, would be defined by the general principles of the system to be the head of a phrase analysed by the grammar as Σn. Similarly for 'intransitive' verbs, which have the categorial classification Σn. However, as we have already remarked, the question of transitivity is more complex than we have so far indicated. No current system of transformational grammar handles all the facts correctly. We return to this point in the following chapter.

7.6.9   Categories and features

The purpose of the above discussion of categorial and phrase-structure grammars was not merely to focus attention upon a rather important difference between the deep-structure combinatorial properties of the major parts of speech relative to one another, on the one hand, and their various inflexional and transformational characteristics, on the other.

We have seen that the difference between what are traditionally distinguished as 'verbs' and 'adjectives' in English is rather complex, involving differences of aspect ('state' v. 'action') and differences of inflexion. But we have also seen that the inflexional and aspectual characteristics do not always coincide. 'Adjectives' and 'verbs' are similar in the way in which they combine with nouns to form bracketed strings of constituents in deep structure; and this might be appropriately referred to as their *categorial* function. The transformational, aspectual and inflexional differences associated with particular subclasses of this 'second-degree' category are more satisfactorily specified in the lexicon by means of *features* which differentiate the subclasses.

Current transformational grammars, formalized according to the system recently proposed by Chomsky, make use of such features, but only at the lowest level of constituent-structure. Our discussion of the minor parts of speech and the secondary grammatical categories in this chapter would suggest that tense, mood, aspect, number, definiteness, etc., are associated with constituents of various levels.

Such categories cannot be regarded as universal categories of human language (although they can be defined in universal terms within the general theory of syntax). Languages vary in respect of the 'selection' they make from the total set of secondary grammatical categories recognized in general syntactic theory: and the way in which the oppositions within these categories are realized in surface-structure also varies considerably from language to language. What may be universal in human language are the combinatorial properties of the major categories relative to one another (as suggested in the theories of Jespersen and Hjelmslev). If this is so, we can envisage the possibility that the base-component of a transformational grammar for any language will comprise two 'subcomponents'. The first (whether it is formalized in terms of rewrite rules or not) would be truly universal and would account for the categorial combination of lexical items. The second would contain rules associating features of tense, mood, aspect, number, definiteness, etc., at various levels of the constituent-structure generated by the categorial subcomponent.

7.6.10 *Grammatica est una...*

The suggestion that has just been made should be regarded as extremely tentative: it may not be technically feasible, and it may rest upon insufficient empirical evidence. But one point should be stressed. A few years ago the majority of linguists would have rejected the possibility of constructing a universal theory of grammatical categories. This is no longer so. As Chomsky has pointed out: 'modern work...has shown a great diversity in the surface structures of languages', but 'the deep structures for which universality is claimed may be quite distinct from the surface structures of sentences as they actually appear'. It follows that 'the findings of modern linguistics...are not inconsistent with the hypotheses of universal grammarians'. Once again Roger Bacon's famous statement about universal grammar is being quoted with approval by linguists: 'Grammar is substantially the same in all languages, even though it may vary accidentally' (cf. 1.2.7). The scholastic terms 'substantially' (*secundum substantiam*) and 'accidentally' (*accidentaliter*) may yet be given an acceptable syntactic interpretation in terms of the formalization of the distinction between deep and surface structure.

8

GRAMMATICAL FUNCTIONS

8.1 Subject, predicate and adjunct

8.1.1 *Nuclear and extranuclear constituents*

It is a fundamental principle of traditional grammar, and also of much modern syntactic theory, that every simple, declarative sentence consists of two obligatory major constituents, a *subject* and a *predicate*; and that it may contain, in addition, one or more *adjuncts*. Adjuncts (of place, time, manner, reason, etc.: we shall come back later to the various kinds of adjuncts) are optional, or structurally dispensable, constituents of the sentence: they may be removed without affecting the remainder of the sentence.

To illustrate the way in which these terms are applied, we may refer to the sentence *John killed Bill in Central Park on Sunday*. The subject is *John*; the predicate is *killed Bill*; and *in Central Park* and *on Sunday* are adjuncts, of place and time respectively. Either or both of the adjuncts may be omitted without destroying the grammaticality of the sentence: *John killed Bill on Sunday, John killed Bill in Central Park, John killed Bill*. By contrast, neither **killed Bill in Central Park on Sunday* nor **John in Central Park on Sunday* are grammatically complete sentences (for the notion of 'incomplete' sentences, cf. 5.2.3). We will say that the subject and predicate together form the *nucleus* of the sentence. The subject and the predicate are therefore *nuclear*, and adjuncts *extranuclear*, constituents.

8.1.2 *Topic and comment*

It has already been mentioned that, from the time of Plato onward, the definition of the noun and the verb has been closely associated with the distinction of subject and predicate (cf. 1.2.5, 7.6.4). Sapir was merely repeating the traditional view when he said: 'There must be something to talk about and something must be said about this subject of discourse...The subject of discourse is a noun...No language wholly fails to distinguish noun and verb, though in particular cases the nature of the distinction may be an elusive one.' In this passage, Sapir implicitly defines the subject as the person or thing about which something is said, and the predicate as the statement made about that person or thing. But this is only one of the ways in which subject and predicate have been defined by grammarians. Since we shall also be considering some of these other definitions, we will adopt Hockett's now widely accepted terminology for the notions referred to by Sapir: we will call the person or thing about which something is said the *topic*, and the statement made about this person or thing the *comment*.

Hockett introduces these terms as follows: 'The most general characterization of predicative constructions is suggested by the terms "topic" and "comment"...: The speaker announces a topic and then says something about it. Thus *John/ran away*; *That new book by Thomas Guernsey/I haven't read yet*. [The oblique stroke in the sentences used as examples indicates the major constituent-structure break.] In English and the familiar languages of Europe, topics are usually also subjects and comments are predicates: so in *John/ran away*. But this identification fails sometimes in colloquial English, regularly in certain special situations in formal English, and more generally in some non-European languages.'

Two points may be made with reference to the passage quoted from Hockett. First, 'subject' and 'predicate', as syntactic notions, are distinguished from 'topic' and 'comment' (although they are said to coincide with 'topic' and 'comment' in the most frequently-used declarative sentences of 'English and the familiar languages of Europe'). Second, Hockett appears to imply that the topic necessarily precedes the comment: he goes on to say, in connexion with his second example, '*That new book by Thomas Guernsey* is spoken first because it specifies what the speaker is going to talk about: it is the topic of the sentence, though not its subject. The topic is at the same time the *object* of the verb *haven't read* (*yet*), and the subject of that verb is *I*, part of the comment of the whole sentence.'

The topic–comment distinction is frequently glossed (though not by Hockett) in terms of contextual dispensability or predictability: the topic, or 'subject of discourse', is described as that element which is *given* in the general situation or in some explicit question to which the speaker is replying; and the comment as that part of the utterance which adds something *new* (and thus communicates information to the hearer). By this criterion, we cannot say what is the topic and what is the comment in a particular utterance (or indeed whether it can reasonably be divided into topic and comment) unless we know what is contextually 'given'. For example, if *John ran away* answers the question, explicit or implicit, 'Who ran away?', then by the given–new criterion *John* is the comment, and *ran away* is the topic. If the explicit or implicit question is nothing more specific than 'What happened?', then merely the past tense is contextually predictable, and all the rest of the utterance is 'new'. Only if the statement *John ran away* answers the explicit or implicit question 'What did John do?' is *John* the topic and *ran away* the comment according to the given–new criterion (and more precisely, it is *ran away* minus the tense-specification that is 'new'). The terms 'given' and 'new' are taken from Halliday, who distinguishes various other notions involved in the analysis of sentences into topic and comment.

Typically, the utterance *John ran away* would not be used in reply to an explicit question in which either *John* or *ran away* was 'given', but rather *He ran away* ('What did John do?') or *John (did)* ('Who ran away?'). In English, and possibly in all languages, the given–new criterion finds its principal application, not in the determination of the syntactic structure of *sentences*, but in the establishment of the conditions of deletability and pronominal substitution in the 'situationally-bound', elliptical *utterances* of connected discourse (for the distinction of sentences and utterances, cf. 5.1.2).

In many languages, by the use of one word-order rather than another or the employment of a particular particle, the speaker can indeed make it clear that he is 'announcing a topic' (not necessarily 'given' in the situation) and then 'say something about it'. This is only possible to a limited degree in English. It is one (among many) of the factors involved in the choice of a passive construction (cf. 8.3.3). But it does not operate in the determination of the form of *John ran away*. Such alternatives as *What John did was run away*, *It was John who ran away*, *The one who ran away was John*, as well as *Jóhn ran away*, *John rán away*, etc. (where the acute accent indicates contrastive or emphatic stress), are 'marked' for a complex set of other distinctions (which we will not go into here). *John ran away* is in fact structurally 'unmarked' for the distinction of topic and comment: it exemplifies the most 'neutral' form of the English sentence.

And yet, if we were presented with this sentence, in isolation from the context in which the corresponding utterance had occurred or might occur, we would no doubt agree with Hockett (and most linguists and logicians since the time of Plato) that something is being said about John, rather than about running away. What motivates our choice in the case of such 'unmarked' sentences is an interesting question. It leads us to the other main approach to the definition of subject and predicate found in traditional grammatical and logical theory. It is this second approach which, as we shall see, also underlies the traditional 'notional' definition of the noun as 'the name of a person or thing'; and it may be the only way of defining both 'subject' and 'noun' (interdependently) that is universally applicable. We have already hinted at this in the section on the parts of speech (cf. 7.6.9).

8.1.3 *Universals and particulars*

At this point we must return to the Aristotelian doctrine of the 'categories' of predication (cf. 7.1.2). It has been mentioned that the first category of *substance* was taken to be logically more fundamental than the remaining *accidental* properties: substances were persons or things of which the accidental properties (of quantity, quality, relation, action, place, state, etc.) could be predicated (or asserted) in logically well-formed propositions. According to this view, *John ran away*, *He is in London*, *My friend is tall*, etc., are logically well-formed: *John*, *he* and *my friend* denote substances (in these instances, persons); and *ran away*, *is in London*, and *is tall* make predications ('say something') about these substances—predications of action, place and quality, respectively.

Now, proper names, as well as pronouns and phrases which identify a definite person or thing (like *John*, *he* and *my friend*, in the examples of the previous paragraph) are to be regarded as the most 'substantival'—the most truly 'nominal'—of the expressions in a language (hence the traditional term 'substantive' for 'noun'). They are *particular* (or 'singular') terms, denoting some definite, *individual* substance. Other words and phrases, including indefinite 'common' nouns (*man*, *book*, etc.) and 'abstract' nouns (*goodness*, *beauty*, etc.), as well as verbs, adjectives and adverbs, are *universal* (or 'general') terms: they do not of themselves denote individual substances (unless they are syntactically determined, in the descriptive specification of an individual, e.g. *the man over there*), but they denote either a class of individuals or qualities, states, actions, etc., which may be associated with individuals.

Some logicians distinguish two kinds of universal terms (and, for convenience of exposition, we will adopt this terminological distinction): (i) *sortal* universals, which serve to group individuals into classes (whether these classes are thought to be definable on the basis of some inherent properties of their members or not), and (ii) *characterizing* universals, which refer to qualities, states, actions, etc. Typical sortal universals are the 'common' nouns of traditional grammar; typical characterizing universals are 'abstract' nouns, verbs, adjectives and adverbs.

On the basis of these distinctions, we can formulate the following important principle of traditional logic: whereas universal terms are found in both subject and predicate position in well-formed propositions, particular terms are restricted to subject position. Stock examples of propositions constructed out of a particular and a universal term are *Socrates is a man* (sortal) and *Socrates is wise* (characterizing); and of a proposition composed of two universal terms, *Men are wise*. (We will not go into the further traditional principle that, of two universal terms, it is the less specific term that is predicated of the more specific.)

The traditional distinction of particular and universal terms can be drawn independently of the Aristotelian and scholastic notions of substance and accidents. It rests upon the recognition, in the perceptual world, of a number of discrete, temporally-enduring 'entities' (persons, animals and things), of the principles of identification and classification, according to which these 'entities' may be named (as individuals) or 'sorted' into classes by means of the lexical conventions of the language in question, and of a set of recurrent properties, states, actions, etc., which may be associated with the 'entities'. There is no reason to doubt that (whatever its philosophical status) this everyday notion of 'entity' is applicable in a sufficient number of instances in the investigation of the vocabulary and syntactic structure of various languages, provided that we respect the distinction between 'notional' and 'formal' criteria (cf. 7.6.1).

8.1.4 *Congruence of logical and grammatical criteria*

It should now be clear why 'subject' and 'noun' are indissolubly associated in traditional grammatical and logical theory. The most typical nouns (to which the standard 'notional' definition applies without any trace of circularity: cf. 7.6.1) are those which denote individual persons and things. Their normal syntactic position in sentences containing just one such item combined with a non-noun (a verb, in the widest sense of this term: cf. 7.6.4) is that exemplified in *John ran away*. And the term 'subject' was defined in the first instance on the basis of such sentences.

What this means, in effect, is that the traditional grammarian or logician, like 'the man in the street', when confronted with *John ran away* and asked the topic–comment question 'What is being said about what?', will assume (in default of any contextual indications to the contrary) that the individual person, John, is more likely to be the focus of the speaker's interest, rather than the activity of running away. And confronted with *Horses are vicious animals* or *Virtue is rare*, he will say that the topics are *horses* and *virtue*, because of their syntactic parallelism with sentences composed of a particular and a universal term (*John ran away*, or *John is good*), which most clearly satisfy the conditions for the application of the traditional principles for determining the subject and the predicate. In other words, the traditional topic–comment criterion was implicitly determined by the substance–accidents distinction in the case of simple sentences containing a particular and a universal term; and the application of the topic–comment criterion to sentences consisting of two universal terms was determined by their overt grammatical structure.

In the definition of 'subject' and 'predicate' (as in many other matters) traditional logic and traditional grammar leaned heavily upon one another. They both made appeal to the Aristotelian doctrine of the categories of predication, which gave a philosophical basis to the view that the world is populated with individual persons, animals and things (substances) and that these substances are either the initiators or the victims ('agents' or 'patients') of activities and processes, are endowed with certain qualities, are situated in particular places at a particular time, are subject to change, and so on. The degree to which this view of the world is determined in detail by the grammatical structure of the classical languages is a vexed question, which we need not go into here. It suffices for the validation of the notion of 'subject' in general syntactic theory that the categories of logic and grammar should be seen as necessarily coincident with one another in the case of simple declarative sentences containing just one nominal expression.

Every language may be assumed to have, as its most typical sentence-type of minimal syntactic structure, a class of sentences whose nuclei are composed of a nominal and a verb (the term 'nominal' is intended to include nouns, pronouns and noun-phrases; and the term 'verb' is to be understood in the wider sense which also embraces adjectives: cf. 8.1.1, 7.6.4). The notions of 'subject' and 'predicate' are first defined, as we have seen, with reference to such sentences. They are then extended to sentences of more complex syntactic structure. It is in the course of this extension that a certain conflict may arise between various kinds of logical and grammatical criteria for identifying the subject.

8.1.5 *'Actor' and 'goal'*

Consider the English sentence *John kills Bill*, the nucleus of which consists of two nominals and a verb. In earlier chapters of this book, we have accepted the traditional view of the syntactic structure of such sentences, according to which (in the present instance) the subject is the noun *John* and the predicate is the phrase *kills Bill*, composed of the transitive verb *kills* with the noun *Bill* as its object (cf. 6.2.3, 7.6.4). The main reason for taking this view is that there is a grammatical parallelism between the noun *John* in *John kills Bill* and the subject in an intransitive sentence and between *kills Bill* and the predicate of an intransitive sentence (the terms 'subject' and 'predicate' being defined in the first instance, as we have seen, in relation to intransitive sentences, containing just one nominal). In both *John kills Bill* and *John runs* (*away*) there is concord between the singular noun *John* and the verbs *kills* and *runs*; and the number of the object-noun *Bill* is irrelevant for the rules of concord in English. If pronouns are substituted for the nouns, the pronoun standing for *John* will assume the same form (the 'nominative' case: cf. 7.4.5) in both the transitive and the intransitive sentence: *He kills Bill, He runs away*. The pronoun standing for *Bill* in the transitive sentence will assume a different form (the 'accusative'): *John kills him*. Furthermore, the two sentences may be co-ordinated in either order and one occurrence of *John* deleted from the resultant compound sentence: *John kills Bill and runs away, John runs away and kills Bill*. The transformational rules of co-ordination require that the constituent-structure of *John kills Bill* be identical with that of *John runs away* at the level accounted for by the rule $\Sigma \rightarrow NP + VP$ (to give this rule in its customary formulation: cf. 6.6.4). And there are many other transformational rules of English which depend upon the identification of *John* as the subject and *kills Bill* as the predicate in *John kills Bill*: cf. *I deplore John's killing Bill*: *I deplore John's running away*, etc. Finally, both *John kills Bill* and *John runs away* can be extended with *that's what he does*, where the 'pro-verb' *do* stands for either *kills Bill* or *runs away*, but not simply for *kills*.

This last fact is connected with another aspect of the traditional theory of subject and predicate, which has not so far been mentioned.

Both intransitive and transitive sentences in English may answer the implicit question 'What does X do?', where X is a nominal expression and *do* (in its second occurrence in the question) is a 'pro-verb' which brings together intransitive verbs, on the one hand, and transitive verbs + their objects, on the other. Whenever this condition holds (and it does not hold for either transitive or intransitive stative verbs: cf. 7.6.4), the subject may be described as the 'actor' (or 'agent'). By contrast, the object-noun in transitive sentences is the 'goal' (or 'patient'). The 'notional' interpretation of the subject as 'actor' and the object as 'goal' often conflicts with some of the other criteria referred to in the previous paragraph. For example, in the sentences *Wealth attracts robbers* and *Riches attract robbers*, the subjects are *wealth* and *riches* (according to the criterion of subject–verb concord), but *robbers* is the only noun that could be reasonably described as fulfilling the role of 'actor'. Nevertheless, for English (and a number of other languages, including Latin and Greek) there is some truth in the traditional view that the subject of an active, transitive sentence is the initiator of the action, and the object the 'patient' or 'goal'. The structure of the vocabulary reflects this, in that most transitive verbs tend to occur with an animate noun as their subject in active sentences, whereas the subject of an intransitive verb and the object of a transitive verb is relatively indifferent to the distinction between animate and inanimate nouns.

8.1.6 *Conflict between criteria*

Outside the Indo-European family, there are very many other languages (Basque, Eskimo, Georgian, etc.), where there is a systematic conflict, as it were, between the principal traditional criteria for the identification of the subject in active sentences containing a transitive verb. We will illustrate this from Eskimo. If the sentences listed as (1) and (2) below are compared (the inflexional endings have been shown as distinct from the stems—*qimmi-*, 'dog'; *agna-*, 'woman'; *taku-*, 'see'—by means of hyphens), it will be observed that one noun in each sentence is marked with the suffix -*q* and the other with -*p* (we are not here concerned with the verbal suffixes):

(1) *qimmi-p agna-q taku-b-a-a*, 'The dog sees the woman';

(2) *qimmi-q agna-p taku-b-a-a*, 'The woman sees the dog'.

We may say that, in transitive sentences, -*p* marks the 'actor' and -*q* the 'goal' of the 'action'. By this criterion, therefore, *qimmi-p* is the subject of sentence (1) and *agna-p* of (2). But in the translations of sentences like 'The dog runs away' and 'The woman runs away' (with an intransitive verb), the nouns *qimmi-* and *agna-* would have the suffix *-q*. This syntactic parallelism between the 'goal' of a transitive verb and the subject of an intransitive verb is generally referred to as 'ergativity'. We shall return to it later in connexion with the notion of 'transitivity', which we are taking for granted for the moment (cf. 8.2.3).

Here it is sufficient to point out that the traditional notion of 'subject', as it applies to transitive sentences, is partly dependent upon the grammatical structure of Latin and Greek (and other Indo-European languages), in which the following two conditions hold. (i) One of the two nouns in transitive sentences (and, where the 'notional' category of 'actor' is clearly applicable, it is the noun which denotes the 'actor') is marked with the same case-inflexion (the 'nominative': cf. 7.4.5) as the subject of intransitive sentences. (ii) The number (and person) of the verb is determined by the subject-noun of intransitive sentences and the 'actor'-noun of transitive sentences. Both of these conditions may be exemplified from English, if we use pronouns rather than nouns: *He sees them, They see him, He runs away, They run away*. (In Latin and Greek, as well as in various other Indo-European languages, the case-distinction manifest in *he* v. *him* and *they* v. *them* is also shown in non-neuter nouns: cf. 7.4.3.) As we have seen, in languages with an 'ergative' construction, the syntactic feature of case (and sometimes concord, although we have not illustrated this) would determine the 'goal'-noun of a transitive sentence as the subject. But this conflicts with the notion of the subject as the 'actor', rather than the 'goal' (or 'patient'); and, in practice, most linguists treat the 'actor'–'goal' distinction as dominant for languages, like Eskimo, with an ergative construction. They would say that the object of a transitive verb has the same case-inflexion as the subject of an intransitive verb.

In English, as also in Latin and Greek, the 'actor'–'goal' criterion is in systematic conflict with other grammatical criteria for defining the subject in passive sentences. In the sentence *Bill is killed by John*, the 'actor' is *John* and the 'goal' *Bill*. In this respect, *John kills Bill* and *Bill is killed by John* are identical. But, whereas *John* is traditionally regarded as the subject of the former, it is *Bill* that is taken to be the subject of the latter. The reasons include the following: (i) the case of the 'goal'-noun in passive sentences is 'nominative' (in English this can only be shown by means of pronouns: cf. *He hits*

them, They hit him, He is hit, They are hit); (ii) the 'goal'-noun of a
passive sentence determines the verb as singular or plural, in the
same way as does the subject of either a transitive or intransitive
non-passive sentence (cf. *Bill hits them, They hit Bill; Bill runs away,
They run away; Bill is hit, They are hit*); (iii) the 'goal'-noun of a
passive sentence may be identified with the 'actor'-subject of either
a transitive or an intransitive non-passive sentence for the purpose of
co-ordination (e.g. *Bill challenged John to a duel and was killed, Bill
fell downstairs and was killed*).

A further reason for saying that the 'goal', rather than the 'actor',
is the subject in passive sentences is that the 'actor' is an optional,
extranuclear, constituent (it is 'outside' the nucleus, at least in surface-
structure). *Bill was killed* is a complete sentence, whereas **John
killed* is not. The phrase *by John* in *Bill was killed by John* is traditionally regarded as an 'agentive' adjunct, syntactically comparable with
the 'instrumental' adjunct *with a knife* in *Bill was killed with a knife*
(cf. 7.4.5).

8.1.7 *Various kinds of subject*

We will discuss the relationship between active and passive sentences
below (cf. 8.3.3). At this point, it may be observed that many linguists
have drawn a distinction between the 'grammatical' and 'logical'
subject of passive sentences; saying that in *Bill was killed by John* the
'grammatical' subject is *Bill* and the 'logical' (or underlying) subject
John whereas in the corresponding active sentence *John killed Bill* the
noun *John* is both the 'grammatical' and the 'logical' subject (and
Bill the object).

The terminological distinction between a 'grammatical' and a
'logical' subject has recently been adopted by Chomsky. He has
further suggested: 'Topic–Comment is the basic grammatical
relation of surface structure corresponding (roughly) to the fundamental Subject–Predicate relation of deep structure. Thus we might
define the Topic-of the Sentence as the leftmost NP immediately
dominated by S in the surface structure, and the Comment-of the
Sentence as the rest of the string.' There is some plausibility in this
suggestion. But the topic cannot simply be identified with the
surface-structure, 'grammatical' subject. In terms of Chomsky's
proposal, the phrase *this book* would (quite reasonably) be identified
as the topic in both the active sentence *This book millions of people
have read* and the passive sentence *This book has been read by millions*

of people: it is only in the passive sentence that it is a 'grammatical' subject. Furthermore, one might wonder whether the notion of 'topic' should be restricted to nominal expressions (unless the notion 'topic' is restricted by appeal to the substance–accidents distinction). In the Russian sentence, *Bežal Ivan*, 'John ran (away)', the occurrence of the verb in initial position might be taken as an indication that it is the topic of discourse ('announced by the speaker': cf. 8.1.2), although *Ivan* is presumably both the 'logical' and the 'grammatical' subject. And in the Latin sentences *Interfectus est Caesar*, 'Caesar was killed', it could be maintained that the topic is *interfectus* (*est*), which is identical with neither the 'grammatical' subject *Caesar* nor the 'logical' subject (some unspecified 'actor').

Consideration of the examples given in this section shows that there are far more distinctions involved than can be accounted for by the simple dichotomy of 'grammatical' and 'logical' subjects. Even a three-way distinction of 'psychological' subject (the topic), 'grammatical' subject (in surface structure) and 'logical' subject (in deep structure) fails to capture all the distinctions which, at one time or another, have been associated with the notion of 'subject' in grammatical and logical theory.

The principal aim of this section has been to show that the distinction between subject and predicate is universally and clearly applicable only in sentences whose nuclei consist of one nominal expression and an intransitive predicate; and, in such sentences, the definition of the subject depends ultimately upon the same criteria as those which define the noun in general syntactic theory. As we have seen, in passive sentences and in sentences with more than one nominal in their nucleus, the traditional criteria tend to conflict with one another in their application to various languages. It is worth pointing out, however, that most of the more strictly 'formal' criteria that have been mentioned for distinguishing the subject have to do with such 'surface' phenomena as case, concord and co-ordination. In the following section, we shall consider the distinction between the subject and the object of a sentence from a somewhat different point of view. But first we must briefly consider the notion of 'adjunct'.

8.1.8 *Adjuncts*

An adjunct is by definition a 'modifier' attached to a 'head', upon which it is dependent and from which it can be 'detached' without any consequent syntactic change in the sentence (for the terms 'modifier' and 'head', cf. 6.4.2). We are here concerned with what are normally regarded as sentence-adjuncts, rather than with the modifiers of lower-level constituents (such as adjectives modifying nouns within the noun-phrase, adverbs modifying verbs within the verb-phrase, etc.). Examples of sentence-adjuncts have been given at the beginning of this section (*in Central Park* and *on Sunday*, in the sentence *John killed Bill in Central Park on Sunday*).

Sentence-adjuncts may be of various ranks (clauses, phrases or words). For example, the clause *as soon as his wife arrived*, the phrase *three hours later*, and the word *immediately* can all be attached as adjuncts to the nucleus (which is itself a complete sentence) *John left for the office*. Furthermore, adjuncts fall into various classes according to their semantic function: they may be adjuncts of time, of place, of purpose, of result, of condition, and so on. Not all these different classes are manifest at all ranks. But we will not go into these details here. In this section, we will restrict our attention to adjuncts of time and place, which have a particularly interesting place in the structure of language.

8.1.9 *Adjuncts and complements*

The first point to notice about temporal and locative adjuncts is that at the rank of the word and the phrase (though not at clause rank) they are frequently identical in internal structure with temporal and locative *complements* (for this sense of 'rank', cf. 5.5.1). So far the term 'complement' has been employed only in relation to nominal or adjectival expressions which combine with the 'copula' in such sentences as *Mary is a beautiful girl* and *Mary is beautiful* (cf. 7.6.2). In traditional grammar, the term is used to refer to any word or phrase (other than the verb itself) which is an obligatory constituent of the predicate: for instance, the object of a transitive verb (cf. *the ball* in *John caught the ball*). The predicative complement is syntactically required, in order to 'complete' the structure of the predicate (hence the term 'complement'). More particularly, the term 'complement' is used of such 'adverbial' expressions as *in Central Park* or *on Sunday* in sentences like *The parade was in Central Park* or *The demonstration was on Sunday*. The temporal and locative phrases in these two sentences are obviously not adjuncts (since **The parade was* and **The demonstration was* are syntactically incomplete). The difference between an adjunct and a complement is, in principle, quite clear: the former is an optional (extranuclear) constituent, and the latter an obligatory (nuclear) constituent of the sentence.

In practice, the distinction between sentence-adjuncts and predicative complements is often far from clear. As we have just seen, the same class of words or phrases may occur as a locative or temporal adjunct in one set of sentences and as a complement (of the copula) in the other. This fact alone would be of small consequence. But consider now a sentence like *The demonstration occurred on Sunday*. In traditional accounts of English grammar, *occur* is regarded as an intransitive verb (which, by definition, combines with a nominal to form a sentence-nucleus, and requires no complement). This classification of *occur* implies that *The demonstration occurred* (unlike **The demonstration was*) is a complete sentence, and therefore that *on Sunday* is an adjunct. On the other hand, the semantic relationship between *The demonstration was on Sunday* and *The demonstration occurred on Sunday* would tend to suggest that *was* and *occurred* are elements of the same type, and therefore that *on Sunday* is a predicative complement in both instances.

It has already been proposed that the copula is not a lexical item in such sentences as *Mary is beautiful*, but a purely grammatical 'dummy' serving as the 'locus' for the indication of tense, mood and aspect (cf. 7.6.3). We may now extend the application of the same principle to the analysis of sentences in which *be* is found with a temporal or locative complement (e.g. *on Sunday* or *in Central Park*); and there seems to be no reason why such 'verbs' as *occur*, *happen*, *take place*, etc., should not also be treated as temporal and locative copulas in such sentences as *The demonstration occurred on Sunday*, etc.

8.1.10 *Locative and temporal complements*

To account for the underlying constituent-structure of sentences like *The demonstration was (occurred, etc.) on Sunday* and *The parade was (took place, etc.) in Central Park*, the following two rules, (1) and (2) would seem to be required

   (1) $\Sigma \rightarrow$ Nominal + Time

   (2) $\Sigma \rightarrow$ Nominal + Place

in addition to rule (3), which underlies at least the intransitive nuclei (including the 'adjectival' nuclei) of non-locative and non-temporal sentences

   (3) $\Sigma \rightarrow$ Nominal + Verbal

Some of the implications of this treatment will be examined later (8.4.2 ff.). But a number of questions arise at this point in connexion with the distinction (if there is any clear distinction) between adjuncts and complements.

There is an important condition which must be imposed upon the class of nominals which occur with temporal complements under the application of rule (1). Such 'sentences' as *John was yesterday, *The dog occurred on Sunday, etc., must be excluded as ungrammatical. Let us therefore draw a distinction between what we will call *first-order* and *second-order* nominals in English, and say that only second-order nominals may occur in sentences whose underlying structure is Nominal + Time.

First-order nominals might well be called substantival nominals, since in the most obvious instances they denote persons, animals, things or places: in 'notional' terms, they are the most 'noun-like' nominals (cf. 7.6.1). By contrast, second-order nominals do not denote 'substances'. Some of them may be items listed in the lexicon (cf. 4.3.1): e.g. *accident*, *event*, etc. But the majority can be transformationally derived from sentence-nuclei generated by means of rule (3). Our example, *the demonstration*, is of this type.

Once we take note of this characteristic of second-order nominals, the syntactic distinction between temporal adjuncts and temporal complements seems to be even less satisfactory. What is the deep-structure difference, we may ask, between *The demonstration took place on Sunday* and *They demonstrated on Sunday* (not to mention *They held the demonstration on Sunday*, etc.)? If there is any difference at all, it is not illuminated by invoking a constituent-structure distinction in the deep structure: Nominal + Time, on the one hand, and Nominal + Verbal + Time, on the other. It would seem rather that the two sentences have the same underlying constituent-structure, with or without additional syntactic features determining the selection of one surface-structure 'version' or the other. This indicates that we should introduce into the grammar a rule which transforms the output of Σ → Nominal + Verbal (this rule for nominalization is required anyway) and embeds it in the subject-position of the structure generated by Σ → Nominal + Time.

Transformationally-derived second-order nominals may also occur in sentences with a locative complement, as well as in those with a temporal complement: cf. *The demonstration took place in Central Park*, *The death of Churchill has occurred in London*, etc. It is to be observed, however, that not only second-order nominals, but also

fully substantival (first-order) nominals, occur with locative complements: cf. *John was at home* v. **John was on Sunday*.

The difference between first-order and second-order nominals is
also relevant to an interesting asymmetry in the distribution of the
locative and temporal copulas other than *be* (semantically, the most
'empty' of all copulas in English). Neither **John occurred on Sunday*,
nor **John took place at home* is possible (except of course by means of
a conceivable, but unusual, 'recategorization' of *John*, such that it is
understood as 'The birth of John', etc.—and the fact that such
'recategorization' can be effected and interpreted *ad hoc* depends
upon the difference we are discussing between the two classes of
nominals). The asymmetry that has been referred to lies in the fact
that *be* is found with second-order nominal subjects with both
locative and temporal predicates, but not with first-order nominal
subjects and temporal predicates; whereas *occur, take place, happen*,
etc., are restricted to second-order nominal subjects with both
temporal and locative predicates. These distributional facts may be
summarized as follows (using *occur* to represent the class which also
includes *take place, happen*, etc.):

	Temporal	Locative
First-order:	**John was on Sunday*	*John was in Central Park*
	*John occurred on Sunday	**John occurred in Central Park*
Second-order:	*The demonstration was on Sunday*	*The demonstration was in Central Park*
	The demonstration occurred on Sunday	*The demonstration occurred in Central Park*

There may be semantic differences between predicates containing
occur, happen, take place, etc., in various contexts. But these predicates have one thing in common, and it is crucial to the point at issue:
they are non-stative (cf. 7.6.4). Since first-order nominals tend to
denote 'entities' (enduring through some time-span, although they
may move or be moved from one place to another) and second-order
nominals tend to refer to 'events' (with 'punctual' location in space
and time) the fact that *occur*, etc., are found with the latter, but not the
former, in the surface structure of locative and temporal sentences is
readily explained. The locative and temporal predicates of first-order
nominals are necessarily stative.

But the difference between first-order and second-order nominals
does not suffice, of itself, to account for the non-occurrence of such

sentences as *John was on Sunday. It is not simply the shortness of the time-span referred to by on Sunday which renders this sentence unacceptable, since *Socrates was in the fifth century B.C. is also impossible. Instead, we would say Socrates lived in the fifth century B.C. (in the fifth century B.C. being correctly regarded as a predicative complement in traditional grammar). Similarly, instead of *This building has been for thirty years, we would say This building has existed for thirty years. This suggests that live and exist (the former restricted to animate subjects) are the temporal copulas occurring with first-order nominal subjects. Like be in locative sentences, they are purely grammatical 'dummies'. But the argument will be taken up again from this point in a later section (8.4.3).

8.1.11 Tense and temporal adjuncts

All the instances that have been cited here of grammatical sentences containing what would be traditionally regarded as temporal adjuncts have tacitly respected a condition of compatibility between the adjunct and the tense of the sentence. If this condition of compatibility is broken, the sentence to which the adjunct is 'attached' is rendered ungrammatical: e.g. *John killed Bill next week v. John killed Bill last week. This point need not be laboured. It should be noted, however, that it casts doubt upon the traditional notion of the temporal adjunct as syntactically independent of the rest of the sentence. It is true that the temporal adjunct is in general 'detachable' from a sentence in which it occurs (cf. 8.1.1), but the generative rules of 'attachment' must make the adjunct and the tense and aspect of the sentence compatible in the first place. In most current transformational work on English (and on other languages which have tense), the rules are ordered in such a way that the prior selection of a particular tense subsequently restricts the choice of a temporal adjunct; and this may well be the best way of handling the necessary conditions of compatibility in a system of generative rules. The point is that the temporal adjunct is bound by conditions of compatibility to the obligatory (nuclear) category of tense.

We will now take up the discussion of the distinction between 'subject' and 'object' and of various other topics connected with this. We shall go into considerably more detail than is customary in general books on linguistic theory. The reason for this is that problems connected with 'transitivity' and 'voice' are leading to important revisions in the theory of generative grammar at the present time. Some indication of one possible line of development will be provided in 8.3.6. But first we must consider the data and traditional approaches to these questions.

8.2   Transitivity and ergativity

8.2.1   *One-place and two-place verbs*

At this point it will be convenient to introduce a classification of verbs in terms of the number of nominals with which they combine in the nuclei of sentences. According to this classification, we will say that a verb like *die*, which requires only one nominal, is a *one-place* verb: e.g. the one 'place' associated with *die* is 'filled' by *John* to form the nucleus of the sentence *John died*. A transitive verb (e.g. *kill*) is a *two-place* verb, one of the places being filled by the subject and the other by the object: cf. *John killed Bill*. Some verbs (e.g. *give* or *put*) are *three-place* verbs, combining with a subject, a direct object and an indirect object (or 'directional' locative: cf. 7.4.6): cf. *John gave Bill the book* (where *the book* is the direct object and *Bill* the indirect object) or *John put the book on the table* (where *the book* is the direct object and *on the table* is a directional locative). We will return to three-place verbs, indirect objects and directional locatives below (cf. 8.2.14).

8.2.2   *The term 'transitive'*

The traditional 'notional' view of transitivity (and the term itself) suggests that the effects of the action expressed by the verb 'pass over' from the 'agent' (or 'actor') to the 'patient' (or 'goal'). There is no need to emphasize the inappropriateness of the 'notional' definition of transitivity in respect of many English sentences. As Robins puts it: 'The weakness of semantic definitions is well illustrated here: *hit*, in *I hit you* is syntactically a transitive verb, and is often chosen as an example because the action referred to may plausibly be said to "pass across" via my fist to you; but *hear* in *I hear you* is involved in exactly the same syntactic relations with the two pronouns, and is regarded as a transitive verb, though in this case, the "action", if any action is in fact referred to, is the other way round; and who does what, and to whom, in the situation referred to by the syntactically similar verb in *I love you*?' As far as it goes, this criticism of the traditional notion of transitivity (which has often been expressed) is correct.

Once again, however, we must be careful to draw a distinction between 'formal' and 'notional' definition. It suffices that the semantic, or 'notional', definition is applicable to the majority of two-place verbs for the whole of this class of verbs to be called 'transitive'. It was by tacit appeal to this principle (which we have already discussed in connexion with the traditional notion of the noun as 'the name of any person, place or thing': cf. 7.6.1) that we described *agna-*, 'woman', as the 'actor' and *qimmi-*, 'dog', as the 'goal' in the Eskimo sentence *qimmiq agnap takubaa*, 'The woman sees the dog' (8.1.6). Furthermore, it might be maintained that the grammatical form of an English sentence like *I hear you* or *I see you* (its parallelism with *I hit you*, etc.) influences speakers of English to think of hearing and seeing as activities initiated by the person 'doing' the hearing and seeing. Whether this is a correct account of perception, from a psychological or physiological point of view, is irrelevant. If the native speaker of English (and other languages in which verbs meaning 'hear', 'see', 'smell', etc., are syntactically parallel with 'notionally' transitive verbs like 'hit' or 'kill') tends to interpret perception as an activity which 'proceeds' from an 'actor' to a 'goal', this fact of itself would suggest that there is some semantic basis for the traditional notion of transitivity. (In fact, *see* and *hear*, as well as *love*, are not completely parallel with *hit*, *kill*, etc., in English. They are 'non-progressive', stative verbs; and, unlike the 'verbs of action', they do not typically occur in sentences answering a question of the form 'What is X doing?': cf. 7.6.4.) Although the class of syntactically transitive verbs undoubtedly includes many verbs (both in English and in other languages) which cannot reasonably be said to refer to actions the effects of which 'pass over' from an 'actor' to a 'goal', it is nevertheless true that the traditional 'notional' account of transitivity is clearly applicable to many, if not most, syntactically (or 'formally') transitive verbs.

8.2.3 *The term 'ergative'*

In the previous section, various criteria were discussed for deciding which of the two nominals is the subject of a two-place verb. It was pointed out that the 'actor'–'goal' criterion is in systematic conflict with criteria of case and concord in languages with an ergative construction, and far more generally in passive sentences. We will leave passive sentences out of account for the moment; and we will consider the relationship between transitivity and ergativity in some greater detail.

The first point to be made is that there are many verbs in English which may combine with either one or two nominals in sentence-nuclei (*move, change, open*, etc.). Consider the following sentences:

(1) *The stone moved*

(2) *John moved*

(3) *John moved the stone*

In (1) and (2) *move* is intransitive, whereas in (3) it is transitive. Moreover, there is an important relationship between (1) and (3). With reference to the information conveyed by (1), we might well ask 'Who moved it?'—i.e. 'Who was the "actor" or "agent" responsible for the movement of the stone?'. And, if this question is put explicitly, the answer might be 'John did' (an utterance derived from the sentence (3) *John moved the stone*). The term that is generally employed by linguists for the syntactic relationship that holds between (1) and (3) is 'ergative': the subject of an intransitive verb 'becomes' the object of a corresponding transitive verb, and a new *ergative* subject is introduced as the 'agent' (or 'cause') of the action referred to. This suggests that a transitive sentence, like (3), may be derived syntactically from an intransitive sentence, like (1), by means of an ergative, or *causative*, transformation. (The term 'ergative' was coined from a Greek verb meaning 'cause', 'bring about', 'create'.) It will also be observed that the causative, or ergative, agent in (3) is an animate noun: we have already noted the tendency for the subjects of transitive verbs to be animate. We will return to this point.

8.2.4 Causatives

The verb *move* illustrates one of the ways in which intransitive and transitive sentences may be related by means of the notion of causativity: the *same* verb enters into sentences of both types without modification of the verb itself. But we also find pairs of *different* verbs between which the same syntactic (and semantic) relationship holds in corresponding intransitive and transitive sentences. Consider the following two sentences:

(4) *Bill died*

(5) *John killed Bill.*

In such instances, we may say that the relationship of the transitive to the intransitive is 'lexicalized'. It is a matter of the lexical structure of English that we say *John killed Bill*, rather than **John died Bill*. The

syntactic and semantic relationship between *kill* and *die* is one that
the child learning English must come to appreciate, just as he must
come to appreciate the relationship between the transitive and intransitive uses of the class of verbs including *move*. For the present we may
call *kill* and *die* two 'different' verbs. Later, we will consider the
implications of treating them as alternative, syntactically-conditioned,
phonological realizations of the 'same' verb.

In many languages, there is a productive grammatical rule for the
formation of causative verbs. We will illustrate from Turkish and
French. The English sentences (4) and (5) may be translated into
Turkish as

(6) *Bill öldü*

(7) *John Bill-i öldürdü*

Here, the suffix *-dür-* (which varies in form according to vowel-
harmony: cf. 3.3.13) converts the intransitive stem *öl-* 'die' into a
transitive stem *öl-dür-* in the derivation of a sentence like (7). (The
suffix *-dü* marks past tense; and the *-i* attached to the 'goal'-nominal
in (7) marks the object of the transitive verb, when the object is
definite—all proper names and personal pronouns being inherently
definite in Turkish: cf. 7.4.4. Both the tense suffix and the object
suffix are variable in phonological form according to vowel-harmony.)
As another example from Turkish, we may take

(8) *Patlïcan pişiyor* ('The eggplant is cooking')

(9) *Ahmet patlïcanï pişiriyor* ('Ahmet is cooking the eggplant')

Once again, the two sentences are syntactically related in the same
way as the English sentences (1) and (3), or (4) and (5). (The suffix
-ir- is a less common variant of the causative suffix. Which of the
variants, or 'allomorphs', occurs with a particular verb-stem is in
general determined by a classification of verbal stems for this purpose:
in other words, the distribution of the causative suffixes is not a
matter of free variation, but of lexical conditioning: cf. 5.3.5. The
suffix *-iyor-* marks the continuous, or 'progressive', aspect. Without
the objective suffix—i.e. with *patlïcan* rather than *patlïcanï*—(9)
would be translatable as 'Ahmet is cooking (some) eggplant'. Since
the distinction between a definite and an indefinite nominal is not
marked for the subject in Turkish, (8) is in fact indeterminate
between 'Some eggplant is cooking' and the translation given above.)
It will be observed that the English verb *cook* may be used either
intransitively or transitively. Furthermore, there is an alternative

translation possible for (8): 'The eggplant is being cooked.' The difference between the intransitive *is cooking* and the passive (of the transitive) *is being cooked* will be discussed below (cf. 8.2.13).

In French, as in English, the relationship manifest in (6) and (7) is lexicalized in the two different verbs *mourir* and *tuer* (cf. *Bill est mort* v. *John a tué Bill*). But (8) and (9) may be translated into French, as (10) and (11), in a way which illustrates the operation of the French causative construction.

(10)　*Les aubergines cuisent*

(11)　*Ahmet fait cuire les aubergines*

(Actually, in the present instance, *Les aubergines sont en train de cuire*, 'The eggfruit is in the process of cooking' as it were, is contextually more probable than (10). But (10) is possible.) In French, the intransitive verb *cuire* is made transitive, not by means of morphological modification (with a prefix, suffix, infix, etc.), but by use of the auxiliary 'verb' *faire* ('make', 'do'). This is comparable with the English *make*, as exemplified in

(12)　*John makes the brass shine*

which, like

(13)　*John shines the brass*

is syntactically derivable from the intransitive

(14)　*The brass shines*

However, the English construction with *make* commonly introduces an implication of force or coercion (though not in the example given here). This is not generally so of the French construction with *faire*, which is far more extensively employed.

Causative constructions, comparable with those illustrated here from Turkish and French, are extremely common throughout the languages of the world. They would seem to provide us with a satisfactory general framework for the discussion of transitivity and ergativity.

8.2.5　*The 'ergative' in the Indo-European languages*

Let us now look at the English 'ergative' constructions from the point of view of case and concord. For reasons which will become clear immediately, we will use symbols rather than nouns in the model sentences. The symbols are to be interpreted as follows: *A* is the subject of a transitive verb (we will assume that A is necessarily animate), and B is either the subject of an intransitive verb or the object of a transitive verb; since B may be animate or inanimate (in either or both of the syntactic positions in which it occurs) we will use the subscripts a and i to mark this distinction—B_a denotes an animate and B_i an inanimate nominal. Given these conventions, the sentences (1)–(3) cited above (8.2.3) may be 'translated' as

(1a) B_i moved (cf. *It moved*)

(2a) B_a moved (cf. *He moved, She moved*)

(3a) A moved B_i (cf. *He moved it, She moved it*)

There is also a fourth possibility, by virtue of the distinction between inanimate and animate objects:

(3b) A moved B_a (cf. *He/She moved him/her*)

which, for the moment, we will assume is related to (2a) in the same way that (3a) is related to (1a).

If we now identify the categories of 'neuter' and 'inanimate', in the Indo-European languages which are traditionally said to have three genders (cf. 7.3.3), we may say that English is typical of most Indo-European languages in two respects: (i) Although the case of B_i in (1a) is usually said to be 'nominative' and the case of B_i in (3a) 'accusative', the occurrence of B_i in subject or object position is never in fact associated with an inflexional difference in B_i. The inflexional difference between a 'nominative' and an 'accusative' form of nouns and pronouns is relevant only to animate nominals (cf. 7.4.3: in English, of course, it is relevant only for pronouns). Thus, *It moved, A moved it: He moved, A moved him.* (ii) The case of B_a in a sentence like (2a) is identical with the case of A: cf. *He moved, He moved it/him*, etc. Furthermore, if there is number (or gender) concord between the verb and one of the nominals, B_a in a sentence like (2a) determines the number (or gender) of the verb in precisely the same way as does A in (3a) or (3b), but B_a has no such effect in a sentence like (3b): cf. *He moves, He moves it/him: They move, They move it/him.* It is mainly because of the features of case and concord mentioned under (ii) that the Indo-European languages are not generally regarded as 'ergative' languages (cf. 8.1.6). However, once we take into account the distinction between animate and inanimate nouns mentioned under (i), these features of case and concord lose a good deal of the importance attributed to them in traditional descriptions of the Indo-European languages.

There is some evidence to suggest that the Indo-European system of case-distinctions did in fact develop from an earlier system in which the 'nominative' was an 'agentive', or 'ergative', suffix (typically -*s*) found only with animate nouns. We will not go into this question from the diachronic point of view here. It is noticeable, however, that as far as the case-distinctions of subject and object are concerned, the difference between, say, English and Eskimo reduces to the relatively minor fact that in (2*a*) B_a has the agentive case in English, but the non-agentive case in Eskimo. That is to say, if we think of the 'nominative' in English (and in the Indo-European languages generally) as the case of the 'actor' (like the Eskimo suffix -*p*), we can introduce a rule into the grammar of English which has the effect of attaching this case, not only to the 'actor' rather than the 'goal' with two-place verbs, but also to animate nominals with one-place verbs. In other words, *He moves* can be derived by an obligatory transformation from **Him move* (using *him*, like *it*, as an 'unmarked' (non-agentive) form, neutral with respect to the distinction of 'actor' and 'goal').

8.2.6   An 'ideal' ergative system

But a distinction between 'agentive' and 'non-agentive' can in fact be drawn with one-place verbs, 'notionally' at least. Consider a sentence like *John flew through the air*. This might answer either of two implicit questions: (i) 'What did John do?' or (ii) 'What happened to John?'. If it answers (i), *John* is an 'agent' (he might be flying an aeroplane, for instance); if it answers (ii), *John* is not regarded as an 'agent' (he may have been thrown across the room by someone else). Some intransitive verbs in English will hardly admit of an 'agentive' interpretation: cf. *John died*. Others will hardly admit of interpretation with a 'non-agentive' animate nominal: cf. *John jumped from the roof*. And others will tend to either an 'agentive' or a 'non-agentive' interpretation with animate nominals, although the less normal interpretation is also conceivable in certain circumstances. For example, *John fell* is probably more normal as a 'non-agentive' sentence; but the other interpretation is certainly possible. By contrast, *The chimney fell* (with an inanimate subject) is necessarily 'non-agentive'.

On the basis of the 'notional' distinction between 'agentive' and 'non-agentive' (relevant only for animate nominals), we might construct a theoretically 'ideal' system for one-place and two-place verbs of the kind illustrated by the following 'sentences' (in which *he* stands for an 'agentive' and *him* for a 'non-agentive' animate nominal: n.b. these are not sentences of English, but pseudo-English representations of an 'ideal' set of distinctions):

(1 a) *It moved*

(2 b) *Him moved*

(2 c) *He moved*

(3 a) *He moved it*

(3 b) *He moved him*

If these are compared with the four English sentences given in 8.2.5, it will be seen that the only difference, as far as the distribution of the cases is concerned, is that (2 a) of the earlier set has now been split into (2 b) and (2 c). This is intended to reflect the possibility, in principle, of a 'non-agentive' and an 'agentive' interpretation of a sentence like (2) *John moved* (8.2.3). This theoretically 'ideal' system is not realized in English (or in any of the Indo-European languages). Nor is it realized in languages which are traditionally described as having an ergative construction. It will be observed, however, that we can arrive at either the English or the Eskimo system by a simple 'merger' of (2 b) and (2 c). If the 'merger' takes place in one direction

$$\left.\begin{array}{l}(2b)\ \textit{Him moved}\\ (2c)\ \textit{He moved}\end{array}\right\} \rightarrow \textit{He moved}$$

the outcome (as far as the category of case is concerned) is the typically Indo-European system for the masculine or feminine subject of an intransitive verb. If the 'merger' operated in the reverse direction

$$\left.\begin{array}{l}(2b)\ \textit{Him moved}\\ (2c)\ \textit{He moved}\end{array}\right\} \rightarrow \textit{Him moved}$$

the result would be an ergative construction, characteristic of Eskimo and many other languages.

8.2.7 *Transitivity and animacy*

This 'ideal' system for the distribution of an 'agentive' case with one-place and two-place verbs is not being proposed as a necessary part of the grammars of English and Eskimo, but merely as an aid to the understanding of ergativity and transitivity. These two languages have been taken as examples of what are often regarded as radically different syntactic types. The general conclusion to be drawn from the discussion is that in both languages the case-inflexion of the subject of an intransitive verb is of secondary importance. Both languages agree in the following respects: (i) they distinguish the 'actor' and the 'goal' of transitive sentences by means of a difference of case (as 'agentive' and 'non-agentive', respectively); (ii) they employ the same form (the 'non-agentive') for the subject of intransitive verbs as they do for the object of transitive verbs, provided that the subject of the intransitive verb is inanimate; (iii) they do not distinguish by case-inflexion between 'agentive' and 'non-agentive' subjects of intransitive verbs. In each language, the 'agentive' (the 'nominative' in English, the 'ergative' in Eskimo) may be regarded as the 'marked' term of the opposition of case. The difference between the two languages lies in the fact that English generalizes the use of the 'agentive' form to all animate subjects (whether they are 'notionally' agentive or not); and Eskimo generalizes the 'non-agentive' form. We have not discussed the difference between the two languages in respect of concord. But it should be clear that this difference also is a matter of surface-structure, and can be handled in much the same way as the distribution of case-inflexions.

Although English has been used here to exemplify the use of the 'nominative' and 'accusative' in the Indo-European languages, it is in many respects an untypical example. First of all, the case-distinction of 'nominative' v. 'accusative' is not relevant to nouns, but only to pronouns, in English (*he* v. *him*, *she* v. *her*, *they* v. *them*, *who* v. *whom*, etc.). More important, the correlation between 'grammatical' and 'natural' gender is far greater in English than it is in most of the other Indo-European languages (cf. 7.3.4). In such languages as Latin and Greek, as far as the case-inflexions are concerned, the distinction of 'agentive' v. 'non-agentive' is 'automatically' extended to inanimate nouns if they are masculine or feminine in gender. But this fact does not invalidate the deep-structure distinction between 'agentive' and 'non-agentive' nominals in transitive and intransitive sentences. In a Greek sentence like *líthoi píptousin ap' ouranoû*, 'Stones fall from [the] sky', *líthoi* ('stones') is in the 'nominative' case; although an inanimate noun, it is masculine, and therefore takes the 'nominative' inflexion in subject-position. But *líthoi* is no more 'agentive' here than is *stones* in the corresponding English sentence. Conversely, in the German sentence *Das Kind öffnet die Tür*, 'The child opens the door', *das Kind* ('the child') is neuter in gender: it cannot therefore take the characteristically 'agentive' inflexion (cf. *Der Mann öffnet die Tür*, 'The man opens the door'; cf. also *Das*

Kind sieht den Mann v. *Der Mann sieht das Kind*, 'The child sees the man' v. 'The man sees the child'). The deep-structure distinction of 'agentive' v. 'non-agentive' is nevertheless applicable in German to animate nouns of neuter gender, as well as to masculine and feminine animate nouns.

Transitivity is bound up, then, with the distinction of animate and inanimate nominals; and in the 'ideal' system the former may be either 'agentive' or 'non-agentive' (in both transitive and intransitive sentences), the latter only 'non-agentive'. The detailed development of this thesis for particular languages would take us too far from the main line of argument. We will assume that the general points that have been made are tenable for at least a considerable number of the transitive and intransitive sentences of the languages referred to. At the same time, we must accept that what we are regarding as the 'notional' basis for the system of transitivity has superimposed upon it in various languages many transitive constructions which do not satisfy the conditions of the 'ideal' system. For example, *Wealth attracts robbers* is a perfectly acceptable transitive sentence of English, in spite of the fact that *wealth* is an inanimate noun. It may very well be that sentences like this (and they are much more common in English than they are in some other languages, e.g. Greek) should be thought of as 'parasitic' upon the more 'normal' type of transitive sentences with an animate subject. However that may be, we shall concentrate here upon transitive sentences which fulfil the 'normal' conditions.

8.2.8 *'Causative' verbs in English*

We have seen that there is a class of verbs in English (to which we gave the label 'ergative verbs': 8.2.3) which occur in both intransitive and transitive sentences; and that the two-place, transitive construction is derivable from the one-place, intransitive construction by means of a causative operation which has the effect of introducing an 'agentive' subject. The example used in the illustrations was *move*. Other members of this class of verbs are *change, grow, develop, open, close, start, stop, begin, break, crack, split, tear,* etc. They may differ according to their selection of an 'agentive' or 'non-agentive' subject in their intransitive usage, but they are 'normal' in that they usually have an animate subject with the transitive construction. In addition, there are certain transitive verbs in English, syntactically related as 'causatives' to corresponding intransitive verbs and (from a historical point of view) derived from them by what were once more or less productive morphological processes (cf. the Turkish causative verbs illustrated above: 8.2.4). Examples are *lay* ('make to lie'), *fell* ('make to fall'), etc. (which are, however, more specialized in their selectional possibilities than the corresponding intransitives). In particular, there are a large number of transitive verbs morphologically related to intransitive 'adjectival' verbs: *enrich* (*rich*), *soften* (*soft*), *strengthen* (*strong*), *actualize* (*actual*), etc. Most of these morphological patterns of formation by prefixation and suffixation are no longer productive in modern English (with the notable exception of *-ize*, which is suffixed, not only to verbal stems, but also to nominals: cf. *computerize*, etc.). These morphological causatives fall between the two extremes of 'lexicalization', on the one hand (cf. *kill*: *die*, discussed above: 8.2.4), and the use of the 'same' verb (e.g. *move*) in both transitive and intransitive sentences, on the other. By contrast with 'lexical' and morphological causatives, the transitive verbs *move*, *change*, *grow*, etc., may be described as being derived from the corresponding intransitive verbs (identical in phonological form, and for that reason referred to above as the 'same' verbs: 8.2.4) by means of a morphological process of 'zero modification'. It is worth pointing out that many of the forms which are traditionally said to occur both as 'adjectives' and 'verbs' fall within the scope of this classification: e.g. *He warms the milk* is related to *The milk is warm* (which contains the intransitive, 'adjectival' verb *warm*) in the same way as *He moves the stone* is related to *The stone moves*. Morphologically, the transitive verbs *move* and *warm* are 'derived' from the intransitive verbs *move* and *warm* by 'zero modification'.

8.2.9 'Object-deletion'

Apart from the class of verbs exemplified by *move*, there are various other classes of verbs in English which would seem to be used transitively or intransitively. Consider the following sentence:

> (15) *We never eat at five o'clock.*

The verb *eat* is here being used without an object. Whether it should be described as an intransitive verb is, however, a moot point. Many traditional grammarians would say that it is a transitive verb which may be employed either with an object or 'absolutely'. The 'absolute' usage (without an overt object) is illustrated in (15). If this sentence is compared with

> (16) *We never eat caviare at five o'clock*

it will be clear that the relationship between the transitive and the 'absolute' usage of *eat* is quite different from that which holds between the transitive and the intransitive usage of *move*. There is no **Caviare never eats at five o'clock* (but rather the passive *Caviare is never eaten at five o'clock*) corresponding to (16). It seems reasonable to say that *eat* is inherently transitive, but that its object may be deleted (in the pseudo-intransitive, 'absolute' construction). The deletion of the object may be contextually determined (and recoverable for the purpose of semantic interpretation) in particular utterances. But it may also be a feature of the lexical structure of the language. For example, *I spent the morning painting* is susceptible of at least two distinct interpretations: (i) '...painting pictures' or '...painting the house (the garden fence, etc.)'. And the 'deletion' of the object in each case (in the first interpretation it is an 'object of result': cf. 9.5.3) is determined by the lexical structure of English: there need be no contextual indication of an object of the verb *paint*, which the hearer will feel obliged to infer in order to understand the sentence. In many languages, there is far less freedom in the matter of 'object-deletion'. For instance, the Turkish translation of the English 'absolute' sentence *He is writing* requires a 'dummy' object (morphologically related to the verb 'to write'): *Yazï yaz-ïyor*, 'He is writing writing', as it were (cf. *Mektup yaz-ïyor*, 'He is writing a letter').

8.2.10 Reflexives

Another class of verbs in English which, *prima facie*, are used both transitively and intransitively is illustrated by *shave* in the following two sentences

(17) *The barber shaved ten men before lunch*

(18) *He never shaves before lunch*

Of these, (17) is a straightforward transitive sentence, with an 'agentive' subject, *the barber*, and a 'non-agentive' object, or 'goal', *ten men*. But (18) is ambiguous: it might mean 'He never shaves (anyone) before lunch' or 'He never shaves (himself) before lunch'. The first of these interpretations is accounted for under the term 'object-deletion', discussed in the previous paragraph. It is the second that concerns us here. Under this interpretation, (18) might well be described as implicitly reflexive.

A *reflexive* construction is one in which the subject and object refer to the same person (or thing). Many languages, like English, have a set of reflexive pronouns distinguished for person and number (*myself, yourself, himself*, etc.); others, like French, German, or Latin, draw a distinction between reflexive and non-reflexive objects only in the third person (cf. French, *Maman me lave*: *Je me lave*, 'Mummy is washing me': 'I am washing myself'; *Maman la lave*: *Maman se lave*, 'Mummy is washing her': 'Mummy is washing herself'); and there are other languages which use the same reflexive pronoun with all persons and numbers (e.g. Russian uses either the suffix -*sja* or the pronoun *sebja*, under conditions which we will not go into here). An explicitly reflexive sentence is one in which the identity of subject and object is overtly marked, either in the form of the object pronoun or in some other way (e.g. by the use of a particular suffix, prefix, or infix, attached to the verb-stem). Thus *He killed himself* (by contrast with *He killed him*) is explicitly reflexive. So too is *He washed himself*. But it is a characteristic feature of English that many verbs can be used in reflexive sentences without the occurrence of an object pronoun. *He never shaves before lunch* exemplifies this usage; and it is for that reason described as implicitly reflexive. In fact, *shave* is very rarely used in explicitly reflexive constructions—most commonly perhaps in sentences like *I don't mind shaving others, but I never shave myself*, where the occurrence of *myself* is required for the contrast with *others*. (It may be noticed in passing that, out of context, *I never shave myself* is syntactically ambiguous: (i) 'As for me, I never do any shaving' (object-deletion), (ii) 'As for me, I never shave (myself)' (implicitly reflexive), (iii) 'I always get someone else to shave me' (explicitly reflexive). Under the interpretations indicated by the glosses in (i) and (ii), *myself* is not the reflexive pronoun, but an emphatic 'adjunct' to the subject of the sentence, which may occur in various positions in surface-structure: *I myself never shave, I never myself shave*, etc.)

The implicitly reflexive construction is commonly found with *wash*, which may also be explicitly reflexive; but not, for instance, with *dry*. *He dried in the sun* is interpretable as an intransitive sentence ('non-agentive') or as a pseudo-intransitive sentence with object-deletion (e.g. 'He dried the dishes' or 'He dried the clothes'), but probably not as implicitly reflexive, equivalent semantically to *He dried himself in the sun*. Unlike object-deletion of the more general kind, implicit reflexivity (which may of course be regarded as a special type of object-deletion) would seem to be restricted in English to a relatively small class of verbs. Moreover, it is not always clear whether a particular sentence exemplifies implicit reflexivity or the more general kind of object-deletion. For instance, *change* is not only found as an 'ergative' verb (like *move, grow, open*, etc.) in corresponding intransitive and transitive sentences, but also in sentences like

(19) *I'll just slip upstairs and change before dinner*

The interpretation that is intended here is the one suggested by the insertion of *my dress* or *into a more respectable suit* between *change* and *before dinner*. (A sentence like *I have changed* is of course ambiguous as between the interpretation we are now considering and the 'ergative' interpretation: 'I have undergone some kind of physical, intellectual, moral, etc. transformation.') The question is whether the second clause of (19) is implicitly reflexive. Notice that the following three sentences are acceptable:

(20) *I'll change the baby*

(21) *I'll change the baby's dress*

(22) *I'll change my dress*

but not

(23) **I'll change myself*

(i.e. explicitly reflexive, in the intended sense). The semantic parallelism between (20) and (21), on the one hand, and (22) and *I'll change*, on the other, might be taken as an indication that *I'll change* is implicitly reflexive—automatically transformed from *I'll change myself* by deletion of the overtly reflexive object. Alternatively, *I'll change* might be regarded as an instance of object-deletion of the more general type, related to sentences like (22) as (15) is related to (16) above (8.2.9). The question would seem to be syntactically undecidable; and semantically it makes no difference (by contrast with the two relevant interpretations of a sentence like *I'll wash before lunch*).

8.2.11 'Pseudo-intransitive'

So far we have discussed three classes of verbs in English which may be used (with 'zero modification') in both transitive and intransitive (or pseudo-intransitive) constructions. The important syntactic characteristics of verbs belonging to these three classes (exemplified by *move, eat* and *shave*)—together with the characteristics of three other classes, which will be mentioned below—are shown in Table 12. It will be observed that classes 2 and 3 (*eat* and *shave*) differ from class 1 (*move*) in a number of ways. In the right-hand side of the table,

Table 12. *Some English verbs*

	Transitive			(Pseudo-)Intransitive		
	Subject	Verb	Object	Subject	Verb	(Object)
1.	A: +ag	*move*	B: −ag	B: ±ag	*move*	
2.	A: +ag	*eat*	B: −ag	A: +ag	*eat*	(≠ A)
3.	A: +ag	*shave*	B: −ag	A: +ag	*shave*	(= A)
4.	A: +ag	*walk*	B: +ag	B: +ag	*walk*	
5.	A: +ag	*build*	B: −ag	B: −ag	*build*	
6.	A: +ag	*sell*	B: −ag	B: −ag	*sell*	

they are both shown with an entry under ('Object)' and they have A, rather than B, in the subject-position. This defines classes 2 and 3 as pseudo-intransitive verbs, since A indicates the subject of the corresponding transitive construction and the parentheses in the third column of the right-hand side mark the 'deletion' of the object of the transitive. The difference between 3 and 2—and we have seen that this cannot always be drawn in particular instances—lies in the identity (= A) or non-identity (≠ A) between the 'deleted' object and the subject of both the transitive and pseudo-transitive constructions. By contrast, class 1 is shown as having the 'ergative' characteristics discussed above (8.2.3). The distinction between '+ag' ('agentive', or 'plus-agentive') and '−ag' ('non-agentive', or 'minus-agentive') is not crucial to the distinction of 'ergative' verbs from verbs with 'deletable' objects. Although *move*, as a one-place verb, may take either an 'agentive' or 'non-agentive' subject, provided that the nominal in question is animate (*move* would therefore be shown in the lexicon with the classification '±ag', 'plus-or-minus agentive': cf. 4.3.3, 8.2.6), it is here assumed that a transitive sentence like *John moved Bill* (e.g. to another desk in the office) is more directly related to the 'non-agentive' interpretation of *Bill moved* than to the 'agentive' interpretation. It would seem that the more usual realization of *John*: +ag, *moved*, *Bill*: +ag (with *John* as the 'causative' subject and the 'agentive' *Bill moved* as its 'predicate': we will come back to the formalization of this notion) is *John made Bill move* or *John got Bill to move* or *John had Bill move*.

8.2.12 *Agentive objects*

However, there is at least one class of verbs in English which may be used with an 'agentive' object (cf. class 4 of Table 12). It is exemplified by *walk* in the following sentence

(24) *John walked the horse*

which is in other respects related to

(25) *The horse walked*

as *John moved Bill* is to *Bill moved*. Other members of this highly-restricted class are *gallop, run, jump*, etc. One difference between (24) and the more common type of 'double-agentive' sentence *John made the horse walk* would seem to be that (24) implies that John is the 'direct' agent (that he himself led the horse, or rode it). *John made the horse walk* does not carry this implication. But the distinction between a 'direct' and an 'indirect' agent cannot be made in this way with most English verbs. Not only is *John made Bill move* (like *John made the horse walk*) neutral with respect to the distinction of 'direct' and 'indirect' agent (as applied to *John*), but so also is *John moved Bill*. The most common way of expressing 'indirect' agency in English is exemplified by *John had a house built*, which is 'marked' as 'indirectly' agentive. Not only are the limits on the use of the construction illustrated in (24) unclear: it is also uncertain, in particular instances, whether the relationship between a pair of corresponding transitive and intransitive sentences is that exemplified in (24) and (25) or the more common 'ergative' relationship holding between *John moved Bill* and *Bill moved*. One might well hesitate, for example, in respect of the following two sentences:

(26) *The aeroplane flew from London to Paris*

(27) *The pilot flew the aeroplane from London to Paris*

The bird flew through the air has an 'agentive' subject ('What did the bird do?') and *The stone flew through the air* has a 'non-agentive' subject ('What happened to the stone?'), but (26) would seem to be somewhat indeterminate in this respect. In clear cases, however, the differences between class 1 and class 4 can be referred to the difference between 'non-agentive' and 'agentive' nominals as the subject of the intransitive or the object of the transitive. Apart from this difference, class 4 verbs are 'ergative'.

8.2.13   *Other pseudo-intransitive constructions*

Classes 5 and 6 of Table 12 are also rather restricted in their employment. The constructions in question are illustrated in the following two sentences:

(28) *The house is building*

(29) *Detergents sell well*

Both of these sentences are 'non-agentive', and relatable to transitive sentences of the most common type (*They are building the house, They sell detergents*). But they differ from intransitive 'ergative' sentences (e.g. *The house is moving, Grass grows well*, etc.) in that they 'presuppose' an agent. In this respect, they are similar to passive sentences in English. In fact, the more normal 'version' of (28) in contemporary English is probably *The house is being built*. But (29) exemplifies a much more common type of construction, and one that cannot be converted into an equivalent passive 'version' in such a straightforward fashion.

According to Halliday: 'This type is especially frequent in simple present tense (*this material washes*), particularly in negative potential, where however the form is *don't/won't* and not *can't*: *this material doesn't/won't wash*; it is not however restricted to these verbal forms, and may in fact occur with any tense, especially with certain *-ly* adverbs, as in *the clothes washed easily, these books are not going to sell quickly*. Underlying all these is a feature of characterization of the process as such, either a qualification of it or a generalization about its feasibility; so that we may call the type "process-oriented" in contradistinction to the "agent-oriented" type *the clothes were washed*.'

This difference between what Halliday has aptly distinguished as 'process-oriented' and 'agent-oriented' sentences can be brought out by comparing the following three examples:

(30) *The books sold quickly*

(31) *The books were sold quickly*

(32) *They sold the books quickly*

Of these: (30) is definitely 'process-oriented': it would seem to imply that it was by virtue of some quality of the books that they were quickly disposed of. ('The books sold themselves', as it were; and it is noticeable that in certain languages, e.g. French, the equivalent of (30) could take the form of a reflexive.) By contrast, (31) might be described as 'agent-oriented': it certainly admits of the interpretation that it was the (unspecified) agent who was responsible for the rapidity with which the books were sold. It is, however, (32)— the active sentence—which carries this implication in a more definite form. One should perhaps say that sentences like (30) are 'marked' as 'process-oriented', whereas the passive is 'unmarked' for this distinction. There are many instances of paired 'process-oriented' and passive sentences (e.g. *She doesn't frighten easily*: *She isn't easily frightened*) which would seem to be semantically equivalent. The passive 'version' may occur with an 'agentive' or 'instrumental' adjunct (cf. 7.4.5): e.g. *She isn't easily frightened by burglars/threats*. But here also one would tend to the 'process-oriented' interpretation. And the reason seems to be that the non-past tense in English (without any 'marking' of aspect) is interpretable as 'habitual' (cf. 7.5.7): the indefiniteness of the adjunct (*burglars*, *threats*) supports this interpretation in the present instance. By contrast, *She wasn't easily frightened by the burglars/threats* is more readily taken as 'agent-oriented'.

The analysis of sentences like (30), containing verbs of class 6, is somewhat problematical. Although the limits imposed on 'process-oriented' sentences are far from clear (and many 'sentences' of this kind are definitely unacceptable: **The first edition exhausted in three days*, **Caviare never eats at five o'clock*, etc.; or doubtful: ?**The music heard well at the back of the hall*, etc.), they are nevertheless of very frequent occurrence in English. Within the general framework established in this section, they are pseudo-intransitive: But they differ from verbs of classes 2 and 3, in that their subject in the pseudo-intransitive usage is the same as their object in the transitive construction. In this respect they are like passive forms of the verb (cf. 8.3.3).

All pseudo-intransitive sentences (classes 2, 3, 5 and 6 of Table 12) are to be transformationally derived from transitives. On the other hand, as our earlier discussion of causative constructions suggests, true intransitives (cf. classes 1 and 4 of Table 12) may be taken as the 'source' for the generation of transitive sentences. The order of derivation is therefore intransitive—transitive—pseudo-intransitive. Before taking up the formal consequences of this proposal, we must briefly consider three-place constructions: i.e. sentence-nuclei with a subject, a direct object and an indirect object (cf. 8.2.1).

8.2.14   Three-place constructions

The general point to be made is that, as two-place constructions can be derived from one-place constructions by means of the notion of 'causativity', so three-place constructions can be derived from two-place constructions by means of a further application of the same notion. As *John moves the stone* is to be related, syntactically, to *The stone moves*, so (33) is to be related to (34):

(33) *John gives the book to Mary.*

(34) *Mary has the book*

For the present, *the book* may be regarded as the object of *have* in the 'possessive' sentence (34). The argument of this section is unaffected by the fact that (34) is not a transitive sentence, as we shall see later (cf. 8.4.4).

It will be more illuminating to discuss three-place verbs with reference to a language that has a productive causative construction applicable both to transitive and intransitive nuclei: and we will use French for this purpose. The two sentences cited in the previous paragraph, (33) and (34), may be translated into French as follows

(35) *Jean donne le livre à Marie*

(36) Marie a le livre

The French causative construction, which has been illustrated above in relation to the derivation of transitive sentences from intransitive nuclei (cf. 8.2.4), may also be applied to transitive nuclei for the generation of three-place constructions. This is exemplified by

(37) *Jean fait manger les pommes aux enfants*

in relation to

(38) *Les enfants mangent les pommes*

(The translation of (37) is 'John makes the children eat the apples'; and of (38) 'The children eat the apples'. The grammatical structure of (37) may be indicated by means of the quasi-English gloss 'John makes-eat the apples to the children'.) The structural parallelism between (35) and (37) is obvious. As *le livre* is the direct object and *à Marie* the indirect object of the 'simple' three-place verb *donne* in (35), so *les pommes* may be regarded as the direct object and *aux enfants* the indirect object of the 'complex' three-place verb *fait manger* in (37). This parallelism is confirmed by the fact that one may frequently choose between a 'simple' and a 'complex' three-place verb in French. For example, the following two sentences are semantically equivalent as translations of 'John shows the book to Mary'

(39) *Jean montre le livre à Marie*

(40) *Jean fait voir le livre à Marie*

(The second of these may be glossed in quasi-English as 'John makes-see the book to Mary'.) This would suggest that, as *kill* is the 'lexicalized' two-place causative form of *die* (cf. 8.2.4), so *montrer*

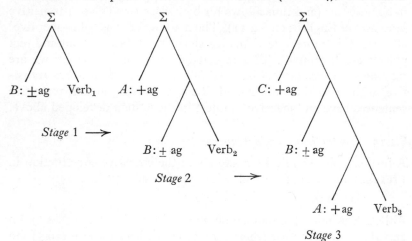

Fig. 19. Transitivity and causativity.

('to show') is the 'lexicalized' three-place causative of *voir* ('to see'). Similarly, one may frequently choose in French between a 'simple' and a 'complex' two-place verb: e.g. *Jean appelle le docteur* ('John calls the doctor'): *Jean fait venir le docteur* ('John makes-come the doctor'). The difference between *donner*, 'make-have' = 'give', in (35) and *montrer*, 'make-see' = 'show', in (39) lies, therefore, in the difference between obligatory and optional 'lexicalization' in three-place constructions.

It is a characteristic of the causative construction in French (as also in certain other languages, including Turkish and Hindi) that the subject of the underlying two-place nucleus is transformed into an indirect object with three-place causative verbs, whether 'simple' (i.e. 'lexicalized') or 'complex' (with the auxiliary *faire*) whereas the object of the underlying two-place nucleus remains as the direct object in the three-place causative construction. The full three-stage 'cycle' is illustrated in Fig. 19, where *B* is the subject of the underlying intransitive nucleus (at stage 1), A is the subject of the two-place transitive nucleus (at stage 2), and C is the subject of the three-place causative construction (at what, for the moment, we may regard as the final stage of the 'cycle'). The subscript on the symbol 'Verb' at the right-hand terminal node of each tree corresponds with the number of nominals which 'fill' the places associated with the verb. (We will introduce labels for the intermediate nodes presently.) It will be observed that the figure marks B as 'plus-or-minus-agentive' in all positions (and thus allows for both class 1 and class 4 transitive sentences of English: cf. 8.2.11). The marking of A as 'plus-agentive' at stage 3 is more questionable, since it implies that all indirect objects are 'agentive'. This is certainly not so. But so far we are treating sentences like 'A have B' (e.g. *Mary has the book*) as transitive, with A as the subject and B as the object; and all transitive sentences have an 'agentive' subject in the system developed above.

8.2.15 *Syntactically ambiguous constructions*

A further point should be made about the causative construction in French. Sentences of the following type are ambiguous:

(41) *Jean fait manger les enfants.*

Although in normal circumstances (41) will be interpreted as 'John gets the children to eat (their dinner, etc.)', it can also mean 'John gets the children eaten'. The ambiguity results from the fact that *manger* ('to eat') admits of object-deletion (cf. 8.2.9). Underlying (41) in its more normal interpretation, is the pseudo-intransitive sentence *Les enfants mangent* ('The children eat'): the fact that *les enfants* in (41) has the form of a direct, and not an indirect, object would suggest that pseudo-intransitives behave like true intransitives under the operation of the causative transformation. The rule for the deletion of the object must therefore operate before the causative transformation that results in (41). Furthermore, (41), in the interpretation 'John gets the children to eat', cannot be accounted for as a stage 3 construction derived from a stage 2 nucleus, but rather as a stage 2 construction which has been derived from another stage 2 construction ('reinterpreted' by the rules of the grammar as a stage 1 nucleus after object-deletion). By contrast, in the interpretation 'John gets the children eaten (e.g. by the lion at the zoo)', (41) is a stage 3 construction with deletion (or non-realization) of the node labelled A in Fig. 19. The ambiguity of (41) is somewhat similar therefore to the ambiguity of such English phrases as *the shooting of the hunters* (one of the examples of syntactic ambiguity that has been discussed by Chomsky). The verb *shoot* is transitive in *X shoots the hunters* (where *X* stands for the unspecified actor), but pseudo-intransitive in *The hunters shoot* (cf. *eat*, 8.2.9). Since the general principle for the interpretation of English noun-phrases of the form *the V-ing of NP* would seem to be that they are 'subjective' if the verb in question (*V*) is intransitive, but 'objective' if the verb is transitive, it follows that pseudo-intransitives operate like true intransitives in the rule which generates phrases like *the shooting of the hunters* from the underlying nucleus of *The hunters shoot*. It may be noted in passing that the ambiguity found in (41) is also present in comparable Turkish sentences (cf. *Ahmet çocuk-lar-ï ye-dir-di*, 'Ahmet the-children made-eat'); and the ambiguity found in the English phrase *the shooting of the hunters* also occurs, apparently, in such simple Eskimo sentences as *agna-q takubaa* ('Someone sees the woman' or 'The woman sees someone').

It is interesting to note that all these instances of ambiguity (between an 'objective' and a 'subjective' interpretation) depend upon the fact that in the constructions in question the 'agentive' nominal is structurally optional (i.e. an 'adjunct': cf. 8.1.1). The 'objective' interpretation is determined by the occurrence of *au lion* in (41)—*Jean fait manger les enfants au lion*, 'John gets the lion to eat the children' or 'John gets the children eaten by the lion'; by the occurrence of *by the gamekeeper* with the *shooting of the hunters*; by the occurrence of *qimmi-p* in the Eskimo sentence (*qimmi-p agna-q takubaa*, 'The dog sees the woman': cf. 8.1.6). Since the optionality (or absence) of the 'agentive' is one of the principal characteristics of passive sentences—cf. *The hunters were shot* (*by the gamekeeper*), *The children were eaten* (*by the lion*), *The woman was seen* (*by the dog*)—there may be some justification for the view that all the ambiguous constructions mentioned in the previous paragraph are neutral as between an active ('subjective') and passive ('objective') interpretation. We must now take up the discussion of the distinction between active and passive sentences in terms of the traditional category of 'voice'.

8.3 Voice

8.3.1 *The term 'voice'*

The term 'voice' (Latin *vox*) was originally used by Roman grammarians in two distinguishable, but related, senses: (i) In the sense of

'sound' (as used in the 'pronunciation' of human language: translating the Greek term *phōnḗ*), especially of the 'sounds' produced by
the vibration of the 'vocal cords': hence the term 'vowel' (from
Latin *sonus vocalis*, 'a sound produced with voice', *via* Old French
vouel). (ii) Of the 'form' of a word (that is, what it 'sounded' like)
as opposed to its 'meaning' (cf. 7.1.2). The first of these two senses
is still current in linguistics in the distinction between voiced and
voiceless 'sounds' (whether as phonetic or phonological units:
cf. 3.2.4). In the second sense, 'voice' has disappeared from modern
linguistic theory. Instead, the term has developed a third sense,
derived ultimately from (ii) above, in which it refers to the active and
passive 'forms' of the verb. (The traditional Latin term for this third
sense was *species* or *genus*. In the course of time, *genus* was restricted
to the nominal category of 'gender'; and the somewhat artificial
classification of the 'forms' of the different parts of speech in terms
of genera and species was abandoned.) The traditional Greek term
for 'voice' as a category of the verb was *diathesis*, 'state', 'disposition',
'function', etc.; and some linguists prefer to use 'diathesis', rather
than 'voice', in this sense of the term. However, the risk of confusion
between the phonetic or phonological sense of 'voice' and its
grammatical sense is very small. In this section we are of course
concerned with voice as a grammatical category.

It is not only the traditional terminology that is confusing, or
potentially confusing, in theoretical discussions of the category of
voice. The Greek grammarians failed to appreciate the true nature of
the distinctions marked by the verbal inflexions which they referred
to as 'active', 'passive' (i.e. signifying the *state* of 'being acted upon'
or 'suffering the effects of the action') and 'middle'; and this has left
us with a legacy of contradictory statements about the role of voice,
not only in the classical languages, but also in English and other
modern languages, the description of which has been strongly
influenced by traditional grammar. As far as English is concerned,
one finds such statements as the following (by McKerrow): 'If we
were now starting for the first time to construct a grammar of modern
English, without knowledge of or reference to the classics, it might
never occur to us to postulate a passive voice at all. It seems to me
that it is questionable whether in spoken English of to-day there is
really any such thing, and though, as a matter of convenience, it may
be well to retain it in our grammars, I doubt whether it ought to
occupy quite so prominent a position as it sometimes does.' (This
passage, together with statements made about the passive in English

by other grammarians, is quoted by Svartvik in a recent comprehensive and illuminating study of the whole question.) Paradoxically,
it might also be maintained that what the Greek grammarians said
about the passive voice, and its opposition to the active, is more
directly applicable to modern English than it is to classical Greek!
Although this point will not be developed here in detail, its simple
assertion will serve as an indication that the interpretation of voice
is a matter of considerable controversy, both at the present time and
in the Western grammatical tradition.

8.3.2 'Active' and 'middle' in Greek

Reference was made in the previous paragraph to the three Greek
voices: 'active', 'passive' and 'middle'. As the term suggests, the
middle was thought of as intermediate between the primary opposition
of active and passive (signifying either an 'action', like the active, or
a 'state', like the passive, according to the circumstances or the
inherent meaning of the verb in question). In fact, the passive is not
distinguished from the middle in most of the inflected forms of the
Greek verb; distinct passive inflexions are found only in the future
and the aorist (cf. 7.5.6); of these the former did not develop before
the classical period, and the latter, with certain verbs at least, could
also have a 'middle' sense (what is meant by this we shall come to
presently); finally, the verbal forms that could be used either in
'middle' or passive sentences are far more frequently to be interpreted as middle than as passive. In short, the opposition of voice in
Greek is primarily one of active v. 'middle'. The passive was a later
development (as it was in all the Indo-European languages); and it
was at first relatively infrequent.

The implications of the middle (when it is in opposition with the
active) are that the 'action' or 'state' affects the subject of the verb
or his interests. One class of sentences that fall within the scope of
this notion are reflexive sentences (cf. 8.2.10). For example, the
English sentence *I am washing myself* (or its implicitly reflexive
'version', *I am washing*) might be translated into Greek as *loúomai*
(v. the active, *loúō*, 'I am washing (something)'). But the middle may
also be used in a transitive sentence with an object that is distinct
from the subject: e.g. *loúomai khitôna*, 'I am washing (my) shirt'.
Here, the implication of the use of the middle voice rather than the
active is that the 'action' is being carried out by the subject for his own
benefit or in his own interests. It is interesting to note, at this point,

that French has a rather similar construction: cf. not only *Je me lave*, 'I am washing myself', but also *Je me lave une chemise*, 'I am washing (myself) a shirt'. The reflexive implication in sentences like this might be described as 'benefactive' ('for the benefit of', 'in the interests of'): cf. *I got myself a new suit*. In other instances the sense of the Greek middle can be best conveyed in English by means of what may be described, rather clumsily, as a 'causative-reflexive': cf. *misthô*, 'I hire' *v. misthoûmai*, 'I get myself hired' (i.e. 'I take a job', 'I sign on as a mercenary soldier', etc.); *didáskō*, 'I teach' v. *didáskomai*, 'I get myself taught'.

Although one can distinguish other senses of the Greek middle (and in a fuller treatment various factors would come up for discussion), what has been said will suffice to illustrate the general character of the 'middle' voice in sentences in which it is opposed to the active. From the glosses that have been attached to some of the examples it will be clear that the subject of the 'middle' can be interpreted as 'non-agentive' or 'agentive', according to the context or the meaning of the verb; and, if the subject is taken as 'non-agentive', it can also be identified in certain instances with the object of a corresponding transitive sentence in the active voice. Under these conditions, the distinction between the middle and the passive is 'neutralized'.

This point may be illustrated, in fact, from English (where a number of constructions with the auxiliaries *have* and *get* manifest the same kind of ambivalence). Consider a sentence like

(42) *I am getting shaved*

in contrast with each of the following two sentences

(43) *I am shaving*

(44) *I am being shaved*

If the subject of (42) is taken as 'non-agentive', but as otherwise 'interested' in the 'action', (42) is semantically equivalent to (44)—a passive sentence; if there is an 'agentive' adjunct in the sentence (e.g. *I am getting shaved by the barber*), then of course only the passive interpretation is possible (cf. 8.2.15, on *the shooting of the hunters*, etc.). If, however, the subject of (42) is understood as 'agentive', the sentence is more or less equivalent to (43)—a pseudo-intransitive sentence.

8.3.3 *The passive*

The point being made is that the 'middle' voice can 'merge' with
the passive under the 'non-agentive' interpretation of the subject;
and this seems to have been the *point de départ* for the subsequent
development of passive constructions in the Indo-European languages.
Grammars of Latin recognize only two voices, 'active' and 'passive';
but there are many functions of the Latin 'passive' which are closer
to those of the Greek 'middle' than they are to those of the passive
voice in its traditional interpretation. Particularly interesting is the
opposition between the active and the 'passive' with verbs like
'move' and 'turn'. We have already seen that the English verb *move*
is 'ergative': *B moves* v. *A moves B* (cf. 8.2.3). In corresponding Latin
sentences, we find *B movetur* ('passive') v. *A movet B* (active, transitive). But *B movetur* can be translated in two ways: (i) as '*B* moves'
(with *B* either 'agentive' or 'non-agentive'); or (ii) as '*B* is moved'
(with an 'agentive', other than *B*, implied). Only the second of these
interpretations is passive, rather than 'middle'. The first can be
glossed as 'there is movement, and *B* is affected (whether *B* is the
cause, or agent, of the movement or not)'.

We have already noted that the 'middle' could be used in Greek
(with certain verbs) in what we would translate into English as
explicitly or implicitly reflexive sentences. Conversely, in many
modern European languages (French, German, Italian, Spanish, etc.)
the reflexive construction is employed in sentences in which one finds
the 'middle' voice in Greek, the 'passive' in Latin, and an 'ergative'
intransitive or a pseudo-intransitive in English (cf. *move, shave, sell*
in Table 12, p. 364). Furthermore, the Russian passive (except for the
past perfective) has developed from, and to a certain degree is still
'merged' with, the reflexive construction; and in Spanish also (more
strikingly than in the other Romance languages) the reflexive can be
employed in place of the passive in a wide range of sentences.
Limitations of space prevent us from going further into the complex
interrelationships which exist between the 'middle', the reflexive,
the passive, and various kinds of intransitive and pseudo-intransitive
constructions in particular languages. At this point, we must discuss
what is meant by 'passive', an understanding of which we have so far
taken for granted.

Of the following four sentences, it would generally be agreed (in
accordance with traditional views of the structure of English: we have
already seen that certain grammarians have expressed doubts about

this point, cf. 8.3.1) that (45 *a*) and (46 *a*) are *active* and (45 *b*) and (46 *b*) are *passive*; furthermore, that there is some sense in which active sentences are more 'basic', so that (45 *b*) may be regarded as the passive 'version' of (45 *a*), and (46 *b*) the passive 'version' of (46 *a*):

> (45 *a*) *John killed Bill*
>
> (45 *b*) *Bill was killed by John*
>
> (46 *a*) *Bill killed John*
>
> (46 *b*) *John was killed by Bill*

This relationship between corresponding active and passive sentences was traditionally accounted for in some such terms as these:

(i) The object of the active sentence becomes the subject of the corresponding passive sentence. Thus, *Bill* is the object of (45 *a*) and the subject of (45 *b*); *John* is the object of (46 *a*) and the subject of (46 *b*).

(ii) The verb is 'active' in 'form' in the more basic (active) 'version', and 'passive' in 'form' in the less basic (passive) 'version'. Thus, *killed* ('active') v. *was killed* ('passive').

(iii) The subject of the active sentence is not necessarily 'expressed' (overtly represented) in the passive 'version' of the 'same' sentence; but, if it is 'expressed', it takes the form of an adjunct marked as 'agentive' by means of case-inflexion or by the use of a particular preposition (cf. 7.4.7). Thus, *by John* and *by Bill* in (45 *b*) and (46 *b*). The 'agentless' passive sentences corresponding to (45 *b*) and (46 *b*) are *Bill was killed* and *John was killed*. We have seen that the relationship between corresponding active and passive sentences in English can be formalized in terms of transformational rules operating upon the same underlying 'kernel' string (or kernel structure): cf. 6.6.4.

It will be observed, however, that the terms 'active' and 'passive' were used in two different senses in the traditional formulation of the three conditions listed in the previous paragraph. In (i) and (iii) they were applied to sentences, whereas in (ii) they were applied to the 'forms' of the verb (and, for that reason, put in quotation marks). The point is that, although the three conditions will coincide in the clearest instances of the distinction between corresponding active and passive sentences, they are to some degree independent of one another. Intransitive 'ergative' sentences (e.g. *The stone moved*) and various kinds of pseudo-intransitive sentences (e.g. *The books sold quickly*, *The house was building*, etc.) might be held to satisfy the first of the three conditions (cf. *John moved the stone*, *John sold the books quickly*, *John was building the house*, etc.), but not the second (the verb is 'active' in 'form': *moved, sold, was building*, etc., rather than *was moved, were sold, was being built*, etc.) or the third (there is no possibility of 'expressing' the subject of the corresponding transitive 'version' by means of the most typical 'agentive' adjunct-construction: **The stone moved by John*, **The books sold quickly by John*, etc.).

The possibility of conflict between 'the form of the passive voice' and its 'function' (the conversion, or transformation, of a sentence in which the subject is represented as 'acting' into a sentence in which it is represented as 'being acted upon', or 'suffering the effects of the action') is well recognized in the theory and practice of traditional grammarians. In Latin and Greek there are many verbs which are said to be 'passive (or middle) in form, but active in meaning' (they are traditionally referred to as 'deponent', since they are thought of as 'laying aside' the 'meaning' normally associated with the 'passive' voice). An example is the Latin verb *sequor*, 'I follow', which occurs in active, transitive sentences despite its 'form'. Conversely, though more rarely, a verb which is 'active' in 'form' may occur in the corresponding passive 'version' of an active sentence. Consider, for example, the following two Greek sentences, of which (47*b*) is the normal passive 'version' of (47*a*):

(47*a*) *hoi Athēnaîoi apokteínousi Sōkrátēn*, 'The Athenians kill Socrates'

(47*b*) *Sōkrátēs apothnḗiskei (hupò tôn Athēnaíōn)*, 'Socrates is killed (by the Athenians)'

The verb that is translated in (47*b*) as 'is killed' may also be translated as 'dies' in other contexts; and it is 'active' in 'form'. It will be observed that, unlike the intransitive 'ergative' sentences and pseudo-intransitive sentences of English referred to in the previous paragraph, (47*b*) satisfies both (i) and (iii), but not (ii), of the conditions listed above.

One cannot talk sensibly of a 'conflict' between 'form' and 'function' in particular instances unless there are other instances, more numerous and taken as typical, in which there is no 'conflict'. The traditional conception of the distinction between an active and a passive voice rests upon the assumption that the three conditions mentioned above will generally coincide. For example, if it were the case in English that the equivalents of (45*b*) and (46*b*) were

(45*c*) **Bill killed by John*

(46*c*) **John killed by Bill*

with *by John* and *by Bill* as optional 'agentive' adjuncts; and, if this were not merely a feature associated with *kill* and a relatively small number of other transitive verbs, but typical of the relationship between pairs of sentences in which the object of the one 'becomes' the subject of the other, one would not say that English had an active and passive voice, but rather that the English verb was 'voice-neutral' and could occur with either the 'actor' or the 'goal' as its subject. This situation obtains in a number of languages (including Eskimo: cf. 8.2.15).

8.3.4 *'Agentless' sentences*

In the statement of condition (iii), it was said that the ('agentive') subject of the active sentence is not necessarily 'expressed', or overtly represented, in the passive version. English is in fact rather unusual, among languages that have a passive voice, in that the 'agentive' adjunct occurs quite freely. But even in English, sentences like *Bill was killed by John* are of less frequent occurrence than sentences like *Bill was killed*. If there is any one function that is common to the passive in all the languages that are customarily said to have a passive voice (and in certain languages this seems to be its sole function: e.g. in Turkish), this is that it makes possible the construction of 'agentless' sentences: e.g. *Bill was killed*.

But there is another way of constructing 'agentless' sentences in English (apart from the pseudo-intransitive constructions discussed earlier). This is by means of a 'non-specific' subject in the position that would be filled by the word or phrase referring to the 'actor' in a corresponding sentence in which the 'actor' was specified: cf. *John killed Bill* v. *Someone killed Bill*; and *Bill was killed by John* v. *Bill was killed (by someone)*. There are therefore five possibilities: active with a 'specific' agent; active with a 'non-specific' agent; passive with a 'specific' agent; passive with a 'non-specific' agent (*Bill was killed by someone*); and passive without mention of the agent (*Bill was killed*). Of these, the passive with a 'non-specific' agent is unusual in English: but there are circumstances in which it might be found.

There are other languages, however, in which only three or two of these five possibilities are realized. For example, Turkish has the structural equivalents of *John killed Bill*, *Someone killed Bill* and *Bill was killed*, but not of *Bill was killed by John*. (Although it is possible to add to the passive sentence an adjunct which might be translated into English, in certain circumstances, as 'agentive', it is not strictly comparable with *by John* in English sentences like the above.) And there are languages in which there are no passive sentences, but rather an opposition between a 'specific' and a 'non-specific' active sentence (cf. *John killed Bill* v. *Someone killed Bill*).

In particular languages, there may be a choice between different kinds of 'non-specific' subjects in 'agentive' position. For example, the Latin pronouns *quidam* and *aliquis* can both be translated as 'someone' in English; but the former might be used when the 'unspecified' person is known to the speaker ('a certain person that need not be identified'), the latter when he is not ('someone whose identity is unknown to me'). There is a somewhat similar distinction in Russian between *kto-to* and *kto-nibudj*. And in many languages there is what might be most appropriately described as a 'dummy-subject' pronoun. Its function is quite distinct from that of the 'non-specific' pronouns (which are, in any case, not necessarily restricted to subject position). This may be illustrated by means of the French *on* or the German *man*, in such sentences as *On parle anglais* or *Man spricht englisch*, 'English is spoken' (or, using the English pronoun *they* with the same 'dummy' function, 'They speak English': i.e. 'in this shop', 'in Jamaica', etc.). It is noticeable that the most usual English translation of such sentences takes the form of a passive. There are other languages, in which it tends to be reflexive (or pseudo-reflexive): e.g. Spanish *Se habla inglés*.

Finally, one should mention what is traditionally described as the 'impersonal' use of the passive with intransitive verbs. So far we have assumed that the passive voice is defined by the coincidence of the three conditions listed in 8.3.3. But the first of these restricts the passive to transitive verbs. Although this restriction holds for English and, on the whole, for most of the Indo-European languages, the passive is regularly found with intransitive verbs in certain other languages. For example, corresponding to the Turkish active sentence (*O*) *Istanbula bu yoldan gider* ('He Istanbul-to this route-by go', i.e. 'He takes this route for Istanbul') there is the 'impersonal' passive 'version' *Istanbula bu yoldan gid-il-ir* ('Istanbul-to this route-by is gone', i.e. 'This is the route for Istanbul' or 'One takes this road for Istanbul': the same suffix, *-il-*, marks the passive voice in Turkish, whether the verb is transitive or intransitive). A similar construction is found, though less commonly, in German: *Es wird heute abend getanzt* ('It will be this evening danced', i.e. 'There will be dancing this evening'). Occurrences are also attested in Latin (*pugnabatur*, 'It was fought', i.e. 'There was some fighting'). Indeed, it is probable that 'impersonal' forms of the verb were 'merged' with the 'middle' to form the 'passive' of classical Latin (cf. 8.3.3).

'Impersonal' constructions of the kind that have been illustrated here clearly do not fulfil the conditions given above for the definition of the passive. For these conditions rest upon the assumption that passive sentences are derived from active transitive structures. On the other hand, 'impersonal' sentences are similar to what we may think of as 'true' passive sentences in two respects: first, they are 'agentless', and we have seen that the most typical function of the passive is that it makes possible the construction of 'agentless' sentences; second, they have a 'form' of the verb which is overtly marked, inflexionally or otherwise, as 'passive'. In languages in which they occur with 'true' passives they are presumably to be related to these syntactically.

8.3.5 *The formalization of transitivity and voice*

The various phenomena that have been discussed in this section under the rubric of 'transitivity', 'ergativity' and 'voice' present the linguist with considerable problems, both practical and theoretical. By 'practical' problems I mean the difficulties of deciding what the 'facts' are in the analysis of particular languages, what are the implications of the choice of one 'version', or one construction, rather than another. These problems are formidable enough (although we have frequently glossed over certain difficulties of interpretation in our necessarily simplified discussion of the topics that have been raised). But the theoretical problems are far greater.

In the field of syntactic theory at the present time one thing is clear. Although great advances have been made in the understanding and formalization of the relationships between sentences of different types, none of the models of transformational syntax that have yet been proposed (the best known of which is that developed by Chomsky and his associates) is capable of handling the complex interrelationships between the many kinds of constructions referred to in this chapter in a systematic and intuitively satisfactory way (cf. 6.5.7, on 'strong adequacy'). Linguistic theory develops of course on the assumption that all the 'facts' are in principle formalizable within a consistent general framework. And a good deal of work is now being published which is directed towards the formalization of such 'facts' as we have discussed here in an elementary and informal manner.

We shall make no attempt to summarize any of the alternative technical proposals that have been made or to discuss their merits and viability. Instead, we will conclude this section by drawing out some of the theoretical implications of our earlier discussion of 'causativity' (cf. 8.2.4 ff.).

8.3.6 *A tentative transformational account of transitives and causatives*

Let us assume that the base-component of the grammar of English contains, amongst other rules, the following:

(i) $\Sigma \to \text{Nom} + \text{Pred}$

(ii) $\text{Pred} \to \begin{cases} \text{Verb} \\ \Sigma \end{cases}$

(The symbols 'Nom' and 'Pred' may be taken as abbreviations for 'Nominal' and 'Predicate'.) Both of these rules are recursively applicable an indefinitely large number of times (cf. 6.2.6).

If rule (i) is applied, followed by the option 'Pred → Verb' in rule (ii), the 'output' is the constituent-structure framework for the nucleus of a simple intransitive sentence; and the noun or noun-phrase that is inserted in the nominal position is, by definition, the subject of the sentence (cf. 8.1.4). As we have seen (8.2.6), the subject of an intransitive verb may be 'agentive' or 'non-agentive': the nominal will therefore be given the feature 'plus agentive' ('+ag') or 'minus agentive' ('−ag') to indicate this option. One-place (intransitive) verbs must be classified in the lexicon according to their potentiality of combination with nominals in terms of the following threefold distinction: (*a*) 'either agentive or non-agentive'; (*b*) 'agentive only'; (*c*) 'non-agentive only'. We will assume that the verbs *move, jump, die* exemplify this classification. Consequently, *Bill moved* will be susceptible of interpretation as either '+ag' or '−ag'; whereas *Bill died* will be '−ag', and *The horse jumped* will be '+ag' (cf. 8.2.11). The underlying constituent-structure of the nuclei of these sentences is represented diagrammatically in Fig. 20.

But the option 'Pred → Σ' may be taken in the first application of rule (ii). In this case, the symbol 'Σ' must be expanded again into 'Nom + Pred' by a further (recursive) application of rule (i). And the conditions now hold for a second application of (ii). If the option 'Pred → Verb' is taken at this point, the 'output' is the constituent-structure framework for two-place nuclei.

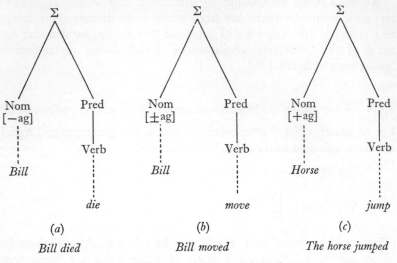

Fig. 20. Some one-place constructions.

Two alternatives present themselves, when we consider the question of 'filling' this two-place structure. The first of these alternatives is to think of the second application of rule (i) as equivalent to the development of the predicate constituent generated by the first application of rule (i), with the nominal constituent generated by the first application of rule (i) held constant, as it were. This would have the effect of determining the subject of a two-place nucleus as syntactically equivalent to the subject of a one-place nucleus. In other words, under this interpretation of the recursive application of rules (i) and (ii) the constituent-structure assigned to transitive sentences (apart from the embedded nodes 'Σ' and 'Pred') would be the same as that assigned by the following two rules:

(a) $\Sigma \rightarrow \text{Nom} + \text{Pred}$

(b) $\text{Pred} \rightarrow \begin{cases} \text{Verb} \\ \text{Nom} + \text{Verb} \end{cases}$

This is the approach to the generation of transitive constructions that has been adopted in most transformational work so far (cf. 7.6.8). But we have decided, in our discussion of transitivity and ergativity in this section, that the sense in which the subject of a transitive construction is syntactically equivalent to the subject of an intransitive construction is largely a matter of such relatively superficial features as case and concord: and these can be handled by later transformational rules (cf. 8.2.7).

If we wish to capture the general principle noted above, that the object of a two-place nucleus corresponds to the subject of a one-place nucleus, we must take the second of the two alternatives. We must embed the one-place nucleus as the predicate of the two-place nucleus. This raises certain rather difficult, but probably not insuperable, technical problems, which we will not go into here. We will assume that they can be satisfactorily resolved, and consider their further implications.

For simplicity, we will make use of a rather *ad hoc* device at this point. When the one-place nucleus is embedded as the predicate of a transitive construction, we will assume that a feature 'causative' is attached to the verb (marked as ' + caus'). This feature will be interpreted differently according to various conditions.

Let us first consider the situation in which the embedded nucleus contains an 'agentive' nominal. There are two possibilities. The verb that is selected may be marked in the lexicon as belonging to that small class of English verbs (*jump, walk, gallop*, etc.: cf. 8.2.12) which may have an 'agentive' object. In this case, the result is what would normally be regarded as a transitive construction: e.g. *John jumped the horse*. This implies that '*jump*: + caus' is realized (on the basis of the information given with the one-place verb *jump* in the lexicon) as *jump*: by a 'process' of 'zero-modification' (cf. 8.2.8). But in the majority of instances, the co-occurrence of 'Nom: + ag' and 'Verb: + caus' in the embedded nucleus will 'trigger off' the application of the rules for the productive causative constructions with the auxiliary verbs, *make, get, have*, etc. The eventual 'output' of the grammar will be such 'overtly' causative constructions as *John made Bill sing, John got Bill to come*, etc.

If the embedded nucleus contains a 'non-agentive' nominal, it fulfils the more normal conditions for transitivity. There are a number of relevant factors. (1) The verb selected from the lexicon may be 'ergative': e.g. *move* (cf. 8.2.3). In this case, it is inserted in the surface structure of the resulting sentence without morphological modifications (with 'zero modification'). However, since the two-place verb is an instance of 'Verb: + caus', the resulting transitive sentence will be determined by the grammar as the causative of the corresponding intransitive ('non-agentive'). Thus, *John moved Bill* will be given a syntactic analysis which makes it readily analysable, semantically, as 'John was the agent (directly) responsible for Bill's (non-agentive) movement'. (2) The verb selected may be one which has associated with it a morphologically distinct two-place form: e.g. *soft* (an 'adjectival' verb, in this particular instance: cf. 8.2.8). The entry in the lexicon for *soft* must therefore contain the information which permits the realization of '*soft*: +caus' as *soften*. (3) The verb selected may be one which has an associated two-place 'lexicalized' form: e.g. *die*. In this case, the appropriate two-place form is substituted for 'Verb: +caus'. For example, '*die*: +caus' is realized in surface structure as *kill*. (4) There may be no corresponding morphological or lexical form, and the verb selected may fail to satisfy the conditions for 'zero modification' (these conditions, it may be observed, are far from clear: it is doubtful whether the 'ergative' verbs of English constitute a determinate and closed class). In this case, 'Verb: +caus' once again 'triggers off' one of the productive, 'overtly' causative constructions: *John made Bill fall*, *John made Bill responsible* (*for the administration of the department*), etc.

Some such approach to the generation of transitive sentences in English (and other languages) would seem to be required, if we are to succeed in formalizing the relationships which undoubtedly hold between the various classes of sentences that have been illustrated. (Sample underlying constituent-structure analyses are given in Fig. 21.) At the same time, it is clear that there are many transitive verbs which do not lend themselves very happily to analysis as realizations of 'Verb: +caus'. They may be called 'basically transitive' verbs. Examples are *eat* and *read*. Little purpose would be served by treating *eat* or *read* as the two-place realizations of 'dummy' one-place verbs, meaning respectively 'be eaten' and 'be read'. The 'non-agentive' one-place sentences *Caviare is eaten* and *The book is read* are not only passive in 'form' (cf. 8.3.3), but, like *Bill is moved* and unlike *Bill moves* ('non-agentive'), they presuppose an 'agent' (which may or may not be specified, of course, in passive sentences). Since it would be counter-intuitive, and of no use for semantic analysis, to impose upon 'basically transitive' sentences the syntactic treatment that has just been outlined for what we may call 'derived' transitive sentences, one should perhaps allow a third option in rule (ii) above. If this rule is now amended to

$$\text{Pred} \rightarrow \begin{cases} \text{Verb} \\ \text{Nom} + \text{Verb} \\ \Sigma \end{cases}$$

it might be possible to secure the advantages of both alternatives. The effect of this amendment, it will be observed, is to integrate the more usual approach to the generation of transitive constructions (cf. rules (a) and (b) on p. 382) with the proposal that we have made for the derivation of two-place nuclei from embedded one-place nuclei. However, this amendment, attractive as it is, increases the technical

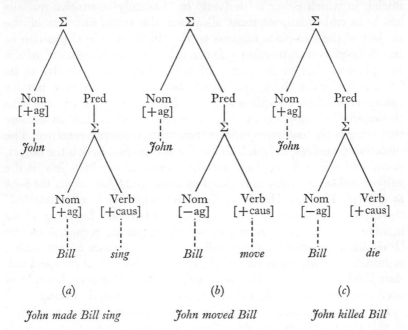

Fig. 21. Some two-place constructions.

problems considerably. If these problems could be overcome, the integration of the two approaches would have the advantage that it formalizes the following propositions: 'Some transitive constructions in the language are basic in the sense that they have both a deep-structure subject and a deep-structure object. Others are derived; and their object is a transformed, one-place, non-agentive subject.' This proposition, or at least the second part of it, expresses a point of view that has often been maintained by linguists working within the more informal framework of traditional grammar. The first part of the proposition represents the view of transitivity that has been formalized by Chomsky in recent work. As we have seen, it is desirable that the theory of generative grammar should enable us to formalize both points of view with respect to sentences containing different classes of lexical items.

Little need be said now about three-place nuclei. If rules (i) and (ii) are recursively applicable an indefinitely large number of times, they will of course generate the constituent-structure framework for nuclei with any number of nominal positions. In the case of three-place nuclei, in which either a 'derived' or 'basically' transitive nucleus has been embedded, we must allow for the transformation of the subject of the two-place nucleus to the 'indirect object' position in the three-place construction (cf. 8.2.14). But this 'demotion' of the two-place subject to the status of adjunct (which is similar to its 'demotion' under the operation of the rules which derive passive constructions from two-place actives: cf. 8.3.4) is obligatory only with 'lexicalized' three-place causatives: e.g. *give*, *show*. Let us assume that *Bill sees the book* exemplifies a 'basically' transitive sentence. The underlying nucleus, in which *Bill* is the subject and *book* is the object, is embedded in a three-place causative sentence in which *John* is the subject and '*see*: +caus' is realized as *show*: thus *John shows the book to Bill* (cf. Fig. 22). However, there are relatively few 'lexicalized' three-place causatives in the language. (There are far more if we include such verbs as *persuade*, which might be regarded as the 'lexicalized' causative corresponding to the two-place *believe* with a nominalized sentence as its object; cf. *Bill believed that the earth was flat*: *John persuaded Bill that the earth was flat*. The consideration of such constructions would introduce additional complications.)

In most instances, an 'overtly' causative construction is employed at this third stage in the cycle. Suppose, for example, that the verb selected from the lexicon is *die*, in the position which has been assigned two causative-features by the operation of the embedding rules: 'Verb: +caus, +caus'. There is no lexical or morphological three-place form which corresponds to *kill* in the way that *kill* corresponds to *die*. At the third stage, therefore, one of the causative auxiliaries is introduced. An example of the type of sentence that might be accounted for in this way is *Tom made John kill Bill*. It is interesting to note that, with the causative auxiliaries *get* and *have*, there is an alternative 'active' and 'passive' form of the embedded two-place nucleus: cf. *Tom had John kill Bill* v. *Tom had Bill killed* (*by John*). The 'passive' form is structurally similar to the sentences which occur, typically, with 'lexicalized' three-place causatives, in the sense that the subject of the two-place nucleus assumes the status of an adjunct (cf. 8.2.15, on the French causative construction). Finally, it should be noted that the 'overtly' causative construction (in English, as in many other languages) is indefinitely recursive: cf. *Peter made Harry make Frank...make Tom make John kill Bill.* It was for this reason that rules (i) and (ii) were made indefinitely recursive in application.

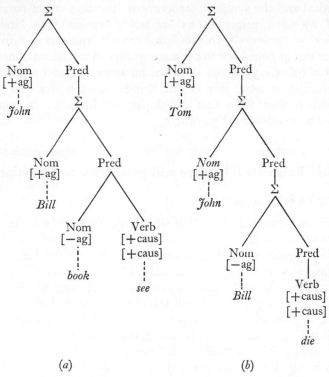

(a)   (b)

John shows the book to Bill   *Tom made John kill Bill*

Fig. 22. Some three-place constructions.

The proposals that have been made in this section, as far as the formalization and more technical details are concerned, must be treated with reserve (cf. 8.3.5). At the same time, it may be pointed out that there are two respects in which they are similar to other proposals that are currently appearing in the linguistic journals and in books on theoretical syntax. First, they presuppose a far more 'abstract' notion of the underlying constituent-structure than was assumed in the earliest work in transformational grammar: in particular, they make free use of such 'features' as ' +ag', ' +caus', etc., which are not constituents in the sense that the auxiliary element 'Pred' or the terminal element 'Verb' is a constituent, but are assigned to such constituents for the correct operation of the transformational rules or the rules of lexical realization. Second, the proposals that have been made here presuppose or imply that both the lexical and the syntactic structure of language are in part determined by such principles as 'agency', 'causativity', 'state' (*v.* 'activity' or 'process'). In this latter respect, theoretical syntax has to some extent gone back to the assumptions of traditional, 'notional' grammar (cf. 4.1.3). It has done so, however, without surrendering (in principle at least) any of the standards of rigour and precise formulation that were first developed by linguists in conscious opposition to traditional grammar.

8.4 Existential, locative and possessive constructions

8.4.1 *'To be' and 'to have'*

It has been suggested above that what is generally referred to as 'the verb *to be*', in English and other languages, is a grammatical element, devoid of meaning, which serves only to 'carry' the markers of tense, mood and aspect in the surface structure of sentences (cf. 7.6.3, 8.2.10). In this section, we will make the same point with respect to 'the verb *to have*'. For simplicity, we will start by assuming that 'being' and 'having' ('possession') are well-defined and universal notions. It may be pointed out immediately, however, that there are many languages which have neither a 'verb *to be*' nor a 'verb *to have*'. There are others in which there are many different 'copulas', no one of which can be put into one-to-one correspondence with English *be* and *have*.

8.4.2 *Logical analysis of 'the verb to be'*

Nowadays, logicians tend to draw a sharp distinction between the 'existential' function of 'the verb *to be*' and its various 'predicative' or 'copulative', functions. The philosophical importance of this distinction lies in the fact that most modern philosophers would say that existence cannot be predicated of objects in the same sense as their various attributes, or properties, but is presupposed in the identification of objects or in any reference to them. We are not concerned here with the philosophical implications of the distinction between 'existential' and 'predicative' statements. It is worth noting, however, that in English 'the verb *to be*' is not used as freely in existential sentences as it was in Greek: it is such sentences as *God is* (where 'the verb *to be*' is perfectly normal in Greek) that have mainly interested philosophers. What would generally be described as the 'existential' use of 'the verb *to be*' in English is not common except with a locative or temporal complement (cf. 8.1.10). Examples of this usage are: (i) *There are lions in Africa*, and (ii) *The accident was yesterday*. We shall discuss such 'existential' sentences presently.

Among the 'predicative' uses of 'the verb *to be*' logicians customarily distinguish: (*a*) the *identification* of one entity with another ($a = b$: e.g. *That man is John*); (*b*) *class-membership* ($b \in C$: e.g. *John is a Catholic*, 'John is a member of the class of persons characterized as Catholic'); and (*c*) *class-inclusion* ($C \subset D$: *Catholics are Christians*, 'The members of the class of persons characterized as Catholic are included among the members of the class of persons characterized as Christians').

Though logically important, the distinction between class-membership and class-inclusion does not appear to be of any syntactic significance in most languages. The distinction between 'characterizing' and 'sortal' sentences (which we have referred to above: cf. 8.1.3) is, however, of considerable importance: cf. *Apples are sweet* and *Apples are fruit*. The former tend to have an 'adjectival' predicate (in languages where one can draw a distinction between 'adjectives' and 'verbs'), and the latter a nominal predicate. The syntactic analysis of sentences with nominal predicates (e.g. *Apples are fruit*, *John is a soldier*, *Mary is still a very young girl*) is a very complex matter: we shall not go into the question here. We will disregard the differences between various subtypes of nominal predicates and treat them all like 'adjectival' predicates. For terminological convenience, we will refer to both classes of sentences (whether they are 'characterizing' or 'sortal', and regardless of any other differences) as *attributive*.

A further use of 'the verb *to be*' is with *locative* complements. We have already discussed this construction in sufficient detail (cf. 8.1.10); and we shall draw upon that discussion in what follows.

8.4.3 *Existential and locative sentences*

We have distinguished four 'functions' of 'the verb *to be*'. They are 'existential', 'identifying' (or 'equative'), 'attributive' and 'locative'. The last three of these are usually grouped together by linguists as 'copulative' (the 'copula' being a 'link' between the subject and the predicate in traditional logic); the 'existential' use of 'the verb *to be*' is frequently treated as quite different from the other uses.

It has already been pointed out that 'the existential verb *to be*' is rare in English without a locative or temporal complement. But in using the term 'complement', rather than 'adjunct', we are perhaps begging the question (cf. 8.1.9). The point is that the distinction can hardly be drawn with respect to existential sentences. Consider the following two sentences

(1) *There are lions in Africa*

(2) *There is a book on the table*

We might be inclined to say that the first is 'existential' and the second 'locative', on the grounds that the first, but hardly the second, can be paraphrased with a sentence containing *exist*: *Lions exist in Africa*. And one might add that *in Africa* is syntactically 'detachable' (and therefore an adjunct): *Lions exist*. On the other hand, there is an obvious structural similarity between (1) and (2). Moreover, from the point of view of their semantic analysis, existential sentences might be described as implicitly locative (or temporal). The assertion that something exists, or existed, requires 'complementation' with a locative (or temporal) expression before it can be interpreted.

Whether or not this last point is accepted, it remains true that in many languages, as in English, there are obvious similarities between locative and existential sentences. There is little or no difference in meaning between such sentences as *Coffee will be here in a moment* and *There will be coffee here in a moment*: one might suspect that they have the same deep-structure analysis.

Two further points should be noted. Existential sentences typically have an indefinite, rather than a definite, subject: this fact raises the possibility that they should be treated, in a syntactic analysis of their deep structure, as indefinite locatives (with 'locative', in this context, being understood to include 'temporal': cf. 7.4.6, on the 'local' cases). Secondly, the connexion between existential and locative constructions is supported by the employment of what was originally a locative (and more particularly a deictic: cf. 7.2.1) adverb in the existential sentences of a number of European languages: cf. English *there* (in *there is/are...*), French *y* (in *il y a*), Italian *ci* (in *ci sono*, etc.), German *da* (in *ist da*, 'is there' or 'exists': cf. *das Dasein*, 'existence', i.e. 'the being-there').

8.4.4 *Possessive sentences*

What is meant by the term 'possessive sentence' may be illustrated, in the first instance, from English:

(3) *The book is John's*

(4) *John has a book*

These two sentences are strikingly different in surface structure. In (3) the subject is *the book* and the predicate is *John's*, a noun in the 'genitive', or 'possessive', case (cf. 7.4.5). In (4) *John* is the subject; and the predicate is *has a book*, with *a book* as the object of 'the verb *to have*'. At the same time, it is clear that (3) and (4) are transformationally related to the phrase *John's book* ('the book which is John's', 'the book which John has'), and therefore to one another. What, then, is the nature of this relationship?

In the treatment of the 'genitive' in the previous chapter, we drew attention to the 'adjectival' function of the genitive in both adnominal and predicative position: cf. *The book is John's*: *John's book*:: *the book is heavy*: *the heavy book*. (It should be noted, in passing, that *book* in *John's book* or *the man's book* is necessarily definite: 'the book of John', 'the book of the man', as it were. The corresponding indefinite phrases are *a book of John's*, *one of John's books*, etc.) There is a similar structural parallelism between locative and possessive constructions: cf. *the book is John's*: *John's book*:: *the book is on the table*: *the book on the table*. (Whether the adnominal word or phrase, e.g. *John's* or *on the table*, occurs before or after the noun it modifies in surface structure is a secondary consideration.)

In most of the transformational accounts of English syntax so far published, it has been assumed that phrases like *John's book* are to be derived from an underlying structure in which the 'possessive' noun is the subject of 'the verb *have*': in other words, it is assumed that *have* is a deep-structure verb (like *read*, etc.), which differs, however, from the majority of transitive verbs in that (in 'possessive' sentences) it cannot undergo the passive transformation (**A book is had by John*). There are many reasons for believing that this account of the relationship between '*have*-sentences' and possessive phrases is incorrect.

First of all, it will be observed that the parallelism between 'adjectival', locative and possessive constructions referred to above would tend to suggest that in all cases the head of the predicate is transformed to adnominal position. What is required then is some rule which derives *John has a book* from an underlying structure in which *a book* is the subject and *John* is in a predicative relationship with it. Of the two possessive sentences given above, (3) is more similar in surface structure than (4) to what we may take to be the deep structure of (4).

Secondly, it should be noted that relatively few languages exhibit what we may call '*have*-sentences': i.e. possessive sentences in which the 'possessor' is the surface-structure subject of a 'verb *to have*' and the 'possessed object' the surface-structure object of this verb. Even in the Indo-European languages, '*have*-sentences' are of relatively late and restricted development: they are not found in all the Slavonic and Celtic languages. Moreover, in the Indo-European languages in which '*have*-sentences' occur (Latin, Greek, Germanic, etc.) they would appear to have developed independently. In many cases (both in the Indo-European languages and in other languages with a 'verb *to have*') the possessive use of the verb seems to have developed from sentences in which it originally meant 'grasp' or 'hold (in the hand)'.

As Benveniste has pointed out, Latin illustrates the development of '*have*-sentences' in the Indo-European languages particularly well. Consider the following three sentences:

(5) *Johannes habet librum* ('John-nominative'+'has'+'book-accusative')

(6) *Est Johanni liber* ('is'+'John-dative'+'book-nominative')

(7) *Liber est Johanni* ('book-nominative'+'is'+'John-dative')

There is no 'definite article' in Latin, and definiteness is not marked as such in any other way. The difference between (6) and (7) lies solely in the order of words in surface structure; and the choice between one order, rather than another, correlates in Latin (although it is also influenced by other factors) with the selection of one word or phrase as the 'topic', rather than the 'comment', of the sentence (cf. 8.1.2). The 'topic' of the sentence is usually definite, whether it is marked as such in particular languages or not. The normal translation of (7) is therefore 'The book is John's' (*liber* being the 'topic'); and the normal translation of (6) is 'John has a book' (not 'John has the book'). The '*have*-sentence' (5), which is a later development from (6), is translatable as either 'John has a book' or 'John has the book'. Let us now assume that the development of (5) from (6) is the result of what was first an optional, 'stylistic', transformation, the effect of which was to put 'John' in surface-structure subject-position. This is the position which animate nouns normally occupy (as the subject of either the active or the passive); and animate nouns, rather than inanimate nouns, tend to be 'topics'.

At first sight, this comparison with Latin and the diachronic considerations introduced above would seem to have little relevance to the synchronic description of modern English. Notice, however, that (3) and (4) must be related to one another in the syntactic analysis of English, just as (6) and (7) must be related to one another in Latin. Since *A book is John's is to be excluded (we assume) as ungrammatical, it is tempting to do so by means of an obligatory transformation which converts it (or rather the underlying structure) into John has a book.

We can now relate this proposal to a somewhat similar proposal for indefinite locative sentences. Although A book is on the table is acceptable in English, it is a less common sentence than There is a book on the table. Let us therefore say that what is sometimes called the 'expletive' ('dummy') use of there in locative sentences is a syntactic device of English for 'anticipating' the locative phrase in surface structure. It is noteworthy that the 'expletive' there is not generally found in locative sentences with a definite subject (e.g. The book is on the table); and it also serves in 'existential' sentences, which we have already related to indefinite locatives. Once we take into account the distinction between definite and indefinite subjects, we see that there is some parallelism between existential, locative and possessive sentences in English. This parallelism is even more striking in certain other languages.

8.4.5 Examples from other languages

Let us consider the following (Mandarin) Chinese sentences:

(8) *Shū zài zhūo-shàng* ('book'+'be'+'table-top'), 'The book is on the table'

(9) *Zhūo-shàng yǒu shū* ('table-top'+'have'+'book'), 'There is a book on the table'

(10) *Shū shì wǒ-de* ('book'+'be'+'me-of'), 'The book is mine'

(11) *Wǒ yǒu shū* ('me'+'have'+'book'), 'I have a book'

It will be observed that there are two 'verbs *to be*', *zài* and *shì*, and one 'verb *to have*', *yǒu*, exemplified here. But their distribution is different from the distribution of the English *be* and *have*. (The 'postpositional' *shàng* is one of a set of such locative forms: inherently locative nouns, names of countries, etc., occur in sentences like (8) and (9) without any such 'localizing' form. Similarly, 'alienable' possession requires the particle *-de*: cf. (10). 'Inalienable' possession does not: cf. *wŏde shū* v. *wŏ jiā*, 'my book' *v.* 'my home, family'. For the notions 'alienable' and 'inalienable', cf. 7.4.6.) Despite their surface-structure differences, the Chinese and the English constructions can be related as follows. The English *have*-transformation operates upon indefinite possessive structures to bring the 'possessor' into surface-structure position; in Chinese, there is a similar *yoŭ*-transformation, which operates, however, in both possessive and locative sentences, (9) and (11). In the case of definite possessive and locative sentences, the syntax of English generates the '*be*-copula'; in Chinese, *shì* is generated for the one, and *zài* for the other. When we translate from one language into the other, we must take note of the syntactic subclassification of the nouns occurring in the sentences to be translated. We translate (11) as 'I have a book', rather than 'There is a book at me', because *wŏ* is animate; conversely, we translate (9) by means of the existential-locative 'There is a book on the table', because *zhūo* is inanimate. In certain grammatical descriptions of Chinese, a distinction is drawn between an 'existential' and 'possessive' sense of the 'verb' *yoŭ*: but this is surely to distort the analysis of Chinese. It is worth noting that (9) can also be translated into English with a '*have*-sentence' in which the locative is 'anticipated' in surface-subject position and then 'repeated' with a pronoun later in the sentence: *The table has a book on it*. And the transformational relationship that holds in Chinese between such sentences as (8) and (9) is found also in English, over a narrower range of sentences, between sentences with a locative complement and corresponding sentences in which the head-noun of the locative phrase is the surface-subject of such verbs as *contain*: cf. *There is water in the bottle*: *The bottle contains water*.

Although Russian has a 'verb *to have*' (*imetj*), it is not common. The most usual translation of the four Chinese sentences given above would be:

(8*a*) *Kniga na stole* ('book' + 'on' + 'table')

(9*a*) *Na stole kniga* ('on' + 'table' + 'book')

(10*a*) *Kniga moja* ('book' + 'my')

(11*a*) *U menja kniga* ('at' + 'me' + 'book')

It will be observed that in these sentences (unmarked for tense, mood and aspect) there is neither a 'verb *to be*' nor a 'verb *to have*'. *U menja* in (11a) is structurally similar to locative phrases; and the preposition *u* with the 'genitive' (as here) would be translated as 'at' or 'near' if the noun dependent upon it was inanimate. Although the modally and temporally marked 'versions' of the above Russian sentences (e.g. in the past and future 'tense': cf. 7.6.3) would have the same 'verb *to be*' (*bytj*), the negative 'versions' of the possessives and indefinite locatives fall together in that they have the 'existential' negative (*net*, with the 'partitive' genitive). There are very many languages in which the 'possessive' construction corresponding to (11a) is structurally identical with a locative (e.g. Gaelic, Swahili, Hindi).

In Turkish, it is the possessives and the existential sentences which are most obviously connected in terms of their surface-structure similarities. The normal translation of (11a) is

(11b)   *Kitab-ïm var* ('book-my' + 'existent')

where *var* is the 'existential verb'. An alternative translation would be

(11c)   *Ben-de kitap var* ('me-locative' + 'book' + 'existent')

The difference between (11b) and (11c) is brought out by translating the latter as 'I have a book with me' or 'I have a book on me'. Many languages distinguish between an 'ordinary', or 'general', possessive and a 'possessive of availability' in this way: and the second is frequently locative, in terms of the case or preposition used.

Enough exemplification has been given to show that locatives, possessives and existential sentences are interconnected in a variety of languages. One has only to consider the range of sentences in which *have* occurs in English as the 'main verb' to realize that the whole category of so-called 'possessive' sentences is suspect. The one thing that '*have*-sentences' have in common—the one thing that there is in common in '*have*-sentences'—is the fact that the 'subject' of *have* is brought into a position of prominence in surface structure. The syntax of these sentences is very complex, from a transformational point of view; but it seems quite clear that *have* is not a deep-structure verb, any more than *be* is.

8.4.6   *The English perfective*

Most grammars of contemporary English distinguish between the 'full verb *to have*' (used in 'possessive' sentences) and the 'auxiliary verb *to have*', which is combined with 'the past participle' to form the perfective aspect (cf. 7.5.7). Sentences like *I have the book* and *I have done the work* might seem to be quite distinct from one another grammatically: but they are diachronically, and to some extent synchronically, related. The diachronic development can be seen most clearly with reference to the Latin 'possessive' and the Romance perfect constructions with 'have'. (The use of 'have' as an 'auxiliary verb' in the Germanic and Romance languages appears to have been the result of independent development in each group of languages. But it is accounted for by the same general principles.) As we have seen, *Est mihi liber* ('There is to me a book') was replaced by *Habeo librum* ('I have a book') in classical and later Latin. The function of the dative case (e.g. in *mihi*) is frequently subsumed under some general term like 'benefactive' or 'dative of interest'. These are vague terms but they will serve for the purpose of illustrating the point we are discussing here. The Latin sentence *Est mihi liber* can be glossed as 'There is a book with which I am involved or implicated'. In the later stages of Latin, the optional transformation which brings the 'person interested' into surface-structure position (*Habeo librum*) becomes obligatory: the 'verb *habere*' resembles the transitive verbs of Latin in many respects, and the subject of a transitive verb is normally 'agentive' (cf. 8.2.7).

The classical Latin for 'I have done the work' (perfective) is *Feci opus*. But this could be put into the passive as *Opus mihi est factum*, or more commonly with the typical Latin 'agentive adjunct' (*a me*: cf. 7.4.5) as *Opus a me factum est*. The later Latin equivalent of *Feci opus* is *Habeo factum opus* (cf. *Habeo librum*), 'The work is done, and I am involved in its doing (as agent)', i.e. 'I have done the work'. The origin of the English 'perfect with *have*' is similarly explained. It was at first restricted to transitive verbs, and thus preserved its relationship with the perfective passive without *have* (still current in such sentences as *The work is done*, *The house is built*). The subsequent extension of the 'perfect with *have*' to intransitive constructions (e.g. *B has moved* parallel with *A has moved B*) loosens, but does not sever, the link between the transitive, active with *have* and the passive without *have*. A sentence like *John has finished the house* is simultaneously linked with both *John finishes the house* and *The house is finished*. Current transformational grammars of English tend to neglect this particular relationship between the transitive perfective and the passive.

The main point that is being made here, however, is this: it is the same principle which explains both the diachronic development of the 'perfect with *have*' and the 'possessive *have*'. In both cases, the *have*-transformation became obligatory, its original function being to bring the 'person interested' (not necessarily the 'agent') into subject-position in surface structure. This same principle is still operative in English. The relationship between *I had a book on the table* and *There was a book on the table* is the same as the relationship between *I had the work done* and *The work was done*. In neither case can the surface-subject be regarded as other than the 'person interested'. In a sentence like *I had a book stolen* (to use one of Chomsky's examples) the 'person interested' may be either the (indirect) agent or the 'beneficiary' ('I got someone to steal a book' or 'Someone stole a book from me'). In a sentence like *I will have the work done by five o'clock*, the 'person interested' may be either the direct or the indirect (causative) agent ('The work will be done by me' or 'I will get someone to do the work'). Whether such sentences should be described as syntactically ambiguous is, however, a moot point. There would seem to be no more, and no less, reason for saying that *I will have the work done* is derived from two different deep structures than there is for saying that *I built a house by the sea* is derived from two different deep structures. *I built a house* is also interpretable in two ways ('I did the building of the house' or 'I got someone else to build a house for me').

8.4.7 *Static, dynamic and causative*

All the locative, possessive and attributive sentences so far discussed in this section (e.g. *The book is on the table*, *John has a book*, *The book is valuable*) are stative (cf. 7.5.7). It was pointed out, in the treatment of the 'local' cases in the previous chapter, that the opposition of 'locative' and 'directional' (which is found in the case-systems of many languages) is a particular instance of a more general aspectual opposition which might be called *static* and *dynamic*; and that, as locomotion is to location, so acquisition is to possession, and 'becoming' to 'being' (cf. 7.4.6, 7.6.3).

If *be* and *have* are not deep-structure verbs, then it would seem that the following sentences do not contain any verbs in their deep structure either

(12) *John came/went to San Francisco*
(13) *John got a book*
(14) *The book became valuable*

As *be* (*in San Francisco*) is to *come/go* (*to San Francisco*), so *have* (*a book*) is to *get* (*a book*), and *be* (*valuable*) to *become* (*valuable*). In each case we can say that the stative sentence (with *be* or *have*) is 'unmarked', by contrast with the dynamic, which is the 'marked' term of this particular aspectual opposition.

That this is correctly regarded as an opposition of aspect is clear from the following considerations. The perfective of the dynamic implies the (unmarked) imperfective of the static sentence which is in correspondence with it. Thus *John has gone to San Francisco* implies *John is in San Francisco, John has got a book* implies *John has a book, The book has become valuable* implies *The book is valuable*. (This particular relationship has led to the virtual equivalence of *has got* and *has* in many dialects of English.) If these pairs of sentences are treated differently by the base-component of the grammar, then a significant generalization is lost. For example, certain 'prepositional phrases' (e.g. *in the park, at church*) must be analysed as 'locative', others (e.g. *into the park, to church*) must be analysed as 'directional'; then the rules must be written in such a way that *be* does not occur with 'directionals' and 'verbs of motion' do not occur with 'locatives'. But, if these constructions are distinguished in this way in deep structure, such facts as the following remain unexplained (except by *ad hoc* rules): *John went to San Francisco and is still there* is an acceptable sentence, whereas **John went to San Francisco and is still here* is not. The deictic opposition of *here/there* (with respect to speaker: cf. 7.2.1) is not relevant to the grammaticality of *John is in San Francisco*: it is relevant to the choice between *came* and *went* in *John...to San Francisco*; and it is relevant to the conjunction of a 'directional' and a 'locative' in such sentences as those illustrated above. These facts can be systematically accounted for, if we say that the deep structure of e.g. *John is in San Francisco* and *John goes/comes to San Francisco* is identical except for the opposition of static and dynamic. Each of them is also marked in deep structure for 'proximity' or 'remoteness' with respect to speaker (*here* v. *there*: there are certain complicating factors, which we need not go into). In combination with the feature 'dynamic', the feature 'proximate' generates *come* in surface structure and the feature 'remote' generates *go*.

For each of the three classes of sentences referred to above—locative, possessive and attributive—there is a typical three-place causative construction (cf. 8.3.6). Corresponding to (12)–(14), we have

(12*a*) *Bill brought/took John to San Francisco*

(13*a*) *Bill gave John a book*

(14*a*) *Bill made the book valuable*

(The last of these three is perhaps a little odd; but it undoubtedly corresponds to (14) in the way suggested.) The causative construction is dynamic: and *Bill has given John a book* implies *John has a book*, just as *John has got a book* does.

Whether the two-place or three-place dynamic locative construction is used in a particular instance depends upon whether the person or object that 'engages in locomotion' is 'agentive' or not. *The book has gone to London*, though certainly not ungrammatical, is less normal than *John has gone to London*; and it may involve 'recategorization' of *the book* as 'animate' (cf. 7.4.5). *Bill took John to San Francisco* (by contrast with *John went to San Francisco* or *Bill went with John to San Francisco*) marks *Bill* as 'agentive' and *John* as 'non-agentive'.

Finally, it may be observed that possessives and locatives are not always clearly distinguishable in three-place constructions. It would be impossible, and it is perhaps unnecessary, to say whether *Bring me the book* is 'possessive' or locative (whether *me* is the 'indirect object' or 'directional'): we have already drawn attention to the fact that the same case or preposition is used in many languages for both the 'indirect object' and 'motion to' (cf. 7.4.6). Once again, we notice the similarity (and perhaps the ultimate identity) of locatives and possessives. More generally, in this section we have seen that a considerable number of what are customarily regarded as 'full verbs' should perhaps be treated as 'surface-structure verbs', each of them being generated by the grammar to carry distinctions of tense, mood and aspect, with or without such additional features as 'dynamic' or 'causative'.

9

SEMANTICS: GENERAL PRINCIPLES

9.1 Introductory

9.1.1 *The term 'semantics'*

Semantics may be defined, initially and provisionally, as 'the study of meaning'. The term 'semantics' is of relatively recent origin, being coined in the late nineteenth century from a Greek verb meaning 'to signify'. This does not mean, of course, that scholars first turned their attention to the investigation of the meaning of words less than a hundred years ago. On the contrary, from the earliest times down to the present day grammarians have been interested in the meaning of words, and frequently more interested in what words mean than in their syntactic function. A practical manifestation of this interest is seen in the innumerable dictionaries that have been produced throughout the ages, not only in the West, but in all parts of the world where language has been studied. As we have already seen, the categories of traditional grammar were to a large extent determined by their characteristic 'modes of signifying' (cf. 1.2.7).

9.1.2 *Neglect of semantics in modern linguistics*

Many of the more influential books on linguistics that have appeared in the last thirty years devote little or no attention to semantics. The reason for this is that many linguists have come to doubt whether meaning can be studied as objectively and as rigorously as grammar and phonology, for the present at least. Furthermore, whereas phonology and grammar quite clearly fall wholly within the province of linguistics (although the way in which a child learns the phonological and grammatical structure of his language is of considerable interest to the psychologist), what is commonly referred to as 'the problem of meaning' might seem to be of equal, if not greater, concern to philosophy, logic and psychology, and perhaps also to other disciplines such as anthropology and sociology. Philosophers, in particular, have always been interested in meaning, since it is necessarily involved in such vital and notoriously controversial philosophical issues as the nature of truth, the status of universal concepts, the problem of knowledge and the analysis of 'reality'.

9.1.3 *Philosophical and psychological interest in meaning*

It is not difficult to show why meaning is of interest to philosophers and psychologists, and why it is regarded as a controversial 'problem'. Consider the innocent-looking question 'What is the meaning of *cow*?'. It is surely not any particular animal. Is it then the whole class of animals to which we give the name *cow*? All cows are different in some way or other; and, in any case, no one is, or could be, acquainted with each member of the whole class of cows, and yet we would wish to say that we know the meaning of *cow* and are able to use it correctly in referring to particular animals we have never seen before. Is there any one property, or set of properties, which distinguishes cows from all other objects for which we have different words? We soon find ourselves in the thick of the philosophical controversy between 'nominalists' and 'realists' which has endured, in one form or another, from the time of Plato down to our own day. Have the things to which we apply the same name some common 'essential' properties by which we can identify them (as the 'realists' might say) or have they nothing in common other than the name that by convention we have learned to apply to them (as the 'nominalist' might say)? And *cow* is not a particularly difficult case. We might be prepared to grant that cows are definable in terms of a biological classification of genera and species. What about *table*? Tables are of various shapes and sizes, are constructed of various materials and are used for various purposes. But tables, we might say, are at least physically observable and tangible objects; and we might think it possible to draw up some list of defining characteristics. What shall we say then about such words as *truth, beauty, goodness*, etc.? Do all the things we describe as 'beautiful' or 'good' have some common property? If so, how do we identify it and describe it? Shall we say that the meaning of such words as *truth, beauty* and *goodness* is the 'concept' or 'idea' associated with them in the 'minds' of those who know the language to which the words belong—and, in general, that 'meanings' are 'concepts' or 'ideas'? If we say this, we shall find ourselves once again in the midst of philosophical, and psychological, controversy. For many philosophers and psychologists are extremely dubious about the existence of 'concepts', or indeed of the 'mind'. Even if we set these difficulties aside, or refuse to look at them, there are others of a more or less philosophical nature. Does it make sense to say that someone has used a word to mean something different from what it 'really' means? Is there such a thing as the 'true' or 'correct' meaning of a word?

9.1.4   The meanings of 'meaning'

So far we have talked only of the meaning of words. We also say that sentences have a meaning. Is 'meaning' being used here in the same sense? Notice that we often say that sentences and phrases are, or are not, 'meaningful'; we do not normally say that words are not 'meaningful'. Is it possible then to draw a distinction, and perhaps many distinctions, between 'being meaningful' and 'having a meaning'? All these questions, and many other related questions, have been much discussed by philosophers and linguists. It has become a commonplace of semantic theory to draw attention to the numerous meanings of 'meaning'.

In addition to the questions of philosophical interest, there are questions of more particular concern to the linguist. Philosophers, like 'the man in the street', usually take 'words' and 'sentences' for granted. The linguist cannot do this. Words and sentences are first and foremost units of grammatical description; and they are not the only grammatical units he will recognize. He must face the general question of the way in which grammatical units of various kinds are related to units of semantic analysis. In particular, he must investigate whether there is a distinction to be drawn between 'lexical' and 'grammatical' meaning.

9.1.5   Inadequacy of current theories of semantics

No one has yet presented even the outlines of a satisfactory and comprehensive theory of semantics. This point must be made clear in any discussion of the subject. However, the fact that no systematic theory of semantics has so far been developed does not imply that no progress at all has been made in the theoretical investigation of meaning. A brief account will be given below of the more important contributions that have been made by linguists and philosophers in recent years.

We have already defined semantics, provisionally, as 'the study of meaning'; and this definition reflects the one point of agreement among semanticists. As soon as we come to consider particular treatments of the subject, we are confronted with a bewildering variety of approaches to the definition and determination of 'meaning'. Distinctions are made between 'emotive' and 'cognitive' meaning, between 'significance' and 'signification', between 'performative' and 'descriptive' meaning, between 'sense' and 'reference', between 'denotation' and 'connotation', between 'signs' and 'symbols', between 'extension' and 'intension', between 'implication', 'entailment' and 'presupposition', between the 'analytic' and the 'synthetic'; and so on. The terminology of the subject is rich—and rather confusing, since it is used without any high degree of consistency and uniformity between different authors. It is inevitable therefore that the terms introduced in the present chapter will not necessarily carry the same implications as the same terms employed in other treatments of semantics.

We will begin with a brief exposition and some criticism of the traditional approach to the definition of meaning.

9.2 Traditional semantics

9.2.1 *Naming things*

Traditional grammar was founded on the assumption that the word (in the sense of 'lexeme': cf. 5.4.4) was the basic unit of syntax and semantics (cf. also 1.2.7, 7.1.2). The word was a 'sign' composed of two parts: we shall refer to these two components, for the purpose of this discussion, as the *form* of the word and its *meaning*. (It will be recalled that this is but one of the senses in which the term 'form' is used in linguistics; the 'form' of a word as a 'sign', or lexical item, must be distinguished from the particular 'accidental', or inflexionally-variant, 'forms' which it assumes in sentences: cf. 4.1.5). Very early in the history of traditional grammar, the question arose of the relationship between words and the 'things' they referred to or 'signified'. The Greek philosophers of the time of Socrates, and following them Plato, set this question in the terms in which it has generally been posed ever since. For them the semantic relationship holding between words and 'things' was the relationship of 'naming'; and the further question arose as to whether the 'names' we give to 'things' were of 'natural' or 'conventional' origin (cf. 1.2.2). In the course of the development of traditional grammar, it became customary to distinguish between the meaning of a word and the 'thing', or 'things', which were 'named' by it. As the distinction was

formulated by the medieval grammarians: the form of a word (the
vox-part of a *dictio*) signified 'things' by virtue of the 'concept'
associated with the form of the word in the minds of the speakers of
the language; and the 'concept', looked at from this point of view, was
the meaning of the word (its *significatio*). This we will take to be the
traditional view of the relationship between words and 'things'. We
have already seen how this view was made the basis, in principle, for
the philosophical definition of the 'parts of speech' according to their
'modes of signifying' (cf. 1.2.7). Without going further into the
details of the traditional theory of 'signification', we should mention
the fact that the terminology employed did not entirely eliminate the
possibility of equivocation, or confusion, in the application of the
term 'signify': the form of a word could be said to 'signify' both
the 'concept' under which 'things' were subsumed (by 'abstraction')
from their 'accidental' properties) and also the 'things' themselves.
And there was of course considerable philosophical disagreement as
to the relationship between 'concepts' and 'things' (in particular,
and most notably, the disagreement between the 'nominalists' and
the 'realists': cf. 9.1.3). We may neglect these philosophical differences for the present.

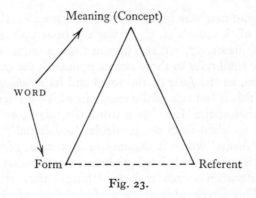

Fig. 23.

9.2.2 *Reference*

At this point it will be useful to introduce a modern term for 'things'
in so far as they are 'named', or 'signified', by words. This is the term
referent. We will say that the relationship which holds between words
and things (their referents) is the relationship of *reference*: words *refer
to* (rather than 'signify', or 'name') things. Granted the distinction
of form, meaning and referent, we can give a familiar diagrammatic

representation of the traditional view of the relationship between them in terms of the 'triangle of signification' (sometimes referred to as 'the semiotic triangle') in Fig. 23. The dotted line between the form and the referent is intended to indicate that the relationship between them is indirect: the form is related to its referent through the mediating (conceptual) meaning associated with both independently. The diagram makes clear the important point that in traditional grammar the word results from the combination of a particular form with a particular meaning.

9.2.3 Synonymy and homonymy

On the basis of this view of the nature of the word, we can account for the traditional semantic classification of words in terms of *synonymy* and *homonymy*. The 'ideal' language, one might say (as did the anomalists: cf. 1.2.3), would be one in which each form had only one meaning and each meaning was associated with only one form. But this 'ideal' is probably not realized by any natural language. Two, or more, forms may be associated with the same meaning (e.g. *hide*: *conceal, big*: *large*—we will assume that they do in fact have the same meaning): in which case the words in question are *synonyms*. And two, or more, meanings may be associated with the same form (e.g. *bank*: (i) 'of a river', (ii) 'for the deposit of money'): in which case the words are *homonyms*. If the language is one for which the orthography is at variance with, or unrelated to, the phonology, then one may of course distinguish further between *homography* (e.g. *lead*, in (i) *a dog's lead* and (ii) *made of lead*) and *homophony* (e.g. *meat, meet*; *sow, sew*: cf. 1.4.2). The important point to notice here is that homonyms in the traditional view are distinct words: homonymy is not difference of meaning within one word. In principle, the association of two or more meanings with one form is sufficient to justify the recognition of two or more words. This follows from the traditional view of the word.

9.2.4 Multiple meaning

The recognition of a distinction between sameness and difference of meaning does not take us very far in semantics. It seems clear that some meanings are 'related' in a way that others are not. The fact that this is so disturbs the symmetry of the simple opposition between synonyms and homonyms. How different must the meanings associated with a given form be before we decide that they are sufficiently different to justify the recognition of two, or more, different words? In their attempts to demonstrate the 'natural' origin of language, the Greeks introduced a number of principles to account for the extension of a word's range of meaning beyond its 'true', or 'original', meaning (cf. 1.2.2). The most important of these principles was *metaphor* ('transfer'), based on the 'natural' connexion between the primary referent and the secondary referent to which the word was applied. Examples of 'metaphorical' extension might be found in the application of such words as *mouth, eye, head, foot* and *leg* to rivers, needles, persons in authority, mountains and tables, respectively. In each instance there is discernible some similarity of shape or function between the referents. Various other types of 'extension' or 'transference' of meaning were recognized by the Greek grammarians, and have passed into traditional works on rhetoric, logic and semantics. Meanings that are more or less clearly 'related' in accordance with such principles are not traditionally regarded as being sufficiently different to justify the recognition of distinct words. The traditional semanticist would not say that the *mouth* of a river and the *mouth* as a part of the body are homonyms; but rather that the word *mouth* has two related meanings. We have, therefore, in addition to synonymy and homonymy, what has come to be called in the more recent development of traditional semantics *multiple meaning* (sometimes called *polysemy*). The distinction between homonymy and multiple meaning is evident in the organization of the dictionaries we customarily use: what the lexicographer has classified as homonyms will be listed as different words, whereas multiple meanings will be given under one entry.

The distinction between homonymy and multiple meaning is, in the last resort, indeterminate and arbitrary. Ultimately, it rests upon either the lexicographer's judgement about the plausibility of the assumed 'extension' of meaning or some historical evidence that the particular 'extension' has in fact taken place. The arbitrariness of the distinction between homonymy and multiple meaning is reflected in the discrepancies in classification between different dictionaries; and this arbitrariness has been increased, rather than lessened, by the development of sounder methods of etymology in the nineteenth century. To give an example: most modern dictionaries of English recognize as two different words (i) *ear*, referring to a part of the body, and (ii) *ear*, referring to parts of such cereal plants as wheat, barley, etc. It so happens that these two 'words' have developed from words which in Old English differed in form as well as meaning (i) *éare*; (ii) *éar*. But how many speakers of English know this? And, if they do, what effect does their knowledge of this fact have upon their use of the language? It would clearly be wrong to assume that *ear* is two words for those (including lexicographers of English) who know the history of the language and one word for the rest of us—unless it were in fact discovered that those who know the history of the language use words like *ear* differently from those who do not know the history of the language. If we discovered that this was in fact the case, we should have to say that the two groups were speaking slightly different languages. Any historical knowledge we might have about the development of the meanings of words is in principle irrelevant to their synchronic use and interpretation (cf. 1.4.5). The distinction of the synchronic and diachronic in semantics is, however, subject to the same general limitations as it is in phonology and grammar.

9.2.5 *Antonymy*

There is a further traditional category of 'relatedness of meaning' which must be mentioned here. This is *antonymy*, or 'oppositeness of meaning'. For the better-known European languages at least, there are a number of dictionaries 'of synonyms and antonyms' available, which are frequently used by writers and students to 'extend their vocabulary' and achieve a greater 'variety' of 'style'. The fact that such special dictionaries are found useful in practice is an indication that words can be more or less satisfactorily grouped into sets of synonyms and antonyms. There are two points that should be stressed, however, in this connexion. First, synonymy and antonymy are semantic relations of a very different logical nature: 'oppositeness of meaning' (*love*: *hate*, *hot*: *cold*, etc.) is not simply the extreme case of difference of meaning. Second, a number of distinctions have to be drawn within the traditional concept of 'antonymy': dictionaries of 'antonyms' are only successful in practice to the degree that their users draw these distinctions (for the most part unreflectingly). Both of these points will be taken up later (cf. 10.4). There is little of value that can be extracted from traditional theoretical discussions of 'antonymy'.

There are a number of criticisms that have been made against traditional semantics in recent years by both linguists and philosophers. The most important of these criticisms will now be discussed.

9.2.6 *Conceptualism and mentalism*

We have already referred to philosophical and psychological controversies about the status of 'concepts' and 'ideas' in the 'mind' (cf. 9.1.3). Traditional semantics makes the existence of 'concepts' basic to the whole theoretical framework, and therefore (almost inevitably) encourages subjectivism and introspection in the investigation of meaning. To quote Haas: 'an empirical science cannot be content to rely on a procedure of people looking into their minds, each into his own'. This criticism presupposes the acceptance of the view that semantics is, or ought to be, an empirical science, which as far as possible avoids commitment with respect to such philosophical and psychological disputes as the distinction of 'body' and 'mind' and the status of 'concepts'. This view will be accepted in the discussion of semantics given in these chapters. It should be stressed, however, that the methodological renunciation of 'mentalism' does not imply the acceptance of 'mechanism', as some linguists have suggested. Bloomfield's 'mechanistic' and 'positivist' definition of the meaning of a word as a full 'scientific' description of its referent is more detrimental to progress in semantics than the traditional definition in terms of 'concepts', since it gives preferential treatment to the relatively small set of words in the vocabularies of natural languages which refer to 'things' describable, in principle, by the physical sciences. Moreover, it rests upon two tacit, and unjustified, assumptions (i) that a 'scientific' description of the referents of these words is relevant to the way in which the words are used by speakers of the language (most of whom have little knowledge of 'scientific' description); and (ii) that the meaning of all words is ultimately describable in the same terms. Indeed, it could be argued that Bloomfield's proposal (which has also been made by others) depends upon a 'realist' view of the relationship between language and 'the world' which is not very different from that of many 'conceptualists': at the very least, it tends to promote the view that since there is, for example, a word *intelligence*, there is also something to which it refers (and this 'something' will presumably be satisfactorily described by 'science' in due course); that since there is a word *love*, there is also something to which this refers; and so on. The position that should be maintained by the linguist is one that is neutral with respect to 'mentalism' and 'mechanism'; a position that is consistent with both and implies neither.

9.2.7 *'Ostensive' definition*

Implicit in the previous paragraph is a further criticism of traditional semantics (and also of certain modern theories). We have already seen that the term 'meaning' itself has many 'meanings' in ordinary usage. When we put to someone the question 'What is the meaning of the word x?' in everyday (non-philosophical and non-technical) discussion, we receive, and are not surprised to receive, answers of a form which varies with the circumstances of the situation in which we ask the question. If we are inquiring about the meaning of a word in a language other than our own, our question will normally be answered by translation. (All sorts of semantically interesting problems are involved in 'translation', which we may neglect for the moment: cf. 9.4.7). More revealing for our present purpose is the situation in which we ask about the meaning of words in our own language (or another language we 'know' at least 'partially'—the whole notion of 'knowing a language completely' is of course chimerical). Suppose we were to ask the meaning of *cow* in the improbable (but, for the argument, favourable) situation in which there were a number of cows present in a neighbouring field. We might be told: 'Do you see those animals over there? They are cows.' This method of conveying the meaning of the word *cow* includes an element of what philosophers refer to as *ostensive definition*. (An ostensive definition is one which defines an object by 'pointing' to it.) But ostensive definition, of itself, is never sufficient, since, first of all, the person interpreting the 'definition' must know in advance the significance of the gesture of 'pointing' in this context (and must know that 'definition', rather than something else, is intended) and, more important, he must correctly identify the object that is 'pointed' to. In the case of our hypothetical example, the words *those animals* limit the possibility of misinterpretation. (They do not eliminate it entirely; but we will assume that the 'definition' of *cow* has been satisfactorily interpreted.) The theoretical importance of this over-simplified, and rather un-realistic, example is twofold: first of all, it makes clear the difficulty of explaining the meaning of any word without using others to limit and make more explicit the 'scope' of 'ostension' (it suggests that it may be impossible to determine, and perhaps also to know, the meaning of one word without also knowing the meaning of others to which it is 'related'—as for instance *cow* is to *animal*); secondly, ostensive definition is only applicable to a relatively small set of words. Consider the futility of trying to explain the meaning of *true*, *beautiful*, etc., in this way! The meaning of such words is typically explained, not always successfully, in terms of synonyms (whose meaning is assumed to be known already to the person putting the question) or by means of rather lengthy definitions of the kind given in dictionaries. Once again, this emphasizes the inevitable 'circularity' of semantics: there is no one point in the vocabulary from which you can start and from which you can derive the meaning of the rest. This question of 'circularity' will come up for discussion later (cf. 9.4.7).

9.2.8 *Context*

Another feature of the everyday situations in which we inquire about the meaning of words is that we are frequently told that 'it depends on the context'. ('Give me the context in which you met the word; and I'll tell you its meaning.') It is often impossible to give the meaning of a word without 'putting it in a context'; and dictionaries are useful in proportion to the number and diversity of the 'contexts' they cite for words. Frequently, and perhaps most typically of all, the meaning of a word is explained by giving a 'synonym' with an indication of the 'contextual' limitations governing the use of the word in question (*addled*: 'bad (of eggs)'; *rancid*: 'bad (of butter)'; etc.). Facts such as these—the diversity of the ways in which, in practice, we state the meaning of words, the 'circularity' of the vocabulary, and the relevance of 'context'—are not given full theoretical recognition in traditional semantics.

9.2.9 *'Meaning' and 'use'*

At this point mention may be made of Wittgenstein's famous and influential slogan: 'Don't look for the meaning of a word, look for its use.' The term 'use' is in itself no clearer than the term 'meaning'; but the substitution of the one for the other has the effect of diverting the semanticist from the traditional tendency to define 'meaning' in terms of 'signification'. Wittgenstein's own examples (in his later work) show that he thought that the 'uses' to which words were put in language were of many different kinds. He did not put forward, or claim to be putting forward, a theory of the 'use' of words as a theory of semantics. But we are perhaps justified in extracting from Wittgenstein's rather programmatic statement the following principles. The only empirical control we have upon the study of language is the 'use' of language-utterances in the multifarious situations of everyday life. Expressions such as 'the meaning of a word' and 'the meaning of a sentence (or proposition)' are dangerously misleading in that they tempt us to go out looking for the 'meanings' they have and to identify as their 'meanings' such entities as physical objects, 'concepts' in the 'mind' or 'states of affairs' in the physical world.

We have no direct evidence about the understanding of utterances, only about their *misunderstanding*—when something 'goes wrong' in the process of communication. If, for instance, we say to someone *bring me the red book that is on the table upstairs* and he brings us a book of a different colour, or a box, or goes off downstairs in search of the book, or does something totally unexpected, we might reasonably say that he has 'misunderstood' the whole or some part of the utterance (other explanations are of course possible). If he does what is expected (goes off in the right direction and comes back with the right book) we might say that he has correctly understood the utterance. What we mean is that (in a case like this) there is good *prima facie* evidence of a 'behavioural' kind to suggest that he has not misunderstood it. It may be that if we continued, rather persistently, to test his 'understanding' of the words *bring* or *red* or *book*, we should come to a point where something he did or said would show that his 'understanding' of these words is somewhat different from ours: that he draws from utterances containing them implications that we do not (or conversely, that we draw implications that he does not), or that he uses them to refer to a slightly different class of objects and actions. Normal communication rests upon the assumption that we all 'understand' words in the same way; this assumption breaks down from time to time, but otherwise 'understanding' is taken for granted. Whether we have or have not the same 'concepts' in our 'minds' when we are talking to one another is a question that cannot be answered otherwise than in terms of the 'use' we make of words in utterances. It would probably be true, but rather pointless, to say that everyone 'understands' a particular word in a slightly different way. Semantics is concerned with accounting for the degree of uniformity in the 'use' of language which makes normal communications possible. Once we abandon the view that the 'meaning' of a word is what it 'signifies', we shall quite naturally recognize that relationships of different kinds have to be stated in accounting for 'use'. Two of the 'factors' to be discussed later will be distinguished as *reference* (which has been mentioned already) and *sense*.

9.2.10 *Indeterminacy of meaning*

As a further consequence of the abandonment of the view that the 'meaning' of a word is what it 'signifies', and that what it 'signifies' is 'transferred' (in some sense) from speaker to hearer in the process of communication, we shall be more ready to accept that it is both un-necessary and undesirable to assume that words have a fully-determined meaning. As we have seen, the way in which language is used in normal situations can be explained on the much weaker assumption that the speakers of the language in question are in sufficient agreement about the 'use' of words (what they refer to, what they imply, etc.) to prevent 'misunderstandings'. This point must be borne in mind whenever we talk of 'the meaning' of words and sentences. We shall take it for granted throughout the following sections of these chapters on semantics.

9.3 'Meaningfulness'

9.3.1 *'Having meaning' and 'significance'*

It was pointed out above (9.1.4) that, although we commonly say that *sentences* or *phrases* are, or are not, 'meaningful', we do not normally say that *words* are not 'meaningful' (for the present we shall continue to adopt the traditional view, according to which words are the minimal 'meaningful' units of language; 'word' is here being used of course in the sense of lexeme: cf. 5.4.4). This fact in itself suggests that the term 'meaningful' may be employed in two distinct senses. We will assume that this is so and, for convenience and clarity, introduce a terminological distinction between *having meaning* and *significance* (or *being significant*). In terms of this distinction, we will say that words have meaning, whereas phrases and sentences may or may not be significant. It should be observed that this statement leaves open the possibility that other units besides words may have meaning; and it does not imply that there is no connexion between 'having meaning' and 'significance'. Traditional semantics (and a number of modern theories) confuse the distinction that is being drawn here by talking of 'signification' in both cases.

In this section it will be argued that having meaning (in the sense in which this notion is to be defined) is logically prior to 'meaning': in other words, that we must first of all decide whether a particular element has meaning before we ask what meaning it has; furthermore, although this may appear paradoxical at first sight, that it is possible for an element to have meaning without having any particular meaning.

9.3.2 *The situational context*

We will start with an intuitive and undefined notion of *context*. Every (spoken) utterance occurs in a particular spatiotemporal situation which includes the speaker and hearer, the actions they are performing at the time and various external objects and events. As we have already seen, there may be 'deictic' features of the utterance which make reference to the situation in which it occurs (cf. 7.2.1). The hearer will not be able to understand an utterance unless he interprets these 'deictic' elements correctly by reference to the relevant features of the situation. However, the context of an utterance cannot simply be identified with the spatiotemporal situation in which it occurs: it must be held to include, not only the relevant objects and actions taking place at the time, but also the knowledge shared by the speaker and hearer of what has been said earlier, in so far as this is pertinent to the understanding of the utterance. It must also be taken to include the tacit acceptance by the speaker and hearer of all the relevant conventions, beliefs and presuppositions 'taken for granted' by the members of the speech-community to which the speaker and hearer belong. The fact that it is in practice, and perhaps also in principle, impossible to give a full account of all these 'contextual' features should not be taken as a reason for denying their existence or their relevance. But it may be interpreted as an argument against the possibility of constructing a complete theory of the meaning of utterances. (The reader will have observed that we are at present talking of utterances, not sentences: cf. 5.1.2.)

9.3.3 *'Having meaning' implies choice*

On the basis of this intuitive notion of 'context' we can now define *having meaning* for utterances. An utterance has meaning only if its occurrence is not completely determined by its context. This definition rests upon the widely-accepted principle that 'meaningfulness implies choice'. If the hearer knows in advance that the speaker will inevitably produce a particular utterance in a particular context, then it is obvious that the utterance gives him no information, when it occurs: no 'communication' takes place. Complete utterances will generally have meaning, since the speaker might in the last resort have remained silent. But there are some socially-prescribed utterances which are highly, if not wholly, determined by their contexts; and such utterances are theoretically interesting in a number of different respects. Let us assume for the sake of the argument that *How do you do?* is the sole socially-prescribed utterance in the context of being formally introduced to someone, and that it is mandatory in such situations. If this is so, then it seems quite reasonable to say that *How do you do?* has no meaning. All that needs to be said about this utterance in a semantic description of English utterances is that it is 'used' in the situations in question. It would be futile to insist that it must 'mean' something over and above its 'use'. But let us now assume that, although it is the sole socially-prescribed utterance in the context of introduction, it contrasts with silence (or a nod of the head, a smile, a surly look, etc.), in the sense that the person being introduced has all these 'choices' open to him. Then, by the definition given above, the result of each 'choice' has meaning—it may *communicate* something to the other person; and we can sensibly go on to ask what meaning each of the potential 'actions' has by contrast with the others.

9.3.4 *Relevance of non-linguistic behaviour*

It is worth while drawing out some further implications of the principle of 'choice' on the basis of this simple example. First of all, utterances interact with, and may be in semantic contrast with, non-linguistic behaviour (including silence, facial expressions and gestures). The utterance *How do you do?*, although itself mandatory in the context, may be pronounced in a variety of ways—'politely', 'casually', 'scornfully', 'condescendingly', etc.—and these different 'modalities' of the utterance may be 'expressed' by 'tone of voice' or accompanying gestures (or both simultaneously). The question that now arises (and it is relevant to all utterances, not merely to those that are socially prescribed for particular contexts) is whether we should say that features such as 'tone of voice' and gestures (of anger, condescension, politeness, etc.) have meaning. In principle, the answer is clear. If such features of the utterance are completely determined (in the sense that the speaker exercises no control over them—no 'choice'), they have no meaning. If, on the other hand, he deliberately wishes to express his anger, his impatience or his 'good breeding', then these 'facts' are indeed 'communicated' by him, and the features of the utterance which serve this purpose have meaning in terms of the definition given above. That the hearer may 'infer' the same facts even when they are not 'communicated' by the speaker (and may not be able to tell whether he is intended to 'infer' them or not) does not affect this question in the slightest. It is quite inappropriate to widen the notion of 'communication' to include all the 'information' which can be 'inferred' from an utterance by the hearer. The principle of 'choice' determines whether utterances and features of utterances have meaning or not.

9.3.5 *Quantifiability of 'having meaning'*

The second point to be made about having meaning is that it is in principle quantifiable with respect to 'expectancy' (or probability of occurrence) in context. From this point of view, having no meaning is merely the limiting case of complete 'predictability'. Any utterance (or feature of the utterance) that is not completely 'predictable' (determined by its context) may be more or less probable than either silence or some other utterance (or feature of the same utterance) with which it is in contrast in the system of communication. And the *less* probable a particular element is, the *more* meaning it has in that context ('element' should here be taken to refer to all the results of 'choice', including silence, permitted by the system of communication for particular contexts). To return to our simple example: if *How do you do?* contrasts with, but is far more probable than, silence (or any other 'element') in the context of introductions, then it has less meaning than silence in that context. It might even be reasonable in such cases to say that the socially-prescribed utterance is 'unmarked', and has meaning only in the rather vacuous sense of contrast (without the communication of any positive 'information'), whereas silence is 'marked' and may serve a positive communicative function. This would appear to be an intuitively satisfying statement of the relationship between the two 'behavioural' possibilities (on the assumption that the facts are as they have been stated). In any case, it is certainly in accord with general, everyday usage to say that the 'meaningfulness' of utterances, and parts of utterances, varies in inverse proportion to their degree of 'expectancy' in context. And this is the sense of 'meaningfulness' that is here being explicated in terms of having meaning. Although it may be possible to say that one element has more meaning than another in a particular context on the basis of their relative 'probabilities of occurrence', it is clear that the precise quantification of having meaning would depend upon our ability to identify the contextual features which determine the 'probabilities of occurrence'. (Strictly speaking, we should not talk of 'probabilities of occurrence' and 'variation in inverse proportion' unless we are able to determine and compute the relevant conditioning factors.) It is very unlikely that it will ever be possible to quantify having meaning in this precise sense. But this is of less importance than one might expect since, as we shall see, *what* meaning elements have in a given context is unrelated to *how much* meaning they have relative to the elements with which they are in contrast. The point to be stressed here is that the question what meaning an element has arises only in the case of those elements which do in fact have meaning (in the sense in which we have defined this notion) in the contexts in which they occur. Although this point has been illustrated so far only for complete utterances of a 'ritualistic' character, we shall generalize it later in the light of the distinction between utterances and sentences drawn in a previous chapter (cf. 5.1.2).

9.3.6 *'Behaviourism' in semantics*

There are two further points to be made about such socially-prescribed utterances as *How do you do?*. They tend to be 'ready-made', in the sense that they are learned by native speakers as unanalysed wholes and are clearly not constructed afresh on each occasion on which they are used in what, following Firth, we may refer to as 'typical repetitive events in the social process'. Since they have this character, it would be possible to account for them in a 'behaviouristic' framework: the utterances in question could reasonably be described as 'conditioned responses' to the situations in which they occur. This fact should not be overlooked by the semanticist. There is a good deal of our everyday use of language which is quite properly described in 'behaviourist' terms, and can be attributed to our 'acting out' of particular 'roles' in the maintenance of socially-prescribed, 'ritualistic' patterns of behaviour. With regard to this aspect of their use of language, human beings behave like many animals, whose 'systems of communication' are made up of a set of 'ready-made utterances' which are used in particular situations. The more typically human aspects of language-behaviour, which depend upon the generative properties of language and also upon the semantic notions of having meaning, reference and sense, are not plausibly accounted for by extending to them the 'behaviourist' notions of 'stimulus' and 'response'. It is nevertheless true that human language includes a 'behavioural' component. Although we shall say no more about this in what follows, we give theoretical recognition to it here.

9.3.7 'Phatic communion'

Mention should also be made in this connexion of that aspect of language-behaviour to which Malinowski applied the term 'phatic communion'. He was drawing attention to the fact that many of our utterances cannot rightly be said to have as their sole, or primary, function the communication or seeking of information, the giving of commands, the expression of hopes, wishes and desires, or even the 'evincing of emotion' (in the loose sense in which semanticists frequently employ this last phrase), but serve to establish and maintain a feeling of social solidarity and well-being. Many 'ready-made' utterances like *How do you do?*, which are socially prescribed in particular contexts, may serve this function of 'phatic communion'. But there are many others which are more or less freely constructed by native speakers, and which simultaneously communicate information and serve in 'phatic communion'. An example might be *It's another beautiful day*, said (we will suppose) as the opening utterance in a conversation between customer and shopkeeper. Quite clearly this utterance is not primarily intended to 'convey' to the shop-keeper some information about the weather; it is an instance of 'phatic communion'. At the same time, it does have a meaning, different from the meaning of innumerable other utterances that might have occurred in the same context and would have served the purposes of 'phatic communion' equally well; and the next 'move' in the conversation will generally be related to the particular utterance on the basis of this meaning. We must therefore distinguish between that aspect of the 'use' of utterances which may be referred to their function in 'phatic communion' and that part of their 'use' which is to be distinguished as their meaning (if they have meaning in terms of our definition). In saying this, we recognize that, even when both of these aspects are present, either one or the other may be the dominant part of the 'use' of the utterance. Malinowski overstated his case when he said that the communication of information was one of the 'most derivate and specialized functions' of language.

9.3.8   *Extension of 'having meaning' to all linguistic units*

So far we have illustrated the notion of having meaning only in relation to whole utterances regarded as unanalysable wholes. For the present, we shall continue to talk of utterances, rather than sentences, and we shall continue to draw upon the intuitive notion of 'context'; but we will now generalize the notion of having meaning in terms of the following principle: *any* linguistic element which occurs in an utterance has meaning only if it is not completely determined ('obligatory') in that context.

It is evident that the notion of having meaning (as it is here defined) is applicable at all levels in the analysis of utterances, including the phonological. There will be many contexts, for instance, in which the words *lamb* and *ram* might equally well occur in otherwise identical utterances. Since these utterances, we will assume, are different in 'meaning (the referents of *lamb* and *ram* are different and the implications 'contained' in the utterances in which they occur are, in general, different), the phonemes /l/ and /r/ not only have meaning, but have a different meaning in these utterances. And there are other utterances, containing words other than *lamb* and *ram*, where the difference in meaning might be carried solely by the phonological opposition of /l/ and /r/. As we saw in an earlier chapter (cf. 3.1.3), the phonological structure of particular languages rests, ultimately, upon this differential property of phonemes (more strictly, of their 'distinctive features') within certain limits imposed by the complementary principle of phonetic similarity. There is therefore good reason for applying the notion of having meaning even at the level of phonological analysis. It is worth noting, however, that in the case of phonetically-distinguishable, but 'similar', speech-sounds, having meaning necessarily implies having a different meaning in at least some contexts. This is not so at the 'higher' levels of analysis. In languages in which the speech-sounds [l] and [r] occur but never distinguish utterances, we say that they are in complementary distribution or free variation (in other words, that they are alternative phonetic realizations of the same phonological unit: cf. 3.3.4). In those contexts in which speech-sounds, elsewhere recognized as distinct phonological units, have the same meaning we may quite reasonably say that they are 'synonymous'. Examples might be the initial vowels of the alternative pronunciations of *economics* (contrast the differential value of the same vowels in *beat*: *bet*, etc.) or the stress-patterns of *cóntroversy*: *contróversy*.

Although the semanticist must give theoretical recognition to the principle of having meaning at the phonological level, he will not generally be concerned further with 'the meaning' of phonological units. The reason is that phonological units never have reference and do not contract any semantic relationships other than sameness and difference of meaning. Furthermore, sameness of meaning when it holds between phonological units (phonological 'synonymy', as illustrated above) is sporadic and unsystematic. It has to be stated in terms of alternative realization rules for particular words; once these rules have been given, there is nothing more of interest to be said. Generally speaking (the qualification is required for cases of 'sound-symbolism'—a semantically interesting phenomenon which limitations of space prevent us from discussing further: cf. 1.2.2), 'the meaning' of a given phonological unit is simply its difference from every other phonological unit (if there are any) that might have occurred in the same context.

9.3.9 Restricted contexts

We have now reached a stage in the argument at which we must draw upon the distinction between utterances and sentences (cf. 5.1.2). Two points must be borne in mind. When we use language to communicate with one another, we do not produce sentences, but utterances; those utterances are produced in particular contexts and cannot be understood (even within the limits imposed above on the interpretation of the term 'understanding': cf. 9.2.9) without a knowledge of the relevant contextual features. Furthermore, in the course of a conversation (let us suppose that it is a conversation) the context is constantly developing, in the sense that it 'takes into itself' from what is said and what is happening all that is relevant to the production and understanding of further utterances. The limiting case of contexts which have not 'developed' in this sense would be those in which the participants in a conversation do not draw upon their previous knowledge of one another or the 'information' communicated in earlier utterances, but where they share the more general beliefs, conventions and presuppositions governing the particular 'universe of discourse' in the society to which they belong. Such contexts, which we will refer to as *restricted contexts*, are comparatively rare, since most utterances depend for their understanding upon the information contained in previous utterances. We must not lose sight of the relationship between utterances and particular contexts.

The second point to be made is this: since sentences are never produced by speakers (sentences being theoretical units established by linguists to state the distributional limitations upon the occurrence of classes of grammatical elements), there can be no direct relationship between sentences and particular contexts. At the same time, utterances have a grammatical structure which depends upon their 'derivation' from sentences; and the grammatical structure of utterances is, or can be, semantically relevant. This is particularly clear in the case of 'syntactic ambiguity' (cf. 6.1.3). Moreover (except for such 'ready-made' expressions as *How do you do?*) utterances are produced by speakers and understood by hearers on the basis of the regularities of formation and transformation determined for sentences by the rules of the grammar. At the present time, neither linguistics nor any of the other sciences concerned with the 'mechanisms' underlying the production of utterances is in a position to make any very definite statements about the way in which a knowledge of the abstract relationships holding between grammatical elements in sentences interacts with contextual features of various kinds to effect the production and understanding of utterances in which the observable 'correlates' of these grammatical elements occur. That there is some interaction between the grammatical structure of the language and the relevant contextual features would seem to be a fact; and we must take account of it.

Since we cannot in general identify either the actual elements 'selected' by the speaker in the production of utterances or all the relevant features of particular contexts, we can make it a matter of methodological decision to do what linguists have generally done in practice; and that is to handle the semantic relationships between utterances in terms of the semantic relationships holding between the sentences from which they are assumed to be 'derived' when they are produced by native speakers in restricted contexts. (The notion of 'restricted context' must still be retained, since, as we shall see below, the semantic relationships that hold between sentences cannot be stated without at least this degree of 'contextualization': cf. 10.1.2.) The features of particular contexts will then be invoked (in what must be, for the present at least, a rather *ad hoc* manner) to account for the 'residual' semantically-relevant aspects of utterances. What has been represented here as a matter of conscious, methodological decision should not be taken to imply any priority of the grammatical over the contextual in the psychological processes of producing and understanding utterances.

9.3.10 *Deep-structure elements have meaning in sentences*

We may now apply the notion of 'having meaning' to the grammatical elements from which sentences are generated by the rules determining the formation and transformation of their bases (cf. 6.6.1). Since having meaning implies 'choice', it follows that no elements introduced into sentences by means of obligatory rules can have meaning in the sense of the definition. (Such 'dummy' elements as *do* in *Do you want to go?* have no meaning: cf. 7.6.3.) Furthermore, if we assume that all the 'choices' are made with respect to the selection of elements in 'deep' structure (these elements being either 'categories' or 'features': cf. 7.6.9), it is clear that the notion of having meaning is not bound to units of any particular rank. First of all, the distinction of such units as morphemes, words and phrases in a particular language is to some degree based on 'surface' structure (6.6.1); and, secondly, there are many 'grammatical categories' (tense, mood, aspect, gender, number, etc.: cf. 7.1.5) which may or may not be realized by morphemes or words, but which constitute systems of 'choices' in sentences. Whether or not one can draw a sharp distinction between 'lexical' and 'grammatical' meaning, in terms of what meaning the elements have, is a question we shall discuss later (cf. 9.5.2). For our present purpose, it is sufficient to point out that the notion of having meaning applies equally to elements of both kinds in the 'deep' structure of sentences. Moreover, this notion is taken into account, explicitly or implicitly, in all recent linguistic theory. Classes of elements (denoted by either auxiliary or terminal symbols: cf. 6.2.2) are established at each point of 'choice' in the generation of sentences.

It follows from what has just been said that no element in a sentence will have meaning unless it is a member of one of the syntactically-determined classes in the 'deep' structure of the sentence: and it is this fact which justifies the almost universally accepted assumption of linguists, logicians and philosophers that the set of elements which have meaning in a particular language is, at least to a very high degree, coextensive with the members of the terminal 'constituents' and 'features' of that language. However, it does not follow that every 'constituent' and 'feature' will have meaning in every sentence in which it occurs. This is an important point which has occasionally been overlooked by linguists, and therefore merits some further discussion.

The whole question turns on the distinction between grammatical and semantic acceptability. As we saw in an earlier chapter (cf. 4.2.12 ff.), grammaticality is that part of the acceptability of utterances which can be accounted for in terms of the rules of formation and transformation specifying the permissible combinations of the distributional classes of elements ('categories' and 'features') in sentences. It is generally recognized that there will be innumerable sentences generated by the grammar of any language which are unacceptable in various ways; and it is traditional to describe at least one type of unacceptability by saying that the sentences in question are 'meaningless' or 'nonsensical'. Let us suppose for example that the following sentences are generated by a grammar of English (and are therefore grammatical):

(a) *John drinks milk* (*beer, wine, water*, etc.)

(b) *John eats cheese* (*fish, meat, bread*, etc.)

(c) *John drinks cheese* (*fish, meat, bread*, etc.)

(d) *John eats milk* (*beer, wine, water*, etc.)

Let us further assume that all these sentences are generated with the same structural description: that the verbs *drink* and *eat*, and the nouns *milk, beer, wine, water, cheese, fish, meat, bread*, etc., are not distinguished in the lexicon by means of any relevant syntactic feature. It seems clear that, in some sense of the terms 'acceptable' and 'unacceptable', utterances derivable from the sentences grouped under (a) and (b) are acceptable, whereas utterances derivable from the sentences grouped under (c) and (d) are unacceptable (in 'normal' circumstances). Whether this kind of acceptability and unacceptability is to be described by reference to criteria of 'meaningfulness' (in the sense of this term which we propose to distinguish as 'significance') is a question to which we shall return presently. The point being made here is that the sets of elements which can occur and have meaning as the verb and the object of these sentences are far smaller subsets of the elements whose occurrence is permitted by the rules of the grammar. Once again the limiting case is that of an element whose occurrence is wholly determined by the context of the other elements in the sentence. An example of complete determination at this level might be the occurrence of *teeth* in *I bit him with my false teeth*. As we shall see later (cf. 9.5.3), this sentence manifests a semantically interesting type of syntagmatic 'presupposition' which is normally latent, but which is made overt when 'syntactic support' is required for a 'modifier' (in this instance, *false*). If the word *teeth* never occurred in sentences other than those in which it is completely determined by its context, it would not have meaning in English; and the semanticist would have nothing to say about it.

The purpose of this argument has been to demonstrate the way in which the notion of having meaning both can, and must, be transferred from the more 'concrete' instances in which it applies to grammatically-unstructured whole *utterances*, on the one hand, and to *utterances* which differ minimally in respect of their phonological structure, on the other, to the more 'abstract' plane on which it applies to the more important far more numerous class of *sentences* generated by the rules of grammar. The notion of having meaning is validated by its reflection of the intuitively-satisfying principle that 'meaningfulness implies choice' in particular contexts. Its transference to the more 'abstract' plane rests upon a methodological decision, the motivation for which is twofold: first, it recognizes the fact that the particular contextual features which influence the production and interpretation of utterances can only be handled in an *ad hoc* manner; and second, it satisfactorily relates the semantic interpretation of sentences to their syntactic description. Given that a particular element has meaning over a certain range of sentences, we can then ask what meaning it has; and this question can be answered in various ways, as we shall see in the next section.

9.3.11 'Significance'

We must now look briefly at the notion of 'significance' (cf. 9.3.1). At first sight, one might be tempted to identify significance with total acceptability, relative to particular contexts for utterances and relative to the more generalized restricted contexts for sentences. But we have already seen that there are many 'layers' of acceptability ('above' the grammatical) which, although they are often described loosely as 'semantic', can be distinguished from what is traditionally described as 'meaningfulness' or 'significance' (cf. 4.2.3). Certain utterances might be condemned as 'blasphemous' or 'obscene'; some might be acceptable in certain uses of language (prayers, myths, fairy-stories, science-fiction, etc.), but unacceptable in everyday conversation. Little purpose would be served by attempting to define 'significance' in such a way that it covered all these various 'dimensions' of acceptability. For example, suppose it were the case that, although the verb *die* was freely used in combination with animate nouns, including the names of persons, in English, there was a generally-respected taboo prohibiting its use in combination with *my father*, *my mother*, *my brother* and *my sister* (i.e. with reference to members of one's own immediate family): so that *My father died last night*, but not *His father died last night*, would be considered unacceptable. It seems quite evident that the correct explanation of the unacceptability of *My father died last night* is one which allows us to say, first of all, that it is 'meaningful', since, if it occurred despite the taboo, it would be understood (indeed it could be argued that the taboo depends upon the possibility of understanding it) and, secondly, that the semantic relationship between *My father died last night* and *His father died last night* is identical with that between *My father came last night* and *His father came last night*, etc. Traditionally, the significance of grammatically well-formed sentences is accounted for in terms of certain general principles of compatibility between the 'meanings' of their constituent elements. One might say, for instance, that *John eats milk* and *John drinks bread* are not significant, because the verb *eat* is compatible only with nouns (as its object) which denote consumable solids and the verb *drink* with nouns which denote consumable liquids. (Notice that in terms of this statement *John eats soup* might be regarded as semantically anomalous, being rendered 'socially acceptable' by a particular convention external to the generalizable rules for the interpretation of English sentences.) There are great difficulties attaching to the notion of significance (one might wish to argue, for instance, that *John eats milk* is 'meaningful', though the circumstances in which it might be employed are somewhat unusual). Nevertheless, the traditional explication of this notion in terms of 'compatibility' seems to be basically sound. We shall discuss some more recent formulations of this notion in a later section (cf. 10.5.4).

9.4   Reference and sense

9.4.1   *Reference*

The term 'reference' was introduced earlier for the relationship which holds between words and the things, events, actions and qualities they 'stand for' (cf. 9.2.2). It was pointed out that, under certain circumstances, the question 'What is the meaning of the word *x*?' can be answered by means of 'ostensive' definition—by pointing to, or otherwise indicating, the *referent* (or referents) of the word (cf. 9.2.7). There are certain philosophical difficulties attaching to the precise definition of the notion of 'reference' which we need not be concerned with here. We shall assume that the relationship of reference (sometimes described as 'denotation') is essential to the construction of any satisfactory theory of semantics: in other words, that there is a sense in which at least certain items in the vocabularies of all languages can be put into correspondence with 'features' of the physical world.

Acceptance of this assumption does not imply acceptance of the view that reference is the semantic relationship to which all others can be reduced; nor does it imply that all the items in the vocabulary of a language have reference. As it will be understood here, 'reference' necessarily carries with it presuppositions of 'existence' (or 'reality') which derive from our direct experience of objects in the physical world. To say that a particular word (or other item which has meaning) 'refers to an object' implies that its referent is an object which 'exists' (is 'real') in the same sense in which we say that particular persons, animals and things 'exist'; and also, that it would be possible, in principle, to give a description of the physical properties of the object in question. This notion of 'physical existence' may be taken as fundamental for the definition of the semantic relationship of reference. The application of the terms 'existence' and 'reference' may then be extended in various ways. For instance, although there are no such objects (we will assume) as goblins, unicorns or centaurs, we can quite reasonably ascribe to them a fictional or mythical 'existence' in a certain kind of discourse; and we can therefore say that the words *goblin, unicorn* or *centaur* have reference in English when the language is used in discourse of this kind. Similarly, we can extend the application of the terms 'existence' and 'reference' to such theoretical constructs of science as atoms, genes, etc.; and even to quite abstract objects. It is important to notice, however, that the source of these 'analogical' extensions of the notions of 'existence' and 'reference' is to be found in their fundamental, or primary, application to physical objects in the 'everyday' use of language.

It follows from this interpretation of the notion of reference that there may be many items in the vocabulary of a language which do not stand in a relationship of reference to anything outside the language. It may be, for example, that there is no such thing as intelligence or goodness to which the words *intelligent* and *good* refer, although it would always be possible for a psychologist or a philosopher to postulate the existence of such entities within the framework of a particular theory of psychology or ethics, and even to claim that their 'reality' is demonstrable by means of some kind of 'ostensive' definition. The fact that there may be disagreement, at various levels of sophistication, about the 'reality' of certain alleged 'objects' does not affect the general principle that reference presupposes existence. To insist that all lexical items must refer to *something* would be futile if it meant that, in certain instances, no evidence could be brought forward for the existence of that 'something' other than the fact that there was a lexical item 'referring' to it.

Two further points may be mentioned in connexion with the notion of reference. By accepting the view that certain lexical items refer to objects and properties of objects outside language we are not logically committed to the assumption that all the objects denoted by a particular term form a 'natural class', in the sense that they 'belong together' independently of the 'convention' tacitly accepted by the speech-community in question to group them together 'under' a common term: in other words, the position maintained here is compatible with either 'nominalism' or 'realism' in philosophical semantics. Second, the reference of a lexical item need not be precise and fully-determined, in the sense that it is always clear whether a particular object or property falls within the scope of a given lexical item: we have already seen that no such assumption is required in order to account for the 'understanding' of utterances in the normal process of communication (cf. 9.2.9). It is frequently the case that the 'referential boundaries' of lexical items are indeterminate. For example, the precise point at which one draws the line between the reference of *hill* and *mountain*, of *chicken* and *hen*, of *green* and *blue*, and so on, cannot be specified. But this does not mean that the notion of reference does not apply to such words. It is a characteristic of languages that they impose a particular lexical 'categorization' upon the world and draw the boundaries 'arbitrarily', as it were, at different places. As we shall see, this is one of the reasons why it is often impossible to establish lexical equivalences between different languages. The fact that the 'referential boundaries' are 'arbitrary' and indeterminate does not normally lead to misunderstanding, since the 'precise' classification of an object 'under' one lexical item or another is very rarely relevant; and when it is, we have resort to other systems of identification or specification. For example, if we wish to refer to one of two persons each of whom might be appropriately denoted by either *girl* or *woman*, we can distinguish them by name, by relative age, by the colour of their hair, by what they are wearing, and so on. Although the reference of *girl* 'overlaps' that of *woman*, the two words are not synonymous; their relative position along the dimension of age is fixed, and there will be many cases in which only one of the two words is appropriate. Far from being a defect, as some philosophers have suggested, referential 'impreciseness' of the kind illustrated makes language a more efficient means of communication. Absolute 'preciseness' is unattainable, since there is no limit to the number and nature of the distinctions one might draw between different objects; and there is no virtue in being obliged to draw a greater number of distinctions than is necessary for the purpose in hand.

9.4.2 Sense

We must now introduce the notion of 'sense'. By the *sense* of a word we mean its place in a system of relationships which it contracts with other words in the vocabulary. It will be observed that, since sense is to be defined in terms of relationships which hold between vocabulary-items, it carries with it no presuppositions about the existence of objects and properties outside the vocabulary of the language in question.

If two elements can occur in the same context, they *have meaning* in that context; and we may go on to ask *what meaning* they have. As we have seen, one part, or component, of the meaning of certain elements may be described in terms of their reference. Whether the two elements have reference or not, we can ask whether they have the same meaning or not in the context, or contexts, in which they both occur. Since sameness of meaning, *synonymy*, is a relation which holds between two (or more) vocabulary-items, it is a matter of sense, not reference. For reasons which we need not go into here, we may wish to say that two items have the same reference, but differ in sense; and we certainly wish to say that items may be synonymous, even if they have no reference. It may be assumed that, for items which have reference, identical reference is a necessary, but not sufficient, condition of synonymy.

Theoretical discussions of synonymy are often vitiated by two unjustified assumptions. The first is that two elements cannot be 'absolutely synonymous' in one context unless they are synonymous in all contexts. This assumption is sometimes supported with an appeal to the distinction between 'cognitive' and 'emotive' meaning. But this distinction is itself far from clear. It is undeniable that the choice of one item rather than another by a particular speaker may be influenced by the difference in their 'emotive associations'. However, this does not mean that these 'emotive associations' are always relevant (even if they are shared by other members of the speech-community). And it cannot simply be made a matter of assumption that words always carry with them the 'associations' which derive from their use in other contexts. We will therefore reject the assumption that words cannot be synonymous in any context unless they are synonymous in all contexts.

The second assumption commonly made by semanticists is that synonymy is a relation of identity holding between two (or more) independently-defined senses. In other words, the question whether two words, *a* and *b*, are synonymous is reduced to the question whether *a* and *b* denote the same entity, their sense. In the approach to semantics being outlined here, there will be no need to postulate the existence of independently-defined senses. Synonymy will be defined as follows: two (or more) items are synonymous if the sentences which result from the substitution of one for the other have the same meaning. This definition clearly rests upon a prior notion of 'sameness of meaning' for sentences (and utterances). We shall return to this question presently. The point being made here is that the relation of synonymy is stated as holding between lexical items and not between their senses. The synonymy of lexical items is part of their sense. To put the same point in a more general form: what we refer to as the sense of a lexical item is the whole set of *sense-relations* (including synonymy) which it contracts with other items in the vocabulary.

9.4.3 *Paradigmatic and syntagmatic relations of sense*

There are many other sense-relations besides synonymy. For instance, *husband* and *wife* are not synonymous, but they are semantically-related in a way that *husband* and *cheese*, or *hydrogen*, are not; *good* and *bad* are different in sense, but more similar than *good* and *red*, or *round*; *knock*, *bang*, *tap* and *rap* are related in a way that *knock* and *eat*, or *admire*, are not. The relationships illustrated here are *paradigmatic* (all the members of the sets of semantically-related terms can occur in the same context). Terms may also be related to one another *syntagmatically*: cf. *blond* and *hair*, *bark* and *dog*, *kick* and *foot*, etc. (For the general distinction of paradigmatic and syntagmatic relations, see 2.3.3.) Whether these syntagmatic and paradigmatic sense-relations can be defined in terms of their 'distance' from synonymy along a scale of sameness and difference of sense (as some semanticists have suggested) is a question we will not go into here: an alternative treatment will be presented in the following chapter. For the present, we will simply assume that at least some vocabulary-items fall into *lexical systems*, and that the *semantic structure* of these systems is to be described in terms of the sense-relations holding between the lexical items. This statement is intended as a more precise formulation of the principle that 'the meaning of each term is a function of the place it occupies in its own system' (cf. 2.2.1, with reference to Russian and English kinship terms).

9.4.4 *Semantic fields*

In recent years, there has been a good deal of work devoted to the investigation of lexical systems in the vocabularies of different languages, with particular reference to such *fields* (or *domains*) as kinship, colour, flora and fauna, weights and measures, military ranks, moral and aesthetic evaluation, and various kinds of knowledge, skill and understanding. The results obtained have conclusively demonstrated the value of the structural approach to semantics, and have confirmed the pronouncements of such earlier scholars as von Humboldt, de Saussure and Sapir to the effect that the vocabularies of different languages (in certain fields at least) are *non-isomorphic*: that there are semantic distinctions made in one language which are not made in another; moreover, that particular fields may be categorized in a totally different way by different languages. This fact is expressed in Saussurean terms by saying that each language imposes a specific *form* on the *a priori* undifferentiated *substance* of the content-plane (cf. 2.2.2, 2.2.3). As an illustration of this notion we may take (as substance) the field of colour and see how it is determined, or 'informed', in English.

9.4.5 *Colour-terms*

For simplicity, we will first of all consider only that part of the field which is covered by the words *red, orange, yellow, green* and *blue*. Each of these terms is referentially imprecise, but their relative position in this lexical system is fixed (and as a set they cover the greater part of the visible spectrum): *orange* lies between *red* and *yellow, yellow* between *orange* and *green,* and so on. It is part of the sense of each of these terms that they belong to this particular lexical system in English and that they contract relationships of contiguity (or, more precisely perhaps, 'betweenness') relative to one another in the system. It might appear that the notion of sense is unnecessary here, and that an account of the reference of each of the colour-terms would be sufficient as a description of their meaning. Consider, however, the conditions under which one might come to learn, or be said to know, the reference of these words. The child learning English cannot first of all learn the reference of *green*, and then subsequently the reference of *blue* or *yellow*, so that at a particular time he could be said to know the reference of one, but not the other. (It is true that he might learn, ostensively, that *green* referred to the colour of grass, or the leaves of a particular tree, or one of his mother's dresses: but the reference of *green* is wider than any particular instance of its application, and a knowledge of its reference involves knowledge also of the boundaries of its reference.) It must be supposed that over a certain period the child gradually learns the position of *green* with respect to *blue* and *yellow*, of *yellow* with respect to *green* and *orange*, and so on until he has learnt the position of each of the colour-terms with respect to its neighbour in the lexical system and the approximate location of the boundaries of the area in the continuum of the field covered by each term. His knowledge of the meaning of the colour-terms necessarily involves therefore a knowledge of both their sense and their reference.

The field covered by the five colour-terms considered so far can be regarded as an undifferentiated (perceptual or physical) substance upon which English imposes a particular form by drawing boundaries in it at particular places and giving to the five areas thus recognized a particular lexical classification (as *red*, *orange*, *yellow*, *green* and *blue*). It has often been shown that other languages impose a different form upon this substance by recognizing a different number of areas within it and drawing the boundaries at different places. To refer to an example used above: the Russian words *sinij* and *goluboj* together cover roughly the same area as the English word *blue*; they refer to distinct, but contiguous, colours and are co-ordinate in the system with the words *zelënyj* and *žëltyj* ('green' and 'yellow')—they are not to be regarded as terms which refer to different shades of one colour, in the way that *crimson* and *scarlet*, with other terms, sub-divide the area covered by *red* in English (cf. 2.2.3).

The relationship between colour-terms and their meaning is not quite as straightforward as we have so far represented it. The difference in the reference of *red*, *orange*, *yellow*, *green* and *blue* can be described in terms of their variation in *hue* (the reflection of light at different wavelengths). Physicists recognize two other variables in the analysis of colour: *luminosity*, or brightness (the reflection of more or less light), and *saturation* (the degree of freedom from dilution with white). The ranges of colour denoted by *black*, *grey* and *white* in English differ mainly in respect of luminosity; and there are other common colour-terms whose reference must be specified according to all three dimensions of variation; e.g. *brown* refers to a range of colour that is between *red* and *yellow* in hue, of relatively low luminosity and saturation; *pink* to a colour that is reddish in hue, of fairly high luminosity and fairly low saturation. Consideration of these facts might lead us to say that the substance of the field of colour is a three-dimensional (physical or perceptual) continuum.

Even this statement is an over-simplification. Not only do languages differ in the relative weight they give to the three dimensions of hue, luminosity and saturation in the organization of their systems of colour-terms (e.g. both Latin and Greek seem to have given greater weight to luminosity than to hue); there are languages in which distinctions of colour are made according to quite different principles. In a classic paper on this subject, Conklin has shown that the four main 'colour-terms' of Hanunóo (a language of the Philippines) are associated with lightness (generally covering white and the light tints of other English colours), darkness (including English black, violet, blue, dark green and the dark shades of other colours), 'wetness' (usually correlating with light green, yellow and light brown, etc.) and 'dryness' (usually correlating with maroon, red, orange, etc.). That the distinction between 'wetness' and 'dryness' is not simply a matter of hue ('green' *v.* 'red': this might appear to be the distinction on the basis of the most frequent English translations of the two terms in question) is clear from the fact that 'a shiny, wet, *brown* section of newly cut bamboo' is described by the term which is generally used for light green, etc. Conklin concludes that 'colour, in a western technical sense, is not a universal concept'; that the oppositions in terms of which the substance of colour is determined in different languages may depend primarily upon the association of the lexical items with culturally-important features of objects in the natural environment. In the case of the Hanunóo words one of the dimensions of the system would seem to derive from the typical appearance of fresh, young ('wet', 'succulent') plants. It is worth noting in this connexion that dictionaries of English frequently define the main colour-terms with respect to typical features of the environment (e.g. *blue* might be said to refer to the colour of the clear sky, *red* to the colour of blood, and so on).

9.4.6 *Semantic 'relativity'*

The field of colour has been discussed at some length, because it is so often used as an example to demonstrate the way in which the *same* substance may have a different form imposed upon it by different languages. We have now seen that even in the case of colour there is good reason to doubt whether one can reasonably postulate an *a priori* identity of 'content-substance'. Conklin's account of the categories of 'colour' in Hanunóo should certainly warn us against assuming that the linguistically-relevant dimensions of the substance of colour are necessarily those selected as criterial by the physical sciences. The general conclusion to be drawn is that the language of a particular society is an integral part of its culture, and that the lexical distinctions drawn by each language will tend to reflect the culturally-important features of objects, institutions and activities in the society in which the language operates. This conclusion is supported by a number of recent studies of various fields in the vocabularies of different languages. Since the natural environments in which different societies live, not to mention their institutions and patterns of behaviour, are so diverse, it is extremely doubtful whether one can talk profitably about semantic structure as the imposition of form upon an underlying (perceptual, physical or conceptual) substance common to all languages. As Sapir has said: 'The worlds in which different societies live are distinct worlds, not the same world with different labels attached.'

Even if it is admitted that different societies live in 'distinct worlds' (and we shall return to this point presently), it might still be maintained that each language imposes a particular form upon the substance of the 'world' in which it operates. Within certain limits this is true (as we have seen, for example, in the case of colour-terms). It is important to realize, however, that lexical systems do not necessarily presuppose an 'underlying' substance. Let us assume for the sake of the argument that the words *honesty, sincerity, chastity, fidelity,* etc., fall into a lexical system with *virtue*. The structure of this system can be described in terms of the sense-relations that hold between its members. From this point of view, the question whether there are any 'substantial' correlations between the lexical items and identifiable traits of character or patterns of behaviour is irrelevant. If there are any such correlations they will be described in terms of reference, not sense. In short, the applicability of the notion of substance in semantics is determined by the same postulate of 'existence' as the notion of reference (cf. 9.4.1).

The assertion that 'the worlds in which different societies live are distinct worlds' is frequently interpreted as a proclamation of linguistic 'determinism'. Whether Sapir (or von Humboldt before him and Whorf after him) believed that our categorization of the world is totally determined by the structure of our native language is a question we need not go into here. It is generally agreed that linguistic determinism, interpreted in this strong sense, is an untenable hypothesis. However, our earlier acceptance of the view that particular languages reflect in their vocabulary the culturally-important distinctions of the societies in which they operate commits us to a certain degree of linguistic and cultural 'relativity'. We must therefore account for the undeniable fact that it is possible to achieve a knowledge of the structure of the lexical systems in languages other than our own, whether in learning them for practical purposes or for the investigation of their vocabularies. Translation from one language to another clearly depends upon this possibility.

9.4.7   Cultural overlap

Cultures (in the sense in which this term is used by anthropologists and sociologists) are not coterminous with languages. For example, many of the institutions, customs, articles of dress, furniture and food, etc., to be found in France and Germany are found also in England: others are peculiar to each country, or to a particular region or social class in each country. (The relationship between language and culture is of course far more complex than this simplified statement would suggest: political boundaries do not coincide with linguistic boundaries, even if we grant that there is some validity in the notion of a unified speech-community; cultural identities may be found between different social classes in different countries; and so on.) In general, it may be assumed that there will be a greater or less degree of *cultural overlap* between any two societies; and it may be the case that certain features will be present in the culture of all societies. Practical experience of learning foreign languages (in the normal conditions in which these languages are used) suggests that we quickly identify certain objects, situations and other features in the area of cultural overlap and learn the words and expressions that apply to them without difficulty. The meaning of other words and expressions are learned less readily and their correct use comes, if ever, only with long practice in speaking the language. We may give theoretical recognition to these facts of experience by saying that entry is made into the semantic structure of another language in the area of cultural overlap; and that, once we have broken into the circle by means of the identification of items in this area (cf. 9.4.7, on the inevitable 'circularity' of semantics), we can gradually develop and modify our knowledge of the rest of the vocabulary from within, by learning the reference of the lexical items and the sense-relations that hold between them in the contexts in which they are used. True bilingualism implies the assimilation of two cultures.

9.4.8 *'Application'*

When items of different languages can be put into correspondence with one another on the basis of the identification of common features and situations in the cultures in which they operate, we may say that the items have the same *application*. The reasons for using this term rather than 'reference' are twofold. First of all, it has been used of the relationship which holds between situations and expressions which occur in them (e.g. of the relationship between *Excuse me*, *Thank you*, etc., and the various identifiable situations in which these utterances occur); this is clearly not a relationship of reference. Secondly, we wish to allow for the semantic identification of lexical items which have no reference: one might wish to say, for example, that the English word *sin* and the French word *péché* have the same application, although it might be difficult, or impossible, to establish this fact in referential terms. It may well be that the second of these reasons for the introduction of the notion of application will disappear with the construction of a comprehensive and satisfactory theory of culture. At the present time, the notion of application, like the process of translation, rests rather heavily upon the intuitions of bilingual speakers. This does not mean that the notion is without any objective foundation, since bilingual speakers tend to be in agreement about the application of most words and expressions in the languages they speak.

Nothing has been said in this section about the way in which paradigmatic and syntagmatic sense-relations are established. Before we discuss the question we must consider the possibility of extending the notions of reference and sense to grammatical, as well as lexical, items.

9.5 'Lexical' and 'grammatical' meaning

9.5.1 *'Structural meanings'*

In our discussion of 'grammatical categories', we made reference to the traditional, 'Aristotelian' view that only the major parts of speech (nouns, verbs, 'adjectives', and adverbs) were 'meaningful' in the full sense of this term (they 'signified' the 'concepts' which were held to constitute the 'matter' of discourse) and that the other parts of speech contributed to the total meaning of sentences by imposing upon the 'matter' of discourse a certain grammatical 'form' (cf. 7.1.3). Strikingly similar views have been maintained by many opponents of traditional grammar.

For example, Fries draws a distinction between 'lexical' and 'structural' meanings which almost exactly reflects the 'Aristotelian' distinction of 'material' and 'formal' meaning. The major parts of speech have 'lexical' meaning; and this is given in the dictionary associated with the grammar. By contrast, the distinction between the subject and the object of a sentence, oppositions of definiteness, tense and number, and the difference between statements, questions and requests—all these distinctions are described as 'structural meanings'. ('The total linguistic meaning of any utterance consists of the lexical meanings of the separate words plus such structural meanings...It is the devices that signal structural meanings which constitute the grammar of a language.')

At least three different kinds of semantic function are subsumed by Fries under the term 'structural meaning': and other linguists have employed the term 'grammatical meaning' (in contrast with 'lexical meaning') in the same sense. The three different kinds of 'meaning' are: (1) the 'meaning' of grammatical items (typically the minor parts of speech and the secondary grammatical categories); (2) the 'meaning' of such grammatical 'functions' as 'subject-of', 'object-of' or 'modifier-of'; (3) the 'meaning' associated with such notions as 'declarative', 'interrogative' or 'imperative' in the classification of different sentence-types. It is important to distinguish these various kinds of 'grammatical meaning'; and we will discuss each briefly in turn.

9.5.2 *Lexical and grammatical items*

Various criteria have been proposed for the distinction of grammatical and lexical items. The most satisfactory (and the only one we will mention here) has been formulated by Martinet, Halliday and others in terms of paradigmatic opposition within either *closed* or *open* sets of alternatives. A closed set of items is one of fixed, and usually small, membership: e.g. the set of personal pronouns, tenses, genders, etc. An open set is one of unrestricted, indeterminately large, membership; e.g. the class of nouns or verbs in a language. In terms of this distinction we can say that grammatical items belong to closed sets, and lexical items to open sets. This definition corresponds quite well with the traditional distinction between the major parts of speech, on the one hand, and the minor parts of speech and secondary grammatical categories, on the other. Unlike a number of other definitions that have been suggested, it is not restricted to languages of one morphological 'type' (e.g. 'inflecting' languages: cf. 5.3.6). For the moment, we will assume that it is correct, and that on the basis of the distinction between closed and open sets all the elements introduced into the deep structure of sentences can be classified as either 'grammatical' or 'lexical'. The question that now arises is whether there is any difference, in principle, between the meaning of grammatical and lexical items.

The first point to notice is that lexical items are traditionally said to have both 'lexical' and 'grammatical meaning' (both 'material' and 'formal meaning': cf. 9.5.1). To employ the terminology of scholastic, 'speculative' grammar: a particular lexical item, e.g. *cow*, not only 'signifies' a particular 'concept' (the 'material', or 'lexical', meaning of the item in question), but it does so according to a particular 'mode of signifying', e.g. as a 'substance', a 'quality', an 'action', etc. (cf. 1.2.7, 7.1.1). Although linguists rarely express themselves in these terms nowadays, this general conception of the difference between the 'lexical' and 'grammatical' meaning of lexical items is still current. Moreover, it would seem to have a certain validity.

For example, there is a well-known poem by Lermontov, which begins: *Beleet parus odinokij*... This is difficult, if not impossible, to translate into English, because it depends for its effect upon the fact that in Russian 'being white' can be 'expressed' by means of a 'verb' (as in *belyj* = 'white', which in temporally, aspectually and modally unmarked sentences would be employed, normally, without 'the verb *to be*', cf. 7.6.3). *Parus odinokij* is translatable as 'a lonely sail' (*parus* being the noun, and *odinokij* an 'adjective'). In traditional terms, the 'verb' represents 'being white' as a 'process' or 'activity', the 'adjective' as a 'quality' or 'state'. The difference between the choice of the 'verb' rather than the 'adjective' in the present instance can be brought out in English only by means of a rather inadequate circumlocution, such as 'There is a lonely sail which stands out (or even, 'shines forth') white (against the background of the sea or sky)...'. Problems of this nature are familiar enough in translating from one language to another. We are here concerned with the theoretical question: can one say that there is a particular 'grammatical meaning' associated with each of the major parts of speech?

We have already seen that the difference between the 'verb' and the 'adjective' in general syntactic theory is a complex matter: in some languages, no such distinction can be drawn at all; in others, there are many syntactic features associated with the distinction, and they may be in conflict in particular instances (cf. 7.6.4). But the principal criterion, and the one which reflects the traditional distinction between 'activity' and 'quality', is the aspectual distinction between 'dynamic' and 'static' (cf. 8.4.7). In Russian this difference of 'grammatical meaning' is 'superimposed' upon the 'lexical meaning' which is common to both the 'verb' *beletj* and the 'adjective' *belyj*. To this extent, the traditional theory of the 'modes of signifying' is correct: it must be reformulated, of course, within a more satisfactory theory of syntactic structure.

At the same time, one must not lose sight of the general principle that 'having meaning implies choice'. If the language that is being described allows the option of either a 'verbal' or an 'adjectival' expression (to restrict ourselves to the distinction illustrated), then the employment of either the one or the other comes within the scope of the semantic analysis of the language. One may then ask whether the two 'modes' of expression have the same meaning or not; and, if they differ in meaning, one may go on to ask how they differ semantically. If this difference can be referred to some deep-structure grammatical distinction (e.g. 'dynamic' *v.* 'static'), it is appropriately called 'grammatical meaning'. But this does not imply that the selection of a 'verb' rather than an 'adjective' is always associated with a difference of 'grammatical meaning'. In many instances, a particular 'lexical meaning' is necessarily associated with one, rather than another, part of speech. In short, on this question, as on many others, linguistic theory should strike a balance between 'notional' and 'formal' grammar (cf. 7.6.1). It should not be maintained that 'denoting an activity' is part of the 'meaning' of every 'verb' or 'denoting a quality' part of the 'meaning' of every 'adjective'.

Lexical items are traditionally said to have both 'lexical' ('material') and 'grammatical' ('formal') meaning. Grammatical items are generally described as having only 'grammatical' meaning. In the previous chapter, we saw that a certain number of items that occur in the surface structure of sentences as 'verbs' can be interpreted as the 'lexical realizations' of aspectual, causative and other 'grammatical' distinctions. Whether these suggestions were correct or not is a question that we may leave on one side. In the present state of syntactic theory, the distinction between grammatical and lexical items is somewhat indeterminate. The reason is that the distinction between open and closed sets of alternatives can only be applied with respect to the positions of 'choice' in the deep structure of sentences; and, as we have seen, there is considerable room for disagreement as to where these positions of 'choice' are.

The main point that must be made here is that there seems to be no essential difference between the 'kind of meaning' associated with lexical items and the 'kind of meaning' associated with grammatical items in those cases where the distinction between these two classes of deep-structure elements can be drawn. The notions of 'sense' and 'reference' are applicable to both. If there is any generalization that can be made about the meaning of grammatical elements (and it will be recalled that certain 'purely grammatical' elements have no meaning: cf. 8.4.1), it would seem to be that grammatical 'choices' have to do with the general notions of spatial and temporal reference, causation, process, individuation, etc.—notions of the kind that were discussed in chapters 7 and 8. However, we cannot assume in advance that such notions, even if they are clearly identifiable, will necessarily be 'grammaticalized', rather than 'lexicalized', in the structure of any particular language.

9.5.3 The 'meaning' of grammatical 'functions'

The second class of phenomena in the structure of English to which Fries (and others) have applied the term 'structural meaning' (or 'grammatical meaning') is exemplified by such notions as 'subject', 'object' and 'modifier'. Fries's book was written before the development of modern transformational syntax, and he was concerned solely with surface structure (from a rather restricted point of view). Consequently, much of what he has to say about these 'functional' notions, though correct, is hardly relevant to semantic analysis. This is also true of most modern linguistic theory.

It is quite clear that certain deep-structure grammatical relationships between lexical items and combinations of lexical items are relevant to the semantic analysis of sentences. Chomsky has suggested that it is the 'functional' notions 'subject-of', 'direct-object-of', 'predicate-of' and 'main-verb-of' which constitute the principal deep-structure relations between lexical items; and Katz, Fodor and Postal have recently tried to formalize the theory of semantics by means of a set of 'projection rules' operating upon lexical items that stand in such relationships within sentences (cf. 10.5.4). Such notions as 'subject', 'predicate' and 'object' were discussed in the previous chapter; and we saw that their formalization in general syntactic theory is not quite so clear as Chomsky has assumed. It follows that the status of the 'projection-rules' which interpret sentences on the basis of these notions is also somewhat dubious.

In our discussion of 'transitivity' and 'ergativity', we pointed out that many of the 'direct objects' of English sentences could be generated by embedding one-place constructions as the 'predicates' of two-place constructions, and introducing a new 'agentive' subject. But we also saw that there were other two-place, transitive constructions which could not be satisfactorily generated in this way. This fact alone would suggest that the relation 'direct-object-of' cannot be given a single interpretation in the semantic analysis of sentences. In traditional grammar, many different kinds of 'direct object' were distinguished. Of these, one may be mentioned here, since (whatever its status in the theory of syntax) it is undoubtedly of considerable importance in semantics. It is the 'object of result' (or 'effect').

The 'object of result' may be illustrated with reference to the following two sentences:

(1) *He is reading a book*

(2) *He is writing a book*

In (1) the book that is referred to exists prior to, and independently of, its being read; but the book referred to in (2) is not yet in existence—it is brought into existence by the completion of the activity described by the sentence. By virtue of this difference, *the book* in (1) is traditionally regarded as an 'ordinary' object of the verb *is reading*, whereas *the book* in (2) is described as an 'object of result'. From the semantic point of view, any verb that has as its object an 'object of result' might be appropriately described as an 'existential causative'. The most common 'verb' in English that falls into this class is *make*; and we have already pointed out that this is also a 'causative auxiliary' (cf. 8.3.6, 8.4.7). This same 'verb' serves, like *do*, as a 'pro-verb' in interrogative sentences. A question like *What are you doing?* carries fewer presuppositions about the 'predicate' in the sentence which answers it (the verb can be transitive or intransitive, but it must be an 'action' verb: cf. 7.6.4). By contrast, *What are you making?* presupposes that the 'activity' in question is 'resultative' and has, as its aim or term, the 'existence' of some 'object'. This difference, it should be noticed, is not so striking in a number of European languages as it is in English. (For example, *Qu'est-ce que tu fais?*, in French, might be translated as either 'What are you doing?' or 'What are you making?'.) But this does not mean that the difference between 'ordinary' objects and 'objects of result' is irrelevant in these languages.

The importance of this notion of 'existential causative' lies in the fact that there is frequently a high degree of interdependence between a particular verb, or class of verbs, and a particular noun, or class of nouns, in sentences that manifest the 'object of result' construction. For example, no satisfactory semantic analysis of the noun *picture* could be given which did not state its syntagmatic relationship with such verbs as *paint* and *draw*; conversely, the fact that these verbs may take the noun *picture* as an 'object of result' is to be stated as part of their meaning.

This notion of syntagmatic interdependence, or presupposition, is of considerable importance in the analysis of the vocabulary of any language (cf. 9.4.3). It is of far wider applicability than can be illustrated here. There are presuppositions holding between particular classes of nouns and verbs, where the noun is the subject of the verb (e.g. *bird*: *fly*, *fish*: *swim*); between 'adjectives' and nouns (*blond*: *hair*, *addled*: *egg*); between verbs and 'ordinary' objects (*drive*: *car*); between verbs and nouns in an 'instrumental' relationship (*bite*: *teeth*, *kick*: *foot*); and so on. Many of these relationships between particular classes of lexical items cannot be stated, except by means of an *ad hoc* set of 'projection rules', within the framework of transformational syntax outlined by Chomsky.

Since there is as yet no fully satisfactory syntactic framework within which to state the various sense-relations in terms of which the vocabulary of languages are structured, we shall make no attempt to formulate a set of 'projection rules' operating upon deep-structure grammatical relations. In the following chapter, we shall discuss a number of particularly important paradigmatic relations between classes of lexical items; and we shall do so in a fairly informal way.

We assume that these relations could be stated more elegantly on the basis of a more satisfactory account of deep-structure grammatical relations.

9.5.4 The 'meaning' of 'sentence-types'

The third class of 'meanings' which are commonly described as 'grammatical' may be exemplified with reference to the difference between 'declarative', 'interrogative' and 'imperative' sentences. In recent transformational theory, there has been a tendency to introduce into the deep-structure phrase-markers of sentences such grammatical elements as 'question-marker' and 'imperative-marker', and then to formulate the rules of the transformational component in such a way that the presence of one of these 'markers' will 'trigger off' the appropriate transformational rule. We are not concerned here with the syntactic advantages of this formulation of the distinction between various 'sentence-types', but with its semantic implications.

It has been suggested (by Katz and Postal) that these 'markers' are semantically similar to the lexical and grammatical elements which occur as constituents of the nuclei of sentences. For instance, the 'imperative-marker' would be listed in the dictionary with an entry 'that represents it as having roughly the sense of "the speaker requests (asks, demands, insists, etc.) that"'. But this suggestion rests upon a confusion in the term 'meaning'. It is to eliminate such confusions that semanticists have drawn distinctions between 'sense', 'reference' and various other kinds of 'meaning'. If we continue to employ the term 'meaning' for all kinds of distinguishable semantic function, we can say quite reasonably that there is a difference of 'meaning' between corresponding statements, questions and commands (which are not necessarily 'expressed' as declarative, interrogative and imperative sentences, respectively—but for simplicity we may neglect this fact). But the question whether two lexical items have 'the same meaning' or not is normally interpreted with respect to the notion of synonymy: sameness of *sense*. This is a paradigmatic relation: i.e. a relation which either holds or does not hold between items that occur in the same context in the same 'sentence-type'. In the following chapter, we shall see that the notion of 'synonymy' with respect to x and y can be explicated in terms of the set of implications which 'follow' from two sentences which differ only in that where one has x the other has y. But these considerations simply do not apply to corresponding declarative and interrogative or imperative sentences (e.g. *You are writing the letter* v. *Are you writing the letter?* or *Write the letter*). Although corresponding members of different 'sentence-types' can be said to differ in 'meaning', they cannot be said to differ in sense. There is no point in trying to formalize the theory of semantics in such a way that the 'meaning' of a 'question-marker' or 'imperative-marker' can be described in the same terms as the 'meaning' of lexical items.

10

SEMANTIC STRUCTURE

10.1 Introductory

10.1.1 *The priority of sense-relations*

In this chapter we shall be concerned with the notion of *sense* (as distinct from both reference and application: cf. 9.4.1–9.4.8). We have already seen that the vocabulary of a language will contain a number of *lexical systems* the semantic structure of which can be described in terms of paradigmatic and syntagmatic *sense-relations*; and we have stressed that these relations are to be defined as holding between lexical items and not between independently-determined senses (cf. 9.4.2).

This last point is of considerable theoretical and methodological importance. It is one of the cardinal principles of 'structuralism', as developed by de Saussure and his followers, that every linguistic item has its 'place' in a system and its function, or value, derives from the relations which it contracts with other units in the system (cf. 2.2.2–2.2.9). Acceptance of the structural approach in semantics has the advantage that it enables the linguist to avoid commitment on the controversial question of the philosophical and psychological status of 'concepts' or 'ideas' (cf. 9.2.6). As far as the empirical investigation of the structure of language is concerned, the sense of a lexical item may be defined to be, not only dependent upon, but identical with, the set of relations which hold between the item in question and other items in the same lexical system. The nature of these sense-relations will be discussed in this chapter.

The methodological significance of the structural approach to the definition of sense may be illustrated by means of a comparison with the proposal made by Russell and other modern logicians for the definition of such notions as length, weight, shape, etc. In traditional logic the question 'Is x the same length as y?' was generally interpreted as if it were secondary to and dependent upon questions of a quite different logical structure: 'What is the length of x?' and 'What is the length of y?' (length being conceived as a property that objects might have more or less of). In practice, the length of an object is determined by comparing it with some conventional standard.

When we say, for example, that x is exactly one metre long, we are asserting that if it were compared with the platinum–iridium bar kept at the International Bureau of Weights and Measures, x would be found to be equal in length to the distance between the two lines marked on the bar (the fact that since 1960 the metre is internationally defined by means of more complex, but more reliable, physical measurements does not affect the point being made). In other words, the question 'What is the length of x?' is answered by means of a procedure which yields an answer to a question of the form 'Is x the same length as z?' (z being the standard). Given two objects x and y, we can compare them directly with one another or indirectly by reference to some third object z (the platinum–iridium bar in Paris, a ruler that has been calibrated in accordance with some agreed standard of measurement, etc.). In either case, 'What is the length of x?' is dependent upon, and indeed reducible to, a set of questions of the form 'Is x the same length as y?' There is no other way, empirically, of determining the length of x; this being so, Russell proposed that length should in fact be defined in terms of the relation 'having the same length as'. (We need not go into the details of Russell's formulation of the definition here. The general principle is independent of this.)

Just as 'having the same length' is a relation which holds between two objects (and not between the 'lengths' inherent in them), so 'having the same sense'—or synonymy—is a relation which holds between two lexical items (and not between the 'senses' associated with them in the minds of the speakers: cf. 9.2.6). The definition of sense is far more complex than the definition of length (or weight, etc.) since there is more than the relation of sameness and difference involved. But there would seem to be no more reason to postulate a set of 'senses' associated with the lexical items in a system than there is to postulate a set of 'lengths' inherent in physical objects. The question 'What is the sense of x?' (and the answer to this question, it will be recalled, is only one part of the answer to the question 'What is the meaning of x?') is methodologically reducible to a set of questions each of which is relational: 'Does sense-relation R_i hold between x and y?'

10.1.2 'Analytic' and 'synthetic' implication

The notion of sense is frequently discussed by philosophers in connexion with the distinction between *synthetic* and *analytic* statements. This distinction may be put as follows: a synthetic statement is one which is true 'contingently'—as a matter of empirical fact which might have been otherwise; an analytic statement is one that is 'necessarily' true, and its truth is guaranteed by (i) the sense of its constituent elements and (ii) the syntactical rules of the language. To take a standard example: the sentence *All bachelors are unmarried* might be regarded as analytic on the grounds that *bachelor* and *unmarried* are semantically-related in such a way that the truth of the sentence is guaranteed.

The validity of the notion of analyticity is open to dispute; and it is possible that it is philosophically indefensible in the form in which it is generally discussed. Fortunately, the semantic analysis of language as it is used in everyday discourse need not wait upon the solution of the philosophical problems attaching to the distinction between contingent and necessary truth. What the linguist requires is a *pragmatic* concept of analyticity—one which gives theoretical recognition to the tacit presuppositions and assumptions in the speech-community and takes no account of their validity within some other frame of reference assumed to be absolute or linguistically and culturally neutral. It was for this purpose that we introduced earlier the notion of the *restricted context*. Any statements that are made in this chapter about the semantic relations that hold between sentences by virtue of the sense of the lexical items in them are to be interpreted in the light of this notion.

Sense-relations are stateable within a framework which includes the notion of *implication*. This notion may be introduced here by way of the prior concepts of explicit assertion and denial. We will assume that in all languages it is possible to establish rules of correspondence between affirmative and negative sentences; and that the correspondence between a particular affirmative and a particular negative sentence is accounted for by the grammar of the language. Thus the negative sentence *John is not married* corresponds to the affirmative sentence *John is married*. We will now say that a negative sentence *explicitly denies* whatever is *explicitly asserted* by the corresponding affirmative sentence; and on the basis of this notion of explicit assertion and denial we can construct the semantically more interesting notion of *implicit* assertion and denial, or implication. One sentence, S_1, is said to imply another, S_2—symbolically, $S_1 \supset S_2$—if speakers of the language agree that it is not possible to assert explicitly S_1 and to deny explicitly S_2. And S_1 implicitly denies S_2—S_1 implies *not* S_2: $S_1 \supset \sim S_2$—if it is agreed that the explicit assertion of S_1 makes impossible, without contradiction, the explicit assertion of S_2.

It should be stressed that implication, in the sense in which it has been defined here, is in principle objectively testable. This does not mean of course that all speakers will necessarily agree that one sentence implies another. As we have already seen, what is normally meant by 'understanding' utterances can be quite well accounted for without making the assumption that all speakers of a language will draw from a given utterance exactly the same set of implications (cf. 9.2.9). What may be assumed is that there is a sufficiently large overlap in the implications that hold for different speakers to prevent misunderstanding in the majority of instances in which they communicate with one another. Semantic theory must allow for a certain degree of indeterminacy in the number and nature of the implications that hold between the sentences of a language.

10.2 Synonymy

10.2.1 *A stricter and a looser sense of 'synonymy'*

One may distinguish a stricter and a looser interpretation of the term 'synonymy'. According to the stricter interpretation (which is the one most commonly found in contemporary semantic theory) two items are synonymous if they have the same sense. It is this interpretation of synonymy that we shall be discussing in the present section.

The looser interpretation may be illustrated by means of a quotation from *Roget's Thesaurus:* 'Suppose we take the word "nice"'...
Under it [in the Index] we will see...various synonyms representing different shades of meaning of the word "nice".' The 'synonyms' given for *nice* in the Index are *savoury, discriminative, exact, good, pleasing, fastidious* and *honourable*. Each of these words itself appears in one of the lists of 'synonyms' in the main body of the text. For instance, turning to the section in which *pleasing* occurs we find 'an array of literally dozens of equivalents...expressing every possible shade of meaning'. So too for *good, exact,* etc. The thesaurus therefore provides us with 'an array of hundreds of words and expressions which are at our disposal to use instead of..."nice" with which we started'. All these words and expressions are 'synonymous' with *nice* under the looser interpretation of the notion of synonymy.

10.2.2 *Proposals for the quantification of synonymy*

It is sometimes suggested that synonymy is a matter of degree; that any set of lexical items can be arranged on a scale of similarity and difference of sense, so that, for example, *a* and *b* might be shown to be identical in sense (strictly synonymous), *a* and *c* relatively similar in sense (loosely synonymous), *a* and *d* less similar in sense, and so on. Various proposals have been made in recent years for the quantification of 'synonymy' along these lines. We shall not discuss any of these proposals here. Even if it were shown that one or other measure of similarity of sense were empirically reliable (applicable by different scholars at different times and consistent in its results) and succeeded in bringing together, as more or less 'synonymous', items which the native speaker felt 'belonged together', we should still be left with the problem of accounting for the differences between the 'synonyms'. (It may be worth pointing out that the practical utility of reference works such as *Roget's Thesaurus* depends upon a prior knowledge of the language on the part of the person using them. Unless he can himself distinguish correctly between the hundreds of 'equivalents' that he is given for *nice* he can hardly be said to have them 'at his disposal'.) There is no reason to believe that, if *b* and *c* are shown to be 'equidistant' in sense from *a*, they are themselves synonymous and related semantically to *a* in the same way. Suppose, for example, that both *mother* and *son* were shown to be 'equidistant' from *father* according to one of the proposed measures of similarity of sense. How would we interpret this result? We should clearly not wish to say that *mother* and *son* were even 'loosely' synonymous. The sense-relationship between *father* and *mother* is patently, and describably, different from that which holds between *father* and *son*. In short, there is no obvious way of deriving the various sense-relations which are known to be of importance in the organization of the vocabulary from a measure of relative 'synonymy'.

10.2.3 *'Total synonymy' and 'complete synonymy'*

It is a widely-held view that there are few, if any, 'real' synonyms in natural languages. To quote Ullmann: 'it is almost a truism that total synonymy is an extremely rare occurrence, a luxury that language can ill afford.' As argued by Ullmann this view rests upon two quite distinct criteria: 'Only those words can be described as synonymous which can replace each other in any given context without the slightest change either in cognitive or emotive import.' The two conditions for 'total synonymy' are therefore (i) interchangeability in all contexts, and (ii) identity in both cognitive and emotive import. We will discuss the validity of the distinction between 'cognitive' and 'emotive' sense presently. For the moment we may take it for granted.

The condition of interchangeability in all contexts reflects the common assumption that words are never synonymous in any context unless they can occur (and have the same sense) in all contexts. We have already referred to and rejected this assumption (9.4.2). Like all sense-relations, synonymy is context-dependent: we will return to this point. The main objection to the definition of synonymy proposed by Ullmann (and others) is that it combines two radically different criteria and prejudges the question of their interdependence. It will be helpful to introduce a terminological distinction at this point. Granted the validity of a distinction between 'cognitive' and 'emotive' sense, we may use the term *complete* synonymy for equivalence of both cognitive and emotive sense; and we may restrict the term *total* synonymy to those synonyms (whether complete or not) which are interchangeable in all contexts. This scheme of classification allows for four possible kinds of synonymy (assuming that only two values are attributed to each of the variables): (1) complete and total synonymy; (2) complete, but not total; (3) incomplete, but total; (4) incomplete, and not total. It is complete and total synonymy that most semanticists have in mind when they talk of 'real' (or 'absolute') synonymy. It is undoubtedly true that there are very few such synonyms in language. And little purpose is served by defining a notion of 'absolute' synonymy which is based on the assumption that complete equivalence and total interchangeability are necessarily connected. Once we accept that they are not, and at the same time abandon the traditional view that synonymy is a matter of the identity of two independently-determined 'senses', the whole question becomes much more straightforward.

10.2.4   'Cognitive' and 'emotive' meaning

Many semanticists invoke the distinction between 'cognitive' and 'emotive' (or 'affective') meaning in their discussions of synonymy. The terms themselves clearly reflect the view that the use of language involves two or more distinguishable psychological 'faculties'—the intellect, on the one hand, and the imagination and the emotions, on the other. One of the points that is frequently emphasized, both in technical treatments of semantics and also in the more popular works on the subject, is the importance of 'emotive' factors in linguistic behaviour. It is often said that, by contrast with the vocabulary of scientific and technical discourse, the words of 'everyday language' are charged with emotional 'associations', or 'connotations', over and above their primary, purely 'intellectual' meaning.

There is no need to discuss here the psychological validity of the distinction between the various mental 'faculties' upon which the semantic distinction of 'cognitive' and 'non-cognitive' meaning was originally based. The term 'cognitive' meaning is employed by many scholars who would not necessarily subscribe to the view that the 'intellectual' is sharply distinct from the 'affective'. As far as the actual use of language is concerned, it is undoubtedly true that one word may be preferred to another because of its different emotive or evocative associations. But the extent to which this is of importance varies considerably from one style or situation to another. For instance, Ullmann cites as examples of English words which are cognitively, but not emotively, synonymous *liberty*: *freedom*, *hide*: *conceal*. It is not difficult to think of occasions when a speaker or writer might deliberately use one rather than the other of these synonyms and make his choice on the basis of these 'connotations' which the words are likely to evoke. But there are also many contexts in which either one or the other might be used without any noticeable difference of effect. It would be wrong to assume that the emotive connotations of a word are always relevant to its employment.

A more important point is the following. The distinction between 'cognitive' and 'non-cognitive' synonymy is drawn in various ways by different authors. But in all cases it is 'cognitive' synonymy which is defined first. No one ever talks of words as being 'emotively', but not 'cognitively synonymous'. This fact of itself would be sufficient to suggest that 'emotive', or 'affective', is being used as a catch-all term to refer to a number of quite distinct factors which may influence the selection of synonyms on particular occasions or in particular contexts. What is required is an account of these factors in terms appropriate to them. No useful purpose is served by employing the undoubtedly relevant category of 'emotive' (or 'affective') connotations for anything that does not come within the scope of 'cognitive' meaning.

Some of the factors which influence or determine our choice between 'cognitively' synonymous words and expressions have nothing to do with sense, reference or anything else that might reasonably be called 'meaning'. Many people deliberately refrain from using the same word more than once in the same utterance, if they can avoid it. Others consciously or unconsciously follow the practice of choosing a shorter word in preference to a longer word, a more 'everyday' word rather than a 'learned' word, an 'Anglo-Saxon' word instead of a Latin, Greek or Romance word, and so on. In writing verse, the particular phonological constraints imposed by the metre or rhyme introduce yet other non-semantic factors.

There are also factors which, though they might well be described as 'semantic', have to do with the situational or stylistic acceptability of particular forms rather than with their sense or reference. We have already seen that there are many 'dimensions' of acceptability that would need to be accounted for in a complete description of linguistic behaviour (cf. 4.2.3). We will say no more about these other determinants of full acceptability here, since we are concerned with the more general principles of semantic structure. It seems preferable to restrict the term 'synonymy' to what many semanticists have described as 'cognitive synonymy'. This is the convention that we will adopt for the remainder of this chapter. As a consequence we shall have no further use for the distinction between 'complete' and 'incomplete' synonymy.

10.2.5 Synonymy defined in terms of bilateral implication

Synonymy may be defined in terms of bilateral implication, or *equivalence*. If one sentence, S_1, implies another sentence, S_2, and if the converse also holds, S_1 and S_2 are equivalent: i.e. if $S_1 \supset S_2$ and if $S_2 \supset S_1$, then $S_1 \equiv S_2$ (where ' $\equiv$ ' stands for 'is equivalent to'). If now the two equivalent sentences have the same syntactic structure and differ from one another only in that where one has a lexical item, x, the other has y, then x and y are synonymous. An alternative way of formulating the definition of equivalence would be as follows: if S_1 and S_2 each implies the same set of sentences, then they are equivalent to one another. The difficulty with a definition of this form, however, is that it falls foul of the principle that the set of sentences implied by any given sentence is indeterminate (cf. 9.2.10). If we define equivalence in terms of bilateral implication, we may assume that sentences which imply one another also imply the same set of other sentences, unless and until this assumption is proved false in particular instances.

10.2.6 *Synonymy and 'normal' interchangeability*

In traditional semantics, synonymy has generally been regarded as a relationship holding between lexical items; and the definition that has just been given takes this view. It is of course possible to extend the application of the term 'synonymy' so that it also covers groups of lexical items that are brought together in a particular syntagmatic construction, as well as single lexical items. One might well say, for example, that the phrases *female fox* and *male duck* are synonymous with the lexical items *vixen* and *drake*, respectively. But it is important to notice that, in making this statement, one is assuming that the phrases and the lexical items are indeed interchangeable in the normal use of the language. By contrast, **male cow* and *bull*, and **female bull* and *cow*, are not normally interchangeable (it may be assumed), even though one can easily imagine a situation in which the simplest way of explaining the meaning of *bull* (to someone who knew the meaning of *cow* and *male*) was by means of the normally unacceptable sentence *A bull is a male cow*. The reason why **female bull* and **male cow* are semantically unacceptable is that neither *bull* nor *cow*, unlike *fox* and *duck*, is 'unmarked' for the distinction of sex (cf. 2.3.7, on *dog* and *bitch*). So much would be undisputed by all semanticists. But the condition of 'normal' interchangeability is here intended to exclude many semantically-compatible (significant) groupings of lexical items, as well as such semantically-incompatible phrases as **male cow*. The phrase *mature female bovine animal* (which might be given as a dictionary definition of *cow*) is undoubtedly well-formed, both grammatically and semantically. But it is probably far less 'normal' a phrase than even the semantically ill-formed **male cow*. The native speaker of English would not 'normally' construct such a phrase as *mature female bovine animal* and use it interchangeably with *cow* in his everyday use of the language. The question of synonymy therefore does not arise in the case of the lexical item *cow* and the phrase *mature female bovine animal*. Alternatively, one might say that the most interesting question that arises in instances of this kind is not whether the relationship of synonymy holds, or how to account for it if it does, but why it is that a lexical item like *cow* and a phrase like *mature female bovine animal* are not in fact freely interchangeable. Many semanticists have failed to see the importance of this question. We will return to it later in connexion with 'componential analysis' (cf. 10.5.5).

10.2.7　*Context-dependent synonymy*

One final point may be made about synonymy: more than any other sense-relation, it is *context-dependent*, and in a theoretically interesting way. It is evident that it is not of itself a structural relationship. All instances of synonymy could be eliminated from the vocabulary without affecting the sense of the remainder of the lexical items. The 'impoverished' vocabulary would offer fewer opportunities for stylistic variety, but everything that could be said with the larger vocabulary could also be said with the smaller synonymy-free vocabulary.

Although synonymy is not essential to the semantic structure of language, it arises in particular contexts as a consequence of the more fundamental structural relations, hyponymy and incompatibility (to be discussed in the following section). It frequently happens that the distinction between two lexical items is contextually neutralized. For instance, the difference between the marked term *bitch* and the unmarked term *dog* is neutralized in a context, like *My — has just had pups*, which determines the animal referred to as female. All sense-relations are in principle context-dependent, but contextually-determined synonymy is of particular importance. It is clear that it can be brought within the scope of the general principle that the same information may be conveyed in language either syntagmatically or paradigmatically (cf. 2.3.8). One can say either *I'm flying to New York* or *I'm going to New York by air*, either *I'm driving to New York* or *I'm going to New York by car*. In the one case the distinction is made by the paradigmatic choice of the verbs *fly* and *drive*, in the other by the syntagmatic modification of the more general verb *go*. If a particular lexical item is very frequently modified syntagmatically in a particular way, this may have the effect, diachronically, of transferring the distinction from the syntagmatic to the paradigmatic and making the overt syntagmatic modification redundant. It is presumably this phenomenon which accounts for the development in the sense of the verb *starve*. At one time, it meant something like 'die' (cf. the genetically-related German *sterben*) and earlier 'to be stiff', but it was commonly modified syntagmatically with *of hunger* and thus acquired the sense it now possesses in modern standard English. (In certain areas of Northern England the typical syntagmatic modification was, and still is, *with cold*, so that *I'm starving* is roughly equivalent to the standard English *I'm freezing*.) The history of the vocabulary of English, and doubtless of all languages, is full of examples of semantic 'specialization' of this kind.

It is important to realize that the contextual determination of a lexical item may be probabilistic rather than absolute. For instance, the substitution of *buy* for *get* in *I'll go to the shop and get some bread* would not generally be held to introduce any additional implications: *buy* and *get* would normally be taken as synonymous in this context. The standard conventions and presuppositions of the society are such that, unless there is some evidence to suggest the contrary, it will be assumed that what is obtained from a shop is obtained by purchase. At the same time, it must be admitted that *get* is not necessarily synonymous with *buy* (even with the syntagmatic support of *from the shop*). The example also illustrates the further point that there is no sharp distinction to be drawn between the probabilistic determination of synonymy by other lexical items in the same utterance and the determination of synonymy by the features of the situation in which the utterance occurs. If one says *I'm just going to get some bread* as one steps into a shop, the context-dependent synonymy of *get* and *buy* is no weaker than it would be if the words *from the shop* occurred in the utterance. Not only is it no weaker, it is no different in kind, since the same set of cultural presuppositions determine the implications in both cases.

10.3 Hyponymy and incompatibility

10.3.1 *Hyponymy*

Hyponymy and incompatibility are the most fundamental paradigmatic relations of sense in terms of which the vocabulary is structured. Although they are very largely interdependent, we shall for convenience discuss them separately.

The term 'hyponymy' is not part of the traditional stock-in-trade of the semanticist; it is of recent creation, by analogy with 'synonymy' and 'antonymy'. Although the term may be new, the notion of hyponymy is traditional enough; and it has long been recognized as one of the constitutive principles in the organization of the vocabulary of all languages. It is frequently referred to as 'inclusion'. For example, the 'meaning' of *scarlet* is said to be 'included' in the 'meaning' of *red*; the 'meaning' of *tulip* is said to be 'included' in the 'meaning' of *flower*; and so on.

This relationship, the 'inclusion' of a more specific term in a more general term, has been formalized by certain semanticists in terms of the logic of classes: the class of entities referred to by the word *flower* is wider than and includes the class of entities referred to by the word *tulip*; the class of entities that may be truly described as *scarlet* is included in the class of entities that may be truly described as *red*; and so on. It will be observed that this formulation of the relationship of 'inclusion' rests upon the notion of reference (since it operates with classes of 'entities' which are named by lexical items). One reason for preferring to introduce the new technical term 'hyponymy' is simply that it leaves 'inclusion' free for the theory of reference and its formalization in terms of class-logic. We have already seen that it is desirable to draw a theoretical distinction between sense and reference. It is important to realize that hyponymy, as a relation of sense which holds between lexical items, applies to non-referring terms in precisely the same way as it applies to terms that have reference.

A more important reason for preferring to use an alternative to 'inclusion' is that 'inclusion' is somewhat ambiguous. From one point of view, a more general term is more 'inclusive' than a more specific term—*flower* is more inclusive than *tulip*—since it refers to a wider class of things. But from another point of view, the more specific term is more 'inclusive'—*tulip* is more inclusive than *flower*—since it carries more 'bits' of information, more 'components' of 'meaning' (cf. 2.4.3, 10.5.1). The difference in the point of view from which one may consider 'inclusion' corresponds to the difference, in traditional logic and in certain theories of semantics, between the *extension* and the *intension* of a term. The extension of a term is the class of entities to which the term is applicable or refers; the intension of a term is the set of attributes which characterize any entity to which the term is correctly applied. Extension and intension vary inversely in relation to one another: the greater the extension of a term, the less its intension; and conversely. For example, the extension of *flower* is greater than that of *tulip*, since the former term refers to more things; on the other hand, the intension of *tulip* is greater than that of *flower*, since the characterization or definition of tulips must make reference to a wider set of attributes than those which suffice to characterize flowers. It may be mentioned in passing that certain semanticists, notably Carnap, have attempted to draw the distinction between sense and reference in terms of the logical distinction between intension and extension. We have taken the view that the difference between sense and reference is of a quite different order (cf. 9.2.2, 9.4.1, 9.4.2). Confusion is avoided by the employment of a neutral, non-metaphorical term like 'hyponymy'. We will say that *scarlet, crimson, vermilion*, etc., are co-hyponyms of *red*, and *tulip, violet, rose*, etc. co-hyponyms of *flower*. Conversely, we will say that *red* is *superordinate* with respect to its hyponyms (the more obvious Greek-based term 'hyperonym' is not sufficiently distinct acoustically from 'hyponym' in English).

Hyponymy may be defined in terms of unilateral implication. (For instance, *X is scarlet* will be taken to imply *X is red*; but the converse implication does not generally hold.) In the most typical instances, a sentence containing a superordinate term will imply either (i) the disjunction of sentences each containing a different member of a set of co-hyponyms, or (ii) a sentence in which the co-hyponyms are semantically 'co-ordinated', as it were. Both of these possibilities may be illustrated with *I bought some flowers*. This sentence might imply the disjunction of *I bought some tulips*, *I bought some roses*, *I bought some violets*, etc. (By 'disjunction' in this context is meant the choice of one from a set of alternatives: if *p* implies the disjunction of *q*, *r* and *s*, then *p* implies either *q* or *r* or *s*.) It might also imply a sentence like *I bought some roses and some tulips*, or *I bought some violets and some tulips*, etc. It is of course one of the most convenient features of the principle of hyponymy that it is enables us to be more general or more specific according to circumstances. It would be quite inappropriate to say that *some flowers* is either imprecise or ambiguous (as between 'some roses', 'some tulips', etc., on the one hand, and 'some roses and some tulips', 'a rose and some tulips', etc. on the other).

10.3.2 *Synonymy as symmetrical hyponymy*

Although a superordinate term does not generally imply its hyponym, it is frequently the case that the situational context or the syntagmatic modification of the superordinate term will determine it in the sense of one of its hyponyms. This is the source of context-dependent synonymy (cf. 10.2.7). And it suggests the possibility of defining the relationship of synonymy as symmetrical hyponymy: if *x* is a hyponym of *y* and if *y* is also a hyponym of *x* (i.e. if the relationship is bilateral, or symmetrical), then *x* and *y* are synonyms. Drawing upon the terminological distinction made in set-theory and the logic of classes, we may refer to the relationship of unilateral, or asymmetrical, implication which holds between *tulip* and *flower* as *proper hyponymy*. All hyponymy is *transitive*, in the sense that if the relation holds between *a* and *b* and also between *b* and *c*, then it also holds between *a* and *c*. Synonymy, as a special case of hyponymy, has therefore the additional property that it is a *symmetrical* relation (it holds between *a* and *b* and between *b* and *a*). And for purely formal reasons it may be defined also as *reflexive*: every lexical item is substitutable for, and is synonymous with, itself in the same context. (Synonymy is therefore an equivalence-relation in the mathematical sense of this term.)

10.3.3   *Absence of superordinate terms*

The main point to be made about the relation of hyponymy as it is found in natural languages is that it does not operate as comprehensively or as systematically there as it does in the various systems of scientific taxonomy (in botany, zoology, etc.). The vocabularies of natural languages tend to have many gaps, asymmetries and indeterminacies in them. For instance, there is no superordinate term in English of which all the colour-words are co-hyponyms. (Logicians frequently cite as an example of analytic implication *If it is red, then it is coloured*. But this implication does not in fact generally hold for all colour-terms in normal English usage. The adjective *coloured* is in contrast with *white* in certain contexts—in sorting out the laundry, in the classification of people according to their race, etc.— and with *transparent* in others: e.g. *There was some coloured liquid in the bottle*—one might also wonder whether *coloured* is in contrast with *white*, as well as with *transparent*, in contexts of this kind.) Similarly, there is no more general adjective of which *square* and *round* are co-hyponyms. On the other hand, there are many words that are commonly regarded as lexical items whose application is so general that they might well be treated as grammatical 'dummies' in 'deep' syntactic analysis: e.g. *come/go, person, thing, event*, etc. At this point, there is a high degree of correspondence between syntax and semantics (cf. 9.5.2).

10.3.4   *Hierarchical structure of vocabulary*

Many semanticists have been attracted by the possibility of describing the vocabulary of the language in terms of a hierarchical, taxonomic classification working from the most general to the more specific categories. We have already mentioned *Roget's Thesaurus*, the most famous attempt to analyse the vocabulary of English in this way; and we shall return to the question of the hierarchical structure of the vocabulary in the section devoted to the principles of 'componential analysis' (cf. 10.5.1; also 4.3.3).

The most important factor in the hierarchical organization of the vocabulary by means of the relation of hyponymy is the structure of the culture in which the language operates and in which it serves as the principal medium for communication. It is a truism that words referring to artefacts cannot be defined except in relation to the purpose or normal function of the objects they refer to: e.g. *school*, 'a building where children are taught', *house*, 'a building where people live'. But this is true of the vocabulary as a whole, which is not only 'anthropocentric' (organized according to general human interests and values), but 'culture-bound' (reflecting the more particular institutions and practices of different cultures). Part of what I have referred to as the semantic anisomorphism of different languages (cf. 2.2.1) is accounted for by the fact that individual languages vary considerably in the extension of 'roughly equivalent' terms. It is often possible to identify (in terms of their application: cf. 9.4.8) the hyponyms of a certain term in one language with lexical items in another language without being able to find an equivalent for the superordinate term. As an instance of this phenomenon, we may consider the word *dēmiourgós* in Greek.

Among the hyponyms of *dēmiourgós* (which is usually translated as 'craftsman', 'artisan') we find a large number of terms, including *téktōn, iatrós, aulētḗs, skutotómos, kubernḗtēs*. For each of these there is a satisfactory English equivalent for the purpose of translating the works of the classical authors: 'carpenter', 'doctor', 'flute-player', 'shoemaker', 'helmsman'. But there exists no word in English that is superordinate to all the translation-equivalents of *dēmiourgós* without being also superordinate to other words that are not translation-equivalents of *dēmiourgós*. The distinction between arts, crafts, trades, professions, and so on, is not relevant to the meaning of *dēmiourgós*. Anyone who had a culturally-recognized occupation which required specialized knowledge or training was a *dēmiourgós*. The meaning of this word can only be described in terms of its hyponyms and in terms of the sense-relations it bears to other words in Greek (in particular, to the verb *epístasthai*, 'to know (as a result of study or training)'). In fact, the translation of many of its hyponyms rests implicitly upon the decision to treat certain classes of people and their 'professional' activities as culturally-equivalent. We identify the application of the English word *doctor* and the Greek word *iatrós* by virtue of our decision to treat the cultural, or social, function of those denoted by these words as equivalent; and this decision involves the tacit recognition that many of the activities characteristic of the 'doctor' and the 'iatrós' are culture-bound and irrelevant to what we regard as their 'culture-invariant' function. All translation from one language to another involves decisions of this kind. It is a sound methodological principle that sense is not held invariant in translation (so that there is no synonymy between words of different languages) but a greater or less degree of equivalence in the 'application' of words. And at the present time semantic theory can do little more than appeal to the bilingual speaker for intuitive judgements of equivalence in the area of 'cultural overlap' (cf. 9.4.7).

10.3.5 *Incompatibility*

Incompatibility can be defined on the basis of the relationship of *contradictoriness* between sentences. If one sentence, S_1, explicitly or implicitly denies another sentence, S_2, then S_1 and S_2 are contradictory (S_1 and S_2 are explicitly contradictory if S_1 negates S_2 syntactically, otherwise they are implicitly contradictory: cf. 10.1.2). If S_2 and S_1 are implicitly contradictory sentences of identical deep-syntactic structure, and if they differ only in that where one has the lexical item x the other has y, then x and y are incompatible.

To take a simple, and familiar, example from the colour-terms in English. If someone says *Mary was wearing a red hat*, this will be understood as implicitly denying *Mary was wearing a green (blue white, yellow*, etc.) *hat*. And the substitution of any one of the terms in the set *green, blue, white, yellow*, etc., for *red* would also be taken as implying the denial of *Mary was wearing a red hat*. The colour-terms therefore form a set of incompatible lexical items.

This is obvious enough. What has not always been quite so clear to semanticists is the fact that the incompatibility of *red, green*, etc., is not a secondary consequence of the sense which each of them has (independently as it were) but is necessarily involved in learning and knowing the sense of each of the terms in the set. As we have already seen, the colour-terms taken together exhaust a referential continuum; and learning where to draw the boundaries within the continuum for a particular term, say *blue*, is dependent upon the knowledge that on either side of the boundary is 'not blue' (cf. 9.4.5). In principle, it is perhaps conceivable that the reference of one of the colours could be learned without knowing the items referring to the areas of the continuum beyond the boundaries of 'blue' (i.e. by contrasting *blue* explicitly with *not...blue*). One could conceive of the language being learned in an environment which did not provide instances of colour at all 'points' in the continuum. But in practice, one may assume, the reference and sense of the most common colour-terms is learned more or less simultaneously, with continual adjustment of the boundaries until they approximate to the norm for the speech-community. Further lexical differentiation is then possible on the basis of hyponymy, *red* being 'subdivided' into *crimson, scarlet*, and so on. But the further differentiation will vary considerably as between individual speakers. Those whose profession or interests require them to draw more numerous distinctions of colour will develop a very rich colour-terminology. But they will do so subsequently to the acquisition of the 'grosser' distinctions characteristic of the non-specialized vocabulary of the community as a whole.

10.3.6 *Incompatibility and difference of sense*

Incompatibility is to be distinguished from mere difference of sense. This is particularly clear in the case of incompatible co-hyponyms of a superordinate term, which are different within some 'dimension' of similarity of sense. For instance, *crimson* and *soft* are different in sense, but not incompatible: both adjectives may be applied to the same object without contradiction. On the other hand, *crimson* and *scarlet* are similar in sense (their similarity being stateable as co-hyponymy with respect to *red*), but incompatible. The 'higher-level' incompatible terms *red, green, blue*, are also similar in sense, although there is no superordinate term of which they are co-hyponyms.

The distinction between incompatibility and difference of sense is less clear in other instances; notably in the case of words which denote physical 'objects' (whether 'natural' or manufactured). The words *chair* and *table* are incompatible (we will neglect the theoretically-uninteresting complications introduced by the consideration of dual-purpose furniture), but we might be inclined to say, and no doubt correctly, that the meaning of the one could be learned independently of the other. Of course, we would not say that anyone knew the meaning of *table* if he used the word to refer to objects which other speakers of English described as 'chairs'. The question is whether there is any 'dimension' of sameness prior to the distinction of the two incompatible terms. The same question can be put in relation to the words *door* and *window*. In the case of *table* and *chair* there is the superordinate term *furniture*; there is no such term which brings together *door* and *window*. But the existence or non-existence of a superordinate seems to be of relatively small importance here. And when we consider such pairs of words as *chair* and *cow* (or a host of other lexical items—to use Lewis Carroll's example, *shoe, ship, sealing wax* or *cabbage* and *king*) which semantically have nothing in common other than the fact that they denote physical entities, there is little point in distinguishing between incompatibility and difference of sense. It is in the case of sets of lexical items which give structure to a continuum that the relation of incompatibility is of crucial importance in both the learning and the use of language. And it would be a mistake to think that the distinction between incompatibility and mere difference does not apply at all to the lexical classification of words which denote persons, animals and physical objects. One has only to think of such sets as *tree, shrub, bush*, etc., to see that the distinction is of importance here also.

One final point should be made in connexion with the notions of hyponymy and incompatibility. We have repeatedly stressed the principle that the same semantic distinctions can be made either paradigmatically or syntagmatically. To give yet another example, English draws a paradigmatic distinction between *brother* and *sister*. Turkish does not: the word *kardeş* is 'unmarked' with respect to the distinction of sex, but may be 'marked' by syntagmatic modification if one wishes to make clear the sex of the person referred to: *kizkardeş*, 'sister' ('girl-brother', as it were). Other languages make a paradigmatic distinction between 'eldest son', 'younger son', etc.

10.4 Antonymy, complementarity and converseness

10.4.1 'Oppositeness' of meaning

Antonymy, or 'oppositeness of meaning', has long been recognized as one of the most important semantic relations. However, it has been the subject of a good deal of confusion, partly because it has generally been regarded as complementary to synonymy and partly because most semanticists have failed to give sufficient attention to different kinds of 'oppositeness'. Synonymy and antonymy, as we shall see, are sense-relations of a very different kind. For simplicity, we will distinguish terminologically between three types of 'oppositeness'; and we will reserve the term 'antonymy' for just one of the three types. A fuller treatment of 'opposites' would draw more distinctions than we have space for here.

10.4.2 Complementarity

The first relation of 'oppositeness' to be discussed is that which holds between such pairs of words as *single*: *married, male*: *female*, etc. We will use the term *complementarity* for this, saying that *single* and *married*, or *male* and *female*, are complementaries. It is characteristic of such pairs of lexical items that the denial of the one implies the assertion of the other and the assertion of the one implies the denial of the other: $\sim x \supset y$ and $y \supset \sim x$. Thus, *John isn't married* implies *John is single*; and *John is married* implies *John is not single*. In the case of those pairs for which we are reserving the term 'antonymy' (e.g. *good*: *bad*, *high*: *low*), only the second of these implications holds: $y \supset \sim x$. *John is good* implies the denial of *John is bad*; but *John is not good* does not imply the assertion of *John is bad*.

Complementarity may be regarded as a special case of incompatibility holding over two-term sets. The assertion of one member of a set of incompatible terms implies the denial of each of the other members in the set taken separately (*red* implies $\sim blue$, $\sim green$, etc.); and the denial of one member of a set of incompatible terms implies the assertion of the disjunction of all the other members ($\sim red$ implies either *green* or *blue* or...). In a two-term set of incompatible terms, there is only one other member. Conjunction and disjunction therefore fall together: 'both y and z' and 'either y or z' amount to the same thing if y and z have the same value. And from this fact there follow the particular conditions of complementarity mentioned above. It would be erroneous, however, to suppose that complementarity is merely the limiting case of incompatibility with the set of incompatible terms reduced, accidentally as it were, to two. Dichotomization is a very important principle in the semantic structure of language. We will take up this point below.

Everything that has been said so far about complementarity and the implications between lexical items which determine this relation presupposes the applicability of the complementary terms. The use of the dichotomous terms *married* and *single* presupposes the applicability of whatever might be the culturally accepted criteria of 'marriageability'. *John isn't married* is hardly less anomalous semantically than *The stone isn't married*, if the person referred to as *John* is not in fact 'marriageable' (by virtue of age and other criteria).

A further point should be noticed in connexion with complementary terms. Although it is *normally* the case that the denial of the one implies the assertion of the other and the assertion of the one implies the the denial of the other, it is generally possible to 'cancel' either or both of these implications. But this fact should not be taken as sufficient to invalidate the normal usage of complementary terms. The point may be made more clearly perhaps by taking the complementaries *male* and *female* as illustrative of the general principle of 'normality' as it is intended to be understood here. Granted the applicability of the distinction of sex, there is a first-level, normal dichotomy into *male* and *female*; and this dichotomy reflects the assumption that a number of different biological and behavioural characteristics will 'normally' be associated in the same person or animal. There are, however, many cases where the dichotomous classification is unsatisfactory either biologically or behaviourally, and then the terms *hermaphrodite* or *homosexual* are available to take account of these 'abnormalities'. Most of the complementary terms in the everyday vocabulary of languages would seem to operate in the same way within the framework of the relevant presuppositions, beliefs and conventions subsumed under the notion of 'restricted context' (cf. 9.3.9). As Moravcsik has pointed out, in a paper devoted to the discussion of the philosophical distinction of the analytic and the synthetic, it is not difficult to think of circumstances in which one might wish to assert of the same person that he was both a *bachelor* and *married* (or neither *single* nor *married*). This situation might arise, if the person in question was not in fact married according to the law and customs of the society, but nevertheless lived and behaved in a way characteristic of people to whom the term *married* is applied 'normally' (living regularly with one woman, having children by her and maintaining a home, etc.). The fact that it is possible to 'cancel' some of the implications of the first-level dichotomous classification means that in such cases the implications can only be regarded as 'normally', and not 'absolutely', analytic. But this principle holds for sense-relations in general.

Not only is it possible to conceive of situations in which the assertion of one term does not necessarily imply the denial of its complementary, but it is also possible to qualify a complementary term, 'abnormally', with *more* or *less*. One can say, for instance, that one person is *more married* than someone else (implying that his behaviour is more typical of what is 'normally' characteristic of married men). This is perhaps unusual, but it is a possibility which semantic theory should allow for. What is involved is the qualification of one or more of the presuppositions which determine the 'normal' interpretation of the term in question. However, in their 'normal' usage complementary terms are not qualifiable, or gradable, in this way.

10.4.3 *Antonymy*

The relation to which we are giving the name *antonymy* (to the exclusion of other kinds of 'oppositeness') may be exemplified by the terms *big* and *small* in English. It is characteristic of antonyms of this class, 'opposites' *par excellence*, that they are regularly gradable. *Grading* (in the sense in which the term is being employed here—it is borrowed from Sapir, to whom we shall refer presently) is bound up with the operation of comparison. The comparison may be explicit or implicit. Explicitly comparative sentences fall into two types. (1) Two things may be compared with respect to a particular 'property', and this 'property' predicated of the one in a greater degree than it is of the other: e.g. *Our house is bigger than yours*. (2) Two 'states' of the same thing may be compared with respect to the 'property' in question: e.g. *Our house is bigger than it used to be*. Actual utterances (taken out of context) may be ambiguous as between the two types of explicit comparison: e.g. *Our house is bigger*, which is presumably derived from a sentence of either one type or the other by the deletion of the phrase or clause introduced by *than*. But they are still explicitly comparative, and can only be interpreted if the other term of the comparison is recoverable from the context.

Both types of explicit comparison may be combined in the same sentence: e.g. *Our house is bigger than yours used to be, He is taller than his father was*. But the semantic interpretation of these more complex comparative sentences does not seem to introduce any additional problems. In fact, each of the two simpler types of explicit comparison may be subsumed under a more general formula which also covers the more complex sentences:

$$Comp \{([NP_1, x]T_i + M_k + A_m) ([NP_2, x]T_j + M_l + A_n)\}$$

In this formula, '*NP*' stands for 'noun-phrase' (denoting the thing or things being compared), '*x*' stands for the particular lexical item which is graded (in English, this is generally realized with the suffix *-er*, e.g. *bigger*, or with the word *more* preceding the uninflected adjective, e.g. *more beautiful*), 'T' stands for 'tense', 'M' for 'mood' and 'A' for 'aspect'. The subscripts distinguish the different values which may be assumed by the noun-phrase and by the markers of tense, mood and aspect. In terms of the formula, the sentence *Our house is bigger than yours used to be* might be analysed as:

$$Comp \{([Our\ house, big]T_{non-past} + M_0 + A_0) ([Your\ house, big]T_{past} + M_0 + A_{habitual})\}$$

This analysis is not definitive, but merely illustrative of the variable factors involved. As we have already seen, the analysis of tense, mood and aspect in English is a complicated matter (cf. 7.5.8). For simplicity of exposition, we have shown tense, mood and aspect as independent variables in the formula: from the syntactic point of view this is quite unsatisfactory, but it does not affect the point being made here. The subscript o ('zero') indicates the 'unmarked' term in a category; the other subscripts are self-explanatory. The corresponding non-comparative sentences are *Our house is big* (modally and aspectually unmarked and non-past) and *Your house used to be big* (modally unmarked, habitual in aspect and past). The reason why the semantic analysis of the comparative sentence *Our house is bigger than yours used to be* does not proceed by way of a prior semantic analysis of the syntactically-embedded sentences *Our house is big* and *Your house is big* will occupy us presently.

In the case of our model sentence, *Our house is bigger than yours used to be*, the two noun-phrases are different (NP_1 does not equal NP_2) and so are the values of T and A ($T_i \neq T_j$ and $A_m \neq A_n$). The two simpler types of explicit comparison can be derived from the formula by imposing a condition of identity either between NP_1 and NP_2 or between i and j, k and l, and m and n. In *Our house is bigger than yours* the second, but not the first, identity holds ($i = j$, $k = l$ and $m = n$, but $NP_1 \neq NP_2$). In *Our house is bigger than it used to be* it is the other way round ($NP_1 = NP_2$; but, although $k = l$, $i \neq j$ and $m \neq n$). If both identities hold simultaneously the result is of course a contradictory sentence: *Our house is bigger than it is.*

Given this formal framework, we can state the most important defining characteristic of the relation of antonymy. If x and y are antonyms, then a comparative sentence containing x of the form

(i) $Comp \{([NP_1, x]T_i + M_k + A_m) ([NP_2, x]T_j + M_l + A_n)\}$

both implies and is implied by a corresponding comparative sentence containing y:

(ii) $Comp \{([NP_2, y]T_j + M_l + A_n) ([NP_1, y]T_i + M_k + A_m)\}$

To exemplify: *Our house is bigger than yours used to be* both implies and is implied by *Your house used to be smaller than ours is*; *Our house is bigger than yours* implies and is implied by *Your house is smaller than ours*; and *Our house is bigger than it used to be* implies and is implied by *Our house used to be smaller than it is* (*now*). The English words *big* and *small* are therefore antonyms in a range of contexts illustrated by these sentences.

10.4.4 'Implicitly graded' antonyms

We may now consider sentences in which antonyms are not explicitly graded. First of all, it may be observed that the denial of the one does not imply assertion of the other. *Our house is not big* does not imply *Our house is small* (although *Our house is big* does imply *Our house is not small*). This is a fact well-known to logicians; and it distinguishes antonyms from complementaries. More important, however, is the fact that sentences containing antonyms are always implicitly, if not explicitly, comparative. This was pointed out many years ago by Sapir, in a passage that deserves to be quoted in full:

'Such contrasts as *small* and *large*, *little* and *much*, *few* and *many*, give us a deceptive feeling of absolute values within the field of quantity comparable to such qualitative differences as *red* and *green* within the field of color perception. This feeling is an illusion, however, which is largely due to the linguistic fact that the grading which is implicit in these terms is not formally indicated, whereas it is made explicit in such judgements as "There were *fewer* people there *than* here" or "He has *more* milk *than* I". In other words, *many*, to take but one example, embodies no class of judgements clustering about a given quantity norm applicable to every type of experience, in the sense in which *red* or *green* is applicable to every experience in which color can have a place, but is, properly speaking, a purely relative term which loses all significance when deprived of its connotation of "more than" and "less than". *Many* merely means any number taken as a point of departure. This point of departure obviously varies enormously according to context.' Sapir goes on to observe, later in the same article: 'contrasting qualities are felt as of a relatively absolute nature, so to speak, and *good* and *bad*, for instance, even *far* and *near*, have as true a psychological specificity as *green* and *yellow*. Hence the logical norm between them is not felt as a true norm but as a blend area in which qualities graded in opposite directions meet. To the naive, every person is either good or bad; if he cannot be easily placed, he is rather part good and part bad than just humanly normal or neither good nor bad.'

The importance of this insight into the nature of antonyms should not be underestimated. Many pseudo-problems have arisen in logic and philosophy as a consequence of the failure to appreciate that such words as *big* and *small*, or *good* and *bad*, do not refer to independent, 'opposite' qualities, but are merely lexical devices for grading as 'more than' or 'less than' with respect to some implicit norm. Plato was troubled, for instance, by the fact that, if one asserted of X that he was 'taller than' Y but 'shorter than' Z, one appeared to be committed to the simultaneous predication of the two 'opposite' qualities 'tallness' and 'shortness' of the same person—that X was both tall and short. A similar pseudo-problem is exemplified by sentences such as *A small elephant is a large animal*. If *small* and *large* are regarded as merely incompatible, or complementary, terms, this sentence should be contradictory (cf. **A male elephant is a female animal*). But it is not; and, however we choose to formalize the rules or principles of semantic interpretation, what should be formalized by the rules is quite clear. The implicit 'size-norm' for elephants is not necessarily the same as the implicit 'size-norm' for animals taken as a whole class. The semantic analysis of *A small elephant is a large animal* should take something like the following form: 'An elephant which is small-rather-than-large by comparison with the norm relevant for elephants is (nevertheless) large-rather-than-small by comparison with the norm relevant for animals'.

It is because explicitly ungraded antonyms are understood as implicitly graded with reference to some relevant norm that a comparative sentence such as *Our house is bigger than yours* (or *Our house is bigger than yours used to be*) cannot be satisfactorily analysed, from the semantic point of view, on the basis of the analysis of the syntactically-embedded sentences *Our house is big* and *Your house is (or used to be) big*. A sentence like *Our house is big* is, semantically, a comparative: 'Our house is bigger than the normal house.'

The implicit grading of antonyms also accounts for the fact that there is no contrast between the two members of a particular pair in 'unmarked' questions (and in various other syntactic functions). For instance, the sentence *How big is it?* does not presuppose that the object of the inquiry will be classed as 'big' rather than 'small', but is completely open, or 'unmarked', as to the expectations of the inquirer. It may be regarded as equivalent to 'Is it big or small?'. The question brings into the discussion a scale recognized by the participants as relevant and asks that the object be measured, as it were, along this scale. The first-level measurement is in terms of the dichotomy 'big-rather-than-small' or 'small-rather-than-big' (by comparison with the norm). If the first-level description as *big* or *small* is not sufficiently precise for the purpose, it is always possible to put the further, 'marked' questions *Hów big is it?* or *Hów small is it?* (which differ in stress and intonation from the 'unmarked' *How big is it?*—this difference is summarized, for the present purpose, in the acute accent on the word *hów?* in the 'marked' questions). The 'marked' questions *Hów big is it?* and *Hów small is it?* carry with them the presupposition that the object in question has already been placed towards one end of the scale rather than the other, and seek further specification of the place of the object on the scale relative to the relevant 'size-norm'.

The opposition between antonyms is 'neutralized', not only in 'unmarked' questions of the kind illustrated in the previous paragraph, but also in various nominalizations: *What is the width of the river? Everything depends upon the height,* etc. The nouns *narrowness* and *lowness* would not occur in such contexts. In general, only one of a pair of antonyms will occur in 'unmarked' contexts (*big, high, wide, good, tall,* etc.); and it is worth observing that many of the nominalizations of these 'unmarked' forms are irregular in English (cf. *big: size, high: height, wide: width,* etc.) by contrast with the less frequent 'marked' forms (*small: smallness, low: lowness, narrow: narrowness,* etc.). The fact that the distinction between antonyms is neutralized in certain syntactic positions contributes, no doubt, to our feeling that one antonym has a 'positive', and the other a 'negative', polarity. We tend to say that small things 'lack size', rather than large things 'lack smallness'. And, in general, the 'unmarked' antonym is used for what is felt as 'more than', rather than 'less than', the norm.

10.4.5 *Converseness*

The third sense-relation which is frequently described in terms of 'oppositeness' is that which holds between *buy* and *sell* or *husband* and *wife*. We will use the term *converseness* to refer to this relation. The word *buy* is the converse of *sell*, and *sell* is the converse of *buy*.

Although antonymy and converseness must be distinguished, there is a parallelism between the two relations. As NP_1 *bought* NP_3 *from* NP_2 implies, and is implied by, NP_2 *sold* NP_3 *to* NP_1 so NP_1 *is bigger than* NP_2 implies, and is implied by, NP_2 *is smaller than* NP_1. In both cases the lexical substitution of one term for the corresponding antonym or converse is associated with a syntactic transformation which permutes the noun-phrase, NP_1 and NP_2, and also carries out certain other 'automatic' changes in the selection of the appropriate preposition (or case-inflexion, in other languages). It may be observed that this 'permutational' feature is also characteristic of the relationship between corresponding active and passive sentences: NP_1 *killed* NP_2 implies, and is implied by, NP_2 *was killed by* NP_1. In English it is possible to form passive sentences in which the 'surface' subject is identical with the 'indirect object' of the corresponding active sentence. *John's father gave him a book* is related semantically to both (i) *John was given a book by his father*, and (ii) *John received a book from his father*. In many languages (including French, German, Russian, Latin, etc.) the 'indirect object' cannot be transformed into the 'surface' subject of a passive sentence in this way; and *John was given a book by his father* would be translated (to use French for exemplification) as either *Le père de Jean lui a donné un livre* ('John's father gave him a book') or *Jean a reçu un livre de son père* ('John received a book from his father').

The consideration of the verbs for 'marry' in various Indo-European languages is illuminating from the point of view of the relation of converseness. (When we say that all these verbs are 'equivalent in meaning' we are, of course, invoking the notion of 'application' and 'cultural overlap': cf. 9.4.8. It is only 'rough' equivalence anyway, as we shall see.) The English verb *marry* is symmetrical, or reciprocal, in that NP_1 *married* NP_2 implies, and is implied by, NP_2 *married* NP_1. (We are not here talking of the transitive, or 'causative', verb exemplified in *The priest married them* and *They were married by the priest*, but of the verb that occurs in such sentences as *John married Jane* or *Jane married John*.) In a number of languages, including Latin and Russian, there are two lexically-distinct, converse, verbs or verb-phrases. In Latin, for instance, *nubere* is used if the subject of the (active) sentence is a woman and *in matrimonium ducere* ('to bring into wedlock') if the subject is a man. In Greek, the active of the verb *gameîn* is employed for the man and the middle (or occasionally the passive) of the same verb for the woman: it is as if one were to say in English *John married Jane* but *Jane got herself married to John* ('middle') or *Jane was married by John* (passive). These three possibilities illustrate the way in which 'the same relationship' between two persons or things may be expressed by means of a symmetrical 'predicator' (like *marry*), by lexically-distinct 'predicators' (like *nubere* and *in matrimonium ducere*) or by the 'grammaticalization' of the asymmetry according to the syntactic resources of the language (as with *gameîn*).

The vocabulary of kinship and social status provides many instances both of symmetry and of converseness. NP_1 *is* NP_2's *cousin* implies, and is implied by, NP_2 *is* NP_1's *cousin*, but NP_1 *is* NP_2's *husband* implies, and is implied by, NP_2 *is* NP_1*'s wife*. Converseness also intersects with complementarity (of sex), so that NP_1 *is* NP_2*'s father* implies either NP_2 *is* NP_1*'s son* or NP_2 *is* NP_1*'s daughter*, NP_1 *is* NP_2*'s niece* implies either NP_2 is NP_1*'s uncle* or NP_2 is NP_1*'s aunt*, and so on.

Other lexical items are 'permutationally' related in the same way as converse terms, although they do not imply one another. For example, NP_1 *asked* (NP_2)... 'expects', rather than implies, NP_2 *answered* (NP_1)...; and NP_2 *answered* (NP_1)... '*presupposes*' NP_1 *asked* (NP_2).... Similarly, NP_1 *offered* NP_3 *to* NP_2 'expects' the disjunction of the complementary sentences NP_2 *accepted* NP_3 and NP_2 *refused* NP_3. 'Expectancy' and 'presupposition' of this kind are ordered with respect to temporal sequence: this is not so, it should be noted, in the case of such converse terms as *give* and *receive*.

10.4.6 *A parallelism between antonymy and complementarity*

We have noted the parallelism between converse terms and explicitly graded antonyms (and the purely grammatical transformation by which active and passive sentences are related). It is no less important to stress the parallelism between antonymy and complementarity. They are alike in that the assertion of a sentence containing an antonymous or complementary term implies the denial of a corresponding sentence containing the other antonym or complementary. This being so, one might envisage the elimination from the vocabulary of all instances of both antonyms and complementarity. Instead of *John is single*, one could say, equivalently, 'John is not married'; and instead of *The house is small* and *The house is big*, 'The house is less big' and 'The house is more big' ('than the norm' being understood). The fact is that we do not; and this, as Sapir pointed out in the article referred to above, is one of the facts which 'so often renders a purely logical analysis of speech insufficient or even misleading'.

The existence of large numbers of antonyms and complementary terms in the vocabulary of natural languages would seem to be related to a general human tendency to 'polarize' experience and judgement—to 'think in opposites'. Although we have distinguished between complementaries, such as *single* and *married*, and antonyms, such as *good* and *bad* (and it is important to draw this distinction), it is noticeable that the difference between them is not always clear-cut in the 'logic' of everyday discourse. If the answer 'No' is given to the question 'Was it a good film?', this will probably be understood to imply, 'It was a bad film', unless the person answering the question goes on to qualify his denial and make clear, as it were, that he is not content to make his judgement in terms of the polarized contrast of *good* and *bad*. It may well be therefore that the gradability of antonyms (though not their implicit reference to some accepted norm of comparison) is 'psycholinguistically' secondary—that is, something which speakers are conscious of and utilize only when a first-level dichotomization into 'yes' and 'no' is insufficient.

10.5 Componential analysis and universal semantics

10.5.1 *Preliminary discussion*

What is meant by the term 'componential analysis' in semantics is best explained by means of a simple example—one that has often been used for this purpose by linguists. Consider the following sets of English words:

(1) *man*   *woman*   *child*

(2) *bull*   *cow*   *calf*

(3) *rooster*   *hen*   *chicken*

(4) *drake*   *duck*   *duckling*

(5) *stallion* *mare*   *foal*

(6) *ram*   *ewe*   *lamb*

On the basis of our intuitive appreciation of the sense of these words we can set up such proportional equations as the following:

$$man:woman:child::bull:cow:calf$$

This equation expresses the fact (and for the moment we may assume that it is a fact) that, from the semantic point of view, the words *man*, *woman* and *child*, on the one hand, and *bull*, *cow* and *calf*, on the other, all have something in common; furthermore, that *bull* and *man* have something in common, which is not shared by either *cow* and *woman* or *calf* and *child*; that *cow* and *woman* have something in common, which is not shared by either *bull* and *man* or *calf* and *child*; that *calf* and *child* have something in common that is not shared by either *bull* and *man* or *cow* and *woman*. What these different groups of words have in common we will call a *semantic component*. (Other terms have also been used in the literature: 'plereme', 'sememe', 'semantic marker', 'semantic category', etc.; references will be found in the notes.)

Let us now introduce some elementary arithmetical considerations. Given a numerical proportion (what the Greek mathematicians and grammarians called an 'analogy': cf. 1.2.3) of the general form

$$a:b::c:d$$

where the first of the four expressions divided by the second is equal to the third divided by the fourth, we can factorize the proportion into what for the present purpose we may call its 'components'; and we can then refer to each of the four expressions as the *product* of a pair of components. (We have already made use of this parallel in our discussion of the distributional definition of the morpheme: cf. 5.3.3.) For example, from the proportion

$$2:6::10:30$$

we can extract the components 1, 2, 3 and 10. The proportion can then be restated as

$$(2 \times 1):(2 \times 3)::(10 \times 1):(10 \times 3)$$

where 2 is analysed as the product of 2 and 1; 6 as the product of 2 and 3; and so on. In this instance, three of the components are *prime numbers*, 1, 2 and 3; the fourth, 10, is not. However, in the case of numerical proportions we can always discover whether a given number is a prime or not; and, if it is not, we can determine its *ultimate components*—the set of prime numbers in terms of which it can be factorized. For the present purpose, we may assume that the process of factorization rests upon the availability of all the relevant proportions. For instance, if we have available the further proportion $1:2::5:10$, we could factorize 10 into the prime numbers 2 and 5; and we could then express our original proportion as

$$(2 \times 1):(2 \times 3)::((2 \times 5) \times 1):((2 \times 5) \times 3)$$

Each of the four expressions is now restated as the product of its ultimate components.

Let us now apply these considerations to the analysis of the English words given above. From the proportion *man:woman::bull:cow*, we can extract four components of sense: we will refer to these as (male), (female), (adult-human), (adult-bovine). At this stage of the analysis, if one were actually analysing the words on the basis of proportional equations, (adult-human) and (adult-bovine) would be regarded as single components. But as soon as we restate the proportion *man:woman:child::bull:cow:calf* as

$$(\text{male}) \times (\text{adult-human}):(\text{female})$$
$$\times (\text{adult-human}):(\text{non-adult-human})$$
$$::(\text{male}) \times (\text{adult-bovine}):(\text{female})$$
$$\times (\text{adult-bovine}):(\text{non-adult-bovine})$$

we can extract the further components (adult) and (non-adult). No one of these components, it should be observed, is assumed to be an ultimate component (a 'prime'): it is conceivable that, by bringing forward for comparison other words of English and setting up further proportions, we should be able to factorize (human) or (male) into 'smaller' semantic components, just as we factorized 10 into 5 and 2. Eventually we might hope to describe the sense of all the words in the vocabulary in terms of their ultimate semantic components. Assuming that the proposed analysis of the few English words given above is correct as far as it goes (and we will presently consider what 'correct' means here), we can say that the sense of *man* is the product of the components (male), (adult) and (human); that the sense of *mare* is the product of (female), (adult) and (equine); and so on.

The componential approach to semantics has a long history in linguistics, logic and philosophy. It is inherent in the traditional method of definition by dividing a genus into species and species into subspecies; and this method of definition is reflected in most of the dictionaries that have ever been compiled for particular languages, and in the organization of such works as *Roget's Thesaurus* (cf. 10.2.1). A number of attempts have been made in recent years to formalize these traditional principles of semantic analysis. We may begin by discussing some of the more important assumptions upon which current componential theories of semantics are based or with which they are frequently associated. The first is the assumption that the semantic components are language-independent, or universal.

10.5.2   *The alleged universality of semantic components*

It has frequently been suggested that the vocabularies of all human languages can be analysed, either totally or partially, in terms of a finite set of semantic components which are themselves independent of the particular semantic structure of any given language. According to this view (which has been a commonplace of philosophical and linguistic speculation since the seventeenth century) the semantic components might be combined in various ways in different languages (and thus yield 'senses' or 'concepts' unique to particular languages), but they would themselves be identifiable as the 'same' components in the analysis of the vocabularies of all languages. To quote Katz, who has put forward this view in a number of recent publications: 'Semantic markers [i.e. semantic components] must...be thought of as theoretical constructs introduced into semantic theory to designate language invariant but language linked components of a conceptual system that is part of the cognitive structure of the human mind.'

Little need be said about the alleged universality of semantic components, except that it is an assumption which is commonly made by philosophers and linguists on the basis of their anecdotal discussion of a few well-chosen examples from a handful of the world's languages.

Chomsky has suggested: 'It is surely our ignorance of the relevant psychological and physiological facts that makes possible the widely held belief that there is little or no a priori structure to the system of "attainable concepts".' The first point that should be made about this remark is simply that the belief that there are few, if any, 'universal, language-independent constraints upon semantic features [i.e. semantic components]' is probably most widely-held among those linguists who have had some experience of the problems of trying to compare the semantic structure of different languages in a systematic fashion: many have tried, and failed, to find a set of universal components. The second point is that, although Chomsky's own work contains a number of interesting, and probably correct, observations about certain classes of lexical items (e.g. 'proper names, in any language, must designate objects meeting a condition of spatio-temporal contiguity', 'the color words of any language must subdivide the color spectrum into continuous segments', 'artifacts are defined in terms of certain human goals, needs and functions instead of solely in terms of physical qualities'), such observations do not go very far towards substantiating the view that there is 'some sort of fixed, universal vocabulary [of semantic components] in terms of which [possible concepts] are characterized'.

It may well be that future developments in semantics, psychology, physiology, sociology, anthropology, and various other disciplines, will justify the view that there are certain 'language invariant but language linked components of a conceptual system that is part of the cognitive structure of the human mind', as Katz has suggested. Such empirical evidence as there is available at the present time would tend to refute, rather than confirm, this hypothesis.

10.5.3   *Componential analysis and conceptualism*

It is obvious that the value of componential analysis in the description of particular languages is unaffected by the status of the semantic components in universal terms. It should also be realized that componential theories of semantics are not necessarily 'conceptualist', or 'mentalistic'. This point is worth stressing, since not only Katz and Chomsky, but also Hjelmslev, Jakobson, and many others who have advocated a componential approach to semantics, have done so within a philosophical and psychological framework which takes it for granted that the sense of a lexical item is the 'concept' associated with this item in the 'minds' of the speakers of the language in question. For example, Katz introduces the notion of semantic components (or 'semantic markers') as follows: 'Consider the idea each of us thinks of as part of the meaning of the words "chair", "stone", "man", "building", "planet", etc., but not part of the meaning of such words as "truth", "togetherness", "feeling", "shadow", "integer", "departure", etc.—the idea that we take to express what is common to the meaning of the words in the former group and that we use to conceptually distinguish them from those in the latter. Roughly, we might characterize what is common to our individual ideas as the notion of a spatially and contiguous material thing. The semantic marker (Physical Object) is introduced to designate that notion.'

We have already suggested that semantic theory should avoid commitment with respect to the philosophical and psychological status of 'concepts', 'ideas' and the 'mind' (cf. 9.2.6). Here it is sufficient to observe that what Katz has to say about the difference between the two groups of words can be stated without employing the term 'concept' or 'idea'. The first group of words denote things which are, or can be, described in English as 'physical objects' (the expression 'physical object' is of course itself made up of English words); the second group of words do not. Whether the correct application of the first group of words to their referents presupposes that the speaker has some 'idea' of 'physical object' in his 'mind' is a psychological question which we may leave on one side. The important question for the linguist is whether there are any facts pertaining to the acceptability or unacceptability of sentences, or to the relations of implication which hold between sentences, which can be described by assigning to all the words of the first group a distinctive semantic component, which we will agree to call '(physical object)'. The answer to this question carries no implications whatsoever for the dispute between various schools of philosophy and psychology about the status of 'mental concepts'.

10.5.4 *Apparent advantages of the componential approach*

At first sight, the componential approach to semantics would seem to have one striking advantage over other approaches: in terms of the same set of components one can answer two different questions. The first question has to do with the semantic acceptability of syntagmatic combinations of words and phrases: whether a given combination is to be generated as significant or excluded as meaningless. The second question is this: what is the meaning (i.e. the sense) of a particular combination of lexical items? We will take each of these questions in turn.

We have said that the significance of grammatically well-formed sentences (and parts of sentences) is traditionally accounted for in terms of certain general principles of 'compatibility' between the 'meanings' of their constituent lexical items (cf. 9.3.11). One way of stating this notion of semantic 'compatibility' is to say that the relevant semantic components of the lexical items in the syntagmatic combination generated by the syntax must not be *contradictory*. Let us assume, for example, that the word *pregnant* contains a component which restricts it to the modification of nouns which contain the component '(female)'. On the basis of this fact ('modification' being interpreted by the syntactic rules of the language) such phrases as *the pregnant woman* or *a pregnant mare* would be generated as significant and such phrases as *the pregnant man* or *a pregnant stallion* would be excluded as meaningless ('uninterpretable'). Whether such phrases as *the pregnant duck* are significant would presumably be decided with reference to further components of sense associated with the word *duck* and further restrictions imposed upon the combinability of *pregnant* with nouns.

There is no doubt that this is an elegant way of accounting for the combinatorial restrictions which hold between lexical items in particular grammatical constructions. It is to be noted, however, that any comprehensive treatment of the significance of sentences in such terms presupposes an adequate syntactic analysis of sentences and satisfactory rules for the semantic interpretation of the relevant grammatical relations. The example that has just been given, which involved the 'modification' of a noun by an 'adjective', is one which has never been regarded as particularly troublesome by semanticists. Its formalization within the framework of current syntactic theory is trivial by comparison with the problem of formalizing the vast majority of the relations of semantic 'compatibility' which hold in the sentences of any language. In the last few years there has been a remarkable concentration of interest upon the problems attaching to the formalization of different relations of semantic 'compatibility' (notably by Katz, Weinreich and Bierwisch). So far the results are not impressive, despite the sophistication of the formal apparatus that has been developed; and it would seem that progress in this area is dependent upon the construction of a more appropriate theory of syntax than is yet available.

The second question that componential analysis sets out to answer is 'What meaning does a given sentence or phrase have?' The general answer to this question is that the meaning of a sentence or phrase is the 'product' of the senses of its constituent lexical items; and the sense of each lexical item is the 'product' of its constituent semantic components. The meaning of a sentence or phrase is therefore determined by 'amalgamating' all the semantic components of the lexical items according to a set of 'projection rules' which are associated with deep-structure grammatical relations. It was suggested in the previous paragraph that current syntactic theory does not yet provide us with a satisfactory account of many of the relevant deep-structure grammatical relationships; and this was the main burden of our discussion of 'grammatical functions' in chapter 8. It follows that we are at present unable to interpret the term 'product' (or 'compositional function'—to employ the more technical term) in the proposed definition of the meaning of a sentence or phrase as 'the product of the senses of its constituent lexical items'.

At the same time, it is clear that many of the semantic relations discussed in the previous chapter might be reformulated within a componential theory of semantics. Synonymy, hyponymy, incompatibility and complementarity are obviously definable in terms of the semantic components of the lexical items in question. (For a componential approach to the definition of these relations the reader is referred to the works cited in the notes.) What must be stressed, however, is the fact that the componential analysis of lexical items rests upon the prior notion of 'implication' with respect to the assertion and denial of sentences. Componential analysis is a technique for the economical statement of certain semantic relations between lexical items and between sentences containing them: it cannot claim to circumvent any of the problems of indeterminacy that were discussed above in connexion with 'understanding' and 'analytic implication' (cf. 10.1.2).

10.5.5 The 'cognitive reality' of semantic components

The most interesting work so far published in the field of componential semantics has come, not from philosophers and linguists, but from anthropologists; and they have recently devoted considerable attention to what they have called the 'cognitive validity', or 'reality', of semantic components. It was this question that we had in mind, when we said earlier that we should have to examine what was meant by 'correct' in the context of componential analysis (cf. 10.5.1).

A good deal of the anthropological discussion makes reference to the analysis of the vocabulary of kinship in various languages. It has been shown, for example, that one can analyse the most common kinship terms of English in various ways. (In particular, *brother* and *sister* can be regarded as having the same component, 'direct line of descent', as *father* and *mother* or *son* and *daughter*, as against *cousin*, which shares the component 'collateral' with *uncle* and *aunt*, and with *nephew* and *niece*; alternatively, *brother* and *sister* can be analysed as having the same component, 'co-lineal', as *uncle* and *aunt* or *nephew* and *niece*, as against *cousin*, which has the component 'ab-lineal'.) The question is which, if any, of the various possible analyses is 'correct'. Each of them is self-consistent; each of them distinguishes every member of the lexical system from every other member of the system; and each of them is 'predictive', in the sense that it provides the anthropologist with a means of deciding, with respect to any member of the family, what his relationship is to other members of the family in terms of the lexical system. But each of the alternative analyses rests upon a different set of proportional equations: either
$$father:mother::son:daughter::brother:sister$$
or
$$uncle:aunt::nephew:niece::brother:sister$$

It is therefore the 'cognitive validity' of one set of proportions, rather than the other, which should decide the question of 'correctness' (if, indeed, this question is decidable). As far as the anthropological analysis of kinship is concerned, the 'cognitive validity' of a particular proportion is determined, presumably, by the social status and roles assigned to the different classes of family-relatives in the society; and this might well be reflected also in the linguistic 'intuitions' of the members of the community.

But we can also consider the question of 'correctness' from a more strictly linguistic point of view. Let us return, for this purpose, to the simple illustration of componential analysis with which we began this section. We assumed the validity of the following proportions

man: *woman*: *child*: : *bull*: *cow*: *calf*

bull: *cow*: *calf*: : *rooster*: *hen*: *chicken*

etc.

On the basis of these proportions, we 'extracted' the semantic components (male) *v.* (female), (adult) *v.* (non-adult), (human) *v.* (bovine) *v.* (equine) *v.* ... (sheep). We may now ask what is the linguistic status of these components.

At first sight, the opposition of the contradictory components (male) and (female) looks satisfactory enough. If we know that someone is an adult, male, human being, then we know that the word *man*, rather than *woman* or *child*, is appropriately applied to him; if we know that a particular domestic fowl is an adult female of a given species, then we know that *hen*, rather than *rooster* or *chicken*, is the appropriate term of reference; and so on. But one might maintain that to differentiate *man* and *woman*, *rooster* and *hen*, etc., in terms of the sex of their referents is to give priority to but one of the many linguistically-relevant features which distinguish them. If one asks a young child (most of whose utterances are perfectly acceptable and manifest the same semantic relationships, as far as one can judge, as the utterances of his elders) what is the difference between men and women, he might answer by listing a whole set of typical characteristics—the kind of clothes they wear, how their hair is cut, whether they go out to work or stay at home and look after the children, etc. A totally unrelated set of criteria might be proposed for the differentiation of *rooster* and *hen*, of *bull* and *cow*, and so on. Why should one suppose that sex is the sole criterion even in adult speech? And how far is it true to say that *woman*: *child*: : *cow*: *calf*: : *hen*: *chicken*, etc.?

Obviously, there is a certain class of sentences, the semantic acceptability or unacceptability of which can be accounted for in terms of this proportional equation: *That woman is the mother of this child*, *That hen is the mother of this chicken*, etc. *v. That man is the mother of this child*, *That woman is the father of this child*, *That woman is the mother of this calf*, etc. And the grammatical phenomenon of gender in English is partly determined by the sex of the referent.

But this does not mean that (male) and (female) are the sole semantic features which differentiate the complementary terms *man* v. *woman*, *bull* v. *cow*, etc. The status of such components as (adult) *v*. (non-adult) is even more dubious: once again, there are sets of semantically-acceptable or semantically-unacceptable combinations that can be accounted for in terms of this opposition, but there are others that cannot.

The problem is undoubtedly related to the anthropologist's problem of 'cognitive reality'. Consider, for example, a society in which the role of men and women is so different that there are very few activities in which both will engage. Assume now that there are two lexical items in the vocabulary of that language, which can be translated into English as 'man' and 'woman' on the basis of their reference to male, adult human beings and female, adult human beings, respectively. Knowing this fact about the reference of the two lexical items, the linguist could apply these terms appropriately to men and women. He would be fairly sure that the translation of English sentences such as 'The man gave birth to a child' (assuming that there is a term that can be satisfactorily translated as 'give birth to') would be semantically-unacceptable. But there might be an enormous range of other sentences, including 'The man cooked a meal', 'The woman lit a fire', etc., which are equally unacceptable. Our own cultural prejudices and our own taxonomic classification of the physical world should not be taken as valid for the analysis of either the culture or the language of other societies, still less of any alleged 'conceptual system that is part of the cognitive structure of the human mind'.

A further point should be made. It is one of the concomitant dangers of componential analysis that it tends to neglect the difference in the frequency of lexical items (and therefore their greater or less 'centrality' in the vocabulary) and the difference between lexical items and semantic components. For example, it is often suggested that *brother* and *sister* can be replaced with the 'synonyms' *male sibling* and *female sibling*. But this is true only in the context of anthropological or quasi-anthropological discussion. The words *brother* and *sister* are extremely common words, known presumably to all speakers of English, whereas *sibling* is a technical term, coined for the convenience of anthropologists; and most English speakers probably do not know it. The fact that there is no common super-ordinate term for the two complementaries *brother* and *sister* is *prima facie* evidence that the opposition between the two terms is semantically more important than what they have in common.

Similarly, the fact that there is a term *horse*, which has as its hyponyms the complementaries *stallion* and *mare*, is relevant to the analysis of the structure of the English vocabulary. Any theory of semantics which encouraged us to believe that the phrase *adult male elephant* stood in exactly the same semantic relationship to *elephant* as *stallion* does to *horse* would be unsatisfactory.

Componential theories of semantics do not necessarily fall victim to inadequacies of this kind. But there has been surprisingly little attention devoted to a discussion of the relationship between lexical items like *male* or *adult* and semantic components like (male) or (adult). One cannot avoid the suspicion that the semantic components are interpreted on the basis of the linguist's intuitive understanding of the lexical items which he uses to label them.

10.5.6 *Concluding remarks*

Limitations of space prevent us from going further into the details of recent componential work in semantics. If our treatment of the subject has been somewhat negative, it should be realized that this has been by deliberate decision. I have tried to draw attention to some of the assumptions upon which componential theories of semantics are frequently based—in particular, the assumption that semantic components are universal. We have seen that the notion of componential analysis rests upon the establishment of proportional equations with respect to the sense of lexical items. The important question, which is not always considered, is the degree to which these proportions are 'cognitively valid'. It is too often assumed that these proportions can be set up simply on the basis of introspection.

Componential analysis has, however, made considerable contributions to the development of semantics. Apart from anything else, it has brought the formalization of syntax and the formalization of semantics (or some aspects of semantics) closer together than they have been in the past. That linguists are once again seriously concerned with the relations between syntax and semantics is due very largely to the impact made by the work of Katz and Fodor, taken up more systematically within the framework of 'an integrated theory of linguistic descriptions' by Katz and Postal, and further developed by Katz in a number of subsequent publications. Although Katz and Postal tended to minimize the value of previous work in componential analysis, they were right to insist upon the importance of specifying the form of the 'projection rules' and the manner of their operation 'within the context of explicit generative linguistic descriptions'. This had not been attempted before.

In a previous chapter, we raised the possibility of a *rapprochement* between 'formal' and 'notional' grammar (cf. 4.3.4); and much of our subsequent discussion of 'grammatical categories' and 'grammatical functions' (in chapters 7 and 8) would tend to suggest that further progress in the formalization of syntax depends upon this *rapprochement*. We may conclude the present work in the certain expectation that the next few years will see the publication of a number of books and articles directed towards this goal.

It is not unlikely also that a greater concentration of interest upon the theory of semantics will bring linguists back to the traditional view that the syntactic structure of languages is very highly determined by their semantic structure: more especially, by the 'modes of signifying' of semantically-based grammatical categories (cf. 7.6.10). If this development does take place, one must be careful not to assume that linguistic theory has merely retreated to the position held by traditional grammarians. All future grammatical and semantic theory, however traditional its aims might be, must meet the rigorous demands of twentieth-century, 'structural' linguistics. Revolutions may be followed by counter-revolutions; but there can be no simple restoration of the past.

10.5.7   *Envoi*

> Ohe iam satis est, ohe libelle,
> iam pervenimus usque ad umbilicos...
> iam lector queriturque deficitque,
> iam librarius hoc et ipse dicit:
> 'ohe iam satis est, ohe libelle'.
>
> MARTIAL

NOTES AND REFERENCES

(Full titles of books and articles will be found in the bibliography)

Notes to chapter 1, pp. 1–52

1.1.4   Quotation from Bloomfield: *Language*, 3.

1.2   Traditional grammar: Many of the standard textbooks of linguistics are unsympathetic and unreliable in their references to traditional grammar (e.g. Bloomfield, *Language*; Jespersen, *Language*; de Saussure, *Cours*). The following may be recommended for further introductory reading: Robins, *Short History*; Dinneen, *Introduction*; Arens, *Sprachwissenschaft*; Kukenheim, *Esquisse*; Leroy, *Grands Courants*; Mounin, *Histoire*; Sandys, *Short History*.

1.2.1   Origins of Greek grammatical theory: cf. Forbes, 'Greek pioneers'; Koller, 'Anfänge'. On the Stoics, the importance of whom is frequently underestimated, cf. Barth, *Stoa*; Barwick, *Probleme*; Pohlenz, *Begründung*.

1.2.3   Analogy and anomaly: For the suggestion that Varro misrepresented the issues, cf. Fehling, 'Varro'; also Dihle, 'Analogie'.

1.2.6   Roman period: For the general background, cf. Collart, *Varron*; Barwick, *Remmius Palaemon*.

1.2.7   Medieval period: For the general philosophical background, cf. Gilson, *History*; Copleston, *History*. On medieval linguistic theory: cf. Dinneen, *Introduction*, 126–50; Robins, *Short History*; Bursill-Hall, 'Medieval theories'; Roos, 'Sprachdenken'. More specialized works: Grabmann, *Mittelalt. Geistesleben*; Heidegger, *Kategorienlehre*; Roos, *Modi Significandi*.

1.2.8   There is an interesting account of seventeenth-century 'rationalist' linguistics in Chomsky, *Cartesian Linguistics*. I may have underestimated the originality of the Port Royal grammarians.

1.2.10   The Indian tradition: cf. Belvalkar, *Systems*; Misra, *Descriptive Technique*; Allen, *Phonetics*; Brough, 'Theories'; Bloomfield, Review of Liebisch; Emeneau, 'India'; Renou's Introduction to Wackernagel and Debrunner, *Grammatik*.

1.3   Comparative philology: The standard work is Pedersen, *Linguistic Science*. It is notoriously deficient in its treatment of subjects lying outside the principal concerns of the 'Neogrammarians', and may be supplemented with Jespersen, *Language*, 32–99; Leroy, *Grands Courants*, 17–60; Mounin, *Histoire*, 152–212; Arens, *Sprachwissenschaft*, 139–337.

1.4   Modern linguistics: This section may be read in conjunction with Gleason, *Introduction*, 1–13; Hockett, *Course*, 1–11, 569–86; Robins, *General Linguistics*, 1–17; Hall, *Introductory*, 3–35; Martinet, *Éléments*, 9–51; Lepschy, *Linguistics*, 17–41; Dinneen, *Introduction*, 1–19; Hill,

[482]

Introduction, 1–12; Sapir, *Language*, 3–12; Malmberg, *Nouvelles Tendances*; Householder, forthcoming book.

1.4.1　Ferdinand de Saussure: De Saussure's own notes have recently been published, cf. Godel, *Sources*; and a critical edition of the *Cours* is now appearing, cf. Engler, *Cours*. For a convenient summary of de Saussure's views, cf. Dinneen, *Introduction*, 195–212; also Lepschy, *Linguistica*, 42–8 (includes a comprehensive, up-to-date bibliography).

1.4.2　Priority of the spoken language: cf. Abercrombie, *Elements*, 1–19; Uldall, 'Speech'; Vachek, 'Some remarks'; Pulgram, 'Graphic and phonic'.

1.4.3　On language-planning: cf. Haugen, 'Linguistics'; Hoenigswald, 'Proposal'.

1.4.7　*Langue* and *parole*: Saussure, *Cours*, 23 ff. (Introduction, chapter 3); cf. Lepschy, *Linguistica*, 45–6; Dinneen, *Introduction*, 196–9; Leroy, *Grands Courants*, 108–10. Chomsky relates his own distinction of 'competence' and 'performance' to de Saussure's distinction of 'langue' and 'parole', cf. *Aspects*, 4.

Notes to chapter 2, pp. 53–98

2.1.3　'Double articulation': cf. Martinet, *Linguistique Synchronique*, 1–35; also Palmer, 'Hierarchy'; Hockett, 'Linguistic elements'.

2.1.4　'Level', 'plane', 'expression', 'content': The terminology used at this point is that of Hjelmslev and his followers, cf. Hjelmslev, *Prolegomena*; Spang-Hassen, 'Glossematics'. The term 'level' is employed elsewhere in this book in a very general sense (to include what Hjelmslev calls a 'plane'). Attention is also drawn to 5.5.

2.2　Substance and form: cf Saussure, *Cours*, 155 ff. (part 2, chapter 4).

2.2.7　Arbitrariness of substantial realization: cf. Householder, 'Uniqueness'.

2.3　Paradigmatic and syntagmatic relations: De Saussure himself does not employ the term 'paradigmatic', but 'associative'. Furthermore, de Saussure's 'associative relations' include non-paradigmatic relations of various kinds: cf. *Cours* 170 ff. (part 2, chapter 5). The term 'paradigmatic' is due to Hjelmslev, cf. Robins, *General Linguistics*, 78. (It is an unfortunate choice of term, since it occasionally leads to confusion with 'paradigm': cf. Index.)

2.3.7　'Marked' and 'unmarked': these terms are associated particularly with the 'Prague School' (cf. Vachek, *Reader*). For a recent discussion: cf. Greenberg, *Language Universals*.

2.4　Statistical structure: cf. Cherry, *Human Communication*; Miller, *Language*; Roberts, *Statistical Linguistic Analysis*; Mandelbrot, 'Theory', Malmberg, *Nouvelles Tendances*, 278–304; Apostel *et al.*, *Logique*.

2.4.1　Functional load: cf. Martinet, *Économie*; Hockett, 'Quantification'.

2.4.2　Information-theory: There is an elementary account in Gleason, *Introduction*, pp. 373–90.

2.4.7.   On 'homonymics': cf. Orr, *Words*, esp. 91–160; Ullmann, *Principles*, 144–52. (Orr and Ullmann give references to the work of Gilliéron and his followers.)

2.4.9   Information about the frequency of English consonants is derived from Roberts, *Statistical Linguistic Analysis*. The most commonly-used list of word-frequencies is Thorndike and Lorge, *Teacher's Word-Book*.

Notes to chapter 3, pp. 99–132

3.2   Phonetics: cf. Abercrombie, *Elements*; Jones, *Outline*; Pike, *Phonetics*; Ladefoged, *Elements*; Fant, *Acoustic Theory*. See Addenda (1), p. 489.

3.3   Phonology: cf. Robins, *General Linguistics*, 121–79; Martinet, *Éléments*, 52–96; Hockett, *Manual*; Trubetzkoy, *Grundzüge*; Jones, *Phoneme*; Malmberg, *Structural Linguistics*, 30–127. See Addenda (2), p. 489.

3.3.9   'Grimm's law': cf. Fourquet, *Mutations*.

3.3.11   For recent developments in distinctive feature theory, cf. Jakobson, Fant and Halle, *Preliminaries*; Jakobson and Halle, *Fundamentals*; Chomsky and Halle, 'Controversial questions'; Fudge, 'Phonological primes'.

3.3.12   Prosodic analysis: cf. Robins, *General Linguistics*, 157–68. A number of 'prosodic' articles are being reprinted in Palmer, *Prosodic Analysis*.

3.3.13   Turkish phonology: cf. Waterson, 'Some aspects'; Lyons, 'Phonemic and non-phonemic'. For a treatment in terms of generative phonology: cf. Lees, *Phonology*.

Notes to chapter 4, pp. 133–169

4.1.3   Quotation from Jespersen, *Philosophy*, 55.

4.1.5   Chomsky's use of the term 'formal' (*v.* 'substantive'): cf. *Aspects*, 27–30.

4.2   Formal grammar: This section draws heavily upon Harris, *Methods*, and Chomsky, *Syntactic Structures*.

4.2.3   Russell's discussion of 'grammatical', but 'meaningless', sentences: *Inquiry*, 170 ff.

4.2.4   'Common core': the term comes from Hockett, *Course*, 332. For a good account of systematic variety in language, cf. Halliday, McIntosh and Strevens, *Linguistic Sciences*, 75–110; Quirk, *Use of English*, 50–63, 79–96, 154–73. On dialects, cf. McIntosh, *Introduction*; also Bach, *Mundartforschung*; Dauzat, *Géographie*.

4.2.5   On 'acceptability' and 'grammaticality', cf. Chomsky, *Aspects*, 10–15.

4.2.14   For the distinction between discovery procedures, decision procedures and evaluation procedures, cf. Chomsky, *Syntactic Structures*, 49–60.

4.3.3   Quotation from Chomsky, *Aspects*, 79–80.

Notes to chapter 5, pp. 170–208

5.1.2 Quotations from Harris: *Methods*, 14.

5.2 The sentence: cf. Robins, *General Linguistics*, 190–292; Hockett, *Course*, 199–208; Fries, *Structure*, 9–53.

5.2.1 Bloomfield's definition: from *Language*, 170.

5.2.5 'Ready-made' utterances: cf. Saussure, *Cours*, 172.

5.2.7 Phonological criteria: Hill, *Introduction*, 336 ff., attempted to define the sentence solely in phonological terms. Once we distinguish between utterances and sentences (and many linguists have failed to draw this distinction) there is no reason to expect that phonological criteria should be definitive. For a discussion of Hill's approach, cf. Haas, 'Linguistic structures'.

5.3 The morpheme: cf. Robins, *General Linguistics*, 201–13; Bazell, 'Problem'; *Linguistic Form*, 51–64; Nida, *Morphology*.

5.3.6 Morphological typology: cf. Bazell, *Typology*. Ratios of morphemes to words: cf. Greenberg, as cited in Mohrmann, *et al.*, *Trends* I, 119.

5.3.7 On Turkish: cf. Godel, *Grammaire*; Swift, *Grammar*.

5.3.8 On Latin: cf. Householder, 'Descriptive analysis'; P. H. Matthews, 'Inflexional component'; Hill, *Introduction*, 441–82.

5.3.9. Quotation from Sapir: *Language*, 124.

5.4 The word: cf. Robins, *General Linguistics*, 193–201; Rosetti, *Linguistica*, 11–46; Togeby, 'Mot'; Sapir, *Language*, 24–41; Bazell, 'Historical source'.

5.4.7 'Potential pause': cf. Hockett, *Course*, 166–9 (n.b. Hockett employs the term 'lexeme' in a different sense from the sense used here).

5.4.8 Semantic definitions of the word: cf. Ullmann, *Principles*, 50–4.

5.4.9 'Minimal free form': cf. Bloomfield, *Language*, 178; also Robins, *General Linguistics*, 194; Bazell, *Linguistic Form*, 67–8; Hockett, *Course*, 168–9.

5.5 'Rank': cf. Halliday, 'Categories'; Pike, *Integrated Theory*; Longacre, 'Fundamental insights'; Lamb, *Outline*; Postal, *Constituent Structure*; P. H. Matthews, 'Concept of rank'; Huddleston, 'Rank and depth'. See Addenda (3), p. 489.

Notes to chapter 6, pp. 209–269

6.1.2 Bloomfield: cf. *Language*, 161 ff.

6.1.3 Grammatical ambiguity of this kind: cf. Wells, 'Immediate constituents'; Hockett, 'Two models'; Chomsky, 'Syntactic Structures', 28.

6.2 Phrase-structure grammar: cf. Chomsky, 'Three models'; *Syntactic Structures*; Postal, *Constituent Structure*; Bach, *Introduction*; B. Hall, *Foundations*. More technical papers in Luce *et al.*, *Readings*, 75 ff., *Handbook*, 269 ff. Also Gross, 'Equivalence'.

6.3 Categorial grammar: cf. Bar-Hillel, *Language*, 99 ff.; also Lambek, 'Calculus'. Attention is drawn to 'dependency grammar', which has certain similarities: cf. Hays, 'Dependency theory'; Tesnière, *Éléments*.

6.4   Endocentric and exocentric: cf. Bloomfield, *Language*, 194 ff., 235 f.; Hockett, *Course*, 184 ff.; Harris, *Methods*, 275 f.; Robins, *General Linguistics*, 234 f.

6.5.4   Concord and government: cf. Hockett, *Course*, 214 ff.

6.5.5   Context-sensitivity: cf. Chomsky, *Syntactic Structures*, 28.

6.6   Transformational grammar: cf. Chomsky, *Syntactic Structures*; *Topics*; Harris, 'Co-occurrence'; 'Transformational theory'; Bach, *Introduction*; Shaumjan, *Strukturnaja*; Lamb, *Outline*; Koutsoudas, *Writing Grammars*.

6.6.1   Deep and surface structure: cf. Hockett, *Course*, 246 ff.; Chomsky, *Aspects*, 16; *Cartesian Linguistics*, 31 ff.

6.6.2   Transformational ambiguity: cf. Chomsky, *Syntactic Structures*, 88 ff.

6.6.3   'Diversification': cf. Lamb, *Outline*, 17.

6.6.4, 6.6.6   Quotations from Chomsky, *Syntactic Structures*, 42; *Aspects*, 98.

6.6.9   Recent developments: cf. Chomsky, *Aspects*; *Topics*; Katz and Postal, *Integrated Theory*; Fillmore, 'Embedding transformations'. For a critical review of these developments: cf. P. H. Matthews, Review of Chomsky's *Aspects*.

Notes to chapter 7, pp. 270–333

My main sources for this chapter on 'grammatical categories' and for chapter 8 on 'grammatical functions' have been works (listed in the bibliography) by Bally, Benveniste, Bloomfield, Boas, Brøndal, Entwistle, Gray, Hjelmslev, Jakobson, Jespersen, Kuryłowicz, Martinet, Meillet, Vendryès.

7.2   Deictic categories: cf. esp. Kuryłowicz, *Inflexional Categories*; also Fillmore, 'Deictic categories', 220 ff.

7.3.5   Swahili: cf. Ashton, *Grammar*.

7.3.8   'Classifiers': For Chinese, cf. Chao, *Primer*. For Vietnamese, cf. Emeneau, *Studies*; Honey, 'Word classes'; Thompson, *Grammar*. For Turkish and Uzbek, cf. Waterson, 'Numeratives'.

7.4   Case: The classic treatments are Hjelmslev, *Catégorie*, and Jakobson, 'Kasuslehre'. Two recent studies of particular interest are Fillmore, 'Modern theory'; 'Case for case'. For Turkish: cf. Swift, *Grammar*; Godel, *Grammaire*. For Finnish: cf. Sauvageot, *Esquisse*.

7.5.1   Tense: cf. Jespersen, *Philosophy*, 254 ff.

7.5.3   Quotation from Palmer: *English Verb*, 111. Quotation from Hockett, *Course*, 237.

7.5.5   Aspect: For Russian, cf. Ward, *Russian Language*, 227 ff. Quotation from Hockett, *Course*, 237.

7.5.7   The term 'mutative' I have taken from Strang, *English Structure*, 146.

7.5.8   The following recent publications (and many others) discuss the categories of tense, mood and aspect with reference to English: Joos, *English Verb*; Ota, *Tense and Aspect*; Palmer, *English Verb*; Ehrman, *Modals*; Crystal, 'Specification'; McIntosh, 'Predictive statements'.

7.6   Parts of speech: cf. Lyons, 'Notional theory'.

7.6.6   References to Jespersen, *Philosophy*; *Analytical Syntax*; to Hjelmslev, *Principes*. References to recent transformational work: cf. esp. Lakoff, *Irregularity*; *Deep and Surface*; Fillmore, 'Case for case'; Postal and Rosenbaum, *Sentence Formation*.
7.6.10   Quotation from Chomsky, *Aspects*, 118.

Notes to chapter 8, pp. 334–399

Main sources for this chapter: see covering note to chapter 7.
8.1.2   Quotations from Sapir: *Language*, 119; Hockett, *Course*, 201. For 'given' and 'new': cf. Halliday, 'Notes'.
8.1.3   For 'sortal' and 'characterizing' universals: cf. Strawson, *Individuals*.
8.1.7   Eskimo: cf. Hill, *Introduction*, 419–40.
8.1.8   Quotation from Chomsky: *Aspects*, 221. For a summary of earlier views: cf. Sandmann, *Subject*; Sechehaye, *Structure*.
8.2.2   Quotation from Robins: *General Linguistics*, 266.
8.2.3   Ergative: cf. Allen, 'Transitivity'; Hockett, *Course*, 235; Martinet, 'Ergatif'; W. K. Matthews, 'Ergative'; Uhlenbeck, 'Agens'; Vaillant, 'Ergatif'.
8.2.13   Quotation from Halliday: 'Notes', *JL*, 3 (1967), 47.
8.3.1   Reference to Svartvik: *Voice*, 2.
8.3.5   For alternative proposals: cf. Anderson, 'Ergative'; Fillmore, 'Case for case'; Halliday, 'Notes'.
8.4   Existential, locative and possessive: cf. Lyons, 'Note'; Graham, 'Being'; Kahn, 'Greek verb'; Benveniste, 'Être'; Bendix, *Componential Analysis*.
8.4.6   Chomsky's example: cf. *Aspects*, 21.

Notes to chapter 9, pp. 400–442

(Much of chapters 9 and 10 is a more systematic and more up-to-date version of what appears as Part 1 of Lyons, *Structural Semantics*.) There is a vast literature on semantics; and there is no book which even claims to cover the whole field. The most comprehensive treatment of previous work in semantics, from the purely linguistic point of view, is Ullmann, *Principles*; cf. also Kronasser, *Handbuch*; Nida, *Translating*. For philosophical semantics: cf. Bar-Hillel, 'Logical syntax'; Cohen, *Diversity*; Warnock, *English Philosophy*; Wells, 'Meaning'. A number of important articles are reprinted in Caton, *Philosophy*; Linsky, *Semantics*. For a criticism of twentieth-century philosophical semantics: cf. Katz, *Philosophy*. For psychological semantics: cf. Brown, *Words*; Bruner et al., *Thinking*; Carroll, *Language and Thought*; Miller, *Language*. For a popular account of philosophical semantics: cf. Salomon, *Semantics*. Also Brower, *Translation*; Austin, *Words*.
9.1.1   The term 'semantics'; cf. Bréal, *Essai*; Read, 'Account'.
9.2.6   Conceptualism and mentalism: Quotation from Haas, 'Defining', 74.

Bloomfield's approach: cf. *Language*, 139 ff.; Fries, 'Meaning'. In my view, the issue has been confused, rather than clarified, by Chomsky, *Aspects*, 193 f.; Katz, 'Mentalism'.

9.2.9 'Meaning' and 'use': cf. Wittgenstein, *Investigations*; Wells, 'Meaning and use'. Misunderstanding: it might be argued that the notion of 'understanding' is on a par with 'misunderstanding' with respect to my argument. Whether or not this is so, there is a considerable methodological advantage in assuming that misunderstanding is more directly testable. Most theories of semantics are vitiated by their assumption that 'understanding' is a matter of the transference of the same 'content' from one person's 'mind' to another.

9.3.6 Quotation from Firth: *Papers*, 203. 'Behaviourism' in semantics: my argument should not be taken as suggesting that the theory of semantics can be satisfactorily developed on the basis of stimulus–response theory (cf. my criticisms of behaviourist semantics in Lyons, *Structural Semantics*, 2 f.).

9.3.7 Malinowski's notion of 'phatic communion': cf. 'Problem', 309 ff.

9.4 Reference and sense: This distinction goes back to Frege, 'Sinn'; a somewhat similar distinction is found in Russell, 'Denoting'. My account is based very largely on Carnap, *Meaning*; and Quine, *Logical Point of View*; cf. also Bar-Hillel, 'Logical syntax'.

9.4.4 Semantic fields: cf. Guiraud, *Sémantique*, 68 ff.; Öhman, 'Theories'; Ullmann, *Principles*, 152 ff.

9.4.5 Reference to Conklin: 'Hanunóo'; cf. also Lenneberg and Roberts, *Experience*; Carroll, *Language and Thought*, 95, 107 ff.; André, *Étude*.

9.4.6 Quotation from Sapir: *Selected Writings*, 162. On linguistic 'determinism': cf. Carroll, *Language and Thought*, 106 ff.; Black, 'Relativity'.

9.5.1 Quotation from Fries: *Structure*, 66.

9.5.2 Reference to Martinet, *Éléments*, 117 (section 4.19); *Functional View*, 50 f.; to Halliday, 'Categories'; 'Lexis'; McIntosh and Halliday, *Patterns*, 5 f. (For criticism of Halliday's distinctions between 'grammar' and 'lexis' and between 'contextual' and 'formal' meaning: cf. Lyons, 'Firth's theory', 298 f.)

9.5.3 Reference to Chomsky: *Aspects*, 71.

9.5.4 Reference to Katz and Postal: *Integrated Theory*, 74 ff.

Notes to chapter 10, pp. 443–481

10.1.1 Definition of 'length', etc.: cf. Reichenbach, *Elements*, 210.

10.1.2 'Analytic' and 'synthetic': cf. Cohen, *Diversity*, 153 ff.; Staal, 'Analyticity'.

10.2.1 Quotation from *Roget*: 'How to use this book', p. vi.

10.2.2 Quantification of synonymy: For a more interesting proposal than most, cf. Sparck Jones, *Synonymy*; cf. also Needham, 'Automatic classification'.

10.2.3 Quotation from Ullmann; *Principles*, 108–9.

10.2.4 'Cognitive' *v.* 'emotive': cf. Ullmann, *Principles*, 96 ff.; Salomon, *Semantics*, 27 ff. For a full and critical account, cf. Henle, *Language*, 121–72

10.3.1 'Hyponymy': As far as I know, this term was first employed by Bazell, 'Logical syntax'—but in a somewhat different sense.

10.3.2 The definition of synonymy in terms of hyponymy is proposed in Staal, 'Analyticity', 78.

10.3.4 The Greek word *dēmiourgós* is one of many related words discussed in Lyons, *Structural Semantics*.

10.4.1 'Oppositeness': One of the best discussions is in Ogden, *Opposition*.

10.4.2 Reference to Moravcsik: 'Analytic'.

10.4.4 Quotation from Sapir: *Selected Writings*, 122. Discussion of such sentences as *A small elephant is a large animal*: cf. Weinreich, 'Explorations', 422 ff.; Katz, 'Recent issues', 184 ff.

10.5 Componential analysis: cf. Bendix, *Componential Analysis*; Bierwisch, 'Hierarchie'; Bolinger, 'Atomization'; Burling, 'Cognition'; Conklin, 'Lexicographical treatment'; Ebeling, *Linguistic Units*; Goodenough, 'Componential analysis'; Hallig and Wartburg, 'Begriffssystem'; Hjelmslev, *Prolegomena*; Katz, *Philosophy*; 'Recent issues'; Kiefer, 'Semantic relations'; Lamb, 'Sememic approach'; Lounsbury, 'Semantic analysis'; 'Structural Analysis'; Weinreich, 'Explorations'.

10.5.2 Quotation from Katz: 'Recent issues', 129. Quotations from Chomsky: *Aspects*, 160; 29.

10.5.3 Quotation from Katz: 'Recent issues', 129.

10.5.5 'Cognitive reality'; cf. Burling, 'Cognition'; Romney and D'Andrade, 'Cognitive aspects'; Wallace and Atkins, 'Kinship terms'.

ADDENDA

1 It was not correct to say that the values of the cardinal vowels are defined by the IPA (p. 104). The IPA established a set of divisions, or ranges, within the articulatory continua. Daniel Jones identified a number of fixed points within these ranges and took these points as 'cardinal'.

2 In the section on neutralization in phonology (3.3.5), it should be pointed out that there is a third possible way of describing the 'facts'. If we abandon the condition of biuniqueness (so that the same speech-sound is always associated with the same phoneme), we can say that /d/ *is realized as* [t] in word-final position and as [d] elsewhere and that /t/ *is realized as* [t] generally. Cf. Fudge, 'phonological primes'.

3 There is a greater difference between Halliday's 'ranks' and Lamb's 'strata' than I have suggested in 5.5.1. It is perhaps only with respect to the distinction of morphology and syntax that they are strictly comparable.

BIBLIOGRAPHY

This list includes all the works referred to in the notes. Periodicals are cited according to the conventions of the *Linguistic Bibliography* of the Permanent International Committee of Linguists, published annually (Utrecht and Antwerp: Spectrum). The following abbreviations are used:

AL	*Acta Linguistica*. Revue internationale de linguistique structurale. Copenhague.
ALH	*Acta Linguistica Academiae Scientiarum Hungaricae*. Budapest.
AmA	*American Anthropologist*. Menasha, Wisc.
ArchL	*Archivum Linguisticum*. Glasgow.
BPTJ	*Biuletyn Polskiego Towarzystva Językoznawczego/Bulletin de la Société polonaise de Linguistique*. Wroclaw and Kraków.
BSE	*Brno Studies in English*. Brno.
BSL	*Bulletin de la Société de Linguistique de Paris*. Paris.
BSOAS	*Bulletin of the School of Oriental and African Studies, University of London*. London.
CFS	*Cahiers Ferdinand de Saussure*, Genève.
CJL	*Canadian Journal of Linguistics / Revue Canadienne de Linguistique*. Toronto.
C & M	*Classica et Mediaevalia*. Revue danoise de philologie et d'histoire. Copenhague.
CPh	*Classical Philology*. Chicago.
CQ	*The Classical Quarterly*. London.
CR	*The Classical Review*. London.
FL	*Foundations of Language*. International journal of language and philosophy. Dordrecht, Holland.
GK	*Gengo Kenkyû*. (Journal of the Linguistic Society of Japan.) Tokyo.
Glotta	*Glotta*. Zeitschrift für griechische und lateinische Sprache. Göttingen.
IF	*Indogermanische Forschungen*. Zeitschrift für Indogermanistik und allgemeine Sprachwissenschaft. Berlin.
IL	*Indian Linguistics*. Journal of the Linguistic Society of India. Poona.
IJAL	*International Journal of American Linguistics*. Baltimore.
IRAL	*International Review of Applied Linguistics in Language Teaching / Internationale Zeitschrift für angewandte Linguistik in der Spracherziehung*. Heidelberg.
JAOS	*Journal of the American Oriental Society*. New Haven, Connecticut.
JL	*Journal of Linguistics*. The Journal of the Linguistics Association of Great Britain. London and New York.

KNf   *Kwartalnik Neofilologiczny.* Warszawa.
KZ   *Zeitschrift für vergleichende Sprachforschung auf dem Gebiete der indogermanischen Sprachen.* (Begründet von A. Kuhn.) Göttingen.
Lg.   *Language.* Journal of the Linguistic Society of America. Baltimore.
Lingua   *Lingua.* International Review of General Linguistics / Revue internationale de linguistique générale. Amsterdam.
MSLL   *Monograph Series on Languages and Linguistics, Georgetown University.* Washington, D.C.
NTS   *Norsk Tidsskrift for Sprogvidenskap.* Oslo.
PF   *Prace filologiczne.* Warszawa.
PMLA   *Publications of the Modern Language Association of America.* New York.
RLing   *Revue de Linguistique.* Bucarest.
SJA   *Southwestern Journal of Anthropology.* Albuquerque, N.M.
SL   *Studia Linguistica.* Revue de linguistique générale et comparée. Lund.
SS   *Slovo a Slovesnost.* Praha/Prague.
StGram   *Studia Grammatica.* Berlin.
TCLC   *Travaux du Cercle Linguistique de Copenhague.* Copenhague.
TCLP   *Travaux du Cercle Linguistique de Prague.* Prague.
TLP   *Travaux Linguistiques de Prague.* Prague.
UCPL   *University of California Publications in Linguistics.* Berkeley and Los Angeles.
VJa   *Voprosy Jazykoznanija.* Moskva.
Word   *Word.* Journal of the Linguistic Circle of New York. New York.

Abercrombie, David. *Elements of General Phonetics.* Edinburgh: Edinburgh University Press and Chicago: Aldine, 1966.
Abraham, S. and Kiefer, F. *A Theory of Structural Semantics.* (Janua Linguarum, 49.) The Hague: Mouton, 1965.
Ajdukiewicz, Kasimierz. 'Die syntaktische Konnexität.' *Studia Philosophica* (Warszawa), **1** (1935), 1–28.
Allen, W. Sidney. *Phonetics in Ancient India.* London, 1951.
    On the Linguistic Study of Languages. (Inaugural lecture.) Cambridge: Cambridge University Press, 1957. (Reprinted in Strevens, *Five Inaugural Lectures,* pp. 3–26.)
    'Structure and system in Abaza.' *TPhS* (1956), 127–76.
    'Transitivity and possession.' *Lg.* **40** (1964), 337–43.
Anderson, John M. 'Ergative and nominative in English.' *JL,* **4** (1968).
André, J. *Étude sur les Termes de Couleur dans la Langue Latine.* Paris, 1949.
Apostel, L., Mandelbrot, B. and Morf, A. *Logique, Langage et Théorie d'Information.* Paris: Presses Universitaires de France, 1957.
Arens, H. *Sprachwissenschaft.* Freiburg and München: Karl Alber, 1955.
Ashton, E. O. *Swahili Grammar.* London, 1944.
Austin, J. L. *How To Do Things With Words.* Cambridge, Mass.: Harvard University Press, 1962.

Bach, A. *Deutsche Mundartforschung: Ihre Wege, Ergebnisse und Aufgaben.* 2nd ed. Heidelberg: Carl Winter Universitätsverlag, 1950.

Bach, Emmon. *An Introduction to Transformational Grammars.* New York: Holt, Rinehart and Winston, 1964.

Bally, Charles. *Linguistique Générale et Linguistique Française.* Paris: Ernest Leroux, 1932.

Bar-Hillel, Y. *Language and Information.* Reading, Mass.: Addison-Wesley and Jerusalem: Jerusalem Academic Press, 1964.

'Logical syntax and semantics.' *Lg.* **30** (1954), 230–7. (Reprinted in *Language and Information.*)

Barth, P. *Die Stoa.* Stuttgart, 1946.

Barwick, K. *Remmius Palaemon und die Römische Ars Grammatica.* Leipzig, 1922.

Probleme der Stoischen Sprachlehre und Rhetorik. (Abhandl. der Sächs. Akad. Wiss. zu Leipzig, Phil.-hist. Klasse, **49**, 3.) Berlin: Akademie Verlag, 1957.

Bazell, Charles E. *Linguistic Form.* Istanbul: Istanbul Press, 1953.

Linguistic Typology. (Inaugural lecture.) London: School of Oriental and African Studies, 1958. (Reprinted in Strevens, *Five Inaugural Lectures,* pp. 29–49.)

'Logical and Linguistic syntax.' *Litera* (Istanbul), **2** (1955), 32–4.

'On the historical source of some structural units.' In *Miscelánea Homenaje I, A André Martinet.* La Laguna, 1957.

'Syntactic relations and linguistic typology.' *CFS,* **8** (1949), 5–20.

'On the neutralization of syntactic oppositions.' *TCLC,* **5** (1949), 77–86. (Reprinted in Hamp *et al., Readings.*)

'On the problem of the morpheme.' *ArchL,* **1** (1949), 1–15. (Reprinted in Hamp *et al., Readings.*)

'The correspondence fallacy in structural linguistics.' *Studies...English Department, Istanbul University,* **3** (1952), 1–41. (Reprinted in Hamp *et al., Readings.*)

'The sememe.' *Litera* (Istanbul), **1** (1954), 17–31. (Reprinted in Hamp *et al., Readings.*)

'Three misconceptions of grammaticalness.' *MSLL,* **17** (1964), 3–9.

Bazell, Charles E., Catford, J. C., Halliday, M. A. K. and Robins, R. H. (eds.). *In Memory of J. R. Firth.* London: Longmans, 1966.

Belvalkar, K. *Systems of Sanskrit Grammar.* Poona, 1915.

Bendix, E. H. *Componential Analysis of General Vocabulary: The Semantic Structure of a Set of Verbs in English, Hindi, and Japanese.* (Part 2 of *IJAL,* 32.) Bloomington: Indiana University and The Hague: Mouton, 1966.

Benveniste, É. *Problèmes de Linguistique Générale.* Paris: Gallimard, 1966.

'"Être" et "avoir" dans leurs fonctions linguistiques.' *BSL,* **55** (1960). (Reprinted in *Problèmes.*)

Bierwisch, M. 'Eine Hierarchie syntaktisch-semantischer Merkmale.' *StGram,* **5** (1965).

Black, Max. 'Linguistic relativity: The views of Benjamin Lee Whorf.' *Philosophical Review,* **68** (1959), 228–38.

Bloch, Bernard and Trager, G. *Outline of Linguistic Analysis*. Baltimore: Waverley Press, 1942.

Bloomfield, Leonard. *Language*. New York: Holt, Rinehart and Winston, 1933 and London: Allen and Unwin, 1935. (References are to the British edition.)
Review of Liebisch Konkordanz *Pāṇini-Candra* in *Lg.* 5 (1929), 267-76.

Boas, Franz. *Race, Language and Culture*. New York: Macmillan.

Bolinger, Dwight L. 'The atomization of meaning.' *Lg.* 41 (1965), 555-73.
'Linear modification.' *PMLA*, 67 (1952), 1117-44.

Bréal, Michel. *Essai de Sémantique*. Paris: Hachette, 1897. Translated as *Semantics: Studies in the Science of Meaning*. New York: Dover, 1964.

Bright, William (ed.). *Sociolinguistics*. (Proceedings of the U.C.L.A. Sociolinguistics Conference, 1964.) The Hague: Mouton, 1966.

Brøndal, Vigo. *Les Parties du Discours*. Copenhague: Munksgaard, 1948.

Brough, John. 'Theories of general linguistics in the Sanskrit grammarians.' *TPhS* (1951), 27-46.

Brower, Reuben, A. (ed.). *On Translation*. Cambridge, Mass.: Harvard University Press, 1959.

Brown, Roger W. 'Language and categories.' Appendix to Bruner *et al.*, *Thinking*.
Words and Things. Glencoe, Ill.: Free Press, 1958.

Bruner, Jerome S., Goodnow, J. J. and Austin, G. A. *A Study of Thinking*. New York: Wiley, 1956.

Burger, A. 'Sur le passage du système des temps et des aspects de l'indicatif du latin au roman commun.' *CFS*, 8 (1949), 19-36.

Burling, Robbins. 'Cognition and componential analysis.' *AmA*, 66 (1964), 20-8.

Bursill-Hall, Geoffrey, 'Medieval grammatical theories.' *CJL*, 9 (1963), 39-54.
'Notes on the semantics of linguistic description.' In Bazell *et al.*, *In Memory*, pp. 40-51.

Capell, A. *Studies in Sociolinguistics*. The Hague: Mouton, 1966.

Carnap, Rudolph. *Meaning and Necessity*. 2nd ed. Chicago: University of Chicago Press, 1956.

Carroll, John B. *Language and Thought*. Englewood Cliffs, N.J.: Prentice-Hall, 1964.

Catford, J. C. *A Linguistic Theory of Translation*. London: Oxford University Press, 1965.

Caton, Charles E. (ed.). *Philosophy and Ordinary Language*. Urbana, Ill.: University of Illinois Press, 1963.

Chao, Y. R. *Mandarin Primer*. Cambridge, Mass.: Harvard University Press, 1948.

Cherry, Colin. *On Human Communication*. Cambridge, Mass.: M.I.T. Press, 1957. (Reprinted New York: Science Editions, 1959.)

Chomsky, Noam. *Syntactic Structures*. The Hague: Mouton, 1957.
Current Issues in Linguistic Theory. The Hague: Mouton, 1965.
Aspects of the Theory of Syntax. Cambridge, Mass.: M.I.T. Press, 1965.

Chomsky, Noam, *Topics in the Theory of Generative Grammar*. The Hague: Mouton, 1966. (Also in Sebeok, *Current Trends*, vol. 3.)

Cartesian Linguistics. New York and London: Harper and Row, 1966.

'Three models for the description of a language.' 1956. Reprinted in Luce et al., *Readings*.

Chomsky, N. and Halle, M. 'Some controversial questions in phonological theory.' *JL*, **1** (1965), 97–138.

Cohen, L. Jonathan. *The Diversity of Meaning*. 1st ed. London: Methuen, 1962. (2nd ed., 1966.)

Collart, Jean. *Varron, Grammarien Latin*. Paris, 1954.

Conklin, H. C. 'Hanunóo color categories.' *SJA*, **11** (1955), 339–44. (Reprinted in Hymes, *Language in Culture*, pp. 189–92.)

'Lexicographical treatment of folk taxonomies.' In Householder and Saporta, *Problems*, pp. 119–41.

Copleston, Frederick. *A History of Philosophy*. Volumes 2 and 3. London: Burns Oates, 1950 and 1953.

Crystal, David. 'Specification and English tenses.' *JL*, **2** (1966), 1–34.

Curry, Haskell B. 'Some logical aspects of grammatical structure.' In Jakobson, *Structure of Language*, pp. 56–68.

Dauzat, A. *La Géographie Linguistique*. Revised ed. Paris: Flammarion, 1943.

Deese, James. *The Structure of Associations in Language and Thought*. Baltimore: Johns Hopkins Press, 1965.

Diderichsen, P. 'Morpheme categories in modern Danish.' *TCLC*, **5** (1949), 134–55.

Dihle, A. 'Analogie und Attizismus.' *Hermes*, **85** (1957), 170–205.

Dinneen, Francis P. *An Introduction to General Linguistics*. New York: Holt, Rinehart and Winston, 1967.

Diver, William. 'The system of agency in the Latin noun.' *Word*, **20** (1964), 178–96.

Dover, K. J. *Greek Word Order*. Cambridge: Cambridge University Press, 1960.

Ebeling, C. L. *Linguistic Units*. (Janua Linguarum, Series Minor, 12.) The Hague: Mouton, 1960.

Ehrman, Madeline. *The Meaning of the Modals in Present-Day American English*. The Hague: Mouton, 1966.

Elson, Benjamin and Pickett, V. B. *An Introduction to Morphology and Syntax*. Santa Ana, Calif.: Summer Institute of Linguistics, 1962.

Emeneau, M. B. *Studies in Vietnamese (Annamese) Grammar*. (UCPL, 8.) Berkeley and Los Angeles: University of California Press, 1951.

'India and linguistics.' *JAOS*, **75** (1955), 145–53.

Engler, Rudolph. *Cours de Linguistique Générale de F. de Saussure: Édition Critique*. Wiesbaden: Otto Harrassowitz. (Appearing in fascicules, from 1967.)

Entwistle, William J. *Aspects of Language*. London, 1953.

Fant, Gunnar. *Acoustic Theory of Speech Production*. The Hague: Mouton, 1960.

Fehling, Detlef. 'Varro und die grammatische Lehre von der Analogie und der Flexion.' *Glotta*, 35 (1956), 214–70 and 36 (1957), 48–100.

Fillmore, Charles J. 'The position of embedding transformations in a grammar.' *Word*, 19 (1963), 208–31.

'Deictic categories in the semantics of "come".' *FL*, 2 (1966), 219–27.

'Towards a modern theory of case.' (Project on Linguistic Analysis, Report No. 13.) Ohio State University, 1966.

'The case for case.' (To be published in the Proceedings of the 1967 Texas Conference on Language Universals, edited by Bach, E. and Harms, R. J.)

Firbas, Jan. 'Thoughts on the communicative function of the verb in English, German and Czech.' *BSE*, 1 (1959), 39–63.

Firth, J. R. *Papers in Linguistics, 1934–1951*. London: Oxford University Press, 1951.

'Ethnographic analysis and language.' In Raymond Firth (ed.), *Man and Culture*. London, 1957, pp. 93–118.

Fleisch, H. 'Esquisse d'une histoire de la grammaire arabe.' *Arabica* (Leiden) 4 (1957), 1–22.

Fodor, J. A. and Katz, J. J. (eds.). *The Structure of Language: Readings in the Philosophy of Language*. Englewood Cliffs, N.J.: Prentice-Hall, 1964.

Forbes, P. B. R. 'Greek pioneers in philology and grammar.' *CR*, 47 (1933), 105–12.

Fourquet, J. *Les Mutations Consonantiques du Germanique*. Paris, 1948.

Frake, C. O. 'The diagnosis of disease among the Subanun.' *AmA*, 63 (1961), 113–32. (Reprinted in Hymes, *Language in Culture*.)

Frege, G. 'Über Sinn und Bedeutung' (1892). Translated as 'On sense and reference' in Peter Geach and Max Black, *Translations from the Philosophical Writings of Gottlob Frege*. Oxford, 1952.

Fries, C. C. *The Structure of English: An Introduction to the Construction of English Sentences*. New York: Harcourt Brace, 1952 and London: Longmans, 1957. (References are to the British edition.)

'Meaning and linguistic analysis.' *Lg*. 30 (1954), 57–68.

Fudge, E. C. 'The nature of phonological primes.' *JL*, 3 (1967), 1–36.

Gabelentz, Georg von der. *Die Sprachwissenschaft*. Leipzig, 1891.

Geach, Peter T. *Reference and Generality: An Examination of Some Medieval and Modern Theories*. Ithaca, N.Y.: Cornell University Press, 1962.

Ghizzetti, Aldo (ed.). *Automatic Translation of Languages*. (Papers presented at a NATO Summer School, Venice, July 1962.) Oxford, London, New York, etc.: Pergamon Press, 1966.

Gilliéron, Jules and Roques, Mario. *Études de Géographie Linguistique*. Paris: Champion, 1912.

Gilson, Étienne. *History of Christian Philosophy in the Middle Ages*. London, 1955. (Translated from *La Philosophie au Moyen Âge*. Paris: Payot, 1922. Revised edition, 1962.)

Gleason, H. A. *An Introduction to Descriptive Linguistics*. 2nd revised edition. New York: Holt, Rinehart and Winston, 1961.

Godel, Robert. *Grammaire Turque*. Genève: Librairie de l'Université, 1945.
Les Sources Manuscrites du Cours de Linguistique Générale de Ferdinand de Saussure. Genève: Droz and Paris: Minard, 1957.
Goodenough, Ward H. 'Componential analysis and the study of meaning.' *Lg*. 32 (1956), 195–216.
Grabmann, M. *Mittelalterliches Geistesleben*, 3 vols. Munich, 1956.
Graham, A. C. '"Being" in Classical Chinese.' In Verhaar, *The Verb 'Be' and its Synonyms*. Part 1, pp. 1–39.
Gray, Louis H. *The Foundations of Language*. New York: Macmillan, 1939.
Greenberg, Joseph. *Essays in Linguistics*. Chicago: University of Chicago Press, 1957.
(ed.). *Universals in Language*. Cambridge, Mass.: M.I.T. Press, 1963.
Language Universals. (Janua Linguarum, Series Minor, 59.) The Hague: Mouton, 1966.
Greimas, A. J. *Sémantique Structurale*. Paris: Larousse, 1966.
Gross, Maurice. 'On the equivalence of models of language used in the fields of mechanical translation and information retrieval.' In Ghizzetti, *Automatic Translation*, pp. 123–37.
Guiraud, Pierre. *La Sémantique*. Paris: Presses Universitaires de France, 1955.
Haas, William. 'On defining linguistic units.' *TPhS* (1954), 54–84.
'Linguistic structures.' *Word*, 16 (1960), 251–76.
Hall, Barbara. *Mathematical Foundations for Language*. New York and London: Harper and Row, forthcoming.
Hall, Robert A. *Introductory Linguistics*. Philadelphia: Chilton, 1964.
Idealism in Romance Linguistics. Ithaca, N.Y.: Cornell University Press, 1964.
Halle, M. 'Phonology in a generative grammar.' *Word*, 18 (1962), 54–72. (Reprinted in Fodor and Katz, *Structure of Language*, pp. 324–33.)
Halliday, M. A. K. 'Categories of the theory of grammar.' *Word*, 17, 241–92.
'Syntax and the consumer.' *MSLL*, 17 (1964), 11–24.
'Lexis as a linguistic level.' In Bazell et al., *In Memory*, pp. 148–62.
'Notes on transitivity and theme in English.' *JL*, 3 (1967) and 4 (1968). (To be published in three parts.)
Halliday, M. A. K., McIntosh, A. and Strevens, P. D. *The Linguistic Sciences and Language Teaching*. London: Longmans, 1964.
Hallig, R. and Wartburg, W. von. *Begriffssystem als Grundlage für die Lexicographie*. (Abhandlungen der deutschen Akademie der Wissenschaften zu Berlin, 4.) Berlin, 1952.
Hamp, Eric P., Householder, F. W. and Austerlitz, R. *Readings in Linguistics II*. Chicago and London: Chicago University Press, 1966.
Harris, Zellig S. *Methods in Structural Linguistics*. Chicago: University of Chicago Press, 1951. (Reprinted as *Structural Linguistics*, 1961.)
'Discourse analysis.' *Lg*. 28 (1952), 18–23 and 474–94.
'Distributional structure.' *Word*, 10 (1954), 146–94.
'Co-occurrence and transformation in linguistic structure.' *Lg*. 33 (1957), 283–340.

String Analysis of Sentence Structure. The Hague: Mouton, 1962.

'Transformational theory.' *Lg.* **41** (1965), 363–401.

Haugen, Einar. 'Linguistics and language-planning.' In Bright, *Sociolinguistics.*

Hays, David G. *Introduction to Computational Linguistics.* (Mathematical Linguistics and Automatic Language Analysis, 2.) New York: American Elsevier, 1967.

'Dependency theory: A formalism and some observations.' *Lg.* **40** (1964), 511–25.

Heidegger, M. *Die Kategorienlehre und Bedeutungslehre des Duns Scotus.* Tübingen: Mohr, 1916.

Henle, Paul (ed.). *Language, Thought and Culture.* Ann Arbor, Mich.: University of Michigan Press, 1958.

Hill, Archibald A. *Introduction to Linguistic Structures: From Sound to Sentence in English.* New York: Harcourt, Brace and World, 1958.

Hjelmslev, Louis. *Principes de Grammaire Générale.* (Kng. Danske Videnskabernes Selskab., Hist.-Filolog. Medd., 16, i.) Copenhague: Høst & Søn, 1928.

La Catégorie des Cas. Étude de Grammaire Générale. (Acta Jutlandica Aarsskrift for Aarhus Universitet, 9.) Aarhus: Universitets-forlaget, 1935.

Essais Linguistiques. (*TCLC,* **12.**) Copenhague: Nordisk Sprog- og Kulturforlag, 1959.

Prolegomena to a Theory of Language. (Translated from the Danish, 1943, by Francis J. Whitfield.) Bloomington, Ind.: Indiana University, 1953.

Hockett, C. F. *A Course in Modern Linguistics.* New York: Macmillan, 1958.

A Manual of Phonology. Bloomington, Ind.: Indiana University Press, 1955.

'The quantification of functional load: a linguistic problem.' (Memorandum RM-5168-PR.) Santa Monica, Calif.: RAND Corporation, 1966.

'Two models of grammatical description.' *Word,* **10** (1954), 210–33. (Reprinted in Joos, *Readings.*)

'Linguistic elements and their relations.' *Lg.* **37** (1961), 29–53.

'Grammar for the hearer.' In Jakobson, *Structure of Language,* pp. 220–36.

Hoenigswald, Henry M. *Language Change and Linguistic Reconstruction.* Chicago: University of Chicago Press, 1960.

'A proposal for the study of folk linguistics.' In Bright, *Sociolinguistics.*

Hoijer, Harry. *Language in Culture.* Chicago: University of Chicago Press, 1954.

Honey, P. J. 'Word classes in Vietnamese.' *BSOAS,* **18** (1956), 534–44.

Householder, F. W. 'On linguistic terms.' In Saporta, *Psycholinguistics,* pp. 15–25.

'On some recent claims in phonological theory.' *JL,* **1** (1965), 13–34.

'On the uniqueness of semantic mapping.' *Word,* **18** (1962), 173–85.

'Descriptive analysis of Latin declension.' *Word,* **3** (1947), 48–58.

Householder, F. W. and Saporta, S. (eds.). *Problems in Lexicography.* (Publications of Indiana Research Center in Anthropology, Folklore and Linguistics, 21.) Baltimore, 1962.

498 BIBLIOGRAPHY

Huddleston, R. D. 'Rank and depth.' *Lg.* **41** (1965), 586.
Hughes, John P. *The Science of Language: An Introduction to Linguistics.*
New York: Random House, 1962.
Humboldt, Wilhelm von. *Über die Verschiedenheit des Menschlichen Sprach-baues.* Berlin, 1836. Republished, Darmstadt: Claasen and Roether, 1949.
Hymes, Dell (ed.). *Language in Culture and Society: A Reader in Linguistics and Anthropology.* New York: Harper and Row, 1964.
Jakobson, Roman. *Selected Writings I: Phonological Studies.* The Hague: Mouton, 1962.
'Beitrag zur allgemeinen Kasuslehre.' *TCLP*, **6** (1936), 240–88. (Reprinted in Hamp *et al., Readings.*)
'Boas's view of grammatical meaning.' *AmA*, **61** (1959), 139–45.
'Linguistics and communication theory.' In Jakobson, *Structure of Language*, pp. 245–52.
'On linguistic aspects of translation.' In Brower, *Translation*, pp. 232–9.
'Implications of language universals for linguistics.' In Greenberg, *Universals.*
(ed.). *On the Structure of Language and its Mathematical Aspects.* (Proceedings of 12th Symposium on Applied Mathematics.) Providence, R.I.: American Mathematical Society, 1961.
Jakobson, R. and Halle, M. *Fundamentals of Language.* The Hague: Mouton, 1956.
Jespersen, Otto. *The Philosophy of Grammar.* London: Allen and Unwin, 1929.
Language, Its Nature, Development, and Origin. London: Allen and Unwin, 1922.
Analytic Syntax. Copenhagen: Munksgaard, 1937.
Jones, Daniel, *An Outline of English Phonetics.* 8th ed. Cambridge: Heffer, 1956. (First edition 1918.)
The Phoneme: Its Nature and Use. Cambridge: Heffer, 1950.
Joos, Martin (ed.). *Readings in Linguistics.* Washington, D.C.: American Council of Learned Societies, 1957. (Republished as *Readings in Linguistics I.* Chicago and London: Chicago University Press, 1966.)
The English Verb. Madison and Milwaukee: University of Wisconsin Press, 1964.
Kachru, Yamuna. *Introduction to Hindi Syntax.* Urbana, Ill.: University of Illinois, 1966.
Kahn, C. H. 'The Greek verb "to be" and the concept of being.' *FL*, **2** (1966), 245–65.
Katz, J. J. *The Philosophy of Language.* New York: Harper and Row, 1966.
'Recent issues in semantic theory.' *FL*, **3** (1967), 124–94.
'Mentalism and linguistics.' *Lg.* **40** (1964), 124–37.
Katz, J. J. and Fodor, J. A. 'The structure of a semantic theory.' *Lg.* **39** (1963), 170–210. (Reprinted in Fodor and Katz, *Structure of Language.*)
Katz, J. J. and Postal, P. M. *An Integrated Theory of Linguistic Descriptions.*
(Research Monographs, 26.) Cambridge, Mass.: M.I.T. Press, 1964.

Kiefer, F. 'Some semantic relations in natural languages.' *FL*, 2 (1966), 228–40.

Kollar, H. 'Die Anfänge der griechischen Grammatik.' *Glotta*, 37 (1958), 5–40.

Koutsoudas, Andreas. *Writing Transformational Grammars.* New York: McGraw-Hill, 1967.

Kronasser, H. *Handbuch der Semasiologie.* Heidelberg: Carl Winter Universitätsverlag, 1952.

Kukenheim, L. *Esquisse Historique de la Linguistique Française et de ses Rapports avec la Linguistique Générale.* Leiden, 1962.

Kuroda, S.-Y. 'Causative forms in Japanese.' *FL*, 1 (1965), 30–50.

Kuryłowicz, J. *Esquisses Linguistiques.* Wroclaw–Kraków: Polska Akademia Nauk, Komitet Językoznawczy, 1960.

The Inflectional Categories of Indo-European. Heidelberg: Carl Winter Universitätsverlag, 1964.

'Dérivation lexicale et dérivation syntaxique.' *BSL*, 37 (1936), 79–92. (Reprinted in *Esquisses*, pp. 41–50; also in Hamp *et al.*, *Readings II*, pp. 42–50.)

'Ergativnost' i stadial'nost' v jazyke.' *Izv. Akad. Nauk SSSR*, 5 (1946), 387–93. (Reprinted in *Esquisses*, pp. 95–103.)

'La notion de l'isomorphisme.' *TCLC*, 5 (1949), 48–60. (Reprinted in *Esquisses*, pp. 16–26.)

'Les temps composés du roman.' *PF*, 15 (1931), 448–53. (Reprinted in *Esquisses*.)

Ladefoged, Peter. *Elements of Acoustic Phonetics.* Chicago: University of Chicago Press and Edinburgh: University of Edinburgh Press, 1962.

Lakoff, G. *On the Nature of Syntactic Irregularity.* (Report No. NSF-16, Mathematical Linguistics and Automatic Translation.) Cambridge: Mass.: Harvard University Computation Laboratory, 1965.

Deep and Surface Grammar. Cambridge, Mass.: M.I.T. Press, forthcoming.

Lamb, Sydney M. *Outline of Stratificational Grammar.* Washington, D.C.: Georgetown University Press, 1966.

'On alternation, transformation, realization and stratification.' *MSFOu*, 17 (1964), 105–22.

'The sememic approach to structural semantics. In Romney and D'Andrade, *Transcultural Studies*, pp. 57–78. (Special publication of *AmA*, 66 (1964), 57–78.)

Lambek, J. 'On the calculus of syntactic types.' In Jakobson, *Structure of Language*, pp. 166–78.

Lees, Robert B. *The Grammar of English Nominalizations.* Bloomington, Ind.: Research Center in Anthropology, Folklore and Linguistics, 1960.

The Phonology of Modern Standard Turkish. (Indiana University Publications: Uralic and Altaic Series, 6.) Bloomington, Ind., 1964.

Leisi, Ernst. *Der Wortinhalt: Seine Struktur im Deutschen und Englischen.* Heidelberg, 1953.

Lenneberg, Eric H. and Roberts, John M. *The Language of Experience: A Study in Methodology*. (Indiana University Publications in Anthropology and Linguistics.) (Memoir 13 of *IJAL*.) Bloomington, Ind., 1956.

Lepschy, Giulio C. *La Linguistica Strutturale*. Torino: Einaudi, 1966.

Leroy, Maurice. *Les Grands Courants de la Linguistique Moderne*. Bruxelles: Presses Universitaires de Bruxelles and Paris: Presses Universitaires de France, 1964.

Linsky, Leonard (ed.). *Semantics and the Philosophy of Language*. Urbana, Ill.: University of Illinois Press, 1952.

Longacre, R. E. 'Some fundamental insights of tagmemics.' *Lg.* **41** (1965), 65–76.

Lounsbury, Floyd G. 'A semantic analysis of the Pawnee kinship usage.' *Lg.* **32** (1956), 158–94.

'The structural analysis of kinship semantics.' In *Proceedings of the Ninth International Congress of Linguists* (edited by H. G. Lunt), pp. 1073–93. The Hague: Mouton, 1964.

Luce, R. D., Bush, R. R. and Galanter, E. (eds.). *Handbook of Mathematical Psychology*. Volume 2, chapters 9–14. New York and London: Wiley, 1963.

(eds.). *Readings in Mathematical Psychology*. Volume 2. New York and London: Wiley, 1965.

Lyons, John. *Structural Semantics*. (Publications of the Philological Society, 20.) Oxford: Blackwell, 1963.

'Firth's theory of "meaning".' In Bazell *et al.*, *In Memory*, pp. 288–302.

'Phonemic and non-phonemic phonology.' *IJAL*, **28** (1962), 127–33.

'Towards a "notional" theory of the "parts of speech".' *JL*, **2** (1966), 209–36.

'A note on possessive, existential and locative sentences.' *FL*, **4** (1967).

McIntosh, Angus. *An Introduction to a Survey of Scottish Dialects*. Edinburgh: Nelson, 1952.

'Patterns and ranges.' *Lg.* **37** (1961) 325–37. (Reprinted in McIntosh and Halliday, *Patterns of Language*, pp. 183–99.)

'Predictive statements.' In Bazell *et al.*, *In Memory*, pp. 303–20.

McIntosh, Angus and Halliday, M. A. K. *Patterns of Language: Papers in General, Descriptive and Applied Linguistics*. London: Longmans, 1966.

Magnusson, R. *Studies in the Theory of the Parts of Speech*. (Lund Studies in English, 24.) Lund: Gleerup and Copenhagen: Munksgaard, 1954.

Malinowski, B. 'The problem of meaning in primitive languages.' Supplement 1 to Ogden and Richards, *Meaning of Meaning*, pp. 296–346.

Malmberg, Bertil. *Structural Linguistics and Human Communication*. Heidelberg: Springer, 1963.

Les Nouvelles Tendances de la Linguistique. Paris: Presses Universitaires de France, 1966. (Translated from the Swedish, 1962.)

Mandelbrot, B. 'On the theory of word-frequencies and on related Markovian models of discourse.' In Jakobson, *Structure of Language*, pp. 190–219.

Martinet, André. *Éléments de Linguistique Générale.* Paris: Armand Colin, 1960.
(English translation, *Elements of General Linguistics.* London: Faber, 1964.)
Économie des Changements Phonétiques. Berne: A. Francke, 1955.
A Functional View of Language. Oxford: Clarendon Press, 1962.
La Linguistique Synchronique: Études et Recherches. Paris: Presses Universitaires de France, 1965.
'Le genre féminin en indo-européen: examen fonctionnel du problème.'
BSL, **52** (1956), 83–95.
'La construction ergative et les structures élémentaires de l'énoncé.'
Journal de Psychologie Normale et Pathologique (1958), pp. 377–92.
(Reprinted in *Linguistique Synchronique,* pp. 206–22.)
Matoré, G. *La Méthode en Lexicologie. Domaine Français.* Paris: Didier, 1953.
Matthews, G. H. *Hidatsa Syntax.* (Papers in Formal Linguistics, 3.) The Hague: Mouton, 1965.
Matthews, P. H. 'Transformational grammar.' *ArchL,* **13** (1961), 196–209.
'Problems of selection in transformational grammar.' *JL,* **1** (1965), 35–47.
'The inflexional component of a word-and-paradigm grammar.' *JL,* **1** (1965), 139–71.
'The concept of rank.' *JL,* **2** (1966), 101–10.
'Latin.' *Lingua,* **17** (1967), 163–81.
Review of Chomsky, *Aspects,* in *JL,* **3** (1967), 119–52.
Matthews, W. K. 'The ergative construction in modern Indo-Aryan.'
Lingua, **3** (1953), 391–406.
Meillet, Antoine. *Linguistique Historique et Linguistique Générale.* 2 vols.
Paris: 1926 and 1938.
Miller, George A. *Language and Communication.* New York: McGraw-Hill, 1951.
Misra, Vidya Niwas. *The Descriptive Techniques of Pāṇini.* (Janua Linguarum, Series Practica, 18.) The Hague: Mouton, 1967.
Mohrmann, Ch., Sommerfelt, A. and Whatmough, J. *Trends in European and American Linguistics 1930–1960.* Utrecht: Spectrum, 1961.
Mohrmann, Ch., Norman, F. and Sommerfelt, A. *Trends in Modern Linguistics.* Utrecht: Spectrum, 1963.
Moravcsik, J. M. E. 'The analytic and the nonempirical.' *Journal of Philosophy,* **62** (1965), 415–29.
Morris, Charles W. *Signs, Language, and Behavior.* Englewood Cliffs, N.J.: Prentice-Hall, 1955.
Signification and Significance. Cambridge, Mass.: M.I.T. Press, 1964.
Mounin, Georges. *Histoire de la Linguistique des Origines au XXe Siècle.* Paris: Presses Universitaires de France, 1967.
Needham, R. M. 'Automatic classification in linguistics.' *The Statistician,* **17** (1967), 45–53.
Nida, Eugene A. *Morphology: A Descriptive Analysis of Words.* 2nd ed. Ann Arbor, Mich.: University of Michigan Press, 1949.
A Synopsis of English Syntax. Norman, Okla.: Summer Institute of Linguistics, 1960. (Republished, The Hague: Mouton, 1966.)
Towards a Science of Translating. Leiden: Brill, 1964.

Ogden, C. K. *Opposition*. London: Kegan Paul, 1932.

Ogden, C. K. and Richards, I. A. *The Meaning of Meaning*. 8th edition. London: Routledge and Kegan Paul, 1946. (First edition, 1923.)

Öhman, Suzanne. *Wortinhalt und Weltbild*. Stockholm, 1951. 'Theories of the "linguistic field".' *Word*, 9 (1953), 123–34.

Olsson, Yngve. *On the Syntax of the English Verb: With Special Reference to 'Have a Look' and Similar Complex Structures*. (Gothenburg Studies in English, 12.) Gothenburg, Stockholm and Uppsala: Almqvist and Wiksell, 1961.

Orr, John. *Words and Sounds in English and French*. Oxford, 1953.

Ota, Akira, *Tense and Aspect of Present-Day American English*. Tokyo: Kenkyusha, 1963.

Palmer, F. R. 'Linguistic hierarchy.' *Lingua*, 7 (1958), 225–41. '"Sequence" and "order".' *MSLL*, 17 (1964), 123–30. *A Linguistic Study of the English Verb*. London: Longmans, 1965. (ed.). ? *Prosodic Analysis*. London: Oxford University Press, forthcoming.

Pedersen, Holger. *Linguistic Science in the Nineteenth Century*, trans. J. W. Spargo. Cambridge, Mass.: Harvard University Press, 1931. (Republished as *The Discovery of Language*. Bloomington, Ind.: Indiana University Press, 1959.)

Pike, Kenneth L. *Language in Relation to a Unified Theory of Human Behavior*. (Janua Linguarum, Series Maior, 24.) 2nd revised edition. The Hague: Mouton, 1967. *Phonetics*. Ann Arbor, Mich.: University of Michigan Press, 1943.

Pohlenz, M. *Die Begründung der Abendländischen Sprachlehre durch die Stoa*. Göttingen: Vandenhoeck und Ruprecht, 1939.

Porzig, W. *Das Wunder der Sprache*. Berne, 1950.

Postal, Paul M. *Constituent Structure: A Study of Contemporary Models of Syntactic Descriptions*. Bloomington, Ind.: Indiana University Publications in Folklore and Linguistics, 1964.

Postal, P. M. and Rosenbaum, P. S. *English Sentence Formation: Recent Advances in Transformational Analysis*. Reading, Mass.: Addison-Wesley, forthcoming.

Pulgram, E. 'Graphic and phonic systems: figurae and signs.' *Word*, 21 (1965), 208–24.

Quine, Willard V. *From a Logical Point of View*. Cambridge, Mass.: Harvard University Press, 1953. *Word and Object*. Cambridge, Mass.: M.I.T. Press, 1960.

Quirk, Randolph. *The Use of English*. (With supplements by A. C. Gimson and J. Warburg.) London: Longmans, 1962.

Read, A. W. 'An account of the word "semantics".' *Word*, 4 (1948), 78–97.

Reichenbach, Hans. *Elements of Symbolic Logic*. London and New York: Macmillan, 1947.

Roberts, A. Hood. *A Statistical Linguistic Analysis of American English*. (Janua Linguarum, Series Practica, 8.) The Hague: Mouton, 1965.

Robins, R. H. *General Linguistics: An Introductory Survey*. London: Longmans, 1964.

A Short History of Linguistics. London: Longmans, 1967.
'The development of the word class system of the European grammatical tradition.' *FL*, **2** (1966), 3–19.

Roget, Peter M. *Roget's Thesaurus.* Abridged edition, with additions, by J. L. Roget and S. R. Roget. Harmondsworth, Middlesex: Penguin Books, 1953. (Original edition, 1852.)

Romney, A. K. and D'Andrade, R. G. 'Cognitive aspects of English kin terms.' *AmA*, **66** (1964), 146–70.

Roos, H. 'Sprachdenken im Mittelalter.' *C & M*, **9** (1949).
Die Modi Significandi des Martinus von Dacia. Münster, 1952.

Rosengren, Inger. *Semantische Strukturen: Eine Quantitative Distributions-analyse einiger Mittelhochdeutscher Adjektive.* (Lunder Germanistische Forschungen, 38.) Lund: Gleerup und Copenhagen: Munksgaard, 1966.

Rosetti, A. *Linguistica.* (Janua Linguarum, Series Maior, 16.) The Hague: Mouton, 1965.

Russell, Bertrand. *An Inquiry into Meaning and Truth.* London, 1940.
'On denoting.' *Mind*, **14** (1905), 479–93.

Salomon, Louis B. *Semantics and Common Sense.* London and New York: Holt, Rinehart and Winston, 1964.

Sandmann, M. *Subject and Predicate.* (Edinburgh University Publications, Language and Literature, 5.) Edinburgh, 1954.

Sandys, J. E. *History of Classical Scholarship.* Cambridge, 1903.

Sapir, Edward. *Language: An Introduction to the Study of Speech.* New York: Harcourt, Brace and World, 1921.
Selected Writings in Language, Culture and Personality. (Edited by D. G. Mandelbaum.) Berkeley, Calif.: University of California Press, 1949.

Saporta, S. (ed.). *Psycholinguistics: A Book of Readings.* New York: Holt, Rinehart and Winston, 1961.

Saussure, F. de. *Cours de Linguistique Générale.* 5th edition. Paris: Payot, 1955. (First edition 1916.) (English translation, by Wade Baskin, *Course in General Linguistics.* New York: Philosophical Library, 1959.)

Sauvageot, Aurélien. *Esquisse de la Langue Finnoise.* Paris: Klincksieck, 1949.

Schuchardt, H. *Hugo Schuchardt Brevier,* 2nd ed. (Edited by L. Spitzer.) Halle a. S., 1928.

Sebeok, Thomas. *Current Trends in Linguistics. Volume 3: Theoretical Foundations.* The Hague: Mouton, 1966.

Sechehaye, Albert. *Essai sur la Structure Logique de la Phrase.* Paris: Honoré Champion, 1926.

Shaumjan, S. K. *Strukturnaja Lingvistika.* (Akademija Nauk S.S.S.R., Institut Russkogo Jazyka.) Moskva: Izdatel'stvo 'Nauka', 1965. (An English edition is in preparation.)

Spang-Hanssen, H. 'Glossematics.' In Mohrmann, Sommerfelt and Whatmough, *Trends.*

Sparck Jones, K. *Synonymy and Semantic Classification.* Cambridge: Cambridge Language Research Unit, 1964.

Strang, Barbara M. H. *Modern English Structure.* London: Edward Arnold and New York: St Martin's Press, 1962.

Strawson, P. F. *Individuals: An Essay in Descriptive Metaphysics.* London: Methuen, 1959.

Strevens, P. D. (ed.). *Five Inaugural Lectures.* Oxford: Oxford University Press, 1966.

Sturtevant, Edgar H. *An Introduction to Linguistic Science.* New Haven, Conn.: Yale University Press, 1949.
Linguistic Change. Chicago: University of Chicago Press, 1961.

Sturtevant, William C. 'Studies in ethnoscience.' *AmA*, **66** (1964), 99–124.

Svartvik, Jan. *On Voice in the English Verb.* (Janua Linguarum, Series Practica, 63.) The Hague: Mouton, 1966.

Swift, Lloyd B. *A Reference Grammar of Modern Turkish.* (Indiana University Publications, Uralic and Altaic Series, 19.) Bloomington: Indiana University and The Hague: Mouton, 1963.

Teeter, Karl V. 'Descriptive linguistics in America: Triviality vs. Irrelevance.' *Word*, **20** (1964), 197–206.

Tesnière, L. *Éléments de Syntaxe Structurale.* Paris: Klincksieck, 1959.

Thompson, Laurence C. *A Vietnamese Grammar.* Seattle, Washington: University of Washington Press, 1965.

Thorndike, E. L. and Lorge, I. *The Teacher's Word Book of 30,000 Words.* New York: Columbia University Press, 1944.

Togeby, Knud. 'Qu'est-ce qu'un mot.' *TCLC*, **5** (1949), 99–111.

Trier, Jost. *Der Deutsche Wortschatz im Sinnbezirk des Verstandes.* Heidelberg: Carl Winter, 1931.

Trubetzkoy, N. S. *Grundzüge der Phonologie.* Prague: Cercle Linguistique de Prague, 1939. (French edition, Principes de Phonologie, trans. Jean Cantineau. Paris: Klincksieck, 1949.)

Uhlenbeck, C. C. 'Agens und Patiens im Kasussystem der indogermanischen Sprachen.' *IF*, **12** (1901), 170–2.

Uldall, H. J. *Outline of Glossematics* (= *TCLC*, **10**). Copenhagen, 1957.
'Speech and writing.' *AL*, **4** (1944), 11–16. (Reprinted in Hamp *et al.*, *Readings*, pp. 147–51.)

Ullmann, Stephen. *The Principles of Semantics.* 2nd ed. Glasgow: Jackson and Oxford: Blackwell, 1957.
Semantics: An Introduction to the Science of Meaning. Oxford: Blackwell, 1962.

Vachek, Josef. *A Prague School Reader in Linguistics: Studies in the History and Theory of Linguistics.* Bloomington, Ind.: Indiana University Press, 1964.
'Some remarks on writing and phonetic transcription.' *AL*, **5** (1945), 88–93. (Reprinted in Hamp *et al.*, *Readings*, pp. 152–7.)

Vaillant, André. 'L'ergatif indo-européen.' *BSL*, **37** (1936), 93–108.

Vendryès, Joseph. *Le Langage.* Paris: Albin Michel, 1923. English translation, *Language.* London: Kegan Paul and New York: Knopf, 1931.

Verhaar, John W. M. (ed.). *The Verb 'Be' and its Synonyms.* (Foundations of Language, Supplementary Series.) Volume 1. Dordrecht: D. Reidel, 1967.

Vogt, Hans. *Esquisse d'une Grammaire de Géorgien Moderne.* In *NTS,* 9 (1938), 5–114 and 10 (1939), 5–188.

Wackernagel, J. *Vorlesungen über Syntax.* Basel: Emil Birkhäuser, 1920.

Wackernagel, J. and Debrunner, A. *Altindische Grammatik.* (With an Introduction by Renou.) 1957.

Wallace, F. C. and Atkins, J. 'The meaning of kinship terms.' *AmA,* 62 (1960), 58–80.

Ward, Dennis. *The Russian Language Today.* London: Hutchinson, 1965.

Warnock, G. J. *English Philosophy Since 1900.* Oxford, 1958. (Home University Library of Modern Knowledge, no. 234.) Oxford, 1958.

Wartburg, Walther von. *Einführung in Problematik und Methodik der Sprachwissenschaft.* 2nd ed. Tübingen: Max Niemeyer, 1962. French translation, *Problèmes et Méthodes de la Linguistique.* Paris: Presses Universitaires, 1963.

Évolution et Structure de la Langue Française. 5th ed. Berne: Francke, 1958.

Waterson, N. 'Some aspects of the phonology of the nominal forms of the Turkish word.' *BSOAS,* 18 (1956), 578–91. (Reprinted in Palmer, *Prosodic Analysis.*)

'Numeratives in Uzbek.' In Bazell et al., *In Memory,* pp. 454–74.

Weinreich, U. 'Explorations in semantic theory.' In Sebeok, *Current Trends,* vol. 3.

Wells, Rulon S. 'Immediate constituents.' *Lg.* 23 (1947), 81–117. (Reprinted in Joos, *Readings,* pp. 186–207.)

'Meaning and use.' *Word,* 10 (1954), 235–50.

Whorf, Benjamin L. 'Grammatical categories.' *Lg.* 21 (1945), 1–11. (Reprinted in *Language, Thought and Reality,* pp. 87–101.)

Language, Thought and Reality: Selected Papers. (Edited by John B. Carroll.) New York: Wiley, 1956.

Wittgenstein, L. *Philosophical Investigations.* Oxford: Blackwell and New York: Macmillan, 1953.

Ziff, Paul. *Semantic Analysis.* Ithaca, N.Y.: Cornell University Press, 1960.

Zipf, G. K. *Human Behavior and the Principle of Least Effort.* Cambridge, Mass.: Addison-Wesley, 1949.

ADDENDA

Apresjan, Ju. D. *Eksperimental'noje Issledovanije Semantiki Russkogo Glagola.* Moskva: Izdatel'stvo 'Nauka', 1967.

Chomsky, N. 'Remarks on nominalization.' To appear in Jacobs and Rosenbaum (eds.), *Readings in English Transformational Grammar.*

Householder, F. W. Forthcoming book. Englewood-Cliffs, N. J.: Prentice-Hall.

Ruwet, N. *Introduction à la Grammaire Générative.* (Recherches en Sciences Humaines, 22.) Paris: Plon, 1967.

TABLE OF SYMBOLS
AND NOTATIONAL CONVENTIONS

*   asterisk: (1) 'reconstructed form', 31
      (2) ungrammatical, or unacceptable, expression, 142

( )   parentheses: semantic component ('marker'), 471

{ }   brace brackets: (1) morpheme, 184
      (2) extensional definition of a class, 77

[ ]   square brackets: (1) phonetic transcription, 60, 101
      (2) grammatical feature, 166

/ /   obliques: (1) expression-elements, 60
      (2) phonemic transcription, 101

italics: orthographic representation (or transcription), 60

CAPITALS: lexeme, 197

\+   plus-sign: (1) concatenation, 91, 116
      (2) positive value of binary variable, 123

−   minus-sign: negative value of binary variable, 123

<   'is less than', 192

>   'is greater than', 92

=   equals-sign: (1) 'is equal (equivalent) to', 77
      (2) identity of reference, 389

≠   'is not equal (equivalent) to', 77

∈   epsilon: class-membership, 161, 389

→   arrow: (1) 'develops diachronically into', 31
      (2) 'is to be rewritten as', 162

⊂   inclusion-sign: 'is included in', 389

⊃   inclusion-sign: 'includes', used for 'implies', 445

≡   equivalence-sign: bilateral implication, 450

INDEX OF PROPER NAMES

INDEX OF SUBJECTS